FOR GOD AND LIBERTY

For God and Liberty

CATHOLICISM AND REVOLUTION IN THE ATLANTIC WORLD, 1790–1861

Pamela Voekel

OXFORD
UNIVERSITY PRESS

OXFORD
UNIVERSITY PRESS

Oxford University Press is a department of the University of Oxford. It furthers
the University's objective of excellence in research, scholarship, and education
by publishing worldwide. Oxford is a registered trade mark of Oxford University
Press in the UK and certain other countries.

Published in the United States of America by Oxford University Press
198 Madison Avenue, New York, NY 10016, United States of America.

© Oxford University Press 2023

CIP data is on file at the Library of Congress

ISBN 978–0–19–761020–6 (pbk.)
ISBN 978–0–19–761019–0 (hbk.)

DOI: 10.1093/oso/9780197610190.001.0001

9 8 7 6 5 4 3 2 1

Paperback printed by Lakeside Book Company, United States of America
Hardback printed by Bridgeport National Bindery, Inc., United States of America

For Bethany Moreton: Solidarity Forever!

Contents

Acknowledgments

FOR GOD AND *Liberty* was a project of archival recovery across eight countries and more than forty collections, and it would not have been possible without the extraordinary generosity I encountered along the way. It is with profound gratitude and respect that I now get to acknowledge its many debts.

First and foremost, I want to thank to the many archivists and librarians who enabled this book. In the United States especially, their commitment to the free circulation of ideas is increasingly made criminal by legislative acts against uncomfortable historical truths and their expertise is disdained by technophilic solutionism. I am especially grateful to the head of the Archivo Histórico del Arquidiócesis de Guatemala, Mtro. Alejandro Conde Roche. The director of the Biblioteca Nacional in Guatemala City, Licenciada Ilonka Ixmucané Matute Iriarte, and the head of the library's Fondo Antiguo, Manuela Campa, as well as archivist Mirna Izabel Hernández, graciously facilitated my research. I would also like to thank the director of the Archivo General de la Nación in San Salvador, Lic. Luis Roberto Huezo Mixco, and archivist Elsy Alarcón. At the Archivo Documental del Instituto de Investigaciones Históricos de la Universidad Autónoma de Tamaulipas in Ciudad Victoria, Juan Díaz Rodríguez graciously shared his vast knowledge of the region's history and archival sources; mil gracias don Juan. Estoy muy agradecida a los encargados de las colecciones especiales de la Biblioteca 'Florentino Idoate, SJ' de la Universidad Centroamericana José Simeón Cañas en El Salvador por la digitalización y envío del periodico *El Salvadoreño*. Several vowed religious allowed this lowly sinner into Church archives and uncatalogued materials in Mérida and Monterrey and the Parish of Santa Bárbara Martir in Ocampo, Tamaulipas. I thank them and Our Lady of Guadalupe for their intercession, as promised: Hail, Mary, full of grace.

The sage advice and afternoon coffee offered at the Archivo Histórico de la Mitra in Mexico City is rightly famous among researchers. The knowledgeable archivists there have created a uniquely welcoming environment. In Rome, the staff at the Vatican Secret Archive and the Archive of Extraordinary Ecclesiastical Affairs proved especially helpful; they serve a multi-lingual group of researchers with patience and humor. I am also fortunate to count myself among the many historians who owe a huge debt of gratitude to the dedicated archivists and librarians at the Archivo General de Centroamérica; the Archivo del Estado de Yucatán in Mérida; and the Biblioteca Nacional in Madrid. I made numerous trips to the Archivo General de Indias, and I am grateful to the helpful staff and for the opportunity to live in Sevilla.

Kathleen Monahan from Burns Library at Boston College; Cherly Gunselman of the Manuscripts, Archives, and Special Collections division at Washington State University; Jessica Tubis at Yale's Beinecke Library; and Christine Hernández, Curator of Special Collections at Tulane's Latin America Library, all went above and beyond to help a mostly off-site researcher access their rich collections, as did the librarians and technicians at the Bancroft Library at UC-Berkeley. Tulane librarian Aida Schooner located rare El Salvadoran and Guatemalan newspapers; thank you for your doggedness. Legions of researchers will be unsurprised to learn that BLAC Rare Books librarian Michael Hironymous digitalized a set of previously uncatalogued pamphlets he helped me locate, and then catalogued this critical resource and made it visible to scholars. Congrats on your retirement, Michael, and *mil gracias* for going beyond mere duty to transform so many people's projects.

At Dartmouth's Baker-Berry Library, the indefatigable Latin America subject specialist Jill Baron helped me locate resources and understand the book illustration process. The film that she made with Melissa Padilla Vang and others, *Changing the Subject*, helped change the Library of Congress designation for undocumented immigrants—a lasting monument. Thank you especially to my colleagues in access and resource sharing who kept a river of books flowing into my hands even throughout COVID-19: Dave Sturges, Wes Benash, Katharine Bepler, Ross Blain, Brian Courtemanche, Phil Garran, Shane Harper, Patrick Mullins, Emily Weidrick, and Bruce Weidrick. The Dartmouth librarians' dedication to student and faculty researchers is matched only by that of the University of Georgia Russell Library Head of Access and Outreach Jill Severn.

Susan Ferber is everyone's aspirational editor in this business, and when you get to work with her, you understand her towering reputation. Thank you, Susan, for making this a much better book and for your kindness and unflagging encouragement. A special thanks to Jeremy Toynbee and Anupama Gopinath for their patience and skill. I deeply appreciate the scholarly generosity of the book's three anonymous reviewers. They provided valuable comments, suggestions, and encouragement in the midst of a global crisis and I am eternally grateful.

Thank you to Sarah Fouts, Jessica Fowler, Sherri Sheu, and Tracy Goode for indispensable research assistance. And to David Chu, who translated a key document from Latin to English in record time: ego sum tam gratus (I hope that says thanks!).

Mi mayor deuda de investigación es con la infatigable Silvia Méndez. Míl gracias, Silvia; estoy muy agradecida. If there is a better researcher than Silvia, I have yet to meet that person.

While the archival research behind this book could only have been accomplished with the support of Dartmouth College, much of its intellectual groundwork is indebted as well to prior scholarly homes. Thank you to the Women's Studies in Religion program of Harvard Divinity School for crucial research and writing support and the opportunity to learn from their wonderful students. Program director Anne Braude's scholarly generosity is legendary, and she more than lives up to the hype. She has a rare gift for creating nurturing intellectual communities grounded in genuinely democratic exchange. Thank you, Anne, for welcoming us to Cambridge. Wisconsin's lively Institute for Research in the Humanities provided a home away from home for a year of writing and research. Conversations with the Institute's then-director, Susan Friedman, made this a better book. Susan's generous engagement with all of the fellows' work set the tone for a magnificent set of seminars. Eliza Zingesser, Catherine Bates, and Victor Goldgel Carballo have yet to see the light on historicism, but were tons of intellectual fun, and Catherine's moveable feasts were the center of this joyful group.

The National Endowment for the Humanities funded a year of on-site research on this project and I am eternally grateful. A Beinecke Fellowship from Yale University also proved indispensable to the book's completion. The University of Georgia and, especially, Dartmouth College provided key resources at various stages, and the latter offered precious leave time for uninterrupted writing. I especially want to thank my department chairs Matthew Garcia, Cecilia Gaposchkin and Bob Bonner, and Dean John Carey, for their support of this project. I am especially grateful to Dean Matt Delmont for his encouragement and scholarly generosity.

Historian Elliott Young and I co-founded the Tepoztlán Institute for the Transnational History of the Americas 17 years ago. The Institute brings together 100 scholars from throughout the Americas for an annual week-long gathering in Tepoztlán, Morelos, Mexico. I am grateful for time spent with the creative group of scholars that comprise the organizing *equipo* and model the truly collective joy of knowledge production. The Institute's interdisciplinary discussions and multiple opportunities to workshop chapters in progress in Tepoztlán made this a far better book. I especially want to thank some of the long-serving collective members and a few regular or early attendees for creating this high-octane intellectual space: the late María Elena Martínez (La Patrona); my fantasy dean Karen Graubart; Padre Jennifer Hughes; Bianca Premo, Anna More, Ivonne del Valle, Gabriela Soto Laveaga, Micol Seigel, Josie Saldaña, Guadalupe Caro Cocotle, Marisa Belausteguigoitia Rius, Alex Aviña, David Sartorius, Dillon Vrana, Adam Warren, Daniel Nemser, Geraldo Cadava, Osmundo Pinho, Mario Rufer, Laura Gutiérrez, Nicole Guidotti Hernández, Beth Haas, Christin Smith, Reiko Hillyer, Jorge L. Giovannetti Torres, Rosalbaek Sakabelnichim and Jonathan Bird, Magalí Rabasa, Yolanda Martínez San Miguel, Anahi Russo Garrido, David Kazanjian, Lessie Jo Frazier, Enmanuel Martínez, Manuel Roberto Escobar Cajamarca, Shane Dillingham, Jody Blanco, Alexandra Puerto, Tito Lindo del Mar, Rachel Sarah O'Toole, Gabriela Cano, Christin Smith, A. Naomi Paik, Diego Flores Magon, Itza Amanda Varela Huerta, Abeyamí Ortega, Araceli Masterson-Algar, Ben Cowan, Ben Sifuentes-Jáuregui, and Karla Palma. The Institute's longevity is thanks in no small part to Doña Minerva and her family and Doña Sirena and Don Felix de la Cruz and their family; *la Guerra de las Tazas* is surely the only non-religious war in Latin American history. I thank the visionary Matt García, head of the first Latin American, Latinx and Caribbean Studies department in the Ivy League, for securing Dartmouth funds for the Institute. A special shout-out to Laura Briggs, who, like Bethany Moreton and Reiko Hillyer, was indispensable to the Institute's founding and through the years since, and who has donned her Converse to bring provocative ideas and good trouble every time for the forty years I have known her. Her early comments on this work proved indispensable.

My understanding of social movements came in part from association with some of the brave visionaries who make them happen. I had the extreme privilege of working alongside the students who organized Freedom University Georgia and gave the state a lesson in dignity. Fellow FU professor Lorgia García Peña's combination of commitment to students, superb scholarship, and uncompromising courage make her unique in my experience of academe; everyone should read her new book, *Community as Rebellion*. Thank you, Gueya. And thanks to fellow FU profs Betina Kaplan and Bethany Moreton and the many people who created

FU's stimulating intellectual spaces and bold political engagement—the students above all, and also Linda Lloyd, head of the Economic Justice Coalition of Athens, and Beto and Noe Mendoza of the Athens' Immigrant Rights Coalition. Over the years, I have learned a lot about Latin American history and being on the right side of history from my students. I especially want to thank the students who are now or are about to become professors, and those involved with the various iterations of the Mississippi Freedom Writers group and the UGA Living Wage Campaign.

I have been lucky to work with a group of uncompromising scholars, students, and support staff while at Dartmouth and the universities of Georgia and Montana. I want to especially thank Yesenia Barragan, Emilie Connolly, AJ Murphy, Mark Bray, Eman Morsi, Lynn Purle, Laura McTighe, Yui Hashimoto, Cori Tucker Price, Abigail Neely, Derek Aldridge, Christine Castro, Nathalie Batraville, Susan Mattern, Betina Kaplan, Lorgia García Peña, Kimber McKay, Amy Ross, Anya Jabour, Wanda Wilcox, and Reinaldo Román. I continue to appreciate Ken Lockridge's radical feminism and commitment to close reading. Thank you, Ken. A special shout-out to Bruch Lehmann for her indispensable work with the various iterations of the Mississippi Freedom Writers, all of whom made this a much better book in myriad ways.

Matt Garcia, Jorge Cuellar, Marcela Di Blasi, Israel Reyes, Mary Coffey, Desiree Garcia, Julia Rabig, Matt Delmont, Annelise Orleck, Jorell Meléndez Badillo, Naaborko Sackeyfio-Lenoch, Soyoung Suh, Doug Haynes, Paul Musselwhite, Jennie Miller, and Golnar Nikpour are just a few of the many wonderful people in the History and Latin American, Latinx and Caribbean Studies departments at Dartmouth whose scholarly generosity helped me though the long book process. I also want to thank the members of the Dartmouth Consortium for Studies in Race, Migration, and Sexuality for sharing their wisdom on archives and the archival turn. I am especially grateful to RMS leaders Eng-Beng Lim and Kimberly Juanita Brown, as well as Jorge Cuellar, Mingwei Huang, Najwa Mayer, Hazel Carby, and Misty de Berry.

Knowledge is always communal. The field is lucky to have creative and generous thinkers who create spaces for collective engagement with the world, not just the world of ideas. Alexandra Brown; Dalia Antonia Caraballo Muller and Jessica Delgado; Jennifer Hughes; Karen Graubart; Mark Overmeyer Velasquez and Gilbert Joseph; John French, Pete Sigal, and Jocelyn Olcott; Susie Porter; Fanny Muñoz and Tito Bracamonte; Kathryn Sloan; the late María Elena Martínez; and many others extended invitations to share my work. I am forever grateful for the invitation to share early drafts of my chapter on the Sanjuanistas at María Elena's transformative symposium "Race and Sex in the Eighteenth-Century Spanish Atlantic World," which featured a dazzling conversation between her and artist

Jesusa Rodríguez. We should all embrace María Elena's legacy of challenging the social hierarchies and disciplinary boundaries that police freedom in academic spaces and elsewhere.

Scholars at the following salons and institutions made insightful comments that transformed this book, and I am glad of the opportunity to thank them: the Mellon Sawyer Seminar at the University of Toronto; the University of Southern California-Huntington Library Early Modern Studies Institute; the Kellogg Institute for International Studies at Notre Dame University; Wayne State University; the University of South Carolina; the Department of Religion at Princeton University; the University of California Riverside; the Instituto Mora in Mexico City; the Department of History at Duke University; the Department of Gender and Women's Studies at the University of Arizona; the David Rockefeller Center for Latin American Studies at Harvard; Freedom University Georgia; the Dartmouth Consortium of Studies in Race, Migration, and Sexuality; the Department of History at Yale University; the Department of History at New York University; La Universidad de San Carlos and La Universidad Católica in Lima; the University of Utah; Emory University; the University of Arkansas; and the departments of History and Latin American Studies at Cornell University.

Although I'm not sure what it says that close reading and five-minute presentations generate the best discussions, they do, and *For God and Liberty* went in new directions thanks to time at the Patrona Collective for Colonial Latin American Scholarship's archival practicum in Rome. Our collective is named for La Patrona, the late María Elena Martínez. Thank you Bianca Premo, Ivonne del Valle, Jen Hughes, Anna More, Jessica Delgado, David Sartorious, and Dean Karen Graubart, as well as Rome stalwarts Jessica Fowler, Alan Malfavon, Kelsey Moss and other symposium participants, for critical engagement with each other's work and collective archival prowling. Thanks Bianca and Karen for your critical intercession at exactly the right moment.

Not all the support that this book and its writer relied on was institutionally based. My friends in the Woodbridges Group, especially Gale Whittier, Leila Balise, Kay Schmaier, Karen Roberts, Renee Lewis, and Teresa Renaker provided a critical lifeline to the world during the COVID crisis and the final years of book-writing. Teresa saved my mother from some capitalist viciousness and I am eternally grateful. Jody Pavilack and Cyrus Cohea are the last best people in the last best place. Hannah Waits, thanks to you and Lance for keeping us close no matter what was separating us. Leslie Abadie and John, Thea, and Thomas Boyne made Bethany and me feel at home in Madison, yet again. I am forever grateful for our year with y'all.

Our pack is a constant source of support and happy chaos. To John Patrick and Kirsten: after all of these book years, the next two decades of tickets to the Thorns and Storm games for Tuuli are on us. For Elliott and Jen: Arachne is yet more evidence that Moreton women are a gift to the world; here's to many years of not-to-be-missed narration. To Lope and Joel Bob: may every day be a tea dance at Russian River or a walk on the Wales coastline. For Haley: thanks for your preternatural calmness and sly humor; you are our radiant center. For Hank, Dolly, and Boris H.: a thousand river swims. To Frere, Ulrike, Jacob, and Helena: the hoop is in the driveway; camping is just down the road; and Bethany's book is always already almost finished. For Susana: next year in Chico. For our matriarch, Hilda Gail Swenson, your two-stepping rodeo romp stomp self will forever be at the center of our pack; thanks for always having the biggest heart even when words fail you—I could never have written this book without you.

For the beautiful Bethany Moreton, my great love and the pack's provisionary: Solidarity Forever!

FOR GOD AND LIBERTY

Introduction: Empire of Faith

AT THE HEART of the Age of Revolution in Spanish America was a transatlantic Catholic civil war. Each side of this religious divide operated from within a self-conscious intercontinental network of like-minded Catholics. The traditional narrative of the transition from monarchy to independent republicanism as a process of secularization misses completely the warring factions in the church who vied to define humanity's relation to God and, therefore, the proper order of temporal authority. For its central protagonists, the era's crisis of sovereignty provided a political stage for a religious struggle. The blood-soaked history that emerged both before and after independence is more legible in light of these sacred stakes.

This theological and ecclesiastical rivalry fired imaginations in the Spanish-speaking Atlantic world. Its networks of ideas and actors undergirded the Age of Revolution and framed the lasting divisions that would define much of Latin America's nineteenth century. The two sides defined themselves along a theological fault line centuries in the making. But the particular permutations of this division in colonial Latin America and then the independent nations of Mexico and Central America responded directly to the historical contingencies of this chaotic period. Alliances were scrambled and new ones made, unintended consequences of state policy begat novel horizons of ideology, and everywhere local interests intersected with transnational currents. The New World's sacred vision of liberty is revealed in the enormous archive of reformist theology, republican

For God and Liberty. Pamela Voekel, Oxford University Press. © Oxford University Press 2023.
DOI: 10.1093/oso/9780197610190.003.0001

advocacy, and official reports of often bloody confrontations that marked this religious civil war.

The contours of the intra-Catholic conflict were self-evident to its combatants. Reformers passionately corresponded with one another, evoking the martyrs and intellectual luminaries of the Reform Catholic International.[1] Their opponents, who operated within the Ultramontane International's networks, cleaved to Rome and its global field of power. For all their cosmopolitanism, however, these identities were not static imports to Latin America; rather, the unique context of the Spanish New World made such seemingly marginal sites as El Salvador or the Yucatán into the centers of this intra-Catholic battle and gave rise to its most radical realizations. Prior to the Cádiz Cortes (1810–1813), and particularly during the reign of Charles III, the reformers had enjoyed the active patronage of the Bourbon state, who saw in them a powerful ally for the project of asserting monarchical power over the vicar of Rome. Expelling the pope's loyal Jesuits from the Spanish Empire in 1767, the Bourbons institutionalized Reform Catholicism's decentralized notions of ecclesiastical sovereignty and its embrace of church history as the guide to the proper ordering of power. But when Ferdinand VII became a captive of Napoleon's invading army in 1808 and left a vacuum of authority, the same reform theology and ecclesiology that had bolstered the monarchy in earlier decades fueled radical experiments in political representation. A generation of clergy and elite laymen had been shaped by the Bourbon-sponsored reform curriculum. With the throne vacant, these reformed Catholics brought their distinctive sacred concepts of representation and conciliar debate to the work of crafting a constitution for the empire and instituting it in New Spain, the Kingdom of Guatemala, and New Granada—all still in the name of loyalty to the absent monarch. Drawing on the Reform Catholic justification for decentralized power in the church, they modeled for the orphaned empire elections and deliberations on the ecclesiastical traditions they had championed against Rome's claims of ancient prerogative.

Ferdinand's return from French captivity in 1814 precipitated a rupture and set Reform Catholicism on the path to a far more radical politics and theology. The monarchy, formerly the patron of the reformers when the centralized power at stake had been that of the pope, instead sought to claw back the authority that the constitution had dispersed to elected bodies. The King's new allies were the same Jesuits and their champions whom the Bourbon state had suppressed half a century earlier. The pope was no longer a rival autocrat but the ideological keystone to centralized authority and corporate identity that the Spanish throne found itself defending against the reformists' theologically justified claims to citizenship and conciliar decision-making. This religious divide fueled two civil wars and defined the two major political parties battling for control of the region for the rest of the nineteenth century. The Reform International and the Ultramontane International, in short, permutated into the liberal and conservative sides on the battlefield and, ultimately, into the liberal and conservative parties in Latin American political spheres, from the *municipios* to the congresses and presidential palaces. At no point in this process did either side lose its religious grounding.

MATÉRIEL IN THE CATHOLIC CIVIL WAR

A representative episode from New Spain's tumultuous final decade suggests how unlikely its leading protagonists would have found a secular interpretation of their struggle. In April of 1817, an intrepid company of 235 soldiers disembarked at the small town of Soto la Marina, just upriver from the Gulf of Mexico in northern New Spain, today's Mexico. The polyglot band intended to rally locals to their side and march inland to deliver munitions to the rebel forces, mostly comprised of indigenous and mestizo peasants, then battling a royalist army whose victory seemed close.

The leader of the expedition, Spanish liberal Xavier Mina, was a formidable veteran of the cause. In 1808, he had successfully led guerilla skirmishes against the French after Napoleon's army swarmed over the Spanish border, taking King Ferdinand VII hostage and leaving patriots across the empire to improvise sovereignty in the King's absence. Mina was therefore critical to the dramatic experiment in republicanism that erupted in the vacuum: the Cortes de Cádiz, a constitutional congress that assembled representatives from throughout the empire between 1810 and 1814. After fighting the French invaders, Mina had defended the Cortes' signature accomplishment, the 1812 Constitution, against a restored and autocratic King Ferdinand VII in 1814. The liberal hero's advocacy for the democratic document had further burnished his revolutionary reputation—and landed him in exile.[2]

The itinerary that brought the famed Mina expedition to the mouth of the Santander River in the spring of 1817 reveals the map of the revolutionary Atlantic that historians have illuminated in all its dense interconnection and political ferment. Mina had initially conceived of the expedition while sojourning in Liverpool and London, in consultation with the community of fellow Spanish exiles who formed an important network of resistance to the autocratic repression of the restore King Ferdinand. Backed by sympathetic merchants and bolstered by favorable press reception in the United States—technically neutral in the disputes between Spain and its restive colonies—the expedition's leaders assembled vessels and matériel in the Virginia port of Norfolk and added local recruits before sailing south.[3]

Their destination on the first leg of the voyage likewise reflects the revolutionary geography that was upending imperial Europe's pride of place. Leaving Norfolk, the expedition made for the Republic of Haiti, the Atlantic world's revolutionary epicenter. Haiti had in 1814 saved Simón Bolívar's cause of Colombian independence after both the United States and Britain spurned his entreaties. The only country on earth that offered freedom to any slave who struggled to its shores had then supplied South America's liberator with seven ships, crewed and captained, and thirty thousand pounds of gunpowder to continue their war of liberation in New Granada. President Alexandre Pétion's one condition in aiding Bolívar's rebellion was "to see that those who tremble under slavery's yoke are free: liberate my brothers and that will be payment enough."[4] Haiti was thus on Mina's itinerary in order that he could consult with Simón Bolívar and especially Pétion, patron of the revolutionary Caribbean and guardian of the world's most radical written constitution.[5]

Although the expedition to Soto la Marina also received Pétion's imprimatur, Mina could not afford to provision the three armed battalions of Black soldiers that the Haitian president offered him for the liberation of Mexico. Meanwhile, a hurricane had damaged two of Mina's ships and delayed the voyage, giving many North American recruits time to rethink the mission and desert. Their ranks were replenished in Haiti, however, by Haitian volunteers, the Afro-Caribbeans who had overthrown slavery, asserted the truly universal rights of man, and joined the growing armada bent on liberating New Spain.[6] Also adding to their numbers were champions of independence from the Caribbean coast of South America then clustered in the southern Haitian port of Les Cayes. Between 1811 and 1815, this multiracial, cosmopolitan band of rebels had sustained the independent state of Cartagena de Indias as a catalytic force in the Caribbean basin, a wide-open center of radicalism and a rallying ground for the defeated founders of the first Venezuelan Republic. But Spanish imperial retribution quickly followed King Ferdinand VII's restoration, and the revolutionaries turned refugees, accepting the offer of asylum in the free-soil Republic of Haiti.[7]

Having drawn fresh recruits from this island refuge of independence, the expedition next sailed to the Texas port of Galveston Island. There the French-born privateer Louis Michel Aury, who had successfully run the Spanish blockade of Cartagena in the final days of the doomed state, had declared the island for independent Mexico and was planning a drive into the interior in support of the growing rebellion. The merging of forces, however, was riven with rival claims to leadership, and Mina's variegated company set sail from Galveston under a cloud—literal as well as figurative, for their voyage down the coast was dogged by stormy weather. At last the assorted champions of Mexican independence arrived at their strategic destination, from which they expected to rally followers to their cause and defend "God and liberty" in New Spain.[8]

After long years of planning, months of fevered preparation, and a circuitous route, the expedition initially met with success on its inland march, scoring stunning victories on the route west from Soto la Marina throughout the summer and early fall. But in late October, a formidable cavalry loyal to Spain's restored monarchy defeated the invaders at Venadito, and this chapter of Mexican independence came to a close on the battlefield. Bolstered by the revolutionary Caribbean and animated by its crisscrossing revolutionary traditions, the Mina expedition is just one of the many multilingual and multiracial errands of liberation, a single miscarried episode in the fierce drama of New World independence.[9]

But a closer look at this doomed undertaking reveals a further dimension of the broad conflict, a map of the revolutionary Atlantic that overlay and animated the struggles over sovereignty. An empire of faith extended across the Catholic Atlantic, giving sacred meaning to the political cause, of which the Mina expedition was a single representative node in this vast communion. Mina the cosmopolitan guerilla fighter and defender of the 1812 Constitution was not the most infamous man on the ill-fated 1817 venture, nor the one that the monarchy's loyalists most feared. That distinction belonged instead to a brilliant and prolific creole cleric, Fray Servando Teresa de Mier, who would go down in history as the intellectual author of Mexican independence. Although Mina had stocked the growing fleet with munitions, Mier had stowed far more explosive cargo on the expedition's eight ships: intellectual seeds of rebellion in the form of three large crates of papers, pamphlets, books, and manifestos.

Mier accepted the royalists' offer of amnesty to all who abandoned the mission, but instead found himself clapped in chains and his arm broken. He was then forcibly marched with his cache of seditious literature to the Inquisition in Mexico City—an institution all too familiar to the renegade cleric and to many of the authors of the works in his portable library.[10] Mier's crates contained an eclectic and multilingual library of liberty: constitutions and manifestos penned by South America's fledgling governing bodies; a memoir by cleric and Cortes de Cádiz deputy Miguel Ramos de Arizpe detailing the economy of several regions of northern New Spain; a single issue of newspaper from the Yucatán, *El Misceláneo*; a guide to sword and drill exercises for cavalry.[11]

One group of readings in his essential library of liberty stood out both for its numerical representation and for its consistency: works in the powerful transatlantic current of Reform Catholicism, of which the Yucatán newspaper was but one representative. That the rebels welcomed the guns and gun powder Mier brought ashore is beyond dispute; that the rank-and-file soldiers of the insurgency would have thrilled to Mier's reformist Catholic library seems highly unlikely. These armed insurgents had their own carefully crafted notions of community at odds with the individualism at the heart of reformist Catholicism.[12] The Reform Catholic International comprised an educated elite, its particular religio-political ideology distinct from the plebian currents of alternative Atlantic cosmopolitanisms or more local ideologies that drove popular movements. It was the insurgent newspapermen, not the anonymous foot soldiers, who shared Mier's reformist commitments.

Father Mier's portable library and the reaction it sparked among his royalist enemies offers a glimpse of the dense ties that bound together these elite rebels of the empire of faith. Consider the religious authorities' response to the spiritual threat that the Mina expedition posed alongside its military challenge. When in April of 1817 Mier arrived in Soto la Marina as the chaplain to Mina's forces, the region's ecclesiastical hierarchy mobilized to prevent his baneful influence over the faithful of New Spain. Mier lacked permission from the Council of the Indies to perform Masses and baptisms, they reported. Most alarming, the hierarchs feared that their flock lacked the education to understand Mier's "crimes and perversity" and that he stalked the flock as a "wolf" among sheep; they promised to excommunicate anyone who knowingly received the sacraments from him or even so much as communicated with the renegade friar.[13]

As the liberatory expedition's forces turned inland and moved toward San Luis Potosí, and a shackled Mier and his seized cache of publications were dragged to Mexico City by an armed escort, the area's jittery ecclesiastical hierarchy issued a severe warning that "infamous tracts" that skewered the monarchy were circulating freely in the region. At the top of their list of dangerous tomes was Cortes de Cádiz librarian Bartolomé José Gallardo's Diccionario crítico—burlesco, which had caused a sensation among deputies at Cádiz when it first appeared in 1811.[14] Gallardo asserted in his dictionary that faithful Spanish Catholics who objected to the Jesuits on principled grounds of doctrine and morality were being wrongfully smeared as impious French Jansenists. He declared himself "horrorized" by Jesuit doctrine, particularly their notion of the pope's infallibility and superiority over kings, councils, and canons. The order's theologians, he roundly concluded, had been the worst corrupters of Christianity.[15] Mier supported the "impious and scandalous" ideas contained in tracts like the Diccionario crítico-burlesco, asserted the Cathedral Chapter in Nuevo Leon in its 1817 edict banning the dictionary and other seditious works.[16]

Far from being picayune doctrinal disputes, the points of open conflict sparked by the Mina expedition hint at the full gulf of ideology separating Reform Catholics—the future liberal combatants and liberal parties of independent Latin American republics—from their ultramontanist fellow believers, later the heart of the region's conservative political parties. At the center of the dispute between the vast transatlantic networks of Catholic rivals lay radically opposed notions of how man connected to God and the related questions of the proper channels and mechanisms of authority within the church, or its ecclesiology, as well as the proper balance between Church and state authority.

"MONSTERS OF SEDITION"

One indispensable document that the friar Mier hauled ashore alongside works from the Yucatán and elsewhere was the 1790 French Civil Constitution of the Clergy. This revolutionary document had suppressed the tithe, nationalized church lands, converted clergymen into salaried functionaries of the state, slashed the incomes of the upper clergy, decimated the regular orders, and established lay elections of clerics through the auspices of departmental or district assemblies across France. Under its terms, new bishops wrote to Rome to inform the pope of their appointments as a courtesy, not to seek the Holy Father's permission. In 1791, parish clergy were required to swear a public oath to this new French constitution, placing the church under state auspices and under the sovereignty of the laity and lower clergy. Recalcitrant clerics lost their benefices and often suffered organized community ostracism. At the center of this earthquake of reform stood the Abbé Gregoire, the first cleric in France to sign the oath. Mier's chests contained three of the French reformer's works.[17]

This French declaration of independence from Rome was a powerful influence within the Reform Catholic International, but Grégoire's was only one voice in this Atlantic conversation. Mier's chests of contraband held works by Latin Americans similarly intent on returning the church to its earlier, more democratic conciliar structure before the ascendancy of the papacy—a vision of national rather than Rome-centered churches. As the fate of the Mina expedition suggests, the Age of Revolution's military and political upheavals cannot be understood without the theological ammunition of figures like Mier. Certainly their royalist foes recognized the powerful hold of this democratic ecclesiology on the Spanish Empire's many literate rebels. These men strove to return the usurped sovereignty to the people—a group who would increasingly be envisioned theologically as individuals, not members of corporate groups like municipalities.[18] This temporal goal could not be separated from their sacred aim of restoring the pope's illegitimate religious authority to the lower clergy and laity. The monarch's defenders systematically detained reformers and relegated them to dank cells, transporting them to Spain and its North African territory whenever the supply of ships allowed. For their part, reformist Catholics in the new republics after independence saw no distinction between their state-building projects and their reform of the church, and they suffered retribution accordingly.

By momentarily expanding consideration of the Mier contraband from the printed works themselves to the personal ties their citational practices represented, this interdependence becomes more evident. When the friar Mier and the general Mina set sail from Galveston, they left behind not only the privateer Aury, but also Father Mier's "good friend" Juan Germán Roscio, one of Simón Bolívar's inner circle of conspirators and the principal author of the 1811 Act of Declaration of Independence of Venezuela.[19] When in 1815 the returned King Ferdinand VII sent an expeditionary force of 10,000 men to besiege the revolutionary movements in New Granada, and Simón Bolívar fled to Haiti, the drama unfolded in religious terms as well as naval ones. After landing at Santa Marta on July 6th, the expedition's iron-handed leader, Pablo Morillo, re-established the Inquisition and took up residence in its former building. He quickly made himself as dreaded as the tribunal itself: his 116-day siege of the port of Cartagena reduced his captives to eating oxen, dogs, and shoe leather; fully a third of the population perished. After seizing the exhausted city, in January of 1816 Field Marshall Morillo issued a manifesto warning New Granadans that the Crown's legitimacy rested on God's authority, and thus the king would summarily discipline dissident clergy as the critical purveyors of revolutionary impiety.[20] This was no idle threat. The mixed-race Roscio was among the group Spanish officer Domingo Monteverde, the Morillo of Venezuela, labeled the "eight monsters" of sedition. The group was hustled aboard a Cádiz-bound ship and ultimately entombed in the dreaded penal fortress in Ceuta, bordering Morocco.[21]

While imprisoned for his pro-independence activities, Roscio wrote El triunfo de la libertad sobre el despotismo (The Triumph of Liberty over Despotism), a Reform Catholic exercise in biblical exegesis that he published in Philadelphia in 1817, following his release from Ceuta.[22] This intellectual trajectory, whereby the author of the Venezuelan constitution spent his ensuing punishment shedding the light of Catholic theology upon the goal of republican liberty, continued upon his release. With undiminished loyalty to Bolívar, Roscio spent the final years of his life as finance minister and president of the Angostura Congress that established the independent Republic of Gran Colombia. He prefaced this renewed service to political independence with further theological contributions to the rebellion in the empire of faith. He translated into Spanish a 1797 homily by the then-Bishop of Imola that argued that there was no contradiction between democracy and Catholicism: "Christian virtue makes men good democrats," the bishop had written in terms that Roscio offered up to the Hispanophone world. "Equality is not an idea of philosophers but of Christ . . . Do not believe that the Catholic religion is against democracy."[23] This Christmas message from 1797 also had been translated into French by the Abbé Grégoire, the head of France's Constitutional Clergy. Both Grégoire and Roscio found in the bishop's homily powerful ammunition for their cause, for the bishop of Imola had become Pope Pius VII. Both the Reform Catholic clerics were anxious to advertise how the Holy Father's newfound support of absolutism belied his prior connection of Catholicism and democracy in the 1797 work. For his New World audience, Roscio invidiously contrasted the pope's earlier democratic inclinations to his 1816 encyclical *Etsi longissimo terrarum*, which called on Spanish American priests to oppose the movements for independence. In the same year that Roscio was meeting with Mina's liberatory expedition in Galveston and a year before he was to preside over the Angostura Congress, therefore, he was publishing theological arguments that found an eager readership among the champions of independence.[24]

The authors Fray Servando Teresa de Mier transported on that seditious mission were connected to each other beyond just their representation in his makeshift library. Many of them formed important nodes in the self-conscious Reform Catholic International, a transnational network of reform-minded clerics and laity who corresponded with each other, drew sustenance from the same corpus of reformist authors, and celebrated the movement's martyrs and luminaries, as well as its high-water moments, like the Synod of Pistoia of 1786.[25] Roscio's career is representative. Not only was he the comrade of Father Mier during much of the Mina expedition, but Father Ramos de Arizpe, a deputy to the Cortes of Cádiz and another of the authors in Mier's cache, championed reformist clerics Roscio and José Cortés de Madariaga when the bedraggled captives landed at Cádiz with the other "monsters" who had so rattled the royalists in New Granada. Ramos de Arizpe then wrote to Mier personally to lament the two imprisoned Reform Catholic clerics' fate. In the same missive, the veteran of the Cortes detailed the movements of royalist troops and praised the opposing army of New Spain's rebel chieftain, José María Morelos. Both Ramos de Arizpe and Mier associated with the Abbé Grégoire during stints in Paris, and Ramos de Arizpe later accepted Grégoire's request to relay information to the radical reformist bishop of Havana, Juan José Díaz de Espada y Landa. Ramos de Arizpe administered last rites to Mier in a public ceremony attended by Mexico's liberal president Guadalupe Victoria in 1827. He went on to lead a full reformist assault against Rome's authority over the

Mexican church as minister of justice in Valentín Gómez Farías' Reform Catholic administration of 1833.[26] He even chaired the committee that created Mexico's first constitution in 1824. In a very real sense Grégoire was not the only "constitutional cleric" whose work crowded Mier's small library.

This transatlantic circle of reformist Catholics, although unusually prolific, cosmopolitan, and influential, was but one small node in a vast network of reformers who championed the Cortes de Cádiz. Collectively they provided a religious imprimatur for new forms of political representation and, like Ramos de Arizpe, emerged after independence waving the banners of liberal political parties and causes in the young republics. The reformist wisdom represented in Mier's captive library was not a novel import grafted onto Latin America direct from the French Revolution. Rather, the Reform Catholic International's ideas had been percolating across the Spanish Empire in the Americas for decades, achieving institutional influence long before the storming of the Bastille.[27] During the century that preceded Mexico's independence in 1821, urban elites of New Spain developed a new political subjectivity through their embrace of Reform Catholicism. Rejecting the Baroque inheritance of external, mediated, corporate Catholicism, these eighteenth-century reformers turned inward. Their new emphasis on self-discipline, moderation, and direct access to the divine ultimately splintered the social order of estates into one of internally regulated individuals, with all the limits to imagination and licenses to violence that critics of liberalism have charted in the bloody wake of universal Man. Although this process is most commonly taken as evidence of secularization, these early heralds of liberal individualism in New Spain dismantled the ancient régime's fixed hierarchies and mercantilist constraints in the name of "true religion" in the Augustinian tradition. Rejecting ascriptive status and corporate political actors, this nominally egalitarian theology spoke in the liberatory idiom of liberalism; and, like its rationalist cousin, it provided new bases for exclusion and domination. It did so, however, not to free rational Man from the superstitious bonds of the church, but rather to free the illuminated interior conscience from restraints to its development, and to free the church herself from the centuries' corrupting accretions. The notion of a society comprised of individual citizens who elected their representatives was not a French import.[28]

In the later eighteenth century, reformers lobbied successfully for the study of ecclesiastical history and church councils in Spanish imperial centers of learning, subjects that were systematically added to theology curricula across the empire after the expulsion of the Jesuits in 1767.[29] Charles III surrounded himself with formidable intellectuals of the Catholic reform and appointed reformist bishops throughout his dominions. From them and their parish-level clerics, the

Augustinian ideas of Catholic reform reached even the illiterate majority of the faithful by way of the pulpit. Parish churches, not salons or coffee houses, constituted a central site of the public sphere; priestly homilies were the newspapers of an empire virtually devoid of printing presses and the freedom to operate them.

The introduction of reformist authors into empire-wide university and seminary curricula after the expulsion of the Jesuits from the empire, and the reformist campaigns these Crown-appointed ecclesiastics and bureaucrats led, would have dramatic but completely unintended consequences. Reformist bishops, authors, and bureaucrats demoted Rome and supported the authority of church councils and Spanish bishops. They certainly saw no role for the laity or the lower clergy in church and state governance. Once released, however, the genie of deliberative conciliar authority proved impossible to return to the bottle. In Spain's far-flung empire, the lower clergy who would be touted as the fathers of their countries' independence would insist on the complete devolution of power back to the lower clergy and the flock through the process of democratic elections for leaders of church and state. Basing their claims on the church's glorious early centuries, they forged a sacred imprimatur for democratic notions of sovereignty based on new notions of representation out of an eighteenth-century reformist ecclesiology meant to halt the downward flow of sacred power at the level of Spanish bishops.[30] According to both sides in this intra-Catholic conflict, the temporal battlefields and war of words of the Age of Revolution in Latin America were but one plane of an intercontinental religious war.[31]

This, then, was not a battle between progressive modernizers and backward-looking traditionalists, still less one between closet secularists and unchanging church adherents. Both sides demonstrated considerable intellectual and cultural creativity, and both relied on precedents to justify their positions. In the decades leading up to independence, literate urban lay and clerical reformers throughout the Spanish Empire transformed the Reform Catholic but decidedly regalist doctrines of earlier reformist Catholics, many of them well-placed ecclesiastical and state officials, into a transnational reformist movement hostile to Bourbon absolutism. During the course of the eighteenth century, reformist Bourbon bishops and statesmen crafted an absolutist defense of the sacralized monarchy's prerogatives over those of the Holy Father and championed notions of conciliar authority that reduced the pope's writ.[32] The next generation of Catholic reformers, many of them humble parish priests, embraced these earlier Bourbon reformers' campaigns to decenter the pope in church ecclesiology, but also gradually took aim against the absolutism of the monarchy itself. They squared off against the pope's champions, the ultramontane forces who increasingly supported the concept of absolutist monarchy and embraced reformist Catholics' biggest foes: the Jesuits, who had been expelled from the empire in 1767, and who had, ironically, earlier crafted elaborate theories of the rights of the people to resist tyrants. During the time of the Cádiz Cortes (1810–1814), new free speech laws and new printing presses provide an early glimpse of the centrality of the two transatlantic church currents to opposing regional and national political parties, liberals and conservatives, that would continue to spar over matters religious and political throughout much of Latin America's nineteenth century.

SACRED LIBERTY

Historians of Latin America have missed the magnitude of religious conflict and its decisive impact on Latin Americans' notions of sovereignty and the proper balance of ecclesiastical and civil power in Mexico, El Salvador, Guatemala, and Colombia.[33] Despite the indisputable dominance of the church as a—indeed *the*—global institutional actor in this period, the same nationally conceived studies that foreclose a regional and transatlantic field of action also tend to assume actors' secular motivations and collapse all mention of religion into an unexamined atavistic whole— when in fact it is precisely the rival sides' equally impassioned but profoundly opposed religious attachments that, in their own telling, define their conflict. A reluctance to take these commitments seriously and attend to their theological roots has therefore obscured the religious tensions that erupted into civil wars in Mexico and Central America after independence. *For God and Liberty* argues that the religious ideologies of these rival strains of Catholicism are necessary to explain the long-simmering conflicts that became visible in the Spanish-speaking Atlantic during the Cádiz Cortes. Further, it asserts that this theological dimension is likewise one indispensable dimension of the armed struggles between the nineteenth century's two main political protagonists, liberals and conservatives—later Liberals and Conservatives—in the emerging Latin American republics.

The Age of Revolution has been understood as an era of secularization, giving democratic movements a genealogy that is necessarily hostile to Catholicism. Scholars who assume the secularization thesis have missed that proponents and opponents of absolutism and democracy, and later centralism and federalism, fought their battles under the sacred canopy, not as secularists nor even as nominally religious people increasingly informed by scientific rationalism or modern philosophy. In these works, the church of the late eighteenth and early nineteenth centuries can appear as a monolithic institution dominated by an antiquated scholasticism, an institution assailed and ultimately defeated or hybridized by modern philosophy and scientific rationalism.[34]

The archives tell a different story. The epistemological and cosmological conflict was internal to Catholicism itself: the Reform Catholic International waged a thoroughly Catholic campaign against the Ultramontane International led by the Holy Father. If historians' tendency to treat the church as a monolith, and resistance to monarchical absolutism as an emanation of the secular Enlightenment, has obfuscated the true battle lines that fundamentally ordered new notions of sovereignty for many of Latin America's literate elites, the Reform Catholic International's centrality to the rebellions was not lost on its ultramontanist enemies at the time. The conservative clergy and laity remained loyal to an empire of faith with a firmly temporal head in Rome and a corporeal bureaucratic and administrative body. They extended their allegiance to the pope's shock troops, the Jesuits, after the order was exiled from the empire by Catholic reformers in 1767. Reformers lambasted the Jesuits' theological emphasis on the importance of free will to salvation, while also rejecting the Protestant notion of predestination. Grace was not so immutable for the Spanish Empire's eighteenth-century Catholic reformers. Although God singled out some for salvation, providing them with their "inner light," He also granted or retracted that gift during an individual's lifetime, and thus works had salvific efficacy—although only if inspired by love for God.

Therein lay the rub: love of God came from His previous gift of grace, the "inner light." In 1777, Reform Catholic archbishop Alonso Nuñez de Haro y Peralta neatly summarized his take on Augustinian grace thus: "Given that God is justice, then by essence there is not, nor can there be good intentions without love, and our intentions are more, or less good, according to the greater or lesser extension of this holy love."[35] The laws God inscribed in Christian's hearts, in their souls, were nothing less than the Holy Spirit, and this presence spread *caridad* (true charity or love) in the heart. Without this presence in the soul, no love of God or His laws; without such love no grace. God's freely given grace worked an internal moral transformation in men, who then performed good acts inspired by God's prior love rather than fear of external punishment or desire for earthly glory.[36]

From this emphasis on the individual's relationship to God naturally flowed hostility to worldly spiritual hierarchy and an emphasis on the inviolability of godly conscience. In the late eighteenth century, reformers had added church history to university curriculums throughout the Spanish Empire. They wielded the results of their novel and relentless historical research to demonstrate Rome's dramatic usurpation of authority that had rightly belonged to bishops, the lower clergy, and even the laity in earlier centuries. A central tool of their craft was the authentication of church documents. Reformers in the Hispanophone Atlantic world returned with well-nigh obsessive glee to the false decrees of Isidore Mercatur, showing how base forgeries had set in motion a monstruous usurpation of sovereignty.

These ninth-century documents, they maintained, had wrongly aggrandized the Holy Father's authority at the expense of bishops and church councils by claiming the pope's suzerainty over both before the fifth century. This false claim and the inauthentic documents it claimed as evidence had, according to the reformers, transformed a Christian republic into a papal monarchy and threatened the survival of true Christianity.[37] "Damned decretals of San Isidoro!" Mier exclaimed. Not the pope but priests and bishops constituted the church's divine tribunal and, moreover, even bishops should act only in consultation with the lower clergy.[38] Having found the origin of the pope's ill-gotten power through their historical mode of proof, reformist Catholics called for a return to the "pristine purity" of the church's earlier centuries, to a church characterized by democratic elections and shorn of its later accretions of sclerotic hierarchies and novel religious cults like the Jesuits' Sacred Heart of Jesus.[39]

Reformers throughout the empire set up juntas to rule in the captive king's name. They rolled back ecclesiastical authority from Rome and its appointed archbishops and bishops, citing as their model the early church's democratic structure, especially lay and clerical elections for church hierarchs. The Colombian region of Socorro in the viceroyalty of New Grenada elected a bishop at the same time it elected a ruling junta and it produced a native son, Juan N. Azuero Plata, who would go on to write a justification for local control of the church that would be read out loud paragraph by paragraph in El Salvador's parishes and in the halls of power in Central America during the early years after independence.

Similar efforts to reclaim the people's sovereignty over the church and to wield government entities like city councils and juntas against more centralized authorities occurred throughout the empire starting in 1808, when the French held King Ferdinand VII captive. Reform Catholic factions mobilized to create juntas or emboldened city councils, while simultaneously calling for more local control, sometimes even elections, of bishops and other hierarchs throughout the empire, including in San Salvador; the Yucatán; Barcelona, Venezuela; and La Paz. Reformers' insistence on the early church's democratic and decentralized structure provided a Catholic theological justification for reclaiming sovereignty from centralized powers and establishing new notions of representation based on individuals, not corporate groups, sacralizing a particular notion of democracy and local rule while simultaneously desacralizing the papacy and the monarchy; ruling juntas emerged side by side with schismatic churches. The empire's seminaries and universities produced priests and laymen who ably championed reformist doctrine and causes and participated in dramatic ways in the campaigns of the Reform Catholic International, in part by citing its luminaries, invoking its martyrs, and rallying against its common enemies.

With the monarchy vanquished after independence, reformist Catholics organized in liberal political parties emerged waving the banners of liberal federalism—as proponents of regional rather than central power—and championed the establishment of state churches largely independent from Rome. Given reformist Catholics' belief in God's gift of grace to the soul, and consistent with reformers before them, they advocated to reduce the church to the purely spiritual in part by placing many of its functions under state auspices. Reformers met stiff resistance from conservatives who clung to Rome and to notions of centralized, corporate political hierarchies sanctified by God. This account charts these reformed Catholics' transformation into political liberals, as well as the concomitant development of traditional papal loyalists into the conservative parties in the new republics.

For God and Liberty follows the circuits of thought, affiliation, and dramatic action among reformist and ultramontanist Catholics in the Atlantic world to demonstrate that religion lay at the center of the era's conflicts. It does so across eight chapters. Chapter 1 relates how tensions between reformist and ultramontane Catholics burst dramatically into the public eye during the Cortes de Cádiz. As delegates to the congress from across Spain's vast empire debated in the Spanish port town of Cádiz, a group of reform-minded laymen and lower clergy from the Yucatán—known to themselves and others as the Sanjuanistas, after their gathering place at the small church of San Juan in the city of Mérida—championed this representative body's signal accomplishment, the 1812 Constitution. They encountered fierce resistance from the *rutineros*, a conservative group of Catholics loyal to the pope. These conservative—or "ultramontane," a reference to Rome's location "over the mountains" from France—Catholics rejected the Sanjuanistas' radically democratic notions of church and state governance, and instead championed Rome and the absolutist monarchy under King Ferdinand VII. Ironically, perhaps, these conservatives pledged their allegiance to the Jesuits, whose perhaps most influential theologian, Francisco Suárez, had devised a theory of popular resistance to tyrannical, absolutist rulers. Where once the reformist Bourbon state and ecclesiastical hierarchs had embraced regalism and conciliar church authority as a hedge against the pope's claims to power, now conservatives embraced the absolutist power of both crown and scepter, while liberals like the Sanjuanistas embraced radicalized notions of conciliarism and radical forms of democratic representation in both church and state. Both groups recognized their membership in transnational networks that weighed in on the Cortes' church and state reforms. The two groups' tensions played out in the press and in the streets, creating an elaborate paper trail of reports and denunciations, as Bourbon bureaucrats and church hierarchs scrambled to contain the threat of the increasingly radicalized Sanjuanistas.

The theo-political battles that erupted onto the streets of Mérida during the Cortes were far from an anomaly in the Spanish-speaking Atlantic world. Chapter 2 shows that the battles between the two church factions wracked the Kingdom of Guatemala (present-day Costa Rica, Nicaragua, El Salvador, Honduras, Guatemala, and the Mexican state of Chiapas) and the viceroyalty of New Granada (present-day Colombia, Ecuador, and Venezuela) during the decade before independence. Religious passions intersected seamlessly with regional political and economic interests. In Central America, El Salvadoran indigo planters infused with reformist sentiment sparred with elite Guatemalan merchants who set prices and controlled necessary capital—and who deployed Rome's spiritual authority in defense of their own economic dominance. In the king's absence, Colombian, Venezuelan, and El Salvadoran reformers sought to establish ecclesiastical and political elections in the face of overweening papal and and monarchical authority.

This chapter introduces the deeply transatlantic networks underlying both sides of the conflicts by way of a particularly compelling group of prominent protagonists. Over the course of the decade, these religious actors gradually transformed into the respective leadership of the opposing liberal and conservative political parties that engulfed Central America in a series of bitter civil wars after independence.

Chapter 3 delves deeply into the intersecting local and transatlantic religious tensions that fueled Central America's holy war, the Civil War of 1826–1829. At the center of the conflict stood parish priest José Matías Delgado's bid to create a bishopric and serve as the bishop of El Salvador.[40] The laity indirectly chose Delgado through the region's elected city councils and the government later appointed him to the post, incurring the enmity of Rome and Central America's battle-tested archbishop, Ramón Casaús y Torres. This rivalry reached beyond the rarefied circles of leadership and intellectuals into rural and urban parishes. For many of El Salvador's rural lay Catholics—often of mixed racial heritage—conflicts between the two rival Catholic Internationals were realized in the theater of the parish church as struggles over the local pulpit. Their identities thoroughly grounded in the *municipios*, the majority of the faithful connected with the transnational circuits of theological thought through homilies and sacraments, or, on dramatic occasions, through public demonstrations of their contrasting loyalties to the cause or a particular parish priest.

For God and Liberty is not, however, a granular regional chronicle divorced from the Atlantic context. Chapter 4 shifts from the dramatic battles in San Salvador and the Central American countryside to follow reformers' struggles back across the ocean to Rome. When El Salvador's hand-picked emissary arrived in Rome in 1826 to seek the pope's blessing for the new reformist national church, he got a chilly reception. This was hardly surprising. The Vatican had successfully recouped some of its authority lost after 1789, but the long-brewing challenges to its unilateral authority over the church erupted from powerful political coteries of reformist Catholics in the United States and Latin America, particularly Central America. These American reformers found inspiration in late eighteenth-century efforts to build national churches in Spain and Portugal and cited the learned apologists for these earlier bids for national autonomy. The fourth chapter therefore details New World challenges to papal authority in the 1810s and 1820s and demonstrates the continuing salience of rival transatlantic epistolary networks for both reformist and ultramontanist Catholics. After reclaiming some of the ground lost to revolutionary and Napoleonic France, the Vatican saw the center of gravity of the Reform Catholic International shifting to Spain and her former empire during this period, greatly radicalizing the International in the process. The papacy threw its weight behind Central America's conservatives, both lay and clerical, pouring gasoline on the fire that had ignited in the West.

Chapters 5 and 6 demonstrates that neither the liberals nor the conservatives were secular political actors, and the theological and devotional commitments that infused actors on both sides of the conflict rendered compromise unthinkable. As tensions mounted, would-be liberal or conservative state-builders who sought to stand on the rock of the church found only shifting sand, plunging the region into a civil war from 1826 until the Liberal victory in 1829. In a rural world of small municipalities, nationalist sentiment proved far too fragile a container for religious passions, which overflowed national, regional, and municipal boundaries. The numerous Central American clerics and statesmen who churned out pamphlets and editorials in the debate engaged in a modern iteration of a centuries-long theopolitical battle, here fought behind the banners of Central America's two political parties, the reform-minded liberal federalists and the ultramontane conservative centralists. To propose their rival visions of the future, each side reached past the secular philosophes of the Enlightenment to draw upon authoritative Christian antecedents and metaphors. In a battle in which both sides passionately advocated for the church but warred over its essential nature, the winning argument could only come from within the sacred canopy. Historians are lost without sources, and Chapter 5 relies on virtually untapped correspondence among ecclesiastics to demonstrate the ubiquity of religious struggle. Chapter 6 provides the first systematic analysis of the actors' own paper trail, analyzing pamphlets and tracts culled from multiple archives and libraries.

Chapter 7 demonstrates that even after their 1829 victory liberals fought tirelessly to transform the state—not to suppress the faith and shackle the church,
as the historiography uniformly suggests, but to bring both in line with Reform
Catholic principles and thereby create a truly godly republic. Because of the centrality of religious currents within the church to the region's conflicts, religious
proclivities became fundamental to delineating notions of civilization and barbarism that replaced the *ancien régime*'s sclerotic racial and social categories after
independence. In later years, conservative ultramontane forces backed by Rome
would ultimately forge an uneasy alliance with the majority, the region's indigenous peoples—who saw through their liberal Reform Catholic would-be-tutors'
rationales for social leadership and refused their religiously inflected notions of
civilization and barbarism.

The book's final chapter moves forward in time to Mexico's civil war of 1858
to 1861 to argue that Mexican Liberals—and their committed allies in places like
Philadelphia, Lima, and Bogotá—were thoroughly suffused with Reform Catholic
principles, which in turn animated their claims to political legitimacy. Historians
of Latin America's mid-nineteenth-century liberals have concluded that the
movement's program of church-state separation amounted to a self-evident secularization drive. Between their initial success in the 1850s and their ultimate displacement by conservative forces allied with the French invaders, the Liberals
placed birth, death, and marriage rites under state auspices; ended the church's
special civil prerogatives; and banned religious expression from the streets, corral-
ling it into private homes and church buildings themselves.

A closer look at the actors' own paper trail suggests a radically different interpretation of their motives. Far from seeking to remove religion from national life, they were instead consumed with refashioning the Catholic Church
from within, with paring down its hierarchy, curbing its luxurious ceremony,
and simplifying its liturgy without eliminating its central mysteries. In place of
Romish excess they envisioned not a secular society but a godly alternative in
the Augustinian tradition. Liberals' well-recognized embrace of republican simplicity and austerity to legitimate their power evolved out of their specific theological critiques of luxury's enervating effects. Nowhere is this better illustrated
than in the 1859 establishment of a Mexican schismatic Catholic Church under
state protection.

By this route, *For God and Liberty* demonstrates the influence of two powerful
transatlantic currents in the church. Reform Catholicism helped to desacralize
the monarchy and elevate conciliar forms of authority, thus making democracy
a holy crusade. By taking seriously the religious motives to which the actors so

passionately testified, the book charts these Catholics transformation into political liberals, and the concomitant development of traditional papal loyalists into the conservative parties in the new republics. The divide that so consistently defined the region for the rest of the century had its basis in warring visions of a sacred polity.

1

Drawing the Religious Battle Lines

BEGINNING IN 1808, a crisis of sovereignty arose after Napoleon's troops seized Madrid. The French emperor's victory led to King Ferdinand VII of Spain's abduction and exile to France, where he was carefully monitored. Spanish resistance to French rule remained fierce. In January of 1810, 60,000 French reinforcements poured across the Pyrenees and drove the defending armies south. Abandoning Seville, the Supreme Central Junta fled to the utmost redoubt of Cádiz. Primed by weeks of agitation, crowds in Seville took to the streets, denouncing the despised Central Junta as traitors and clearing the way for Seville's regional junta to declare itself the empire's legitimate government. Barely a week passed, however, before Seville in turn fell to the French, leaving only Cádiz as the base of Spanish patriot rule. Bowing to the inevitable, the remaining members of the Central Junta dissolved the larger body and named as its successor a five-man Council of the Regency of Spain and the Indies to rule in the place of the absent king. The British ambassador grumbled that this was a distinction without a difference, an improvement only in the sense that he now had but "five blockheads to transact business with instead of thirty-four."[1] But the dissolution of the Central Junta, under threat of complete defeat by the French, catalyzed independence movements in Spanish America. Regional juntas began forming in anticipation of peninsular capitulation to Napoleon. The *Cortes* that the Central Junta had announced months before

For God and Liberty. Pamela Voekel, Oxford University Press. © Oxford University Press 2023.
DOI: 10.1093/oso/9780197610190.003.0002

would now meet in a besieged city on a sand spit at the farthest edge of Iberia, under a different authority altogether.

From 1810 to 1814, this empire-wide constitutional convention in Cádiz, Spain, created an unprecedented window of political experimentation.[2] During this time, an influential group of highly literate reformist Catholic laymen and lower clergy from Mérida, Yucatán, championed the Cádiz Cortes and its signature achievement, the liberal 1812 Constitution. Under the iron hand of the monarchy and the Inquisition, religious fault lines had been fiercely contained, but the Cortes' guarantees of free speech and a free press allowed them to surface. The Sanjuanistas, as they came to be called, threatened to upend Church and secular hierarchies in the name of individual liberty and their understanding of early church history. These theological rebels squared off against ultramontanist Catholics led by a pro-Jesuit bishop. Organized under the banner of the *rutineros*, these conservative clerics and laymen supported monarchical and papal absolutism, while simultaneously creating novel conservative networks and alliances. Importantly, these ultramontanist Catholics supported King Ferdinand VII after their Sanjuanista reformist enemies turned permanently against the monarchy in 1814. The Sanjuanistas, like reformist Catholics throughout the empire's urban areas in this period, transformed the decidedly regalist and episcopalist Reform Catholicism of prior Bourbon state and church officials into a far more democratic doctrine, one that provided a justification to decenter not just the pope—a cause many reformist Catholic statesmen and ecclesiastical hierarchs under King Charles III ardently supported—but the absolutism of the monarchy itself. The experience of the conflict transformed its content in ways that neither side could have predicted, but that laid down some of the tracks on which the coming decades would run in the region.

The deep history of Reform Catholicism in the Spanish Empire helps explain the Sanjuanistas' support for new notions of sovereignty undergirding the Constitution of 1812. Constitutional innovations represented a rupture with earlier forms of representation: the Constitution of 1812 declared all men who could claim lineages in Spanish possessions to be citizens and gave them the right to vote for electors who then chose deputies to the Cortes de Cádiz.[3] As well, citizens were eligible to vote for members of the new constitutional city councils to be established in every town of at least 1,000 people and for representatives to another Cádiz Cortes innovation, the regional Provincial Deputations.[4] That access to citizenship required evidence of lineage in Spanish possessions essentially meant that Afro-descended men were not citizens, although Article 22 did specify that "virtuous" Black men could appeal to join the ranks of the enfranchised.[5] Representation in the Cortes itself was based on population numbers, the number of individual citizens in a given region of the empire; the corporate *municipio*—and other corporate groups—were not the fundamental constituent of politics in this nineteenth-century governing body. This notion of a society of equal male individuals was home grown in New Spain and the larger Spanish Empire, made possible because it was culturally conceivable to the adherents of the individualistic, reformist current of the church embraced by many urban elites in the late eighteenth century.[6] The reformers' enemies, the conservative *rutineros*, invoked the long-exiled Jesuits, who had never had a stronghold in the Franciscan-dominated Yucatán, and actively spread the Jesuits' signature cult, the Sacred Heart of Jesus. However, they rejected Jesuit Francisco Suárez's theological justification for popular overthrow of a benighted monarch set out in his 1613 *Defensio fidei*. They also rejected the centuries-in-the-making myth of the Jesuits as enthusiastic regicides and rejected the earlier Bourbon state's belief that the Jesuits represented a dangerous state-within-the-state, a threat to monarchical absolutism.[7] These novel conditions produced novel religio-political amalgams on both sides. By the time of King Ferdinand VII's 1814 return from exile in France, the regalist and reformist Catholicism of the late eighteenth century, with its absolutist defense of the sacred monarchy's prerogatives over those of the Holy Father, was not the Sanjuanistas' Reform Catholicism, or that of their allies throughout the empire. And indeed it was the pope's champions, the ultramontanist *rutineros*, who now backed the absolutist monarchy. Mérida's new printing presses and the Sanjuanistas' contretemps with their ultramontane *rutinero* enemies provide an early glimpse of the centrality of church currents to opposing regional and national political parties—to liberal federalists and conservative centralists—that would continue battling over matters religious and political throughout much of Latin America's nineteenth century.

Context was critical to this early rehearsal of a long-term fissure. The sudden power vacuum triggered an intertwined political and religious debate on the nature of sovereignty in the monarch's absence. The Regional juntas (1808–1809) and the empire-wide Spanish Cortes of Cádiz (1810–1814) rose to fill the void, calling into question where sovereignty resided during the king's absence. But merely posing that question permanently altered the terms of debate. Even if the king were to be restored, the genie of popular sovereignty could never fully be returned to its bottle. The stakes could not have been higher for the participants on all sides, for they were arguing not simply about temporal power, but rather about the nature of God's authority on earth. The Cortes de Cádiz—and the empire-wide debates it engendered—was as much a church council as it was a parliamentary body.

When their impassioned arguments are read in tandem with the writings of pro-independence insurgents who, like Andrés Quintana Roo, were their peers or immediate biological as well as ideological heirs, the Sanjuanistas illuminate the theological doctrines supporting individualism, this-worldly asceticism, and democratic, conciliar church authority based on elections involving, perhaps, even the laity.[8] On the opposite side of the theological and political divide, the *rutineros* championed collective identities, baroque Catholicism, and papal and monarchical prerogatives against democratic challenges of any sort. This transatlantic battle of ideas, so characteristic of the late eighteenth-century university reforms, thus permutated into more radical and democratic programs, especially in the New World. With nothing less than the divinely sanctioned ordering of Christendom at stake, no clear line divided theological opinion from political action. The battle raged in the press and in the pulpits, but also in the streets and schools. Seemingly obscure interpretative differences about church ecclesiology could lead to enclosure in monasteries or imprisonment. Reformist Catholic and highly regalist bishops in Spain and America had conspired with Charles III's ministers to end Jesuit control over the universities and implement a theology curriculum centered on reform-minded authors well-versed in direct biblical exegesis and the church's conciliar history in general and in the Spanish councils in particular, firmly against the moral laxity of Probabilism associated with the Jesuits, and in favor of a simple ethical piety shorn of baroque excesses and historical accretions. The Sanjuanistas joined the intellectual leaders of anti-colonial struggles, men like Fray Servando Teresa de Mier.

The Sanjuanistas, then, coalesced as an identifiable faction in the midst of the political ferment of the Cortes of Cádiz, but they were not latecomers to the heady mix of reformist piety and democratic politics swirling around the Spanish-speaking Atlantic world. The group met in Mérida's small church of San Juan Bautista. Reformist cleric Vicente María Velázquez had become the church's curate in 1802 and served many of the well-educated and restless members of this small city of around 28,500 people.[9] Immediately before the full effects of the Cortes were felt in Mérida, in 1811, the small church had proven itself a focal point of resistance to overweening authorities. When Lorenzo Ignacio de Argaez, for example, found himself detained for failing to pay proper public respect to the interim governor in 1811, four key Sanjuanista leaders—José Matías Quintana, José Francisco Bates, Lorenzo de Zavala, and Pedro Almeida —led a crowd of forty men into the streets to demand the prisoner's release and the removal of the interim governor. The governor ordered the troops out of their barracks, promptly dispersed the street protesters, but prudently awaited the arrival of his replacement rather than confront the powerful pens and pulpits of the Sanjuanistas directly.[10]

With a record of protest already behind them, then, Father Velázquez and a core of about fifty of the town's reform-minded citizens met regularly in 1812

FIGURE 1.1 The Church of San Juan Bautista in Mérida, Yucatán. The small church gave its name to the Sanjuanista movement of Reform Catholic clerics and elite laymen who met regularly to continue the debates underway at the Cortes de Cádiz (1810–1813). The public sphere in this early phase of Mexican liberalism, in other words, was squarely within the sacred sphere. Fierce champions of the Cortes' Constitution of 1812, the Sanjuanistas are memorialized as fathers of Mexican independence, though that was not their aim at the time. Photograph by Gina Kelley/Alamy Stock Photo, 2019; used by permission.

and 1813. They gathered to discuss the 1812 Constitution and to participate in the empire-wide debates about church and state in light of their reformist Catholic principles. Roughly a dozen secular priests, many of them former classmates from the Tridentine Seminary of San Ildefonso, which also educated laymen, regularly attended meetings. So did José Matías Quintana, a prosperous newspaper editor and merchant; his intertwined democratic religious and political legacy would become clear by 1813, when his son Andrés Quintana Roo would win a place in Mexico's later pantheon of independence heroes by assuming the editorship of the insurgent publication *El Semanario Político*. Other figures who became central to Mexico's early nineteenth-century liberals are found in the pious debates of the little chapel, including Lorenzo de Zavala.[11] Zavala, like Quintana, took immediate advantage of the freedom of the press granted by the Cortes' declaration of 1810. A printing press had been imported to Mérida several years before, and these men of letters around Father Velázquez lost no time publicizing defenses of the constitution and other liberal causes.

The tiny hermitage's debates found a wide audience through the newly created public sphere of print. Sanjuanistas controlled five of the city's seven newspapers, and Sanjuanista José Francisco Bates published pamphlets and Cortes' and ecclesiastical decrees with his own press. In this new space for debate, the sides quickly took shape: the group that had coalesced over perhaps years of devotional study squared off against the equally religious vision of the *rutineros*, the conservatives who defended the traditional church and the monarchy against what they saw as the heretical threat of the liberal elements of the imperial Cortes and the local Sanjuanistas.

In this novel competition for public hearts and minds, both sides minutely parsed the Cortes' published deliberations, the widely circulating news and tracts responding to events at the Cortes, and the 1812 Constitution itself—all in light of their version of Catholicism's core truths and proper church ecclesiology. Neither group could know that in 1814 the king would return to power, abrogate the constitution, and end free speech. For a brief window between 1810 and 1814, reformers and ultramontanists both operated under the incrementally democratic rules of a freer press. Their seizure of this new space brought the theological debate that had roiled so much of the Catholic world—with all its clear political implications—to the entire Yucatán Peninsula.

While the king was absent and the Cortes held sway, the Sanjuanistas enjoyed the upper hand. They controlled the local censorship board from 1812 through much of 1814 and held definitive influence in Mérida's newly created constitutional city council. When their democratic theology was challenged, moreover, the radical Catholics could look to Cádiz for reinforcements. In this period of their ascendance, the Sanjuanistas flooded Mérida and the Yucatán Peninsula with their intertwined arguments on church and state governance. Their ideals met robust opposition from the conservative *rutineros*. For example, when in 1812 the Cortes abolished obventions (*obvenciones*)—the traditional personal services that Indians were bound to provide to their local parish priests—the Sanjuanistas clearly sided with this emancipatory measure. However, their position cost them much loyalty among lowly parish priests in the countryside, whose potential embrace of the democratic theology ran up against their personal dependence on Indian agricultural labor.[12] For a few short years around the Cortes and the promulgation of the 1812 Constitution, then, the Catholic world's competing views of grace and free will played out as a pitched battle between this radical reformist Catholic cell, the ultramontane *rutineros*, and conflict-averse Bourbon officials.

REFORM CATHOLICS AND THE CONSTITUTION OF 1812

Although the Sanjuanistas were politically active prior to the empire-wide crisis of sovereignty, two events launched their period of maximum influence: the publication in the Yucatán of the new Spanish constitution, and the Cortes' decree of press freedom under the auspices of new *Juntas de Censura* rather than the Inquisition. When news of the 1812 Constitution reached the Yucatán Peninsula, church and Crown authorities dragged their feet rather than proclaim its authority—even after official copies arrived in the hands of Mérida's own returning Cortes deputy Miguel González y Lastiri in late July of 1812. In the months following the promulgation of the document in Spain, lamented Sanjuanista spokesman Father Pedro Almeida, Mérida's officials failed to celebrate with even a single cannon volley or a peal of the bells—both routine ways to mark "even the most trifling, common, and trivial" events. In response to these delays, the Sanjuanistas took the Cortes' mandate to proclaim the document's contents to the public into their own hands. In early August, over fifty Meridians signed a letter requesting that Governor and Captain General Manuel Artazo y Barral officially recognize the new liberal legal code.[13] In late September, a boisterous crowd gathered in the atrium of the Chapel of San Juan for a public reading of several chapters of the constitution. Overcome with joy, revelers spilled out into the nearby streets, accompanied by the din of musicians, firecrackers, and the exuberant crowd itself.[14]

The reaction from Mérida's conservative Bishop Pedro Agustín Estéves y Ugarte was swift and unyielding, clearly making the connections between the theological debates and the struggle over temporal governance. The unofficial celebration of the constitution in the church atrium was merely the most visible expression of the seditious nocturnal gatherings at the small chapel. The hermitage of San Juan, the bishop charged, hosted regular gatherings of people known for their "restless spirits" and "authorship of pasquinades, calumnies, and inflammatory writings." Most alarming to the ultramontane bishop, however, the Sanjuanistas' impious propositions about the Immaculate Conception of Mary—a key point of contention in earlier but ongoing doctrinal wars between the Jesuits and their ultramontane supporters, on the one hand, and, on the other, reformist Catholics.[15] In maligning this doctrine, the bishop reported, the Sanjuanistas promoted the heretical opinions of authors known for their "atheistic, Jansenistic, and libertine proclivities." Bishop Estéves y Ugarte offered no specific evidence that the Sanjuanistas denied the Immaculate Conception—that is, the doctrine that Jesus' mother was herself the only human sexually conceived without original sin, so that she could later serve as a sinless vessel for the Son of God. However, he was certainly right that Jansenist and other reformed Catholic authors remained skeptical about her sinless conception in St. Anne's womb; indeed, this assertion would only become official church dogma in 1854, a move that did not end centuries of controversy around the notion of a "pre-purified" Blessed Virgin Mary. While never denying that Mary should be honored above the saints, eighteenth-century reformist Catholics had promoted Christocentric worship.

Reformist Catholics engaged the as-yet unsettled question of Mary's conception in light of their opposition to an expanded Mariology more generally—the latter a cherished project of the Jesuits. Thus the campaign to have the immaculate conception declared dogma formed a part of the wider struggle between reformers and ultramontane Catholics. Mérida's conservative bishop could logically assume that the local Sanjuanistas would have come down on the reformist Catholic side and could expect to rally opposition to them on that basis. Hoping to end the "scandalous" meetings at the hermitage, the bishop ordered the gatherings to stop on pain of excommunication for attendees, clerics, and laymen alike. By his order, the edict was read in every church during the next three major days of celebration and affixed to every church door in the city.[16] The bishop's very public collapsing of conception and constitution indicates the Sanjuanistas' intertwined theology and politics.

With such weighty issues hanging on the outcome, Mérida's ultramontane supporters joined their bishop in striking back against the reformers' rowdy public embrace of the constitution and their control of Mérida's new Constitutional City Council. To counter this representative body's heretical bent, a group of mostly clerical electors unveiled a bold plan to ensure that conservative *rutineros* would dominate the new Provincial Deputation, a regional governing body created by the Cortes. Their strategy was to discredit the Sanjuanistas by painting them as pro-independence insurgents, rebels who sought not a constitutional monarchy for the Spanish Empire but a wholly independent New Spain. This accusation was designed to galvanize Spanish officials into immediate and drastic action, in the context of the incipient independence movement taking shape in part under clerical leadership in the less heavily Indian population centers of New Spain. Parish priest

Miguel Hidalgo y Costilla and, following his grisly execution, his fellow priest José María Morelos were just two of the important leaders of a mestizo and indigenous insurgent peasant army aligned against royalist forces in the heart of New Spain in 1810 that won major battles. As the debate heated up in Yucatán—with its potentially explosive numerical dominance of Mayans—this armed rebellion transformed into an outright anti-colonial struggle; its ultimate outcome was far from clear in 1813.[17] Similarly alarmed, other conservative accusers joined the ultramontane clerical electors in their campaign of guilt by association: three of the region's elected representatives to the Cortes also insinuated that insurgent leader José María Morelos was involved with the Sanjuanistas. The deputies also accused the group of advocating that the people were authorized to execute the Cortes' decrees "by tumult" if necessary.[18]

In Mérida, the Sanjuanistas quickly gained control of the new constitutional city council, completely locking the *rutineros* out from the new institution. Somewhat ironically, in order to promote their conservative vision of both temporal and divine authority, the *rutineros* would need to embrace the constitutional innovations in democratic governance. As the elections for one of these new governing bodies, the Provincial Deputation, approached, these conservatives went on the offensive. In a letter of March 16, 1813, directed to Captain General Artazo, *rutinero* clerics Francisco de Paula Villegas, Ángel Alonso y Pantiga, and Manuel Pachecho (the editor of the conservative paper *El Sabatino*) and others complained that a "league of fractious men" sowed discord by raising the standard of rebellion, proclaiming independence, and following in the footsteps of the Hidalgos and Moreloses and other American dissidents—a decidedly false but nevertheless effective claim. These Sanjuanistas, the conservatives reminded the Captain General, had created a scandal in the streets the previous September with their rowdy public celebration of the constitution—a sure indication of their seditious intent, in the rather hazy logic of the constitution's foes. Sanjuanistas, they further alleged, served as emissaries to carry secret instructions and enigmatic letters about the elections to Yucatán's far-flung hamlets. This clandestine organizing centered on controlling the upcoming elections for the Provincial Deputation; these nine *rutineros*, eight of them clerics, therefore advised the Captain General to thwart the alleged plot by speeding up the election of the election committee (the electors chosen by citizens who then chose the deputation's members) and ordering a military presence on election day. This latter measure was an absolute necessity, they assured the military commander, because of the machinations of José Matías Quintana; José Francisco Bates; Lorenzo de Zavala; Lorenzo's brother, the priest Agustín de Zavala; Pedro Almeida; and Pablo Moreno, who all acted under the protection of Cortes deputy Miguel González y Lastiri.[19]

Captain General Artazo proved skeptical of the insurgency charges floated against the Sanjuanistas, noting that the September "scandal" had been little more than a group of musicians and followers who issued from the church of San Juan Bautista into nearby streets. The leaders had read aloud a couple of articles of the 1812 Constitution, and the whole gathering quickly retreated into the church at Artazo's request. That the group displayed a disconcerting "party spirit" was undeniable—elections were supposed to be placid affairs—but Artazo found no evidence of independence sentiment among these Sanjuanistas. He called on their clerical accusers to clarify their facts. Characteristically, Quintana waxed more dramatic than the cautious Captain General Artazo: if he became a prisoner because of these libelous accusations, he avowed, his blood would expiate the patria from the false accusations brought against him.[20]

While Artazo proved unwilling to tar the Sanjuanistas with the brush of insurgency in 1812, he took the conservatives' broader call for caution more seriously for the Provincial Deputation election in Mérida. He posted troops in the Plaza of the Constitution and throughout the city and ordered cannons readied around the central square. The election proceeded without incident, but the Sanjuanistas' worst fears came to pass: three conservative clerics were elected to the new institution. All three priests were energetic opponents of the reformers and valued members of the ultramontanist entourage around Bishop Estéves y Ugarte. The Sanjuanistas were down but not out, however. Controlling as they did five of the city's seven newspapers, these reformist Catholics took their grievances about the new elected body directly to the city's reading public. Lorenzo de Zavala's *El Aristarco* ran a letter from a reader lamenting the "horrible qualities" of two of the clerical members of the deputation and lambasting the third as cruel and avaricious. As evidence of this un-Christian cruelty, the Sanjuanista paper referred its public to a letter in which the priest-politician promised to extract what the Indians owed him in "pure lashes."[21]

Sanjuanista city council lawyers (*sindicos*) José Matías Quintana and the printer Josef Francisco Bates took their grievances all the way to the Minister of Governance of Overseas Territories (Ministro de la Gobernación de Ultramar). They had rightly feared that conservative priests would be elected to the Provincial Deputation, which violated the constitutional ban on clerical participation in the new governing bodies. They did not shrink from naming names, lamenting that ultramontanist stalwarts Father Diego Hore (Valladolid), Father Manuel Pacheco (Tihosuco), and Father Francisco de Paula Villegas (Calkini) won seats despite being parish priests in their respective towns. This happened in part, Quintana and Bates reported, because eight ultramontanist clerics reduced the Sanjuanistas' credibility by tarring them as revolutionaries in the style of Morelos.[22] According to the version Artazo provided for adjudication in Spain, the priests had arrived in the peninsula as part of the bishop's entourage and enjoyed his protection, which emboldened them to indulge their baser instincts. One of them, for example, beat an Indian in front of his other parishioners; he lacked appropriate gravitas in other ways, too, dancing in public with considerable enthusiasm. Another, Artazo reported, had collaborated with the third to constitute a group intent on oppressing the Indians. None of the three, in short, had earned the support or approval of the captain general.[23]

THE OBVENTIONS DISPUTES

The Sanjuanistas' urgency to represent their side of the story was spurred by one of their greatest concerns: that clerical members of the Provincial Deputation would conspire to overturn a Cortes law of 1812 that freed the Indians from any obligation to provide personal service and goods, obventions, to priests—an extension of an 1810 edict that had liberated Indians from tribute payments.[24] Although this religio-political battle raged within the tiny urban creole minority, their dispute had direct implications for the indigenous majority.

The law on obventions was indeed a flash point. In May of 1813, numerous clerics—including the *rutinero* priests Villegas, Pacheco, and O'Horán serving on the deputation—gave their permission for Father Raymundo Peréz and others to request that the regency reinstitute a secure revenue flow to sustain worship.[25] The end of personal service and obligatory payments, this group of alarmed rural clerics relayed to the bishop, had decimated church adherence by indigenous Mayans with "electrical velocity." The payment of fees for church baptisms, marriages, and burials had therefore summarily disappeared. Overnight, the pastors found themselves destitute. Moreover, a Sanjuanista-led press barrage called them "immoral, ambitious and the authors of acts so criminal their very mention horrorized the hearer."[26] The battle over the payments raged in the press and in the streets.

In the tumultuous years of King Ferdinand VII's exile, then, the obventions debate between the Reformed Catholic Sanjuanistas and the conservative *rutineros* pivoted around their distinct assessments of the Indians' core nature and the purpose of the priesthood. These were religious questions of the most fundamental order. The Sanjuanistas adhered passionately to the classic reformist notion that, with proper education, Indians could be like Spaniards, defined as people who responded to opportunities for economic self-aggrandizement through work. The *rutinero* clergy—many of whom toiled in vineyards with majority Mayan parishioners, far from the large Spanish populations of Mérida and Campeche and Valladolid—were less sanguine about Mayans willingness to work or support the church without considerable force. By their lights, the Indians should remain a separate group, the República de Indios, with their own privileges and duties, like tribute payments and obventions. The *rutineros* therefore resisted the Cádiz Cortes inclusion of indigenous men in the polity as equal citizens. Both creole parties to the debate, of course, took it for granted that the Indians desperately needed their tutelage.

An anonymous reformist priest laid out the fundamental link between Indian education and an improved work ethic in an 1802 essay first published in the *Gazeta de Guatemala*. Granted, Indians were lazy, ungrateful, stubborn, and drunk. Yet, this was not an innate condition, the priest reported. "Give them the same education as us," he informed the papers' enlightened readers, "and they will be as dedicated to work, compassionate, thankful, educated and sober as we are—or should be."[27] The principal incentive to work, of course, was to obtain basic sustenance: clothing, food, and, in the Indians' case, obligatory tribute. Many reformers feared the Indians had no appetite for work beyond that needed to meet these basic needs. But if Indians craved Spanish comforts, they would work harder, the priest reported; and the key to inculcating this desire was education because, after all, "erudition and knowledge spurred civility," *El Redactor Méridano* pronounced.[28]

While reformist Catholics identified education as key to the Indians' energetic pursuit of a comfortable life and voluntary payment of church extractions and state taxes, the ultramontanist *rutineros* proved reluctant to part with physical punishment as a motivator. Sanjuanista pundits carped incessantly about abusive priests' violence toward recalcitrant Indians, taking advantage of the relative freedom of the press that reigned from 1810 to 1813 to excoriate their opponents.[29] A letter printed in Zavala's *El Aristarco* noted that individual liberty was the true path to the development of the *pueblos*. Would a man who ordered Indians to receive a thousand lashes in his presence be a "good protector of individual liberty?" he asked rhetorically of a recently elected deputy to the Provincial Deputation whom he accused of this barbarity.[30]

Outnumbered in Mérida's public sphere of letters and challenged at the imperial level during the brief Cortes period, the ultramontanists nevertheless managed to loom large in elite debate over Indians' status in the Yucatán. Their eloquent and prolific spokesmen, parish priest of Hoctún, Raymundo Pérez y González, intervened with particular flair. When Lorenzo Zavala's paper *El Aristarco* accused Pérez of whipping two Indians who resisted paying the obventions and the new tithe proposed by the Provincial Deputation, Pérez denied the accusation, but also pursued a surprising defense: *had* he flogged the Indians, he would have been well within his rights and proper duties. Clerics had a tacit contract with their flock, Pérez asserted as they provided spiritual sustenance in exchange for physical sustenance. If Indians resisted this pact, he could force payment by any legal means necessary. Was a system tyrannical if its judges used fear to encourage legitimate payments, he asked rhetorically and presumably in response to *El Aristarco*'s assertion of exactly that point. What priest did not eat of the vine he cultivated, after all, Pérez concluded in his typically dramatic fashion.[31]

In fact, Pérez did have a record of forceful extractions from his charges. During a routine inspection of his former Tabasco parish in 1804, his Indian flock produced a litany of complaints centered mostly on unpaid labor, exorbitant fees, excessive corporal punishment, and Pérez's insistence that they hunt alligators as tribute payments.[32] Not surprisingly, given this reputation, he proved nonplussed by the Cortes' edicts abolishing the obventions and continued to exact this tribute from his Hoctún-area flock. He was not afraid to use force. When a group of Indians refused to pay the eggs and castor beans demanded for their children's classes in church doctrine, Pérez summarily jailed them and then defended himself from his Sanjuanista detractors in the Mérida press.[33] Pérez's heavy hand was but one among many, and in the paper debate the ultramontanists could often be found forthrightly defending their violent extractions. In 1813, for example, Yaxcabá's priest proudly told the bishop that after fifteen years of lashings, little superstition remained in his parish, although diviners still used crystals to see the future. Reform newspapers like *El Aristarco* and *El Miscelaneo* gleefully reproduced conservative pastors' orders to flog Indians who refused to pay the fees and services.[34]

Summing up the obventions debate some ten years later, several critics of the Sanjuanistas noted that, while most parties to the dispute agreed that Christians should be obliged to give to the cult and its ministers, one group thought otherwise. These "emboldened ironic spirits, these turbulent geniuses, these proud ignoramuses, these nineteenth-century innovators wanted prodigious virtue to descend from the heavens to visibly sustain religion's economic edifice, or, better put, they use this pretext to destroy that what they pretend to uphold."[35] Though vituperative, this statement is also essentially accurate. At the heart of Sanjuanista and Reformed Catholic theology lay the notion of efficacious grace, of the need for God's prior gift of salvation to the soul. This gift in turn created virtue, embuing its recipient with the ability to resist the temptations of the world. If the Indians did not exhibit this asceticism and self-mastery, then reformers felt they should rightly be under the tutelage of those who did.

THEOLOGY AND POLITICS

As the violent public debate over obventions suggests, the Sanjuanistas' support for Cadiz's radical democratic reforms paralleled and indeed sprang from their reformist theology. The arguments of religion were their assumed arsenal in the war of ideas that the unstable political moment unleashed. Two sources of authority in particular were central to their vision of Christianity and, therefore, the polity: the Bible and the early church councils. Thanks to changes in the regulation of print culture and education that took root in the late eighteenth century, both of these potentially explosive resources had been more widely disbursed than ever before in the Catholic Spanish Empire.[36] Yet at the original moment of cautious liberalization of access to sacred writings, neither side could have foreseen their long shadow across the constitutional period.

Their most powerful tool against the hierarchy, reformers were confident, was their knowledge of the Bible. In a newspaper passage about his son the insurgent newspaperman Andrés Quintana Roo, held captive and tortured by the royalists, the grieving Quintana waxed ecstatic on the Bible's importance. "Holy scripture, the pure and inexhaustible fountain that we must drink, the clear water that purifies our souls and makes us capable of sublime and heroic acts" were for him the most "chaste delicacies," and he wished that the Bible study that typified the early church would be restored.[37]

The Bible was available for this kind of impassioned appropriation because of a pair of policy reversals by the Inquisition a generation earlier. In 1783, the Inquisition allowed the Bible to be read in the vernacular, and in 1789 it granted official permission for the publication of a Castilian Bible. These moves cracked the clerical monopoly on religious interpretation, opening the way for individual evaluation of dogma, although certainly not encouraging it.[38] Unmediated access to the Word became a powerful justification for protest in Mérida as across the Christian world. In this direct access to scripture, unleashed thirty years before and taken for granted by the 1810s, the reformers embraced the Bible as a critique of hierarchs.

With equal zeal they also drew upon the models of the early church councils, the deliberative bodies that regalists, and reformist Catholics agreed could eclipse the pope's authority in most situations. The Sanjuanistas operated with a conception of ecclesiastical authority based on the serious study of the Church Fathers and the early councils. In the late eighteenth century, reformers throughout the empire had lobbied successfully for the study of ecclesiastical history and early church councils and discipline—especially councils held in Spain—all of which were added to university theology curriculums throughout the empire.[39] These curricular changes were part of a larger movement led by Charles III and his enlightened ministers and prelates to shore up the empire's moral fiber—a movement centered on ending Jesuit control of university education and replacing what they saw as Jesuit moral "laxism" with a focus on moral rigor and reason. Much of the controversy centered around the Jesuits' promotion of the moral system of Probabilism, which the reformist archbishop of Mexico in 1767, Francisco Antonio Lorenzana, denounced as the "greatest evil of the century" in a pastoral letter dedicated in its entirety to the theme.[40] In essence, probabilists counseled that, when in doubt about an action's lawfulness, following a solidly probable opinion backed by a church authority was acceptable even if an opposing view was more probable. The rigorist position held by reformist Catholics like Lorenzana (sometimes confusingly referred as "probabiliorists") shot back that it was always unlawful to follow an opinion regarded as less probable under any circumstances, for "the Church Fathers and pious men always looked to do what most conformed to reason, which is what the law of God and natural law ascribe."[41]

The campaign to substitute this rigor for the moral laxity of Probabilism included not only expelling the Jesuits from the Spanish Empire in 1767 and banishing probabilist thought from university curricula but also systematically replacing probabilist authors with Reform Catholic authors. The reformist ranks included moral theologians like Natal Alexander, Zeger Bernhard van Espen, Claude Fleury, Daniel Cóncina, and Melchor Cano, who would, according to a royal order of 1768, "uproot laxness in moral opinions . . . and re-establish Christian morality in its purity. . . so that faith and truth be defended as is just."[42] Reform-minded prelates shared Charles III's enthusiasm for this moral crusade. "Let us read authors like Cóncina, who in our time have declared war with laudable force and zeal against scandalous laxism," the Bishop of the Canary Islands Antonio de Tavira y Almazán enthused in a typical response in 1792.[43]

Cóncina's 1743 work *Storia del probabilismo e rigorismo* was translated into Spanish by 1772. Directed against the Jesuits, it quickly became a touchstone for reformers throughout the empire. Cóncina was safe, in part, because he carefully distanced himself from French Jansenists, noting in no uncertain terms that "he didn't need Pascal or Arnaud or any Jansenist" to understand Probabilism's errors. Instead, he carefully spelled out his fellow reformists' fundamental position on the weight of grace and free will in salvation. As "the great Augustine taught," real truth came from a "sweet delectation" infused in our hearts by God alone, by means of which we are made capable of obeying the law and divine precepts.[44] Reformers felt that probabilists, on the other hand, amplified the freedom of the will and restricted obedience to the law, reducing its yoke and diminishing its obligation.

Cóncina and the rigorists might thus appear to be discouraging human freedom in broad terms. Certainly this was the interpretation by regalists across the Catholic world. Bourbon champions of kingly authority found in the rigorists' argument a powerful antidote to what they felt was the relativism that emboldened the probabilist Jesuits to justify even regicide itself. But the ramifications of rigorist arguments were not so clearly contained on one side of the larger war of ideas. Although the intended emphasis was on how grace provided men with the ability to obey, this gift of grace to the heart implied as well that the bearer was infused with natural reason—the same quality, that is, that emboldened the laity and the lower clergy to rely on their own knowledge of the Bible and the Church Councils to challenge sanctified hierarchs. Grace was a dangerous power in the wrong hands. By the late eighteenth century and especially later during the period of the Cádiz Cortes and into the early republican period after independence, reformist Catholics had forged a theory of sovereignty and representation based on the individual as society's fundamental constituent and out of the conciliar forms of authority stressed by reform Catholic Bourbon bureaucrats and churchmen and the cultural sea change in Catholic theology and practice wrought by this individualist current of the church among urban elites.[45]

The constitutional monarchical Sanjuanistas and a huge swath of more decidedly pro-independence insurgents from around the empire made this danger concrete. These Reform Catholic Yucatecans imbibed the new learning in the Seminario de San Ildelfonso. Many of the most prominent Sanjuanistas, including laymen like Lorenzo de Zavala and José Matías Quintana, had passed through the seminary on their way to Velázquez's salon in the tiny church of San Juan. In 1785, seminary rector Nicolás de Lara, backed by organized student protesters who led a strike, lost a battle against Bishop Piña y Mazo to reform the curriculum. Lara had incurred the conservative bishop's wrath because of his belief in the "superiority of the Church, together in a council, over the pope, its visible head." He was forced to flee to Mexico City, where the reformist Archbishop Alonso Núñez de Haro y Peralta sheltered him.[46]

The stakes were clear in any number of specific struggles between the reformers and the *rutineros*. The Sanjuanistas took particular aim against Ultramontane Catholicism's celebration of miracles, those anomalous infusions of the divine into the profane world. God was a legislator of laws, by their lights, not a worker of miracles. The *Redactor Méridano*, the voice of the Sanjuanista-dominated 1813 city council, sardonically announced that the credulous were reporting new miracles at an absurd rate. A dove appeared in a Mercedarian convent and was immediately taken for an angel—until its worried owner came to claim it. And a rock long known as the "Rock of Pleasures" was given the title of Virgin of Pleasures—a scandal in itself, and one that drew cult followers who claimed the Virgin responsible for numerous miracles in the Church of San Benito. When would true piety take the place of witchcraft, superstition, and greed, the paper wondered rhetorically.[47]

Hostile to the ostentatious display of authority, reformist Catholics like the Sanjuanistas also sought to topple the church's own hierarchies in the name of restoring the early institution's purity, radical democracy, and episcopal or national (rather than papal) prerogatives. Writing in insurgent publications, reform-minded intellectuals provided deeply historical justification for these campaigns. The excommunications imposed on the Mexican rebels proved one of the flashpoints. The thirty-two Sanjuanistas who signed a letter in protest of Estéves y Ugarte's excommunication threats against them noted that the practice redounded against the souls of its executors and that the church Councils of Orange, Orleans, and Seurs had prohibited its use except in grave cases.[48] In 1812, the rebel paper edited by José Matias Quintana's son Andrés Quintana Roo, the *Semanario Patriótico Americano*, also underscored the historical novelty of excommunication for anything except mortal sins, warning pastors they imperiled their own salvation by punishing minor offenders. So prevalent had denial of the sacraments become in recent centuries that during France's second national council regalist bishops produced a catechism protesting the "frightful practice." That abuse had migrated to the Americas, where Michoácan's bishop-elect excommunicated rebel priest Miguel Hidalgo y Costilla and declared the entire insurgency he headed heretical. The Gallican Church, the rebel paper noted, had roundly rejected excommunication, citing its non-existence in the early church and late emergence in the twelfth century. This unfortunate practice sprang from the papacy's ninth century self-elevation from appeals judge to universal bishop. Priests and bishops, after all, constituted the real church, and the bishops were rightfully constrained by the presbyterium formed by city curates. They had no authority to act independently. Lest anyone doubt these facts, the article reported, the erudite theologian Zeger Bernhard van Espen had carefully documented this history.[49] Van Espen's authority—often cited by reformist Catholics—was another ironic legacy of the late-eighteneeth-century efforts to inculcate piety through encouraging religious study. In 1791, some of his works received official permission to circulate in the Spanish Empire, and his most cited work, a book on canon law, exalted the authority of bishops against the popes.[50]

Two central ideologies informed and emboldened critique of ecclesiastical hierarchs and hierarchies by the reformers across the empire prior to the Cortes de Cádiz: regalism, or the elevation of the king and nation above Rome's prerogatives;

and conciliarism, or the faith in church councils to arrive at truth through debate and consultation. Sophisticated arguments for the authority of church councils provided some members of the literate intelligentsia of the insurgency with ammunition against this sort of hostility from the upper clergy, and ample justification to resist the church hierarchy—even the Holy Father. An 1817 insurgent decree recommended that these loyalist clerics be forced to read regalists like Pedro de Campomanes and embrace the teachings of the Holy Book and the general church councils; only then would they cease to interfere in the dispute "so heroically maintained against our oppressors."[51]

Insurgent intellectuals frequently lamented that the centuries' accretions of rank had corrupted the church's core democratic structure. When inquisitors asked a captured priest from the insurgent hotbed of Tecpan about the rebels' intentions, specifically whether they wished the king good riddance, he replied, "Well, that's what we want, that there be no king and no pope."[52] Josef Eduardo de Cardenas, the erudite parish priest from Tabasco concerned with luxury's enervating effects, called for a national ecclesiastical council—Pistoia being the most famous one in recent memory—and noted that over the centuries the church had added cardinals and other hierarchs to its early egalitarian core structure and should now return to that more glorious time.[53] In the context of a rebellion led in part by excommunicated priests, this call to return to a less hierarchical church took on renewed urgency.

An 1813 debate called in Oaxaca by the rebels, for example, focused on the insurgency's relation to the church. It featured a local parish priest and former seminary vice-rector who insisted on the rebels' right to create ecclesiastical structures without the permission of the church hierarchy—which would most assuredly not be forthcoming. Clerics and the men and women of all classes who comprised the "Party of the American Nation," Manuel Sabino Crespo asserted at the debate, constituted the "real Church of Jesus Christ."[54] His most vocal opponent likened Crespo to Thomas Kramer, the English bishop imprisoned by Mary, and accused him of fomenting a schism. After hearing his arguments for radical democracy, forty-two of the gathering eighty-five electors voted for him in an election in Oaxaca's cathedral attended by the city's ecclesiastical and secular councils; he came in second in this vote for a representative to a larger insurgent council.[55] That this radical cleric's arguments were seriously entertained, historian Ana Carolina Ibarra persuasively argues, can be attributed to the numerous reform Catholic tracts that had circulated among Oaxaca's clergy in the years leading up to the rebellion.[56] Others echoed Crespo's concerns: "Renegade Dominician Fray Servando Teresa de Mier advised that the laity in company with their clergy—not the pope or even the king—should select bishops."[57]

Sanjuanistas like Quintana shared the insurgents' radical piety and much, but not all, of their politics, proving particularly enthusiastic about a trans-oceanic Spanish polity under the constitution rather than American independence from the Motherland. Quintana's ultramontanist *rutinero* detractors, however, placed him firmly in the rebel camp. Certainly he shared the radical reformist Catholic sensibility so favored by rebel intellectuals. His own son Andrés Quintana Roo was involved in three of the most important 1812 rebel publications: as an editor of the *Semanario Patriótico Americano* and as a contributor to *El Ilustrador Nacional* and *El Ilustrador Americano*. The elder Quintanas' critiques of public officials like Viceroy Venegas—he called him an animal and a beast, citing the Spanish Academy's definitions of these terms—expressed the extreme angst of a father forced to bear his rebel son's risk of capture and execution, his daughter's death by natural causes, his future daughter-in-law's confinement in a nunnery for her defense of his valiant son.[58]

But Quintana's was not a crusade for Mexican independence. The very year his son Andres presided over the insurgents' National Constitutional Assembly that declared their quest for Mexico's autonomy in 1813, Quintana penned a mock letter to rebel leader José María Morelos that suggested that the 1812 Constitution rendered the insurgent's struggle pointless. He even noted that without the constitution "ten years of despotism was preferable to ten minutes of anarchy." He and the rebel leader "would not be friends," he warned, until Morelos swore his allegiance to the great document.[59]

That said, Quintana did heed insurgent Carlos María de Bustamante's plea to publish in Quintana's newspaper *Clamores* a letter explaining Bustamante's loyalties and some musings on governance.[60] Bustamante rightly feared that he was about to meet the same grisly fate as other rebels. Eager for the public to read these exonerating documents, he also urged Quintana to disseminate the documents to papers in New Orleans, Baltimore, and Philadelphia and to send copies to Spanish exile, and reformist Catholic intellectual Juan Blanco White, who published the influential *El Español* in London.[61] And the Yucatecan editor expressed his sorrow over Viceroy Venegas' unjustifiable arrest of fellow newspaperman and reformist stalwart El Pensador Mexicano (The Mexican Thinker), Joaquin Fernández de Lizardi, after he politely asked the viceroy to reconsider his decision to try the colony's many rebel priests in secular courts—essentially a death sentence.[62]

In the pages of *Clamores*, Quintana provided a *tour de force* of erudition on Reform Catholic tenets on the scriptures, the Church Fathers, and the early church councils. Girded in this intellectual armor, he parried openly with ecclesiastical dignitaries. In an irony that repeated itself throughout the empire, reformist Catholic bishops found themselves lashed by a whip in part of their own making, publicly excoriated by an emboldened laity and lower clergy who found in conciliar authority a weapon against papal infallibility and even episcopal prerogatives—and who were fast distancing themselves from Bourbon churchmen's regalism episcopalism and embracing a more radical ecclesiology. Andres Quintana Roo supported Fray Servando Teresa de Mier's call to expand the Gallican idea of collective clerical infallibility to include the lower clergy, a provocative assertion that priests as well as bishops were legitimate judges of the faith. Quintana also advocated such a radical devolution of infallibility, and by his public invocation of conciliar authority, he engaged in a similar decentralization of theological reasoning. The results could be equally radical. A dramatic example emerged in his crusade against the archbishop of Mexico City when the latter endorsed the 1810 excommunication of rebel leader Miguel Hidalgo y Costilla and other rebel priests. Even those "barely versed in the canons, and in the firm facts of Spain's ecclesiastical history," could see that the Fourth Toledan Council that the bishop cited to justify excommunication for the rebels actually prescribed the exact opposite: Venegas the usurper, not Hidalgo the rebel, should bear the brunt of the church's anathamas.[63] The council, any careful reader would divine, actually ruled for a rebel who toppled a usurper to the throne, just as Hidalgo struggled to overturn not the legitimate king Ferdinand VII, but "a gang of evil-doers" who had risen without the king's authority; Viceroy Venegas was the usurper in New Spain's drama. So that his readers could grasp this truth, he noted that he included the "infallible voice of the councils so that they understood bishop Abad y Queipo's unpardonable flights of fancy."[64] If the councils were not enough to persuade readers, they could look to Church Fathers like Augustine, who found clear scriptural commands for withholding the sacraments but not for corporal removal of the faithful from the church.[65]

Insurgent intellectuals and supporters of the Cortes de Cádiz like Quintana knew full well that their embrace of the early church councils, their vernacular biblical exegesis, and their reformist ethics in opposition to Jesuit "laxism" placed them on the side of the Reform Catholic International within larger Catholic currents in the Atlantic world. The insurgent paper edited by Andrés Quintana Roo, the *Semanario Patriótico Americano*, noted that the nefarious Spanish banned all manner of political and religious books to better serve "ultramontanist pretensions." Here ultramontanism referred to clerics and laymen enthralled to the Holy Father, who literally resided "over the mountains" from France. Under the pope's direct authority, and with their extra vow of obedience to the Holy Father, the Jesuits were, by reformers' lights, the ultramontanist force par excellence, and the insurgent paper raked over the Jesuits' historical contretempts with reformers to identify their own precursors and enemies. In a famous 1747 case, the *Semanario Patriótico Americano* reported, the Spanish Inquisition, at the behest of King

Ferdinand VI and his Jesuit advisors, put French Jansenist intellectuals Nicole, Dugnet, and Arnaud on its list of prohibited books, where they remained as of its 1812 publication.[66]

Although later in the century Charles III would embrace Spain's large anti-Jesuit faction, in 1747 it was Pope Benedict XIV who defended the Jansenists from the ultramontanist Jesuits backed by the Crown. The insurgent paper noted that the Holy Father sent a spirited defense of the "erudite Cardinal Noris" to the king—who ignored it, polarizing Spain's inchoate religious factions. Italian Cardinal Enrico Noris' seventeenth-century *Vindicae augustinianae* and *Historia pelagiana* had carefully delineated the differences between Jansenism and Augustinian Catholicism.[67] That the insurgent paper championed these prohibited Jansenist writers, decried "ultramontanist pretensions," and defended Noris' subtle Augustinianism against the Jesuits' Molinism, indicates not only their awareness of these religious factions, but their forthright allegiance to the reform camp.

In the late eighteenth century, reformers had lobbied successfully for the study of ecclesiastical history and early church councils and discipline in university theology curriculums throughout the empire.[68] Charles III also reformed clerical education through a royal cedula of 1768 that created new diocesan seminaries headed by secular clergy. These seminaries prohibited Jesuit theology, focusing instead on reformist works.[69]

Behind their adoration of the early councils lurked a barely disguised attack on papal pretensions. With their numerous clerical, and even lay, participants these church councils arrived at truth through heated debate and discussion and thus implicitly challenged the pope, as well as scholastic respect for authority generally. Thus, reformers' oft-repeated injunctions to "return to the pristine purity" of the early church, with its conciliar authority structure, struck a blow against the very pinnacle of the church hierarchy: the Holy Father.[70] Insurgent mouthpiece the *Semanario Patriótico Americano* noted that two novelties fraudulently introduced in the church since the ninth century had proved particularly pernicious: universal bishops (the popes) and their insistence that they were kings of kings.[71]

In this the Sanjuanistas and rebel intellectuals swam happily in prevalent and powerful Reform Catholic currents. By the late 1780s, as Eamon Duffy points out, kings and princes in Catholic states controlled much of church life, vetting the publication of papal bulls and appeals to Rome, setting feast-day calendars, and even appointing bishops and abbots.[72] In this climate, papal nuncios provoked distrust, their power to ordain, confirm, and hear appeals considered a threat to royal prerogatives and the truth that lay in early church councils.

TRANSNATIONAL INTERNATIONALS

A trio of disputes serves to map the emerging transatlantic religious cohesion galvanized by the debates of the Cádiz Cortes. The case of the celebrated Bishop of Orense, Pedro Benito Antonio Quevedo y Quintano, provided a lightning rod for the ecclesiological rifts over sovereignty in Mérida's new press. The bishop had already achieved fame as a standard-bearer for the conservative cause among patriots fighting the French with his protests of the abdications of Charles IV and Ferdinand VII. When Napoleon abolished the Spanish Inquisition in 1808, the Central Junta defied the French order by appointing the Bishop of Orense to the position of inquisitor-general. Two years later the bishop became the president of the Council of the Regency of Spain and the Indies, the five-man successor body to the discredited Central Junta. From this position he argued vociferously against the convocation of the Cortes, then found himself presiding over it as a duty of his presidential office.[73]

If this were not visibility enough, the inaugural debate of the Cortes rendered the Bishop Orense a minority of one. On September 24, 1810, the deputies from Extremadura introduced a decree that simultaneously declared the monarchs' abdications void and the Cortes a legitimate, sovereign assembly empowered to reform the government. In an exuberant vote, the fundamental principles of absolutism were upended. The Bishop of Orense promptly resigned his presidency. When he also refused to swear allegiance to the Cortes as the decree required, he was briefly detained, and a flurry of vituperative pamphlets took up his cause. "It appeared," grumbled one of the bishop's opponents, "that the Bishop of Orense counted for more than the whole of the nation." In the face of such clamour for clemency, the prelate was permitted to return to his diocese, still defiant.[74]

The entire drama repeated itself in 1812, by which time Mérida's press was primed to join the increasingly harsh new journalistic tone. The trigger this time was the bishop's refusal to swear allegiance to the constitution, as mandated by the Cortes in highly choreographed empire-wide ceremonies that October. Swearing allegiance to the constitution meant accepting the limits it placed on the monarchy, another violation of the absent monarch's divine right. While citizens should obey the constitution as the law of the land, the bishop informed the regency, they should not be forced to endorse it as a positive good, and certainly not as a condition of employment. The Cortes' deputies were a gaggle "little despots" who forced ideological conformity, far more dangerous than a single despot. His candor was not appreciated: this time the Cortes voted four to one to banish him from Spain.[75]

The dispute was widely aired on both sides of the coalescing divide, aided by the Bishop of Orense's stature and his history of dramatic stances. It flared again with the Cortes' decree to abolish the Inquisition. When the Bishop of Orense backed his cathedral chapter's decision to not publish the decree, authorities detained the clerics and systematically removed his edict from church doors.[76] Other hierarchs also pushed back: the bishops of Santander, Oviedo, and Astorga refused to publish the abolition decree and fled their dioceses to avoid punishment.

Conservatives circulated the Bishop of Orense's work in Mérida, where the Sanjuanista-controlled constitutional city council declared it a "tapestry of contradictions, chicanery, and sophisms" that openly denied the constitution's validity. Not even rebel leader José María Morelos was as rebellious or revolutionary as the Bishop of Orense, Quintana declared in his exhortation to the city council to track down and punish whoever had reprinted the seditious work in the Yucatán.[77] As in Spain, the bishop became a villain for the liberal Sanjuanistas and a hero to the conservatives. After the king's return from exile, Mérida's conservative Provincial Deputation issued a widely circulating manifesto claiming they had been slandered by the liberal press, and that liberals had provoked the "tenebrous chaos of civil discord." The virtuous prelate, they explained, had been similarly persecuted for standing up to the Cortes' assault on royal authority.[78]

The new privilege of voting also produced disputes between the coalescing sides. In early 1813, the election for Cortes deputies from the Yucatán became a flashpoint between the Sanjuanistas and the conservative Provincial Deputation. The clash reveals each group's profoundly transatlantic allegiances and the close twinning of religion and politics. An electoral committee appointed by the deputation blocked a handful of Sanjuanistas from participation as electors. The group responded by dispatching cleric Agustín de Zavala to Cádiz to air their grievances. While their spokesman made the journey across the Atlantic, the constitutional city council boycotted the deputation's swearing-in ceremony, and both groups refused to sit next to each another at religious functions.[79]

Once in Cádiz, Zavala quickly found an ally from within the constellation of Reform Catholics. Father Miguel Ramos de Arizpe, a former professor of canon law at the seminary in Monterrey and a correspondent of both Mier and Grégoire, relayed the Sanjuanistas' cause to the Cortes, urging a formal investigation of the electoral infractions.[80] The liberal *El Conciso* lauded Zavala's defense of the constitution and the Cortes' willingness to entertain his appeal.[81] Although the election results ultimately stood, the Cortes praised Zavala and his associates for their patriotism.[82]

But this hardly settled the issue. From Mérida, Bishop Estéves y Ugarte dispatched reports to the minister of grace and justice in Cádiz giving the conservatives' version. According to His Eminence, Zavala had engaged in electoral irregularities himself and an ecclesiastical tribunal had charged him with disturbing the peace for his antics. Hinting that Zavala might be suspended and even excommunicated, the bishop asked imperial authorities to return him to Mérida.[83]

The city's partisan newspapers eagerly drew the connections for their readers. Liberal writers accused the bishop of acting on orders from the notorious Bishop of Orense and labeled his plans "servile, arbitrary and despotic."[84] Like the Bishop of Orense, too, the local bishop did not respect the constitution. They also linked the question of electors to the abolition of the Inquisition, one of the perennial issues dividing the two factions: the Yucatecan deputies who had won seats in Cádiz, the liberal Mérida papers reported, planned to bring back the Holy Office.[85]

However, the nascent liberal press was no match for the steady stream of denunciations flowing to imperial authorities from Yucatán's conservatives. They likened the Sanjuanistas to rebel parish priests Hidalgo and Morelos and glossed the conflict as a revolt against Bishop Esteves y Ugarte.[86] Father Zavala had defied his bishop, and although Cádiz hosted reform-minded Catholics from throughout the empire, it also housed the reformers' ultramontanist opponents. Apprehended by these ecclesiastical authorities and escorted through the streets in chains in full daylight, Agustín de Zavala was secreted to a Capuchin monastery in Cádiz to await a boat home, where he would face his bishop's judgement. Instead, he escaped and went into hiding in 1814. Zavala's advocate Ramos de Arizpe would prove less fortunate. He was apprehended in Ferdinand VII's roundup of liberals in 1814, and spent twenty months in a dungeon before being secluded in a Carthesian monastery in Valencia for four years.[87]

Electoral politics and the Bishop of Orense galvanized both sides of the empire-wide religious dispute. A third issue also divided Catholics on both sides of the Atlantic. In February of 1813, the Cádiz Cortes secured a long-sought goal of Reform Catholics by voting to abolish the Inquisition and replace it with Tribunals of the Faith (*Tribunales Protectores de la Fé*) under the direction of Spain's own bishops. The decision was to be publicized immediately from pulpits around the empire.[88] The question of how the church would police heresy and apostasy, like so many of the contentious issues that the Cortes addressed, was at heart a question of Roman versus episcopal and royal authority. The Inquisition's ultimate independence from the bishops and rulers of Spain had made it the target of resentment from eighteenth-century clerical reformers and regalists, who were themselves most often one and the same. Arguing with the tools of history, particularly their gloss on the early church, rather than abstract philosophical reason, reformers identified the Inquisition as an institution of recent vintage, a rupture with historical tradition rather than its continuation. Reformers' regalist and episcopalist arguments bore the influence of reformist luminary Juan Antonio Llorente. On the other side of the issue, conservatives had consistently supported the Inquisition's role in preventing the fragmentation of the faith by policing an orthodoxy ultimately defined by the Vatican. Accepting the historicist epistemology, they simply argued to opposite conclusions: the Inquisition carried with it the weight of tradition.[89] Conservatives rallied to its defense, making the mechanism for guarding the Catholic faith into a critical point of contention defining the two coalescing factions on both side of the Atlantic.

The underlying question of authority quickly became explicit in the controversy. The papal nuncio to Spain, Pietro Gravina, was caught urging the cathedral chapters of Malaga, Grenada, and elsewhere to resist the controversial decision. The Cortes retaliated by banishing the meddling Roman representative from the country, seizing his possessions, and issuing an empire-wide circular denouncing him for inciting a "civil war." The regency's circular evoked the monarchy's constant struggles with the papacy and reminded readers that the king had long exercised the right of refusal of papal edicts and utterances. By acting around the now-sovereign Cortes rather than through it, Gravina had overstepped his jurisdiction.[90]

As all the participants understood, however, this dispute was not confined to the territorial boundaries of peninsular Spain. Gravina's exile did not remove him as an active and widely recognized opponent of the Cortes' action against the Inquisition, for these affected the universal church as a whole. From Portugal he spelled out the ecclesiological claims that it indexed. First, his own expulsion was not an insult against the nuncio himself but an abrogation of papal authority. The pope, as the bishop of all the bishops, could not be overruled by territorial authorities on the question of who was to represent him in Spain, or anywhere else. Further, the Inquisition—the substance of the original dispute—was not a matter for the Cortes to decide; it was foundational to the unity of the church headed by the pope in Rome and affected all Christendom. The Inquisition impeded "schisms that flowed from the removal of the Pope from the Church's center." Without a single central enforcer of orthodoxy, the church could not hold together, and it was not some Spanish prelates' prerogative to open the universal church to this threat. Gravina's arguments also raised the epistemological markers of the wider debate: if, as the reformers contended, church history proved the Inquisition's recent vintage, the nuncio demanded to know how centuries of Spanish savants had failed to notice this fact: surely their documented support was also historical evidence. It was his detractors who promoted newly minted doctrines sprung from their own imaginations, he lamented; in what previous century had Spain not recognized the pope's writ? Gravina resisted reformers' oft-repeated assertion notion of a Spanish church: he himself was not a foreigner, an Italian, as they accused, but the representative of the universal church. Geographic divisions were irrelevant to the empire of faith. The papal diplomat exhorted his many readers to continue to pray for the captive Pope Pius VII and to remember the rallying cry "Long live religion and long live the king!"[91]

With the fundamental issues both legible to the broad literate public and unambiguously critical to the shape of the constitution under construction in Cádiz, the Gravina dispute became an episode deserving of wide public circulation on both sides of the religious divide. Conservative papers leapt to amplify the nuncio's arguments. One helpfully directed readers to Madrid's centrally located Brun bookstore, where they would find the nuncio's manifesto, his account of his exile, and documentation pertaining to his case. Liberal and bitingly satirical, the Cádiz paper *El Duende de los Cafes* (*The Café Elf*), in contrast, offered its readers an imagined visit to a conservative salon ("*tertulia de los serviles*"). In this fictional gathering, the correspondent purported to find "friars, clerics, and ex-inquisitors" raising a toast to Gravina's happy travels and vowing to send the poor exile gifts of "macaroni"—a barbed reference to the Italian nuncio's foreignness despite Rome's claims of universality. The *Gazeta de Valencia* denounced Gravina's insult to the Cortes' authority and pointedly offered the nuncio a boat to his next destination—which would certainly not be Spain.[92]

But in a sign of the transatlantic intellectual and theo-political communities forming around these debates, the Gravina dispute entangled a cast of New World players. For example, articulating the Regency's official position on Gravina was the responsibility of the interim minister of grace and justice, Manuel Antonio García-Herreros. A prominent leader of the Cortes' liberal faction, García-Herreros had roots on both sides of the Atlantic: born in the disputed region of La Rioja, he been sent at the age of eight to the household of an uncle in New Spain, and went on to study theology at Mexico City's Royal College of San Pedro, San Pablo, and San Ildefonso. He later returned to the peninsula, where he received a doctorate in canon law from the University of Alcalá de Henares.[93] In his denunciation of the nuncio, he turned his daunting erudition onto ecclesiology, placing the Cortes in the role of defender of the proper ordering of church governance. He raked over Spanish history to demonstrate that Gravina's high-handed circumvention of the Cortes' decision to abolish the Inquisition infringed on the king's traditional prerogatives over the church. In particular, the nuncio's rejection of the new Tribunals of the Faith violated the sovereign power's right to vet papal proclamations before their publication in Spain; that right had passed to the Cortes in the king's absence. Further, the prominent liberal asserted, nuncio Gravina's defense of the papacy violated the innate rights of bishops, the group that the

Cortes had appointed to direct the new tribunals. The Cortes had responded ap-
propriately by banishing him, and thus exiled, Gravina was no longer the pope's
representative to Spain.[94]

The opponents of the Inquisition feared that zealotry like Gravina's would lead
to the "blood-letting" plaguing other countries. Their apprehension proved prescient, although they did not anticipate that the violence would come from the
very monarch in whose name they were defending Spain's sovereignty against
Rome.[95] When the now decidedly absolutist and ultramontane Ferdinand VII disbanded the Cortes on May 4, 1814, García-Herreros, along with the regents and
twenty-four leading liberal Cortes delegates, were detained within the week. But
García-Herreros' personal experience of the Spanish religious turmoil was only
beginning. After five years in prison, García-Herreros served again as minister of
grace and justice during the Liberal Triennium. In 1823, the Holy Alliance's troops,
the famed One Hundred Thousand Sons of Saint Louis, restored Ferdinand VII's
absolutist authority. The king promptly exiled García-Herreros and 10,000 others.
He returned to Queen Regent María Cristina de Borbón's more liberal Spain in
1834, and, again minister of grace and justice, published the orders to expel the
Jesuits and close religious houses with fewer than a dozen residents, effectively
shuttering 900 monasteries.[96] Throughout these years, he stood firmly on the reformist side of the religious divide, a zealot himself in a conflict that continued to
divide peninsular Spain.[97]

Gravina's dispute with the Cortes, with all its ramifications, likewise made
headlines in Mérida, where readers read the conflict through the framework
of international church-state relations. El Miscelaneo, an organ of the radical
Sanjuanista-dominated constitutional Mérida city council, reprinted from
Havana a portrayal of reformers as defenders of the faith, martyrs besieged
by ultramontane fanatics whose actions discredited the worldwide church. In a
fatal decision for English Catholics, the article noted, tales of Spanish nuncio
Gravina's "scandalous conduct" proved decisive in Catholics' bid to serve in
both houses of England's parliament. The speaker of the House of Commons
had intervened particularly forcefully, citing Rome's constant meddling in civil
affairs and violation of state sovereignty. One MP had declared that Catholics'
blind obedience to the clergy and pope rendered them unfit members of a free
state, and had cited Gravina's antics as evidence. But for the pseudonymous
author, the reform currents were showing the way to redeem the good name
of Spanish Catholicism: wise Spanish clerics no longer tolerated the Pope's
usurpations of Spanish jurisdiction over the church. After all, it was a group
of priests that had reported Gravina's pro-Inquisition scheming to the civil
authorities.[98]

The abolition of the Inquisition similarly divided opinion in Mérida. The Sanjuanistas understood that a religion centered on conscience could not abide an institution like the Inquisition, and that the institution had not existed in the early church. They eagerly followed the Cortes' order, celebrating a solemn mass in the hermitage of San Juan to give thanks for the institution's abolition—exactly as was done in Cádiz churches several months earlier. Religious dignitaries, the military corps, and the Capitan General attended the ceremony. Although all the city's dignitaries received a cordial invitation to the event, droves of citizens could not disguise their opposition to the measure and stayed home in a silent show of support for the Inquisition. For weeks there was public grumbling about the Cortes' controversial decision and its implications for the rights of bishops against an overweening pope. The Sanjuanistas countered that the abolition announcement actually enhanced the decorum and purity of the faith, demonstrating the godliness of the constitution.[99] Quintana found proof of the constitution's worthiness in this action abolishing the Inquisition; rebelling against the constitutional government—even in the name of independence rather than ultramontanism—was defying the constitution's spirit of evangelism, the heart of the true religion that the Spanish nation should respect.[100]

THE SANJUANISTAS AND RADICAL DEMOCRACY

In a pattern that would repeat itself throughout Latin America, *El Miscelaneo* echoed Spanish reformers' call to curb papal prerogatives over Spanish bishops and sovereigns. But the Mérida paper also went beyond the regalism and episcopalism of Bourbon reformers to champion the authority of parish priests. Over the centuries, its pages warned, the lower clergy's prerogatives and revenues had been usurped by the ecclesiastical hierarchy. Did Gravina really imagine that Spaniards would abandon the precious liberties of their church—liberties decreed by Spanish councils through the centuries and backed by the holy doctors of the church who had flourished there? Who gave the nuncio the right to overrule the will of the nation, as expressed by the elected Cortes deputies? Did he think that the riches and privileges people of his class enjoyed made him superior to the people? If so, this prince of the church was gravely mistaken. These riches would last only until the Cortes mustered the will to elevate parish priests and redirect revenues to their pockets, thereby ending the misery that the "canonical aristocracy" had imposed.[101]

The Sanjuanistas' spiritual leader, Father Velázquez, had a solution to the "canonical aristocracy" savaged by *El Miscelaneo*. Taking a page from the controversial Council of Pistoia and France's constitutional clergy, he called for the popular

A la NACION ESPAÑOLA *que apoyada en la* RELIGION *y excitada por la* LIBERTAD *derriba el edificio de la Inquisición. Huyen despavoridos la* SUPERSTI- *cion, el* FANATISMO *y la* HIPOCRESIA; *y la* VERDAD *aparece triunfante en el ayre.*

FIGURE 1.2 In a pamphlet publicizing its decree of 1813 abolishing the Inquisition, the Cádiz Cortes (1810–1813) explained this allegorical image to readers as a guide to its contents: "The Spanish nation, supported by RELIGION and excited by LIBERTY, demolishes the building of the Inquisition. SUPERSTITION, FANATISM and HYPOCRISY flee in terror; and the TRUTH appears triumphant in the air." Many delegates to the Cortes understood themselves to be acting on behalf of "true religion" in authoring the empire's first constitution and encouraged this conjoining of religion and liberty in the tradition of the ancient church councils. By Manuel Alegre y Pedro Nolasco Gascó, after a painting by Antonio Rodríguez Onofre, in Cortes de España, *Discusión del proyecto de decreto sobre el Tribunal de la Inquisición* (Cádiz, ES: Emprenta Naciónal, 1813). Biblioteca Nacional de España.

election of bishops. Velázquez's demand for a more democratic church was revealed by cleric Juan Esteban Rejón, a Sanjuanista sympathizer, during an interrogation led by the emboldened vicar general of the bishopric, Juan María Herrero, in 1814, the year of the king's return and the abrogation of the Constitution of 1812. Rejón conceded that he had indeed attended *tertulias* (salons) in San Juan Bautista chapel. As he faced a high-stakes inquiry into the group's actions, he scrambled to save himself.

He had parted ways with the Sanjuanistas after attending a sermon given by conservative cathedral canon Leonardo Santander de Villavicencio, he explained. In retaliation, Velázquez shunned him and spread rumors about his loyalty. Santander clashed frequently with the Sanjuanistas. Bishop Esteves y Ugarte appointed him to a coveted theology chair at the local seminary. He later insinuated to imperial authorities that a Sanjuanista had attempted to assasinate the cathedral canon in his home after his sermon on the Day of Purification of Our Lady. In addition to wisdom on Mary's immaculate conception, the sermon had included some fire and brimstone against "subversive doctrines."[102]

Rejón remembered Velázquez saying that the people should elect their bishops, a precept that formed part of this Sanjuanista leader's larger democratic project, which included the elimination of ancien régime hierarchies. But elected bishops and the equality of citizens were not the only reformist themes batted about in this church salon: the Sanjuanistas spoke ill of ecclesiastical hierarchs, and they encouraged Indians in Mérida and neighboring towns to refuse the new tithe payments to the church.[103] When some Indian leaders from the neighborhood surrounding the hermitage referred to Velázquez using an honorific before his name, he shot back that "the time of those humiliations had passed. . . you should not call anyone Señor Whoever, just Whoever, especially when addressing clerics." Velázquez also dined at the same table with Indians and even with mulattoes and blacks and held the Inquisition in contempt, Rejón reported to his interrogators.[104]

Rejón may well have embellished his story to save himself, but the gist of it rings true: a year before, in 1813, the conservative clerics of the Cathedral Chapter had reported to the Council of the Indies that Velázquez connived with Mérida's Sanjuanista-dominated city council. These *rutineros* noted that Velázquez pointed to popular acclaim to justify an appeal to become the diocese's bishop; as absurd as this might sound, they elaborated, it was made all the more ridiculous by Velázquez's lowly position; the aspiring bishop currently served as a chaplain in the hermitage of San Juan and had been censored by the reigning bishop. The times were "fecund with odd occurrences," the *rutinero* clerics marveled, but the council should regard any forthcoming appeal from the lowly cleric with suspicion.[105]Although he failed to elucidate specific examples, Velázquez's clerical

nemesis Francisco de Paula Villegas also underscored the priest's "constant failures to pay rightful respect to the prince and prelate of the Church." This track
record of disrespect for church hierarchs, and his radical ideas about church ecclesiology rendered Velázquez's apology for failing to pay homage to the pope at a recent Holy Thursday celebration in the cathedral disingenuous, Villegas insisted.[106]

As well, Rejón insisted that Velazqúez stood idly by as his sidekicks Lorenzo
de Zavala and Quintana denied the church's doctrine on hell and purgatory. This
was a stock accusation against rebel priests, and a not entirely illogical concern
given reformed Catholics' pared-down piety and near-total dependence on God's
grace for salvation. At its most extreme, the reform movement could be read by
its enemies as at least implicitly representing a subtle critique of the Doctrine of
the Keys—the church's necessary mediation between the soul and God. In his
1810 public proclamation against the Inquisition's charge that he denied hell, rebel
leader Miguel Hidalgo y Costilla tied them up in their own logic: "They say that
I deny hell, but then they say I said a Pope was in hell—how can it be both?"[107]

The Sanjuanistas' dominance of Mérida's public sphere of letters during the brief
heyday of the 1812 Constitution, and the religious convictions they shared with
the liberals of the Cortes de Cádiz, emboldened them in their battle with *rutinero*
authorities. In control of Mérida's official censorship board and the constitutional
city council, these reformist Catholics erroneously remained confident they could
defend their religious and political advances under the constitution even after the
return of King Ferdinand VII in 1814. Sanjuanistas on the city council and the
censorship board openly leapt to the defense of the imperiled constitution upon
the King's return to power, and in so doing sealed their fate. The Sanjuanistas
were no longer regalists but the king most certainly was: Ferdinand VII sought to
restore monarchical absolutism to the empire, and unlike his Bourbon absolutist
precursor Charles III, he was no reformist Catholic. The king would now support
the regalist ultramontanism now associated with the Jesuits.[108]

SANJUANISTA DOMINANCE UNRAVELS

Their candor would prove their undoing. In a public declaration signed by the
Sanjuanistas on the censorship board, the men insisted they would not respect
a king who disavowed the constitution and noted that the document's guarantee
of press freedom "allows us to confront tyrants." Reformist Catholicism had now
outrun its regalist twin. They would give their last drop of blood before seeing the
great document "violated even slightly."[109] City council members also decried the
restoration of absolutism in statements printed in the Sanjuanista press. Two city
councilmen—both avowed Sanjuanistas who had granted Pedro Almeida power of

attorney to represent them against the bishop's earlier allegations of their scandalous and irreligious behavior— joined Father Almeida in noting that for themselves and for the people, they would disobey any order that contravened the 1812 Constitution. The reform-minded city councilmen asserted that "they had sworn to sustain a government system that assures our rights" and would resist "attacks that intended to enslave them afresh." "Are we by chance the playthings of despots? . . . Have we not embraced our dignity? Sacred Constitution! Extraordinary Cortes! Death to tyrants!" they exclaimed.[110]

Not six days later, on July 26, 1814, more prudent city-council minds came to the fore. Rutinero stalwart Pacheco had underscored the danger represented by the circulation of Ildefonso Montoré, Almeida, and García Sosa's pledge to disobey the king if he failed to swear allegiance to the constitution, the city council noted. And the Deputation Provincial insinuated that neither Almeida nor García Sosa had displayed any love of their sovereign prior to their dramatic pledge to uphold the constitution. These two miscreants should be removed from their council positions, the captain general suggested. The city council's more conservative members also expressed their satisfaction at receiving Lorenzo de Zavala's retraction of his support for the Junta de Censura's published excoriation of tyrants and defense of the constitution. The stone inscription lauding the constitution had been reduced to fragments on the morning of July 23, and the council urged the creation of a new monument with the royal insignia and the king's name in gold letters. The council minutes also reported that henceforth the political labels liberal, *rutinero*, and Sanjuanista would not be allowed in public gatherings or published works, and no meetings would be held at the Hermitage of San Juan by order of the captain general. With the return of absolutism, party affiliations were considered an affront to the king's sovereignty.[111]

Mérida's more cautious city councilmen were right: the theo-political winds had shifted with the king's return. By a decree of July 21, 1814, Ferdinand deemed it fitting that the Holy Office of the Inquisition should resume its exercise of powers.[112] In Spain, the manifesto of the Persians signed by *rutinero* stalwart and Yucatán Cortes Deputy Alonso y Pantiga contributed to the dramatic arrest and detention of liberal Cortes deputies on the evening of May 10, while Ferdinand moved to remove reformers and place conservative clergy in prebends and episcopal sees.[113]

The round-ups of reformers in Yucatán followed closely the persecution of Cortes' liberals in Spain. The crackdown on the Sanjuanistas extended beyond Mérida. Upon receiving the news of Ferdinand's abrogation of the constitution, an edict officially issued on May 4, 1814, a clutch of male and female revelers in the town of Izamal sallied forth into the streets on July 23, singing and shouting "*¡Viva!*" to King Ferdinand VII after each stanza. Their celebrants later repaired to a private home a block from the town's plaza, where one Father Castillo joined them on his guitar. Liberal city councilman José Joaquin Rivas and three constables arrived on the scene and violently seized a reveler, declaring his shouting irreverent; Manuel Lope demanded to know if it was a crime to shout "*¡Viva!*" to his sovereign. As Lope languished in prison, news of his travails trickled back to Mérida. Captain General Artazo ordered an elaborate investigation. The witnesses labeled Rivas a notorious liberal and a friend of Sanjuanista Pedro Elizalde and denounced several other liberal office holders who had menaced the town during the constitution's reign. Artazo removed Rivas from his position as first city councilman.[114]

On July 30, 1814, Artazo seized printer Josef Francisco Bates and packed him off to Campeche and then to San Juan de Ulua prison off the coast of Veracruz.[115] He used the pretext of a political commission to lure an unsuspecting Lorenzo de Zavala and then summarily dispatched him to the dungeon of the public jail, clapping him in chains—all without legal niceties. The charges centered on Zavala's authorship of the damning censorship board and city council documents that had pledged allegiance to the constitution. Writing from prison in Veracruz and striking a cautious note, Zavala did not admit to authorship of either document, merely membership in both bodies, and protested the extralegal conduct of his case. How, asked the imprisoned editor of *El Aristarco*, could his tormentors "take a subject from the bosom of his family, manhandle him, and put him in the dungeon of a fortress without first taking his confession?"[116] The same day of Zavala's arrest, Artazo seized Quintana, chained him in Mérida's public jail, and encircled him with bayonet-wielding guards; he later whisked him off to Campeche, where he was held for fifty-seven days before being transported—still in chains—to San Juan de Ulúa.[117]

The Sanjuanista–controlled Junta de Censura dramatically declared in July of 1814 that the king had an obligatory duty to the constitution. The Sanjuanista clerics affiliated with this challenge faced the wrath of ecclesiastical authorities while the laymen fell under the jurisdiction of the secular state apparatus. After a hearing in front of an ecclesiastical tribunal in early August, the vicar general of the bishopric ordered the arrest and confinement of Junta de Censura member Father Manuel Ximenéz Solis. Although not a signatory to the daring manifesto, and although under intense questioning he fingered Lorenzo de Zavala as its principal author, Ximenéz spent the next three years confined to the Franciscan Convent of the Mejorada.[118] Less than a week before Ximenéz Solis' sentencing, Vicente María Velázquez was dragged before a tribunal that included Captain General Artazo and a slew of witnesses who attested to his radically democratic notions of church governance.[119] He too was whisked to seclusion in the Franciscan convent. In 1815, a royal order demanded the two men's transportation to Spain, but with few boats, and corsairs menacing off the coast, they remained secluded within the Franciscan monastery. Three years later, an increasingly blind and sick Ximenéz, and an exasperated Velázquez, feared perpetual seclusion and implored the vicar general to at least pronounce a fixed time sentence. Aid came in the form of a letter from Asesor General Gavilán to Captain General Castro y Ataoz dated around May 24, 1817. After careful examination of the cases in front of the ecclesiastical tribunal, Gavilán concluded that Junta de Censura members had been ignorant of the king's May 4, 1814, order abrogating the constitution and that Ximenéz and Velasquez had renounced their error. By August 17 of 1817, Herrero ordered Ximenéz's release. The exact date of Velázquez's freedom is unclear.[120]

Both the Council of the Indies and King Ferdinand VII would ratify Captain General Artazo's decision to imprison the three Sanjuanistas. Based on reports from the nearby town of Campeche's city council, as well as an earlier report from one of Yucatán's representatives to the Cortes, the Council of the Indies concluded that the Sanjuanistas had ignored the bishop's orders against nocturnal meeting, wielded too much influence over government, and should cease to convene; they recommended a more thorough investigation be conducted into their machinations. When King Ferdinand received—in or around June of 1815— the city council and censorship board's incendiary publications, he ordered the authors' immediate arrest and prompt transportation to Spain.[121]

Bishop Estéves y Ugarte and the ultramontanist *rutinero* forces' 1814 victory would prove to be shortlived. Even from the formidable fortress prison of San Ulúa, Sanjuanista pens would not be stilled; and indeed for the three imprisoned Sanjuanista stalwarts, liberation was near. In July and August of 1816, Bates, Zavala, and Quintana fired off appeals to a confident and firmly entrenched Ferdinand VII. All of them underscored their longstanding loyalty to the king: Bates had published and energetically distributed the glad tidings of Ferdinand's 1814 liberation and had donated a large load of grain to the royalist troops in 1808, he reported. Zavala and Quintana reminded their sovereign that it was not the Sanjuanistas but their tormentors, Captain General Artazo and Bishop Estéves y Ugarte, who had ordered the removal of his image from Mérida's Franciscan church when his 1808 captivity became officially known to Yucatecans. And Quintana reported that the perfidious Captain General Artazo even ordered Meridians to remove the king's image from their hats, while he, in contrast, dedicated an 1814 edition of his newspaper to His Highness.[122]

The three Sanjuanistas also seized the opportunity to decry inhumane treatment and the absence of any semblance of proper judicial procedure during their initial arrest and later confinement. Their letters rehearsed a litany of horrors. He had languished, Quintana reported, for 732 days shackled and incommunicado in the notorious prison off the coast of Veracruz. He had indeed been a supporter of the constitution, the Sanjuanista newspaper editor proudly admitted, but so too had the king, after all; it had been the law of the land. Leniency had marked the king's response to the traitors who had gathered at the Café Lebante in Madrid to conspire against the throne in 1815, Quintana further underscored, so he expected nothing less for a faithful vassal like himself. Against all odds, the bedraggled Sanjuanistas had struck the right note, and on September 20, 1816, with the approval of the Council of the Indies, the King ordered them released.[123]

The Sanjuanistas' appeals for clemency revealed that they understood themselves as part of a polity riven into two warring factions. Quintana's son, the priest Tomas Domingo Quintana Roo, reminded His Excellency that throughout the empire, not just in Merida, two parties had emerged during recent years. Given Captain General Artazo's spies and mysterious nocturnal proceedings, witnesses proved loath to testify for fellow party members, to the detriment of men like his father.[124]

City councilman Ildefonso Montoré, Father Velázquez, and Sanjuanista spokesman and cleric Pedro Almeida had also apparently fallen victim to the revived *rutinero* forces during their giddy first months back in power after the king's 1814 return. Montoré appealed to Captain General Artazo in early 1815, claiming to have been imprisoned in Mérida's Ciudadela de San Benito since September of 1814; the city councilmen who authored the pamphlet urging the king to swear allegiance to the constitution, he underscored, had doubted the veracity of the news of the king's abrogation of the constitution on May 4, 1814. When Bishop Estéves arrived in October of the previous year, he asserted, he had gone to him to retract his loyalty to the constitution and pledge his allegiance to Ferdinand. In 1820, the liberated Quintana and Velázquez would use their new positions on the Deputation Provincial to demand cleric José Almeida's release from the Inquisition, which the new Cortes (1820–1823) had again banned.[125]

THE SACRED HEART OF JESUS: THE ULTRAMONTANISTS IN POWER

From the safety of 1815, with king and pope restored, the constitution abrogated, and the Sanjuanista leadership in chains, Bishop Estéves y Ugarte and clerics from the cathedral chapter had no problem fingering the San Juan Bautista hermitage as the site of a church schism. During the time of the constitution, the church not only hosted gatherings of avowed liberals, the clerics lamented, but sponsored an unofficial Confraternity of the Blessed Sacrament—a signature devotion of reformist Catholics throughout the empire. Reformist Catholics founded numerous

such confraternities during the late eighteenth century as part of their campaign
to focus worship on Christ's sacrifice and the mediation of holy people whose acts
were detailed in the scriptures rather than on the plethora of saints from later centuries. As well, every Sanjuanista cleric turned up for the funerals and other life
events of the liberal faithful. Yet these reformist clerics never asked the cathedral
chapters' permission to perform these ceremonies and refused to turn over fees
rightly belonging to other clergy. The bishop was determined to stop the financial
hemorraging. He prohibited chaplains in the town's hermitages and chapels from
saying mass or participating in a funeral without a license and prior payment of
parish fees, and threatened recidivists with removal from their posts.[126]

With the *rutineros* in firm control of church and state again, the obventions
dispute came to a temporary end. When the restored King Ferdinand VII ordered
a report on each of his provinces in June of 1814, former Yucatán Cortes deputy
Ángel Alonso y Pantiga seized the opportunity to tell his sovereign of the crisis
confronting that peninsula's rural priests.[127] Alonso y Pantiga was a conservative
stalwart. He had been one of José Matías Quintana's principal accusers and was
no stranger to the king: earlier that year he and sixty-eight other conservative
Cortes deputies had penned a manifesto of allegiance to his majesty to celebrate
his return to Spain. Democracy, they assured the Ferdinand VII, was unstable and
excluded the nobility, destroyed hierarchy, and left society without splendor; that
the Cortes had made overseas subjects equal and declared press freedom also came
in for criticism from the sixty-nine signatories.[128] So moved was Fernando VII by
Alonso y Pantiga's implorings that he took the case to the Council of the Indies
himself in 1814 and issued an edict in January of 1815 reinstating the obventions.[129]

Yucatán's ultramontanists also sought to seize the moment of conservative
ascendance in 1814 to win back Christians' hearts and minds through popular allegiance to conservative cults, in particular the Sacred Heart of Jesus. In 1675,
as French visitationist nun Margaret Mary Alocoque contemplated the Blessed
Sacrament, a miracle occurred: Jesus appeared and displayed his heart to her.
"Behold this heart," he exclaimed, "which has loved men so much . . . and in return
I receive from the greater number nothing but ingratitude."[130] She promised him
she would set aside the Friday after the Feast of Corpus Christi for honoring his
heart. The celebration's date and the location of her vision were significant: the
late seventeenth century was the height of the Jesuits' contretemps with the
Jansenists about the frequency of absolution, the pinnacle of the debate between
attrition and contrition. Jansenists like Saint Cyran and Antoine Arnauld wanted
to delay absolution to impress upon the penitent their dependence on God's
grace; Jesuits counseled frequent communion in keeping with their emphasis on
the importance of the church's sacraments and the individual will to salvation.[131]

The Sacred Heart's eucharistic overtones sanctified the Jesuits. As well, authors praising the Sacred Heart employed the sensual language and imagery of the baroque piety so anathema to austere reformers. Juan de Loyola's popular 1739 *Meditaciones del Sagrado Corazon*, for example, compared Christ's heart to a divine sun spinning off fire and light to ignite the world in the flames of divine love—an image worthy of the sensorial experiences of hell and Christ's passion depicted by Jesuit founder Ignatius Loyola himself in the *Spiritual Exercises*.[132] Through her own doggedness and with the help of her Jesuit confessor, Mary Margaret quickly made her vision of the wounded, flaming heart surrounded by a crown of thorns into one of the Jesuits' signal devotions, ubiquitous in Catholic Europe and New Spain and a potent symbol of the besieged order in the eighteenth century.

Indeed the cult's popularity was immense. From 1690 to 1740, the faithful established 700 confraternities dedicated to the Sacred Heart in the papal city.[133] In New Spain, the first Sacred Heart confraternity sprang up in 1733 in Mexico City, with establishments soon following outside the capital.[134] Under the direction of the Jesuits, public devotion to the image grew. Increasingly bedeviled by enlightened despots and religious reformers, who worked in tandem in the Spain of Charles III and were indeed one and the same, in 1771 the Jesuits struck a characteristically dramatic blow against their austere, ceremony-adverse enemies. That May they hosted a spectacle in Rome's Amphitheater of Titus featuring a large image of Jesus with a gaping aperture in his breast. The hole revealed a bleeding heart spewing holy wafers, one of which Christ offered to Mary Margaret Alacoque. Later the same day, the order distributed many thousands of small medals to the populace bearing the images of the hearts of Jesus and Mary.[135] In 1765, just two years before their expulsion from the Spanish Empire, Pope Clement XIII approved the first official liturgy for the Sacred Heart and renowned artist Pompeo Batoni painted an eye-catching painting of the devotion for the Jesuits' main church, Il Gesú in Rome.[136] In France, too, the cult became a symbol of the Jesuits and of papal and regal authority. Peasants in the rebellious Vendée area stitched Sacred Heart emblems into their clothing before taking up arms against the revolution, and bore banners with the image into battle.[137] Nuns in New Spain sported badges on their chests with the emblem to mark their devotion to the cult and to the Jesuits after their expulsion from Spain and her empire.[138] Others displayed their support for the banished order more discreetly, donning small metal lockets about the size of pocket watch with illustrations of the Sacred Heart painted on copper, wood, shell, or bone.[139]Batoni's image that hung in Il Gesú was a particularly popular locket in New Spain after the Jesuits' 1767 banishment from the empire.[140]

FIGURE 1.3 Beginning in the late seventeenth century, the Sacred Heart became a potent focus of the extravagant devotionalism that so distressed reformist Catholics. It was a favorite of the Jesuits, with its eucharistic associations, but also widely popular as a representation of divine compassion for suffering humanity. Mexican artist José de Páez's painting, circa 1770, depicts the Sacred Heart of Jesus with Saint Ignatius of Loyola and Saint Louis Gonzaga. World History Archive/Alamy Stock Photo.

Evidence suggests that the faithful kept the memory of the Jesuits and their signature cults alive in New Spain well after the expulsion. Not only did nuns sport badges with the Sacred Heart, but prophecies and revelations of their impending return were also legion in the years immediately after 1767, particularly among religious women. Miraculous occurrences linked to their return agitated the faithful. The most famous case involved the crippled four-year-old son of a Mexico City merchant who walked perfectly one day, according to astonished family members, and exclaimed that the Jesuits would soon return—rumors of the good news circulated widely.[141]

Dressing as a Jesuit also became a viable way for imposters to incite public generosity. A notorious case arose in Toluca, where Jesuits had led a 1763 mission to win devotees to one of their signature causes, the Marian cult of Our Lady of Light. This advocation of Mary was specifically denounced by regalist bishops in 1771 at the Fourth Mexican Provincial Council, but its devotees were not easily swayed and became the prey of a faux Jesuit named Antonio who claimed to be one of the missionaries. Antonio maintained himself by beseeching *pulqueria* (tavern) patrons for alms in the 1780s. Similar swindles proliferated where the Jesuits' supporters forged on even in their official absence.[142]

For the same reasons that the Sacred Heart became a rallying point for the embattled Jesuits and their supporters throughout the Catholic world, it was an object of ferocious criticism by their reformed Catholic opponents. In the late eighteenth century, Scipione de' Ricci, the bishop of Prato and Pistoia who presided over the controversial Reform Catholic 1786 Synod of Pistoia, decorated his dining room with a painting of Emperor Joseph II of Austria ripping up a pious picture of the Sacred Heart.[143] In a 1781 pastoral letter, Ricci linked rejection of the cult to Christian manliness, underscoring that "Christians have made themselves a laughing stock to unbelievers by their mass of fantastical, womanish, and ridiculous devotions . . . Rome only at the last minute permitted it but did not encourage it."[144] French constitutional cleric Henri Grégoire dedicated an entire chapter of his 1810 *Histoire des sects religieuses* to ridiculing the cult of the Sacred Heart and elsewhere noted that it served to "consecrate despotism."[145] The Fourth Mexican Provincial Council held in 1771 and presided over by regalist bishops fretted over the proliferation of Jesuit-led cults like the Sacred Heart and Our Lady of Light. King Charles III issued a 1767 edict ordering the removal of images of the Sacred Heart from all churches under Spanish political jurisdiction.[146]After the Jesuits' expulsion from the Spanish Empire and before handing one of their Madrid churches over to the reformist stronghold that was the Colégio de San Isidro, Crown minister Manuel de Rodo explained that removing images of the Sacred Heart and Our Lady of Light from the premises was essential to the project of "erasing the memory of these people and their superstitions."[147]

Objections to the cult most frequently included its novelty—no such devotions appeared in the Bible or the writings of the Church Fathers—and its association with the mystical, sensorial piety exemplified for reformist Catholics by the Jesuits and the cult's most renowned visionary, Marguerite Mary Alcoque. In the late eighteenth century, the empire's reform-minded and regalist bishops and the king himself were well placed to influence popular piety, but the cult of the Sacred Heart proved well-nigh intractable to their extirpation campaigns. It again became a rallying point for ultramontanist forces throughout the empire with the 1814 return of the Spanish king and the pope from their respective exiles and with the increasingly cosy relationship between crown and scepter, dramatically represented by King Chares IV's welcoming reception of Pius VII back to Rome on May 24, 1814.[148]

Back in the Yucatán, the powerful and condensed meanings of the Sacred Heart were not lost on Bishop Estéves y Ugarte. Even with king and pope firmly entrenched, with the Sanjuanista leadership slowly creeping back into the city from their trials, the bishop feared another uptick of reform piety and democratic politics and sought allies. Even a dungeon-wearied Quintana or a chastened Velázquez was not to be underestimated. Or perhaps as a dutiful shepherd he simply saw an opportunity to return his flock to ultramontane Catholic orthodoxy. Either way, Bishop Estéves Ugarte knew to focus attention on the Sacred Heart—and even to reach out to the Jesuits, who had never had a particularly secure toe-hold in the Franciscan-dominated Yucatán but who had been formally restored to the empire in 1815.[149] So Bishop Estéves y Ugarte wrote to the Holy Father, asking him for the blessings needed to advance the cult. Pius VII responded with plenary indulgences and remission of sins: a whopping 200 days of reprieve from penalties for the penitents who visited a church with an image of the Sacred Heart and confessed and received communion every month for a year, beginning on the Friday after Corpus Christi. So that everyone could partake of this gift from the church's warehouse of grace, he ordered images of the Sacred Heart placed in every church in the Yucatán.[150] As they did throughout New Spain, nuns proved enthusiastic allies in the cult's promulgation, and the bishop established a confraternity dedicated to the Sacred Heart in the church of the Monasterio de Religiosas Concepcionistas.[151] Overcome with joy upon the king's return, the subdelegate of the town of Mama, Juan Antonio de Castro y Toledo, penned a lengthy poem of praise to the Sacred Heart and dedicated it to the bishop. To show his appreciation, Estéves y Ugarte granted forty days of indulgences for each stanza.[152]

The Holy Father, too, had been battered by regalists and more radical reformist Catholics alike in recent years, nowhere more than by the Cádiz Cortes and by Latin America's fledgling decolonization movements. So Estéves y Ugarte brought the church's treasures of grace to bear on restoring Rome's centrality to the faith. The holy stairs opposite Rome's Basilica of Saint John Lateran, a former papal palace, had captured the imagination of the faithful and in particular numerous popes: here, the church taught, were the very twenty-eight steps that Jesus ascended on his way to trial by Pontius Pilate. At the top of the stairs, pilgrims

peered into a small chapel known as the Holy of Holies, a private oratory of medi-
eval popes. Replicas of the steps graced Christendom, including, apparently, the
Yucatán, and Estéves y Ugarte offered forty days of indulgences for ascending the
extant replicas of the stairs in the peninsula, as well as forty days for ascending
the ones he had appealed to the pope to establish. The bishop reiterated that the
popes had always supported the cult and that Pius VII had amplified and expanded
the indulgences granted to pilgrims.[153] A year later, in September of 1817, Pius VII
granted those who ascended the stairs on their knees nine years of indulgences
for each step. Another pamphlet that circulated in the Yucatán in 1816 began with
paeans to Saint Peter as the first apostle openly to acknowledge Christ's divinity;
Estéves y Ugarte offered forty days of indulgences for reciting the prayers contained therein.[154]

Miracles, processions, Mary's immaculate conception, unchecked papal power,
and the regular orders—these flashpoints of ultramontanist piety received renewed attention during the brief interlude of conservative dominance after
the dismissal of the Cortes de Cadiz in 1814 and the Sanjuanistas' banishment
from Mérida's streets and churches. During these years, the Sanjuanistas, who
had briefly dominated Mérida's lively public sphere of letters, ceded their pride
of place to more ultramontanist pamphleteers—with Bishop Estéves y Ugarte's
blessing. Just outside Mérida lived the miraculous Virgin of Ytzmal. Our Lady had
herself chosen to reside in the pueblo, a 1816 publication that circulated in the area
reported: when conquistadors tried to remove her to Valladolid, she had refused
to budge, rendering herself immobile. She had, however, consented to be escorted
into Mérida at least three times over the course of the centuries, most memorably
in 1630 when she helped rescue the city from plague. To show their gratitude, the
author of the 1816 pamphlet recommended that the city's faithful participate in a
novena to the Immaculate Conception, nine days of acts of contrition and confession prior to the happy day of her birth.[155]

The regular orders were also a significant rallying point for conservatives.
Estéves y Ugarte told a sympathetic King Ferdinand VII that it was as an old man
with a bitter heart that he had read the November 1813 news in the *Gazeta of the
Regency* that the Cortes had ordered the regular orders to cede their parishes to the
secular clergy—a move that in one blow had destroyed the noble Franciscans who
had led the spiritual conquest of the Yucatán Peninsula and continued to serve its
majority Mayan population.[156]

Estéves y Ugarte used one of his most effective tools to shore up respect for
the Holy Father's absolute authority: the pulpit. In a sermon to his Mérida flock,
the bishop recounted the European side of the great drama in which they were all
involved. French troops had occupied Rome in January of 1808, rendering Pope

Pius VII a prisoner in his own palace with eight French cannons aimed at his windows. He spent four years in an episcopal palace on the Italian Riviera before being whisked away for a twelve-day journey to Fountainebleu, where he signed over his temporal powers in 1813 at Napoleon's behest. But on May 24, 1814, the bishop reminded his listeners, the carriage of the liberated pope reached Rome's gates to great fanfare. In 1815, the Congress of Vienna returned to him almost all of the lands previously lost.[157] Vile Jansenists had taken advantage of the pope's seven-year captivity to suggest the church could easily forge ahead without him, Estéves y Ugarte further informed his Mérida audience. During this unfortunate time, atheists, Jansenists, *philosophes*, and Calvinists had cavorted with Satan and spent huge sums on their suspect agendas. Love of novelty and disobedience to the pope had fueled numerous heresies, the bishop roundly concluded. The pope was back, however, and he had returned the Jesuits to their rightful place in the church. Also back was Ferdinand VII. Estéves y Ugarte had triumphed over his Sanjuanista enemies; and, at least temporarily, the bishop had friends in all the right places.[158]

Contemporaries readily saw the intimacy between religion and politics. A pamphlet describing the pope's travails during his captivity circulated in the Yucatán in 1816 and made explicit the religion of politics and the politics of religion. The French author asserted that he "could not help but notice" the affinities between religious proclivities and the state during the French Revolution. In 1791, the presbyterianism of the church could not be separated from the democracy of the state; in 1793, the destruction of the religious cult mirrored the collapse of government; and in 1795 a fractured government found its counterpart in a vague and anemic piety. Happily, the Frenchman noted, in 1800 Catholicism and the monarchy emerged triumphant, the head of the church and of the state regaining their power to dictate faith and politics. Imagine, this ultramontanist Catholic proposed, what we could be done with the Holy Father back![159]

The Sanjuanistas' reformist Catholicism could not be separated from their democratic sensibility and support for the 1812 Constitution. Reform Catholicism provided a sacred imprimatur to conciliar, democratic authority, and it emboldened the laity and lower clergy to spar with hierarchs based on their knowledge of the democratic practices upheld at national church councils throughout the centuries, particularly in Christianity's early centuries before false decretals aggrandized the popes' authority and demoted that of bishops and councils. And it provided an intellectual justification for a religion of conscience, not of force— hence reformers' abhorrence for the Inquisition and of the violence wreaked on recalcitrant Indians. Reformist Catholics throughout the Empire supported the Cortes de Cádiz because the Cortes brought worship and the church structure in line with their beliefs—in supporting the Cortes they were not supporting a secular government, but one dominated by priests and passionately religious laymen intent on transforming man's relationship to God. But reformers deemed women incapable of the new patriotic and republican austerity that marked a man as eligible to lead his male equals and to guide women whose extravagance marked them as in need of tutelage. And if the ultramontanists seemed timeless and anti-modern, they were anything but—what we perhaps what is brewing in Yucatán foreshadows a new power base in women.[160]

Throughout the nineteenth century, women would prove conservative stalwarts, peopling the pews and organizing in defense of ultramontanist causes. Mérida witnessed an adumbration of this powerful new conservative alliance in its early stages. While the Sanjuanista leadership embraced the constitution and eventually defended the document from the king, an organized group of Mérida women sprang into motion to welcome Ferdinand VII back to the throne in 1814. On July 26, several of the city's most prominent women appeared before the city council to request permission to hold a church function in honor of the monarch and ensure the presence of the troops and the city's other official bodies. The Provincial Deputation and the *rutinero* paper of record, *El Sabatino*, recounted the joyous tumult that occurred the next day; the events were later reported by ultramontanist papers in Spain.[161] The huge crowd spontaneously encircled the portrait of Fernand VII in the city council building and insisted on carrying it to the cathedral—but not before clerics, religious communities, and other authorities lined up in hierarchical order, the *ancien régime*'s social categories on display for the edification of all. The city's women carried the heavy portrait, even after the chivalrous tried to remove it from their "beautiful and delicate hands," and the daughters of Mérida's elite flung flowers taken from trays held by "distinguished subjects" at the image. Especially noticeable, the paper reported, was the "majestical solemnity" with which the marchers shredded the constitution into small bits.[162] They were not alone in their iconoclasm: two days before, *rutinero* official Basilio María Argaiz and priest Manuel Pacheco had dealt the first hammer blows to a plaque commemorating the constitution housed in the city council building. A swirling crowd reduced it to rubble. A crowd escorted a statue of the king to the cathedral.[163]

The event of July 26th had been publicized in advance by the parading through the city's streets of a figure dressed in old rags of various colors and festooned with firecrackers and multiple copies of the constitution. The parade throng paused periodically at the sound of a bugle to read the sentence to the motley figure: he was to burn in the public plaza by the cemetery. The effigy represented Agustín de Argüelles Álvarez, one of the 1812 Constitution's principal authors, nicknamed "The Divine" for his powerful oratory during the Cortes of Cádiz, particularly his speeches in favor of the abolition of slavery and against torture as a judicial process. Like Quintana, Zavala, and Bates, Argüelles' enthusiasm for the 1812 document had landed him in prison in 1814.[164] At the end of the event, many of Mérida's well-heeled elite proceeded back from the cathedral to the city council in their carriages. Inspired by their success, the city's distinguished women proposed to use the surplus money collected to serve the city's prisoners and poor a "splendid meal" with their own hands.[165]

The Sacred Heart–loving poet and subdelegate of the Sierra Baja town of Mama ensured that his town's celebration of King Ferdinand VII's abrogation of the Constitution of 1812 rivaled that of Mérida. He donned ceremonial garb and sallied forth to read the May 4 edict to the gathered public. A band then struck up some martial music, and the assembled processed through the streets. Indians played bugles and other loud instruments. Overcome, Castro could not hide his tears. Arriving in the main plaza, he called for silence. His wife led the ¡*Vivas*! for Ferdinand VII. She then grabbed a copy of the 1812 Constitution and shredded it, as did the women accompanying her. Not to be outdone, one woman stood in the doorway of her house masticating the hated document with her teeth. A dance that evening was punctuated by renewed choruses of ¡*Que vivan*! to pope and king.[166]

Organized women would form a strong column in the conservative parties of the nineteenth century; reformed Catholic men would provide the intellectual ballast for the liberals. Sanjuanista spawn Andrés Quintana Roo, for example, served as minister of justice in 1833 under militant reformist Catholic president Gómez Farías, who oversaw a radical restructuring of church and state that would perhaps have shocked even the reformist Catholic authors in Mier's makeshift Mina Expedition library. Yucatán's delegate to Mexico's first Constitutional Congress in 1823 championed the church's early centuries as a font of wisdom for the new legislators grappling with the tithe question. During that glorious time, he argued, the faithful only gave money to the church voluntarily, not by force of law, and it was only in the sixth century that misguided bishops had begun to insist on mandatory tithe payments—thus his contemporaries mistakenly believed God himself demanded tithing. He roundly concluded with a Catholic, not secular, justification for state control of the church: the church's early centuries demonstrated that the civil powers should control a voluntary tithe and pay ministers a salary.[167] Manuel Cresencio Rejón was anything but a provincial eccentric in the deliberations in Mexico City.[168] A commission on the *patronato* led by Fray Servando Teresa de Mier tackled the question of who controlled ecclesiastical appointments—the Mexican state or Rome—and enthusiastically rehearsed centuries of papal usurpations of civil prerogatives and the perfection of the democratic early church. Mexico had inherited the *patronato* from the Spanish Crown and should appoint ecclesiastical officials, the report concluded, but the country's control of the church also sprang from early church precedent.[169]

Throughout the empire, reformers imbued with reformist teachings supported the Constitution of 1812 and ultimately the devolution of power away from central authorities like popes, kings, and central governments. Reformers called for the devolution of sovereignty to local and regional juntas or city councils in the king's absence and, often at the same time, for the lower clergy and the laity's participation in elections for ecclesiastical hierarchs like bishops, and for civil authorities. For literate urban elites across the Spanish-speaking Atlantic world, Reform Catholicism sanctified these efforts, grounding them in Catholic theology and fueling decolonization and the establishment of novel forms of representation centered on individual citizens rather than corporate groups after independence. These reformers faced stiff opposition from ultramontanist Catholics, especially after the king's return in 1814 and into the early decades of the young republics. It is to those conflicts that we now turn.

2

The Rivals Muster

IN THE OPENING years of the new century, the monarchical crisis provided a window of opportunity for religious antagonists in the Yucatán who vied to enact their intertwined religious and political agendas. Reformist Catholics responded to the chaotic power vacuum of 1808 by insisting that authority devolved back to the people in the king's absence. Their notions of proper church governance mirrored their particular form of representational politics with its emphasis on the participation of citizens in elections for municipal and provincial deputation officials. The individual male citizen—not the *municipio* or the *común*—was the fundamental constituent of these elections. Reformers' support of church councils was intertwined with their enthusiasm for the Cortes de Cádiz and local, elected political bodies like the new city councils over the power of the popes and monarchs favored by the ultramontane. The elections involving even the laity and the distrust of hierarchy they found in the church's early centuries sanctified reformers' bid to return to the sovereignty of the people organized in councils in the monarch's absence. The novel freedom of the press ushered in by the 1812 Constitution, moreover, allowed the debates between the two Catholic currents to enter the public sphere of letters in unprecedentedly explicit terms before the backlash of the restored monarchy in 1814.

As the dynastic monarchy cracked open and the "loyal rebellions" filled the new political space in the years between 1808 and 1814, this religious partisanship

For God and Liberty. Pamela Voekel, Oxford University Press. © Oxford University Press 2023.
DOI: 10.1093/oso/9780197610190.003.0003

stirred conflicts in other parts of Spain's New World empire as well. During the second decade of the nineteenth century, reformers centered in San Salvador championed local political and ecclesiastical control against secular and religious hierarchies, as well as against economic elites clustered in Guatemala City engaged in large-scale merchant trade across the Atlantic. Enraged by the predatory loans of these big merchants, indigo growers in and around San Salvador developed an *esprit de corps* and formal advocacy organizations. The local political and ecclesiastical control necessitated by the Bourbon abdications in addition became a theater of experimentation in governing the municipalities as well as the churches. The organized El Salvadoran dye growers demonstrated a decided affinity for Reform Catholicism's democratic ecclesiology and the Cádiz Cortes' secular and religious reforms. These El Salvadoran reformers did not yet have a printing press, so their adherence to the reform cause, while strong, was less clearly expressed than that of the Sanjuanistas under the leadership of their prolific newspaperman José Matías Quintana. But to their south, the crisis of sovereignty of 1808 introduced the men who would later be regarded as the founding fathers of El Salvador and Colombia—committed reformist ecclesiastics like José Matías Delgado and José Simeón Cañas, radical friar Juan de Dios Campos Diez, and parish priest Juan Nepomuceno Azuero Plata. They would all go on to provide the intellectual and political leadership of the reform forces that would square off against their ultramontane enemies—led by Archbishop Ramón Casaús y Torres—on the literary barricades and the literal bloody battlefields of Central America in the five years after the region's formal declaration of independence in 1824.[1] But in the century's second decade, they and their supporters struck fear into Bourbon officials and ecclesiastical hierarchs alike and, like the Sanjuanistas, ultimately paid for their rebellious spirit with jail terms and monastic seclusion after Ferdinand VII's 1814 return to the throne. Economic tensions between El Salvadoran indigo growers and Guatemalan merchants intertwined with these religious conflicts. Ideological, spiritual, and economic interests would remain decidedly connected and dependably consistent across the first four decades of the new century.

REGIONAL RIVALRIES: THE INDIGO GROWERS OF SAN SALVADOR AND THE MERCHANTS OF GUATEMALA CITY

The religio-political cleavages that would later erupt into open warfare in Central America in the 1820s intersected in complex ways with the region's economy. The harvesting of wild indigo plants called *xiquilite*, whose rich blue dye enlivened the region's textiles, predated the arrival of the Spanish in the region. In a region devoid of precious metals like the silver found in Potosí and the lucrative mines of northern New Spain, the Spanish invaders rapidly re-focused their dreams of vast riches on the plant, and ultimately forced Indian workers to work in the dangerous indigo processing vats. For the first hundred years of colonization, the Crown had exempted Indians from this lethal work, as the plant contained toxins that became life-threatening with extended exposure. In the late eighteenth century, the city councils of San Salvador, San Vicente, and San Miguel reported a labor shortage. In 1784, the Crown responded with a plan for forced labor drafts of indigenous and *casta* workers.[2] The hue had quickly won over the European market, where it eclipsed more costly colorants from East Asia and outsold northern Europe's inferior products. By 1600, indigo ranked as the region's leading source of wealth. And by the late eighteenth century and through the years immediately after independence, colorants set the contours of Central America's export, domestic, and spiritual economies. In 1803, a report submitted to the Council of the Indies noted that indigo provided the bulk of the tithe money that supported the archbishopric and Guatemala City's impressive cathedral.[3] The crop's epicenter was the El Salvadoran areas around San Miguel, San Vicente, and San Salvador. Large indigo *haciendas* as well as small farms owned by *poquiteros* dotted the countryside around these towns. Indigo's economic centrality in Central America, however, extended beyond its importance as an export crop: the vast tracts of land and numerous people engaged in monocrop production spurred the demand for vegetables, wheat, and textiles from the Guatemalan highlands and for cattle, sheep, and horses from the areas around Leon, Tegucigalpa, and Comayaga. The region's entire export economy flourished around or faltered on the blue dye.[4]

Credit is often the cruel scourge of rural planters, and Central America in the late eighteenth and early nineteenth centuries was no exception. Regional elites engaged in indigo cultivation in El Salvador, textile and food production in Guatemala's highlands, and livestock raising in Costa Rica, Nicaragua, and Honduras—and all of them required capital. Only Guatemala City's wealthy merchant houses could provide it, but it came at a high cost. Led by Juan Fermín de Aycinena and his extensive family, merchants' tentacles reached across the region, sending credit coursing through the countryside and ensuring that the profits from the vast Atlantic trade were pooled in Guatemala City, Cádiz, and northern Europe, not San Salvador and Tegucigalpa. As indigo poured into Europe, a river of European, Latin American, and Asian imports flowed through the Central American countryside: British cloth, Valencian silks, Dutch linens, Chinese cinnamon and earthenware, Mexican leather and textiles, and Peruvian and Chilean wines.[5] Perennially in debt, regional elites were largely at the mercy

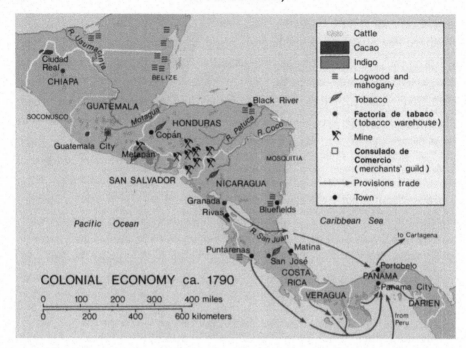

FIGURE 2.1 Before the development of synthetic dyes in the later nineteenth century, indigo cultivation was the chief source of wealth-generation of Central America. Relations of labor, land-owning, and credit were shaped by its production and mapped significantly onto the growing divide between reformist and ultramontanist Catholics. © 2003 University of Oklahoma Press. Reprinted by permission of the publisher.

of the Aycinena clan who were unaffectionately known simply as "The Family." The resentments made for a volatile situation in Central America, against the larger backdrop of a credit crisis in Spain's New World as a whole. Accumulating deficits from the almost continual state of war since 1793, the Spanish Crown began printing unbacked paper money, the infamous *vales reales*. In order to retire this constantly depreciating currency, in 1798 the state ordered public and religious institutions to sell off some of their property and turn over the proceeds to the treasury; in return they would receive three percent annual interest. On the peninsula, the properties to be consolidated were largely in real estate. But in 1804, Charles IV extended this decree of consolidation to the colonies, where the affected wealth was principally in the form of loans by the religious institutions to merchants, planters, and miners. Forced to call in the loans in order to underwrite the Crown's consolidation of the *vales reales*, the lenders drove many indebted men of affairs into bankruptcy and intensified the credit crunch across the Spanish New World. Fifteen million pesos were ultimately collected from the colonies, and the Bourbons earned themselves the lasting resentment of many subjects.[6]

Tight credit was particularly burdensome for the region's indigo growers. Merchants extended credit to El Salvadoran indigo growers in exchange for their crops at a fixed, pre-season low price that guaranteed the lenders vast profits in the Atlantic market and kept a cadre of rural indigo growers forever trapped in a cycle of debt. Failure to pay up resulted in land forfeiture. Lest there be any confusion on their willingness to seize the collateral in the event of default, the Aycinena family's many properties ringing San Salvador provided a chilling reminder.[7]

"The Family's" presence was ubiquitous in El Salvador and their economic power as lenders of seed money was only compounded by their position as merchants of imported goods sold on credit during the growing cycle. In the 1760s, Aycinena had worked closely with the *alcalde mayor* (regional magistrate) of San Salvador and other Crown officials to force the consumption of European goods at inflated prices in exchange for Indian and Ladino small producers' harvests. At the height of the patriarch's powers a quarter century later, Aycinena perhaps controlled a full quarter of Central America's commerce.[8] Regional growers' long-simmering resentments began to boil over at the end of the eighteenth century. At the same time—and despite the ideological and religious conservatism of "The Family"— the Crown had good reason to look askance at such an agglomeration of economic and political power among such a cohesive group of colonial elites. Thus as indigo farmers increasingly moved from harboring individual grievances to redressing them collectively, they did so with the king's blessing despite their own decidedly reformist leanings. The result was a long-running debate over political economy conducted in the religious terms set by Reform Catholicism.

At the center of these collective efforts stood the Crown-backed Society of Indigo Growers, established in 1782 to provide an alternative and less exploitative source of credit to farmers.[9] San Salvador's beleaguered indigo producers tapped Pedro Delgado to represent them at the society's Guatemala City meeting in 1794. Over the Easter holidays, the executive committee of the indigo growers' collective deputized Delgado to represent San Salvador. The aging patriarch, a respectable city councilman, replied that, although anyone as brittle-boned and busy as him preferred to stay at home, he would gladly sacrifice himself for the "good of the guild (*gremio*)" and for the "interests of this province." But to leave his large family and fund a journey to the city with his servants and horses required money—and he had none to spare, despite his attempts to sell his fruit harvest and dyes to raise it. When the society's executive committee ignored his request for a travel subsidy, he wrote to the Kingdom of Guatemala's captain general with the identical request; the outcome of his quest remains unknown.[10] Although Guatemalan and Spanish merchants in attendance at the 1794 meeting voiced their opposition to the society, the captain general and the Audiencia voted for its continuance. The captain general explained his support thus: loans favored capitalists, and capitalists traded imported goods and silver for crops with prices set well below the prices offered at large regional trade fairs. Truth be told, the society's report concluded that while loan sharks grew fat "not one man had grown rich from growing indigo and doing nothing else."[11]

The *Consulado de Comercio*—the official merchants' guild, established in 1793—apparently diverted attention from its members' predatory credit dealings by detailing what it saw as the self-sabotaging and morally reprehensible behavior of its indigo-growing debtors.[12] Their debt and dependency, and the "notorious decadence" of these provincial elites, the merchants sneered, sprang from their love of luxury and ostentation, not their coerced participation in a parasitic loan system. The Indigo Growers Society retorted that this accusation had no factual basis: luxury meant lavish decoration and extravagance, and Guatemala City far outdid rural El Salvador in both. Provincial Indigo growers, they parried, lived frugally but nevertheless remained mired in poverty, despite ever-more robust harvests and rising prices in Europe.[13]

"THE MONSTER OF LUXURY"

It may seem puzzling that a dispute between powerful Guatemala City merchants and plucky regional indigo growers would be expressed in a language that contrasted the moral valence of luxury and austerity, frippery, and carefully cultivated restraint. The choice of terms was no accident: Reform Catholic intellectuals had successfully cast luxury in opposition to their austere Augustinian piety. They regarded simplicity, restraint, and the rejection of baroque excess as signs of the efficacious grace that allowed them to resist worldly temptations.[14] This religious sensibility suffused economic thought and become a powerful rhetorical tool applied against national, class, and regional enemies. Its ubiquity, however, did not preclude its flexibility as a rhetorical device; rather, the pervasive critique of luxury set the terms for debate between supporters of free trade and defenders of mercantilism.

In a 1769 tract that helped establish the parameters of the discourse, Spaniard Antonio Muñoz found luxury's threat so overwhelming that he broke it into two parts: factual luxury and luxury of opinion. Factual, or absolute, luxury emerged when people consumed more than custom prescribed for their social class, a definition clearly rooted in the traditionally defined status hierarchy. But his definition of luxury of opinion placed him squarely in the dominant current of the late eighteenth century: excessive esteem for pomp characterized luxury of opinion regardless of who engaged in it. Over time, the opulence that had signaled the nobility's military valor and utility to the state descended into a mere representation of wealth. America's bounty magnified this problem, as return migrants basked in a level of luxury beyond that of the European nobility and, alarmingly, initiated a preference for rare foreign baubles. The nobility should distinguish itself by state service centered on merit, not mark their status through luxury consumption. A nation under the influence of luxury of opinion could not help but aspire to riches and devalue civic virtues. Fortunately, Muñoz explained, a solution was at hand: luxury was not any excess above mere subsistence but specifically the consumption of foreign goods. The state should prohibit imports and insist that even industries' primary materials spring from Spanish soil. Here Augustinian austerity made a powerful argument for the closed imperial mercantilist system versus free trade.

In a series of letters published in Madrid's *Memorial Literario* in 1789, economist Manuel Romero del Alamo likewise denounced all arguments for luxury's salutary effects, particularly claims that it stimulated supply and demand and thus filled state coffers. To the contrary, excessive luxury created celibates and thus reduced the population that formed the state's greatest resource. Ironically, his argument was itself rather baroque: marriage costs had skyrocketed for everyone; a rich laborer outspent a typical gentleman of fifty years prior on his progeny's nuptials. Titled subjects bought jewels, shoes, fans, and even lavish gifts for maids and others in attendance, borrowing from foreign creditors at markups of up to 60 percent. Middling families succumbed to these same deceivers, who flattered their vanity to sell them their trifles, even two gowns for one bride, and relieve them of their precious metals. All of this expenditure, Romero del Alamo lamented, led to the bride and groom's sterility or had devastating effects on their offspring; or worse, many fathers condemned their children to celibacy in convents and monasteries to avoid these ruinous outlays altogether. Like money, reproductive members of society should circulate and beget more people and more money, not be accrued to the church or the idle rich. In a reversal of folkloric beliefs in sterile people who represent sterile capital, here capital misspent on sterile luxury rather than productive investment leads to sterile people. The resulting population decrease injured the national economy while benefitting the Dutch, French, and English merchants who enriched themselves by "throwing fuel on the fire of Spanish luxury." Population decrease, of course, was not to be taken lightly, as population eclipsed precious metals as the measure of wealth for many late eighteenth-century economic thinkers; as the greatest wealth of a state, Gaspar Melchor de Jovellanos noted, consisted in "an abundant population." Like Muñoz, Romero del Alamo branded foreign goods as morally treacherous, even concluding that the French preference for French fashion, based as it was on principles of moderation, benefited France, and that the Spanish monarchy should ban foreign goods entirely.[15]

Gaspar Melchor de Jovellanos, an economist and historian who briefly served as Minister of Grace and Justice in 1797, shared Romero del Alamo's economic protectionism but was more adamant about blaming the wealthy for foreign consumption. Wines and liquors, clothing laden with precious stones, jewels and paintings—the ultra-wealthy imported these luxury items from other provinces, mostly foreign ones, to the great detriment of local manufacturers. He instead recommended the production of ordinary manufactured goods that appealed to a wide swath of the population.[16] He closed by juxtaposing the wealthy's capricious appetite for novelties to the virtuous customs of the people—and the people did not include the landed or the rich.

By 1820, the luxury debate had evolved to the point where some reformers saw anyone who engaged in opulent display or elaborate ceremony as betraying the *patria*. Simplicity, austerity and the use of Spanish goods were the mark of a true patriot, although the rise of new consumer values like comfort, utility, and naturalness and their attachment to particular commodities meant that one could consume a great deal before falling into the anti-patriotic category.[17] The emerging notion of *buen gusto* (good taste) meant that while reformers deemed ostentatious baroque display distasteful, carefully cultivated sensibility could indeed find public expression. One anonymous author who coupled patriotism with strictly Spanish attire emphasized that he did not wish to deprive his countrymen of both sexes of "the good taste (buen gusto) in elegance of clothing, but to foment this good taste with articles from Spain."[18] As baroque display of group status receded in the face of more widely available consumer goods, carefully cultivated individual aesthetic sensibility came to the fore as a marker of social distinction and patriotism.

This same author was so optimistic that good taste would prevail that he entitled his pamphlet "Spain Triumphant over Decadence, Luxury and Other Preoccupations."[19] To be sure, Spain needed to process its own primary products, and it was still too dependent on foreign imports, but if everyone engaged in this consumer boycott, the country could recover from its recent tribulations. The author called on his countrymen to eschew the "immoderate luxury" that fed foreign fortunes and instead embrace simplicity in the form of "patriotic fashion." To do so was to reject luxurious equipages in favor of graceful and comfortable carriages, to don clothing made of Spanish cloth and devoid of gold and silver trinkets, and to replace the "pompous exterior" that many affected to win over the gullible with virtue and personal merit.

If those who wallowed in foreign luxuries sabotaged the *patria*, so too did vaga-
bonds and others without a work ethic. The same anonymous 1820 author cast a
skeptical eye on Mandeville's bees, oft-cited beings whose many vices, including
the immoral pursuit of personal wealth, paradoxically redounded to the economic
benefit of the whole hive. The author noted in passing that actual bees killed the
lazy among them to guarantee their overall productivity. Individual initiative, he
thus implied, could not be relied upon to stimulate the economy. Instead, the state
should collect lay-abouts in workhouses or assign them to public works and re-
ward the wealthy for investing in factories. God obliged men to work for a living.[20]
Here the wealth that Muñoz's 1769 tract decried as threatening to civic virtue was
redeemed: it could be invested in productive factories rather than consumed in
vain display. It was not wealth itself that endangered, but hoarded or lavishly displayed riches.

As described by Muñoz, Romero del Alamo, and especially the anonymous 1820
pamphleteer, protectionism strengthened the country's moral fiber by shielding it
from luxury's enervating effects. As well, at least by 1820, new consumer values,
and new concepts like *buen gusto* and *urbanidad* would make individual discernment and allegiance to values expressed in particular consumer goods central
to social distinction. The new language of luxury cast aspersions on the ancient
regime's ascriptive privileges like nobility and on opulent display, and threw up
virtue and patriotism in their wake.

On the other side of the debate, luxury held more positive connotations for the
advocates of free trade who abounded in Spain's New World, especially in coastal
trading ports. Over the course of the late eighteenth century, the monarchy promulgated a spate of legislation challenging Mexico City's dominance of New Spain's
trade. The opening initiative was New Spain visitor General José Bernardo de
Gálvez Gallardo's 1767 measure allowing Veracruz interests to funnel European
merchandise directly to the Yucatán and Campeche rather than forcing them to
pass through peninsular ports. A cascade of deregulation legislation soon followed: in 1774, the Crown permitted the exchange of products among New Spain,
Peru, and Grenada, provided they did not compete with Spanish imports; in 1789
free trade within the empire, which had been in effect in most of Spain's other colonies since 1778, was extended to New Spain; and in 1791 Spain's allies obtained
entree to the New World's markets, a privilege that was quickly extended to the
allies' colonies in 1795.[21] But open trade with the world, particularly the powerful
English market, was not part of the reforms—and it was access to those markets
that the colonists sought.

Free trade advocates often extolled their cause's virtues in the language of
luxury. In an 1814 tract, Yucatán's provincial governing body turned the peninsular

Spanish literature on luxury and protectionism on its head, separating patriotism from national consumption. The desire for luxury had created a mutual interest in commerce. The area's henequen, copal, wax, cotton, grain, rice, and medicinal plants could form the core of a prosperous trade with the world and stimulate the peninsula's industry. National rivalries impeded the wealth of nations and should be removed.[22]

Other free-trade advocates underscored different virtues in luxury. It could, for example, stimulate work. In a series of musings published in the *Gazeta de Guatemala* in 1802, a reform-minded Yucatecan priest echoed the era's ubiquitous concerns with laziness and sloth, finding it particularly prevalent in the region's majority Mayan population, who worked only the exact amount required to eke out a living and pay tribute obligations. But in his examination of the reasons men work, he deviated slightly from his brethren in Spain, concluding that the desire for luxury could be a salubrious stimulus. "How many men were there who to hear the silk of their garments rustle, let their intestines rumble with hunger?" he asked rhetorically. No one was so foolish, just as few of the century's philosophers lived in shacks or threw their fortunes into the sea. Rather, knowledge and culture encouraged civility, which engendered *buen gusto*, which begat luxury—specifically a desire for luxury that could only be indulged with increased labor. Thus a desire for luxury tempered by good taste could cultivate the work ethic so sorely lacking among the Maya.

Coupling as they did protectionism with virtue, and virtue with flamboyant austerity and good taste, these new free-trade critiques of luxury linked patriotism to consumption for the first time. In reversing the villains and heroes of the economic drama, however, they argued within the terms of Augustinian restraint. Luxury found no defenders; rather, the combatants fought to define a term of universal opprobrium. Its new critics cast aspersions on sclerotic old regime hierarchies and on ostentatious display as a means to support status. In their place, the theorists proposed simplicity and adherence to new values like restraint—the sort of this-worldly asceticism made possible by the efficacious grace at the core of reformist Catholicism's notion of how man knew God. The consumer revolution and the attendant concerns with luxury thus constituted a source of the social shuffling occurring in Enlightenment Spain and empire, simultaneously a powerful moral solvent for old identities expressed by ostentatious display and moral glue for emerging ones. Free-trade advocates also found luxury a moral provocateur by imbuing laborers with an improved work ethic and stimulating global free trade. Laborers who refused luxury's siren call were cast as irrational. That said, luxury's real revolutionary potential is best seen with the Sanjuanistas and the Mexican insurgency (1810–1821) where it provided the rebels with a powerful religious language to critique the colonial relationship.

REFORM CATHOLICISM, LUXURY, AND THE INSURGENCY

The rebellion in New Spain emerged in part as a result of an empire-wide sovereignty crisis. In 1808, French troops spilled over the border into Spain and forced both Ferdinand VII and Carlos IV to renounce their rights to the Spanish throne, which Napoleon promptly bestowed on his brother Joseph. Although no one yet called for independence or even an end to royal rule in New Spain, the episode shook traditional notions of sovereignty to their core. Delegates from Spain's provincial juntas descended on the colonial capitals seeking recognition as the new legitimate authorities. Rather than recognize these officials, the Mexico City Council urged the viceroy to establish a separate junta to rule in the king's name; a group of peninsular merchants responded by violently deposing Viceroy Iturrigaray and replacing him with their own candidate until an official replacement, Francisco Javier Venegas, arrived in 1810. At this juncture, parish priest Miguel de Hidalgo y Costilla emerged at the head of a peasant army determined to wrest sovereignty from these peninsular usurpers. His program grew increasingly radical in the crucible of battle, and by 1810 some rebels were calling for independence and the expulsion of all Spaniards. The rebels failed to rouse the peasantry in the Central Valley, however, and Hidalgo's planned attack on the capital dissolved into retreat, desertion, and ultimately a grisly execution of the principals. On the heels of this disaster, another parish priest, José María Morelos y Pávon, convened a congress in Chilpancingo in 1813 after several years of hard-won victories by Morelos' peasant army; Guatemalan officials feared his movement would spill over into the Kingdom of Guatemala. As the 1813 Congress of Chilpancingo, the rebels declared Mexico's independence and called for a representative government and an end to the legal caste system. The fighting continued after Ferdinand's restoration in 1814 until Mexico's independence in 1821.

In the midst of the battles that raged during this period, the insurgent press utilized the evils of luxury in its battle to demoralize the Spanish, in both senses of the term.[23] The press blamed the idle rich, Spaniards, and cities as the source of this contagion. Carlos María de Bustamante's 1813 musings on rebel virtue, published in the insurgent paper the *Correo Americano del Sur* (The American Messenger of the South), provide a case in point. To convince Puebla's city council of the righteousness of the cause, and perhaps to alleviate their trepidations about provisioning the troops, insurgent leader and intellectual Bustamante limned his brothers-in-arms' virtues, proposing a geographical map of luxury along the way. Because of his troops' "frugality and peasant origins," rebel encampments sustained themselves at little cost. This was particularly true because his hearty lads had never known the "indispensible necessities" demanded by enemy troops. The Royalist troops, recruited from both Spain and New Spain, and "spawn of the pampered and luxurious cities they were recruited from," might be an expensive undertaking, but bivouacking the virtuous who comprised the rebel ranks was not.[24]

While Bustamante contrasted decadent cities saturated by luxury to virtuous countryside, the insurgent paper the *Ilustrador Americano (American Illustrator)*, under the leadership of cleric Francisco Lorenzo Velasco de la Vara, provided a map of class propensities. "Middle class of the country, the deserving and enlightened class," the paper declared in 1812, "your sacrifices in helping us from the center of the repression have elevated you to the true nobility that rightly elevates the citizen."[25] And "for those of you for whom luxury, vice, and prostitution have led you to tie yourself to despotism's carriage . . . [for those of] you who kiss the hand that secures your chains," remember that the future *patria* will only recognize valor and virtue and will revile the wealthy whose coffers might have helped the cause.[26] The *Seminario Patriótico Americano* echoed Bustamante on the virtue of honest work, noting that thanks to the "enlightenment of our time," labor and civic virtue elevated men to the peaks of real hierarchy. The paper also gave thanks for the end of "the barbarous centuries" when nobility had been tied exclusively to the splendor of vain titles and the distinction of birth.[27] Just seven years after independence, Lorenzo de Zavala would echo this analysis, blaming the young republic's woes on the traffic in titles carried out under the monarchy. The traffic had fomented a Spanish-grandee level of luxury and ostentation, he lamented, and forced title holders to purchase the vast tracts of land that could have sustained the many instead of the few.[28]

An 1812 insurgent publication entitled "Political Steps that the Leaders of the American Armies should take to obtain their Goals by Safe and Secure Methods, Avoiding an Effusion of Blood" provides a perfect case in point. What were these steps? First, insurgent officers should be clear on who constituted "tyranny's addicts," or the nation's enemies: the rich, nobles, and employees of the first order, whether Creole or Gauchupine (Spanish). These people's wealth should be immediately distributed to the poor. Then the rebels should seize the church's gold and silver to destroy "overseas luxury" and its debilitating effects on every virtuous village in New Spain.[29] Miguel Hidalgo y Costilla, in his 1810 retort to the inquisition, had savaged the Spanish along many of these same lines: their God was money, they triturated everyone in their frenzy to enrich themselves, their blind avarice drove them to steal lands and make Americans vassals. Finally, the father of Mexican independence noted that "men nourished by these sentiments cannot maintain sincere friendship with us."[30] This juxtaposition of artifice and sincerity was constantly rehearsed: the *Semanario Patriótico Americano* argued that the sacred tenet of the sovereignty of the people came with a logical set of corollaries, including that governments should be judged by their sincerity and simplicity.[31]

A slow river of critique of urban luxury, the titled, and the idle rich flowed from insurgent intellectuals. For the "Mandarins of Cadiz" and other trade monopolists, however, they unleashed a veritable torrent of invective. These merchants prohibited the local manufacture of tobacco, salt, and mescal; centralized trade in themselves and one port; halted the planting of grapes and the making of vine in Hidalgo's town of Dolores; and obstructed America's real source of wealth—industry.[32] The *Semanario Patriótico Americano* reported American industry was so stifled that "metal came out of our mountains for no other purpose than to tighten our chains and to attract an ever multiplying number of oppressors."[33] One Yucatan paper concluded in 1814 that "no pen could possibly represent the pool of blood in America caused by the avarice, pride and spirit of monopoly demonstrated by Cadiz, Mexico City, and Veracruz."[34]

But if the insurgent press deployed the morally charged language of luxury to tar their enemies, they did so regardless of the author's stance on independence or the Cortes. In a piece typical of the genre, the characters Vanity and Luxury were the subjects of an 1811 fable printed in the *Diario de México*, which had the largest circulation of the capitol's new periodicals and exhibited little or no support for the insurgency.[35] Born in the populous city of "Vanidopolis" in the province of "Showiness," Luxury's parents were Laziness and Insanity, his running mates and instructors Self-Love and Novelty. Seduced by a foreign girl named La Moda (Fashion) and known particularly for her significant investments in expensive clothes, Luxury marries and gives birth to little Dueda (debt) and Trampa (deception). The good queen, Healthy Conscience, finally ends the tale by expelling the family from her dominions.[36]

This readily available theme packed a moral wallop: it was sanctified by the reformed element of the church, one of the major fonts of antipathy to luxury and of enthusiasm for the worldly asceticism thought to be a sign of God's efficacious grace. The mouthpiece of reformist Catholics, and a paper well connected to fellow travelers across Europe, Madrid's *El Censor* (1781–1787) fabricated a facetious letter and attributed it to a certain benighted confraternity majordomo baffled by his parish's recent arrival: a dedicated Reform Catholic priest. It seems that *El Censor's* hero, the priest, had banned or sold off most of the church's ornamentation, including blond wigs for an image of the baby Jesus, a silver staircase, wooden angels, and a parade float with life-sized representatives of Christ's passion. The

befuddled majordomo lamented that, in his crusade for "moderation," the new
priest had prohibited his flock from dressing an image of the Virgin in a lavish silk
and gold dress bequeathed by a grateful noblewoman. The Virgin should provide
an example of real Christian virtue, *El Censor's* editor lectured this stubborn trad-
itionalist, and thus her clothing should be simple; the senses should not be excited
by luxurious display, particularly not in church.

El Censor was not alone in its religious critique of luxury. To set a spiritual example of moderation and good taste, the ecclesiastical hierarchy throughout the
empire rejected the extravagance that had formerly characterized pastoral visits.
In 1771, Mexico's Fourth Provincial Council, presided over by Mexican Archbishop
and later Spanish Cardinal Francisco Antonio Lorenzano, noted that "moderation edifies the faithful" and equipages and other hoopla constituted a scandal.
Like other reformist hierarchs at the time, Mexico's Archbishop Nuñez de Haro y
Peralta banned the customary triumphal arches, fireworks, and dances from his
pastoral visits; as had other hierarch during this time, he insisted on humble ac-
commodations uncluttered by special pillows or wall hangings and a modest table
rather the customary lavish banquet.[37]

In cleric José Eduardo de Cárdenas, the Sanjuanistas had a fellow traveler to
represent them in the Cortes; this erudite priest had attended Merida's seminary
with many of the San Juanista faithful. Cardenas opened his address to that august body in 1811 with direct reference to this burning issue: in his home region of
Tabasco "devastating luxury," that terrible monster that should be enchained and
sent back to Asia, was virtually unknown.[38] And thank goodness, he thundered
in the Cortes, because all who truly prostrated themselves before Christ detested
sumptuous palaces and churches. The viceroys, he informed his fellow delegates,
misunderstood the colony's laws and ignored its customs. Their only purpose was
to provide the people with an example of luxury and enormous scandal. What ret-
inues! What sumptuousness! What ostentation! He told his no doubt sympathetic
audience that "crown officials sported Persian pomp, and the noble and majestic
Spanish simplicity has been slowly disappearing, including among ecclesiastical
dignitaries."[39] Spain needed a national church council, Cárdenas concluded, that
would purify the clergy of both Spains.[40] Here Cardenas echoed the wisdom of the
reformist Sanjuanistas, who found in the bible "arms to defend the people from
clerical avarice."[41] Society should maintain priests, to be sure, but over the centuries priests had abused this privilege to insist on excessive wealth. The Cortes
had embraced this same biblical principle when it prohibited fathers from giving
pious bequests to convents or confessors, a San Juanista paper reported. As it
rousingly concluded, it was clear that the bible demonstrated that "enriching the
ministry was never one of the dogmas of our divine religion."[42]

For Cárdenas as for critics across the empire, the "monster of luxury" was a decidedly feminine beast. After contrasting the virtuous but hungry poor to the opulent rich, the erudite parish priest declared that "today more than ever good patriots should be aghast at the gap between practice and moral maxims, between preening and coiffed *petimetres* (effeminate male fops, swishes, dandies) and austere and manly soldiers."[43] In his discussion of the region's economy, he extolled the virtues of agriculture and the trades, but noted that hairdressers, perfume vendors, and designers were "superfluous" and that happily the region housed few of them.[44] The *Diario de México* similarly cast *petimetres* as virtue's foil. In a mock interview between a tribunal of *petimetres* and a prosperous laborer, the group of effeminate men facetiously asks the good peasant, the story's hero, if he would don tight pants that accentuated his plump thighs and whether he would squeal out catcalls to distinguished persons in the street.[45]

The theme of luxury and femininity was constantly rehearsed. The insurgents' *El Despertor Americano* lambasted Spaniards' "decadence and effeminacy," which sprang from their "immoderate luxury and excessive wealth, their insatiable greed and vast treasures."[46] Luxury was the alter-ego of patriotism, nationalism, and political legitimacy, all of which were sanctified by the reform currents in the church that rejected opulence and sensuality as a path to God. As political legitimacy for reformers in particular became grounded in austere Catholic manliness, wealthier, whiter women's association with luxury proved fatal for their inclusion as citizens in the nations that were to come.[47] After independence, Central America's branch of the Reform Catholic international would continue to brand their enemies as luxury's proponents, as moral saboteurs who threatened a patria build on reformist virtues that manifested themselves in republican simplicity.

Guatemalan merchants and the El Salvadoran indigo growers who exchanged insults about who was most mired in luxury, then, were hardly an anomaly in the late Spanish Empire. But relations between the two groups became increasingly fraught. The growers' union reported that their situation was steadily worsening, as dyes from India edged out indigo in the English market, depressing demand for the Central American product. Poor but virtuous, El Salvador's growers exerted little control over crop prices in the vast Atlantic market. Although Pedro Delgado and others received generous loans, the growers' union never accumulated enough capital to fully free El Salvadoran growers from the grasp of Guatemalan lenders. Still less could these provincial landowners make barren metal breed, as did the powerful Aycinena clan. Their biological spawn would, however, carry their parents' resentments into the new republics. Pedro Delgado's zeal to advance his province's interests in the late eighteenth century would be inherited by his sons, especially the priest José Matías Delgado. Delgado the younger would go down in history as an important instigator of El Salvador's independence from Spain, Mexico, and Guatemala. He would be a central protagonist in the leadup to a three-year religious war fought by El Salvadorans against a Guatemalan army led by a scion of the House of Aycinena in the 1820s. The beginning of the second decade of the century found José Matías Delgado manning San Salvador's central parish; two of his brothers sat on the governing board of the growers' union in San Salvador.[48] He energetically participated in the town's bid for more political and ecclesiastical autonomy, and orchestrated the elaborate celebrations of the 1812 Constitution in ways that mirrored the Sanjuanistas determined support for the Cortes de Cádiz's democratic reforms.

THE FIGHT FOR POLITICAL AND RELIGIOUS AUTONOMY IN CENTRAL AMERICA, 1811–1814

José Matías Delgado was all too familiar to the Kingdom of Guatemala's highest-ranking official, Captain General Bustamante, who had been kept apprised of the parish priest's frenetic activity during San Salvador's small-scale uprising of November 1811. On the evening of November 4, San Salvadorans learned that cleric Manuel Aguilar had been detained in Guatemala City and that his brother Nicolás would soon face a similar fate; a rumor swirled that Spaniards had threatened to kill their beloved parish priest, José Matías Delgado. That evening, as a crowd gathered outside the intendency building, shouts against Spaniards rang out. The next day, armed men surrounded the intendent's house and the city council building while pockets of people stoned Spaniards' homes. Over the next twenty-eight days, the rebels controlled the city, and riled San Salvadorans pledged fealty to the king but replaced the intendent with an ad-hoc ruling junta and demanded the removal of all peninsular authorities and immediate elections for a new city council.[49] Theirs was a movement for more local political autonomy, not a declaration of independence from the Spanish king or the Cortes of Cádiz. Under parish priest Delgado's sage leadership, the rebels quickly exchanged amnesty from prosecution for acceptance of the Creole officials Captain General Bustamante wisely dispatched to San Salvador to restore order.[50]

Although Delgado had been more a conciliator than a provocateur in the tumult of November of 1811, his brothers and his cousins the Aguilar brothers—the priests Manuel, Nicolás, and Vicente—had loomed large in the commotion, and Delgado's enthusiasm for the Cortes' democratic promises and the social leveling at the heart of its system of representation was an open secret.[51] The Cádiz political body had joined together philosophy and religion to produce over 200 salutary articles, Delgado preached from his San Salvador's parish church a few days before Christmas in 1811; thankfully the "impetuous torrent of popular convulsions" that shook San Salvador in early November had passed, and his parishioners would now "rest not on the weak shoulders of a particular person or personality no matter how elevated, but on the shoulders of the largest, most illustrious, wisest, most just, and most august congress that the centuries had yet witnessed."[52]

The subtle jab at ancien régime hierarchies and the plaudits for democracy and congressional and conciliar authority were hardly a casual slip of the tongue. In the same sermon, Delgado referred to himself as "your pastor, your co-citizen, your natural brother," and assured his flock of his concern for "the poorest and most miserable individual—a person in God's eyes as respectable and precious as the wealthiest, most opulent citizen."[53] Surely the captain general shuddered when he heard Delgado's call for horizontal co-citizenship and fraternity and recalled the 1811 San Salvador uprising's tempered but nevertheless decidedly anti-Spanish tenor—Spaniards' homes stoned by swirling crowds, the removal of *chapetones* from the city council, and the devolution of sovereignty away from royal officials.[54]

If Delgado proved a mediator rather than an energetic instigator of these disturbances, the long-time parish priest of San Salvador proved indefatigable in his enthusiasm for winning hearts and minds to the 1812 Constitution. Delgado and Miguel José Castro y Lara, the parish priest of tiny Texaguangos, turned the public oath of allegiance to the 1812 Constitution into a multiple-day event. They spared no expense. A Central American representative to the Cortes boasted that, in celebrating the document, El Salvador had mustered "more pomp than any other country," and that the names of the virtuous patriots Delgado and Castro were "forever emblazoned in residents' minds." The two parish priests had received a copy of the constitution in mid-September, but since most city councilmen were tending to their indigo crops on their haciendas outside town at that time, they postponed the celebrations until October. Bull fights, an orchestra, and fireworks enlivened a series of evening events, which culminated in a Sunday sermon and Delgado's careful reading of every word of the constitution following Castro's mass.[55]

Delgado's enthusiasm for the 1812 Constitution paralleled his ongoing bid for El Salvador's ecclesiastical freedom from Guatemala's archbishop, a move deeply influenced by his own and his coterie's reformist sensibilities. At the city council's request, El Salvador's representative to the Cádiz Cortes proposed the establishment of a new bishopric for the region and placed himself in the influential reform camp in that deliberating body by stressing that his fellow Cortes' deputies well knew that bishoprics had multiplied in the church's early centuries, "those happy times of Christianity's resplendence."[56] The 1813 San Salvadoran constitutional city council answered Archbishop Casaús' fear of the potential tithe losses to a new bishopric with a reformist ultimatum to the hierarch to eschew luxury and return to the simplicity of the early centuries, noting that "in apostolic times" copious funds and magnificent cathedrals had not existed. The church could exist without the "ostentation and luxury and all the other things that some find necessary, but not without the bishops and priests that sustain and promote it."[57] Delgado, San Salvador's constitutional city council, and the area's Cádiz representative rehearsed the core Reform Catholic tenets of simplicity and equality, while carefully careful parsing the history of the church's early centuries rather than the contemporary pope's pronouncements. In San Salvador, Captain General Bustamante faced dissidents girded in the armor of the word and carrying the torch of church history.

Bustamante was rightly concerned. The reformed Catholics he faced were clustered in San Salvador and emboldened by the Cádiz Cortes, but he understood the reformers' ubiquity, transnational ties, and deep roots in the region. The Inquisition case against Simón Berguño Villegas provides an articulate exemplar of the argument: during the tumult of 1808, the authorities charged the *Gazeta de Guatemala* editor with sedition. He ran afoul of the Inquisition for allegedly saying that, while church councils might be infallible, he distrusted many of the pope's pronouncements, as the pontiff was subject to error like any man.[58] Banishing the unreliable editor to Spain, the Audiencia auctioned off Bergaño's goods to pay for his boat passage, including his ample library. This practical necessity proved the further undoing of the luckless journalist: among his eccentric possessions that thereby came to light was a screed he wrote against monastic vows, addressed to the Holy Father. A wise pope who embraced his ideas would cover himself in glory, he argued; his proposed reforms were as righteous as the rationale for expelling the Jesuits. His work pivoted around reform Catholic notions of virtue and the will. Naive young people regarded the cloister as a barrier to vices, ignoring that "true virtue, like happiness, is not about external circumstances." Virtue came from following godly conscience and the cloister denied the will the liberty needed to act virtuously; monks followed their hierarchs, who followed Rome, not their consciences. As well, these cloistered clerical intellectuals denied nature its course, wrongly attributing physical urges to the Devil's workings. Following this logic, he elevated marriage to the pinnacle of sexual virtue, deposing celibacy from its former pride of place, a move not unrelated to the growing conviction that populations not minerals indexed a nation's wealth; chastity vows, after all, ill-served nuns whose hearts burned for the joys of conjugal life and the children it produced. He urged the Holy Father to raise the age of vows to twenty-five, to declare vows non-binding, to allow religious outside the walls at least four times a year, and to decree that nuns teach girls rather than withdraw into community life.[59]

In a pattern repeated throughout the empire, in Havana the feisty Bergaño y Villegas sparred in print with Havana's reformist Bourbon bishop Juan José Díaz de Espada y Landa, who shared much of the exiled Guatemalan's reformist theology. Bishop Espada's firm episcopalism, however, left him with little patience for challenges from the lower clergy or a laity emboldened by the Cortes' declaration of free speech. Authority might lay with the bishops not the pope, but it stopped there—and most certainly did not include Bergaño y Villegas' right to debate with his hierarch in an egalitarian "republic of letters." The Guatemalan gadfly had challenged the sexual double standard in his *Correo de las Damas* (*The Ladies Mail*). Espada issued a pastoral letter calling the piece a license to lasciviousness and himself the newspaperman's rightful teacher not his fraternal equal in a public battle of wits.[60] While Bergaño y Villegas' prose lacked the lyricism of Mexico's Tenth Muse on the topic of the sexual double standard, his argument that "the seducer is more malignant that the seduced" provided a solid defense of a woman scorned for forfeiting her honor to a rake. His widely circulated response to the bishop's censure was published by a prolific reformist press in Palma de Mallorca, an island town outside the Spanish peninsular territory under French control. In it he recognized "no other teachers than Jesus and the universal church," which of course included the laity and the lower clergy, and noted that Espada was not infallible. That honor belonged instead to the councils, which were comprised of more than one bishop.[61] With the Inquisition reinstated in 1814, Bergaño y Villegas' *Manifesto* made it onto a short list of banned works to be immediately confiscated. The list featured reformist luminaries like Llorente, Villanueva's lengthy intervention on the Inquisition's abolition during the Cortes, and liberal newspapers like the satirical *El Duende de los Cafes*.[62] Tagged by the Inquisition as one of the empire's biggest threats, Bergaño y Villegas had first flexed his reformist erudition as the editor of the *Gazeta de Guatemala*. The threat was home grown, transnational, and not confined to San Salvador.

Further fraying the captain general's nerves was another of the political innovations emanating from the Cádiz Cortes, a provincial deputation that first met in Guatemala City in September. The new governing chamber promised to diverge significantly from its equivalent body in Mérida; rather than a conservative bastion, elected delegates from across the region included reformers like El Salvador-born clerics José Simeón Cañas and José Matías Delgado.[63]

Captain General Bustamante quickly realized that the Provincial Deputation's delegates disrespected authority, in particular his. Furthermore, the deputation's many clerics—five of the seven men elected—boded ill; throughout the empire, he rightly noted, the utopian visions of "misguided" churchmen had escalated the turbulence after the French invaded the Spanish Peninsula in 1808. He pleaded in particular for the nullification of the Sonsonate election that had seated cleric José Simeón Cañas.[64] As rector of the University of Guatemala in 1802 and again in 1810–1811, the reform-minded Cañas had led the charge against scholasticism in the curriculum and promoted the Cortes de Cádiz and the 1812 Constitution; many of the region's reform-minded citizens, both clerical and lay, studied under Cañas.[65] By late October, Bustamante sighed that his premonitions about the new governing body had been accurate. Cañas served as the unofficial leader of a body intent on demoting the king's appointed rulers and elevating into sovereignty the Provincial Deputation itself, a *junta* of men elected by the region's new constitutional city councils. The deputation was particularly adamant about diminishing Captain General Bustamante's authority. The captain general himself would be one voting member among many, not the body's leader; meetings would happen at the city council building, not the palace; the captain general would attend only selected meetings, not all official gatherings; the rebels from Granada, Nicaragua, held in the city's jail could appeal directly to the deputation, circumventing the captain general's prying eyes; the new governing body, not the king's men, would police infractions of the 1812 Constitution; and the deputation's deliberations would be published and disseminated in accordance with the Cortes' dictums on governmental transparency and press freedom.

While dripping sarcasm about the wisdom of these radically democratic reforms that pulled authority away from king, Bustamante assured the Regency that he had demonstrated proper respect for the new governing body, guaranteeing that all seven men sat "with pillows at their feet" in church at the king's official birthday celebration. Although happy to chirp in the Regency's ear, Bustamante was chagrined to read in Madrid's liberal newspaper *El Universal* that the deputation had complained about him to the Cádiz Cortes, underscoring his crack-down on the press and his fear that Guatemala's Cortes representatives would publicly malign his conduct unchallenged.[66] Accustomed to unilateral rule and the ceremonial display of ascriptive precedence, in 1813 Bustamante faced powerful and organized opponents, many of them dissident priests.

Fortunately for Captain General Bustamante, he did not face men like Cañas and San Salvador's reform cleric-led malcontents alone. The church wielded far more influence in predominately rural Central America than did the state, and the divided church was headed by powerful conservatives like Archbishop Ramón Casaús y Torres—who had arrived in 1811 Guatemala City fresh from his contretemps with Mexican rebel priest Manuel Hidalgo y Costilla. When New Spain's Viceroy Francisco Xavier Venegas had needed to throw some serious theological shade on a manifesto issued by the Reform Catholic Hidalgo in 1800, he had tapped Casaús, who delivered a lacerating take-down: the wayward cleric "drank, danced and whored" at fiestas he hosted in his home while sacraligious clerics danced with the holy oils hanging around their necks in his church. He later wrote a series of denunciations of the rebel leader published in the Mexico City press. Later he described Hidalgo as "a priest and apostate who rises against bishops, who pursues them like a ravenous wolf, who wants all of Christendom to join in his projects," all the while claiming to be Catholic—"an unheard of monstrosity!"[67]

Archbishop Casaús tacked a subtler course with El Salvador's more small-scale rebels than he had with the Mexican rebel priest Hidalgo, cajoling, coopting, and inciting divisions rather than outright condemning the San Salvadorans. He counseled Guatemalans to combat the rebels by recommitting to timeworn cults like that of Our Lady, who had an enviable history of smiting heretics. The wily archbishop questioned priests Nicolas and Manuel Aguilar after the November commotion in San Salvador. When pressed to reveal "those who sowed the fatal seeds of disunion and disloyalty," Casaús informed his San Salvadoran flock in a pastoral letter, the two rebel leaders betrayed their countrymen. Take note, Casaús advised readers and listeners hearing the pastoral letter read from pulpits: "miserable troublemakers" claimed the two influential clerical brothers supported their cause, but at Casaús' urging the Aguilars had copped to detesting the rebels' "frenzy" and "machinations." The voice of religion had prevailed over "sacrilege" and "absurdity," the wily archbishop reported. The hierarch presented the rebellious Aguilars as traitors to their own cause.

In a more theological vein, Casaús insisted that attacks on hierarchical authority constituted an attack on Christianity's core tenets—a definition of the faith diametrically opposed to Delgado's gloss on the Christian mission of the Cortes' 200-article draft for what would become the 1812 Constitution, and the parish priest's sense of horizontal brotherhood and citizenship that he conveyed in his sermon. Casaús sincerely hoped to avoid hurling the anathemas the church rightly reserved for traitors to the king and his representatives.[68] Gentle persuasion was his public stance, and he sent missionaries like José Mariano Vidaurre to preach obedience in San Salvador. Vidaurre did not disappoint, seizing the opportunity of a funeral elegy to exhort San Salvadorans to "open your eyes" and see the horrors wrought by popular revolutions in Mexico and Caracas—revolutions born of ambition and greed.[69] To his Guatemala City flock, Casaús advocated redoubled devotion to the Rosary as a weapon against insurgency and warned them against reformist Catholics like those of the Synod of Pistoia who had revived Calvin's critique of the devotion as superstitious rot.[70]

A RENEGADE FRIAR ON THE RUN

In the waning months of 1809, a friar named Juan de Díos Campos Diez took his concerns about shady dealings around a Franciscan monastery election all the way from Nicaragua to the Audiencia, the high court in Guatemala City. He appears to have remained in the city for three years. Although the dissident friar roomed in at least three separate monasteries, he preached in numerous churches and even served as a chaplain in La Concepcion. He later fretted that his superiors back in Nicaragua deployed news of his decidedly worldly preaching to discredit him.[71] With its population of some 25,000 souls—over twice the size of roughly 12,000-person San Salvador, the kingdom's second largest urb—Guatemala City appears to have appealed to Campos' restless spirit, and he apparently lingered to imbibe its bustle and political ferment. It was perhaps not until 1813 that Captain General Bustamante issued him a passport for safe passage to a monastery in Panama.[72]

Captain General Bustamante's desire to rid Guatemala City of restless ecclesiastics like Friar Campos was far from irrational. By late 1812, rebel Mexican priest José Maria Morelos' troops controlled Oaxaca and threatened to push into Chiapas, then part of the Kingdom of Guatemala. Fearing that a rebel presence on Guatemala's border would embolden internal dissidents, Bustamante ordered 700 soldiers into Mexico. After several royalist victories, Morelos' troops soundly defeated the Guatemalans, and the bedraggled survivors stumbled back across the border. Bustamante had failed to consult with Guatemala City's constitutional city council before dispatching the troops, and this new Creole stronghold demanded an accounting after news of the defeat trickled back into the city.[73]

More alarmingly still, some of El Salvador's malcontents appeared to entertain Morelos as a potential ally. In May of 1813, José Matías Delgado's brother Miguel and two others wrote to the intrepid Mexican rebel leader, assuring him of their loyalty to his just cause. This letter to Morelos was reportedly found in Miguel Delgado's papers, and he spent at least four and half years imprisoned for his role in the 1814 San Salvador uprising, which included hosting a gathering of malcontents at his home starting at ten at night.[74]Part of the El Salvadorans' appreciation of this Mexican insurgent may have stemmed in part from their common Reform Catholic sensibilities.

If clerics like San Juanista Velasquez, Friar Campos, and university rector Cañas and laymen like Miguel Delgado and newspaperman Bergaño y Villegas had been an anomaly, Captain General Bustamante could have easily ignored them, but with Morelos' troops advancing toward Guatemala, he felt himself surrounded. His fears of radical reform-minded priests were not exagerated: calls for political and ecclesiastical democracy were fast becoming ubiquitous, as the San Salvadoran

Delgado coterie's support for the Cádiz Cortes, reformist invocations of the early church's democratic decentralization, and repeated pushes for more political independence signaled. The news out of the Cortes was particularly alarming for an autocrat like Bustamante. To name just one representative example of the dominant Reform Catholic current in the deliberative body, Cádiz deputy José Eduardo de Cárdenas, who had informed the Cortes of his concern with luxury's enervating effects, called for a national ecclesiastical council, and noted that over the centuries the church had added cardinals and other hierarchs to its early egalitarian core structure and should remove them and return to that more glorious time.[75]

In the context of a rebellion led by excommunicated priests like Miguel Hidalgo y Costilla and José María Morelos, the rebels' call to return to a less hierarchical church had taken on renewed urgency. Rebel Mexican troops threatening to spill into Guatemala; reformist priests leading armies into battle and promoting their radically democratic ecclesiology: it was in this fraught context for Spain's empire that the prolix friar Juan de Díos Campos Diez wended his way out of Guatemala City en route to Panama—at Captain General Bustamante's behest. Jittery military authorities in León, Nicaragua worked with the energetic Bustamante to piece together evidence of the friar's transgressions during his wanderings, compiling a voluminous report based on the testimony of scores of witnesses.

In May of 1813, they found, Campos passed through the small El Salvadoran town of Tepetitlán, near San Vicente, where he acted as a veritable advanced propaganda machine for Morelos' army, which he depicted to his listeners as poised to invade within weeks. A clutch of illiterate women flocked to the parish church to hear the friar's gloss on the news. The Mexican rebel army was traveling between Oaxaca and Quezaltenango and would arrive in Tepetitlán shortly, the friar enthused, but they should not fear. Morelos was an honorable man and would place guards at the nunneries and evacuate girls from towns to protect them from the natural depredations of soldiers. The insurgent priest had gifted Oaxacan Indians and widows with money, Campos assured listeners in the town, and only killed declared enemies, like the Central American troops Captain General Bustamante had ordered into Mexico.

The friar proved more circumspect with an ecclesiastical judge in Santa Ana. He told Manuel Cárcamo that the royalist troops had faced fierce opposition from Morelos and tendered that, if the rebels arrived in Guatemala in great numbers, he would advocate for neutrality. Cárcamo shot back that neutrality was nowhere near good enough: he would defend the just cause of Spain. As to the charge that he had seduced the naïve with tales of the rebel priest Morelos' supporters who grew corn that miraculously ripened in fifteen days, Campos assured his military inquisitors he would never traffic in such obvious superstition.[76] Tellingly, the Spanish Regency later rewarded Cárcamo and fellow loyalist priest Dr. Manuel Antonio Molina of San Vicente—who also informed against Campos—with the titles of honorary canons of the Metropolitan Cathedral of Guatemala.[77] The two were clearly royalist stalwarts: Captain General Bustamante had lauded Molina and Cárcamo as critical to the San Salvadoran rebels' December 1811 defeat in a letter to the Council of the Regency.[78]

Perhaps most alarming to his military inquisitors was the sober report that Campos had met with clerics in San Salvador who asserted with "deep senti-ment" that the province was home to 6,000 "aggrieved people" who might rally to Mexican rebel priest Morelos. Equally troubling, priest Manuel Aguilar had hosted Friar Campos and a group of unspecified local clerics for a soup lunch in San Salvador.[79] Casaús had detained Aguilar for sedition in October of 1811, spe-cifically for alleged possession of correspondence with Morelos. Aguilar's detain-ment and false rumors that José Matías Delgado had received death threats were galvanizing events in the November uprising of 1811 in San Salvador.[80] Thus, when called to testify against Campos, caution born of experience with royal authorities tempered Aguilar's responses. Government authorities questioned Aguilar about his conversations with Campos only months after the El Salvadoran priest's re-lease from detainment. He had mentioned aggrieved people, Aguilar confessed, but not the number of aggrieved people nor their timetable to avenge their griev-ances. Having barely tasted liberty, he was in no hurry to return to confinement. His cryptic answers were devoid of revolutionary sound and fury.[81]

But as the Sanjuanistas' tribulations demonstrated, confinement often galvan-ized rather than intimidated prisoners and their communities. Manuel Aguilar would later throw caution to the wind. After the defeat of a second short uprising in San Salvador in January of 1814, a new, more conservative *ayuntamiento* invited the priest to bring the still-smoldering town a message of peace. He instead riled up a San Salvador parish crowd by pronouncing that "without justice there can be no peace."[82] He then laid out the festering injustices that justified the second uprising: men left languishing in prison for days, months, or even years with no formal charges; the glorious 1812 Constitution spurned; the arbitrary seizure of property; girls stolen and prostituted by royalists.[83] Alarmed Intendent José María Peinado relayed to Captain General Bustamante that Aguilar had likened him-self to Christ, promising to martyr himself for the cause. Insurgent assignations hosted in Aguilar's house; his incendiary sermon; his grandiosity—to meet this challenge, Bustamante should detain the priest immediately, the intendent urged.

Shortly thereafter, the captain general would open official sedition cases against Manuel Aguilar and his two brothers. Nicolas had preached an "ambiguous" ser-mon the day before his brother's incendiary remarks and conservative city council members would not invite the brothers to take the pulpit again.[84] Restless reformers like Friar Campos Diez and José Matías Delgado's brothers and cousins were forced into exile, dank prison cells, and the solitude of the monastery, as Ferdinand VII's triumphant return to the throne and 1814 disbandment of the Cortes sealed their fate. As in the Yucatán, in Central America this 1814 monarchical ascendency was ultramontane ascendency. An elated ecclesiastical hierarchy led by Archbishop Casaús and backed by the conservative faithful giddily promoted the Jesuits' signature cult, the Sacred Heart of Jesus. In Central America the cult would find an able champion indeed.

1814–1820: THE ULTRAMONTANE OFFENSIVE IN CENTRAL AMERICA

On the day of the Feast of the Sacred Heart of Jesus, June 21, 1816, God sent an important message to the Kingdom of Guatemala. The medium for such fervently desired communication was a nun in a state of holy ecstasy, Teresa de Aycinena. She was the daughter of Guatemala's most prominent merchant, Juan Fermín de Aycinena, whose credit networks had so enraged El Salvadoran growers that they had dispatched the elder Delgado, Pedro, the father of priest José Matíias, as their representative in 1794.

On this day dedicated to the Sacred Heart of Jesus, an image of a heart painted in blood appeared on a cloth wrapped around Teresa's head. News of the miracle spread and Teresa began to proffer more heart-shaped images on cloth to the faithful. The angels that painted the hearts had set up a veritable cottage industry, producing heart images with the characteristic flames of the Sacred Heart of Jesus, as well as other less ornate, poorly wrought heart images, that, as Teresa explained to skeptics, were destined for the less worthy among her supplicants. The angels also provided her with several particularly large images of the magnificent hearts of her confessor and of Archbishop Casaús, who frequented her bedside in the Descalzed Carmelite convent in Guatemala City. The angel band wet their brushes with blood from Christ's heart and his seven wounds, a salutary reminder of His passion, as He carefully explained to her. Around the same time, the Son of God also revealed to Teresa that the Jesuits' 1767 exile from the empire had been a mistake. Children had learned obedience from the Sons of Loyola, she explained to her clerical audience, and in their absence loyalty to church and state had diminished; slight reform, not exile, should have been their lot.[85]

Teresa's spiritual authority, her direct line to the Almighty, translated into political influence. After King Ferdinand VII's return in 1814, the capital's city council fell into the hands of conservatives. Facing mounting criticism from displaced

Creole city councilmen, the new conservative body fished for some divine sanctification of their charge, sending three blank handkerchiefs to Teresa through
Casaús. If the city council or the populace itself harbored any lingering doubts
about the Lord's preferred piety and politics, the handkerchiefs they received back
through the mediation of the archbishop surely disabused them of them: the angel
band had painted the Sacred Heart of Jesus with his own blood, not once but three
times on each handkerchief.[86]

Teresa parlayed her spiritual powers in dramatic political interventions that rever-
berated far beyond convent walls. In an 1817 proclamation, the nun insisted that God
wanted a letter from the king to Guatemala's high court, the Audiencia, to remain
sealed.[87] This incident soon had Guatemala city teetering on the brink of violence,
with the nun the epicenter of a showdown between the city's political and economic
elites, people like Teresa's own family, and royalist administrators. Creoles smarting
from Captain General Bustamante's autocratic regime felt sure that the unopened
missive contained the Crown's vindication of their many grievances, particularly
their desire to reclaim city council seats that an 1815 royal order had removed from
them. As the letter lay unopened, tensions simmered. Bustamante posted troops
around his palace. Ever the prophet, Teresa foresaw a civil war and swayed her confessor and Casaús to throw their weight against airing the document's contents lest
tensions boil over. The two religious did manage to delay the big reveal, but it happened soon enough: the 1817 royal order opened in 1818 lambasted Captain General
Bustamante's regime and restored offices to the Creoles he had spurned.[88]

Here was manly, austere reformers' worst nightmare: a miracle-working nun
promoting the Sacred Heart and insinuating herself and her patron Casaús into
political decisions best left to reform-minded men. In his memoirs, Fray Servando
Teresa de Mier recounted a conversation with an alienated former Jesuit, who
told him he sedulously avoided Rome's Piazza Colonna, a Jesuit hangout where
the brothers talked of nothing but "the visions of nuns and pious women." In response, Mier lamented that otherwise enlightened people proved credulous on
the topic of holy women, a subject "which has caused endless scandals and fiascos
in the Church." One such holy woman in turn-of-the-century Madrid, he warned,
had led the faithful astray with her widely circulated solution to France's revolutionary upheavals and Europe's ills: the return of the Jesuits and the elevation of
the feast of the Sacred Heart of Jesus to a high holy day.[89]

THE EMPIRE RECLAIMS SOVEREIGNTY

Reformist Catholics in both Central America and the Yucatán responded to the monarchical crisis of 1808 by insisting that in the absence of the monarch, sovereignty

should be decided by the citizenry through the medium of elections. These impassioned reformers' ecclesiology mirrored their democratic political leanings, and they championed both church councils and the Cortes de Cádiz, as well as favoring local political bodies like the new city councils and Provincial Deputations over the power of the popes and monarchs favored by the ultramontane.

These religious conflicts and the Reform Catholic sanctification of new forms of representation centered on elections were not unique in the fracturing Spanish Empire, as reformist sensibilities elsewhere contributed to even more profound devolutions of power to local governing bodies. As early as 1809, in La Paz, Bolivia, Vicente Pazos Kanki enthused to readers, reformers had established a governing junta to rule in the king's name and the laity had taken the first steps to electing their own bishops; the pope served only as the bishop of Rome, he offered by way of explanation, and early church history demonstrated the validity of popular elections for ecclesiastical hierarchs.[90]

Reformers in the viceroyalty of New Grenada (at the time encompassing present-day Colombia, Ecuador, Guyana, and parts of modern Brazil, Peru, and Suriname) set up ruling *juntas* to govern in the captive king's name. At the same time they reclaimed ecclesiastical authority from the Rome-centered hierarchy, citing the early church's democratic structure as their model. This twinned assertion of popular sovereignty would have decisive reverberations both in New Granada and, ultimately, far beyond it as well. Two critical figures from this early experiment in independence went on to sow the seed of Christian revolt in new ground in the years that followed, with momentous results. The Colombian region of Socorro in the Viceroyalty of New Grenada elected a bishop, Andrés María Rosillo y Meruelo, who fomented subversion. The same mutinous region also produced Juan Nepomuceno de Azuero y Plata, who would go on to write one of the foundational documents of Central American independence and state building, a justification for local control of the church that would be read aloud paragraph by paragraph in El Salvador's parishes and in the halls of government in Central America. The viceroyalty of New Grenada, too, would produce priests and laymen who ably championed reformist doctrine and causes in print and participated in dramatic ways in the campaigns of the Reform Catholic International. Following the lines of solidarity and even literal descent brings into high relief the religious networks undergirding the political rivalries that independence loosed across the former colonies.

The Schism of Socorro that elected Rosillo as bishop took place in Azuero's eponymous hometown, and it seems to have strengthened the cleric's convictions about the simple, ethical, and anti-hierarchical Catholicism he championed, or at least exposed him to the heady arguments adduced by both sides. Father Andrés

Rosillo, the schismatic bishop at the center of the movement, was a cathedral prebendary who resided in Bogotá but hailed from Socorro. On December 10, 1810, the
Junta Suprema de Socorro, which had seized sovereignty, voted unanimously to
establish a bishopric, a move that came close on the heels of their declaration of
control of the *patronato*. The next day, Rosillo received forty-four votes for bishop
to just a few each for his competitors. In short order, he was provisionally "consecrated" by local clerics and lay people in an ad-hoc public ceremony. The *junta*
immediately penned a report of the election and issued a call for all of the region's
clerics to sign a loyalty oath to the newly elected bishop. As the pressure mounted
for clerics to sign, the persecutions of those who refused proliferated, and the regions' parishes became theaters for fractious showdowns between partisans and
detractors of the schismatic bishop. Tensions ultimately dissipated when Rosillo
was elected as a deputy to the first national congress and embroiled himself in government rather than shoring up the new bishopric, but the trail they left mapped
the deep theological fissures that rent the ex-empire politically as well.[91]

Understandably, the decision by Socorro's Junta Suprema to erect a bishopric
for the area's 160,000 souls pleased some of the faithful while gravely shaking others. Socorro's Junta chose the parish priest of Bituima, Manuel Plata, to promote
the elected bishop and the new bishopric itself to fence-sitters and opponents in
Santa Fé de Bogotá. Accordingly, Plata teamed up with lawyer Ignacio de Herrera
to fire off a pamphlet intended to allay the fears of the faithful: the Socorro Junta's
representatives had consulted apostolic tradition and studied the church's early
history before launching the new bishopric and would be submitting their chosen
bishop to the pope for official anointment.[92] Despite striking a cautionary note
about the Holy Father's ultimate authority to embrace or reject the new bishop,
parish priest and appointed schism propagandist Plata also took the opportunity
to assert that the church's core practices had been corrupted by Rome over the
centuries. By shedding these historical accretions of hierarchy, the Socorrans were
returning to a lost time when the people not only attended clerical elections, but
actively voted in them. From the dim recesses of the past could be rescued a heritage that would inform their future, and the reform-minded Socorrans were its
heralds. Thus even while acknowledging the pope's authority, the Socorrans were
advocating for something far from orthodox, and ultimately more threatening to
Rome: a more democratic church, and an ecclesiology that sanctified a more democratic polity by extension.[93]

The wisdom of the church's early centuries, the Church Fathers, and the democratic past that justified the democratic future were all stock Reform Catholic
ideas, powerful pillars of ideology in El Salvador, Cádiz, and the Yucatán. The
junta's belief that reciting these tenets would win hearts and minds to the new

bishopric indicate that a fair number of Socorrans may have embraced these tenets. Here, as elsewhere, those advocating for democracy relied on a consistent and shared gloss on the church's history for justification.

But in Socorro, as throughout the Spanish Empire, reformed Catholics' every campaign, every small victory, incited a coordinated ultramontane response, and their opponents often commanded far greater resources and a near monopoly on the tip-top positions in the ecclesiastical hierarchy. The advisory cathedral chapter of clerics in Bogotá, the de facto governing body of the bishopric in the archbishop's absence, issued a pastoral letter opposing the Socorro schism and gave clerical participants like Manuel Plata forty days to come to heel.[94] The Vatican "prepared its lightning bolts," ready to impose the highest punishment against 160,000 souls, the pastoral letter warned. In response to these alarming threats, Manuel Plata parried that the faithful fervently desired their own bishop not to distance themselves from religion and the church, but to draw closer to it—and, importantly, to reclaim their tithe money for their own unfortunate neighbors. After all, why should their alms continue to succor the hordes of beggars who entreated Bogotá's ecclesiastical hierarchy rather than their own impoverished but at-task neighbors?[95]

Plata and Herrera's ringing defense of the new bishopric incited a spate of conservative recitations of the fatal errors the schismatic Socorrans committed. The conservative parish priest of Tabio, some 280 miles to the south, likened the Socorrans' assertion of their right to appoint a bishop to the Synod of Pistoia's second proposition, condemned as heretical by the bull *Auctorem Fidei*. Father José Antonio de Torres y Peña further ridiculed the Socorran call to return to the church's early discipline as a cynical and distorted reading of its history. In an erudite ninety-page pamphlet published just shortly after Rosillo assumed the mantle of the new Socorro bishopric, the Tabio cleric savaged the notion that the church formerly held popular elections for its personnel.[96] Elected bishop Rosillo would later accuse Father Torres of reporting on him to dreaded Spanish commander Pablo Murillo, of labeling him a schismatic, and of forwarding on to authorities in Spain a pro-schism manifesto he had circulated.[97] Archbishop of Santa Fé Juan Bautista Sacristán y Galeano expressed his displeasure with events in Socorro to ecclesiastical hierarchs in Bogotá and to the errant Bishop Rosillo himself. Rifling through the church's repertoire of responses to schisms, he seized upon Pius VI's response to the French Constitutional Clergy, the 1791 breve *Quod aliquantum*, making it clear the extreme measures the church was prepared to take against schismatics.[98]

The schismatic crucible of Reform Catholic militancy in Socorro also nurtured a young parish priest whose dramatic biography connects Socorro's restive local past to the regionwide rebellious future. While Father Juan N. Azuero Plata's revolutionary pedigree did not quite rival that of José Matías Delgado or Andrés Quintana Roo, it was impressive: on his mother's side, he claimed kinship with the legendary Antonio Santos Plata and other illustrious captains of the Comuneros, an anti-tax but pro-monarchical movement that drew upwards of 6,000 rioters into the streets of Socorro in 1781 and rippled outward to neighboring areas.[99] Father Azuero himself seems to have been drawn to the conflict early on, displaying the same incendiary mix of piety and liberal political leanings as the priests and laymen who comprised Delgado's inner circle and the core of the San Juanista faithful. In 1809, Azuero attended a reunion of armed men contesting vice-regal authorities. The viceroy and the Audiencia (high court) detained him for this dalliance with rebels, and he spent six months imprisoned.[100]

He might have languished longer in jail, but when Napolean's forces conquered southern Spain in May of 1810, the Supreme Central Junta in Sevilla disbanded. Claiming an equal right to govern in the king's absence as their peninsular counterparts, juntas sprang up in Cartagena de Indias, Calí, Pamplona, Socorro, and Santa Fé de Bogotá.[101] The pro-junta crowds in Bogatá's plaza swelled to upwards of 8,000 people on July 20, 1810, and by noon the next day the upstart Bishop Rosillo was free. Rosillo had been held in the Capuchin Convent surrounded by armed guards—guards that Viceroy Amat had earlier claimed were brought in for the cathedral prebendary's protection.[102] The jubilant crowds who released Rosillo paraded him through the city's crowded streets to the central plaza. Church bells pealed, musicians struck up rousing tunes, and residents bedecked balconies with decorative silk cloth.[103] Father Azuero was also liberated during these heady days and demonstrated a preternatural energy, rallying the crowd in streets adjacent to the main plaza to stand firm against a patrol that appeared to disperse them.[104]

Both Azuero and his fellow Socorran Rosillo manned the new ruling junta. Among the other members of this thirty-five-man body was lawyer Ignacio Herrera, who had served as Manuel Plata's co-conspirator on the pamphlet they penned in defense of the Schism of Socorro.[105] Both Rosillo and Azuero served on this ruling junta's committee for ecclesiastical affairs, bringing their reformist sensibilities to the body's debates and demonstrating the centrality of Reform Catholic thought and action to the push for local democracy and ultimately decolonization.[106]

Sadly for Azuero, the Junta was short-lived, his reprieve from persecution brief. During the Spanish "reconquest" led by the iron-handed military commander Pablo Morillo from 1815 to 1819, Azuero returned to the fray, leading a rebel unit of mixed cavalry and infantry troops against the royalists. On the run, hiding in grottos and canyons, he was eventually captured and condemned to the notorious prison fortress in the Spanish North African outpost of Ceuta. However, he managed to elude his captors en route to the Africa-bound ship as it lay in the harbor, and lived disguised and undercover in Nueva Granada until Independence in 1819.[107] He later served in congress for twenty years. At his death in 1857, a graveside eulogizer paid him a fitting compliment, with all the bombast characteristic of the epoch: "He grasped that nothing separated the Holy Books from democracy, because democracy is the Good Word applied to the public affairs of men."[108]

Archbishop Coll y Pratt would later report that he had smothered the Socorro activists in their nest, before the movement could grow wings, only to see another schism take flight in the province of Barcelona, Venezuela, in 1811. There the governor had placed priest and liberal political player Manuel Antonio Pérez Carvajal in charge of the region's ecclesiastical affairs, a move confirmed by a court and later accompanied by preparations for a democratic vote of the people for a new bishop. Pérez headed up Barcelona Americana's Sociedad Patriótica at its inception in 1811. Coll y Prat bragged that his swift intervention had kept these schismatic sputterings inchoate as well. But this claim should be taken with caution, as his 1822 report to a suspicious King Ferdinand VII was meant to defend his actions in Venezuela as archbishop; thus the report was less a careful analysis of the schism's causes, successes, and failures, and more a deliberate magnification of his own importance to outcomes advantageous to the king.[109]

Indeed, the Schism of Socorro petered out in large part because Rosillo himself, a prebendary in the powerful Cathedral Chapter of Santa Fé de Bogotá, lacked an outsider's monomaniacal fervor and aversion to compromise. Over time, it became clear that, despite his reformist convictions, Rosillo was an organization man, a church hierarch with much to lose during this tumultuous time. Pragmatism about keeping his position often tempered his radicalism—perhaps by preference, perhaps by dint of his inescapable obligations as a cathedral canon. While members of Santa Fé's Supreme Junta, keen to control church revenues, banned the ultramontane Archbishop Juan Bautista Sacristán from traveling inland to Bogotá to claim his post in December of 1811, Rosillo championed the cause of this Crown and Scepter-approved appointee, noting among other things that he was neither—as his opponents labeled him—an agent of Napoleon, nor a threat to the new government. Ironically, Rosillo, imprisoned by the Audiencia and the Viceroy in 1809 for his supporting role in an armed conspiracy and only liberated by Bogotá's pro-junta crowds, now felt the archbishop would be a salutary counterweight to the region's revolutionary priests, many of them armed, some of them military leaders.[110] And Rosillo committed to print that he was no fan of government seizure of tithe funds; these were rightfully controlled by the church.[111] Rosillo later noted to the king that the rebel congress had whisked him to Calí with the intention of banishing him to a deserted island for supporting the monarch

and church hierarchs in November of 1815; he was already in trouble with the upstart government when he got caught in Morillo's dragnet and exiled to Spain.[112]

Although Rosillo wrote flattering letters to the peripatetic Archbishop
Sacristán, and the hierarch praised his advocacy, the officially appointed archbishop doubted that Rosillo's interior sentiments truly matched his exterior words
and actions. Indeed, the cathedral prebendary's revolutionary past would prove
too well documented to hide: along with roughly four dozen other ecclesiastics,
Rosillo was marched to the coast for transportation to prison in Spain by order
of Spanish commander Pablo Morillo. One of his fellow clerics detailed the horrors of the forced exodus: the almost-raw meat doled out with their meager ra-
tions, the forced silence, the sweltering stint in a cramped below-ground cell while
awaiting embarkation. Eleven clerics died from such hardships.[113] Despite Rosillo's
back-peddling of his rebellious tendencies, once in Spain his part in the Schism of
Socorro landed him squarely in the crosshairs of the Inquisition. The Vallodolid
Inquisition charged him with three serious faults: embracing Luther's error of
conceding spiritual matters to the people and the secular authorities, leading a
schism, and being a patriot.[114]

Rosillo's appeals for clemency during his ordeal in Spain were frequent, but
the king's ear came at a price, and the savvy Ferdinand VII insisted that he report on how the monarchy could recover its dissident vassals in New Granada.
Underscoring the poor health his imprisonment had occasioned, Rosillo nevertheless spun a lengthy response to his sovereign. If the crown wanted peace, he stated
forthrightly, it must end the royalist atrocities committed under Pablo Morillo's
leadership and terminate the machinations of the National Congress and Simón
Bolívar.[115] In 1817, Rosillo's brother Miguel waxed optimistic about an abbreviated
sentence for his sibling, referencing his detailed report to the king and elliptically
noting that a "famous Spaniard" had recently described Rosillo as a "martyr and
defender of the King's cause"; furthermore, the queen had birthed an heir and in
celebration the king was pardoning political prisoners, including the many clerics
suffering in Caracas.[116]

In 1818, the Council of the Indies recommended Rosillo's inclusion in the
General Amnesty of 1817—the same pardon that had likely freed Sanjuanistas
Quintana and Zavala as well as the protagonists of San Salvador's uprisings. The
Socorro Schism had quickly fizzled out, the council argued. Moreover, its demands
were not unambiguously heretical: the church's early centuries demonstrated that
control over the *patronato* had indeed varied over time. After all, Spain had recently witnessed governing juntas' insistence on control over the *patronato*—and
no one considered these reformers schismatics.[117] Rosillo later praised the Council
of the Indies' efforts to convince the king of his orthodoxy. But the king whisked

Rosillo to the Inquisition against the council's recommendation in July of 1818, underscoring his pro-schism manifesto and his insurgent activities.

By 1821, however, Rosillo again resided in Santa Fé de Bogotá. In his view, his happy repatriation happened because during the Liberal Triennium of 1820–1823, a reform-minded representative assembly met, restored the constitution, and again abolished the Inquisition—the institution though which Ferdinand had "wreaked vengeance on those who opposed his despotism."[118] Of course before long neither Ferdinand VII nor the new *cortes* of 1820 to 1823 had reason to fear a repatriated Rosillo: on August 7, 1819, Bolívar's troops staggered over the Andes to deal the death blow to Spanish forces at Boyacá. The liberator soon stood atop an empire larger than that of modern Europe. Rosillo returned from his inquisition cell in Spain to the independent republic of Gran Colombia.[119]

Even after his return from exile, Rosillo's radicalism coexisted uneasily with his high church status: now the challenge was emphasizing his Reform Catholic roots rather than downplaying them as he had in Spain. When the liberal Colombian Congress called in Reform Catholic opinion leaders to guide the public on the *patronato* question in 1823, Rosillo held pride of place, along with Ignacio de Herrera. Authorities had fingered both Rosillo and Herrera as among the prime movers of the 1809 plot to establish a governing junta in Santa Fé inspired by that of Quito.[120] Rosillo played up these connections. His original report to the august congress reminded them of his dark days sparring with his Spanish inquisitors in Vallodolid. His Spanish tormentors had found no evidence in church history of popular elections for bishops and other hierarchs, but in Rosillo's retrospective account, he himself had bravely insisted to his Spanish interogators that the church's first eight centuries abounded in ecclesiastical elections. The good people of Colombia rightly held the *patronato*, a right best exercised through their congressional representatives. Here Rosillo reappeared as the defender of the reformist faith.

Only days after Rosillo, Herrera, and their fellow travelers submitted these impassioned musings to congress, the cathedral chapter Rosillo presided over submitted a report to congress brimming with ultramontanist sentiments—and they signed Rosillo's name to it. Their tormented argument that Colombia's *patronato* still belonged to the Holy Father was an impressive example of what reformers labeled Jesuitical casuistry: the "schismatic and Lutheran" authors who persuaded reformers like Pereira and van Espen to exaggerate secular authority over the church—both authors who loomed large in Ignacio de Herrera's report—constituted a tiny and benighted fraction of Catholic dissidents, they opined.[121]Warming to their subject, the ultramontanist clerics traced the inheritance of the precious *patronato*: if the people never willingly ceded sovereignty to the Spanish conquistadors, as the rebellious reformers maintained, then Colombia could not inherit the *patronato* from Spain. At best it could recuperate the sovereignty that its pagan people unjustly lost to their Spanish conquerors; but obviously the pope had not ceded the *patronato* to these pagan precursors—and so the *patronato* safely rested with the Holy Father in Rome. The cathedral chapter rounded out its rehash of key ultramontanist arguments by declaring any denial of the papal prerogatives a heresy condemned a thousand fold, pure "Jansenist" claptrap adopted by wayward clergy. The title of the report claimed Rosillo as its principal author—unlikely indeed as it systematically contradicted his earlier report. More likely, the clerical advisory board wielded enough power over Rosillo to ensure his compliance, or at least his silence.[122]

Reformist Catholics Rosillo, Azuero, Herrera, and Plata stand out in the historical record for their highly dramatic acts of defiance in Colombia during the crisis of royal authority. However, their fundamental views were far from anomalous among the region's clergy, many of whom advocated openly for the new juntas and later for independence from Spain. A case in point is José Cortés de Madariaga, a Chilean-born priest and doctor of theology who taught for six years at Santiago's Royal University of San Felipe, before beginning his more peripatetic life.[123] Sent to Bogotá as a Venezuelan government representative to craft a friendship treaty with the region's new junta in 1811, Father Cortés de Madariaga's faith that another world was possible never wavered. His account of his overland and river journey from Bogotá back to Caracas beginning in June of 1811 crackles with Reform Catholic cosmopolitanism and sentiment. He and his entourage of ten men undertook nothing less than a new geography for their new world, naming the crocodile-infested water features and landmarks after the revolutionary heroes of the Americas: an unnamed river cove became Miranda Bay after the worldly Venezuelan patriot Francisco Miranda; that same day, the group dedicated a small tributary to "our brothers from oppressed Mexico in honor of the inimitable *restaurador* Hidalgo."[124] A stream was reborn the Nariño River, after the New Granadan patriot Antonio Nariño, who had languished "sixteen years in chains."[125] But they outdid themselves commemorating the treachery of the hated Jesuits: the decaying fort on the Parausa River originally constructed by the Society of Jesus was re-christened "the Trench of Monastic Despotism."[126]

Dramatic, public, and bold, Cortés Madariaga's democratic fervor was not lost on royal authorities. His most famous act of defiance came on April 19, 1810, at the crowded main plaza in Caracas. On a balcony overlooking the plaza, the priest was among those arrayed behind the unpopular Captain General Vicente Emparán y Orbe as the official asked the assembled population below whether he should remain their ruler. As a result of Cortés Madariaga's energetic signaling from behind Emparán, the crowd thundered back a resounding "No!" to the Captain General—a defining moment in the formation of an independent ruling junta, as Emparán stood down.

The reform-minded Cortés Madariaga became notorious among authorities throughout the region as he promoted the cause. On his way to Bogotá to press for the friendship treaty, he stopped long enough in the town of Timotes to register his disrespect for ecclesiastical authorities by removing two edicts signed by the bishop of Merida from a church door and other locations; Bishop Hernández Milanés declared him excommunicated if he refused to return the edicts and repent publicly. By July 12, 1810, authorities had issued a royal order calling on everyone to be on the lookout for the rebel priest; six months later, Lima's authorities were rifling through the passports of travelers to their region in pursuit of the Chilean-born Caracas cleric.[127] Not surprisingly, when he attempted to flee into exile after Francisco Miranda's famous capitulation to the Spanish on July 25, 1812, the royalists pursued him. The fugitive priest almost escaped their grasp in the company of his traveling companion, his young nephew. But at the last possible moment the king's soldiers snatched him off the departing ship's deck.[128]

What happened next would give pause to even the most skeptical critic of the Black Legend of Spanish cruelty. Cortés Madariaga's fate at the hands of his royal captors demonstrates the power and ubiquity of reformist Catholic clergy and laymen in decolonization struggles across the empire. The Spanish first flung the priest into one of coastal La Guaira's dungeons, where he festered for two and half months. From the cell he was then packed below deck and shipped to Cádiz alongside seven of the region's most renowned patriots, whom the draconian Spanish officer Domingo Monteverde—the Pablo Morillo of Venezuela—denounced as "the eight monsters." Upon arrival, they were transferred to a jail at Cádiz to await a final move to prison in Ceuta.

Undaunted by his trials, Cortés Madariaga appealed to Britian's Ambassador Wellesley from his jail cell, composing an elaborate memorial that detailed Venezuela's and his own suffering. Wellesley promptly forwarded the account to the British cabinet—at least initially, it appears, to no avail. Neither the British nor the Spanish Cortes de Cádiz empathized with the detained American rebels, Madariaga concluded.[129] But Wellesley's advocacy may have worked: looking back on his heroism and his misfortunes from the vantage point of 1817, Cortés Madariaga elliptically noted that divine providence working "through a great nation" had saved him, and it did so "so I could work until my last breath in the cause of Independence and to consolidate the magnificent edifice of our hard-won liberties." He had, he noted, "put the first stone in this edifice in Venezuela." Chile, by contrast, had been afflicted with the "malignant fever of fanaticism" and the habit of "servility."[130]

Whatever role divine providence or Britain played in his ultimate freedom, however, Madariaga was only partially right about the indifference of the Cortes de Cádiz to his petition. The deliberative body was no monolith and some delegates very much sympathized with the detained Americans. Mexican deputy Miguel Ramos de Arizpe from Coahuila, New Spain, wrote to Fray Severando Teresa de Mier in March of 1813 that the "eight unfortunate prisoners" from Venezuela had not yet departed for Ceuta and still languished in the Cádiz jail. Recall that Arizpe had earlier championed San Juanista priest Agustín de Zavala's crusade to curb *rutinero* power over elections when the cleric landed in Cádiz to make his case. And Arizpe was connected to the Reform Catholic International through his friendship with Mier; he would later visit with the Abbé Gregoire in Paris. A Cortes de Cádiz commission had sentenced the "Eight Monsters" to remain in jail until they could be transferred to Ceuta. The legislative body was slated to reconsider the prisoners' fate in a week, but a pessimistic Arizpe held little hope for their release. He did, however, enthuse to Mier about Mexican rebel leader José María Morelos' leniency towards his royalist prisoners while his troops briefly held the town of Orizaba in 1812. Furthermore, Morelos' troops had shown exemplary restraint, he informed the famous friar: not one home sacked nor a single resident roughed up. In perhaps an even more telling indication of where his loyalties lay, Ramos de Arizpe meticulously detailed for Mier the movement of Spanish troops and armaments from the peninsula to America, particularly to Montevideo and Buenos Aires.[131]

As Spanish authorities tried to confine the carriers of rebellion in brigs and cells, they were fighting as well the infectious ideas of a radicalized reformist Catholicism. Juan Germán Roscio was one of the "monsters" sentenced and transported to Spain alongside Madariaga. The principal author of Venezuela's 1811 Act of Declaration of Independence, and one of the two co-authors of the 1811 Federal Constitution, Roscio wrote magisterial ruminations on the politics of religion that provide yet another illustration of the pervasive influence of Reform Catholicism and its centrality to decolonization struggles and democratic sensibility in the Spanish Atlantic world.[132] A former conservative and royalist, Roscio had fallen in with some of Reform Catholicism's most influential proponents and displayed the zeal of a recent convert. He exchanged letters with Blanco White and Juan Antonio Llorente in 1811, for example, and delegates to the rebel's 1813 Congress of Chilpancingo may have consulted Roscio, although the details of that consultation remain somewhat murky.[133]

Roscio's work found a wide audience in Latin America. In a February, 1823, diary entry Carlos María de Bustamante chastises the bishop of Oaxaca for reading "second-rate" religious writings that advocated obedience to political authorities rather than Roscio's rousing call for democracy. Likewise, on a bookselling junket to Mexico City in 1821, a publishing agent from the Philadelphia press that brought out a second edition of *The Triumph* sold 190 copies of the work compared to only 160 of Rousseau's *The Social Contract* and 75 copies of Thomas Paine's *The Rights of Man*. The work was reprinted in Mexico City in 1824.[134]

The Triumph did not mince words while championing core radical Reform Catholic tenets. The ultramontane party insisted on the pope's infallibility, Roscio lamented, but luckily French Catholicism had sustained the opposite with ineluctable arguments. Those learned priests had championed the truths that Jesus said welled up from the body of his church rather than falling from on high, as from the lips of the pope alone. The Holy Book was crystal clear that Jesus championed democracy, not autocracy. How was it that evangelizers in the age of feudalism had so distorted this clear maxim? Rocio pointed to their construction of the thicket of baroque practices that reformers like himself attempted to prune back: the fables, romances, and wild analogies spun from the simple scriptures; the invention of extraordinary happenings and mystic unions; the miraculous infusions of the divine into the mundane world. Like the Yucatán's Matias Quintana, Roscio found in the Bible the simple ethical maxims that formed the core of the religion and clear support for the sovereignty of the people. He declared a highly individual and divinely illuminated conscience indispensable to biblical exegesis, a conscience characterized not by blind and servile obedience, but by enlightenment and rationality.[135]

A schismatic bishop appointed by secular and ecclesiastical radicals; a flurry of written public contestation between ultramontane and reformed Catholics on the question on church governance in the new republics; his own armed opposition to royalist troops; a resolute and wily archbishop, Coll y Prat—this was the tempestuous context in which Azuero came of age and joined the priesthood. Having grown up in the midst of the abortive Socorro Schism, he would go on to be a principal intellectual influence over the much more momentous split between reform and ultramontane forces in Central America. This revolt was led by parish priest José Matías Delgado in El Salvador, and it would help infuse the deadly discord between Liberals and Conservatives with its religious fervor. Central America's front of the Reform Catholic International would be led by Delgado and his coterie, inspired in part by the Colombian Azuero; they would plunge the region into fifteen years of religious struggle over the fundamental nature of authority.

Simeon Cañas would leap to the intellectual barricades of the public sphere of letters in Delgado's defense; Miguel Castro, Delgado's helpmeet during the celebrations of the 1812 Constitution, would edit San Salvador's weekly reformist newspapers in 1824 and again in 1828, and prove thoroughly undaunted by his ultramontane interlocutors; Morelos enthusiast Campos Diez, who had met San Salvador's militant ecclesiastics as he wended his way through the region, would serve as the chaplain of a liberal army that fought in a holy war against the ultramontane, renting the region asunder from 1826 until the liberal victory in 1829.

3

The Sacred Polity

IN 1823 AND 1824, Central America emerged from three centuries of Spanish rule and a brief dalliance with Mexico to become a federation made up of five independently sovereign states: Costa Rica, El Salvador, Guatemala, Nicaragua, and Honduras. The Federal Republic of Central America, as it came to be called in this period, lasted from 1824 to 1839. While political tumult wracked most Latin American nations in the post-independence era, Central America's fissiparous tendencies proved particularly pronounced, in part because of the competition for resources and influence between the federal and state governments, particularly over the all-important tobacco monopoly revenues.[1] Regional and even municipal elites jockeyed to advance their interests, which, as Salvadoran Pedro Delgado's defense of El Salvadoran dye-growers' concerns demonstrated, were often opposed to those of Guatemala's entrenched merchant families, led by the powerful Aycinena clan. Once the dust had settled, it quickly became apparent that crisscrossing these regional, state, and municipal loyalties was a political division between liberals and conservatives.[2] That Central America would experience twenty major conflagrations in the sixteen years between formal independence and 1840 can be attributed in large part to the liberals and conservatives with opposing religious beliefs. Their allegiances were never separate from their ideas about the proper relationship between church and state, and the proper demarcation line between the sacred and the profane. As the new nations came into being, Central

For God and Liberty. Pamela Voekel, Oxford University Press. © Oxford University Press 2023.
DOI: 10.1093/oso/9780197610190.003.0004

American ultramontanist and reformist Catholics picked up and marched behind
conservative centralist and liberal federalist banners, respectively—this was not
a battle between secular liberators and religious traditionalists, but between two
factions of the Catholic Church.

The salience of these religious tensions came sharply into focus thanks to bolstered press freedoms and increased access to printing during the early independence period. New printing presses made visible reformist ecclesiology's pride
of place in the desacralization of *ancien régime* authorities and the "transfer of
sacrality" from pope and monarch to electoral democracy, as well as in disputes
about the relationship between church and state. Indeed, as evident from both the
Sanjuanistas and Mexico's pro-independence rebel literati, reformist Catholicism's
conciliar ecclesiology was one of the most important ideologies animating those
who sought the devolution of power to representative bodies like the Cortes de

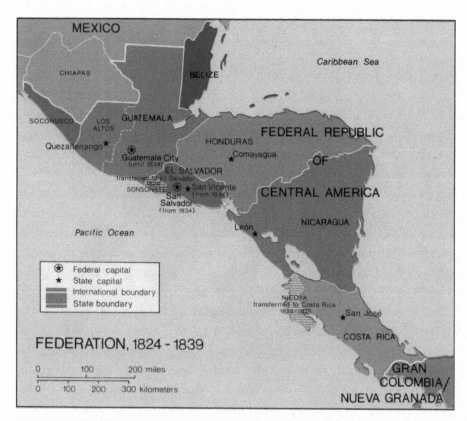

FIGURE 3.1 The Federal Republic of Central America united the former territories of New
Spain's Captaincy General of Guatemala until the process of dissolution that began with
Nicaragua's defection in 1838 was made official by El Salvador's declaration of an independent
republic in 1841. © 2003 University of Oklahoma Press. Reprinted by permission of the
publisher.

Cádiz and literate elites who debated passionately about sovereignty and representation in places like San Salvador and Mérida.

Both reformist Catholics and their ultramontane opponents readily identified
themselves and each other. They displayed their local and international *esprit de
corps* through dramatic confrontations in muddy streets and plazas; vituperative
debates in deliberative bodies from municipal councils to the federal government;
running arguments in the burgeoning public sphere of letters, one of whose major
outlets remained the parish; and often violent show-downs over the region's all-
important pulpits, regarded as a—perhaps the—key resource in the battle for
hearts, minds, and revenues. These religious passions proved so divisive and disruptive in part because partisans of each camp existed throughout the region, although each side had geographical pockets of strength at particular times, such as
the reformist stronghold of San Salvador and the El Salvadoran state throughout
the 1820s, and the conservatives' hold over the Guatemalan and federal government during the civil war of 1826 to 1829.

EARLY RUMBLINGS OF THE RELIGIOUS CIVIL WAR TO COME

In 1823, a federal governing body for Central America was created. The new
Asamblea Nacional Constituyente (ANC), or National Constituent Assembly, was
peopled by representatives from all five states in numbers proportional to their
populations. For the first head of this federal assembly, charged with penning
a constitution and establishing the federal government, the delegates selected
Father José Matías Delgado. The well-qualified parish priest from San Salvador
had served in a number of government bodies and participated in the 1822
Provincial Deputation of San Salvador that declared El Salvador a diocese; indeed,
he was named its first bishop.[3]

Although one of the region's most visible religio-political leaders, Delgado was
far from the only Reform Catholic stalwart seated at the ANC, which steadily
churned out legislation deeply disturbing to the region's ultramontane forces. The
simmering religious tensions that would reach a boil in the civil war were already
very much present. When in 1823 the ANC required ecclesiastics and government
officials alike to swear their allegiance to the new federal governing body, the
region's ultramontane cadres saw the writing on the wall: they refused the oath,
setting up dramatic showdowns around its administration throughout the region.

Nicaraguan Bishop Friar Nicolás García de Jeréz was well positioned to lead this
movement of the region's ultramontane Catholics, and in September of 1823 he
and a group of clerics in León refused to swear their fealty to Central America's

ANC. García de Jeréz feared his signature would sanctify a set of policies slowly coming into focus. The bishop of Nicaragua rightly surmised that the governing body was poised to have an energetic go at the ultramontane church, and he had no intention of lending his name to those efforts.[4]

His worries sprang from reformers' obvious ascendency across the region. García de Jérez was well aware that in July the liberal-dominated Guatemalan state had adopted laws that contravened the church's sacred canons and discipline. Perhaps most alarmingly, he felt they had taken these laws from the Cortes de Cádiz playbook, attacking clerical immunity from secular courts (clerical *fueros*), advocating for the suppression of the monastic orders, and pushing for the increased power of the secular over the regular clergy. Bishop García de Jérez knew that the Guatemalan government's Cadiz-like reforms boded ill for the ANC's emerging legislative agenda. The capital's liberal press only fanned his fears: a liberal Guatemala City paper, *La Tribuna*, lauded the great "century of reforms" that the ANC capped. Bishop García de Jeréz, his supporters reported, would rather "die a thousand deaths" than embrace such a century, a century of what they interpreted as virulent anti-church sentiment, not needed reforms.[5]

These Nicaraguan conservatives understood themselves as ultramontane Catholics squaring off against regional representatives of the Reform Catholic International. Two clerics wrote to the ANC in Bishop García Jérez's defense, displaying a strong familiarity with—and hostility toward—the theo-political genealogies of the reformers like Delgado and Isidro Menéndez who peopled the ANC. Bishop García Jeréz's reluctance to lend his imprimatur to the ANC's still somewhat inchoate policies, they argued, was more than justified. They lived in dangerous times; the immorality of the *philosophes* circulated promiscuously; and, most importantly, Pietro Tamburini and the Synod of Pistoía had described and circulated the civil power's long historical genealogy of rightful dominance of the church, threatening to turn the Lord's lushly cultivated vineyards into a secular wilderness.[6] Led by Bishop García Jeréz, then, León's conservative clerics rightly regarded these state-run churches as the heart of Llorente's "infernal plan."

Given the international and regional scope of Reform Catholic intellectual networks, Archbishop Jeréz's champions argued, no one should fault the ultramontane clerics of León for their reluctance to pledge allegiance to the ANC, nor question their distrust of liberal politicians who so brazenly menaced their immunity from secular courts. The many Delgado-like figures who peopled the ANC denied the pope's power and prerogatives. To a man, these reform-minded delegates were Riccians from Pistoía, Febronians—in short, Jansenists. Fortunately, the two ultramontane apologists explained, martyrs loyal to the true Catholic Church had lit the path forward: France's refractory clergy who had refused to sign the Civil Constitution of the Clergy particularly fired these Nicaraguans' imaginations. But other ultramontane exemplars provided inspiration, such as Saint Thomas of Canterbury, who had refused to sign Henry II's Constitutions of Clarendon weakening clerical fealty to Rome. They would imitate him, they rhapsodized, and when men rose against them, God would be on their side.[7]

The ANC's special commission established to coax Jeréz into a public proclamation of loyalty fired off a detailed defense of reformers' core principles. Its liberal majority could not let ultramontane clerical opinion leaders go unchallenged, especially not in Nicaragua. There, the inchoate state's loyalty to the federal government was uncertain, and liberal stronghold Granada and a conservative León under Jeréz's leadership engaged in ever-escalating violence. The battles in the two gracious cities threatened to tear asunder the barely unified federation of Central America.

To combat Garcia Jeréz's coteries, the ANC's Ecclesiastical Commission flashed the reform movement's favored epistemology: the careful study of church history, particularly the early councils. Indeed, the ANC's reply to the ultramontane bishop of Nicaragua's two champions expertly rehearsed many of the oft-invoked moments in reformers' revisionist history: the murky epoch after the popes' false decretals that removed secular oversight of the church; the church's glorious early centuries marked by frequent councils and a monk-less clergy, a Roman bishop with a limited writ; theologians who promoted conciliar authority like Juan Antonio Llorente and the Flemish Jansenist Zeger-Bernard van Espen; the Cortes de Cádiz's radical reforms—all of these Reform Catholic shibboleths were lovingly detailed in the ANC commission's report. If that were not enough, they summarized every station of the cross of the reformist church.In the fourth century, the monk Graciano introduced the idea of clerical immunity, van Espen documented and the ANC commission repeated, but the Church Fathers unanimously insisted on clerics' subjection to the secular authorities. In the thirteenth century, wise kings fought to recreate the early centuries' pared-down, purely spiritual church; far from introducing threatening innovations, the Cádiz Cortes had merely embraced these wise king's earlier interventions.[8] Van Espen's star had risen in Spain after the Jesuits were expelled in 1767, when a determined Crown replaced Jesuit authors with Reform Catholic texts in university curriculums; the Flemish theologian featured prominently in the canon law curriculum at many Spanish universities.[9] Bishop García de Jérez, the ANC report sighed, was their cross to bear, a particularly resolute and talented member of the Ultramontane International in their midst. He was Central America's Bishop of Orense, they proposed, invoking the refractory cleric who had thumbed his nose at the Cádiz Cortes, scandalizing Mérida's Sanjuanistas and reformist Catholics throughout the empire. The ANC would declare Roman Catholicism the official state religion, hoping to foster unity. But as the struggle over the oath already demonstrated, the church was deeply divided—nowhere more so than in Central America.

For all its reformist zeal, the ANC's reformist cadres knew that clerics like Jeréz were among the region's most important opinion leaders and thus had to be placated, not provoked. This they did somewhat reluctantly and not particularly well. The ANC prudently assured Bishop Jeréz de García that his fears of their church and state reforms were unfounded. He should relax; comfortable with the religion of their forefathers, the ANC commission rejected the Calvin- and Luther-like measures that had brought the church "to tears." Instead, they assured León's refractory clerics, ANC policies would benefit the *pueblo* by "enlightening" their customs. They also boasted that they sought equality under the law and positions open to all regardless of color or origin, a world where virtue and virtue alone determined rank. Virtue, in this case, was a reform-inflected class and race-based concept that would in the short and long run alienate the region's majority.[10] The ANC's reply to the Nicaraguan bishop's refusal to swear the oath was nowhere near truly conciliatory. The authors lobbed insults: León's ultramontane clergy were "degenerate sons of the country" who dangerously depicted the new "system of liberty" as an affront to religion.

Despite Jeréz's misgivings, he swore his allegiance to the ANC on December 10, 1823, as did the vast majority of León's clerics. Leon's *jefe politico* (regional governor) felt the ANC Commission's report had swayed the bishop to repent, and he praised the "sincerity" of the "Citizen Father Archbishop," as he titled Jeréz.[11] García Jeréz's future actions, however, belied any claim to sincere repentance. Perhaps the federal Ecclesiastical Commission's detailed historicism and farrago of citations of reform Catholic authorities simply wore the conservative Spanish bishop down. For García Jeréz to continue to refuse to sign would mean committing to endless defense of his position, close exegesis of church history, and recitation of ultramontane wisdom, which would be exhausting in the midst of civil strife and his leadership of Nicaragua's conservative faction. Whatever his reasoning, the bishop's capitulation would prove a temporary reprieve for the federation's reformers. Jeréz would yet spoil their gossamer dream of a Central America governed by reform principles. By early 1824, liberal and conservative Nicaraguans had resumed their duel; in the midst of a fratricidal civil war, the bishop, located in Managua, chronicler Alejandro Marure reported, remained the very soul of the party that opposed the new system.[12]

Bishop Jeréz understood the dominant religious proclivities of ANC members. For their part, reformers in this federal governing body readily identified Jeréz as a dangerous member of a transnational ultramontane conspiracy. In response to

Jeréz and his refractory clergy in León, the ANC's ecclesiastical affairs committee leaned on the wisdom of multiple renowned Reform Catholic intellectuals. In both Guatemala and Nicaragua religious tensions ran high in 1824 as these two deeply self-conscious factions dug in, invoking a long history of religious antagonism as they did so.

Jeréz's distrust of the reform-dominated ANC proved prescient. As the legislative body lumbered into action in 1824, a handful of ultramontane stalwarts attempted to hold back the reformist tide, the large and determined group of Reform Catholic deputies. Reformers issued a raft of measures adapted from the Cortes de Cádiz and other Reform Catholic deliberative bodies, as well as from the works of the International's intelligentsia. Although perhaps outnumbered, the ultramontane made a valiant showing in the new federal legislative body, in no small part because of the indefatigable representative from Sacatepeque, Friar Fernando Antonio Dávila. Dávila was elected president of the ANC in 1823, served on the editorial team of the conservative paper *El Indicador*, and happily brought ecclesiological issues to the floor during ANC meetings.[13] He had help from fellow *El Indicador* editor and ANC representative José María Castilla. During one memorable exchange, Dávila insisted on the church's right to act without the permission of civil authorities; Castilla chimed in that the Pope appointed bishops in Spain and had summarily dismissed the Cortes' elevation of reformer José Espiga to a bishopric, a case that quickly became a Reform Catholic cause celebre.

Some of the region's most erudite and polemical reformers rose in response. Future Guatemalan head of state Mariano Gálvez flipped Dávila's wisdom on its head, arguing for the civil powers' near complete control over the church. El Salvadoran priest Isidro Ménendez argued to limit the church's jurisdiction to the purely spiritual and to end ecclesiastical *fueros*, clerics' exemption from secular courts. The reformers' closer was Domingo Dieguez, who asserted that Spanish emperors had adjudicated clerical disputes throughout history, so Menéndez was right to call for the end of special ecclesiastical courts. He also echoed Gálvez's support for civil power over the church in dramatic fashion: the ANC was fully within its rights to remove bad clerics from their benefices.[14]

Although Dávila and Castilla put up a spirited defense, the ANC's legislative agenda reflected the will of its reform-minded members. Early decrees formally abolished the Inquisition; declared that papal bulls required government approval to circulate; set 23, not 16, as the minimum age of entry to convents and monasteries and 25 as the minimum age to profess; and required the archbishop to obtain government sanction of priests prior to their appointment. It insisted the state vet and approve pastoral letters and other ecclesiastical utterances before their mass circulation, tithes were reduced by 50 percent, and the children of priests and nuns obtained the rights of inheritance enjoyed by all children.[15]

The reformist Catholic liberals' religio-political priorities were also on display in their campaigns to extinguish the "Mayan language," using secular priests to advance that agenda.[16] During the early centuries of the colonial period, Crown officials depended on the finely tuned language skills of the mendicant orders, who conscientiously learned the languages of their charges; the monolingual state officials and the monolingual secular clergy had virtually no access to many indigenous communities without the friars' mediation. But this all changed in the mid-eighteenth century, as the Bourbon state sought to wrest control of the church from ultramontanist forces. A 1753 Royal Order had removed the regular orders from their *doctrinas* and from parishes, and subsequent orders from church officials and the Crown in 1754, 1770, and 1778 insisted that all religious instruction be in Spanish, and that schools be established in every town to teach the language. The Crown expelled the Jesuits in 1767, and dealt a further blow to ultramontanist pretensions when Pius VII was pressured to concede a May 15, 1804, bull *Inter gravioris* that established a vicar general for all of the Spanish Empire chosen by the king and resident in Madrid. Despite Bourbon Hispanization efforts, however, many indigenous towns in the western highlands of Guatemala remained in the hands of the Dominicans and Franciscans throughout the 1820s; and indeed secular clerics had only replaced the regulars in Quetzaltenango's parishes in 1815.[17]

Significantly, throughout the colonial period, the secular clergy had overwhelmingly predominated in the parishes of eastern Guatemala and El Salvador, and, relatedly, these regions were home to majority Spanish-speaking populations, despite El Salvador's population being roughly 52 percent indigenous, 4 percent white, and 44 percent ladino or free black. Indigenous people in Guatemala's highlands remained the vast majority in that region and remained overwhelmingly monolingual throughout the colonial period.[18] The ANC tied clerical promotions to energetic indigenous language eradication, perhaps with a full understanding that eradicating the popular religiosity that had long-vexed reformers was dependent on reformist educational projects like the *tertulias patrioticas*. The ANC nevertheless waxed pessimistic about the campaign's outcome given contemporary clerics' ambition and greed, so tragically distant from the "purity and disinterest" that marked the church's early centuries. Reformist luminaries José Simeon Cañas and José Antonio Alcayaga, and Mariano Gálvez served on an auxiliary commission of theologians tasked with commenting on the project.[19]

THE TENSIONS IN THE STREET: EL SALVADOR, 1824

In Central America's first year of independence, it proved to be El Salvador where tensions between ultramontane and reformist Catholics would radically tear the church apart at all levels of society. Delgado's May 4, 1824, investiture as bishop without Casaús' or the pope's approval proved a flashpoint, with ultramontane enemies coming from both within and without the country. The two sides fought bitterly to control El Salvador's parishes, as Delgado sent his fellow travelers—many of them resolute reformist Catholics who poured into El Salvador from other areas of Central America to defend the schism—to replace Casaús' loyal appointees. As the home-grown bishop and his government allies sat atop an extensive network of willing informants and loyal state bureaucrats, Delgado's loyalists readily ferreted out and expelled clerics unwilling to bend their flock's opinion to the "Good Cause." As the parish-by-parish skirmishes escalated into violence, literati cited either reform or ultramontane authorities and movement shibboleths that left no doubt where their loyalties lay. A pamphlet war raged. On the reform side, consistent with a religiosity that centered ethical maxims and the written word, Delgado's university educated coteries disseminated key reformist texts. These counteracted the Archbishop's pastoral letters and the ultramontane squibs flying off of Guatemala City's conservative-controlled presses.

The ANC and state governments naturally turned to priests to serve as crucial intermediaries between the federal government and the towns. Through its parish priests and vicars, the church was the only supra-municipal entity with the capacity to influence hearts and minds at the local level. In most towns the parish priest was the only representative of an outside entity; the new states had regional *jefes politicos*, but not lower-level officials. But the region's priests and a small slice of the laity had long been split into hostile reform and ultramontane factions, and lined up behind liberal and conservative parties, respectively. This theo-political divide would surface repeatedly in the coming decades and thwarted efforts to establish stable federal and state governments. State-builders with no real bureaucracy of their own looked to stand on the rock of the church—and found only shifting sand.

Even as early as January of 1824, this fundamental cleavage among the region's literate Catholics roiled the small towns and more populated urbs of El Salvador. Reformist Catholic priests teamed up with *jefes politicos* and like-minded municipal councils and lay radicals to rid the country of Archbishop Casaús' suffragan. Adding to the volatility was a laity that often proved attached to their priests, less, perhaps, because of these clerics' particular stances on church ecclesiology and worship or the proper relationship between church and state and more for their long and dutiful service in the town.

The town of Santa Ana was a case in point. Parish priest José Crisanto Salazar was the single biggest reason that the "spirit of servilism" proved so intractable in the area, a Delgado-appointed priest reported to the sympathetic *jefe politico*. Salazar, he continued, was no friend of Delgado's regime; the conservative priest had spread the rumor that Spanish troops were amassing nearby and that Guatemalans supported them, and he had long opposed El Salvador's independence. The *jefe politico*'s report detailing Salazar's "sedition" soon landed on Delgado's desk. The bishop and El Salvador's chief of state gave Salazar three days to leave the country. A state order to exile a priest, Salazar fumed, contravened canon law; moreover, he answered only to the church hierarchy and his secular persecutors violated his ecclesiastical *fuero*, his right to be judged only by religious authorities in church courts.

As would become all too familiar in El Salvador, escalation trumped reconciliation. Santa Ana's *jefe politico* assured the Head of State that he would crush the town's servile civil authorities if they tried to protect Salazar from state justice. The *jefe politico* swore to rid the area of the gadfly priest post haste. Salazar departed Santa Ana. That an armed guard escorted him out seems unlikely. By April of 1824, Salazar was confessing parishioners alongside the parish priest of San Pedro Pustla. He may have been biding his time until the conservative hierarchy again needed a stalwart foot soldier: they suggested him as Ignacio Perdomo's replacement in Ahuachapán on April 23, 1824. By May 10, Ahuachapán city officials and Salazar had both received an order from Mariano Prado instructing Salazar to vacate the parish within twenty-four hours.[20]

Ahuachapán had already experienced conflict on the ground between the two religious factions. In March of 1824, a group of 300 men gathered in this liberal stronghold and decided to oust parish priest Ignacio Perdomo from the town. Perdomo had been done in by a small and unrepresentative group of back-biters led by the municipal council, who had gone house-to-house to drum up support for his forced departure.[21] Ultramontane stalwart Perdomo most likely underestimated his own unpopularity: in 1823, the ANC had officially declared Ahuachapán a Very Loyal Town (*Muy leal villa*) for its role in the independence struggles and its "liberal sentiments in a time of great oppression."[22] The vicar replaced Perdomo and implied that he would not be sent back to Ahuachapán to face his agitated detractors.[23] The banished Perdomo instead lobbied in writing against Delgado's reform-minded appointees.[24]

The religious clashes in San Salvador's small towns intensified, and the state increasingly responded with force. In May of 1824, two conservative priests in charge of the ten-thousand-person pueblo of Isalco provoked what state authorities rather enigmatically referred to as "a commotion" in the streets, then fled the scene. The "commotion" had a backstory: two hot-headed clerics with diametrically opposed theo-political loyalties manned the town's two parishes, which were divided by the main road. Just eight days after Delgado's official inauguration as bishop, Tomás Miguel Pineda y Saldaña preached a ringing jeremiad against the schism. The other parish priest, a liberal, alerted state authorities to the sermon's content; soldiers dispatched from San Salvador rushed to Isalco to arrest Saldaña. Luckily for him, armed parishioners came to his defense, providing cover for a dramatic escape. The local *jefe politico* and the six soldiers then pursued conservative priests Miguel Muñoz and Saldaña across the border into Guatemala.

There fellow ultramontane cleric Francisco Estevan López and his riled Jutiapa parishioners rode in and confronted the armed squadron as it encircled Saldaña's hiding place in a convent in Yupitepeque, just over the Guatemalan border. An emotional López told the soldiers from San Salvador of his willingness to "shed his last drop of blood" to stop a malevolent government that persecuted priests.[25] Although chased by armed representatives of the liberal El Salvadoran state, Muñoz in retrospect attributed the incident to a theological firestorm. The priest who served the other parish in Isalco, the man who had alerted the state to Saldaña's sedition, was "deliriously feverish with liberal frenzy." Indeed Isalco's reform-besotted parish priest, Muñoz sputtered, had assailed the "Church's universal discipline" by arguing for a reformist cause célèbre, clerical marriage, in front of El Salvador's national assembly.[26]

The incident report later sent by an Isalco municipal councilman to El Salvador's government incensed López: it portrayed him as a *belletrist sans merci* who goaded his reluctant flock to confront the soldiers pursuing the two priests. But he voiced no regrets about his armed support for Muñoz and Saldaña. They did the Lord's work by discouraging loyalty to the schismatic bishop. Moreover, as vicar, he was obliged under penalty of excommunication to defend the church's rights, especially against lay judges who overstepped their authority to pronounce against priests. He had not, as the loose-lipped city councilman reported, led his flock into battle merely to protect his friend Saldaña. Defending a loftier principle, he had informed the squadron of the grave punishments the church promulgated against persecutors of its ministers and those who stood idly by. The San Salvadoran soldiers had gotten the message and turned home.[27]

A beleaguered Saldaña instead went into exile, wending his way first to Guatemala City for Archbishop Casaús' blessings, and then to Antigua Guatemala and the peace of the Convent of Belén. As he did so, members of Asunción Isalco's city council and representatives of the town's *comun* pled with ecclesiastical higher-ups for the return of their revered and hardworking priest. After mass, Saldaña heard confessions until midday without even so much as a cup of chocolate to fortify him; then, after a short nap, he heard confessions well into the night. He shared food from his own table with the sick and tirelessly baptized, married, and buried the poor at no charge. The greater glory of God would be served by his return to his community.[28] Isalco parishioners, however, were not the only ones angling for Saldaña's return. El Salvador's government demanded that the triumvirate--the three men who made up the federal government's executive council--extradite the conservative priest to San Salvador. This they were not prepared to do.[29]

Safe in Guatemala in the fall of 1824, Muñoz, Saldaña, and López tapped church coffers to produce and disseminate a trio of pamphlets denouncing the Delgado-led schism, rallying ultramontane literati and the laity to join them. Their most impassioned causes: the perils of democracy and the sanctified unilateral authority of popes and monarchs. This defense of hierarchy stood in stark contrast to their Reformed Catholic opponents, for whom the church's early centuries revealed the sacred origins of participatory democracy, a world of widespread lay and clerical vote-casting for ecclesiastical leaders. El Salvador's liberal congress, Saldaña and Muñoz underscored, even had the gall to argue that the pope should rightfully be elected by the civil authorities.[30] The three exiled clerics refuted any and all attempts to cast hierarchs as usurpers of the people's prerogatives. Their Carta católica noted that, according to the fourth-century Nicene Council, the laity could opine on a bishop's merits, but the right of election lay elsewhere, with the other bishops and with the Holy Father. Deaths, bribes, and fractious sparring sprang from open elections involving the people. The popes had rightly restored the church's original monopoly method of ecclesiastical appointments to avoid these evils.[31] In short, electoral democracy did not have the church's sanctifying imprimatur.

Conservative critiques of federalism couched in secular rather than ecclesiological terms echoed the dangers of open elections, demonstrating yet again the hopelessly intertwined nature of theological and political discourse during this period. The ANC representative from Sacatepeque, Friar Fernando Antonio Dávila, informed the assembly that "it was only natural that governments have one head," and that the establishment of separate, independent states with divergent interests would lead only to anarchy.[32] Popular elections were prone to error and downright dangerous, Dávila proposed, especially when people lacked sufficient enlightenment to "act for themselves." He called for propertied family men or people with a useful profession to serve as electoral representatives.[33]

El Salvador's reformist Catholics felt differently and engaged in obsessive rehearsals of the radical democracy that characterized the early church. The Roman

Curia's centuries-long efforts to occlude the church's democratic past and aggrandize the pope's unilateral authority came in for particular criticism. In response to Casaús' edict of June 21, 1824, condemning El Salvador's new bishopric, the El Salvadoran assembly's ecclesiastical commission applauded a Mexican committee that had argued for the country's patronage rights and for a radically democratic national church.

The El Salvadorans most likely referenced the work of an 1823 Mexican congressional commission on ecclesiastical affairs, led by the flamboyant Fray Servando Teresa de Mier, which had praised the Council of Pistoia and the French Civil Constitution of the Clergy and located patronage with the civil authorities. The 1823 Mexican report also had stressed the imperative to restore the discipline of the early church, particularly a system of ecclesiastical elections. At the lowest level this process would involve even parishioners.[34] El Salvador's congress echoed the Mexicans' logic, noting the laity's participation in clerical elections during the "time of the apostles." Councils like that of Chalcedon demonstrated that, for a prelate to be superior to everyone, he had to be chosen by everyone.[35] Not only did these Central American radicals align themselves with their Mexican counterparts and embrace "organic intellectual" Azuero's wisdom, they also displayed their allegiance to the transatlantic Reform Catholic International by citing reform luminaries from across the Atlantic, such as Juan Antonio Llorente.[36]

The authors of the *Carta católica* did not exaggerate their reformist opponents' love of elections and distrust of top-down authority, whether monarchical or papal. Indeed, no hierarch was immune to criticism from reformers girded in the armor of Reform Catholicism's radical ecclesiology. Even the popes had been elected by the people and confirmed by kings in the church's earliest times, Anonymous declared in the reformist tract *Aviso oportuno (Opportune Notice)*. Over time, the papacy had usurped the people's rights to elect the Holy Father. Reformers' duty was clear: restore the church to its glorious democratic past. Thus did this anonymous author struggle with ultramontane pamphleteers to define the church's essence and to shift sacral authority from monarchical to democratic political formations.[37] The Reformist Catholics like *Aviso oportuno*'s author and members of El Salvador's congress promoted a radical lay conciliarism where the people and their priests held the biblical Keys to the Kingdom. They sanctified this radical democratic vision by locating it in primitive Christianity.

These reformers were the unexpected heirs of the reformist Bourbon upper clergy and Cádiz Cortes liberals whose episcopalism and regalism threatened Rome. El Salvadoran congressional deputies representing San Salvador, laymen Ramón Meléndez and Bonifacio Paniagua, both of them participants in the 1811 uprising, clearly stated that neither crown nor miter held the right to the *patronato*. The church's early centuries demonstrated that the selection of clerics was the people's prerogative—a prerogative usurped by popes and kings alike in subsequent centuries.[38]

The reform-minded Provincial Deputation had demonstrated their enthusiasm for the ecclesiology of the church's early centuries several years before the pamphlet war. In June, July, and August of 1821, El Salvadoran municipalities, residents of San Salvador (*vecinos*), and Archbishop Casaús responded to the Provincial Deputation of Guatemala's request for nominations for bishop of a proposed new bishopric in El Salvador. The nominations were sent to the king. All of the constitutional city councils with the exception of Sensuntepeque recommended Delgado, as did Archbishop Casaús. Sensuntepeque noted an equal number of votes for Delgado and Manuel Antonio de Molina, the priest from nearby San Vicente who we last saw denouncing renegade friar Campos Diez. In their arguments for Delgado, many towns noted that he had popular approval, as evidenced by his election to the Provincial Deputation in both 1813 and 1820.[39]

To appreciate how truly radical this was requires an understanding of the reformist Catholicism's genealogy in Latin America. Ironically, in sacralizing democracy, independence-era reformers and their counterparts in the early republics were the unexpected spawn of the reform-minded bishops and Crown bureaucrats of the late Spanish Empire. These reform-minded upper clergy, and a sizeable number of Crown bureaucrats, most of them Peninsular Spaniards, had sidled towards a Spanish national church by reclaiming bishops' prerogatives from a power-hungry papacy, citing evidence from church councils held in Spain to justify their position. These late Bourbon-era bishops owed their position to the king. For them, the divinely ordained monarch was as close to God as the Holy Father, and thus should take responsibility for reforming the church in his territory in accordance with God's will. These reformist bishops and high-ranking members of the Bourbon state argued for a conciliar ecclesiology and for the Augustinian notion of efficacious grace. Literati like Mier and lower clergy like Sanjuanista Vicente Velásquez and El Salvadorans Delgado and Miguel Castro were therefore the decidedly wayward progeny of these imperial reformers. To be sure, these lower clergy and lay radicals drew inspiration from the bishops' revanchist claims against the Holy Father. But Latin American rebels against the empire and supporters of the Cádiz Cortes alike crafted an ecclesiology beyond anything these regalist bishops and bureaucrats desired or even could have imagined. Rather than vesting the pope's power in the king and bishops, they vested sovereignty in the people and the entire clergy. In doing so, they joined a growing cast of New World actors in sanctifying the democracy of the Cádiz Cortes, the wars of independence against Spain, and democratic governance in the new republics.

THE NEW PUBLIC SPHERE OF LETTERS

The region's fractured religious landscape and the centrality of Reform Catholicism both to Latin America's process of independence and to subsequent republican governance all come sharply into focus in Central America after independence in 1824, in part because of increased access to local printing presses. Being able to communicate their ideas particularly empowered reformers located outside of Guatemala City.

In this climate of increased freedom of the press in post-independence Central America, the *Semanario Político y Mercantil* ably represented San Salvador's reformist Catholics. Delgado had laid the groundwork for the paper in 1824, successfully taking up a collection for the country's first printing press. The *Semanario* started in late July under the editorial leadership of cleric Miguel José de Castro y Lara. Castro had orchestrated San Salvador's week-long celebration of the 1812 Constitution alongside Delgado, participated in the 1811 and 1814 uprisings in San Salvador, spent time in confinement for this "sedition," and then received a royal pardon. He later sat in the 1823–1825 ANC as the deputy from Zacatecoluca, where he served as parish priest, and served a short stint as president of El Salvador's congress in 1826. Castro was yet another example of the pattern of reformist Catholic partisans who fought for the "return" of sovereignty to local political bodies and then emerged from the rubble of the ancien régime's fallen hierarchies after independence waving the banner of liberalism and federalism. Cañas, Delgado, and Isidro Menéndez also contributed to the *Semanario*, which circulated in El Salvador, Guatemala, and Honduras.[40] One foreign visitor summed up the *Semanario*'s editorial slant as inveighing incessantly against the Holy Father, monastic institutions, and clerical celibacy.[41]

San Salvador's *Semanario* denounced Saldaña, Muñoz, and López's *Carta católica* while the pamphlet still lay on the press and roasted the three clerics for declaring El Salvador's bishopric schismatic and for recycling the wisdom of ultramontane authors. Given Muñoz and Saldaña's reputation for "malice" and their "sordid motivations," the San Salvador paper felt readers deserved a fair and balanced explanation of the new bishopric's logic. They were only too happy to provide one. A country of 300,000 souls needed its own bishop, they explained, and Spanish kings had wielded the right of presentation to benefices. El Salvador, they asserted, had inherited that right. They likened the three wrongheaded clerical

FIGURE 3.2 The lifting of censorship laws after
independence encouraged an explosion in print
culture, enabled by the proliferation of printing
presses in the region. The result is immediately
evident in the historical record: religious disputes
were prevalent in the newspapers and pamphlets
that flowed from a dispersed printing landscape.
© 2003 University of Oklahoma Press. Reprinted by
permission of the publisher.

authors to Spaniards like Casaús who had conspired against independence and
prescribed excommunication for New Spain's rebels. *Semanario* readers should
beware the *Carta católica*, for it sought to again yoke Central America to Spain.
Not surprisingly, El Salvador's congress agreed with the city's liberal paper and

submitted the pamphlet to the official censorship board in Guatemala City to prevent its circulation.[42]

Pre-publication denouncements and a government attempt at censorship might seem excessive reactions to a pamphlet, but reformers grasped that the *Carta católica*'s rhetoric ratcheted up the stakes in the battle. Nothing less than salvation—and the nature of church and state in that process—was at stake here. Furthermore, liberals understood that Saldaña and Muñoz circulated their musings through the church's extensive communication mechanisms, including pulpits, and the all-important *cordillera*—the rapid mail system between religious houses and parishes. Most alarmingly, the three conservative priests pulled readers and listeners into the fray by asking them to sign their names to the *Carta* to indicate their support, which they did in droves.[43]

Both sides understood themselves to be in a war to save the church. The *Semanario* rightly feared the *Carta Catolica*'s polarizing rhetoric. They felt that the screed portrayed reformers not as slightly errant but still beloved brothers in Christ, but as the Devil's slavish minions. Indeed Saldaña and Muñoz further escalated the war of words and deeds against the "perverse," defined as people who "vomited infernal ideas," and confused the "power of the keys with the authority of the scepter" thus raising the government above the church. Will you stand idly by, they challenged their readers, as your opponents "rip Jesus Christ's seamless tunic"? Will you let your enemies destroy the Lord's inheritance "without arming yourselves with holy zeal"? For the two clerics, this was a war to save the deceived, whose errors destined them to "perish and perish eternally."[44] In the end times, they warned, some would abandon the faith and attend to the "doctrines of demons." That time had come and the righteous should not countenance the fallen lest they empower them.[45]

The demon's doctrines were so seductive because they were anything but secular. Many of the region's ultramontane authors proved particularly clear-eyed about their enemies, eschewing other Latin American conservatives' penchant for tarring reformist Catholics with the brush of secular *philosophes*. A case in point of their deliberate misrepresentation of their Catholic opponents are the controversies that swirled around the work of Juan Nepomuceno Azuero Plata. Azuero participated in the "Schism of Socorro" and went on to a storied career as a pundit and liberal senator in the new nation. Like Delgado's circle of supporters and influential groups of reformers from Buenos Aires to Philadelphia, Azuero and Bogotá's reformist Catholics engaged in heated public exchanges with conservative Catholic opinion leaders. And like the reform-minded El Salvadorans and Guatemalans, Azuero championed a church shorn of its centuries' accretions of cults and corrupt hierarchs and a state whose prime purpose was the creation of that reformed church.

But in an oft-repeated move, Azuero's conservative detractors rejected his framing of the fight as one between ultramontane and reformist Catholics. This mischaracterization incensed the priest, as it did so many reformers in the early republics of Latin America. This deeply religious man was especially the most maddening part of the ultramontane's slur campaign was this: they disparaged him as a deracinated French philosophe, a new world spawn in an ongoing and pitched battle for hearts and minds between religious belief and secular philosophy, enchantment and a world without God. In one particularly illustrative interchange, a prominent Bogotá doctor lambasted Azuero's ruminations on the raucous religious processions funded by the city council, misrepresenting his criticism as an assault on the church by someone outside its fold. His detractor, Azuero fired back, ran with a benighted crowd: people who clung to ultramontane doctrines contrary to the church's liberty, people who hated independence, and people who maliciously labeled progressive public authorities like himself "masons, heretics, and the impious."[46]

During an acrimonious 1826 exchange on the proper education of Bogotá's youth, Vicente Azuero Plata, Juan's brother and fellow liberal politician, seethed that their enemies portrayed them as religion's detractors rather than its determined defenders. Left unchecked, conservatives would take all but ultramontane books away from impressionable students, Vicente warned, as they accused the champions of an ethics-centered piety and democratic church of being dangerous atheists and heretics. Simply put, the ultramontane contorted reality, equating liberty with heresy and republicanism with impiety. Glorious independence, a crime; tolerance, an affront to religion; the curtailment of the church to spiritual matters, a schism—these, Vicente Azuero insisted, were the conservatives favorite litanies.[47]

Juan Azuero exhorted reformers to the barricades to fight the mischaracterizations. Good Colombian citizens, good liberals, he explained, refused these distortions of the battle lines. They would no longer countenance the charge that their precious independence was the child of Jacobinism or that liberals rejected religion.[48] They were not irreligious; rather they successfully used reason and talent to see through the religious distortions wrought by the Inquisition and the Jesuits, to challenge their monopoly on what constituted orthodoxy. Reformers aimed their righteous fire at reforming the church. City council funds spent to ramp up public processions with dancing, firecrackers, and matachines did not foster devotion, Azuero insisted, but only degraded real religion.[49] Religion had two enemies, the irreligious and the fanatical, Vicente Azuero insisted, and his austere, ethical Catholicism was neither. The ungodly, and worse yet fanatics like his ultramontane detractors, were the real threats. To combat this fanaticism and impiety, he supported the city's first Bible society, where he could "drink holy doctrines untainted by the commentaries of hypocrites."[50]

Central America's ultramontane conservatives could ill afford to misread or underestimate the godly passion animating their reform-minded enemies. López joined the clerical Saldaña brothers—*Carta Católica* author Tomás, and San Salvadoran cleric José Ignacio—to author a more honest analysis of the fault lines than that of the conservative Colombians who so frazzled the pious Azuero brothers in Bogotá.

The Saldañas were particularly motivated ultramontanes in part because of their own family history. Their Spanish father had served the Marques de Aycinena as a high-ranking administrator on his estate near San Salvador, and was killed during the 1811 unrest in the area—unrest led in no small part by the Delgado brothers. Archbishop Casaús had brought the two orphans into his orbit, perhaps even into his Guatemala City palace. Fourteen years later, in the heat of rhetorical sparring with a liberal opponent, José Ignacio suggested that Delgado's band had planned his father's murder and contracted an assassin to carry it out. These heartless conspirators later christened this assassin a "patriot" and granted him a captainship.[51]

The clerical Saldaña brothers had every reason to pursue a deeply personal family vendetta and to support their patron Archbishop Casaús. Instead they saw themselves as frontline combatants in a widespread religious dispute. With salvation and the proper relationship between church and state at stake, these religious enmities proved intractable, the battles' continuance inexorable. The church had indeed survived some determined foes, the Saldañas proposed, but might not weather the current religious crisis. Who would have thought, the two clerical brothers mused, that having triumphed over the Voltaires and "Juan Santiago Rousseaus," the church would now face its stiffest challenge from within its ranks, from its own sons?

The *Semanario*'s editorial team also understood themselves and fellow travelers as sincere reformist Catholics squaring off not only against clerics blindly loyal to Casaús, but a vast network of committed ultramontane opponents. The El Salvadoran paper's opening salvo: the *Carta católica* was little more than a "fastidious" and "poorly crafted" hodgepodge of ideas copied directly from the work of ultramontane luminary Guiseppe Devoti.[52] The Italian theologian certainly offered an arsenal of ammunition against reformist Catholic claims for the righteousness of conciliar authority and a reduced papal writ. The church should be a positively sclerotic hierarchical monarchy; Rome's jurisdiction extended far beyond the purely spiritual; the pope's opinions always trumped decisions made by councils—if not an exact copy of Devoti's musings, the *Carta católica* certainly shared his basic tenets.[53]

Faced with Devoti's razor-sharp rendition of ultramontane tenets, the *Semanario* turned to a Reform Catholic heavyweight: Archbishop of Barcelona Josef Climent, and specifically to his 1769 pastoral letter on the tithe. In the El Salvadorans' estimation, Climent rightly juxtaposed the Christian imperative to succor the deserving poor with the sinful squandering of resources on excessive celebration and sensual stimulants to piety. What would Climent have said, the *Semanario* asked rhetorically, had he known that Central American tithe payments swelled to bursting the central hierarchy's coffers, leaving not even a pittance to alleviate the misery of El Salvador's citizens.[54]

The *Semanario* did not exaggerate: tithe payments flowed out of the provinces and into the cathedral chapter in Guatemala City. The tithe was thus a key grievance animating Delgado's bid for the bishopric. The practice had a long history and was a particular irritant in El Salvador, where the majority of residents were not exempt from tithing. Anxious to remove the new faith from any taint of material interest, the Crown had exempted the indigenous population from the ten percent tax in the early sixteenth century. To fund evangelization efforts, it increased Indian tribute and gave this hidden ecclesiastical tax to the church to administer Indian *doctrinas*, where the friars outnumbered the secular clergy until the middle of the eighteenth century. Originally designed as a temporary measure while the neophytes mustered an enthusiasm for funding the faith, the tithe exemption lived on: the friars who worked closely with the Indians as *doctrineros* thwarted attempts to establish the tax, as it went directly to the bishop and the secular clergy. Regular and secular clergy sparred on the tithe issue, with uneven outcomes across the Spanish Empire. In the Kingdom of Guatemala, the Indians never paid tithes; instead, each *doctrinero* received a standard salary from the "extra" tribute collected from the Indians by the Crown.

Official legislation carefully divided the tithe between the Crown, the bishops, the cathedral chapter, parish upkeep, and the parish clergy, among others. But throughout the colonial period in the Kingdom of Guatemala, the cathedral chapter and the bishop simply usurped the overwhelming bulk of the funds. Clergy both regular and secular gleaned most of their wealth from the *ración*, food or money extracted from the Indians, and through *servicio* (service) labor performed by natives in the sacristy and in the priests' homes and other properties. This service included jobs like haying, wood stacking, cooking, singing, music-making, and making tortillas; some clergy had staffs of upwards of twenty Indians. Indians as well as others also paid fees for baptisms, burials, and marriages. All told, the rural population paid more in parochial fees and donations than in any other single tax.[55]

Thus Delgado's bid for the bishopric was also a bid for the tithing revenue that had long flowed away from local parishes that received little to nothing from the cathedral chapter in Guatemala's capital city—or from Rome. The spiritual economy very much paralleled the world market for indigo, with wealth pooling at the top and among distant elites. And the tithe was only part of the wealth extracted from El Salvador and sent to Guatemala City's hierarchs. The *Semanario* accused the archbishop and the cathedral chapter of extorting fees for marriage dispensations and announcements of impending nuptials, and forcing clerics to purchase holy oils from the Archbishop at exorbitant prices.

THE FRENCH ANALOGY: NEW WORLD REFORMERS AS THE SECOND COMING OF THE CONSTITUTIONAL CLERGY

As the *Semanario*'s discussion of tithe revenues and the *Carta católica* incident demonstrated, rhetorical fisticuffs joined armed soldiers and riled parishioners in a war of words. Although physical conflagrations continued, the ultramontane and the reformed could fight battles by proxy. In one particularly illustrative exchange, their avatars included the Holy Father and a group of radical French clerics.

Central American conservatives readily drew parallels between Pope Pius VI's ringing denunciations of the 1790 revolutionary French Civil Constitution of the Clergy and the church hierarchy's stand-off with Delgado and his supporters. It was an apt analogy, in part because Latin American intellectuals like Mier eagerly imbibed the intellectual production of these Constitutional Clergy, particularly the Abbé Gregoire. The revolutionary French document had suppressed the tithe, nationalized church lands, made clergymen salaried functionaries of the state, slashed the incomes of the upper clergy, decimated the regular orders, and established lay elections of clergymen through the auspices of departmental or district assemblies. New bishops wrote to Rome to inform the pope of their appointments as a courtesy, not to seek the Holy Father's imprimatur or his permission. By 1791, parish clergy swore an oath in front of their parishioners to this new French constitution, with its jaw-dropping reorganization of the church. Refractory clerics lost their benefices and often suffered organized community ostracism. Parish strife ran rampant and factions formed, but the oath proved inescapable: children reenacted it while playing in the streets, poets extolled its sublime merits, playwrights mused about it, and peddlers plied engravings of the oath that partisans hung on their walls next to images of the saints. The names of recalcitrant clerics filled the papers, and, in August of 1792, the government decreed the blanket deportation of all non-jurors.[56]

Faced with this unprecedented affront to church authority from a key majority-Catholic country, Pius VI condemned the French Constitutional Clergy and their followers, but knew to tread lightly. Initially he refrained from fulminating un-equivocal excommunications at the principal actors in favor of threats for failing to desist, fearing a schism along the lines of that of Henry VIII.[57] His April 13, 1791, encyclical *Charitas*, however, prevented juring clerics from exercising their ecclesiastical functions, declared the new bishops to be schismatic, and thundered about the threat the Constitutional Clergy posed to the Church. Pius VI described the new religious structures in France as heretical, schismatic, perverse, and sub-versive of papal authority. Louis Alexandre Expilly, who rose to bishop in the new system without the pope's approval, was particularly criticized by the Holy Father. It seems he had argued that the constitution returned Church discipline to its early pristine purity, a halcyon time when the people had elected bishops and other bishops had then anointed the elected, bypassing Rome entirely. Only the Pope held this right of appointment and anointment, Pius VI reminded him, and Expilly and the other new bishops were illegitimate.[58]

Delgado was Central America's Expilly, and to make sure everybody knew it, his ultramontane opponents rushed out stacks of copies of Pius VI's 1791 brief to clergy for distribution in both El Salvador and Guatemala. El Salvador's congress imitated their heretical French predecessors, these conservatives argued, and the Pope had condemned the French Constitutional Clergy in no uncertain terms. What made these New World schismatics think that the famously reactionary Pope Leo XII would hesitate to condemn them? El Salvador had not even the "re-motest hope" of winning Rome's support for Delgado's little adventure in elect-oral church politics. The French national assembly erected bishoprics and chose bishops for both new and established positions, often forcibly replacing refractory prelates in already existing jurisdictions. The El Salvadoran reformers mimicked this sad precedent, the ultramontane noted while pushing their schism forward knowing full well that a prior pope had already condemned their every move.[59]

This accusation had enormous consequences. The *eminence grise* of reform cir-cles, José Simeón Cañas, needed a bold and clever reply. Rather than attack the Holy Father's authority head on, Cañas insisted that the papal brief the conser-vatives circulated lacked all semblance of credibility. Conservative Guatemalan printer C. Beteta had failed to properly document its provenance or prove the document's authenticity. In the late eighteenth century, reformers had conducted relentless archival research to demonstrate Rome's centuries of usurpations that undermined the rightful prerogatives of bishops, the lower clergy, and even the laity; a central tool of their craft was the authentication of church documents. If the ultramontane replied to Cañas with evidence of the 1791 document's authenticity—even deeply convincing evidence—they entered the debate on his terms. The question then became, who is the better historian, not Rome has spoken and the only response is obedience.

His written treatise was not Cañas' opening salvo in this dispute; he had long been one of the *serviles'* most implacable and prolific enemies. As rector of the University of Guatemala, he had led the charge against scholasticism in the curriculum and promoted the Cortes de Cádiz and the 1812 Constitution. He served as the representative of Sonsonate, El Salvador, alongside Delgado in the Provincial Deputation of 1813 until Ferdinand VII abolished the governing body in 1814, and served again in 1820 and 1821 after its reestablishment. Along with Delgado, he and other members of the ANC proclaimed Central America's absolute independence in July of 1823. When his fellow El Salvadoran Delgado had needed advice about the new bishopric, Cañas made the long journey to San Salvador from Guatemala City on horseback and urged him to press forward.[60]

In a clever rhetorical move, Cañas insisted that he truly championed the papacy while servile pamphleteers slandered Rome's good name by disseminating untrustworthy documents that mocked the papacy's erudition and wisdom.[61] The *Semanario* went further, calling the putative papal letter of 1791 little more than a crude and contradictory mash-up of ideas wrongly attributed to the Holy Father.[62]

Liberals like Cañas were unwilling to challenge papal power head on. It was better to pay lip service to limited papal power and undermine confidence in the pope's unilateral authority, hence Cañas' strategy of raising doubts about the authenticity of Pius VI's pronouncements on the Constitutional Clergy. He cast aspersions on the local boys' ability to accurately represent the Holy Father's will or discern the authenticity of papal utterances. It was a sly argumentative strategy indeed—but ultimately it hardly disguised his true beliefs. Reform Catholics like Cañas quibbled with the ultramontane about the authenticity of particular papal edicts against the French Constitutional Clergy, trapping their opponents in the "discursive pits," that kept them arguing in the reformers' terms, while simultaneously circulating stacks of copies of French Constitutional cleric Grégoire's work.

While Cañas' *Advertencia patriótica* raised doubts about the authenticity of particular papal documents, the work also revealed his distaste for an overweening papacy and his belief in conciliar authority. To make his case, Cañas cleverly quoted Pope Pius V's quip that wrongheaded jurists regularly overestimated the "scope of papal jurisdiction." And he entertained not the "tiniest doubt" that the new bishopric aligned with church practice and underscored Delgado's sweep of state-wide municipal nominations for the post in 1821 as a sound justification for the new bishopric. After all, the former university rector explained, municipal nominations for prelates constituted a timeworn church practice.[63]

Cañas' writings drew other literati into the partisan debate. Basilio Zeceña underscored Cañas' disrespect for the Holy Father, sarcastically noting that reformers gained their fame from copying paragraphs from reformist luminary Juan Antonio Llorente's work and ignoring the wisdom of the Council of Trent. Reformer Victor Castrillo likened Zeceña to a "bloodthirsty wolf" for an earlier written attack on the revered elder and noted that Zeceña's conscience was ruled by phantoms. The region's 1821 independence, Castrillo explained, had triggered his enemies' "political-ecclesiastical nervous system," causing their bad behaviour. Zeceña and Cañas' public sparring, he reported, was the talk of the town of Antigua.[64]

Three conservative co-authors blasted Cañas for his irreverent tone in addressing the Holy Father, suggesting he reduced the Pope to a bureaucratic yesman for government decisions over ecclesiastical personnel. They also schooled readers with some close textual exegesis of the papacy's concessions to the Spanish monarchy concerning the right to make ecclesiastical appointments. The pope, they cautioned, conceded nothing permanently. The three ecclesiastical authors suggested the former university professor and rector memorize this phrase and ponder it often: Rome would not retreat.[65]

Neither would the Central American branch of the Ultramontane International. To refute the region's reformist Catholic coteries, the conservatives rehearsed the arguments of a true ultramontane hero, the French Jesuit Augustin Barruel. A prolific proponent of papal prerogatives, Barruel had honed his arguments in a work that became a best seller among conservatives across Europe. His multivolume treatise denouncing the Jacobins had been translated from the original French into Italian, Spanish, Swedish, German, English, and Russian; and was reprinted in multiple editions in numerous European cities, including Rome, Lisbon, Palma de Mallorca, and London.[66] It was not this imposing tome, but Barruel's *Histoire du clergé pendant la Révolution française* (*History of the Clergy in the Time of the French Revolution*) that Central American conservatives seized upon. They used Barruel to combat the brash aspersions Cañas cast against the authenticity of Pius VI's 1791 invective against the Constitutional Clergy. Meanwhile Archbishop Casaús' crotchety secretary, José Mariano Herrarte, noted that the papal letter was anything but a forgery. The Latin version of the pope's brief was readily available in a collection of his works published in London in 1821, and moreover the Abbé Barruel referenced the document in his history of the French clergy.[67] Cañas, however, proved undaunted by Herrarte's accusations and pointed intervention into the rapidly escalating pamphlet war, declaring that he preferred to "regard the documents as inauthentic rather than attribute to a venerable pontiff letters that contravened my previous ideas about that pope," and warning that all important ecclesiastical documents required government approval to circulate.[68]

Barruel had also exalted the virtues of the vicar-general of Dol, a cleric named Veauxpont, and Central American conservatives followed his lead. It seems the resolute cleric had refused the French National Assembly' offer of a bishopric, noting that the laymen who comprised the bulk of the assembly usurped the pope's unique right to make such an appointment. This story was gleefully reproduced by Delgado's ultramontane clerical detractors, who made the virtuous Dol and the renegade Delgado comparison clear.[69]

If the ultramontane found renowned allies like Barruel to cite and celebrate, so too did Delgado's circle of Reform Catholics. If Delgado's crew sought to defuse accusations that they resembled the French Constitutional Clergy, they failed miserably. The first cleric to sign the ecclesiastical oath in France was the leader of the Constitutional Clergy, Henrí Grégoire, a priest whose energetic letter writing, inspired oratory in the French assembly, and authorial output placed him at the epicenter of the Reform Catholic International's epistolary networks and projects.[70] Ending the Jesuit and ultramontane connivance with monarchy stood at the center of Grégoire's reformist campaigns and he had sought in France to encourage democratic pastor-citizens who would "present to the French the Gospels in one hand and the Constitution in the other."[71]

Using the country's first printing press, the El Salvadoran government published and widely disseminated Grégoire's handbook on creating these two-handed clergy so useful to the state. The head of the Constitutional Clergy exhorted his readers to reactivate their ancient right to elect bishops without Rome's approval. In a similar vein, the Abbé argued that papal nuncios were ambassadors of a foreign power and as such should have no influence over government decisions. The Holy Father should indeed sit at the church's pinnacle, but the councils should be its ultimate governing bodies. Grégoire recommended national church councils as the best way to achieve necessary reforms and as the quickest way to end the upper clergy's "tendency to ally themselves with despotism."[72] Grégoire's hostility was clear to the upper clergy: in an 1807 sermon sponsored by the Inquisition, Casaús described the French cleric as a "bloodthirsty wolf," a pseudo-bishop, and, alongside reformer Claude Fleuri, a purveyor of dangerous sophistries.[73] In a treatise that circulated in Central America, Grégoire lamented the resurgence of monarchy and the persecution of the Constitutional Clergy in 1820s France by the "Jesuitism and ultramontanism" infesting the country. He hoped that "heroic" new world nations would fight for the triumph of "true piety" united with "true liberty" and thereby provide an example for the world to emulate.[74]

Grégoire must have been pleased, for the liberal El Salvadorans were not his only New World aficionados. In 1825, the liberal-dominated Federal Congress issued an official decree thanking Grégoire for his support of the cause of liberty and his enthusiasm for the independence of the new American republics and his gift of his new work on the liberties of the Gallican church. The congress ordered the work translated into Spanish and a copy placed in its library. That same year, the Mexican Constituent Congress passed a resolution honoring Grégoire's book.[75] Just a year before, Grégoire had gushed to Mier about a similar accolade granted to the book by the Cortes Generales founded in 1822 that sat during the Liberal Triennium (1820–1823) in Spain. He was especially gratified that news of the award appeared in the Mexican press, and that Mexicans distinguished between real religion and the "abuses and intrusions" of popes and kings who violated the rights of Christian peoples and the church's early discipline. That Mier and his compatriots understood that political liberty meant deploying state power to reestablish the early practice of election of church hierarchs by the people and their priests particularly delighted Grégoire.[76]

With tracts like Grégoire's issuing from the government press and Delgado's hand-picked ministers occupying ever-more pulpits, escalation was the order of the day. Guatemalan clerics would finally live with "the moderation dictated by Canon law," Cañas insisted in a barely disguised barb, if El Salvadorans' tithe funds stayed in El Salvador.[77] This full-throated threat to diminish the hierarchy's ill-gotten and sinfully spent revenues, and the resultant corrupting luxury, would not go unchallenged.

Father José Antonio Santa María routinely electrified readers with his erudition and fire-and-brimstone prose. Cañas, he lamented, promoted the Apostol Paul's advice to Timothy on clerical remuneration: "and having food and raiment let us be therewith content."[78] In Santa María's view, this advice no longer held: the Catholic Church's golden age of heroically virtuous, abstemious ministers had forever passed, and the clergy rightly swayed the faithful with the splendor of their vestments and the cult.[79] As throughout the former Spanish Empire, El Salvador's Reform Catholics puffed a simple ethical piety undergirded by the efficacious grace that enabled resistance to worldly temptations, especially luxury—and the ecclesiastical hierarchy. Ultramontane Catholics like Santa María countered with the church's necessary and hierarchical mediation with God and the legitimating pomp of liturgical celebration.

In the Central American context, this theological conflict drove political conflict between liberals and *serviles*, federalists and centralists. Divergent economic interests too found their clearest expression in the region's heated theological battles. Santa María, for example, had quoted only a snippet of Paul's advice, but his readers knew well that what followed was one of the Abrahamic religions most powerful condemnations of wealth accumulation:

"But they that will be rich fall into temptation and a snare, and into many foolish and hurtful lusts, which drown men in destruction and perdition. Which while some coveted after they have erred from the faith, and pierced themselves with many sorrows, for the love of money is the root of all evil."[80]

Reformers and ultramontanists used new printing presses to churn out tracts that vied to sanctify their respective notions of government and the proper relationship between church and state; reformers, like the Reform Catholic bureaucrats of the late eighteenth-century Spanish Empire, sought to use the state to enact godly reforms to the church and transform the laity's mores. In these campaigns, the deluge of printed propaganda was mirrored by dramatic confrontations in the streets and plazas. The large crowd of 300 that ousted parish priest Perdomo from the liberal stronghold of Ahuachapán; the forced flight of the *Carta católica*'s eventual authors over the border into Guatemala—these were highly public incidents. With armed soldiers chasing conservative priests in cassocks through the countryside, El Salvador's overwhelmingly illiterate rural denizens saw a church divided and understood that they were increasingly being asked to choose a side. Religious tensions between ultramontane and reformist Catholics mapped loosely onto economic tensions between elite Guatemalan merchant capitalists and scrappy indigo growers and their white-collared scions and other relatives in the provinces.

THE SYMBOLIC POLITICS OF DEVOTION

Although it was not a battle the champions of a simple, ethical piety could win, reformers also understood the power of public ceremony and religious iconography to sway the faithful. Even as early as 1824, it was clear that Delgado's champions extended beyond the circles of reformist literati who obsessively rehearsed the apostolic church's conciliar authority and radical democracy to all who would read or listen. Soldiers in one of San Salvador's civic militias, for example, paraded through the city's streets with a castle sustained by two artillery canons—shimmering atop the structure was a bishop's miter resting on a pillow. A deeply moved observer was inspired to note that these sorts of images were "the best books" to throw at the obstinate, including conservative members the federal government, because "when reason and justice fail it is necessary to resort to force."[81]

Conservatives, too, proved capable of sorties beyond the literary public sphere. Dramatic propaganda incursions deep into enemy territory, including the liberal stronghold of San Salvador, formed part of the ultramontane's tactical repertoire. The shadow author of one particularly brazen gambit was, perhaps, none other than the miraculous nun Teresa de Aycinena. In June of 1824, just three years before her brother would lead 3,000 conservative troops into liberal El Salvador, Teresa received a message from God: the archbishop should dispatch her confessor Anselmo Ortiz into San Salvador. Suffice it to say that Teresa and her confessor Ortiz had been at odds in the preceding weeks, his enthusiasm for her miracles waning, and he had accused her of "a diabolical spirit."[82] Liberals were most likely aware of Ortiz's close connection to the controversial nun; an anonymous pamphleteer sneered that Ortiz had previously manipulated her into proclaiming that God wanted Bustamante to continue as captain general and Guatemala to remain in Spain's thrall.[83] Teresa, then, had perhaps cleverly calculated the risks of Ortiz's trip into Delgado's El Salvador. Understandably, Ortiz balked at such a dangerous mission and scurried to Antigua to appeal to Teresa's brother, Dominican friar Miguel José de Aycinena —but to no avail. Teresa went over Ortiz's head to her advisor, José Buenaventura Villagelin; Ortiz countered, warning Villagelin that "Tertulian had been lost because he heeded the advice of a woman"—but off to San Salvador Ortiz went.[84]

Mounting San Salvador's parish-turned-cathedral pulpit in mid-to late July 1824, Ortiz instead told his audience that the archbishop had ordered him to San Salvador after the venerable priest of Llobasco, Juan José Salázar, had graciously invited him. Ortiz's homily sidestepped the considerable virtues of the feast day's patron, Our Lady of Mount Carmel, in favor of a blistering rant about the heresy of anointing a bishop without the pope's explicit consent. Ortiz also led parishioners through Matthew 7, stressing the dangers of false prophets in sheeps' clothing, those inwardly ravenous wolves whom he insinuated lurked among this flock of El Salvadorans. The archbishop, Ortiz assured the faithful, would soon descend on El Salvador to smite his schismatic enemies.[85] That very week, the archbishop and the bishop, Casaús and Delgado, had engaged in a terse epistolary exchange. Delgado asserted that El Salvador's constitutional congress flexed its "inherent right" to the *patronato* in naming him bishop. Casaús flatly retorted that the investiture violated ecclesiastical laws and that the pope had not conceded the patronato to El Salvador.[86]

Sadly for Ortiz, however, his hero the archbishop tarried, leaving him at the mercy of San Salvador's militants, who quickly detained him. His host Salázar wrote a tearful but rather elliptical letter to Casaús describing how the "city's executive power," potentially *Semanario* editor and priest Miguel Castro, dispatched a picket of soldiers to drag Ortiz from his monastery cell and into confinement in a private home.[87] A week after his arrest, soldiers escorted Ortiz out of the area.[88] That El Salvador's authorities summarily expelled the clerical gadfly probably surprised no one: in addition to his sermon, Ortiz was thought to have disseminated a directive from Casaús that nullified the new bishopric and censored clerics who embraced Delgado's authority.[89] In an emergency legislative session, the El Salvadoran congress ordered the immediate confiscation of every copy of Casaús' order that Ortiz had disseminated, and established a commission to parse the document's contents.[90] The liberal *Semanario* applauded the state's alacrity, underscoring that Ortiz and several priests had conspired—albeit unsuccessfully—to circulate a document "full of excommunications" and calibrated to sow enough discord to render a return to Spanish domination attractive.

Yet acts of individual courage that fail in the moment often accomplish something far more important for long-term outcomes by encouraging others to enter the fray. The very day of Ortiz's exile the liberal paper revealed that "internal enemies" emboldened by the government's "leniency" towards its critics had goaded "gullible women" into hurling insults at city officials. Alarmingly for liberals, San Salvador's conservative women—like their counterparts in Mérida—cast themselves as the defenders of a church besieged. Thankfully, a *Semanario* reader enthused, these women's family members enrolled in the civic militia had demonstrated they had "no other mother than the patria": the soldiers had taken their own mothers prisoner without hesitation.[91] Like the crowds of women in Mérida who shredded the Constitution of 1812 at least some of El Salvador's women proved resolute defenders of the ultramontane church.

Even in San Salvador, the schism's epicenter and a reformist stronghold, religious conflict burst onto the city streets. Early that same day, July 28, 1824, a boisterous crowd swept into government offices in a show of support for Ortiz, who Mexican general Vicente Filísola described as more popular than the civic authorities or the El Salvadorean heroes who had recently battled his own armies. José Salazar, the elderly priest and Casaús supporter from Llobasco, reported a "frightening commotion" as a crowd swept into the building to speak in favor of Ortiz. San Salvadoran officials countered with 500 armed men posted in the city's plaza from nine in the morning until nightfall. The *jefe supremo* then urged state officials to immediately pass a special edict against these sorts of disorders, and promised to punish his obstreperous countrywomen.[92]

At least one priest emerged from the show down in San Salvador with redoubled resolve: Salazar professed he would never recognize the upstart bishop. Nor would his similarly steely replacement in Llobasco's parish, Pedro de Lara, genuflect to San Salvador's radical religious reformers. Delgado yanked dissident priests from their posts, and Salázar understood that prison and exile awaited him. Most of all, Salazar told Casaús in March of 1825, he shuddered to imagine his gentle parishioners in the hands of the "wolf" that Delgado would surely assign to them after his inevitable ouster.[93]

Salazar was prescient. The wolf would come, just not immediately. On December 12, 1825, Llobasco's new priest Pedro de Lara left an ominous note in the parish's baptismal record book. *Jefe supremo* Villacorta had banished him for disobeying Bishop Delgado and for preaching the unity of the Roman Catholic Church and the righteousness of Casaús' authority. His replacements, he scrawled among the list of baptized infants as he scrambled to depart, should know that "if they came here under Delgado's authority, the sacraments they administered would be worthless."[94]

Several years later, in the midst of civil war, Maximo Piñeda, a Delgado appointee, arrived in Llobasco. He had landed in hostile territory indeed, he reported to his bishop in San Salvador, but he promised to soldier on. It seems that at least some of Salazar and Lara's "gentle parishioners" had imbibed their two priests' wisdom, and they resisted the usurper; adding to his woes, priests from nearby towns refused to cooperate with him. It appeared that many saw the sacraments he administered as worthless, as Lara had predicted. Casually asked by a passing cleric in the street if they would be attending mass in town, one family went on a rant: they would rather die than take communion from a priest appointed by the "intruder bishop"; Delgado's emissary to Rome, Castrillo, was a knave who removed his religious habit while in Havana on his way to Rome; no nation had the right to the *patronato* without the pope's prior blessing. When the Holy Father named someone like Salázar or Pedro Molina bishop, they continued, then and only then, would they attend mass and take the sacraments—at present interloper priests offered sacraments "stained with blood."[95]

A strike against the sacraments was a serious and risky venture. The Council of Trent (1545–1563) declared the seven sacraments necessary for salvation and all who denied this truth anathema, and it reiterated that the key rites included baptism, confirmation, the eucharist, penance, extreme unction, holy orders, and matrimony. Archbishop Casaús played this widely known tenet of the faith to devastating advantage, denying Delgado-appointed priests access to the materials and documents required to administer these key rites. The Archbishop prohibited church officials from sending baptismal records and other information essential for marriage applicants to El Salvador's reformist priests and nullified the marriages and even the confessions the Delgado-appointed priests did perform.[96] He also tightened control of the traffic in consecrated oil, ultimately in early 1829 allowing only four clerics to distribute it—among them model martyr Ignacio Perdomo—and providing it only to priests who disavowed Delgado's authority.[97] Casaús loyalists lined up behind their hierarch. When his parishioners married in nearby towns, Pineda raged, clerical officiants declined to ask him for the required documents. He had tried to fix the situation, he told Delgado, with instructive homilies for the "few that attended" mass, and, outside of church, through exhortations to the faithful delivered with both "furor and affection." Alas, all his efforts had been for naught.[98]

Pineda's fervor to control access to the sacraments was far from an anomaly. In a heated exchange, a Casaús loyalist made "citizen priest" and Delgado appointee Mariano Carillo's request for a baptismal certificate for a marriage candidate contingent on proof that he labored in the lord's vineyard with the archbishop's blessing.[99] In a similar vein, Chiquimula's parish priest requested Casaús' permission to send his counterpart in Metapan a baptismal certificate. His conscience and the good of the church, he explained, dictated his decision to communicate with the archbishop about his fellow priest's loyalties.[100]

As Pineda's despair underscores, the battle between the church's two branches for the laity's loyalty was not easily won. Reformers stepped up their efforts to disseminate salutary wisdom. In August of 1824, the *Semanario* happily obeyed a government order to reprint Azuero's 1820 argument for the new nations' right to the *patronato*. The paper lauded the author's views as impartial and praised his argument for government control over ecclesiastical appointments.[101] Reformers then made sure that Azuero's reformist wisdom on church and state ecclesiology circulated among both the highly literate and El Salvador's overwhelmingly rural parishes. The government ordered Azuero's entire pamphlet read at high mass on three consecutive festival days in parishes throughout the country. Opponents noted that the El Salvadorans' media blitz worked: the Colombian's work "scandalously circulated through the hands of the unwary faithful."[102]

Azuero's work proved deeply influential, in large part because the Colombian liberal shared a historical trajectory with Central American reformers. Armed battles with royalist troops; an elected schismatic bishop; a resolutely ultramontane archbishop, Coll y Prat; highly public debates between ultramontane and reformist Catholics Church governance and proper worship in the new republics—Azuero had come of age in this tempestuous crucible. It is little wonder that he produced a pamphlet so useful to Delgado's inner circle in Central America.

Opponents were less sanguine. Refractory Central American clerics described Azuero's contribution to the schism as "preparing . . . the paths of the anti-Christ." His work received similarly negative although less hyperbolic reviews elsewhere in Latin America. A Chilean detractor noted that the authors Azuero cited to justify state supervision of the clergy were all members of "the irreligious Jansenist sect . . . whose works were condemned and prohibited by the Church."[103]

It is easy to see why Azuero's text became such a flashpoint. His 1820 pamphlet was a militant statement of reform principles in general and of the new Latin American nations' right to exercise the *patronato* in particular. And it offered the always rousing frisson of familiarity to reformers, repeating some of their most cherished tropes. Happily, Azuero reported, the tenebrous centuries when monarchs had been under the popes' "haughty power" had ended, and secular control over much of the church had been restored. He called on sovereign elected bodies to place trusted prelates in plum positions, lest conservative priests return to governing with bulls, excommunications, and penitentiary processions, burying society in ignorance and superstition. The divine word, the practice of the church's early centuries, the wisdom of the wisest of the popes, and the public laws of Christian nations all dictated that the church focus exclusively on spiritual matters, narrowly defined as the remission of sins, the direction of consciences, and the teaching of the maxims and virtues required for salvation.[104]

Reform Catholicism's centrality to the sanctification of popular sovereignty and democratic elections was also on full display in Azuero's widely disseminated text, which was reprinted in both Santiago de Chile and San Salvador in 1824 and 1825. In the church's early centuries, clerics and the people enjoyed universal suffrage, he explained, and elected the ministers of the sacred cult; after these peaceful gatherings, bishops merely conferred sacred orders on the chosen candidates.[105] This pristine practice was not to stand. A process that originated with the apostles quickly attracted a multitude of heretical infiltrators and turbulent crowds, who transformed occasions to display democratic electoral principles and civic virtue into roiling anarchy, provoking the church to exercise unilateral control over ecclesiastical appointments to stem the chaos.[106] The time had come to return to that uncorrupted past prior to the church's seizure of its now-overweening power. Azuero certainly shared his French contemporaries' belief that they lived in an age of light, that victory over hierarchical rule was nigh. He found this light not in abstract reason, but shining out from universal Christian antiquity to all who would bore back through the dark centuries to uncover it.

He was hardly alone in this belief. Returning to the church's pristine purity was a rallying cry for reformed Catholic El Salvadorans, Guatemalans, and Yucatecans alike, indeed for reformers throughout the empire. But Azuero's text was not without original twists and turns, especially in comparison to the musings of peninsular Spanish reformers during the age of revolution. Strong regalists, reformers like Valencia's Archbishop Gregorio Mayans, and Minister of Grace and Justice Baltasar Gaspar Melchor de Jovellanos, had strategically glossed the wisdom contained in church councils held in Spain, not elsewhere. The Toledan Council of 589 was a particularly popular fount of wisdom. These reformers created a deeply historical nationalist narrative counterpoint to Rome's prerogatives over the Spanish church.

Azuero provided a different but equally historically and geographically specific rationale for Socorrans' control over church affairs: the ancestors of the country's white citizens had discovered and populated the territory, delivering the indigenous population from their "stupid ignorance," through education and Christianization, and had later formed with them a "national family of brothers." There could be no clearer statement of why reformers were so destined to fail: here the nominal equality of "brothers" was based on a sameness that depended on eradicating "the stupid ignorance" of the indigenous majority. Where the regular orders ruled by maintaining language and other differences, reformers sought a republic ruled by the virtuous—with virtue defined as adherence to reform tenets. How one related to God would be absolutely central to new notions of civilization versus barbarous superstition that emerged after independence and replaced the Spanish caste system. Azuero also stressed the economics of national churches: Columbia's churches had been built not by the king of Spain or Rome but by the toil of his ancestors and their generous donations to the cult.[107] Born in a schismatic crucible, brimming with white creole nationalist sentiment, and laced with intertwined Reform Catholic and liberal principles: the Colombian's treatise proved supremely useful to Central American liberals.

As in Bogotá, in Central America the ultramontane knew a threat to salvation when they saw one. Real Catholics understood, Santa María explained, that heretical innovators both denigrated the church's centuries-built wisdom and persecuted Christ's true vicars. Men like Wyclef and Luther and their minions insisted that Rome was Satan's synagogue, the pope the beast of the apocalypse. Azuero placed himself with these reformers, depicting six centuries of church savants as a "gaggle of stupid animals," Santa María insisted, and the popes as ambitious politicians who routinely usurped civil authority.[108] Azuero's call for lay participation in church governance particularly raised Santa María's hackles: no real Catholic could ignore that Jesus gifted the apostles unfettered jurisdiction over the church's workings. Anyone confused about the church's rightful autonomy from meddling governments should look no further than the Abbé Barruel's published collection of edicts and pastoral letters responding to the "ungodly" 1791 French assembly.[109] Dominican and member of the storied Aycinena clan Miguel José de Aycinena declared it fortunate that no Central American Dominican embraced Azuero's dangerous maxims, which denied the church its independence from the civil authorities.[110]

Perhaps most alarming to ultramontanists like Santa Maria, Azuero's influence was not limited to El Salvador. Although San Salvador was an epicenter of reformist scheming, reform Catholics could be found in the halls of power and in municipal councils throughout the region. In November of 1824, an anonymous observer of Guatemala's liberal-dominated congress bemoaned the lack of stenographers recording the deliberations and took it upon himself to relay the gist of the proceedings to the public in the pages of the conservative *El Indicador*. Theological debate larded with canon law and church history, he concluded, dominated the proceedings. Members wrangled passionately over questions like the *patronato*, abolishing confraternities and seizing their funds, and the government's right to review ecclesiastical pronouncements prior to their publication. Nary a single debate on these issues, *El Indicador* lamented, failed to include an elegy to Azuero's patriotism and erudition, or a verbatim reading from at least one section of his widely circulated treatise. Where the Cádiz Cortes moved cautiously to reform the clergy, the anonymous author reported, the Guatemalan assembly took "lead steps" toward the same end, perhaps, he felt, because some thought the reforms would impoverish clerics and enrich those who would control confraternity funds and the land and goods wrested from the church's "dead hands." But the rationale for these anti-clerical measures was anything but secularization or anti-religious sentiment. Rather, he asserted, reform-minded congressmen felt it "necessary to render ministers of the cult as poor as the very first bishops to make them truly apostolic—apostolic like many of today's faithful that fought to return religion to the purity and simplicity of the early centuries."[111] In Costa Rica, too, reformers in the legislature proclaimed their support for Azuero and Cañas.[112] Although the heirs of Bourbon regalism and episcopalism, impassioned reformers, the vast majority of them lower clergy and laymen, shed both of these justifications to defy papal authority. They instead stressed the democratic origins of church authority, and in doing so sanctified their intertwined church and state-building projects and their own authority to rule.

As 1824 came to a close, Central Americans were increasingly aware that their union was fragile, at best. The church, state, and federal governments, and rural and urban parishes and municipalities were beset with ultramontane and reformist factionalism. It was in this fractious context that Archbishop Casaús planned a trip to El Salvador. His enemies were legion and plotted to poison him or worse, he feared, but the hierarch bravely set off in December of 1824 to heal a flock riven by religious tensions. It was too late to help the shaken Ortiz but perhaps he would be in time to save at least some of the country's fallen brethren. Early into his journey, the archbishop fell gravely ill, but, burning with both righteous and real fever, he persevered, resting briefly in San Vicente. Just a day before the archbishop's arrival in this indigo-growing town, Delgado supporters had paraded a monkey sporting an archbishop's miter through the streets. But Casaús' critics fell silent the day of his actual visit. The ever-faithful Saldaña reported the prelate received a warm reception in San Vicente. He also enjoyed the gracious hospitality of future El Salvadoran head of state José María Cornejo at his hacienda. Too sick to continue—or so he reported—Casaús returned to Guatemala without a showdown with Delgado in the schism's epicenter of San Salvador.[113] Instead, both sides would take the battle to the Holy Father in Rome.

4

The View from the Vatican

IN THE YEAR of Jubilee of 1825, Pope Leo XII was consumed with the opportunity to display the city to its best advantage before an audience of some half a million pilgrims. The ceremonial pomp and the careful policing of public decorum were meant to project the restored power of the papacy after Napoleon's abdication and Pius VII's triumphal return in 1814. But as he displayed the Eternal City for its many visitors, arch-conservative Leo XII pondered the threat represented by Delgado across the ocean in El Salvador and, soon, by the presence of one very unwelcome visitor to Rome. Just after the Jubilee, Delgado's emissary, Victor Castrillo, arrived in July of 1826. To Leo's eye, Castrillo was the spokesman not of an anomalous challenge to his authority from an insignificant little country, nor of a mere idiosyncratic flare-up led by a parish priest suffering from delusions of grandeur.[1] Rather, the pope understood that in Central America the church faced an organized iteration of the highly self-conscious Reform Catholic International with a deep history of antagonism to Rome.

The papacy was, of course, long aware of Spain's history of reform challenges to its authority, particularly recent provocations like a 1799 church "schism" led by a faction in the Spanish court of Charles IV. And it was not lost on Leo that New World revolutionaries eagerly identified with the reformist network. They championed its history, recent councils, martyrs, and luminaries as part of their efforts to forge a future out of a past that was not even past.

For God and Liberty. Pamela Voekel, Oxford University Press. © Oxford University Press 2023.
DOI: 10.1093/oso/9780197610190.003.0005

But the map of rebellion had shifted in the new century. From Rome's perspective, the post-Napoleonic center of gravity of the reformist network had moved from France to the Spanish Empire to the new countries of Latin America. The restoration of conservative order in Europe after more than two decades of revolution, Napoleonic wars, and the Congress of Vienna's return of lost territory to the papal states brought an end to one phase. Moreover, reformist Catholics had been radicalized in the process. During the independence era and in the young republics, the lower clergy, renegade friars like Mier, and emboldened laymen like the Yucatán's Quintana debated with the ultramontane in the new public sphere of letters and battled for the state and local power required to effectively reform the church and thereby create godly republics. New Spain's rebel literati found justification for their decolonization movement in Reform Catholicism's conciliar authority and Augustinian grace—which placed them as close to God as the king and went a long way to desacralizing monarchical authority. That their ecclesiology intersected seamlessly with their class and regional economic interests should not negate the sincerity of their quest for salvation, or their fervent desire to live according to the ethical maxims of Reform Catholicism and to spread its values to the benighted. The late-eighteenth-century Spanish Empire's reformist bishops and Crown bureaucrats had defended their prerogatives from an overweening papacy, drawing on theologians like Pereira de Figueiredo and Bossuet, who had championed a divine-right monarch's rights over the church and episcopolism as a counterweight to the Holy Father. In their place men like Mier, Delgado, Cañas, Azuero, Roscio, and Madariaga provided the intellectual rationale, first, for decolonization, and then for nominally democratic, decentralized church and state where parish priests and the laity elected bishops, statesmen, and city councils—and resisted overweening centralized power. Led by bonafide revolutionaries deeply imbricated in the establishment of a constitutional monarchy and in the continent's decolonization movements, America's reform-minded Catholics simultaneously challenged centralized power; entrenched economic interests like those of the Aycinenas; conservative centralist parties saturated with ultramontane sentiment; and indeed Rome itself. Central America's reformers and their resident ultramontane foes knew themselves to be more than just local theo-political parties. They acted within self-conscious transatlantic networks whose far-flung members acknowledged them by championing their Central American counterparts' causes. And the Central Americans demonstrated their adherence to the Reform Catholic International by invoking its literati and martyrs.

The papacy had no intention of embracing the reduced role of symbolic figurehead assigned to it by their reformist foes' ecclesiology. And in Central America,

FIGURE 4.1 Pope Leo XII, the former Annibale Francesco Clemente Melchiorre Girolamo Nicola della Genga (1760–1829), carries the Eucharist in a procession for the feast day of Corpus Christi, 1824. The pomp of the display was characteristic of Leo XII, who occupied the throne of Saint Peter from 1823 until his death in 1829. A deeply reactionary figure, he and his cardinals confronted the reformist currents in the church with fierce suppression and summary justice. His measures included stripping Roman Jews of the right to own real estate and confining them in the city's ghetto, as well as policing public morals and ruthlessly suppressing political dissent. "In atto di portare il venerabile nella solenne Processione del Corpus Domini l'anno 1824" ("The act of conveying the Pontiff in the solemn procession of Corpus Christi in the year 1824"), artist unknown, c. 1824. INTERFOTO/Alamy Stock Photo.

conservative ultramontane forces backed by Rome would ultimately forge an uneasy alliance with the majority in Central America, the region's indigenous peoples—who saw through their liberal Reform Catholic would-be tutors' rationales for social leadership, refused their religiously inflected notions of civilization and barbarism, and perhaps represented a third Catholic force in the region by the mid-nineteenth century.

The Curia's Congregation for Extraordinary Ecclesiastical Affairs, then, weighed the news of the El Salvador schism in light of a threatening transatlantic movement of reformist Catholics, many of them—like Delgado, Mier, Quintana Roo, and Cañas—recognized leaders in Latin America's recent independence-era struggles and processes. Pius VI had established the congregation in 1793 to confront the French Revolution's shocking demotion of the Holy Father in church affairs through entities like the French Constitutional

Clergy. In the early nineteenth century, the congregation's scope became more global, as France's threat waned and other problem regions like Spain and Latin America came to the fore. The cardinals who peopled the congregation advised the pope on the Holy See's relations with civil powers, drafted agreements "to cancel the effects of revolution," and oversaw relations with Latin America, as well as with Russia and the former Portuguese empire. By the time of the first Cortes of Cádiz and the early independence rumblings in Latin America, the Spanish Empire was fast becoming the new epicenter of radical challenges to the church's hierarchical ecclesiology. In recognition of the threat posed by Spain and Latin America's increasingly radical reformist Catholics, in 1820 Pope Pius VII established a special committee within the Congregation for Extraordinary Ecclesiastical Affairs dedicated exclusively to confronting the danger from Spain during the Liberal Triennium of 1820 to 1823, when the Constitution of 1812 was reinstated. The new committee included representatives from throughout the empire.[2]

This pivot in official concern meant that even an emissary from tiny El Salvador was legible to the Vatican as a substantive problem for a global church. Victor Castrillo arrived in a Rome recently decorated with trophies of classical Roman conquest and stamped with the imposing grandeur of a Baroque flurry of construction following the sack of the city in 1527. The crowning glory of this architectural achievement, St. Peter's Cathedral, visually asserted the church's global sovereignty even while Leo struggled to maintain territorial authority in the rump papal states so recently returned. The pontiff whose attention Castrillo sought was a deeply unpopular reactionary whose signal achievements included the ghettoization of Rome's Jews and the construction of a brutal apparatus of espionage and torture to suppress political dissent. With far less skill and success than his long-serving predecessor Pius VII, Pope Leo XII understood his remit to be restoring papal prerogative. Not surprisingly, Castrillo was not received by the man he had crossed the ocean to meet.

This chapter maps the new terrain of reform and reaction that consumed the church in the 1820s, after the papacy's triumphant 1814 return to Rome following the years of imprisonment and occupation under Napoleon. The conservative order was supposed to usher in an era of consolidating authority and elaborating Rome's ecclesiastical primacy, symbolized by the celebration of the first Jubilee since the French Revolution. Instead, thanks to the New World republics, the long-simmering theological disputes had erupted into the realm of overt contestation. Nothing less than the foundational structures of authority—temporal and ecclesial—was at stake, thanks to the restive American rebels.

FIGURE 4.2 The Rome that Latin America's Reform Catholics challenged in the early nineteenth century was the self-conscious seat of a global ecclesiastical empire as well as the capital of the rump papal states, restored to the pope's control by the Congress of Vienna in 1814. Robert Sands, "Rome," 1820s. View of the city of Rome, Italy, with the dome of St. Peter's Basilica at center. [Fisher, Son & Co., London & Paris]. The Print Collector/Alamy Stock Photo.

VICTOR CASTRILLO: DELGADO SENDS A RADICAL TO ROME

Delgado had chosen Mercedarian Victor Castrillo to plead the case for the new bishopric to the Holy Father.[3] Like his patron, Castrillo had long been a scourge of the conservative hierarchy and held impeccable pro-independence credentials. He had been a key protagonist of the Belén Conspiracy, the foiled 1814 pro-independence plot that had hoped to seize Captain General Bustamante, Archbishop Casaús, and top military officials, and to free a group of Nicaraguan rebels imprisoned in Guatemala City. With that rebellion quelled, Castrillo and his co-conspirators languished in monastic seclusion or prison until 1819.[4] Castrillo was not the only radical in the group. Among the so-called Belén conspirators was Mateo Antonio Marure. Suspecting him of plotting from prison after his arrest, authorities exiled Marure to Spain. Detained en route in Havana, he died in the notorious Cuban prison fortress of El Moro. His orphaned son Alejandro would take his revenge, however, with the pen rather than the sword, eventually becoming Central America's most prolific and renowned liberal historian.[5]

In Castrillo, Delgado had chosen an emissary who survived the crucible of incarceration with his Reform Catholic convictions and revolutionary spirit intact;

he would prove undaunted by Rome's might. Mercedarian friar Castrillo met a less grisly fate than his Belén Conspiracy comrades. Condemned to death for his part in the foiled plot, he instead found himself in seclusion in Guatemala City's Convent of La Merced. Cut off from his "brothers," and burning with religious passion, in December 1817 he implored the captain general to allow him to say the Mass and participate in the cloister's communal activities during Easter festivities and beyond. His superior backed his request, noting his edifying conduct and the benefits of communal life for this "good religious . . . seduced by the perverse" into sedition. Within a month, Bourbon statesman Bustamante granted the provincial's request. In isolation since his 1815 entrance into the monastery, Castrillo enjoyed the company of his fellow friars, at least during Easter week, and initially said Mass in a "secret chapel" in the monastery. The provincial-elect decided that Castrillo was safer with the dead than with the living, however, and he moved his Masses to the monastery's cemetery.[6] Formally released in 1819, he received his doctorate in theology in 1822.

By 1824, the contrite Castrillo had transformed back into a feisty reformer. The Mercedarian provincial reported multiple complaints about him and feared that he incited "anarchic movements that rattle public order" in the highland town of San Marcos. Mixing in politics, he reminded Archbishop Casaús, contravened the church's mission.[7] Castrillo told a different story. Originally called to San Marcos by his religious superiors in December of 1823, he was ejected by the town's duplicitous priest, but sent back to the fractious town by Quetzaltenango's *jefe político*. According to this self-report, the *jefe político* asked Castrillo to create a salon dedicated to the new liberal regime's civic values (*tertulias patrióticas*) and to disabuse the town of the anti-liberal and pro-monarchical sentiments promoted by its former priest.

Founded by the Asamblea Nacional Constituyente (ANC) in 1823 to spread "enlightenment" throughout the republic, the *tertulias patrióticas* provided a space to disseminate the hopelessly intertwined civic and Reform Catholic values cherished by reformers. Castrillo embraced this charge with gusto. The ANC placed these salons under the protection of the region's all-important municipalities, in particular the constitutional city councilmen, the group created by the Cortes de Cádiz's reforms. All citizens could attend the twice-weekly meetings, the founding edict noted, and conversations should center on the ANC's new laws and discourses on special topics presented by the members. Discussions of "religion and dogma" were explicitly prohibited. Given how intertwined politics and religion were in the region, the latter directive may have proved unenforceable. At a meeting of a patriotic salon in Guatemala City in 1826, land surveyor Valerio Ignacio Rivas held forth at length on the government's right to monitor and confiscate church wealth. Rivas would later serve as a representative and as the vice-secretary in the liberal Guatemalan government of 1829, and signed his name to the order extinguishing the regular orders in the state. At the 1826 *tertulia patriótico*, he established his authority on the topic of church wealth on a soaring reformist note, promising to transport himself "in spirit to the Church's early centuries," and then work forward through time to cement his case. His fellow citizens should understand, he emphasized, that the virtuous clerics of the early centuries held no property. This abetted their holiness, as the interest of true religion lay in a clergy who elicited respect for their sanctity, charity, and virtue—not their wealth, luxury, and pretentious insolence. The ignorance and superstition of the people had led them to donate riches to the church, the impassioned citizen declared, and the church in turn had "sold heaven to buy up the earth."[8] A simple, ethical church of conscience had no need of the excess wealth the church spent on enervating luxury and raucous ceremony.

Delgado's emissary to Rome, then, was charged with establishing a vector for reformist Catholic values into the town; he also summoned the town's "honorable residents," lectured them on America's right to self-governance, and, for good measure, taught a free geometry class. These activities provoked Mercedarian provincial Salvador Barrios, who declared Castrillo a revolutionary in a disparaging letter to Guatemala's head of state and then expelled the friar from San Marcos. Clearly at home in a festering nest of enmities, an undaunted Castrillo sought to tar the provincial's reputation and solicited testimony from the liberal city council of Granada, Nicaragua. Barrios, the Nicaraguans fired back, had earlier transformed the Mercedarian convent in Granada into a hive of anti-independence and anti-liberal organizing. Liberal commander Cleto Ordoñez had exiled the divisive provincial from the city.[9]

Castrillo sent the liberal Granada *municipio*'s assessment of Provincial Barrios to Archbishop Casaús and expressed his desire to defect from the Mercedarians to join the secular clergy. The order, he explained, had strayed far from its original purpose of redeeming Christian captives from the Holy Land. Moreover, its respect for external hierarchies like the nobility and its commitment to internal hierarchies and blind obedience to superiors prevented the inculcation of virtue in its members; the Mercedarians were akin to a monarchy. As in any monarchy, favorites emerged. Like many a Reform Catholic polemic, his argument crackled with opprobrium for despots and paeans to unfettered conscience and inalienable rights. He himself suffered under a tyrant, Barrios, who violated his rights because the provincial felt his position entitled him to do so. But if Castrillo rehearsed the Enlightenment's critique of despotism and tyranny and praise for nominal equality, it was not for reading secular philosophes. Like Reform Catholics

everywhere, Castrillo pointed to Saint Augustine the exemplar of "apostolic perfection" and noted that the real virtues he recommended—fraternity, humility,
compassion, and charity—could not be exercised by the order in its present state.[10]
This, then, was the man Delgado named his emissary to Rome in early July of
1825.[11]

Not surprisingly given his "revolutionary" past, Castrillo repaid the trust El
Salvadoran reformers placed in him. His own formal letter included in the packet
to the Holy Father was a creative amalgam of unabashed reform ecclesiology and
polite deference to Leo XII. El Salvador's ambassador detailed the trajectory of reform: In 1823–1824, Central America had held its general council, the ANC, to decide the area's political fate. The fully sovereign state of El Salvador then elected a
bishop, Delgado. Castrillo neither justified nor apologized for this election, imply-
ing that a council or a state, however secular, had a right to hold a vote for an ecclesiastical hierarch. He then gingerly introduced the subject of Archbishop Casaús'
perfidy, particularly his cravenness: the hierarch portrayed independence-seekers
like Mexico's Iturbide and the Constitution of 1812 as diabolical, and then later
praised them when they emerged victorious. The archbishop was a flip-flopper,
not a man of godly convictions. The Holy Father should therefore ignore Casaús'
reports to Rome—reports that excoriated Delgado. Casaús had, after all, earlier
recommended San Salvador's parish priest to the Crown as a worthy occupant of
the country's first bishopric.[12]

In a more candid letter to a friend, Castrillo revealed his allegiance to reform
tenets that had won Delgado's trust. He dropped the obsequiousness to Rome and
acknowledged that electing a bishop was both worthy of comment and a deliberate threat to the pope's writ. Moreover, he noted, many Americans feared that
Spain's King Ferdinand VII intimidated the Holy Father from the shadows, encouraging him to ignore the new nations of Latin America; indeed, His Holiness himself "abhorred the American republics." Given this collaboration between Crown
and scepter, the church's utopian early centuries fired Castrillo's imagination and
gave him the strength to forge ahead. The true faithful should challenge Rome's
authority. "Return, return then, fleeing a bad pope, to the times of the first popes,"
Castrillo importuned his epistolary friend. "How can I be a schismatic, how can
I cease to be Catholic, if I live as in the times of the apostles, if I follow the dominant and most glorious discipline of the Church?" No matter their position, no
one was obliged by conscience to support the pope's machinations, to endure deception from anyone, he exuberantly concluded.[13]

The letters that the radical friar ferried from Delgado and from El Salvador's
head of state Juan Vicente Villacorta to Pope Leo XII detailed Archbishop Casaús'
irrational opposition to independence and tiny El Salvador's rightful inheritance of

the *patronato* from Spain. Delgado noted Archbishop Casaús' hostility to America's "new institutions" and governments, his "inequities and scandals," and his long-standing neglect of his El Salvadoran flock.[14]

Rome, however, already knew of Delgado's bid for the bishopric before Castrillo's arrival. Archbishop Casaús had briefed the Holy Father in 1824, claiming rather hyperbolically that Delgado had intimidated the deputies of the El Salvadoran state assembly with an armed company of 200 men while they deliberated on the new bishopric.[15] Delgado then had the resulting edict establishing the new bishopric read in all of El Salvador's parishes. Casaús had countered with a pastoral letter condemning the new bishopric, but for naught, or so he reported: El Salvador's government threatened force to prevent the circulation of the archbishop's communication with his flock and issued "libelous" screeds against the archbishop.[16] The pope, then, already had this breathless gloss on the schism straight from his ally Casaús before Castrillo arrived in Rome—and it was alarming indeed.

If Casaús' partisan report helped prime His Holiness for Castrillo's errand to Rome, he was not alone. Before Castrillo's arrival in Rome in late July of 1826, José Alejandro de Aycinena, scion of the merchant monopolist who had so vexed Delgado's own father, had secreted schism news to the papal nuncio in Madrid. From his base in Spain, the young Aycinena had served in the Council of the Indies, where he worked to discredit Guatemala's iron-handed Captain General Bustamante, in large part because the officious Bourbon bureaucrat threatened the Aycinena family's contraband trade and sway over indigo credit networks. No stranger to intrigue, José Alejandro was also familiar to radicals in El Salvador, having served as interim intendent there during the tumult of 1811. He had wielded his influence for the return of the Jesuits with the Empire-wide conservative ascendency that followed Ferdinand's 1814 return, and in 1825 he turned his attention to thwarting the order's reform-minded enemies in El Salvador.[17] While reformers mocked his famous half-sister Teresa's miracles and Casaús' thralldom to the nun, it gave Aycinena "special pleasure" to pass along to the Spanish nuncio the Central American federal congress' July 1825 decree upholding the federal government's—not the states'—right to negotiate bishopric cases and the papacy's right to appoint bishops, and condemning the premature investature of Delgado by the El Salvadorans. The Guatemala City cathedral chapter had also chimed in with pro-papal arguments against the El Salvadoran schism, Aycinena happily reported to the nuncio. Victory over the upstart Delgado was at hand.[18]

After this optimistic prior intelligence, Castrillo's presence in Rome and the letters he delivered must have shocked the cardinals manning the Congregation for Extraordinary Ecclesiastical Affairs. Here was a bonafide revolutionary standing before them in Rome as the official representative of a sovereign nation, not moldering in a prison cell. Rome probably seemed equally shocking to Castrillo, although the Vatican's unbridled opulence no doubt ratified the ragtag renegade friar's sense of righteousness.

Rather than dress him down in a direct confrontation, Pope Leo XII assiduously ignored Castrillo. He denied the El Salvadoran ambassador the courtesy of an audience or an official written response. El Salvador's scorned messenger left the Eternal City, fearing he would "grow old there as many aspirants do," but went to Paris to await further instructions from El Salvador. The Holy Father, meanwhile, fired off exhortations to desist to parish priest-turned-bishop Delgado and to El Salvador's *jefe supremo* Villacorta.[19]

The pontiff's reply flared with moral righteousness. How could a congress or an assembly of laymen arrogate to itself the power to elect a bishop, Leo VII fumed to El Salvador's head of state. Villacorta had grievously injured the church, had created a schism, and had committed a grave crime indeed—but the Holy Father promised that if the El Salvadoran leader recanted, he would gladly discuss with him the needs of the country's faithful.[20] Delgado, on the other hand, felt Rome's frightful wrath. Leo XII was especially angered that the upstart bishop expelled priests who bucked his authority and replaced them with his own loyalists. That a parish priest had the gall to request Rome's imprimatur caused the Holy Father to go beyond not approving the new bishopric; he declared every action taken by Bishop Delgado null and void. He had fifty days to step down and come to heel or face excommunication.[21] Leo XII fired off a letter to Archbishop Casaús informing him of his decision. In August of 1827, Casaús relayed Rome's condemnation of the schism to his Central American flock, including his stray El Salvadoran sheep, underscoring that the Holy Father had nullified all of Delgado's acts.[22]

The pope's decided condemnation of Delgado, his tempered warning to El Salvadoran leader Villacorta, and his discourtesy toward emissary Castrillo, were thus entirely foreseeable—and based in part on the troubling news out of Central America. But Rome's alacrity in the Delgado case also sprang from its knowledge of recent Reform Catholic victories in the Spanish Empire and the Vatican's growing unease about ongoing reform campaigns from Philadelphia to Buenos Aires. El Salvador's infernal cheek was a troubling outbreak of a disease Rome feared was a growing pandemic in the New World.

THE THREAT FROM MEXICO

The reports coming out of renegade friar Mier's Mexico particularly worried the Vatican—and troubled the organized transatlantic ultramontane network that championed the Curia. And well they should have. In February 1826, a Mexican senate report tendentiously invoked signal Reform Catholic councils, luminaries, and historical shibboleths, proudly claiming for the newly independent country pride of place in a reform movement with a long history of challenging the Holy See. Delgado's emissary to the Vatican was never going to get anything but a chilly reception given these developments north of its border. The Mexicans openly blamed a sordid history of Vatican power plays for the failure of much-needed church reform, lauding the French Constitutional Clergy and the 361 "wise" Tuscan clerics who defended the Synod of Pistoia's conclusions from the anathema of the papal bull *"Auctorem fidei."* This document condemned the prescriptions for church reform championed by the 1786 Synod, particularly conciliar government, vernacular worship, and state control over the church. By adding American clamor for reform to noble but increasingly anemic European efforts, the Mexicans would restore the real religion the papacy strayed from and cleanse the church of centuries of novel cults and papal usurpations.

In confidently prognosticating the vicar of Christ's own return to the purity of true Catholicism, the 1826 senate report rehearsed reformers' favorite declensionist narrative. Starting in the ninth century, they asserted, the Holy Father had usurped the people's right to elect ecclesiastics, and the bishops' right to confirm those choices, turning "the representative government" of the church into a monarchy of the "most absolutist sort." The forced flow of wealth into Rome through papal control of marriage dispensations and absolutions was born of "obscure passions," the "people's ignorance," and "false decrees"—the latter the conduit for practices unknown by the primitive church.

These New World radicals declared it indispensable to reclaim the power that rightly belonged to bishops—to fail to do so would be to allow "vanity" and "human ambition" to continue to engender hatred toward a religion centered on curbing vices and inculcating virtue. In short, the entire church militant, not just Peter, had received the keys, the Mexicans argued. The church should be shorn of top-down power and returned to its core mission of promoting morality rather than lavish ceremony. The Mexican senate's ecclesiastical affairs committee concluded that the nation's congress held the Patronato rights formerly exercised by the Spanish Crown and indeed should establish diocesan boundaries; moreover, not some but all ecclesiastical affairs should be decided within Mexico—with the papal see's blessing, of course, but not its interference or obligatory imprimatur.[23]

Ultramontane communication networks crackled with the news of Mexico's proposed national church. Even before the country's official emissary to the Vatican Francisco Pablo Vázquez could wend his way from Brussels to Rome, the Congregation for Extraordinary Ecclesiastical Affairs received news from the ultramontane press concerning the militancy of the demands in the February, 1826 Mexican senate committee report—portions of which ran in ultramontane newspapers in Europe as well as Central America. Coverage of Mexican religious affairs in the conservative papers had found its way to the Council in Rome.[24] Thus alerted to the Mexicans' schismatic plans, Pope Leo XII was fully apprised of the threat before the arrival of the country's official emissary. The Council found the Mexicans' spirited attack on Rome's prerogatives and defense of a national church disconcerting, to say the least.[25]

The Vatican, of course, sat atop a global ultramontane empire. And the ultramontane press knew a Reform Catholic conspiracy when it presented itself and readily identified the movement's intellectual leaders. Conservatives understood their Reform Catholic opponents as members of vast, sinister networks of schemers under the sway of men like Grégoire and Mier, and they debated the extent of their influence in the press. According to the French *Ami de la religion et du roi*, many of its loyal ultramontane readers saw the hand of Mexican renegade cleric Fray Servando Teresa de Mier behind the 1826 manifesto against papal prerogatives, or what they termed the Mexicans' "ecclesiastical constitution." The French paper's editors, however, suspected Grégoire, who, they stressed, corresponded regularly with new world radicals, and dreamed of seeing his thwarted "schism" plans realized in the new world. The council duly noted the ultramontane's paper's concerns about Grégoire and Mier and declared the Mexican statement to be "apparently" schismatic and heretical based on reports in the conservative press; the council then sent the information on to the Holy Father for an official decision.[26]

Here the ultramontane intelligence network failed, or perhaps revealed a hope that the rebellions could be laid at the feet of a few outside agitators. In fact, one of the Mexican report's principal authors was Valentín Gómez Farías, who as vice president of Mexico and the country's de facto leader in 1832 and 1833 would initiate legislation designed to align the church with Reform Catholic precepts, including abolishing the tithe and secularizing the northern missions. His right-hand man in this effort, dubbed the First Reform, would be his minister of justice, rebel newspaper editor Andrés Quintana Roo. San Juanista Lorenzo Zavala served alongside reformist Catholic intellectual José María Luis Mora as one of a small handful of Gómez Farías' principal advisors.[27] Gómez Farías' head of ecclesiastical affairs was Ramos de Arizpe, whose work Mier had carried with him in a chest to liberate New Spain with the Mina expedition, and who had succored San Juanista cleric Agustín de Zavala in Cádiz. The agitators, in other words, were home-grown.

Rome increasingly understood that in the Latin American branch of the Reform Catholic International it faced an organized network, not just a few scholarly gadflies well versed in church history. The movement comprised not only prolific intellectuals like Mier but also humble parish priests like Vicente Velásquez and Delgado and organized laymen like Quintana and Villacorta. Mier and Grégoire were merely the most visible members of a vast network of impassioned reformers—men who organized in places like the tiny chapel of San Juan in Mérida and the parish church on San Salvador's muddy plaza. Certainly the Mexican senate committee that wrote the 1826 argument for a democratic national church required no help from foreigners—even beloved foreigners like Grégoire—to craft their searing critique.

Indeed, the Vatican recognized that even the reform movement's most representative intellectuals were not armchair theorists but active participants in liberatory expeditions and printing and epistolary networks. The learned Mier had won fame across the Catholic Atlantic world as much for his defense of reformers, for example, as for his theological challenges to papal authority.[28] Grégoire likewise had long associated with New World revolutionaries, including its most successful ones; in 1796 none other than Touissant Louverture wrote to the head of the French Constitutional Clergy to procure "religious and republican" prelates for the new nation of Haiti and to invite him to help organize the revolutionary young country's religious life. Seeking to end papal appointments to the island and to encourage the growth of a black clergy, a 1797 national Council of the Constitutional Church held in Paris named four constitutional bishops for Haiti, whom they hoped would train black Haitians for the priesthood.[29] Grégoire also met regularly with expatriate intellectuals and politicians like Mier and his countrymen José Francisco Fagoaga and José Miguel Ramos de Arizpe during their stints in Paris.[30] Their shared dream was the papacy's nightmare: that, in Grégoire's words, the true religion that had taken root in the New World would surely cross the Atlantic to save "decrepit Europe."[31]

REFORM CATHOLICISM ACROSS THE AMERICAS AND THE RETURN OF THE LIBERALS IN SPAIN

Leo XII thus decided El Salvadoran parish priest Delgado's fate, and his emissary Castrillo's reception in the context of Reform Catholic challenges to his authority from places as important to the church as Mexico. But he was keenly aware of a sprawling transatlantic network of reformers whose leadership circles included influential intellectuals like Mier and Grégoire. Alarmingly for Rome, the increasing number of Catholics who questioned his writ were connected to the international, particularly its most radical branch. Mier served as an intellectual consultant to a schismatic movement in Philadelphia, and the Vatican was well aware of his involvement in the tempest at St. Mary's Church in the early 1820s.

The Philadelphia schism pivoted around a principled defense of trusteeism. This system of parish governance was widely practiced among the Catholic minority in the United States, where it had the advantage of resembling Protesnt Congregationalism. The trustee system placed funds and clerical appointments in the hands of elected committees of laymen rather than the church hierarchy. Defenders of the system frequently sparred with the more ultramontane bishops and other higher-ups who energetically sought to claw back papal and hierarchical control over clerical appointments and parish resources.[32] When Mier arrived in Philadelphia in 1821, a priest at the center of the turmoil in that city, Father William Hogan of St. Mary's parish, requested the Mexican's intellectual guidance in proving the canonical soundness of trusteeism—a role Mier was only too happy to serve.

In Philadelphia, Hogan looked to end the interference of his arch-rival and fellow Irishman, Bishop Henry Conwell, and prodded Mier to elaborate on how the church hierarchy should properly relate to the lower clergy. The "intellectual author of Mexican Independence" did not disappoint, arguing that no one bishop could stand in judgment of a lower cleric; only a dozen bishops could do so. Indeed in Spain and her empire, Mier asserted, as well as in France, the clergy had recourse to the civil courts of the king to protest decisions made by overweening bishops, who could be fined and even deposed by these secular magistrates.[33] In a subsequent pamphlet, Mier further laid bare his antagonism toward church hierarchs: during Mexico's independence struggle and throughout Spanish America, bishops had declared "emancipation from the Spanish yoke" heretical, crusaded against "patriots," and converted people into ultramontane *fanáticos*. These fanatics caused so much carnage that Mier felt like "if we had not been able to distinguish *the church* from the bishops, and religion from its *abuses*, we should have apostatized from Catholicism as England did."[34]

St. Mary's schism was not an anomaly; as Rome well understood, it was connected to transatlantic Reform Catholic networks. Mier was not the only Luso-Hispanic Atlantic-world intellectual to bring his vast knowledge of church history and Reform Catholic tenets to the trusteeism fight that flared along the East Coast of the United States. John F. O. Fernández, a Portuguese doctor with a past nearly as dramatic as Mier's own, provided intellectual ballast to a lay movement vying to control a parish in Norfolk, Virginia. The godparents of Fernández's children were none other than Portuguese Prince Regent John VI and his wife Carlota Joaquina. The doctor had found himself exiled from Portugal in 1803 after he attempted to protect the reputations of his royal benefactors by simulating the abduction of the princess' maid, widely rumored to be sexually entangled with the Prince Regent. Between 1815 and 1820 Fernández acted as the Norfolk church's spokesman after an ultramontane archbishop appointed a parish priest against the trustees' wishes.[35] His 1816 protest letter to Archbishop of Baltimore Leoard Neale was a model of reformist erudition. The congregation, he explained, founded their "rights" to control parish funds and personnel on the teachings of Jesus, the apostles, and the Holy Fathers, as well in as on the wisdom of early church councils. Saint Bernard loomed large in his citations, and he quoted the Church Father's hope that he would see in his lifetime "the Church of God as in former times, when the apostles threw their seines to catch not gold and silver but souls."[36] Archbishop Ambrose Maréchal of Baltimore summarily dismissed the idea that Norfolk's parishioners had "a natural right" to elect their pastors, noting that "their folly would be less, were they to hope that they can stop the course of the sun, than to hope that the Catholick [*sic*] Church will ever acknowledge in them such a right."[37]

Needless to say, neither the Philadelphia nor the Norfolk schisms sat well with Rome. Baltimore's Archbishop Maréchal kept Propaganda Fide up to date on the trustees' manueverings in Norfolk and described a metastasizing number of people who denounced papal prerogatives as inimical to American democracy.[38] In 1821, St. Mary's trustees sent a series of complaints about their bishop and archbishop directly to Rome and, perhaps more shockingly, accompanied their letters with a robust critique of Propaganda Fide's control over ecclesiastical appointments. When, in 1827, Bishop Conwell made serious concessions to the trustees in their ongoing tug-of-war with him over control of appointments and resources, Propaganda Fide lost patience and immediately circulated the agreement throughout the Roman Curia. The General Congregation repudiated Conwell's concessions on April 30, 1827, and the Holy Father followed suit a week later—the news of the Holy See's unequivocal disapproval of the St. Mary's schism arrived in Philadelphia in early July.[39]

It came on the heels of news that, after advising the Philadelphia radicals, Mier was carrying the germs of schism in Mexico. Despite doing hard time in inquisition dungeons in Mexico City from 1817 to 1820 and a short stint in the infamous San Juan de Ulúa prison Mier, like the St. Mary's trustees, proved willing to spar with the church hierarchy. While the St. Mary's trustees peppered Rome with their requests, back in Mexico Mier penned a brazen response to Pope Leo XII's controversial September, 1824, encyclical *Etsi iam diu* that condemned Independence and called on Americans to renew their loyalty to Ferdinand VII. The cosmopolitan Mexican cleric's missive pierced the papacy's righteousness, suggesting that mammon motivated the Holy Father's exhortation to embrace the conservative king. Spain, he asserted, served as Rome's "milk cow" and could not continue to produce without the American mines that had gilded the churches of Rome and Europe. While in London, Mier claimed, he attended a public debate over who was worse, Ferdinand VII or the Anti-Christ. The king beat the Dark Prince in a landslide.[40]

The troubling tidings from Mier's Mexico and the collaboration of Luso-Hispanic reformist intellectuals with their fellow travelers in the United States combined with the horrors of the Liberal Triennium to place Rome on high alert. El Salvadoran emissary Castrillo was a visible reminder of a Reform Catholic movement that threatened to release the Americas from Rome. Indeed Castrillo's mission had been doomed before his costly transatlantic journey began. In May of 1820, the papacy had faced the threat head on, establishing a special council to confront the Spanish Empire's emboldened reformers, many of whom now gathered together at the second Spanish Cortes. The news from the legislative gathering was so ominous that Spain's papal nuncio urged Rome to "suffocate the reborn monster of Jansenism, that after infecting so many churches in Europe, now attempts to tumble the Church in Spain."[41]

The Congregation for Extraordinary Ecclesiastical Affairs urged the papal nuncio to use prudence in the face of the Cortes' proposal for a national church council, fearing a schism. Although the national council failed to materialize, the second Cortes took sweeping measures to reform the church, including abolishing the Inquisition, prohibiting new religious vows and religious houses, banning the church from acquiring new properties, and tossing the recently returned Jesuits out of the country.[42] Over the course of its four-year existence, the council's new committee dedicated to Spain grappled with such weighty issues as the Cortes' exile of bishops who opposed the Constitution of 1812, the Cortes' attack on the regular orders, and the proposal to raise José Espiga y Gadea and Diego Francisco Muñoz Torrero y Ramírez Moyano to bishoprics. The council even succeeded in persuading the Council of the Index to place two of Llorente's works on the list of prohibited books, as well as one text by Espiga.[43]

Espiga's inclusion on the Index no doubt reminded Rome of an earlier Spanish church schism. Indeed the papacy weighed Delgado's pretensions to a bishopric not only in light of contemporary events but in the context of a deep and oft-cited Spanish Reform Catholic history—a history that gave the reformers the sort of glorious past that any bright future depends upon. Reformers glossed this past to burnish the early church councils, martyrs, intellectuals, and heroes claimed by the Reform Catholic International.

THE DISPUTE OVER MARRIAGE DISPENSATIONS: THE SPANISH "SCHISM" OF 1799

Mexico, Argentina, the United States, Colombia, Cuba, Central America, Spain: Rome faced a dispersed but connected and militant Reform Catholic

International at exactly the time that the scrappy El Salvadorans sent Castrillo to Rome in 1826. The Curia also pondered Delgado's threat in the light of a recent schism in Spain that continued to inspire reformers in the Americas. This history was as relevant to the Vatican as it was the movement coalescing on the ruins of Spain's American empire.

On September 5, 1799, Charles IV issued a decree granting bishops the right to "use their full capacities according to the Church's primitive discipline to issue matrimonial dispensations and related matters." While Rome had previously received ample funds from the fees for these important dispensations, those funds would henceforth stay in Spain. Reformers chose a propitious moment to move against the Holy Father: Pope Pius VI had died the previous week and his successor had not yet been seated. Minister Mariano Luis de Urquio bent the king's ear in favor of the marriage dispensation measure.[44] His right-hand man in this campaign to "return" Spanish bishops' stolen right to grant dispensations, royal chaplain and Reform Catholic party apparatchik José de Espiga y Gadea penned a soaring defense of the decree. In an example of the self-consciously radical gestures so essential to any group's ongoing *esprit de corp*, Espiga joined Spain's many reformist bishops who refused to include the customary phrase "by the grace of the papacy," after their titles; papal authority over appointments, and thus the phrase, were, after all, "unknown in the first twelve centuries."[45] Joaquin Lorenzo Villanueva later reported, "Comrade Espiga" had joined him and "three religious that the Jesuit rabble labeled Jansenists" on a committee that persuaded the Inquisition to approve for publication the works of prolific seventeenth-century French Jansenist Pierre Nicole.[46] Not surprisingly, Espiga had found himself before the Inquisition in 1799, denounced as a Jansenist.[47]

Espiga's and Urquio's fellow travelers across Spain, especially the country's many reform-minded bishops, joined them in arguing that in earlier centuries the Holy Father had indeed controlled marriage dispensations—but only through the bishops' tacit concession. "Concession," of course, meant that the bishops should reclaim their rights and act unilaterally. So too, in many villages, everyone was related, so both ecclesiological differences and considerable revenues drove this marriage dispensation dispute.[48]

Reformist Catholic savants rushed to defend the marriage dispensation edict. These influential ecclesiastics shared Espiga and Urquijo's desire to decenter Rome, establish a national church, and aggrandize bishops' authority. Their carefully crafted rationales would be echoed by the Spanish Cortes in the early 1820s, and were shared by the ever-more-radical Reform Catholic International.

In their defense of the 1799 "schism," Spanish Church hierarchs like Salamanca's Bishop Antonio de Tavira y Almazán decried the "chaos" provoked by the Isidorian decretals, which astoundingly continued to inform the wrongheaded decisions of Crown and scepter, and underscored righteous prior efforts to stanch the flow of revenue to Rome. A professor of ecclesiastical history at Madrid's Colegio de San Isidro, a Reform Catholic stronghold, lambasted the "frivolous controversies" fanned by Scholasticism's adherents. Such people were too lazy to conduct historical research to confirm the papacy's limited writ, he charged. Christians who imbibed the church's "pure doctrine" from scripture and tradition eschewed Scholasticism's "capricious subtleties." Invoking some of the reformers' favorite church historians, Barcelona's bishop lamented the "river of gold" that had illegitimately flowed out of Spain to the Roman curia. Marriage dispensations should be free, or, failing that, the fees should be collected and spent locally by Spain's own bishops.[49]

Llorente demonstrated the ecclesiological stakes of the marriage dispensation debate in two key works: a pro-decree treatise written at Urquio's bequest featuring the testimonials from the sympathetic Spanish bishops and others who had weighed in at the time, published in 1809; and a translation of Portuguese Oratarian priest Pereira de Figueiredo's 1769 exposé of the papacy's tragic history of running roughshod over prerogatives rightly held by bishops and the state.[50] In an intellectual move Latin American reformist Catholics would embrace during the nation-building of the 1820s, Pereira de Figueiredo's *Doctrinam veteris ecclesiae* limited the church's power to the exclusively spiritual and stressed the state's sanctified monopoly over coercive power; the church could not compel people to come in, nor could it shield its personnel from state justice. Portuguese King José I and his minister Carvalho broke off relations with the papacy over the expulsion of the Jesuits in 1759, ushering in a nine-year schism in the church. Pereira provided the intellectual ballast for the break from Rome, decrying Jesuit despotism. His 1766 magnum opus *Tentativa theologica* insisted bishops obey divinely anointed kings over the supreme pontiff, particularly in matters relating to marriage dispensations. In Pereira de Figueiredo's vision, the state acted to protect the bishops' imprescriptible rights from an overweening papacy, just as it rightly held jurisdiction over the clergy. Pereira de Figueiredo stressed the collective ownership of the Petrine keys and the authority of a general church council over that of the bishop of Rome, whilie pledging his allegiance to the Jansenist International centered at Utrecht. In essence, he provided an intellectual justification for divinely anointed monarchs to use the state to reform the church in accordance with Reform Catholic tenets.[51] Central American reformers leaned on Pereira de Figueiredo authority in their own bids for national churches.

Llorente's networks extended well beyond Spain, including American and European reformers in Paris and London and reform-minded Latin Americans. He even collaborated with other intellectuals on major publishing projects designed to discredit Spanish suzerainty in the New World: his celebrated two-volume treatise that translated from the original Latin the sixteenth-century Indian-defender Bartolomé de las Casas' influential writings, also included Grégoire's exculpation of de las Casas' role in the slave trade; Argentine archbishop and reform firebrand Gregorio Funes' letter to Grégoire on the topic; and Mier's report on the same theme. Grégoire, Funes, Mier, and Llorente: here were the intellectual architects of the Reform Catholic International in all of their glory, collaborating to amplify de las Casas' searing critique of Spanish abuse of the indigenous people of Latin America and the Caribbean and thereby discredit their continuing hold on the region. Llorente's towering 1818 history of the Inquisition's depredations, written from primary sources he took with him into exile in France in 1814, rapidly appeared in German, English, Spanish, and Dutch, intriguing readers in both Europe and the Americas.[52]

The 1799 Reform Catholic marriage dispensations victory led by Urquio and Espiga, and later defended by Llorente, triggered ultramontane forces in Spain and Rome in 1800. Conservatives convinced the king to finally publish in Spain Pius VI's 1794 bull *Auctorem fidei*, a scathing take-down of the radical synod of Pistoia and Reform Catholic beliefs more generally. Regalists and reformers had conspired with Charles III to prevent the bull's earlier circulation[53] Minister of State Urquijo perhaps suffered the most in the crackdown on this self-identified group of reform-minded intellectuals and statesmen. Urquio was arrested three days after the marriage dispensation edict's 1799 promulgation and imprisoned in his home city of Bilbao. In March of 1801, the Crown transferred him and his man servant to a room under the floor of Pamplona's fortress prison; denied visitors, his books doled out to him one by one, the beleaguered reformer quickly succumbed to illness.[54]

Mier lamented the injustice done to the minister of state, seeing him as a fellow victim of ultramontane manueverings.[55] The Mexican friar reported arriving in Pamplona just four days after Urquijo's imprisonment; barely escaping arrest himself in what he glossed as a systematic roundup of religious reformers, Mier noted that "this was the crucial period of the persecution carried out against the Jansenists by Godoy (who for this reason was called a pillar of religion in a brief issued by Rome)."[56] As part of the crackdown detailed by Mier, the Inquisition hunted down reformers like Espiga, the intellectual author of the 1799 schism. It also targeted Madrid's Jansenist salonnaire, the countess of Montijo, as well as her husband, head of the Royal Academy of San Isidro in Madrid.[57] The canons of this royal academy had recognized the expatriated Mexican as one of their own and had kept Mier alive during his time in their city, or so the friar reported.

They paid the impoverished refugee six reales to say eleven o'clock Mass. All of these clerics had passed an examination and were "clever," and, as a consequence, Mier argued, were accused of being Jansenists.[58] The countess and a handful of her salon attendees regularly exchanged letters with Grégoire about the glories of the church's primitive discipline and the Jesuits' lax morals. Espiga and other canons of San Isidro, prolific authors like Joaquin Lorenzo Villanueva, frequented the countess' gatherings.[59] During the roundup of reformers, Juan Antonio Llorente, a former secretary general of the Inquisition, advised the countess on eluding the institution's grasp.[60] Spain's persecuted reformers that so captivated Mier would later become the movement martyrs invoked by Central American reformers to invigorate their own *esprit de corp*.

The Rome that welcomed El Salvadoran emissary Castrillo was keenly aware of the schism of 1799, in part, no doubt, because during the Liberal Triennium in Spain (1820–1823), the Cortes had rehearsed themes from the event and invoked its martyrs. In particular, 1820 debates in the legislative body over the wealth hemorrhaged to the Vatican echoed the wisdom of Espiga, Urquio, Pereira de Figueiredo, Villanueva, and Llorente, identifying the false Isidorian decretals and ultramontane machinations as threats to Spanish ecclesiastical liberties and as remnants of an "age of ignorance" that aggrandized the Holy Father. Spain should control marriage dispensations, as Espiga had insisted, as well as the canonization of saints, privileged altars, and even the sale of indulgences, thereby ending the exodus of national wealth.[61] In March of 1821, the Cortes' ecclesiastical commission recommended ending payments to Rome for dispensations and bulls, and placated His Holiness with a small "donation" instead; Rome took umbrage, because, as Villanueva explained, Spain had contributed 24 million pesos to Vatican coffers from marriage dispensations from 1818 to 1820 alone.[62]

The schism of 1799 was a living memory for Rome more than two decades later, but a much more proximate provocation was the Cortes of 1820 to 1823 itself, with its persistent efforts to promote reform causes. In 1821, for example, the legislative body pushed to elevate reform firebrands Espiga and Diego Francisco Muñoz Torrero y Ramírez Moyano to the positions of archbishop of Seville and bishop of Guadix, respectively. In an unusual move, the pope refused to approve their nomination, although he demonstrated a tiny modicum of sympathy for Espiga, who had quickly informed Rome of his commitment to "sane doctrine." The Holy Father's correspondence with Muñoz Terrero, on the other hand, had further revealed his "tenacious adhesion" to "erroneous doctrines," and the pope had urged King Ferdinand VII to nominate another candidate.[63] Few Spanish political players of the early nineteenth century escaped anti-monarchalist Carlos le Brun's satirical pen, and he lambasted Espiga's obsequiousness, accusing him of "abjuring the constitution before the pope by calling it Jansenist." He acknowledged Espiga's noble past as a "man of Urquijo," but lamented him as a fallen hero who lost his moral bearings when tantalized by the opportunity to move up in the ecclesiastical hierarchy.[64] The Philadelphia resident heaved even heftier shafts of ridicule at King Ferdinand, whom he accused of conniving with the French ambassador and the papal nuncio to sway the church against the two reformers.[65]

Enlightened Madrileños talked of nothing else but the pope's perfidy, *El Universal* had reported in July of 1821. The liberal Madrid paper questioned Rome's motivations for denying the promotions and concluded with some bragadaccio about the pervasiveness of reformist sentiment in Spain. Current university students understood the bishop of Rome's limited writ and the rights of peoples better than even theologians from previous centuries, and Spain's constitutional government would resist the Vatican more energetically than had the ministers of Charles V or Philip II, the paper reported.[66]

Reform Catholic opinion leaders weighed in on the Espiga incident across the Atlantic world; the network crackled with the news. Rome rejected Bishop Espiga despite his fawning, the London newspaper *Ocios de Españoles Emigrados* reported in 1824, because of his influential arguments for the earlier Cortes de Cadiz's abolition of the Inquisition; Muñoz Torreros' support for the second Cortes' 1820 law against the regular orders earned him the Holy Father's opprobrium, the London paper reported.[67] Joaquin Villanueva chimed in from exile in England. Papal lackeys had sifted through Rome's dusty files and found his "intimate friend" Espiga's written defense of bishops' rights over marriage dispensations; this was Rome's "recondite motivation" for denying him the proposed bishopric.[68]

The ripple effects of incidents like the "schism" of 1799 were felt throughout the empire, as Rome was well aware. Reformist networks emerged from the split and refashioned themselves at the Cortes de Cádiz. The bishop of Havana for thirty years beginning in 1802, Juan José Díaz de Espada y Landa, owed his plum ecclesiastical appointment in part to schism-author Urquijo's patronage. Espada was well connected in reformist networks. As part of the 1813 debate about the Inquisition held at Cádiz, reform luminary Joaquin Lorenzo Villanueva lauded Espada's support for the 1812 Constitution and his leadership against the Vatican's usurpations and in support of the restoration of bishops' "primitive dignity," which amounted to their autonomy from Rome. In an 1824 missive to Mier, the Abbé Grégoire mentioned rather eliptically that he had sent a special commission to Espada through the mediation of Miguel Ramos de Arizpe, but had not heard back from either man; he sent his regards to Arizpe through Mier. Among his many reformist forays into the tangles of the baroque excess that so irked his co-religionists, Espada oversaw a neoclassical revolution in architecture in Havana, issued edicts against

excessive bell ringing, and built an extramural cemetery. Justifying the controversial change in burial customs from urban churches to the suburban site, he
cited the reform-minded bishop of Barcelona, Josep Climent I Avinent, as well as
renowned Jesuit scourge Antonio Jorge Galbán, a former archbishop of Grenada.[69]
As part of his focused attack on ultramontane piety, Espada banned prayers to
the Sacred Heart of Jesus.[70] In 1830, Espada ran afoul of Rome's Congregation for
Extraordinary Ecclesiastical Affairs, who concluded that Espada's ideas about the
pope's dependency on the bishops were not only similar, but "indeed identical,"
to those of the Jansenists, and that his doctrine overlapped considerably with
doctrines propounded by the repudiated Synod of Pistoia. The congregation considered excommunication a fitting punishment, but the bishop died in 1832 before
the case could wend its way through the papacy's labyrinthian bureaucracy.[71]

Espada surrounded himself with Havana's most enlightened citizens and advanced the career of the young priest Félix Varela, appointing him to teach philosophy in the Seminary of San Carlos in 1811 and to the newly minted position
of Professor of the Constitution in 1820 at the same institution. An avowed proponent of Cuban independence, Varela deployed his resounding but simple rhetoric in the cause of illuminating the absurdity of Scholasticism, finding fellow
travelers in the reform Catholic authors so central to university curricular reforms
of the late eighteenth century. His own prose dripped sarcasm on the topic of the
Schoolmen, and he cited reformer Melchor Cano's equally sardonic lampooning of
questions like "whether God could make matter without form, or if He can create a
lot of angels from the same species of Angel . . . and other things equally useless."[72]
Here Varela, now widely regarded as the apostle of Cuban independence, echoed
Mexico's father of independence Miguel Hidalgo y Costilla, whose prize-winning
early scholarship argued that Scholastic Père Jean Baptiste Gonet's five weighty
tomes could profitably be condensed to one single volume in theology curriculums. Hidalgo noted that one problem with this type of theology, "as Melchor
Cano has signaled, are the ridiculous questions like can an angel be in two places
separated from each other and not be in the middle of them."[73]

The Congregation for Extraordinary Ecclesiastical Affairs, then, weighed the
news of the El Salvador schism in light of the 1799 "schism" in Spain, the Reform
Catholic radicalism of the Cortes de Cádiz and the Liberal Triennium, and an
Americas-wide movement of reformers, many of them—like Delgado, Mier,
Quintana Roo, Hidalgo, and Cañas—recognized leaders in the recent Independence
and autonomy struggles. Not surprisingly, Rome ignored El Salvador's messenger.
Pope Leo XII did, however, hurl anathemas at Delgado, including, eventually, a
definitive decree of excommunication in 1829; and Rome backed the efforts of
Archbishop Casaús and Central America's ultramontane conservatives centered in

Guatemala. Rome and the region's ultramontane would lose the three-year civil war to Central American liberals centered in El Salvador and Honduras, but present throughout the region. But the reformist Catholic victory in this skirmish would prove fleeting, as their state-led reform of the church galvanized a coalition that included the region's majority, the indigenous people, who had largely watched and bided their time as the region's whiter and better off residents plunged Central America into a profoundly religious conflict in the 1820s.

5

Escalation and Confrontation

ACCUSATIONS OF SUPERSTITION and fanaticism came easily to liberals' lips after more than a decade of rhetorical conflicts and armed confrontations. The terms have long been noted by historians; the conservative recapture of Central America after 1838 is rightly understood as a religious resurgence. What has been missed, however, is how these two terms indexed not the liberals' secularism but rather their specific religiosity, positioned in contradistinction to the two perverted forms of Catholic faith: "superstition" stood for what they saw as an essentially pagan folk Catholicism on the part of the *indios*, while "fanaticism" was the term of art for servile fealty to tyrannical papal authority on the part of the ultramontane. Thus the conflict that continued to percolate until the conservative counterrevolution of 1839 was not one of secularizing forces of liberalism ultimately defeated by undifferentiated resurgent religion, but rather the coalescing of interests between the two quite distinct objects of longstanding liberal religious hostility.

That the "superstitious" and the "fanatical" would forge a loose alliance against a common enemy—much less prevail over it—was not a foregone conclusion at the outset of the liberal reign. The process by which religious proclivities became fundamental to political legitimacy and competing notions of national belonging depended on the content of the rival interpretations of Catholicism. As the elaborate Spanish colonial caste system fell to liberal notions of more putatively universal political subjectivity in the early republics, the religiosity of the region's

For God and Liberty. Pamela Voekel, Oxford University Press. © Oxford University Press 2023.
DOI: 10.1093/oso/9780197610190.003.0006

indigenous and rural *campesino* majority increasingly became an index of their backwardness and a central factor—perhaps the central factor—in their racialization. Over the same years, liberals learned to regard conservatives as religious fanatics who thwarted their dreams of a godly Reform Catholic republic.

As historian Jordana Dym has argued, political elites, not the popular classes, plunged the region into well-nigh-endless conflagrations from 1824 to 1839.[1] But these political elites, I have argued, were also religious elites, and their conflicting loyalty to God also doomed the region's unity as well as its liberty. With its fraternal universalism that obliterated difference, the logic of the Reform Catholic faith demanded a uniformity of belief that it could never evoke from the majority, for whom theological and ecclesiological disputation and devotional practice diverged significantly from that of reformist Catholics. In contrast, the ultramontane rallied the majority to their banner not by winning subaltern worshippers to their learned defenses of papal authority but by adopting a more *laissez-faire* attitude to "folk" Catholic praxis, indeed, in certain instances, encouraging the communal, mediated devotion that was anathema to Reform restraint. The rural majority's "superstition" and elite conservatives' ultramontane "fanaticism" rendered them enemies of the liberal configuration of the nation and civilization, barbarian others whose benighted religious sensibilities indexed their utter irrationality and need for liberal tutelage or complete replacement by foreigners, even Protestants, who could be counted on to behave rationally. While Dym further argues persuasively for the increasing significance of the municipal district as the seat of sovereignty in late colonial Spanish America, and for the ways this Bourbon revival in municipal political philosophy and governance set in motion conflicting tendencies in post-independence Central America, municipalities were not only politically significant; in some cases they also represented outposts of two rival religious networks among those elites.[2] Many municipalities, as we have seen, entered these recurring disputes out of impassioned commitment to either reform or ultramontane religio-political ideologies. But these religious tensions among the fractious elites had serious consequences for the poor, mostly indigenous majority in the region whose faith could not claim a voice in the republic of letters. They also impacted rural ladinos engaged in small-scale farming and livestock raising, as in the eastern part of El Salvador. And, to be sure, sometimes municipalities mobilized in defense of personally beloved priests, regardless of their theological orientation—a project that could unite the popular classes behind one or the other elite project on essentially coincidental grounds.

In the judgment of Guatemalan conservative Manuel Montúfar y Coronado, the civil war that wracked Central America for three years beginning in 1826 was the logical outcome of the schism incited by José Matías Delgado. On May 9, 1825, El

Salvadoran hero Manuel José Arce ascended to the presidency of the federation. Arce had paid a steep prize for his participation in the 1811 and 1814 uprising in El Salvador—four years in prison—and had led El Salvadoran troops against Mexico in 1821. The presidency of this revered native son should have cemented El Salvador's loyalty to the federation, but, as Montúfar explained, Arce owed his rise to a backroom deal that won him conservative votes in exchange for his condemnation of his nephew Delgado's schismatic church, angering many El Salvadorans.[3]

The tensions between literate regional elites imbued with opposing ultramontane or reformist sensibilities steadily mounted in 1825, as this chapter details. These tensions culminated in the first Central American civil war in late 1826. Originally orchestrated by the El Salvadoran government, but eventually led by the talented Honduran General Francisco Morazán, the liberal army—named the Ejercito Aliado Protector de la Ley (The Allied Army Protector of the Law) after Morazan knitted together a coalition comprised of El Salvador, Nicaragua, Honduras, and exiled Guatemalan liberals—prevailed over the Guatemalan and federal armies in 1829 and immediately began to impose their reformist agenda on church and state. The liberal agenda, however, would prove deeply unpopular with the region's indigenous majority, who had largely stayed on the sidelines as intertwined religious, political, and economic elites rent the region's fragile municipal, national, and federal balance during the three-year open conflict.

Reformers, of course, faced an uphill battle against ultramontane Catholics who defended the papacy. In Central America, these two church factions, wielding the respective banners of federalism and centralism, liberalism and conservatism, were essentially in agreement about the righteousness—or at least the permanence— of independence from Spain, but still very much divided by religion in their own self-conceptions. Their enmity engulfed the region in interminable conflicts after 1824. These battles were often fought at the granular level of the parish, but also spilled dramatically over the boundaries of the region's all-important *municipios* and inchoate nation-states.

Yet Montúfar overstated his claim: few wars have only a single cause. To say that Delgado's schism provoked anger, or, that religious passions tore Central America apart, is not to say that ultramontane and reform conflicts were the only cause of the region's tensions and conflagrations during the five years after Independence and into the 1830s. Religious proclivities mapping onto regional economic interests was nowhere more evident than in the rivalry between the flush Guatemalan merchant houses connected to Atlantic markets and El Salvador's credit-starved indigo producers. Recall that Delgado's father Pedro represented El Salvadoran interests at the Society of Indigo Growers' 1794 meeting in Guatemala City, and that his family members dominated the growers' union in San Salvador in 1813.

Backed by the Crown, the growers' organization sparred with the Consulado de Comercio, which represented Guatemalan merchant interests, among them those of the powerful Aycinena clan. Delgado and Aycinena scions of the younger generations perfectly embodied the religious differences that closely tracked with their families' warring economic interests. Reform luminary José Matías Delgado championed secular and religious conciliar authority like the Cádiz Cortes and reformers gloss on the simple church of the early centuries after Christ; during the same years, Teresa de Aycinena embraced Archbishop Casaús and the ultramontane's signature cult, the Sacred Heart of Jesus. This alliance between the nun and conservatives would not be forgotten. Commenting on his conservative enemies in his 1841 memoirs, General Francisco Morazán noted that maximizing "their joy and our sorrow, on earth as it is in heaven, they even produced saints from among their own families!"[4] The tensions between Guatemalan elites and El Salvadorans continued after independence, and indeed, as historian Sajid Alfredo Herrera Mena argues, the perceived "barbarity of the Guatemalan aristocracy and its empire of blood and injustice" continued to play the role of stalking alter-ego in the construction of El Salvadoran nationalism through the 1820s if not beyond.[5]

The centrifugal economic tensions continued after independence, as revenue-starved national governments sparred with the federal government—a body dominated, as we have seen, by Guatemalan representatives—for control over the federal government's major funding sources: tobacco and gunpowder monopoly revenues, sales taxes (*alcabala*) and customs duties on maritime trade (the *alcabala marítima*), and the postal system. Another source of tension was the debt to the British House of Barclay and Herring incurred by a desperate federal republic in 1824. The conservative federal government spent most of the loan money during the Civil War of 1826 to 1829. The debt exacerbated tensions between the peripheries and the Guatemala-dominated Federal Republic of Central America, as impecunious states refused to help service the debt. El Salvador declined to turn over its tobacco revenues in 1831, for example, after the federal republic had pledged all of the region's funds to its British creditor.[6]

Only Guatemala relinquished desperately needed revenues to the federal governmet from *alcabala marítima* taxes, already low during this period because of smugglers landing on coastlines the republic could not afford to police. And in 1831 and 1832, two of Arce's former coronels, Vicente Domíngues and Ramón Gúzman, seized the key ports of Trujillo and Omoa, preventing the collection of the *alcabala marítima* from these major ports for a year. In 1832, conservative-led El Salvador refused to pay President Morázan and the republic a "forced loan" to defray the cost of putting down this conservative revolt and shortly thereafter attempted to secede from the federal republic. President Morázan foiled their plans in short order: he led an army into El Salvador, arrested the ringleaders, and replaced them with federal loyalists. Chafing against these imposed authorities and yet another "forced loan," not a year later, in 1833, El Salvadoran rebels deposed the Morázan-appointed interlopers and seized the *alcabala* and tobacco revenues for state use.

This jockeying for much-needed revenues had a desperate tenor. Plagues of locusts, rising competition from India, post-independence political turmoil, and wars with Britain afflicted indigo production, the lifeblood of the economy: the 1.5-million-pound harvest of 1793 declined to roughly 100,000 pounds per year during most of the 1820s. Originally decreed by the Cádiz Cortes in 1812, the abolition of Indian tribute continued in force during the Central American republic's early years and represented a loss of revenues in comparison to the pre-Cádiz period, when Indian tribute had been the state's third-largest revenue source.

While the young republics' instability and the emergence of regional strongmen unwilling to bend to a central government has received much attention, the fundamentally religious causes of these tensions and armed conflicts have been overlooked.[7]

To observe that regional elites with conflicting economic and religious interests brought the region to civil war is not to say that ordinary Catholics had no opinions about the religious disputes that proved a constant strand in the genealogy of the conflicts. Although they may not have read Cañas, Azuero, or Grégoire, parishioners in El Salvador did hear theologians' works read from pulpits and did form particular attachments to their priestly advocates, whom they energetically defended from Delgado's and Casaús' respective tentacular networks. These humbler Catholics who peopled the El Salvadoran countryside fretted about their immortal souls and energetically sought the sacraments from the priests they trusted to hold the legitimate keys to the church's warehouse of grace. Control over the sacraments—over salvation itself—quickly became an explosive flashpoint between reformist and ultramontane factions, generalizing a theological dispute beyond elite circles, escalating the divisions into armed confrontations and, eventually, and in combination with other factors, precipitating a three-year civil war that officially began in 1826.

THE KEYS TO THE STOREHOUSE OF GRACE

Priests on both sides of the conflict battled to control the mundane paperwork that undergirded the church's apparatus. These paperwork scuffles became increasingly virulent, as the ultramontane attempted to deny these crucial documents to Delgado's clerical appointees. A representative heated exchange centered on the baptismal certificate that was required for marriage. When "citizen priest" and Delgado appointee Mariano Carillo requested proof of baptism from a prospective bridegroom's former parish, for example, the other priest demanded evidence that Carillo was serving with Archbishop Casaús' blessing.[8]

Tensions between priests over control of the sacraments soon escalated into armed confrontations. In Santa Ana and nearby Chalchuapa, two Delgado-appointed priests, the brothers Calderón, actively promoted the schism, in part by cajoling the faithful into re-baptizing infants who had been previously christened by the conservative archbishop's appointees. In July of 1825, Casaús ordered his loyal priests in the area to shut down the Calderóns' traffic in false sacraments. Conservative parish priest Ignacio Perdomo sprang into action. To be sure, he was for the moment a one-man army; more circumspect ministers studiously ignored Archbishop Causaús' order. But Perdomo rushed to the area to confront the interloping priests. His campaign proved shortlived, as he was promptly jailed in Santa Ana by *gefe político* Elizondo and later in the national jail in San Salvador.

The episode is a revealing one, thanks to the prisoner's circumspection in expressing himself. Perdomo proceeded to display the fortitude of the true believer, despite his history of personal distaste for Archbishop Casaús. He was no craven sycophant, he felt compelled to explain; to the contrary, his fractious relationship to Archbishop Casaús was common knowledge. But Delgado's schism represented to him a moral earthquake that threatened to plunge his homeland into apostasy, and he supported church unity under the Holy Father. His countrymen might yet label him the archbishop's lap dog. But in deference to Rome's monopoly on salvation, he remained loyal to his rightful hierarch the archbishop despite their personal animosity, as he carefully explained to the hierarch himself in a flurry of letters from his prison cell.[9]

Perdomo's feverish prose, biblical erudition, and ever-stiffening spine quickly made him the ultramontane movement's perfect jailhouse martyr, a status he wholeheartedly embraced. Even his former antagonist Casaús eventually came to his defense. God had winnowed him from the clerical multitude to bear witness to the truth, he informed the archbishop, and he intended to honor that charge. The pamphlets churned from Guatemala City presses, priests who sermonized from the pulpits—these he deemed secondary tools in the struggle, as his imprisonment and suffering bore witness to Delgado's unjust pretensions to the bishopric. Covered in scabies and crawling with lice, sleep-deprived, half-starved, and publicly maligned, the former priest of Aguachapán admitted to periods of "turbulence and anguish." He begged the archbishop to supply him with food and to convince the federal congress in Guatemala to write to El Salvador's state legislature on his behalf. Despite his appeals for help, he yearned for a martyr's death: if beheading were his fate, he willed his tormentors to do it within the hour of the sentence, as he wished to "water the land of El Salvador with his blood." His body, in a state of "humiliation," was the best defense of true religion.[10]

Perdomo's steadfastness won him entry into the bishop's inner circle despite their personal rancor, and Central America's ultramontane network slowly mobilized on the martyr's behalf. Casaús had ignored Perdomo's initial pleas from prison for provisions and patronage and had declined to write to him personally, delegating the correspondence to his loyal secretary, José Mariano Herrarte. The archbishop feared that Delgado's sympathizers would intercept missives, and then increase the priest's torments as retaliation against his meddling. He was probably right to worry: in June of 1825, the conservative *El Indicador* accused leaders of the "farcical" bishopric movement of re-creating Captain General Bustamante's oppressive regime, of systematically opening private correspondence under the pretext of public security.[11] The mail, as Perdomo himself had repeatedly warned, was not a secure medium.[12]

Archbishop Casaús, a Dominican, did prevail upon San Salvador's few remaining Dominicans to deliver much-needed provisions to the jail, prompting Perdomo's lyrical gratitude.[13] None other than Father Anselmo Ortiz, Teresa de Aycinena's confessor, ferried Perdomo's entreaties to the archbishop in early 1827.[14] By 1829, Perdomo was on the short list of El Salvador's priests approved to receive consecrated holy oil from the archbishop, as part of his campaign to cut off at the root Delgado's ministers' salvific powers.

The tensions in Santa Ana eventually erupted into violence, which state troops swept in to curb.[15] Angered by Delgado's edicts and letters, crowds led by a conservative Santa Ana councilman sacked stores and destroyed buildings, assassinated a handful of their enemies, and removed the *jefe político* from his post.[16] In Guatemala, the ultramontane circulated rumors that Santa Ana's anti-Delgado forces had turned back the El Salvadoran troops called to the scene and inflicted two gunshot wounds on their commander, Miguel Elizondo. Elizondo served as the local *jefe político* and had boasted of his invincibility in the face of the town's civic militia. He sequestered Perdomo in Santa Ana in the summer of 1825 while he awaited transfer to San Salvador's jail. The Guatemalan rumor-mongers asserted that the town of Santa Ana had forged an alliance with like-minded factions in nearby Ahuachapán and Sonsonate and that the alliance plotted to attack San Salvador to liberate themselves from Delgado.[17] A conservative federal senator arguing against Delgado's schism feared that if the federal government allowed individual states to claim the *patronato*, the region would erupt in interminable civil wars. Most people would simply not abide such an attack on papal prerogatives; he pointed to El Salvador's threats and attack on Santa Ana to prohibit people's religious preferences, and the town's spirited resistance, as a cautionary tale for governments intent on assailing their populations' deeply held religious proclivities.[18] Conservatives were charged with fabricating reports that Santa Anans preferred to die without the sacraments than receive them from Delgado's illegitimate appointees. An anonymous Delgado supporter, however, read the situation differently, seeing Bishop Delgado's detractors in Santa Ana not as members of a town united against false sacraments, but as an obstreporous minority faction who would taste defeat soon enough.[19]

The conflict in Santa Ana quickly moved from the local and state level to the international arena, as a handful of Santa Ana's ultramontane rebels sought refuge in Guatemala after El Salvadoran soldiers swept into the town. In 1826, Guatemala's congress protected these Santa Ana city councilmen and others from extradition by the El Salvadorans.[20] The same Guatemalan congress ordered refugee Friar Geronimo Zelaya reinstated in the Dominican convent in Sonsonate. President Arce cautioned against forcing Zelaya's return, regarding the measure as a de facto declaration of war, as the friar could only be returned to Sonsonate and protected by force.[21]

An anonymous pamphleteer fingered Casaús and Perdomo as the Santa Ana jacquerie's prime movers and ratcheted up the conflict's stakes, insisting that they acted in tandem with others. The scandalous publications of the "heterogenous mob" of clerics who found refuge in Guatemala, he reported, had inflamed passions. If Casaús and his immigrant priests ignored the public's cries for justice, if they continued to churn out libelous and inflammatory papers, the prescient pamphleteer warned, it would not be "Minerva but Mars that decided the diuturnal question."[22]

THE REFORM OF THE REGULAR ORDERS

As skirmishes over the paperwork required to administer the sacraments morphed into armed arrests in El Salvador, transforming God's humble servants into full-fledged martyrs, liberals escalated tensions by targeting the regular orders, long regarded as the Vatican's shock troops. The perpetual vows taken by the friars marked them as a threat to the freedom of conscience so precious to reformers, and they continued to man most of the parishes in the indigenous Guatemalan highlands, menacing reformers' citizenship-building projects. Adding to the explosive mix was the friars' response to the order to swear allegiance to the 1824 federal constitution, evidenced by García Jerez's spirited resistance to the oath to the federal government from the ultramontane stronghold of León. In many ways,

Nicolás García Jerez proved prescient about the ANC's then inchoate reformist agenda: early decrees of the legislative body abolished the Inquisition; declared that papal bulls required government approval to circulate; set twenty-three as the minimum age of entry to convents and monasteries and twenty-five as the minimum age to profess; and required the archbishop to obtain government approval of priests prior to their appointments. Tithes were reduced by 50 percent, and the children of priests and nuns obtained the rights of inheritance enjoyed by all children.[23] Conservatives were probably outnumbered in the hallowed halls of federal power in 1825: liberals in the federal government handily quashed challenges from the conservatives in the ANC's ranks. In particular, conservatives found themselves helpless to fend off to the El Salvadoran Congress' ruling of April 1825 that penalized clerics with loss of property—including their benefices—for circulating ecclesiastical orders without prior government approval.[24] The liberal-dominated federal government voted to allow the law to stand.

It was in this tense context that on February 19, 1825, the conservative fathers of the Colégio de Propaganda Fide announced an organized preaching mission. Neither these friars nor the regular orders had yet sworn the oath to the 1824 Constitution, and *gefe político* Antonio Rivera's patience had frayed: no oath, no mission, he declared. His confidence was misplaced. Angry crowds amassed in Guatemala City's main plaza, and the supreme executive branch of government called an emergency session that very afternoon, hoping to avert further protests by "simple people" who, they asserted, wrongly saw republican government as incompatible with Catholicism. The people were not appeased. "We want the mission!" thundered the large crowd that escorted Propaganda's leader to the emergency meeting, while smaller groups threaded through the city's center belting out "Long live religion!" "Death to heresy!" and "Death to those who oppose missions!" The executive branch, sensing the well-timed capitulation, greenlighted the mission.[25]

Reformers were unrelenting, but the ultramontane proved indefatigable in defense of the friars. In July of 1826, a Guatemalan legislative decree declared youth ineligible for cloister until age twenty-three and unable to profess final vows before turning twenty-five. These restrictions sent conservative intellectuals into a pamphlet war. Franciscan Manuel García assured Guatemalans of the friars' abiding enthusiasm for national independence from Spain and their studied refusal to meddle in politics. But with so few youth choosing the cloister, he feared that raising the entry age spelled ruin for the regular orders—and that the new law's champions sought that very outcome. When they regained power in 1827, conservatives revoked the decree, arguing that the law further inflamed divisions in the unstable country.[26]

Always in the vanguard of reformist campaigns, El Salvador's government sub-jected friars to heightened scrutiny. Fray Luis Cilloto had fetched up in San Vicente, raising alarms for the authorities. An alleged leader in the 1826 Quetzaltenango riot that ended in the dismemberment and death of liberal Lieutenant Governor Flores, Cilloto could easily seduce San Vicente's "simple people" who "lacked edu-cation," the government warned the area's *jefe político*.[27] The riot provided a cau-tionary tale to Central American liberals, and Cilloto's alleged participation was cause for concern. In 1826, President of the Federal Republic of Central America Manuel José Arce had found himself at loggerheads with Guatemala's liberal gov-ernment. When tensions boiled over and Arce deposed liberal head of state Juan Burrundia, Guatemalan liberals moved the state's government to Quetzaltenango, a conservative bastion—or, as liberal chronicler Marure put it, a decidedly unen-lightened "emporium of fanaticism." It was not lost on the El Salvadorans that the federal government could also move against them. When the Guatemalan state-in-exile enacted a series of liberal laws, including halving the tithe and recognizing priests' illegitimate children as rightful heirs, the city's friars denounced the lib-erals as heretics. Deadly violence ensued. A swirling crowd of men and women tore vice-president Cirilo Flores limb from limb while chanting "Death to the tyrant, death to the heretic, death to the thief!" They then dragged his corpse through the streets to enthusiastic cries of "Long live religion! Death to the heretics in Congress!"[28]

The incident both underscored and foreshadowed a problem that would haunt liberals throughout the nineteenth century: their hostility to popular culture and particularly popular religiosity would more than once prove their undoing. Even before the liberal state government arrival in Quetzaltenango in October of 1826, there was no love lost between the unfortunate Flores and the city's K'iche residents: he had administered a deeply unpopular vaccination campaign during the 1826 smallpox outbreak, and his orders to end church burials and construct a public cemetery had rankled popular sensibilities. Public cemeteries were a signa-ture Reform Catholic project, one animated by both theological and public health concerns, and they drew the ire of folk and ultramontane Catholics alike.[29] That Flores looked to church and confraternity coffers to fund his numerous adminis-trative projects, and to Indian conscripts and taxes for his army, proved particularly galling to Indian-majority Quetzaltenango's organized K'iche community.[30] With the defeat of the liberals—or Liberals, as the organized political forces now some-times called themselves—Arce teamed up with a new conservative-dominated Guatemalan state to send into flight the remaining liberals in Quetzaltenango. Many crossed over the border into El Salvador. The political and theological al-liances in the Quetzaltenango showdown cemented the battle lines for the remainder of the three-year civil war: the conservative Guatemalan state and the conservative-dominated federation would battle liberals centered in El Salvador and Honduras.[31]

State meddling with El Salvador's clerics increasingly extended into the interior decision-making of the regular orders. Officials informed Franciscan Provincial Pedro José Méndez that the state government distrusted the friars he sought to place in monasteries in San Miguel and Sonsonate; these untrustworthy clerics should be sent back to Guatemala immediately. Friar Joaquín Taboada appealed the decision, pledging his allegiance to El Salvador's government and procuring character witnesses from Sonsonate's city council and local residents. El Salvador's vice-jefe initially granted Taboada's request to stay but later retracted his support after receiving repeated reports of his prejudicial behavior. He ordered Sonsonate officials to remand him to Ahuachapán's department head under the false pretext of a routine conversation. They neglected to tell Taboada of the government's real intention: to expel him from the territory.[32]

Actions were accompanied by a torrent of words. The liberal press incessantly rehearsed the invidious distinction between virtuous reformed priests and servile friars. Franciscans in Quetzaltenango collaborated with a group of foreign comics to construct a coliseum, the pseudonymous "Friend of Religion" proclaimed from the reform mouthpiece *El Salvadoreño*; Casaús followed up this folly with a promise of eighty days of indulgences for theater goers. The same paper ran a poem contrasting a virtuous reformed ecclesiastic to a vile friar. The former embraced religious reforms advantageous to virtuous citizens; the later sowed discord and clamored for the return of the Inquisition.[33]

DELGADO PURGES THE PARISHES

It was in El Salvador where disputes between reformers and ecclesiastical conservatives proved most disruptive. Delgado's round-up of refractory priests was uncompromising, systematic, and far-reaching, and it relied on assistance from the El Salvadoran state, which was fully implicated in the schismatic church. The round-up and exile of ultramontane loyalists often left parishes unmanned until Delgado or El Salvador's congress could name a replacement. Casaús loyalist Silvestre Tomé wrote his archbishop for permission to offer the sacraments at an ultramontane cause célèbre, the celebration of Mary's Immaculate Conception, soon to be observed in the port of Conchagua. The news from the town was disheartening, and Tomé was determined to help. The "pseudo-bishop's scandalous schism" had left the areas' faithful bereft of clerics: one, Manuel Torres, had been marched to San Miguel in chains; another, Dr. Manuel Antonio Molina, immigrated; and still another, the area's vicar, had fled. Tomé professed his loyalty to Casaús. "His foot was in the stirrup" to gallop off to "kiss the Archbishop's hand" during the hierarch's earlier trip to El Salvador, Tomé assured his prelate, when he received the bad news that an ailing Casaús had returned to Guatemala City.[34] Such florid sentiments were increasingly the rule in turbulent El Salvador.

El Salvador's government kept careful records of priests' political proclivities, often based on reports from concerned citizens and local officials. Few El Salvadoran or Sonsonatan clerics escaped state surveillance. When Delgado inquired about Doroteo Alvarenga's suitability for a parish in Chalatenango, the government found its file on him: while not a declared dissident, his conduct strongly suggested his opposition to the new bishopric. Tolerating him, the government's note concluded, would prove imprudent, a spur for him to persevere in his wrongheadedness. The vice-jefe therefore declared the parish of Chaletenango vacant and invited Delgado to appoint a trusted minister to the position.[35] In a case that reveals a similarly intrusive albeit informal surveillance network, the head of state reported to Titiguapa's (Titihuapa's) authorities that news of its parish priest's disloyalty had landed on his desk. The priest had three days to leave town and six days to present himself to the government. The local authorities reported back to Delgado that they knew of Sebastián Sanchez's scandals and would send him on to San Salvador.[36] Indeed the chaterati learned the hard way that public spaces were hardly safe. Just after saying the Mass, for instance, Father Eusébio Lanuza repaired to a local store where he allegedly said "scandalous things" about El Salvador's government. The state's vice-jefe ordered the intendent of the unnamed district to interview the three witnesses in the store and whisk Lanuza to prison if their testimony rang true.[37]

This was not a mere face-off between two factions of a bureaucracy, each seeking to occupy or retain plum positions. Towns also demonstrated decided preferences for Delgado's priests over others and refused to recognize the archbishop's appointees. Casaús suspended parish priest Rosal's license so that a priest named Anselmo Llorente could assume his benefice. But the town of Chalchuapa refused to recognize Llorente, announcing on three separate occasions that Rosal would remain in his pulpit and that Llorente had no legitimate claim to the position. Rosal continue to officiate at festivals even after Llorente possessed the keys to the parish. Even ultramontane stalwart Francisco Esteban López warned the archbishop that cracking down on Rosal would unnecessarily agitate townsmen.[38]

Tensions between priests and parishioners in the two camps intensified. One conservative priest left the town of San Miguel Petapa in 1825 rather than continue to serve alongside Delgado appointee Manuel Bolaños, who he alleged had spread rumors that he was the culprit in a series of local robberies.[39] Nearby Santa Inés banned Bolaños from their town entirely; he stirred up rivalries, and he neglected his duties. Had he been present during a recent epidemic, *munici-pio* officals asserted, the sick would have passed without last rites because of his fecklessness.[40]

Adding to the growing tensions was a steady stream of liberal clerics that poured into El Salvador from other states, seeking parish appointments in support of the schism. At the same time, dedicated conservative ministers exiled to Guatemala returned to their El Salvadoran parishes to defend their flocks from the inter-lopers. When Father Tiburcio Hernández arrived from Costa Rica, he requested 400 pesos to defray the cost of his journey to Yayanique; other priests arrived from unspecified Central American countries and immediately directed themselves to El Salvador's government in their quest for a benefice.[41]For their part conserva-tives took risks to advance the ultramontane cause. Knowing that Delgado would replace him with a reform-minded interloper, Martín Torres boasted that he had returned with renewed commitment to his Tecapa parish and his parishioners now enjoyed the attentions of a "legitimate pastor."[42]

THE RETURN OF THE REPRESSED

During the Civil War of 1826–1829, Guatemalan troops faced off against the liberal army of El Salvador and Honduras, united under the designation the Allied Army Protector of the Law. Conservative military victories in this period allowed Casaús to return some of his loyal priests to their El Salvadoran parishes in the liberated territories in El Salvador. In the late summer of 1827, Teresa de Aycinena's brother, Governor of Guatemala Mariano de Aycinena y Piñol, headed up the Guatemalan army, which occupied the El Salvadoran departments of Santa Ana and Sonsonate. With schism supporters at bay, the archbishop nudged cleric Geronimo Zelaya to-ward Sonsonate parish in 1827, bidding him repeat the marriages performed by the previous priest, a Delgado appointee whom Casaús had earlier suspended and who had fled to San Salvador as the Guatemalan troops rushed in. Noting that the occupation guaranteed that legitimate priests could return to the area, Casaús or-dered another loyalist priest back to Apaneca.[43] José Francisco Aqueche celebrated the Guatemalan troops' presence in Santa Ana and Sonsonate and pleaded with the archbishop for a parish appointment in that secure territory. In yet another example of the consistency that partisans on both sides of the Catholic divide demonstrated over many years, in 1837 Aqueche reportedly suggested to his pa-rishioners that the liberal Gálvez government had thrown a sack of venom into a nearby stream, thereby encouraging evil spirits to inhabit the waters. His outraged parishioners leapt to fight the liberal government.[44]

The federal government and Casaús not only sent priests into El Salvador under Guatemalan army protection, they jerked particularly renowned Delgado partisans from their pulpits. El Salvadoran Isidro Menéndez lost his influential pulpit in populated Ahuachapán and was sent back to the tiny backwater of Caluco.[45]

Rarely passive bystanders in the El Salvadoran schism, parishioners pressed for the return of their beloved priests. Cleric Mariano Solís wended his way to Coatepeque from his exile in Guatemala at the behest of his flock and the archbishop. The Guatemalan army had put a stop to the "persecutions that priests endured," he enthused, and the clergy exiled by Delgado returned triumphant to succor flocks left "orphaned and without spiritual sustenance." He stayed until the Allied Army Protector of the Law ran him out. Even then, he pledged to rally obedience to the legitimate prelate, Casaús.[46] With the blessing of region's vicar, in 1828 ultramontane pamphleteer and parish priest Pablo de Sagastume's Isalco parishioners traveled to the town of Sauce to implore him to return to his former pulpit. Once there, he reported to Casaús that he would not be moved, despite the considerable danger all around him.[47]

Casaús' loyal ultramontane priests were determined to save the El Salvadoran souls endangered by the false sacraments that Delgado's appointees had trafficked in, particularly false marriage sacraments. Education was a key strategy: conservatives circulated an anonymous squib written in a straightforward question and short-answer format and in simple prose. The accessible piece did not mince words: only the pope could create bishops and bishoprics or concede permission to a government to do so. Marriages and confessions performed by interloper priests were invalid, and all other sacraments received from those appointed by false hierarchs should be done over immediately by legitimate ministers. Furthermore, parishioners should not turn over the tithe or other funds to imposters, as the Council of Trent prescribed excommunication for those who usurped resources rightly belonging to the church.[48] In this case the marriage cause was urgent, as an unexplained absence of the baptismal records required for marriage meant the church had to improvise creative solutions for these imperiled souls who desired to wed. Thus when Casaús received a request for such documentation in May of 1828, he dispatched a messenger with marriage dispensations almost immediately.[49] It was only one in a flood of such sacramental emergencies.

Evidence suggests that a substantial number of El Salvadorans were terrified that Delgado's clerical thralls proffered worthless sacraments, imperiling their post-mortem fate, as the parishioners who travelled to beseech their former priests to return demonstrated. The poor from far-flung towns flocked to Buenaventura

Guerrero seeking marriage and other sacraments after he was appointed as ñchaplain of the Guatemalan army in El Salvador. Guerrero vociferously pledged his loyalty to ñsaús, and El Salvador's government "monitored him closely."[50]

In 1824, when Father Miguel Muñoz fled El Salvadoran troops into Guatemala with Saldaña, he found a friend in Archbishop Casaús, who placed him in the church home of the Crucified Lord of Esquipulas, the swarthy Christ figure that annually attracted tens of thousands of pilgrims.[51] This popular pilgrimage site was a plum posting, its church one of the most resource-rich institutions in the region. There the priest exuded confidence that victory over the upstart Delgado was nigh: God had blessed his people, Muñoz reported, and removed Satan's noose from their necks; the church would, indeed, prevail against impiety. Deeply sympathetic to the "afflictions they suffer," he had done some advance publicity for Holy Week with El Salvadorans, enticing them to travel to the Guatemalan town's magnificent colonial church for the festivities by promising them he would remediate marriage sacraments performed by imposter priests.[52] In a world of barely inchoate national sentiment but strong municipal and religious attachments, a world where national armies of no more than a couple of thousand men each engaged each other in the civil war, the ultramontane conservative forces proffered a timeworn, powerful path to the Almighty to cement allegiance to their cause: legitimate sacraments from Mother Church, immortal life, access to a warehouse of grace built up by Christ and centuries of martyrs and saints. Esquipulas was part of a religious geography of pilgrimage, one that in this case defied national borders.

The town served as a geographical hotbed of ultramontane organizing. There the erudite and activist Muñoz sheltered fellow travelers during his six-year stint in the popular pilgrimage spot and forged bonds with the popular classes who frequented the site. In 1827, he harbored Father Mariano Castejón, whom Honduran President José Dionisio de Herrera and his Secretary General Francisco Morazán had persecuted for his refusal to support edicts hostile to church authority. Castejón was no stranger to theo-political intrigue, having served in 1826 as one of eight deputies in the national assembly and as the Honduran assembly's provisional president.[53] Muñoz reminded Archbishop Casaús that Castejón had been a favorite son of Nicaragua's and Costa Rica's ultramontane Bishop García Jerez. Anxious to fully incorporate this useful ally into his circle of ultramontane stalwarts in Esquipulas, Muñoz asked the archbishop to "amplify" Castejón's licenses to preach, confess, and celebrate the Mass.[54]

The events in Honduras that sent Castejón into exile provide further evidence that religious tensions roiled not just San Salvador but the entire region, and spilled into municipal and national loyalties. Castejón's pointed opposition to

FIGURE 5.1. The Basilica of Esquipulas, photographed in 1884 by an unknown artist. The wealthy and prominent church eighty miles east of Guatemala City, near the border with El Salvador and Honduras, drew tens of thousands of predominantly indigenous pilgrims annually to visit the image of Christ known as El Señor Crucificado de Esquipulas (The Crucified Lord of Esquipulas). Conservative clerical holdouts under liberal rule successfully used the pilgrimage site as a base of support. Reproduced from William T. Brigham, *Guatemala, the Land of the Quetzal* (New York, NY: Charles Scribner's Sons, 1887).

the liberal Honduran president is understandable. Herrera's measures against the church were nothing if not inflammatory. Factions erupted: the liberals accused church head Nicolás de Irías y Midence of masterminding an attempt on Herrera's life. Irías' brother, Pablo, served alongside Castéjon in Honduras' 1826 assembly, and he too came under suspicion for the dramatic assassination attempt against President Herrera. Overnight on November 2, 1826, bullets shattered the president's bedroom window, narrowly missing the couple and their infant son but killing a guard. After the assassination attempt, rumors swirled, and actions escalated: Irías built wooden cannons and hid them in his house; he branded Herrera a freemason; he plotted a midnight assignation of rebels at a shoemaker's shop in hopes of seizing government arms and deposing the liberals; he rallied fellow clerics to his cause; he excommunicated Herrera.[55]

REFORM ZEALOTS

Ultramontane pundits accused Delgado of replacing conservative priests with inveterate voluptuaries, political refugees, his own addled relatives, and callow opportunists who overlooked his shenanigans to advance their careers. In truth, most of his appointees were true believers not opportunists. The ideological consistency among Delgado's appointees was apparent to his more astute theological foes, including the imprisoned priest Ignacio Perdomo. From San Salvador's jail, Perdomo wrote to Archbishop Casaús about the fate of his former parish of Ahuachapán. Perdomo himself, he reported, had been replaced by Father Juan de Dios Campos Diez, who, Perdomo warned his archbishop, only *appeared* to be a true "son of the Church," but was actually part of Delgado's zealous cadre of some thirty reformed clerics, a significant number in a country with fifty-five parishes, although not all were parish priests. This duplicitous Campos had read his new parishioners Delgado's edict requiring their recognition of his bishopric, Perdomo reported, and they had shamelessly accepted the imposter. Perdomo suspected that the effectiveness of such efforts owed much to the significant influence of prolific theologian José Simeón Cañas. Specifically, Cañas stressed the patriotism of schism supporters—a ploy that Father Perdomo felt gave people with "limited talents" an identity.[56]

Campos' talents and determination, of course, were anything but limited. Like Perdomo, he had survived the crucible of incarceration, albeit alone in monastery cells.[57] During his 1813 travels Campos had met with the Kingdom's most infamous rebels, and was thus no stranger to El Salvador's Reform Catholic militants in the 1820s. When Delgado nominated Campos to replace the imprisoned Perdomo in Ahuachapán, he chose a man like himself, a man with an impressive record of resistance to theological and political conservatives like Archbishop Casaús. He was an impassioned stalwart in the reformist camp, neither opportunistically currying patronage nor enthralled by Delgado's personal charisma.

By December of 1827, Campos' proven piety and politics made him the liberal army's perfect spiritual guide; he served as an army chaplain. But even from this lofty position, he continued to offer his services selflessly wherever needed. Military brass asked Campos to assume Isidro Menéndez's Aguachapán pulpit during a brief moment when the Reform Catholic intellectual's loyalties were in doubt. Federal President Arce, a heroic son of El Salvador, was also the nephew of Delgado and a friend of Menéndez.[58] Like many El Salvadoran statesmen, Menéndez had enjoyed Arce's friendship before the Independence hero promised to thwart Delgado's bid for a bishopric in exchange for conservative's support of his successful 1826 presidential campaign.

But the El Salvadoran leadership was quickly disabused of its suspicions of Menéndez. It eagerly sought both this towering intellectual and the tried and true Campos to man the parish barricades of the "Just Cause." Menéndez's erudite support for the schism was a matter of public record, and he may have secreted information on conservative "projects and resources" to Delgado, as federal army officials accused.[59] What is clear is that the liberal town of Aguachapán that had forcibly ousted Perdomo clamored for Menéndez's return. He continued in the parish.

In an 1828 letter addressed affectionately to "Tata P. Campos" and signed "one who loves you," the influential Juan de Dios Mayorga offered to help Campos find a pulpit in any parish he pleased.[60] Like Campos, Mayorga had earlier run afoul of Captain General Bustamante and been imprisoned for his leadership of uprisings. The letters between these two veteran rebel priests, Campos and Mayorga, fell into conservative hands, and they circulated them as evidence of the "base sentiments" spurring liberals to beguile their countrymen into "the abyss of political and religious evils" that currently beset them.[61] In late March of 1827, the very month El Salvadoran troops first crossed into Guatemala, a grateful government wrote to Campos Diez, noting his service to the "Just Cause" and thanking him for promising a 1,000 peso donation to the public treasury for the war effort.[62] With Campos offering spiritual succor to El Salvadoran soldiers or spreading the good word in the pulpit, conservatives saw their worst fears realized: in 1825, an anonymous pamphleteer had declared that "the blood of the Saviour is trampled and profaned by El Salvadoran and suspended Nicaraguan priests who have appeared in our parishes."[63]

SECOND THOUGHTS: RECANTATIONS AND RETRACTIONS

The Catholic Church was a formidable foe, and, as its displeasure with Delgado became hard to ignore, a handful of the upstart's early supporters retracted their allegiance. Pablo Sagastume had served with schism stalwart Miguel Castro, the editor of San Salvador's reform mouthpiece *El Semanario Politico y Mercantil*, on the ecclesiastical affairs council that recommended Delgado as the new bishop to El Salvador's congress in 1824. Sagastume had even sung the Mass at Delgado's subsequent swearing-in ceremony. Shortly thereafter, the San Salvadoran priest publicly recanted and named Cañas as the solo author of the El Salvadoran congressional committee's favorable report on the bishopric of Delgado. The dearth of "wise and judicious" men on this committee had enhanced Cañas' charisma, by contrast, Sagastume explained. The El Salvadoran congress had unanimously passed the measure appointing Delgado, which Sagastume attributed to Cañas' towering reputation. The contrite cleric depicted a harried group of legislators who blindly trusted Cañas, the former University of San Carlos rector. In contrast, he had been disabused of his errors through reading alternative interpretations of the controversial investiture. He assured readers he had abandoned his parish and worldly goods to distance himself from Delgado and repair his conscience and public honor. Furthermore, he emphasized that he avoided the nocturnal carousing that so undermined public morality in San Salvador, and eschewed all official state functions and even routine correspondence with his potentially compromised compatriots.[64]

The wise counsel of Ultramontane International intellectuals also loomed large in San Salvador cleric José Ignacio Saldaña's public retraction. Initially convinced that Archbishop Casaús, Guatemala's cathedral chapter, and perhaps even the pope would support Delgado's pretensions, Saldaña had signed an 1821 congressional call for what basically amounted to a public referendum on the investiture issue. He did an about-face, he claimed, after reading Herrarte's 1824 response to Cañas' pamphlet *Advertencia patriótica*, in which Herrarte had denounced Cañas' assertion that Pius VI's letters condemning the Constitutional Clergy were apocryphal.[65] The *Gaceta Diaria de México* printed Saldaña's apologetic retraction, which cast the Delgado brothers as intriguers who employed their connections to rally support for their sibling. The public should disregard his own and the other clerical signatures that these schemers had procured, Saldaña intoned, and instead read the many tracts denouncing false authorities like the Colombia pamphleteer Azuero.[66]

Not all retractions were so dramatic. Father Eusébio María Menéndez repented for succumbing to Delgado's authority in less public form, by quietly appealing to Casaús for forgiveness in 1827. Earlier, Fray Juan de Dios Campos Diez had effused to Delgado about a meeting with Menéndez where the priest professed his obedience to the new bishop, provoking an exuberant Campos Diez to envelop Menéndez in "the arms of love."[67]

This Father Menéndez was already known to the archbishop: Ignacio Perdomo had earlier warned the hierarch of his rebellious spirit.[68] He was sentenced to perform penance in the Colegio de Cristo Crucificado in Guatemala City.[69] In response, a clutch of city councilmen from Aguachapán, where Menéndez briefly served after Perdomo's dramatic ouster, came to his defense, attesting that the dedicated clergyman neither provoked controversy nor fanned factionalism. To bolster their credibility with Casaús, the town reminded the archbishop they had decided to exile Perdomo without any encouragement from El Salvador's government. Whatever his prior loyalties, Menéndez proved a penance virtuoso. His extreme enthusiasm for midnight services, the Colegio's prior boasted, left him sleep-deprived, imperiling his physical health but of course augmenting his spiritual health; moreover, he energetically confessed his sins.[70] Retractions, of course, are typical casualties in a battle for hearts and minds, and not surprisingly ultramontane pamphleteers used the official church's vast resources to produce lengthy pamphlets designed to bring clerical and other renegades to heel.

Delgado certainly lost some early supporters as ultramontane writers brought the dramatic implications of this theo-political battle into sharp focus. At stake were salvation and proper government, and each side portrayed the other as a menace to both. But Delgado did not rely on persuasion alone, driving many of his clerical detractors into exile in Guatemala and filling the resulting vacancies with reformist Catholic pastors. One anonymous conservative pamphleteer provided a "catalogue of priests" who had fled or been expelled from El Salvador by 1825, totaling thirty-seven clerics. Ironically, he reported, liberals painted these exiled ecclesiastics as schismatics, "imputing their crimes to us when they are the real authors of the schism. They call us immigrant cowards when it is their mandarins that expel us, threatening us with prison or death to seize our benefices and destroy our authority." A Cañas or a Miguel José Castro or the "fanatical cabal of twelve clerics" proclaim themselves the "oracles of the new Salvadoran Vatican," the author marveled. Pray for your spiritual enemies, reclaim your real pastors, "open your eyes and see the wolves," he thundered, "for they have taken off their sheeps' clothing."[71]

While well aware of Catholic intellectual currents swirling around the Atlantic, both sides, however, demonized local malefactors to distill their theo-political differences for popular consumption and practical political victories. Liberals, of course, pilloried Casaús as the author of the clerical exodus from El Salvador.[72] He vehemently denied the charge, insisting that he called his loyalists to steadfastness, not retreat—or at least steadfastness until the violence became unsupportable, a state that, sadly, he believed had come to pass by early 1826.[73] Men devoid of "morality, religion, and proper authority" occupied these important clerical positions, the Archbishop lamented.[74]

THE ULTRAMONTANE CHURCH SUPPORTS THE CONSERVATIVE WAR EFFORT

The church threw its influence behind the conservatives' war effort. Guatemala's vicar general in 1827 praised a war so "gloriously begun." He amplified the archbishop's order to parish priests: exhort your flocks to enlist in the militia troops that the state was mustering from each province; lead public prayers and ceremonies to entreat God's favor for the Guatemalan army.[75] These calls circulated on the *cordillera*, the church's rapid written-communication network that reached every secular parish in Guatemala as well as parishes and houses controlled by the regular orders, many of which were in the highlands of western Guatemala. Their urgings did not fall on deaf ears: In April of 1827, the parish priest of San Juan Sacatepéquez responded to an order to raise at least 300 troops for the cause: even better, he had "armed every single person capable of bearing arms."[76] In 1828, the parish priest of Cobán, Friar Miguel Moscoso, preached in both Spanish and a "language the Indians understand" their duty to give their persons and resources to the war effort. Father Moscoso dutifully read government edicts from the pulpit; he preached on the El Salvadorans' ravages on both women and churches; he warned that failure to aid the government spelled ruin. As the El Salvadorans approached the town, he led rogations through the streets with the images of the parish saints and ordered a three-day jubilee, penitent processions, and attendance at pastoral talks. He then convened confraternity members to urge them to engage in more street demonstrations with the images of those saints images that they—not he—controlled.[77] If Cobán fell to the invaders, it would not be for lack of celestial allies.

The martial spirit sometimes exceeded such pious public displays: In Guatemala City, the United States' ambassador reported, "priests ran through the streets exhorting people to take up arms" as the El Salvadorans closed in, while friars led crowds of knife-wielding women who "swore destruction to all who attempted to overturn their religion." The women wielded the knives as spears, fastening them to sticks. With the El Salvadorans put to flight on the morning of March 23, 1827, the capital's residents celebrated the victory in the streets with fireworks. The church threw its full weight behind sanctifying the victors: Archbishop Casaús himself orchestrated the elaborate burials of soldiers, the regular orders attended the funeral ceremonies en masse, and the city's nuns wove garlands of flowers for the "martyrs."[78]

While knife-wielding women backed the conservatives in Guatemala, the archbishop reached heights of rhetorical drama in his sermons urging the faithful to martial heroism, as a foreign visitor noted: his flock must fight to remain "in the divine bark of the fisherman, lest we make shipwreck of the faith and become the plaything of the waves, or the unhappy victim of piratical mariners." He warned of "malicious men, who would cast America out of this ship, and leave her to be tossed in the tempestuous sea of every heresy," and bade his audience to hail Mary and implore her intercession.[79] From the cathedral pulpit, Casaús declared Delgado's supporters "a sterile branch cut from the tree of life and destined to eternal fire" and informed listeners that the pope had given Delgado fifty days to step-down or face excommunication. The archbishop declared September of 1827 a month of freely given absolution—after that he would apply the "pastoral rod" to all schismatics.[80]

Of course no one could hope to compete with the ultramontane church's ability to lionize heroes, causes, and martyrs through elaborate public ritual. If the official church went toe-to-toe with liberals in the pamphlet war, it had a decided advantage in the ceremonial sanctification of its people and policies. Many of Guatemala City's formal religious and civic organizations turned out in force to speed to glory the immortal soul of Manuel Antonio Molina, the exiled priest of San Vicente who had "refused to kiss the new bishop's ring."[81] As Delgado's rival for the bishopric, Molina had incurred considerable wrath from the liberals, and his hacienda was among those burned to the ground.[82] In posthumous tribute to his heroism, the capital's religious, political, and military leaders accompanied Molina's body through the streets to the cathedral, where Casaús himself presided over his "sumptuous" funeral. The conservative and moderate press sang his praises, noting his service in the Guatemalan legislative assembly and reminding readers that some adoring parishioners had nominated him to occupy a "real bishopric," earning him the areas' ultimate conservative imprimatur: Delgado's enmity. That the El Salvadoran liberals, that "miserable anarchist faction," celebrated his passing was his most fitting eulogy.[83] Reformers inveighed against street spectacles as dangerous distractions from the simple ethical piety they advocated and the this-worldly asceticism that sprang from efficacious grace, leaving the church to claim the power of ceremony to sanctify its martyrs.

The church also willingly succumbed to state orders to raid its deep coffers and sell its treasures for the cause. It also supported the war effort unbidden. Casaús instructed the religious orders to "donate" their silver objects for sale to cover war expenses. Guatemala's state government lauded these efforts and thanked the archbishop for the generous donations received to fight the El Salvadorans.[84] In response to the government's call for a "patriotic loan" from Guatemalan parishes, priests pitched in amounts ranging from 25 to 300 pesos each, depending on the size and wealth of their parishes.[85] Two priests from the pilgrimage town of Esquipulas sent 2,000 pesos to the archbishop for him to distribute to conservative El Salvadoran priests in exile, resolute defenders of the faith, and the rest of the clergy—in that order.[86] As the region veered toward war, it became clear that the Catholic Church would tap its resources to fund its ministers and support the increasingly cohesive ultramontane faction.

In an example of the sort of ironies that emerge in wartime, however, the church may have inadvertently funded both armies. Neither Delgado nor the Protective Allied Army of the Law had a legitimate claim on Rome's bounty and they could not, like Archbishop Casaús, legitimately transform sacred chalices into mules and materiél. But the liberal army certainly could pilfer holy objects from churches in towns it controlled, and Delgado's hands could reach into church funds through the mediation of his own appointed parish priests. Evidence in the form of elliptical instructions to his appointees suggests that Delgado and El Salvador's reform-minded government drew from parish coffers for their projects: Delgado casually noted to a provisional parish appointee in Cojutepeque that he should focus on the sacraments, but also "keep close track of incoming funds and turn over a third of them to the government."[87]

The question of using sacred treasures to pay for the war was clearly a vexed one for the liberals, who could not claim papal sanction. One unusual case suggests just how volatile the issue might have been: although chaplains ministering to soldiers were not normally subject to military courts, head of the liberal army General Francisco Morazán himself pursued charges against a Franciscan friar in an extraordinary military tribunal. The friar, he charged, was warning the liberal army soldiers that they were courting damnation by accepting salaries funded through the appropriation of sacred church objects. The normally self-assured Morazán engaged in uncharacteristic hand-wringing, fretting that religious conservatives in contact with his own army might provoke a mass exodus from the ranks with these stories of stolen treasures. He proposed relocating dangerous clerics to a single location to better surveil and silence them. The Franciscan was guilty of sedition, General Morazán insisted, and thereby forfeited the protection of his ecclesiastical *fuero*.[88]

While the liberals were forced to negotiate such pitfalls, the official Catholic Church put the whole panoply of its powers into play in support of the conservative Guatemalan army, with the archbishop and the Holy Father himself leading the charge. Casaús forwarded on to his suffragan a government directive to engage in public prayers for the success of the Guatemalan army. But he went much further, ordering *causa belli* Masses and litanies said in every parish in the state.[89] The pope, of course, held the best hand, and he played it to devastating effect: in 1827, the president of the federation issued Pope Leo XII's generous jubilee year (1825) remission of sins to everyone in Central America, except those who recognized Delgado as Bishop of El Salvador, a measure that sent El Salvadoran reformers scrambling to prevent the news from crossing the border and reaching the country's faithful.[90] On December 1, 1826, the Holy Father roundly declared that Delgado had appropriated Rome's right to create bishoprics and name bishops, and had summarily exiled clerics who rejected his illegitimate authority from the territory. Casaús circulated this papal declaration on September 14, 1827, including the pièce de résistance: that Delgado had fifty days to renounce all pretensions to the bishopric or face excommunication.[91] But this was not a battle the increasingly besieged Holy Father was destined to win, at least not in the short term. Passions would escalate and find outlets in an explosion of written propaganda. It is to that story that we now turn.

6

The Literary Barricades

SO FAR, WE have established that the church lent its powers of suasion and its considerable resources to the conservatives' war effort. While Casaús' coterie certainly lost key El Salvadoran parish pulpits during the tumultuous 1820s, reducing their influence over the faithful, they simultaneously redeployed their resources into churning out numerous and often-lengthy treatises. They faced a talented and highly motivated contingent of reform-minded pamphleteers and newspaper men. The Central American Republic of Letters was born in a religious crucible. Not putatively universal secular reason but knowledge of church history, biblical exegesis, and other religious justifications entitled literate men to participate in public debate. One such religious justification was reason, but this reason sprang from God's gift to the soul not nature.[1]

The pamphlet deluge continued into 1825. Few works went unchallenged, creating a constant vitriolic dialogue; as a prescient reformer noted in 1825, "the actual war is one of papers, but it threatens to end with bayonets."[2] The polarization of opinion intensified and left little room for equivocation or gentle persuasion; empathy for opponents waned decidedly, and hyperbole and calls for violent action became commonplace. An anonymous pamphlet charged that in 1811 Casaús and his clerical minions had abused the pulpit to suffocate "the seed of our glorious Independence." El Salvadorans had forgiven them. In 1821, the critic continued, Casaús' team had preached loyalty to "the Tyrant of Anahuac"—that

For God and Liberty. Pamela Voekel, Oxford University Press. © Oxford University Press 2023.
DOI: 10.1093/oso/9780197610190.003.0007

is, General Agustín de Iturbide, then in the process of transforming himself into the emperor of Mexico—and again the people forgave him. In 1825, Archbishop Casaús demonized regional elites who advocated for federalism—strong state governments rather than federal power centralized in Guatemala. And he allied with the ultramontane intellectuals who churned out inflammatory pamphlets. To forgive the archbishop again, the anonymous author declared, would be criminal.[3]

Ultramontane intellectuals echoed the anonymous reformer's call to rain vengeance upon their enemies rather than forgive them their trespasses. In turn, they mockingly imitated the structure of the anonymous squib, sharing their own inspiring tales of vengeance from the annals of history. When Mani challenged the church in the third century, they offered, Persian troops dismembered him alive and threw his body to wild beasts. In the fourth century, seventy bishops summarily drummed the upstart schismatic Donatus from the church. These were examples of appropriate responses to the church's enemies. By contrast, when Delgado riled the faithful under the pretext of Independence, Spain forgave him; when he resisted Mexican rule in 1822, the Mexicans oozed compassion; when he declared himself bishop in 1824, the church offered gentle paternal counsel. The upstart bishop had responded to these olive branches with redoubled fervor, the conservative pamphlet explained, exiling dissident clerics, ignoring church laws, and seizing the *patronato*. El Salvadorans had a duty to smite this "Manes (Mani), the author of your misfortunes."[4]

In this way accusations flew back and forth, becoming increasingly hyperbolic, both before and during the civil war. One conservative cleric noted that Delgado divvied up vacant parishes among his loyalists in August of 1826 and that he threatened clerics who refused to travel to San Salvador to receive their benefices directly from him. This pamphleteer fingered Castro and Cañas as the schism's prime agents, along with former Guatemalan Cortes de Cádiz deputy Mateo Ibarra, just back from a failed recruiting trip to Nicaragua without any new clerical adherents. The conservative critic reserved his most damning accusation for Cañas, who, he claimed, had said point blank that "priests are not necessary for the salvation of souls, because if a soul is well with God, then the priest is superfluous, and if the soul is not well with God, then no amount of confession could save it from condemnation." God would surely intervene to stop such rank heresy, but to be safe, he urged Archbishop Casaús to continue the campaign against Delgado.[5] Other ultramontane influencers likewise deployed fiery rhetoric that escalated tensions and polarized public opinion. One pamphleteer wondered if conservatives could remain serene as "we witness our holy religion and its altars brought down while the idols of Luther, Calvin, and Epicure and all their impious monsters are elevated over its ruins?"[6] Inaction in the face of such an enemy would surely bring

God's wrath upon us, he thundered, just as the biblical prophet Ezekiel warned the Israelites that abandoning the battlefield to the impious would lead God to rain justice upon them and strike them from the records of Israel.[7]

For its part, the San Salvadoran reformist Catholic mouthpiece *El Salvadoreño* warned its readers in 1828 that a "group of ambitious clerics" peopled Guatemala's conservative state government. Nonchalant about their ministerial duties, these clerical politicians instead dedicated themselves to releasing "fogs of fanaticism and ignorance," and championing inquisitorial practices. Shifty and conspiratorial, they contorted "the religion of Christ" into a theater of intrigue and fraud and a "shadowy system of despotism." Antonio García Redondo, who had earlier penned an eighty-two-page pro-Vatican history of the church against Delgado's pretensions to the bishopric, earned honors from *El Salvadoreño* as the leader of this sorry assortment of authoritarians.[8] Alongside the increasingly heated rhetoric, the use of force against God's ministers seemed only to increase. The El Salvadoran government openly advocated for shows of force to discourage "public disturbances," in one case ordering that four dissident priests who operated in the San Miguel area without government permission be brought at gun point to San Salvador by local soldiers and in shackles if necessary.[9]

Casaús became a particular target of reformers' wrath. One author called for an end to his pernicious influence in dramatic terms. He proposed two options to deal with the meddling prelate: exile him from Central America, or kill him outright. The federal government, he argued, should enact one of these plans, so that the public would have the satisfaction of seeing the "iniquitous and blood-thirsty" prelate removed from the community. This was too much for the archbishopric's two ecclesiastical lawyers, one of them a scion of "The Family," Juan José de Aycinena, who argued that it was unconstitutional to menace ministers of the faith. He called upon elected representatives to denounce violence against clerics.[10]

In January of 1826, members of Guatemala's congress argued that Casaús' role as the prime destabilizer of Delgado's schism threatened to plunge the region into civil war. Patience had begun to fray within the liberal-leaning Guatemalan state government: the archbishop demanded his El Salvadoran suffragan and the layity reject Delgado's authority; his hand-picked priests incited "popular commotions;" the federal executive power ignored the El Salvadorans' repeated pleas for succor. Congress insisted the archbishop desist.

But if Guatemala's reformist Catholics sought to intimidate the archbishop, they woefully underestimated him. Casaús relished public furors. He had, after all, spewed bombast at Miguel Hidalgo y Costilla, and he was by now a virtuoso, capable of both paternalism and subtle behind-the-scenes maneuvering. The archbishop commanded a range of public tones, from the sorrowful scoldings of a betrayed patriarch to hardline ultimatums. Tactically, he held the upper hand. Through his parish priests, the archbishop knew, his reach was far longer than that of the federal government, which had neither a real army of its own, nor agents in the countryside. Towns and governors, the *jefes políticos*, reported to state rather than federal officials and operated under state legislation.[11] A confident Casaús responded to the Guatemalan government that he answered only to God and church. Prescient liberals surely saw the writing on the wall: the hierarch in charge of the region's most extensive bureaucracy was tightly allied with their "servile" foes, and he flouted the liberals' authority. Equally portentous, Casaús' reformed enemies were quite clear that their cause was righteous, that they fought not to topple the church but rather to save it from Rome. The heirs of centuries of reformers before them, they were a formidable force.

As rhetoric increasingly became a weapon to demonize opponents, the nun with a direct line to the Almighty become a flashpoint for reformers bent on discrediting their ultramontane rivals. Woe to those who underestimated the ecstatic Sor María Teresa de Aycinena, the editors of the reformist El Salvadoran *Semanario Político Mercantil* implicitly cautioned readers. Teresa's father, José Fermín de Aycinena, was of course known to El Salvadorans as head of Guatemala's most economically powerful family. One of Teresa's half-brothers, José Alejandro de Aycinena y Carrillo, ferried evidence against the El Salvador schism to Spain's papal nuncio in Madrid. Teresa's full brother, Mariano de Aycinena y Piñol, presided over the conservative federal government and army during much of the Civil War of 1826–1829.

Teresa herself was the perfect symbol for reform-minded malcontents to invoke. Her body was a conduit for the infusion of the Divine into the mundane world—an act of mediation highly prized by the ultramontane and just as highly suspect to the reformed. She also represented her family's storied history in the region. Reform-minded critics stressed the Aycinena daughter's distinctly gendered political influence: she ruled some men from the shadows and served as the political pawn of others.

A case in point was Archbishop Casaús, whose authority radical El Salvadorans assailed by underscoring his longstanding enthrallment to the influential nun. Casaús had whiled away entire days in Teresa's Carmelite convent, seduced by her apocryphal, scandalous miracles. His attention to Teresa had paid off, his detractors reported: during one of her frequent ecstasies, the nun saw Casaús' name shimmering in gold letters in the Book of God's Chosen (*el libro de la predestinación*). This news had raced like wildfire through her networks, which stretched all the way to Mexico. But her machinations did not end with relaying God's election of Casaús. Nary a conservative *cause célèbre* lacked her imprint, reformist muckrakers asserted. Anselmo Ortiz, her spiritual guide, persuaded her to declare that God willed the unpopular Bustamante to continue as captain general of a Guatemala forever yoked to Spain.[12]

The archbishop's coterie fought back. Ignacio Saldaña had been present along-side Casaús in 1817 when Teresa returned the city council's handkerchiefs inscribed with the image of the Sacred Heart of Jesus rendered in the blood of Christ Himself. He noted that liberal pundits accused the archbishop of tendentious readings of the Holy Book and the Church Fathers in his condemnation of independence-era heroes like Hidalgo, Mina, and Morelos. Worse yet, the archbishop's detractors accused him of promoting Teresa's false miracles to the unsuspecting. Overcome, Saldaña "could say no more" as his hand shook to recall such "scandalous and impious" accusations against his beloved hierarch.[13] Santa María reminded a re-formist interlocutor that he had indeed divulged Teresa's miracles and revelations, and reiterated that her exemplary life made her a "Christian privileged by God," one whose prayers contributed much to the current tranquility. José

Sister Teresa drove her critics to intemperate vitriol. An anonymous liberal ended his pamphlet with a direct attack on the nun and an ominous message to her supporters, men like Santa María who "offended religion and Christian re-publics." In these dark days "the devil had become an angel of light" to delude the "weak of head and heart" into reading deliriums as revelations, artificial wounds and paintings as miracles, and jealously and rage as holy zeal to resist the legit-imate authorities.[14] *Semanario* editors also reminded readers of Teresa's 1817 proc-lamation that God wanted a letter received by Guatemala's *audiencia* from the king to remain sealed.[15] The liberal El Salvadoran newspaper's rehearsal of one of Teresa's major missteps, of course, was part of a larger offensive against ultramon-tane piety. In this case the reformist forces sought to stanch the steady drip of "precious drops of God's mercy" into the mundane world, especially mercy medi-ated by a would-be holy woman promoting the sort of popular cult so despised by reformers—and the Jesuits' signature devotion, no less. Teresa had largely fallen silent in the 1820s, having turned her attention to convent reform, but the Sacred Heart's utramontanist promoters continued to promote the cult's merits: one 1823 pamphlet urged redoubled devotion to the Sacred Heart, including the dedication of the first Friday of each month to the cult.[16]

No hierarch was immune to criticism from reformers girded with Reform Catholicism's radical ecclesiology. Even the popes had been elected by the peo-ple and confirmed by kings in the church's earliest times, and this was no time to consent to the clerical machinations prevalent in the dark centuries, an an-onymous author declared in in the 1824 pamphlet *Aviso oportuno* (*Opportune Notice*). The church had systematically usurped these rights, acquiring property, jockeying with temporal powers, and deploying spiritual authority to overthrow legitimate sovereigns. Theological disputes had bathed their universe in blood, yet pamphlet writers like the ultramontane Father José Andrés Santa María proclaimed that governments had no legitimate control over ecclesiastics, a doctrine that threatened to embroil the country in civil war. Anonymous implored Central Americans to place the church firmly under government authority, especially concerning ecclesiastical appointments, and reminded them that they held the *patronato*, as even monarchical power originated with the people. In reality they had always been its rightful executors, as the *patronato* had passed to the new nations at Independence. Furthermore, as a Spanish friar, Santa María was deeply suspect, motivated by his desire for Ferdinand VII's return and a church free from the whims of El Salvador's independent government. Without firm secular supervision, the anonymous author prophesied, Santa Maria and other friars would march forth with images of Christ in one hand and "carabines in the other" to open fire on those who refused the authority of the Spanish king; the anonymous author counseled that if they were truly Christ-like these clerics would humbly submit to the public authorities and would cease to spew in favor of "false doctrines." More than anything, he feared that if Santa María and his friends had their way, "our government will end up enslaved to the Roman Pontiff by means of his loyal soldiers and satellites."[17]

Santa Maria's criticisms aside, *Aviso oportuno* was no secular attack upon Catholicism but a deeply theological call for church reform. Critics like Castrillo identified Christianity's real core tenets that ecclesiastics like Santa María ignored: poverty, equality, and hatred of riches and the rich. For the anonymous author, the apostles' virtue lay precisely in their refusal to save for tomorrow, their material poverty, and their decided lack of hierarchy. They had imbibed the Savior's message that he came to serve rather than to be served, that the last should be first. Yet the church hierarchs who claimed to be the apostle's successors wanted to be first, to command rather than obey commandments, unaccountable to legitimate governments.[18] Within the church itself, in its glorious early centuries, priests and bishops had been elected, and then approved by kings before exercising their offices. The pamphlet, then, made a strong case not only for El Salvador's right to exercise the *patronato* based on the church's early democratic institutions—not the Spanish monarchy's prior possession of this right—but also for the country's existence as a virtuous Christian republic. Did it not, by rejecting corrupting luxury, prove itself a truly Catholic polity, a nation purified of a distant and hierarchical ecclesiastical structure?

Thus this unnamed champion of reform struggled with ultramontane pamphleteers to define the essence of the church and to shift sacral authority from monarchical to democratic political formations, and from the flamboyantly wealthy like the Aycinena merchant clan to those with less. The ultramontane intellectual Santa María fully understood the stakes of this battle, asking rhetorically whether the people were sheep or shepherds. Sheep, he roundly concluded—and as such unqualified to vote for their shepherds, who were rightly appointed by legitimate pastors. Even the most virtuous laymen ranked below the clergy in the spiritual hierarchy. While historically church councils had consulted with kings about mutual concerns, monarchs could not meddle in council affairs or overturn their rulings. He rightly concluded that his enemies preferred a church reduced to its teaching role, with no real right to pass laws or commanded obedience. As for the exaltation of poverty and hatred for the rich, Santa María noted this merely exhumed the heresy of the proto-Protestant theologian John Wycliffe, who in the fourteenth century denied the church's right to property. The ultramontane cleric put a decidedly Central American spin on his praise of church riches: Anonymous, Santa Maria accused, read the holy scriptures as a paen to poverty because he was akin to "the parrot in your house, making them say what he wants them to say and not what they actually mean."[19] Only the heretical denied that the church was rightly an unequal society of superiors and prelates, inferiors and subjects.[20] Were people sheep in need of shepherds, or were they democratic citizens who chose their rulers, both ecclesiastical and secular? Was the church entitled to temporal wealth to support its ministers and an elaborate cult of worship? Should Catholicism be austere and focused on teaching simple ethical maximums found in the Bible? Santa María and his anonymous interlocutor fell on opposite sides of these key questions.

The numerous Central American clerics and statesmen who churned out pamphlets and editorials in the debate engaged in a modern iteration of a centuries-long theo-political battle, here fought behind the banners of Central America's two political factions, the reform-minded liberal federalists and the ultramontane conservative centralists. To propose their rival visions of the future, each side reached past the secular philosophes of the Enlightenment to draw upon authoritative Christian antecedents and metaphors. In a battle in which both sides passionately advocated for the church but warred over its essential nature, the winning argument could only come from within the sacred canopy. Although the heirs of Bourbon regalists and episcopalists, Central American reformers who connected the patronato to the people's usurped rights would not have been recognizable to their intellectual precursors.

The erudite Santa María was a master of the debate. When a liberal editorialist proposed that only the whole Church Militant, and not the Holy Father, could declare a Christian schismatic, Father Santa María evoked the schismatic church of Utrecht, a thoroughly legible example for both parties: a century earlier, Pope Clement XI—acting alone on his own authority—had declared the Dutch archbishopric of Utrecht dissident for its persistent Jansenist heresy. Referencing this notorious episode, Father Santa María branded his anonymous interlocutor a Jansenist in unmistakable terms.[21] As all the principals in the American dispute were well aware, a group of émigré French priests based in Utrecht had been at the epicenter of international Jansenism in the eighteenth century. These avowed Jansenists had corresponded with fellow travelers across the continent, clerics like Grégoire and Scipione de'Ricci, and Catalonian archbishop Josef Climent, whom the El Salvadoran reform mouthpiece the *Semanario* turned to for wisdom on the tithe. Utrecht's side of the dispute had appeared in its newspaper *Nouvelles ecclésiastiques*, which promoted a radical conciliar ecclesiology: bishops, priests, and even the laity gathered together were, by these heretical lights, worthy counterweights to papal authority. The Utrecht schismatics had likewise promoted the neo-Augustinian theology of selective grace that undergirded their more democratic governance and distrust of unilateral papal authority. All of these recommended reforms could be found, of course, in the church's primitive, apostolic early centuries, as *Nouvelles Ecclésiastiques* frequently reminded the faithful.[22] This heritage—not the secular French Enlightenment—and Spanish Bourbon episcopalism and regalism was the shared frame of reference in Spain's restive former colonies.

GOD IN GOVERNMENT

The novel public sphere of letters provided a critical venue where the two sides of the religious divide sparred; the hallowed halls of government supplied another. In 1828, El Salvador's legislature, for example, discussed the "counterfeit" papal utterances the federal government had ordered Casaús to circulate during the civil war. Clerical "fanatism and ultramontane ideas" imbibed in seminaries and colleges had mired the region in conflict, legislators argued, and Delgado's bishopric scandalized the benighted who embraced the Roman curia's fabrications as the legitimate laws of the church. The El Salvadoran government should not only exile conservative priests but replace them with an educated cadre of clerics imbued with an accurate understanding of church history. By these means, reform-minded El Salvadorans could defuse the growing power of those who worshipped the Vatican and its centuries of usurpations of the people's prerogatives. The El Salvadoran legislature rehearsed these and other shibboleths before launching into their critique of the false papal condemnations of the schism—documents circulated surreptitiously by both the federal government and by Casaús and his supporters. Even if these papal edicts were authentic, legislators insisted, no American government should willingly succumb to the curia's machinations or give up its right to self-government.[23]

One critical theater of conflict was the federal government, which sought to hold together the restive states of Central America's federation during the 1820s. It offered an arena for reformers like Father Isidro Menéndez, who, as a deputy to the ANC, had argued together with its president, José Matias Delgado, the reformist side in the debates over a constitutional project for a united Central America, finalized in October of 1824[24].

On 18 July, 1825, this canon lawyer, Reform Catholic firebrand, senator from Nicaragua, and loyal son of El Salvador rose in the federal congress in Guatemala City. He regaled his fellow deputies with a speech justifying the new nations' right to the *patronato de Indias* formerly held by the Spanish crown, and defended El Salvador's 4 May 1824 decree that named Delgado as head of the new bishopric.[25] The El Salvadoran government later published his lengthy remarks in pamphlet form. Many of his fellow congressmen disagreed with the El Salvadoran statesman representing Nicaragua and formally declared that as representatives of the Central American Federation, they, not El Salvador's own congress, should grapple with the thorny question of the *patronato* and Delgado's bid for the bishopric, and that the Roman pontiff had the last word on presentations to benefices and the creation of diocesen boundaries.[26] Menéndez disagreed. His speech exemplified the hopelessly intertwined relationship between Reform Catholic ecclesiology, with its insistence on decentering the papacy through conciliar authority structures, and liberal federalist arguments against concentrating too much power in a central government. His speech and subsequent pamphlet were a *tour-de-force* of reform Catholic erudition, bristling with citations of works deeply troubling to Rome.

Menéndez found particular inspiration in an 1823 Spanish Cortes' report on the proper balance between state and church authority.[27] His enthusiasm for the document was hardly surprising: the report's author, a Cortes ecclesiastical commission, opened with a rousing cry to rid Spanish territory of "the vestiges of despotism, vestiges still covered with the sacred veil of religion."[28] The commission juxtaposed its own liberatory knowledge of the church's early discipline, the Church Fathers, and the Bible, to the usurpations of the Roman clergy, those "constant enemies of the light," who had seized power during a previous "time of darkness." The nation and the nation alone held the right to draw ecclesiastical boundaries and expel prelates who disrespected state authority. Certainly the church should control all things spiritual, the commission proposed, but territorial demarcations had nothing to do with basic dogma. Territorial demarcations were a classic example of the church's external discipline that should rightly be under state auspices. Furthermore, the only ecclesiastical hierarchy the nation should recognize was that of its own national church; after all, all of the apostles, not just Peter, received their divine mission from Jesus Christ.[29]

CONNECTING WITH THE INTERNATIONAL

Menéndez's citation practices revealed his identification with the Reform Catholic International, specifically reform luminary Juan Antonio Llorente. Llorente too had praised the Cortes commission's knowledge of ecclesiastical history and their noble efforts to regenerate Spain's clergy and restore the canonical discipline of the early centuries. The commission's targeted pruning of the ecclesiastical calendar in particular provoked Llorente's approval, for intriguing reasons: in the church's early centuries people rested only on Sundays, and even then they only rested during the hours dedicated to the cult. But the proliferation of festival days was an incitement to inertia, Llorente declared, invoking Protestant political economist Jean-Baptiste Say, whose treatises had valorized productive work as the key to the wealth of nations and derided the "time lost in adoration" by "superstitious nations" in their idolatry of "saints and madonnas."[30] Llorente further insisted that civil society preceded ecclesiastic society—good news indeed, as nations could therefore rightly recuperate their old rights over the church, as he had previously argued at length. The primary sources included in Llorente's 1810 *Disertación's* appendix, Menéndez noted, indicated that the early *usos y costumbres* (customs and traditions) of Spain's church pivoted around unfettered regal control over diocesan boundaries and clerical appointments. It was this royal authority over the church that El Salvador had inherited from the Crown after independence.[31]

Thus while the reform Catholicism of Menéndez certainly was wielded in the federal congress in defense of El Salvadoran interests against economic powers centered in Guatemala City and ecclesial authority based in Rome, it was anything but provincial. Rather, Central American reformist Catholics moved in a wider Atlantic intellectual sphere—a sphere whose enthusiasts evoked the Cortes' reform-minded ecclesiastical councils and Llorente's wisdom as the relevant precedents, and rallied to each other's defense as they conducted the business of state.

Menéndez's fellow El Salvadoran deputy in the federal government, Ciriaco Villacorta, matched his countryman's passion—and demonstrated a similar command of transnational Reform Catholic tenets and luminaries. His opening salvo took aim at a vast ultramontane conspiracy: those who opposed El Salvador's new bishopric sought to "submit the nation to a despotism covered with the sacred veil of religion—a despotism that would subject us to the Spanish yoke, or to the whims of the Holy Alliance, who would seize every opportunity to destroy our political system."[32] Somewhat hyperbolically, Villacorta proposed that even the most obstinate ultramontanist wavered more than his intransigent federal opponents on the national governments' right to erect a bishopric. All who read the pamphlets that now "fly from hand to hand" knew that the church's early history contravened arguments for papal control of the *patronato*. Although Villacorta argued that "monstrous fanaticism" animated the Central American federal commission's "hyper-ultramontanism," he knew the more skillful pens of his reform-minded comrades would prevail. Like his fellow El Salvadoran Menéndez, he also enthusiastically cited the 1823 Cortes' report on the Spanish clergy, quoting its assertion that in the "time of ignorance" Rome controlled all ecclesiastical appointments, dispensations, and indulgences based on "fabricated decrees" composed by counterfeiters who aggressively advanced the clergy's mutual interests, not God's will. Happily, in this current age, people understood God's word and readily discerned false documents and doctrines. El Salvador was well within its rights to appoint Delgado.[33]

While reformers like Menéndez and Villacorta harkened back to the texts produced by reform-minded Cádiz deputies, conservative Central Americans cited the publications of Cortes conservatives. Although in the minority, conservatives, or "*serviles*" as the liberals dubbed them, were present in both sessions of the Cádiz Cortes. Central Americans were part of the highly self-conscious transnational networks of reformist and ultramontanists that the Cádiz congresses had nurtured and strengthened by bringing together delegates from throughout the empire. A conservative Central American pamphleteer who wrote under the pen name the Friend of the Truth (*Amigo de la Verdad*) signaled his piety and politics to the cognoscenti by lauding the truths of "rancid philosophers," referring to the Filósofo Rancio, Francisco Alvarado, the scourge of Cortes liberals. Alvarado's numerous writings defended papal prerogatives, scholasticism, and the Inquisition and tarred even moderate reformers with the brush of Jansenism. In one of his numerous scraps with reformers, Alvarado took on Cortes delegate Agustín de Argüelles, who argued that the Cortes had the right to encumber the tithe for its own purposes. The rancid philosopher found this proposition preposterous, but he replied succinctly: in coveting the tithe for the Cortes, Argüelles did not compromise his standing as a Catholic—he terminated it.[34] That the Friend of Truth larded his tract with ultramontane wisdom from the likes of the rancid philosopher demonstrates that Central American conservatives, like their liberal opponents, drew from a transatlantic corpus of works to add historical and intellectual depth to their deepening divide at the local level. The importance of church currents to this decidedly political identity formation could not be clearer.

If Central America's literati claimed membership in these transnational ultramontanist or reformist networks, these networks happily claimed their El Salvadoran brothers in the struggle: the periodical *El Nivel* of Guadalajara, Mexico ran Ciriaco Villacorta's lengthy defense of the schism over multiple issues. The militant Reformed Catholic paper consistently inveighed against the ultramontane perversions of the church so often cited by reformers: vowed celibacy and monasticism, proliferating saints' cults, enervating luxury, fanaticism, popular superstitions, and, above all, the historical usurpations of an overweening papacy. *El Nivel* also contributed to the anti-Jesuitical critique produced by the Reform Catholic International.[35] The titular saints' festivals so important to local identities and indigenous culture came in for particular criticism. Revelers processed with up to fifteen or twenty different images of Christ, and cargo cults funded festivities with names like "the Dance of Our Lord" or the "Comedy of San Francisco" or "Refreshments by Santiago." Although completely peripheral to these popular celebrations, priests did receive money for Masses and for sermons during these riotous occasions. They therefore stayed mum about the excesses of festivals whose costs would easily feed and clothe many families for a year.[36]

While the two El Salvadoran reformers struck a chord with fellow travelers in Mexico, their speeches in the federal congress also incited spirited attacks from their ultramontane enemies closer to home. An anonymous pamphleteer penned a vituperative hundred-page pamphlet against the schism and rebuked the Cortes' controversial 1823 document. A "jansenistic spirit" animated the august assembly's ecclesiastical commission, and the Cortes was nothing less than a gathering of Jansenists intent on creating a church schism.[37]

Father José Antonio de Santa Maria published a garrulous response to Menéndez. Mier, Llorente, and the Cortes held during the Liberal Triennium (1820–1823)— Senator Menéndez's pantheon of reform militants were not learned exemplars of the church's valuable traditions, but rather hucksters of a dangerous secularism that threatened the church's prerogatives and the laity's salvation. The waywardness of reformers like Menéndez and Villacorta was almost too much to contemplate, but he could not do otherwise since the two El Salvadorans' attack on papal primacy in particular rendered them outside the church's fold rather than loyal if idiosyncratic internal critics. Rome should not abide them. The Apostolic Canon dictated excommunication for clerics who claimed their positions came from the people, and the faithful should disavow bishops and abbeys who cited the laity's participation in the selection process as a justification for rule. Ordaining Delgado, "the Mier of El Salvador," constituted a sacraligious violation, the heavyweight ultramontanist concluded in another work that same year.[38] Nor could the civil powers tamper with clerical immunity; and indeed "no sincere Catholic" even seriously entertained such an idea. The 1794 bull *Auctorem fidei* finally promulgated by the Spanish crown in 1800 in part in response to Espiga and Urquiqo's 1799 marriage dispensation challenge, Santa Maria insisted, had made the sanctity of clerical immunity from civil courts abundantly clear. Furthermore, if the "Jansenistic mob, worldly politicians, and charlatan armchair lawyers" argued for the civil powers' jurisdiction over ecclesiastical appointments and life they were "neither wise nor Catholic."[39]

Santa Maria was set on winning hearts and minds to the ultramontane cause and fretted that the reading and listening public would not persevere through his labyrinthian and highly erudite denunciation of Menéndez. So he rushed out an abbreviated version of his pamphlet, a short question-and-answer catechism to highlight Menéndez's errors. To the question of with what right San Salvador and Cartagena's secular authorities had appointed bishops, the catechism roughly responded "might does not make right" and called the act heretical.[40] To a query on the validity of the election that brought Delgado to power, Santa María snapped back that valid elections required legitimate electors, designated places and times, and presiding authorities; who but a vile schemer would survey the haphazard canvassing of homes that he claimed brought Delgado to power in El Salvador and declare it a canonical election? Nor did the new American states hold the *patronato*. Many of the Spanish Monarchy's prerogatives did indeed pass to the new nations, but the *patronato* was not one of them: it had been conceded to the Spanish Crown by the Holy Father, and the new nations could not claim the right without his express permission.[41]

The response to Santa Maria's catechism revealed the vituperation and ad-hominim attacks that increasingly characterized the debate. The Dominican friar, a liberal pamphleteer announced, was a monarchist and the archbishop's poodle, a man who if given the chance would transform Central Americans into the "slaves of Ferdinand VII." Moreover, he favored the fantastic stories and false miracles of the nun Teresa de Aycinena. The liberal author suggested that Santa Maria pray and repent for the scandals he and the archbishop fomented, which were well known in the republic and the church. Perhaps most galling to the pseudononymous author who signed his work "*Un Prógimo*," Santa María deemed Delgado an intruder. To this he fired back that the fully sovereign state of El Salvador had declared Delgado the bishop, and sovereign states were the legitimate heirs of the Spanish *patronato*.[42]

Here history was not unambiguously on the side of the reform-minded Un Prógimo or that of the ultramontane Santa María. That the Spanish Crown had chosen and presented ecclesiastical hierarchs to the pope for his approval and set diocesan boundaries in its American territories was an unassailable truth. That this patronage over the church inhered in secular political bodies that succeeded the Crown after independence was debatable. A 1501 papal bull granted the tithe to the Crown, which used royal treasury officials to collect the money and spent the funds on churches, hospitals, and the clergy. A papal bull of 1508 "conceded" the patronage of the church to the Spanish monarchs, with the implication that the concession could be rescinded; and, until the reign of Philip II, the Crown claimed its rights over the church affairs exclusively by dint of papal concessions. By the end of the sixteenth century, however, a tripartite justification for Crown appoint-ment of church officials and other matters had emerged. Philip II informed New Spain's viceroy in 1594, for example, that Spain held patronage because of its dis-covery of the new world, its expenditure on churches and monasteries, and papal concession. The laws of the Indies stipulated that viceroys, governors, and other new world officials could exercise the patronato on the king's behalf. Two bulls issued by Benedict XIV in 1753 etched into law the right of the *patronato* based on endowment, papal concession, and other legitimate title, and these justifica-tions oft-cited by regalist and later nationalist reformers. The erudite Menéndez invoked the 1753 law as precedence for civil oversight of the church.[43]

Central American reformers of the immediate post-independence period knew that Ferdinand VII regarded papal communication with a new world no longer under his sway as a violation of the *real patronato de Indias* and that he lobbied the Vatican to deny recognition to the new nations. Reformers like Menéndez and Villacorta rightly worried about the Holy Father's propensity to favor the Spanish king, to support monarchy against the fledgling democracies. In 1816, Pius VII had issued the encyclical *Etsi longissimo* to church hierarchs in the Americas, urging them to exhort obedience to the Crown.[44] And in 1824, Leo XII granted a request from Spanish King Ferdinand VII, issuing an encyclical that encouraged prelates to preach loyalty to the king over national independence.[45] But as it dawned on Rome that the New World would not return to the fold, the Vatican began to deal directly with emissaries from Latin America, although they resolutely reeled the *patronato* back under the church's control, refusing to "concede" it to the new nations, and pointing to their original "concession" of the *patronato* to Spain as justification for papal control over ecclesiastical appointments and jurisdictions.[46] In 1828, Pope Leo XII appointed bishops to vacant positions in Colombia, side-stepping the Spanish king.[47]

The *patronato* issue divided reformers and conservatives across Latin America's young republics. The debate in Mexico was particularly heated. Sanjuanista María Alpuche e Infante, who had attended classes in Mérida with the core of the

Sanjuanista leadership, promoted his 1827 congressional proposal for the *patronato*, confident that it would restore the church to its resplendent "first times . . . when the apostles cast their nets to capture souls, not silver and gold."[48] Mexican reformers, he waxed optimistic, would serve as the chosen sons of the "afflicted and enslaved" Mother Church, to be emulated by all Catholic nations and ultimately lauded by an awakened Rome. Clerical abuses had caused an exodus from the pews; reformers' pared-down democratic national church would call them back to the fold. Alpuche knew "fanatics" would tag him a Jansenist, an atheist, or a Protestant, but he pledged not to falter. Mexican reformers were poised to remove the church's centuries-old shackles, and the Sanjuanista, like so many reformist Catholics before him, expressed sorrow for his enemies blinded from the truth and bereft of Christian charity. Sanjuanista Alpuche drew on some Reform Catholic heavyweights to make his case for the patronato and a national church to Mexico's public: Cádiz Cortes firebrand Francisco Serra; prolific canon of San Isidro and Countess of Montijo salon-goer, editor, and writer Joaquin Lorenzo Villanueva; and ultramontanist scourge Friar Benito Oberhauser, who argued for the separation of the marriage contract from the Church's marriage sacrament.[49] Alpuche was not the only Sanjuanista to bring reformist arguments to this iteration of the patronato debate: a greying José Matias Quintana also sought to decenter Rome.[50]

THE TRANSNATIONAL PUBLIC SPHERE OF LETTERS

Effective and highly mobilized, the reform-minded El Salvadorans who championed Delgado's schism threw the region into a decade of religious conflict. But they were certainly not anomalies in the early republics of Latin America and formed part of a constellation of reformers connected to each other through the burgeoning public sphere of letters. Mexican intellectuals and public figures vigorously debated the El Salvadoran conflict as immediately relevant to their own fledgling independence. Zacatecan priest José Guadalupe Gómez Huerta, for one, reiterated took arguments for the era's most radical ecclesiastical reforms, proposing that not the nation of Mexico but the state of Zacatecas should exercise the *patronato*—with negligible papal oversight. Like many of the area's passionate federalists, Gómez Huerta found inspiration in the writings of Llorente, and he held a doctorate in canon law to give weight to his words. Local control over marriage dispensations, the elimination of obligatory tithing, state funding of clerical salaries and liturgical expenses—these were just a few of Gómez Huerta's suggestions. In 1827, the priest even proposed that Zacatecas establish its own bishopric to free itself from the fiscal extractions of the diocese of Guadalajara.[51]

The proposal created a national furor. One buoyant critic publicly analogized him to the reformist forces holding sway in El Salvador and pondered whether the Zacatecan firebrand would usher into Mexico, "our beloved *patria*," all the "inconsolable tears" and the "horrors" experienced by the unfortunate Salvadorans who endured Delgado's schemes.[52] He was right to worry: many Mexicans believed that a purified church and polity was on the horizon. Gómez Huerta displayed the chiliastic fervor exclusive to those convinced of God's imprimatur: he rehearsed in elegiac tones the tragic loss of the decentralized and democratic political purity of the church's early centuries, but also soared to heights of optimism for the reform's prospects. After all, as he explained, "Tamburini, Llorente, the Liberties of the Spanish Church in both worlds, and works of this nature are now common in the new nation."[53] Booksellers attested that hundreds of copies of these authors' passed through their hands—and that readers eagerly devoured them.[54]

Guadalajara's *El Defensor de la Religión* found the learned Zacatecan's arguments so dangerous that it subjected them to minute, line-by-line critique—the hallmark of the indefatigable paper's rebuttals to Reform Catholic intellectuals more generally. The reformist works, *El Defensor* insisted, did not entice readers because of their illuminating arguments but because Gómez Huerta dazzled his unsophisticated public, lovers of novelties enthralled to fashionable opinions. But truth was truth no matter what public opinion declared. Llorente and his devotees seized on the Roman curia's human flaws to elevate bishops above the pope and the civil powers above the church in matters religious—both unpardonable offenses.[55]

The conservative *Defensor* rejected the authorial maxim that a few dramatic examples persuade best, instead launching a forensic dissection of every line that only narrowly skirted the histrionic. Over the course of 1827, the ultramontane mouthpiece shredded Gómez Huerta's treatise, tackling three paragraphs per issue. One issue of *El Defensor*, for example, disabused readers of any lingering enthusiasm they might harbor for paragraph 26 of Gómez Huerta's work. If the people had historically participated in ecclesiastical elections, as the schismatic Huerta argued, some sage hierarch had wisely ended this practice. Popularly elected pastors were wolves and mercenaries, their faux marriage dispensations turned real couples into concubines, they could not absolve sin—these were just a few of the *Defensor*'s points.[56]

The *Defensor* paid microscopic attention to the foundational publications of reformist luminary Juan Antonio Llorente, often in the same issue. To Llorente's parry that only the entire Church Militant and not just the hierarchy could rightfully legislate on matters of faith, the *Defensor* sardonically noted the logistical impossibility of gathering all Catholics together. This sort of gathering had not even occurred at the Council of Jerusalem in 50 CE, which had abolished the practice of Hebrew circumcision—surely an issue calculated to attract maximum popular interest.

Several years after Menéndez and Villacorta's dramatic speeches in the federal assembly and the flurry of ultramontane retorts they occasioned, Archbishop Casaús issued an edict banning thirty-two dangerous works, blasting them as "impious and perverse." Among them was Llorente's 1820 advice on a "religious constitution," a rigorous manifesto declaring that the use of God-given rationality trumped blind obedience to superiors. New national churches that claimed lineage from Saint Peter were Catholic regardless of the pope's approval, Llorente proclaimed, and legislative power in the church resided with the Church Militant, not the Holy Father. The church's first two centuries, when bishops acted autonomously from Rome, provided a blueprint for these and other radically decentralizing measures.[57] Dangerous tomes like Llorente's circulated in Central America, and the archbishop implored the faithful to "rip them up with their own hands or burn them along with the infamous and obscene paintings that destroy innocent souls with a single glance."[58] Here Casaús seems to have been admirably up-to-date on Rome's most burning concerns: an energetic Spanish nuncio, taxed with the quixotic task of thwarting the 1820s Cortes' anti-Rome agenda, had enthusiastically reported on the pope's decision to place Llorente's work on the Index, noting his pleasure at "suffocating the resurgent Jansenist monster, which had infected so many vibrant European churches and now threatened Spain."[59]

Mexican newspapers' divergent interpretations of the El Salvador schism indicate that doctrinaire positions on the matter became shibboleths for reformist Catholics and their ultramontane detractors as their theological divisions shaped the political sphere in the former Spanish Empire. The radical Salvadorans' quarrels with their ultramontane foes were but one skirmish in a larger transatlantic religious battle, and the Mexican press lent solidarity to their respective sides. Guadalajara's conservative *El Defensor* and Mexico City's *El Sol*, mouthpiece of the ultramontane Scottish Rite Masons, both reprinted the Guatemalan *El Indicador*'s 1827 analysis of the schism. *El Indicador*'s conservative editors portrayed Guatemala's liberals as turncoats and argued that the miter conflagration was the prime cause of the three-year civil war. San Salvador's Reform Catholic mouthpiece *El Salvadoreño* noted that not a single issue of *El Indicador* failed to cite an expert from Mexico's *El Sol*. The editors of *El Sol* merited a plank in the pantheon of heroes who had resisted frontal assaults on Catholic unity, *El Defensor* enthused. The conservative paper concluded that Central America's religious upheavals demonstrated the threat to national unity represented by Gómez Huerta, their own homegrown Delgado.[60]

The proxy war in the Mexican press continued: *El Sol* ran Archbishop Casaús' pastoral letter condemning Delgado, along with a stern warning from Pope Leo XII to the upstart bishop—both of which had appeared in Guatemala's *El Indicador*. In his letter, Casaús thundered that the abominations of schismatics like Donatus and Delgado had plunged the Catholic world into darkness. Characteristically, Casaús left a path to redemption open for the object of his wrath, vowing to embrace a penitent Delgado like the Prodigal Son upon the surely imminent return of legitimate sacraments to El Salvador. In December of 1826, Leo XII likewise granted Delgado room to maneuver, but threatened excommunication if he failed to come to heel within fifty days. The Holy Father reserved his most searing condemnation for Delgado's persecution of refractory priests and his most withering sarcasm for his attempts to coax Rome's imprimatur for his nonsense through the medium of Castrillo, but the pontiff also reserved space in which to denounce Delgado for usurping Rome's monopoly over the lucrative marriage dispensations.[61] While neither approach had any discernible effect on Delgado, the Mexican paper's conservative readers no doubt thrilled to the knowledge that Rome could still smite its enemies. Though they were surrounded in the public sphere of letters by countrymen who shared with this schismatic "Mier of El Salvador" an enthusiasm for federalism and a positive ecstasy for the return of the church's primitive discipline, those Mexicans loyal to Rome could bring powerful voices into the debate, and perhaps prevent Mexico from becoming another El Salvador with the force of words.

As El Salvador's contributions to the global intra-Catholic battle became a central topic in Mexico's vibrant new public sphere of letters, few wielded more influence than José Joaquín Fernández de Lizardi, remembered as one of the most important voices of liberalism and as a reformist stalwart.[62] The Reform Catholic Lizardi weighed in against Archbishop Casaús' coterie from Mexico's capital. Lizardi could claim an unbroken record of bold activism, first imprisoned on charges of smuggling arms to Miguel Hidalgo's troops and then incarcerated again in 1821 for defending Mexican Independence, excommunicated by Pope Pius VII for his 1822 defense of free masonry and critique of papal infallibility, and a clangorous hawker of pamphlets outside the very doors of Mexico's senate.[63] Lizardi's 1827 tract *Horrifying Attacks by a Faction of Guatemala's Clergy* noted liberal clerics' salutary influence while bringing the Central American conflict to the heart of literate Mexico's concerns. Importantly, his was not a broadly anti-clerical rant by an Enlightened secularist, but specifically an attack on ultramontanist clerics. He focused on the "servile" clergy's support for monarchy and their savagery during Nicaragua's earlier independence struggles. Singled out for critique was Nicaraguan priest Dionisio Crespin, who served as a chaplain in the conservative

Guatemalan army during the three-year civil war. Lizardi noted that, during an unspecified earlier engagement in Nicaragua, Crespin had severed the ears, testicles, and scrotum of a liberal soldier in a public plaza. He described a special 8,000-member confraternity that funded this butcher. An unspecified cleric, according to the Mexican Thinker, had created the religious brotherhood specifically to amass bribes for luring the undecided into conservative ranks.

While Lizardi was prone to exaggeration for dramatic effect, this choice of Crespin for specific attack shows that he was well informed about the religious conflict wracking Central America: Father Crespin indeed had a knack for putting himself at the service of conservatives. At one point he occupied an El Salvador parish, from which Delgado expelled him in 1824, and he was an appropriate target for a Reform Catholic commentator. Lizardi further demonstrated his knowledgeable partisanship in the southern theological conflict: El Salvador's *Semanario Político Mercantil* had recently run an article suggesting that Casaús—a "friar as infamous as the Devil"—deserved exile, even death for his machinations. The *Pensador* of Mexico pronounced the sentence "insolent and harsh," but insisted that the archbishop's "criminal excesses" had rightly exasperated El Salvadorans.[64] José María de Aza, a Mexico City pundit undaunted by Lizardi's swagger and just as capable of creative name-calling, fired back with a pamphlet accusing the Mexican Thinker of obfuscating the key context of the violence in Central America: the bishopric controversy that occasioned the attack on Archbishop Casaús.[65] In short, even the most illustrious of liberal public intellectuals found the specifics of the debate between Reformed and ultramontane Catholics in Central America critically important for Mexico's own political future.

POPULAR RELIGION AND THE INDIGENOUS MAJORITY

Looking back on the tumultuous 1820s, prominent ultramontane opinion leaders blamed the three-year war on reform-besotted priests and politicians, particularly those involved in Delgado's schism, and fingered authors like Llorente and Grégoire as the fonts of their opponents' misguided zeal. Guatemalan conservative Manuel Montúfar y Coronado, an editor of *El Indicador* and author of an 1832 memoir that quickly became one of two definitive guides to the region's tumultuous previous decade, granted Llorente's work a prominent niche in the causes of both militant federalism and the Civil War. He regarded the Delgado-led schism as the prime cause of the three-year bloodfest. A member of the Aycinea clan, or "The Family," as critics dubbed it, Montúfar headed Guatemala's state government in 1825 and served as a coronel in Guatemala's cavalry and then as Arce's second-in-command during Guatemala's first invasion of El Salvador. Cut off from supplies, he surrendered to the El Salvadorans in 1828 outside of San Salvador.[66]

Delgado's vision of the church, Montúfar argued, sprang from a dangerous confection of his own demagoguery, the church's primitive discipline, and "all of the new ideas of Grégoire and Llorente." By his lights, this incendiary mixture ignited the three-year armed struggle that engulfed the region. During and prior to this time, federalism and the new bishopric had hopelessly intertwined, Montúfar asserted, and Central America's religious antagonists proved far more averse to compromise and reconciliation than politicians guided by more mundane concerns. Clergymen divided along party lines, towns riven and scandalized, degenerate priests appointed by an upstart bishop, laymen who refused the sacraments from Delgado-appointed priests, turncoat Guatemalan legislators who abetted El Salvadoran liberals: all this Montúfar blamed on Delgado's schism and Central American liberals' ham-fisted interpretations of the early church—interpretations inspired above all by Grégoire and Llorente.[67]

But victors spin history, and the conservative Montúfar's party lost the war in 1829. Predictably, the Reform Catholic victors uncorked a spirited rebuttal: in 1833, ascendant liberal leader Mariano Gálvez commissioned historian Alejandro Marure to pen a primary-source driven response to Montúfar's influential tract. If liberals supported Delgado's bishopric, they did so primarily to diminish Casuas' creditability and, to a lesser extent, to back a politician who shared their priorities. The battle over the bishopric did not by itself, according to Montúfar, compel people into the fray. Marure, whose Belén-conspirator father had died en route to forced exile in Spain, lauded Delgado's personal austerity and heroism in El Salvador's early independence struggles and heaped fulsome praise on the statesman's patriotic service to Central America, especially his presidency of the ANC. But Delgado's pretensions to the bishopric elicited snickers, and if conservatives denounced his exploits, they did so to whip up their base, to alarm "the ignorant" into opposing the federalists. The schism was indeed a prime cause of the civil war, but it was at best a secondary factor, albeit one that engendered impassioned pamphlets and boldly seditious acts like Ortiz's sermon in San Salvador. Marure concluded that an investiture controversy alone could not have compelled men into battle; the miter conflagration intersected with politics and therein lay its power to move men.[68]

Central America's indigenous majority did not participate in the war in significant numbers, at least not on the Guatemalan side. The near absence of indigenous soldiers in the war was a legacy of the colonial period. The Spanish Crown had made it illegal for Indians—fully two-thirds of the population— to bear arms. Colonial militias and the Royal Army in the Kingdom of Guatemala had therefore been comprised of creole, ladino, Black, and mulatto soldiers. Even in K'iche Quetzaltenango, where Indians fully controlled the only city council until 1806, and where they retained control of one of the two councils after that, Ladinos and whites manned the militias deployed against rebellious Indians, most famously those of the 1820 Totonicapán rebellion.[69] East of Guatemala City, in Chiqimuila, where the repasturing of cattle dominated the economy, and day laborers and muleteers dominated the labor force, blacks and mulattoes filled the militia ranks. Although after independence Indians gained the right to bear arms, and although a handful of *caciques* in Los Altos established Indian militias, most of the soldiers in Guatemala's fighting force during the civil war hailed from the center and east of the country, not the indigenous highlands, and few Indians fought overall.

Indeed war efforts most likely antagonized the indigenous population. In one particularly brutal instance, the federal army reduced a Totonicapán department town to ashes for refusing to muster up men and resources.[70] During the war's early days, the deposed liberal Barrundia's partisans attempted to recruit Indians into the fight against Arce's federal troops. In several instances at least, officers raided Indian confraternity treasuries, and commandeered valued objects from churches to pay for these new militias and for supplies like gunpowder.[71] It strains credulity to imagine that these confiscations of sacred resources fostered the "popular liberalism" found among the Mexican peasantry during a slightly later period; indeed, the liberal aversion to Indian religiosity did little to ingratiate them with K'iche and other indigenous groups, as Cirilo Flores realized too late. Neither do Indians appear to have flocked enthusiastically to the conservative Guatemalan or federalist armies. In 1828, Secretary of State José Francisco Córdova reported few Indian soldiers in the centralist ranks and high desertion rates.[72]

Regardless of the role of indigenous Central Americans, by 1829 reformers had emerged victorious in the three-year civil war and had their hands firmly on the reins of state. Their passionate commitment to deploying the state to reform the church and their fellow citizens' religiosity would prove their undoing.

7

"Religious Passion Tore Us Apart"

IN MAY OF 1829, victorious liberal general Francisco Morazán revealed a strategy that ensured that his and fellow liberals' reign in the Federal Republic of Central America would last less than a decade. Following Delgado's precedent, the Guatemalan government ordered Casaús to remove conservative priests and replace them with adherents to the liberal reformist cause, and to send conservative stalwarts to Antigua to await further orders.[1] Over the course of the next several years, as liberals held power in the federal, Guatemalan, and Honduran governments, they would banish Archbishop Casaús to Havana; exile the regular orders (with the exception of the Bethlehemites) and seize their property; drastically reduce the number of religious holidays; ban religious processions from the streets; issue edicts to move burials from churches to suburban cemeteries; and attempt to end required clerical celibacy.[2] Under the motto "God, Union, Liberty"—a devout riposte to the secular trio of "Liberty, Equality, Fraternity"—these reformed Catholics wrote their religious priorities into law, and, in so doing, sealed their fate.

Indeed, the effects of these measures hostile to Rome and popular religiosity on the liberals' long-term control of the region can safely be called disastrous. Their political hold lasted less than a decade, as their two most abhorred moral saboteurs—the "fanatical" ultramontane and the "superstitious" indigenous and ladino majority—crafted uneasy alliances to oust them from power and usher in the long reign of a swarthy swineherd named Rafael Carrera. Factions of Carrera's

For God and Liberty. Pamela Voekel, Oxford University Press. © Oxford University Press 2023.
DOI: 10.1093/oso/9780197610190.003.0008

indigenous and poor ladino power base fought in part in the name of preserving their hopelessly intertwined religious and political configurations from the on-slaught of religious reformers throughout the decade. In 1839, the new alliance of popular and ultramontane Catholics ended the liberals' firm hold on the reins of state for the next thirty years.

The decade from 1829 to 1839, then, represents not a final resolution of the religio-political conflict that came before, but rather its continuation by other means. The religious war that tore Central America apart in the 1820s regularly broke out into open hostility after the liberals' nominal victory in 1829. National loyalties continued to be far too fragile to contain these religious passions. Even some of the key protagonists remained fully embroiled in the struggle: Casaús and Rome fought on against Delgado and the reformers as the wily archbishop continued to exercise outsized influence with the ultramontane even from exile and in their darkest hour. After Delgado's death, his lay and clerical coterie would eventually fade as the reformist vanguard in Central America, to be replaced by energetic Guatemalan reformers underMariano Gálvez's leadership. Only death could end the erstwhile bishop's machinations: neither an excommunication de-cree from the Holy Father in 1831, nor a resurgent ultramontane faction in El Salvador bolstered by region-wide reinforcements, could end his pretensions to the bishopric, and his fellow travelers continued to defend him from his detractors from San Salvador to Rome. Thus bracketed on one end by the political victories of first the liberals and on the other by the conservatives starting in 1838, the re-ligious tensions that had previously rent the region asunder and plunged it into a three-year civil war would continue to render the polity deeply unstable. As be-fore, the actors themselves continued to understand their conflicts as pervasively religious and their politics as the logical extension of ultimate concerns about man's relation to God.

That the religious roiling of the young republics had not ceased with the formal end of hostilities was immediately apparent after the liberals' 1829 military vic-tory. The war's end punctuated but did not resolve specific skirmishes. And some familiar faces resurfaced to grant their imprimatur—and God's—to their side's cause.

The ongoing struggle in Esquipulas serves as an illustration. Recall that Archbishop Casaús placed ultramontane stalwart Miguel Muñoz in the church in Esquipulas, near Guatemala's borders with both Honduras and El Salvador. The town was the home of the famed "Black Christ" of Esquipulus, the dark crucified figure that annually attracted tens of thousands of mostly indigenous pilgrims.[3] There the erudite Father Muñoz sheltered ultramontane fellow travelers during his six-year stint. In 1827, as the war raged, he harbored priest Mariano Castejón, whom the liberal Honduran President José Dionisio de Herrera had persecuted for his refusal to support edicts hostile to Vatican authority.[4] President Herrera was a Reform Catholic true believer, a veritable *"come-ultramontane-curas,"* and his measures against the church were nothing if not inflammatory.

In response to these anti-Romish measures, factions of the ultramontane mounted organized resistance. Attempting to stanch this criticism and tar its authors with sedition, liberals accused the vicar general of Comayagua, Honduras, Nicolas Irías, of masterminding a failed attempt on the president's life.[5] In a conservative coup d'état, President Herrera was deposed in May of 1827 and sent to prison in Guatemala.

With the liberal army's 1829 victory, General Francisco Morazán freed the captive Herrera. He leaned hard on the now vulnerable Archbishop Casaús to appoint reformist Catholic enthusiast Francisco Antonio Márquez to head the Honduran church.[6] From exile in Havana, Casaús was forced to contemplate the outrage: Márquez was appointing clerics in his own image and sending them out to dispense the sacraments among the flocks.

But welcome news reached the exiled archbishop. Despite the official banishment of Irías in 1829, Casaús learned that he was in fact surreptitiously directing the Honduran diocese from a mountain redoubt near Esquipulus. From Cuba Casaús relayed his blessings for this happy development. He called for the resignation of the liberal, reformist Catholic pretender Márquez and urged Irías to order his loyal clerics to revoke sacraments received from Márquez's own illegitimate clerical appointees. With his hands effectively tied, Márquez resigned. Comayagua's Cathedral Chapter promptly named Bruno Medina in his place; when he died soon after, he was replaced by Mariano Castejón—the very priest whom Muñoz had so carefully sheltered from Herrera's wrath in the pilgrimage town of Esquipulas.[7] Muñoz later boasted that he had served as the main liaison between the unbowed ultramontane Honduran priests fighting behind enemy lines in the early 1830s and their prelate Irías in Esquipulus, and thus helped the ultramontane church survive the misrule of the liberal reformers.[8]

As this dramatic series of reversals and subterfuges suggests, Morazán and his reform cadre were well aware they needed the region's clerics to sway hearts and minds. Their ultramontane rivals, however, were playing the long game, building alliances as they maintained underground networks. As in Esquipulas, these would ultimately carry the day in the region as a whole. But the road to that ultramontane victory was never a straight one in the 1830s.

THE ATTACK ON THE REGULAR ORDERS

As the tangled story of Esquipulas' ultramontane resistance demonstrates, throughout their fragile reign the liberal forces of Reform Catholicism fought an unrelenting battle to quash their religious rivals in the secular clergy. At the same time, liberals took drastic action against the region's vowed religious friars—excepting only the Bethlemites, spared for their national utility as pedagogues. There were not a lot of religious—fewer than three hundred in all of the United Provinces, according to one contemporary—but they still controlled most of the parishes in the western highlands and regularly received the pious bequests of the ultramontane faithful. For the reformers, however, three hundred friars was three hundred too many.[9]

The issue of the regular orders had long divided reformed and ultramontane Catholics the world over. In the region itself, furthermore, the 1829 decision to expel the regular orders from Central America had a long backstory. Before the sweeping 1829 banishment of the regular orders, state and regional governing bodies had issued a spate of laws designed to raise the minimum age for monastic vows from sixteen to twenty-five, citing early vows as a threat to the "liberty and discernment" so foundational to religion.[10] More generally, Reform Catholics engaged in some serious rhetorical hyperbole at the friars' expense, laying the havoc wrought by the civil war at their feet. Guatemalan president Mariano Gálvez noted that "always howling," fanaticism was the principal instrument of the perverse, who accused their liberal enemies of heresy and labeled their heartfelt defense of the church's true mission an attack on religion. Ex-friars had teamed up with vulgar and superstitious old women, a newspaper supportive of Gálvez reported, to continue their defense of absolutism and inquisitorial scheming.[11] Government pronouncements deviated from routine information transmission to rehearse the regular orders' errors: monastic institutions suffocated equality, the regular orders embroiled the region in bloody revolutions, they hated independence, they refused to swear allegiance to the laws of the land, and they goaded the ignorant into atrocities like the mob lynching of Liberal leader Cirilo Flores in Quetzaltenango—Guatemala's head of state included this gloss in a widely circulated decree about the expulsion of the regular orders in 1829.[12]

The expulsion decree brought this high-flown rhetoric down to earth. Though few in number, the members of the regular orders were real people, and the harshness of their banishment disturbed even some liberals themselves. In their efforts to avoid exile, the religious and their supporters summoned an array of persuasive tactics, stressing both their political innocence and their personal attachments. The specter of expulsion incited parents to plaintive pleas for their childrens' exemption from exile; even friars, after all, had families. In these petitions, the parents begged for mercy on grounds both political and personal. One father stressed the cruelty of the order and also offered proof of his son's loyalty to the government: the twenty-six-year-old Dominican was seized in Salamá and marched to the coast of Sonsonate in El Salvador, where he lay on a sick bed awaiting recovery and then a boat ride to banishment. If these hardships did not move the supreme government to pity, the father hastened to reassure the liberals that his son's generation of Dominicans embraced modern ideas and the current political system; and indeed José Rosa y Aguirre's superiors had "persecuted and tormented" him and his youthful friends because of their advanced ideas. Nor had this beloved son participated in the tumult of regime change in 1826. This "aging father" hoped to bend the "humane and just" heart of the *jefe supremo* toward the return of his offspring.[13] The mother of another friar stressed ringing endorsements for her son from "illustrious patriots" as well as her boy's principled neutrality in war time. Further, a classic plea: she was a lonely, destitute widow, he was her sole support and comfort.[14] These were powerful arguments. The acting head of the regular orders, José Antonio Alcayaga, the vicar general appointed by Morazán, advised the government to allow the friars to doff their robes, don secular priestly garb, and remain with their families. What damage could these repentant and isolated friars do, he asked rhetorically, given that politicians and liberal clerics, not the regular orders, would be overseeing them?[15]

Appeals from family members were particularly heartfelt, but the petitions drew upon the threatened friars' larger circles as well to make the case that rumors of their conservatism were greatly exaggerated. When the government offered amnesty to friars willing to break their vows and join the secular clergy, Dominican Jose Clemente López set off immediately for the capital; decidedly agnostic during the war, he confessed, he eagerly sought secularization. The government, however, required corroboration of his political leanings, which he provided: during the time of the "darkest despotism," one of his character witnesses proffered, López had opposed the conservatives and fervently supported the Constitution of 1824's restoration; another witness attested to the friar's "better and more liberal sentiments" during the conflagration and noted that, unlike his convent brothers, López had not scandalized "men of good sense" by collaborating with the intruders, or by arming himself to inspire his flock into the fray.[16]

If the argument for clemency had been limited to these highly personalized petitions by the friars and their parents, the central government might have had an easier decision to make. The problem lay with the much broader support that the regular orders commanded as symbols of the conflicting religious visions. Indeed, the government felt compelled to bolster troop numbers in areas where they feared "*fanáticos*" would protest the friars' forced exile, and ordered their overland march under armed guard to the coast of Sonsonate to avoid Guatemala City and the former capital of Antigua, with their potential for angry crowds.[17]

SECULAR CLERGY UNDER FIRE

Because of the way they crystallized key differences between the rival theologies, and because they had direct links to the indigenous population reformers sought to reform, then, the regular orders served as a flashpoint disproportionate to their actual representation in Central America. But the attempted purge of the ultramontane during the liberal reign was not limited to the vowed religious; it included the public-facing secular clergy—that is, parish priests, the only face of the church encountered by the overwhelming majority of the faithful. Casaús and Delgado had battled each other to control this all-important conduit to hearts and minds, and for the liberal moment Delgado held the whip hand. Thus the dragnet cast for friars also encircled conservative members of the secular clergy, and the same arguments were put forth to launder questionable reputations.

In the effort to ensure a unified Reform Catholic voice for the liberal-era church, no one escaped scrutiny. Some sailed through, their earlier allegiance rewarded in this moment of victory: Victor Castrillo's credentials as a "liberal" cleric were beyond reproach, for example, in large part because of his official visit to Rome on Delgado's behalf, and moreover he had left the Mercedarians to become a secular cleric. In 1829, the newly liberal Guatemalan state itself proposed him for a plum benefice, informing Vicar General Antonio Alcayaga of the "important services" he had rendered to the republic and "the Cause."[18] The state was right to put its faith in him: in 1838, the new conservative-controlled state approved the town of Zacapa's decision to jail Castrillo for his active support of Mariano Gálvez's liberal government.[19]

Other clerics who tried to burnish their reformist credentials under the new dispensation, however, seemed to be emulating the vicar of Bray. Cleric Ramón Solis was a case in point. His service as a deputy in congress under the conservatives landed him in the liberals' crosshairs in 1829.[20] A host of witnesses rushed to his defense, attesting to his neutrality during the civil war and the generosity he had shown to liberals. A British traveler had met Solís at an 1827 Corpus Christi party hosted by the wealthy Gutiérrez family in Guatemala City. Solís, the family's confessor, was the life of the gathering, his mellifluous voice and mastery of the guitar and piano as impressive to the traveler as the distinctly Spanish feast served.[21] Similarly accused of disloyalty to the new government, the parish priest of San Juan Amititlan, José Serapio Sánchez, also mustered key witnesses: mother María Dolores Roma's son Pedro deserted his conservative artillery unit in 1826 to defect to the liberals, she explained; parish priest Sánchez had graciously gifted him clothes to replace his uniform and thereby escape undetected.[22]

As became clear after the reversal of 1839, however, the petitions could indicate influence and connections rather than genuine sentiments: those with friends in high places were able to summon impassioned defenses of their liberal sympathies, but later showed their true colors. Basilio Zeceña y Fernández de Córdoba, for example, only barely escaped exile despite his thoroughly suspect past. In 1824, this doctor of theology had joined the ultramontane chorus against José Simeón Cañas' controversial pamphlet. Zeceña's 1824 pamphlet had defended the Holy Father's exclusive right to appoint bishops, and ridiculed Cañas' claim that the erudite Pius VI could not possibly have authored such wrongheaded documents. A sarcastic Zeceña had fired back that surely the erudite Cañas had not penned such a wrongheaded pamphlet—had some lesser being forged his name?[23] El Salvador's emissary to the Vatican, Victor Castrillo, criticised Zeceña for his attack on this revered elder.[24] Not surprisingly, then, the ultramontanist heavy appeared on the May 1829 list of priests Gálvez ordered removed from their parishes and replaced by "liberal clerics."[25] Despite the thick file against him, Zeceña managed to escape exile by raising a vigorous defense. In August, he took his case public in a pamphlet stressing his protagonism during earlier peace negotiations with El Salvador, his neutrality in the recent war, and his protection of "patriots" persecuted during the unfortunate violence.[26] In September, he appealed for reinstatement to the parish of San Juan Sacatepéquez with the help of Vicar General Juan Antonio Alcayaga; the secretary general of Guatemala approved his request.[27] The liberals would rue the day they forgave Zeceña: he went on to serve as the secretary of justice, ecclesiastical affairs, and foreign relations after conservative Rafael Carrera's 1844 rise to power.[28]

Sometimes the vetting process worked as intended. Priest Dionisio Crespin, for example, had created an elaborate transnational paper trail. Lizardi depicted the cleric as a cruel butcher of Nicaraguan liberals in his 1827 screed *Horrorosos atentados de una parte del clero de Goatemala* [sic] (*Horrifying Attacks by a Faction of Guatemala's Clergy*). Crespin was a party man who dispatched to where his swagger was most needed: he had at some point left Nicaragua to serve in a parish in Chinameca, El Salvador. A conservative pamphleteer listed him as one of the priests that "El Salvadoran terrorists" forced into exile during the civil war; his firm opposition to Delgado's bishopric, he argued, provoked his petty tormentors into exiling him. Crespin was picked up in Morazán's dragnet of ultramontane clerics after the Allied Army Protector of the Law's 1829 victory. His considerable political nous led him to confess to entering onto the battlefield in his role as a chaplain in Guatemala's conservative army, as many eyewitnesses could confirm. But he vehemently denied wielding arms. Despite Crespin's pleas of priestly passivism, Morazán held him in the Convent of Belén for several months before ordering his deportation.[29]

Regardless of the efficacy of the process, the overarching goal of promoting the spokesmen for reformist Catholic ecclesiology and campaigns against popular excesses was a critical counterpart to the liberal victory—indeed, for some it was the point of the war itself. As in El Salvador earlier, in 1829 liberals across the United Provinces demonstrated the inseparability of their religious and political convictions. In the new federal republic's self-presentation, God came first, before both unity and liberty, and it was in God's name that both sides continued the struggle throughout the decade.

ARCHBISHOP CASAÚS LEADS THE OPPOSITION

Casaús proved undaunted by the new Liberal federation and Guatemalan government, especially when it concerned itself with his old nemesis, Delgado. In early April of 1830, he retracted his appointment of Vicar General José Antonio Alcayaga, who had angered him by appointing Delgado as Vicar of El Salvador; Cañas had presided over Delgado's public swearing in ceremony for the post.[30] As with so many of Central Americas' clerics, Alcayaga's Reform Catholic loyalties were longstanding, and Morazán's choice of Alcayaga to lead the church probably came as no surprise to the defeated conservatives or to Casaús, who continued to lead them. During the civil war, conservatives had intercepted and then circulated Alcayaga's personal correspondence to demonstrate his "base sentiments" and the "hypocrisy" with which the reformed had plunged El Salvador into a roiling cauldron of religious and political problems. In a letter to a female friend or relative that detailed his overland trip to El Salvador, Alcayaga boasted of enough valor to die for the cause and exuded confidence that a just God would prevent tyrants from ruling eternally. When entering El Salvador he rejoiced to be "in the land of the free." In Guatemala, he explained, fanatics and toadies languished under the yoke of their "blasted leader," who Alcayaga "despised for his unjustness." Now in El Salvador, he told "Nela," he was a proud citizen of a free republic.[31]

Morazán had pressured the archbishop to appoint the reform-minded Alcayaga, but, safely in Cuba, Casaús followed his druthers. Alcayaga, the exiled archbishop carefully explained to Rome, supported Delgado and other enemies of the Catholic Church, men widely regarded as "Jansenists and York Rite Masons." Sanjuanista

Lorenzo Zavala edited the organ of the York Rite Masons, *El Aguila Mexicana* (The Mexican Eagle). Casaús knew his enemies. By 1831, the Council of Extraordinary Ecclesiastical Affairs had heard enough and ordered Alcayaga's removal. Whether the exiled Casaús still wielded sufficient sway to depose Alcayaga remained unclear.[32] Nonetheless, Alcayaga worried that the archbishop's disapproval of him would embolden conservative El Salvadorans angling to unseat the increasingly unpopular Delgado.

The test of Casaús' ongoing influence never happened: Alcayaga became a deputy in the federal congress rather than continue as vicar general. Immediately after stepping down, he received an order from Casaús removing him from the post he had just abandoned. He had some choice words for the archbishop. He was not the prelate's slave, but a proud subject who enjoyed the laws and constitution of his country; Casaús had no right to remove him. To discredit Casaús, Alcayaga dredged up a *cause célèbre* of Central American liberals, a dark moment when one of their own had died at the hands of a mob putatively riled into action by local friars: the archbishop had no credibility, for he had failed to punish the "pharisees" of Quetzaltenango who brutally assassinated Deputy Governor of Guatemala Cirilo Flores. Recall that Flores had moved the remnant of the liberal government dissolved by President Arce to Quetzaltenango in 1826. As well, Alcayaga charged, Casaús had encouraged friars and other clerics to fight in the conservative's army, the army that opposed the constitution. Yet the archbishop moved with alacrity against Alcayaga, who sought only to protect real religion: a people so recently "scorched by the devouring fire of fanaticism" had entreated him to name Delgado head of El Salvador's church, Alcayaga reported, and they were right to do so, as the "enemies of liberty" who assailed these good El Salvadorans had previously invalidated marriages and other sacraments to incite revolt against El Salvador's liberal government.[33]

When the Cathedral Chapter moved to choose a new vicar general to replace Alcayaga, their actions ignited passions in El Salvador, where ultramontanists felt the Cathedral Chapter took a decision that still rightly belonged to the unjustly exiled Casaús.[34] The Cathedral Chapter mounted a collaborative and decidedly tempered defense of the secular power's right to control appointments in the archbishop's absence. This move provoked a spirited 1834 rebuttal from ultramontanist Miguel Muñoz, who strategically read the sober canons as reformist radicals. Father Muñoz sounded the alarm by underscoring the ecclesiastics' connections to the Reform Catholic International. The Cathedral Chapter, he argued, had cribbed from reform firebrand Félix Amat de Palau y Font's *Observaciones pacíficas (Peaceful Observations)*, a weighty tome on ecclesiastical jurisdiction and the evils of the Jesuit Order that appeared serially in Barcelona, Spain, from 1817 to

1822. Pope Leo XII repeatedly condemned the work for lionizing civil power over that of the church.[35]

Muñoz chose his evidence soundly: Amat was indeed a Reform Catholic luminary. None other than Joaquin Villanueva underscored his intellectual influence over the latters own defense of Espiga. Amat's reform pedigree deeply impressed Villanueva. As a student, Amat had resided in the home of Barcelona's Jansenist archbishop Josep Climent y Avinent, the cleric who had loomed large in San Salvador's *Semanario Político Mercantil's* defense of the tithe. Villanueva fondly recalled visiting with Amat in Barcelona in 1823. Amat had been "devoured with anxiety about the reform of the Roman Curia," Villanueva reported.[36]

Thus the cathedral canons co-authored their lengthy justification of just where the authority to appoint churchmen lay given the archbishop's forced exile. When Alcayaga departed from the vicar general position to pursue a political career, Casaús seized the opportunity to act. The archbishop cancelled Alcayaga's appointment of Delgado as Vicar of El Salvador, naming Friar José Ignacio Ávila in his place, and prompting the newly victorious liberals to investigate Casaús' ongoing political machinations.[37] An alarmed Spanish nuncio reported to the pope what happened next: the Guatemalan state assembly—a lay institution—had the temerity to seize the archbishop's goods and formally condemn him to perpetual exile. The assembly also systematically violated clerical immunity, seized the tithe, and shut down the monasteries.[38] Representative Calixto García Goyena accused Casaús of corresponding with his secretary about raising an invasion army.[39] In light of this and other accusations, Guatemala's state government officially banished the Havana-based Casaús, noting that his meddling threatened to provoke a "religious war," and declared him a traitor to the *patria*. The archbishop had conspired against the country's independence; the state declared his bishopric unoccupied.[40]

The Spanish papal nuncio labeled Alcayaga's choice of Delgado to lead El Salvador's church "a detestable abuse." Sadly, he continued, the list of impious Central Americans extended beyond Delgado and his coterie: among others, the list included Sagrario cleric Mariano Méndez as well as Morazán, both of whom championed the "new system." A sympathetic Pope Gregory XVI promised to whisk the information on Delgado to the appropriate Vatican committee, presumably the Congregation for Extraordinary Ecclesiastical Affairs, and reply to the nuncio immediately.[41] The Holy Father had barely been on the job a month, but the nuncio probably predicted the tenor of his response to this iteration of the Reform Catholic challenge to Rome: the future pontiff's 1799 work *The Triumph of the Holy See and the Church Against the Assaults of the Innovators* had sealed his stellar ultramontane credentials. The anti-reformist polemic argued for papal infallibility years before its official declaration in 1870.[42]

Close on the heels of Casaús' formal banishment in 1830 came the federal assembly's July debates about whether to imitate the Honduran government's controversial edict against clerical celibacy.[43] An alarmed Spanish nuncio relayed the shocking development to Rome.[44] The issue of clerical marriage had long divided reformists from ultramontanist Catholics. Summing up the wisdom of the reform camp with his characteristic interpretive flair, Fray Servando Teresa de Mier noted that neither Christ nor the apostles ordained celibacy—perhaps Saint Paul did not get the memo?—and the church's support for the practice had created innumerable scandals through the centuries. Clerical celibacy was a late and dangerous accretion to the purity of early church doctrine and praxis. Even Spanish bishops married during the church's early centuries. Although Pope Siricius' decretal to the bishop of Tarragona had officially criminalized these unions, Mier explained, the salacious had continued to defy the edict, and it became a general law only in the fifteenth century.[45]

Mier's opinion on clerical celibacy was anything but whimsical or opportunistic: the three crates of books he traveled with on the Mina Expedition contained Bolivian Aymara speaker Vicente Pazos Kanki's translation of an earlier French reformist tract on the topic, as well as an additional essay by an American that deployed an elaborate parable to decry the pope's authority.[46] Central American conservatives disagreed with the renegade friar, finding no precedence for the practice of clerical marriage in church history. Alarmed foreign observers joined the chorus of local conservative critics, warning against the explosiveness of the clerical marriage issue, vacant bishoprics, and illegitimately appointed vicar generals. Central America's radical church reformers, their opponents warned, marched precariously over "an abyss full of thorns not flowers, and they marched deceived."[47]

The warning about the volatility of the Reform Catholic assault on the church would prove prescient. Behind Head of State José María Cornejo, El Salvadoran conservatives rallied to Casaús and against Delgado and the federation's evermore radical reformers. In August of 1830, eleven months after the promulgation of the decree expelling the regular orders, widespread conservative resistance in El Salvador continued to stymy the friars' departure.[48] Although Delgado apparently no longer claimed the bishopric, he continued to don his bishop's regalia, and satirical writings lampooning his preening and his rumored attempts to depose Cornejo in the state assembly appeared on San Salvador's buildings with regularity.[49]

Once a refuge for dissident reformist priests from Nicaragua, Guatemala, and Honduras, El Salvador had become a magnet for ultramontane stalwarts fleeing Morazán's wrath and seeking succor from the ever-more-conservative Head of State Cornejo. Over the course of the next year, Delgado's old clerical nemeses trickled back into the country, despite the federation's mass deportations of both friars and the more flamboyantly ultramontane members of the secular clergy. In July of 1831, Guatemala's liberal government received alarming news. Conservative clerics José Ignacio Saldaña, José León Taboada, Pablo María Sagastume, and Crisonate Salázar had embarked for El Salvador without government permission, and without passports. Despite a federal order to deny them benefices, El Salvador's new vicar had apparently placed them in parishes, presumably with exiled Archbishop Casaús' blessing. El Salvador's conservative government, the report noted, had been corresponding with the exiled archbishop since March.

All four priests graced an earlier list of clerics who had left or been expelled from El Salvador by Delgado. Saldaña and Sagastume ranked among the most dogged of the region's ultramontane pamphleteers. Salazar had thoroughly unnerved Delgado's loyalists in Santa Ana. Taboada had professed his hatred of Delgado's coterie and loyalty to Casaús in 1825, and was available to travel to El Salvador because Guatemala's state government had earlier removed him from Quetzaltenango, where, government officials reported, he and three clerical co-conspirators worked to foment "bloody fanaticism" and undermine liberalism. The government knew Taboada from his earlier exploits, and his former parishioners in Quezaltepeque, El Salvador, continued to speak ill of him, citing his "perverse opinions."[50] The arrival of these battle-tested ultramontane priests in El Salvador, indicates that Delgado was increasingly surrounded, but also demonstrates the lasting destabilizing power of the ultramontane versus Reform Catholic disputes, and the continued centrality of ecclesiastics on the front lines of the battle for hearts and minds.

As he wended his way through El Salvador, a weary Sagastume must have reveled in the ascendant conservatives' warm embrace. He had lost hope of ever returning to his Dolores Isalco parish, he had lamented to Archbishop Casaús in 1827. His penury and the dangers of the times meant he barely eked out a living in the "miserable" Guatemalan parish of Zacualpa; he had earlier implored the archbishop to find him a more comfortable post.[51] Adding to his travails, in 1830 he had fallen victim to the systematic purge of conservative parish priests, despite Zacualpa's concerted efforts to prevent his replacement by a government-approved cleric.[52]

These conservative clerics probably received a warm welcome in the troubled nation if the group of 370 El Salvadorans who broke their silence to condemn Delgado indicates the prevalent mood. The group wanted nothing more than a return to the peace shattered by the "ecclesiastical madness" Delgado had unleashed when he elevated San Salvador's parish to a cathedral in 1824. "The patriots," as they dubbed themselves, denounced the divisive bishop as the prime mover of the three-year war with Guatemala; they bewailed Delgado's violence toward even neutral apolitical priests who failed to energetically support him; and they decried the corrupt doctrines circulated by his clerical appointees. The Delgado-appointed interlopers should be forced out, these patriots insisted, and the sacraments they administered done over by clerics with the hierarchy's imprimatur. The patriots had originally remained silent, they explained, in hopes that ambassador Victor Castrillo's visit to Rome, which had cost El Salvadorans a pretty penny, would sway the Holy Father to approve the new bishopric. They later guarded their tongues out of fear of Delgado's wrath. But when the pope's decision against the new bishopric leaked back into El Salvador, the upstart bishop had simply ignored Rome's emphatic "no." More alarming still, the affrontery continued. Delgado simply ignored Casaús' order removing him from the vicarship of El Salvador. If this was not enough, the patriots reported, the rebel priest schemed to deprive the regular orders of their property and chaplaincies, throwing El Salvador into a "horrifying anarchy." The assembly should remove Delgado from both posts, insist he return his bishop's salary, and oust his clerical minions immediately.[53]

A group of eight clerics shared the patriots' desire to be rid of Delgado. When revolutions assault religion, they explained to El Salvador's state assembly, silence equals criminal misconduct. Every man should soldier in God's cause, and clerics' special mandate to defend the church perforce compelled them into the fray; they would no longer be silent. The 1824 El Salvadoran congress that named Delgado bishop had trespassed on the pope's writ. Clerics elected by the people or appointed by the secular powers fit the Council of Trent's very definition of interlopers; moreover, the perverse Delgado continued to proffer marriage dispensations. Only the conservative assembly's alacrity could stop these outrageous abuses.[54] The El Salvadoran legislative body embraced the task. On the last day of January in 1831, they nullified the Assemblea Extraordinaria's appointment of Delgado as El Salvador's ecclesiastical vicar from September of 1829. In his stead they offered to submit three candidates for the post to the legitimate ecclesiastical authority—presumably Casaús—who they declined to name. They did, however, indicate that the liberal Guatemalan or federal governments were not legitimate ecclesiastical authorities.[55]

Delgado's star was fading but reformist Catholics dominated both the federal and Guatemalan state governments, and the erstwhile bishop still had powerful allies in El Salvador. A new newspaper sympathetic to the Gálvez administration, *El Siglo de Layfayette*, excoriated Delgado's enemies. It informed readers that "intolerance and religious frenzy had powered the avenging arm of a fanatical leader," El Salvador's Cornejo, who had exiled a multitude of clerics and citizens and engaged in electoral fraud. While Guatemala had passed a spate of laws to contain the scandals fanned by friars, the paper further intoned, conservative El

Salvadorans by contrast cozied up to a Spanish bishop, Casaús, to better persecute their countrymen. El Salvadorans, formerly the "most defanatisized people"
of Central America, were increasingly in thrall to *fanáticos*. Cornejo and his fellow
travelers wanted to return to friars, chapels, and tyrants, and represented the return of "servility" and superstition, the reformist Catholic paper warned.[56]

Guatemalan liberals like the powerful Mariano Gálvez had his back, but Delgado
also counted on the support of old friends and countrymen. Reform Catholic
luminary Isidro Menéndez went on an anti-ultramontane rampage in his bishop's defense, citing Reform Catholic wisdom from the previous half century and
skewering the state's "fanatical *serviles*." These conservatives exercised outsized
influence, spewed ultramontane doggerel, and embraced Casáus and even the yoke
of Spain. The exiled archbishop's bid for continued authority in Central America
particularly alarmed the venerable El Salvadoran statesman. Was Delgado the first
government-appointed bishop to exercise his position without Rome's approval,
he asked rhetorically? He was not! The Holy Father had vetoed the constitutional
Spanish state's elevation of Espiga and Muñoz to bishoprics, but they remained
in their posts awaiting the outcome of their appeals—or so Menéndez asserted.

That Menéndez referenced the Holy Father's contretemps with the Spanish
Cortes in the Espiga affair a decade earlier recalls the movement's deep history
and transatlantic self-conception. Espiga stood at the epicenter of the 1799 reformist coterie persecuted by what Minister of State Urquijo described as a Jesuit
court faction around Charles IV. The reformers met regularly at the countess of
Montijo's Madrid salon. Montijo corresponded with Grégoire, and her gathering
boasted bright reformist lights like Joaquin Villanueva and Juan Antonio Llorente.
Tellingly, Sanjuanista Lorenzo de Zavala's Mexico City newspaper, an organ of the
York Rite Masons called *El Aguila Mexicana*, also evoked this reformist cell. In 1825,
the paper noted that the Count of Montijo had languished in an inquisition dungeon until freed during the Liberal Interregnum in 1820.[57] In evoking these movement martyrs, especially Espiga, Menéndez linked Delgado to a celebrated cause
that his readers knew had sent shock waves through Reform Catholic networks
just a decade earlier.

With Llorente in hand, and Espiga's martyrdom fresh on his mind, Menéndez
nudged El Salvador towards a state-run church. Only the Vatican's lackeys puffed
doctrines that contravened the rights of nations, Menéndez insisted, and Casáus
lost his ecclesiastical authority when Guatemala's legislature declared him a traitor
to the nation and he accepted a salary from another country, Spain, while in Cuba.
How could he serve as bishop in a territory where he was not a citizen?[58] Should
Central Americans obey an archbishop resident in Spain's hopelessly decadent
empire over the orders of the properly authorized patriot Alcayaga? Certainly no

nation should publish a papal edict without thorough government vetting, the equivalent of the exequatur previously held by Spanish monarchs.[59]

Menéndez ventured into the backwaters of the Reform Catholic ecclesiology swirling in Central America's radical 1830s. These currents of ecclesiastical reform ran deep and wide. He tapped the Synod of Pistoia's wisdom and Reform Catholic publishing networks to justify his attack on the papacy's jurisdictional creep. The Holy Father, he conceded, stood as the visible head of the church, but spoke only for himself when he legislated unilaterally. Papal briefs dispensed by the pope alone were his personal opinions, not laws of the church.[60]

Menéndez noted that he imbibed this radical ecclesiology in part from the Synod of Pistoia's theological mastermind, Pietro Tamburini, author of the *Vera idea della santa sede (True Idea of the Holy See)*. The work's anonymous Spanish translator had crowned its author the most ferocious fighter against the ultramontane's "exorbitant pretensions." Tamburini's anti-curial screed decried the "fatuous" notion of the papacy as an infallible absolute monarchy and argued for the return of the authority stolen from bishops by false decretals like that of Isidore of Seville. The church's supple conciliar governing structure involving even humble parish priests particularly fired Tamburini's imagination, starkly contrasting with the papacy's sclerotic hierarchy.[61] Tamburini's thought synchronized perfectly with that of his comrades convened in Pistoia: "It is you as well as I who rule in the Church and must share in the reform," Scipione de' Ricci told the 230-plus Synod of Pistoia attendees: "The Kingdom of Jesus Christ is not a despotism or a monarchy."[62]

Tamburini was no stranger to Spanish-speaking reformers like El Salvador's Menéndez. Baltasar Melchor Gaspar María de Jovellanos—statesman, author, and frequent participant in the salons of countess of Montijo—had enthused that all of the University of Salamanca's youth were "Port Royalists of the Pistoian sect," avid readers of the works of Tamburini, Zola, and Obstraet. These works were in "everyone's hands," Jovellanos rhapsodized: after the books were banned, only one of three thousand copies had been dutifully turned over to inquisitors. When the Inquisition demanded that Salamanca's elite students relinquish their copies, they refused to do so. An ecstatic Jovellanos noted that their bravery boded well for Spain's future, when "those who now obey will give the orders." This aptly named exemplar of Reform Catholicism's pared-down Christocentric worship thus echoed the ecclesiology and liberalism of many of the Cortes de Cádiz's members and of Latin America's early liberals.[63]

But if Tamburini and the Synod of Pistoia inspired the venerable El Salvadoran statesman Menéndez and linked him to a previous generation of reformist radicals, it was not the Italian author of *Vera idea della santa sede* but rather the book's mysterious Spanish translator that Menéndez quoted at length. Be Christians without superstition, the stealthy translator exhorted American readers; be Catholics without ultramontanism, be devout but tolerant religious practitioners. Align the church's external discipline to civic needs and the church's early centuries. And if you falter, if you doubt, learn from the disasters wrought by superstition and fanaticism in Spain, where "sterile families" of lazy friars and arrogant clergy dictated to the throne and beguiled the addle-brained into ever-more opposition to rational religious reforms. Americans, he concluded, should guard their homelands from these scourges and the attendant indignities of dependent ultramontanism.[64]

This text yields up further connections to the larger world of ideas animating Central America's godly reform movement. The publisher of the incendiary book, exiled Spanish liberal Mariano Calero, occupied a pivotal position among transatlantic reformers. His London press published the last two years of the newspaper *Ocios de Españoles Imigrados*. It glowingly reviewed Tamburini's *Vera idea della Santa Sede*, insisting that Latin Americans should be grateful for the translation: among the many threats to their liberty stood the Court of Rome with its "ambitious parasites," who deviously set spiritual snares under the pretext of religion and respect for the Church of Jesus Christ. Tamburini showed these Americans where to draw lines between temporal and spiritual authority, the paper enthused.[65] The London-based editors of *Ocios*, the clerical Villanueva brothers Joaquín and Jaime, and other reformist Catholics exiled from Spain to London's Somers Town neighborhood discussed the Atlantic world's intertwined religion and politics at literary salons, including one presided over by an uncle of guerilla fighter and expedition leader Francisco Xavier Mina.[66]

Promoting Tamburini among the Hispanophone exiles and immigrants of London was only part of the Villanueva brothers' contribution to the international cause of Reform Catholicism during Central America's decades of religious turmoil. The editors had undertaken an ambitious tour of Spanish churches to uncover the nation's liturgical rites from antiquity to the present. A critic had poked fun at the brothers' big archival dig by describing Joaquín as a falcon-like man of letters, with big hands and "fingers like a necromancer's," with which he "scratches, extracts and compiles."[67] Jaime's siftings through church cabinets groaning under the weight of moldering documents and Joaquin's cataloguing of their findings hardly represented disinterested scholarship: Reform Catholic historicism was an epistemology, a sanctified path to truth. Their research provided a scientific foil to Rome's gloss on church history and canons, and a justification for a uniquely national Spanish church whose "external discipline" sat firmly under state auspices.[68]

Thus did Dr. Menéndez's defense of Delgado tap the wisdom of reformers, each tendril connecting the Central American schism to a transatlantic network of ideas and actors. His deeply held liberal and Reform Catholic commitments would prove life-long and unwavering in the face of Rome's clear disapproval. In 1831, he crafted a tract that defended Delgado from an El Salvadoran legislative assembly law that declared him unfit for any ecclesiastical office without a formal pardon from the Vatican. This was most certainly not forthcoming, as the pope had in fact formally excommunicated Delgado in 1829 at Casaús' behest, and in accordance with the recommendation of the Commision for Extraordinary Ecclesiastical Affairs. Sharing the news with the canny archbishop, Pius VIII cited Delgado's ongoing schism and his commandeering of control over marriage dispensations as his reason to exile the erstwhile El Salvadoran bishop from Mother Church.[69]

If Menéndez knew of Delgado's excommunication, he studiously ignored it in his spirited defense of his friend. Rome's clerics had colluded with the Spanish court to suffocate Americans' spiritual demands, he charged. The "Enemy of Independence" had prodded the pope to reject the new bishopric. Rome constantly conspired to extend its putative universal jurisdiction and advance its ultramontane agenda. No "independent-minded American," this El Salvadoran reformed Catholic intellectual concluded, should trust an edict against Delgado given these precedents.[70]

Reflecting on the constant turmoil of the previous decade, in 1831 *El Siglo de Layfayette* declared that "religious passion had torn us apart." It was simply naive to imagine Central Americans living harmoniously given this recent history of religious enmity. After independence, an "exclusive religion" had proclaimed itself opposed to republican principles, but the republicans had triumphed nonetheless, demonstrating to the people that rights and religion could march cheek-by-jowl. Alas, victory proved fleeting, as "infamous atheists" collaborated with "fanatics," the "ignorant masses," and the corrupt faction of the clergy to resist democratic innovations and dethrone liberty. Tragically, even with the expulsion of the friars after the liberals' 1829 victory, remaining "fanatics" continued to cast reformers as heretics and schismatics. The paper urged fellow citizens to support new laws guaranteeing religious tolerance as the only means to permanently end fratricidal blood-letting.[71]

Lest readers think their endorsement of religious toleration signaled their atheism rather than their deep adhesion to the Reform Catholic International, the liberal reformist Catholic paper called upon a tried and true reformer. The paper entreated the "august ghost of Grégoire" to depart its tomb and urge congressmen to embrace republican firmness, enlightened piety, and the zeal for the public good. If they were true Catholics or even secular philosophes, the paper intoned, these representatives would find in Grégoire a guiding light on the proposed religious toleration law. The "independents, republicans, and

federalists" in Guatemala's new government would surely welcome this venerable French reformer, the paper enthused, as they owed their seats to the liberal restoration of 1829 that had "broken the scepter of religious fanaticism."[72]
Subsequent events would prove that the "scepter of religious fanaticism" was
anything but broken.

8

The Long Shadow

MEXICO'S *REFORMA*

THE COMBATANTS HAD withdrawn from the literal field of battle in Central America by the middle decades of the nineteenth century, but the fundamental conflicts over theology and ecclesiology could still bring the opposing sides to arms. Mexico's signal moment of constitutional conflict, the War of the Reform that rent the country from 1857 to 1860, was animated by many of the same concerns.[1] The divisions remained salient in that war's continuation, the French imperial intervention of 1861 to 1867, when the ultramontane church actively supported the foreign empire.

For more than forty years, the homeland of Fray Servando Teresa de Mier had been both denounced and championed throughout the Atlantic World as a critical breeding ground of the Reform Catholic International. The explosively dangerous cache of literature that had landed this father of Mexican independence in chains back in 1817 was, above all else, a portable library of Reform Catholic literature and of national constitutions and federalist writings. Mier would have recognized Mexico's 1857 Constitution as the heir of this sacred intelligence. So did many of the constitution's own champions at the time.

Their interpretation has been underrepresented in subsequent historical literatures. Instead, historians of Latin America's mid-nineteenth-century liberals have concluded that the movement's program of church-state separation amounted to an unambiguous secularization drive.[2] Certainly the means suggest

For God and Liberty. Pamela Voekel, Oxford University Press. © Oxford University Press 2023.
DOI: 10.1093/oso/9780197610190.003.0009

this end: between their initial success in the 1850s and their subsequent displacement by conservative forces allied with the French invaders, the liberals placed birth, death, and marriage rites under state auspices; ended the church's special privileges and prerogatives; and removed religious expression from the streets and corralled it into the home or the church building.

But a closer look at the actors' own paper trail suggests a radically different interpretation of their motives. Far from seeking to remove religion from Mexican national life, they were instead consumed with refashioning the Catholic Church from within, with paring down its hierarchy and simplifying its liturgy without eliminating its central mysteries. In place of Romish excess they envisioned not a secular society but a Godly alternative.

As we have seen, Reform Catholicism as far back as the early eighteenth century had advocated for civil control over the church, not out of animosity to religion but in order to create more godly empires and states. Central American reformers had imbibed this wisdom from such reformist luminaries as Pietro Tamburini and the Synod of Pistoía, who had described and circulated the civil power's long historical genealogy of rightful dominance of the church.[3] Mexico's liberals formed a central node in the mid-century Reform Catholic International. They were anything but secular, and, like El Salvador's reformist Catholic liberals we saw earlier, exhibited as much if not more religious passion than did the conservative forces they battled during Mexico's War of the Reform.[4]

The centrality of Reform Catholicism to Mexican liberalism of the mid-century is brought into high relief by the 1859 establishment of a schismatic Catholic Church under state protection—the opposite of state-driven secularization. Prominent liberals cast their newly created Constitutional Clergy as critical messengers of a simple, ethical piety that blossomed in the Christian fraternity and God-given sentiment required to bind the fractured nation together. In so doing, they echoed reformist advocates of constitutionally constituted church authority that we have seen in previous chapters. Sanjuanista founder Father Vicente Velázquez in Mérida, El Salvador's heroes of independence José Matías Delgado and José Simeón Cañas, and cleric and liberal editor Miguel José de Castro y Lara—all promoted the sacred polity envisioned by Mier and briefly realized in Mexico at the end of the 1850s.

This schismatic national church would prove a resounding failure.[5] With its stress on individual and unmediated conscience and its cult of masculine sensibility, its creed sanctified the male laity's leadership. In effect, with their very fervor for lay individualism, the reformed church's leaders put themselves out of a job. Their rapid disappearance combined with liberalism's subsequent and undeniably more secular career has misled observers into ignoring the liberals' own interpretations of their fight. Mexican liberalism certainly spawned idol-smashing secularists, but it was born Christian.

CHURCH AND STATE IN POST-INDEPENDENCE MEXICO

The period between Mexican Independence and the US invasion of 1847 is famously one of political chaos: fifty military regimes, the products of a relentless series of coups; invasions by Spain and France and, decisively, by the United States; breakaway states in the north and gulf south.[6] On paper, Mexico emerged from its war for independence with a constitution marked by two provisions that would come under cross-cutting pressures over the next three decades. First, it asserted that "The religion of the Mexican nation is and shall be perpetually the Catholic, Apostolic, Roman religion." Second, rather than echoing the radical demand of equal law for every individual that had marked the insurgent constitution of Apatzingán of 1814, the new ruling document sought to cement the allegiance of the military and the church by preserving their respective corporate privileges, or *fueros*.

The 1824 constitution underwent a series of amendments and revisions, first in 1836, alongside official recognition of Mexican independence by both Spain and the Holy See, and then again in 1841–1842. This latter constitutional convention produced a draft that retained the Roman Catholic religion as Mexico's official faith but resurrected the demand of individual rights and equal standing before the law, effectively a liberal revocation of the *fueros*. The army promptly defended its corporate interests by shutting down this congress and in its place the acting president summoned a reliable body of conservative clerics, jurists, and landowners. A new constitution was penned that dropped any reference to liberal individual rights and even left the door open for the importation of a European monarch to assume control of Mexico. This document remained in effect only briefly before falling victim in turn to the turmoil of simultaneous civil war and territorial defense against the United States in 1846: the ubiquitous General Antonio López de Santa Anna, restored to power, promptly revived the 1824 constitution.

At the conclusion of the Mexican-American War in 1848, then, the constitutional order of a quarter-century earlier had been restored. Meanwhile, the liberal argument for disentailment of church properties had percolated through the dizzying series of alternating administrations and military strong-arm rule since Independence. In 1831, the reformist priest José María Luis Mora, father of Mexican liberalism, had won a prize for his essay on the respective property rights of the church and the state. His plan offered a principled, ideologically liberal argument for divesting the church of ownership of resources it could control but not develop. He had an opportunity to put some of these principles into action two years later when General Santa Anna, his independence-era heroism refreshed by his expulsion of the 1829 Spanish invasion, was elected president. The duties of governance, however, did not suit him, and policy fell to his liberal vice-president, Valentín Gómez Farías, an ally of Mora's. Several reformist Catholic goals were achieved under their guidance: civil enforcement was removed from tithing and from monastic vows, so that now both forms of pious sacrifice became entirely voluntary. Further, with an eye to possible future forced liquidation of church real estate, the sale of such properties by the regular orders— the chief landowners within the church—was declared illegal and past transfers voided. The goal here was to prevent cut-rate transfers of title to church allies among the wealthy laity.[7]

Liquidating the property that was monopolized in the "dead hands" of the church, then, was a liberal economic goal as well as a Reform Catholic principle. However, in the years leading up to the War of the Reform, the political realities became increasingly complicated: both conservatives and liberals needed the frozen assets of the church to run their alternating military campaigns against invaders, against indigenous rebellions in Yucatán and the Northern deserts, and against each other. Santa Anna in particular—vacillating between the two political camps as he rotated between power and exile—became adept at playing church fears of complete disentailment off against only slightly less coercive pressures for loans that were unlikely ever to be repaid to their ecclesiastical creditors.[8]

Santa Anna's final tour of duty in the presidency elevated the conservatives' priorities. Between 1853 and 1855, the general superordinated the church, appointing the archbishop as state councillor and welcoming the Jesuits back to Mexico. In a move that was to have unforeseen reverberations, the president also exiled the former liberal governor of Michaocán Melchor Ocampo, an eloquent advocate of religious toleration and critic of the high fees that poor parishioners were forced to pay for priestly services. During his two years in New Orleans, Ocampo befriended and radicalized his fellow exile Benito Juárez, the Zapotec Indian and devout, austere Catholic who would ultimately become president of the Mexico in 1858.[9]

After the final overthrow of Santa Anna in 1855—the end of his eleventh turn in power—a new generation of liberals came to positions of influence within the succeeding government. Most had spent some portion of their youth exiled or imprisoned, and had all imbibed Mora's systematic liberal program. In power under the presidency of the relatively non-ideological General Juan Alvarez, they instituted a liberal program in keeping with Mora's own vision.

"IN THE NAME OF GOD:" THE CONSTITUTION OF 1857 AND THE REVOLT OF THE CHURCH

The first of the Laws of the Reform was named for its author Benito Juárez, the Zapotec minister of justice. The 1855 Juárez Law abolished the privilege of clerical immunity before civil law: by restricting the jurisdiction of the ecclesiastical courts to purely ecclesiastical matters, it asserted civil authority over clerics. The response was immediate: under the slogan *"religión y fueros"* (religion and corporate privileges) bands comprising priests, army officers, and conservative catholic laymen rose of in revolt against the Juarez Law in scattered actions around the country. In January of 1856, the conservative rebellion seized the city of Puebla and set up a rival government. It was overpowered by federal forces and the church's collusion in the rebellion punished with confiscation of property, However, this would proceed with some care, given the scale of the original reaction.

The next step in liberal reform was therefore the Lerdo Law of June, 1856, named for Minster of Finance Miguel Lerdo de Tejada. This required the church— in practice, mostly the rent-collecting regular orders—to sell its real estate to the tenants at an attractive discount. If the tenants declined the purchase, the government would then sell it at public auction. Further, the church was prohibited from acquiring property in the future. The church reacted with defiance and non-compliance.

Finally, José María Iglesias, successor to Juárez as minister of justice, authored his eponymous law of April 1857. The Iglesias Law prohibited parish priests from collecting fees for baptizing, marrying, or presiding at the deaths and funerals of the poor, or refusing to provide those sacraments for free to those unable to pay. The church again refused to comply.

These three laws were the prelude. The main act was the constitutional congress that was meeting in 1856 and 1857, at which many of the leading lights of Mexican liberalism came into their own. The church was the central issue dividing liberals from conservatives in these debates, but not because one side was secular and the other religious.

Opening with the words "In the name of God and the authority of the Mexican people," the 1857 Constitution was largely the crowning achievement of Mexican liberalism. Their deliberations suffused with prayer and invocations of faith, the constitutional congress sought the purification of the state by restoring of the simple interior piety of Reform Catholicism. For the first time the governing document dropped the identification of Mexico as a Catholic country and asserted "freedom of conscience." The Juárez Law and the Lerdo Law were largely incorporated into the new constitution. And the old claim of equality before the law, asserted in the symbolic 1814 Apatzingán constitution, was now the law of the land. The *fueros* were abolished, civil protections extended, debtors' prisons abolished, habeas corpus and the right to defense established. Universal manhood suffrage was declared, except for vagrants and prisoners.[10]

In December of 1857, conservative army units in Mexico City rebelled against the constitution. They dissolved the congress, arrested Juárez in his capacity as president of the supreme court—and thus legal successor to the deposed president—and installed General Félix Zuloaga. Juárez managed to escape to Querétaro, where he assembled his rival government. The war was on.

With mass support in many cities and some rural regions, the liberals were able to assemble an army. As their manifesto of July, 1859, asserted, the war was the fault of the church, and by rebelling against the government it had made itself subject to a new wave of reforms: confiscation of all church property, now including capital as well as real estate, the completely voluntary payment of fees for priestly parish services, the official separation of church and state, and the abolition of monasteries and of novitiates in nunneries.[11]

After almost exactly three years of civil war, the liberals were to prove victorious over their opponents, those champions of "*religión y fueros.*" The hierarchy loyal to the pope had enlisted the ultramontane church as an unabashed combatant in a civil war, and they were now the vanquished traitors to the republic. "Eminent liberals literally picked up axes to destroy altars, church facades, pulpits, and confessionals," summarizes Enrique Krauze. "Images of saints were decapitated, shot full of holes, burned in public *autos-da-fé*; Church treasuies were robbed, archives were plundered, ecclesiastical libraries went up in flames. Bishops were stoned to death and Church property was auctioned off."[12] When in 1861 France took the opportunity of Mexican debt and a United States distracted by its own civil war to invade Mexico, its imperial mission found ready allies in the conservative church and the elite laymen loyal to the pope. The War of the Reform continued in a new guise for six more years.

HIERARCHY VERSUS CONSCIENCE

Their own archives reveal that literate liberals had a decidedly transcendent sense of mission: they were fighting an epic battle in the larger religious war that had wracked the Christian world for centuries. Like earlier reform-minded Catholics in Mexico and throughout the Atlantic world, Mexican liberals distrusted religious hierarchy in general and reserved their most vituperative fire for the pope in particular, contrasting his opulent earthly empire to the simplicity of the primitive church. Saint Bernard knew that "the popes were created to serve, not to give orders," they insisted, and Christ would certainly have agreed with him; and furthermore "with their pretensions to monarchy the popes imitated Constantine but not Peter."[13] With the pope's fall, the church would cease to be the instrument of worldly ambition and the old councils and assemblies would be reborn amidst the glorious efflorescence of Christianity's heroic age, they predicted: "The modern revolution that ushered in liberty and equality under the law, would now reconcile itself with Christianity, which had brought liberty and equality to conscience."[14] Conscience was the enforcer of moral order that liberals offered in place of the hierarchy's authority.[15]

By the radical liberal reformist Catholics' reckoning, the pope represented a feudal relic in a world aflame with democratic passion, a despot leagued with those twin enemies of progress: aristocracy and divine-right monarchy. After noting that the church preached fidelity to the cross but not to Christ, liberal Pedro T. Echeverria satirized the classic catechism. Taking on the voice of a mock conservative, his pamphlet begged the pope to liberate Mexico from the liberal heretics in the name of that unholy trinity, "the aristocracy, tyranny, and Mammon."[16] Other public champions of liberalism noted that absolute power was simply anachronistic in the nineteenth century: the world needed a pope willing to declare that democracy and the Bible shared the same spirit.[17] To the conservative assertion that despotism reigned supreme in non-Catholic countries, they pointed to the sad state of affairs in Rome, where the nobility had united with the papacy and a swarm of parasites lived from their abuses.[18]

Just as they devalued priestly access to the Divine, these reformist Catholics likewise denied reports of communication with Heaven through saints and miracles. In a typical instance, liberal journalists took on the supposed miracle of lush vegetation surrounding a cross in a dry little town. Their investigation revealed the hidden tubing that brought water from a nearby convent, and they proudly publicized the subsequent dehydration that occurred when they disconnected the pipe.[19] Likewise, the liberal army's official paper ridiculed the conservative troops' "superstition," noting that they attributed their successful defense of a particular plaza to the intervention of San Francisco.[20] Orations to render prisoners invisible to guards, miraculous powers attributed to Santiago's horse, chants to invoke lost objects or rid oneself of unwelcome guests—all this scattered devotion rightly belonging to God alone and distracted from the valuable lessons to be learned from the saints' virtue and compassion.[21]

Moreover, a God who oscillated wildly between avenging wrath and miraculous mercy contravened the ethical truths found in scripture, which all men imbued with reason and conscience could read for themselves. "Millions of souls will

divorce themselves from the bad clergy," the liberal press predicted, but not to become secular rationalists: to the contrary, they would "conserve the most powerful
connection, the belief in just one Book."[22] All of the ambitious church councils,
fatuous monarchs, the Vatican, canons, and even the eloquence of the Church
Fathers were not worth the science, truth, love, and, indeed, liberalism found on
just one page of the Bible.[23]

The church's continuous emphasis on the exterior cult of worship constituted
the biggest threat to this purified piety that would bind the nation together. Why
give alms to an institution when they could go directly to suffering humanity and
simultaneously make visible one's inner experience of God? And why give to a
church that would most likely squander the money on useless distractions like
the cult of the saints or elaborate decorations, unbridled luxury—with all of its
enervating effect? Why indeed, thundered Ponciano Arriaga from the wellspring
of his soul and the pages of the liberal Mexico City paper the *Monitor Republicano*:

> It would be bitter indeed to see inside a church on the day of its patron saint
> celebration curtains of rich silk, chasubles, gilded objects, ornaments of pure
> gold, branches of bright silver, incense holders, and chalices of emerald and
> other precious stones while there exists in the portices of the same temple
> dedicated to the God of Love (*Díos de la Caridad*) a multitude of blind men,
> lepers, and the sick pallid with hunger, exhausted by misery, pulling them-
> selves along the ground and extending their squalid hands for a handout, for
> the charity that one asks for in Christ's name and in the name of the same
> saint in whose honor they pay the noisy orchestra, Italian singers, and fire
> works . . . cover your face, Holy Charity! . . . nothing is true, nothing is just,
> nothing correct, nothing legitimate, especially not for the Christian clergy,
> without love (*caridad*) and good works.[24]

The message also emerged in literature. Ignacio Manuel Altamirano's short story
La Navidad en las montañas (Christmas in the Mountains), for example, united
the aesthetic of simple reformist Catholicism with republicanism, ostensibly as a
tale told to the author by a soldier in the liberal ranks one Christmas night. In a
small village, the soldier had stumbled across an exemplar of the reformed clergy.
The good brother-priest collected no money for baptisms, weddings, and Masses
and had founded schools, improved agriculture, and introduced the mechanical
arts. Overcome by this news, the soldier dismounts from his horse, embracing
the priest and affirming that he loved Christianity "when I find it as pure as it
was in the first magnificent days of the gospel."[25] Stripped of side altars to the
saints, the humble parish church held only a small altar adorned with a manger

scene, which the narrator described as a concession to "the parish's tender imagination, which was not yet entirely free of old inclinations."[26] Bare walls and sturdy benches greeted the parishioners, who listened with rapt attention but exhibited no "servile cringing" to the good brother. During services that evening the priest recounted the simple story of Christ's birth, adding some "consoling and eloquent reflections on human brotherhood and charity."[27] All of the brother-priest's democratic goodness was contrasted with the bad former town priest, who had supported the conservative army and devised a series of small festivals to new saints to profit from the faithful's donations.[28]

As liberals fought the last remnants of the corporate privileges of Mexico's colonial society, particularly those of the church, they proposed a new religious *esprit social* to replace the *esprit de corps* that had formerly reigned: simple Christian love and charity, a form of Christian humanism, catapulted believers above petty corporate and mere party interests into a world of natural, God-given bonds between all men, a universal rather than particularistic ideology. Or, as the *Monitor Republicano* more eloquently put it: "Christian charity, now emerging from the fonts where it had been hidden, would overflow hearts and fertilize a new society"; it would save religion from an old society "grown so hopeless from the yoke of fanaticism that it wanted to break all religious bonds."[29]

This national sentiment manifested itself in republican simplicity, in the asceticism that made public the believers' relationship with God. Echoing the calls for simplicity and antipathy to baroque Catholicism of Bourbon church and state reformers and independence-era insurgent publications, as well as the centrality of luxury to economic debates at the turn of the nineteenth century, in a description entirely typical of liberal hagiography, an anonymous writer made explicit this link between sentiment, simplicity, and the virtue that marked a man eligible to lead his fellow citizens. When Juárez arrived in Veracruz from exile to join his compatriots, the author explained, they escorted him to a reception room decorated "not with the luxury and ostentation that palace courtiers deploy to flatter princes and tyrants, but with the simplicity and decency appropriate to republicanism." Veracruz had eschewed triumphal arches and fireworks, because "these exteriorities disgust the true republican." Men deserved public acclaim for "their elevated principles, their pure sentiments, and the rectitude of their actions"; sensual ceremony was no way to express public approval for liberal leaders.[30]

Indeed, Mexican liberals read even the great rallying cry of the French Revolution "Liberty, Equality, and Fraternity" through a decidedly Christian lens. "Christ emancipated the spirit . . . and placed at the font of all morality the sacred dogma of human liberty. . . . [B]ecause of this, from the first instant that this doctrine entered the conscience, one felt this great movement of emancipation that would end until Christianity triumphed as a social doctrine. Equality, fraternity, and liberty are the core of Christianity's message."[31] And lest anyone doubt this, the Liberal *Monitor Republicano* reminded readers of the biblical case for fraternal over hierarchical bonds: "Whosoever will be great among you, let him be your servant. And whosoever shall be chief among you, let him be your servant (Mathew 20: 26-27)." Who could fail to see in Christ's simple instructions the transparent message of "fraternity and the principles of republicanism and democracy upon which the Church was founded?"[32]

Thus reformers aflame with a desire to return to the church's pristine democratic purity confronted an ultramontane institutional church sidling towards papal infallibility and energetically promoting pilgrimage, the saints, and the cults of Mary and the Sacred Heart of Jesus; here were the battlelines in Mexico in the mid-nineteenth century.[33] Although often demonizing the liberals as atheists and even communists, the conservative clergy also read reformers' attacks on the church not as philosophical secularism but rather as a specific religious misinterpretation, specifically what they termed the heresy of eighteenth-century Jansenism, in actuality a Mexico-specific branch of the Reform Catholic International.[34]

Their campaigns demonstrably affected the laity's pious sensibilities. Mid-nineteenth-century testators echoed reformist Catholic intellectuals' invidious contrast of true charity and benevolence with the frivolous and spiritually void exterior cult. The pious bequests contained in 350 wills from each of the three periods of 1710–1720, 1810–1820, and 1850–1860 tell a story of steadily increasing concern for the poor and declining support for the pomp and splendor of the cult of worship. Whereas during the period of 1710–1720, only 33 of the 138 testators who made pious bequests gave specifically to the poor, a hundred years later 49 of the 65 testators who left gifts did so. By mid-century, a full 67 percent of Mexico City residents leaving bequests designated the poor as recipients, with over half of these giving exclusively to the destitute. The candles, bells, and rich cloth to adorn the saints faded from the wills to be replaced by gifts given directly to the indigent.[35] Whether mid-century testators concerned with the poor definitively shared the liberals' theology and politics remains uncertain and perhaps ultimately unknowable, for to tacitly acknowledge *caridad* as an important social value was not necessarily to recognize radical liberals as its definitive exemplars. As well, to reject the baroque religiosity still prevalent in the late eighteenth century was not necessarily to reject the mid-nineteenth century Ultramontane International, whose identity was based more on its Rome-centered ecclesiology and its promotion of Marian cults and the Cult of the Sacred Heart than on elaborate baroque ceremony. In 1870, the decree *Pastor aeternus* declared the pope infallible. In 1854, Pope Pius IX declared the Immaculate Conception of Mary official dogma, an event enthusiastically celebrated in Mexico City's cathedral in 1855; Juan José de Aycinena reported on a similar ceremony in Guatemala City that year. In 1860, exiled ultramontane priests returned to Mexico and energetically promoted the cult of the Sacred Heart. The devotion represented a critique of liberal modernity.[36] In 1864, the pope beatified Margarita María Alacoque, the founder of the cult of the Sacred Heart of Jesus, and issued the encyclical *Quanta cura*, which declared the Sacred Heart a remedy against the church's many enemies.[37]

MEXICAN LIBERALS AND THE REFORM CATHOLIC INTERNATIONAL

Like their predecessors in Latin America and Spain, Mexico's reformist Catholics had deep intellectual and social roots in their own country, but they were also in conversation with a Reform Catholic International that spanned the Spanish-speaking Atlantic world. Religion and liberty were inextricably linked but clerical ignorance thwarted this simple truth, noted *El Constitucional*, citing such champions of liberal Catholicism as Abbé Felicité de Lamennais and Père Lacordaire.[38] In 1830, Lamennais and Lacordaire founded the journal *L'Avenir*, whose motto "God and Liberty" summed up the tenor of the entire venture. The pope forced the men to make a statement of doctrinal submission in 1833 and Lamennais lived out his remaining years a bitter man, refusing to cede to papal authority while Lacordaire went on to found *L'Ere Nouvelle*, which staunch ultramontane Louis Veuillot sarcastically tagged "erreur nouvelle."[39] When asked his opinion on the separation of church and state, Lacordaire quipped that "It was not with a cheque drawn on Caesar's bank that Jesus sent His Apostles out into the world."[40] *El Heraldo* offered for sale to its readers Italian Giuseppe Mazzine's *The Pope in the Nineteenth Century*.[41] Their enthusiasm for this illustrious father of Italian nationalism is not difficult to fathom. In an 1834 letter to Lamennais, Mazzine rehearsed fundamental Reform Catholic tenets: "The thought of the time rejects every intermediary between humanity and the source of life. In our epoch, humanity will forsake the pope and have recourse to a general council of the Church—that is to say, of all believers. The papacy has destroyed religious faith through materialism far more degrading and fatal than that of the eighteenth century."[42]

If *El Heraldo* found Europe's reformist Catholic intellectuals inspiring, *El Siglo Diez y Nueve* found fellow co-religionists closer to home. Giant of Peruvian liberalism Francisco de Paula González Vigil opined on the evils of papal pretensions and the virtues of Christianity's early centuries in the Mexican paper in 1857, displaying the reform movement's familiar juxtaposition of simple biblical ethics to the church's overweening power and unbridled hoarding of riches.[43] On receiving

Vigil's eight-volume magnum opus *Defensa de la autoridad de los gobiernos y de los obispos contra las pretensiones de la Curia Romana* (*Defense of the Authority of Governments and Bishops Against the Pretensions of the Roman Curia*) Pius IX is said to have exclaimed "How is it that even in the land of St. Rose they persecute me? Well, to the *Index* with the diabolical work!"[44] An 1851 papal brief prohibited the book and excommunicated Vigil. But Rome, a frustrated Vigil lamented, had mistaken his intentions: he merely wanted to separate Catholicism from "curalist pretensions so that it would remain Christian and humanitarian," not "de-Catholize Peru."[45] In a work published in Guadalajara in 1856, cleric José Ignacio Victor Eyzaguirre denounced Roman Catholicism's detractors the world over, and joined Peru's ultramontane Catholic press in accusing González Vigil of heresy. He laid the blame for the small country's "twenty years of anarchy" squarely at the feet of Peruvian liberals' fondness for "rationalism and Jansenism."[46]

As historian Frederick B. Pike points out, in questioning papal authority and in vaunting apostolic Christianity as the only real religion, González Vigil and his fellow liberals were less secular reformers than religious heretics who sought to mold the church's interior workings to their own democratic ideals. Peruvian Liberals' decidedly religious heresy, Pike convincingly argues, added a measure of vindictiveness and bitterness to the country's political struggles, which became, in essence, religious ones.[47]

THE CONSTITUTIONAL CLERGY OF MEXICO

The explicit link between the longstanding global battle within the church and the larger War of the Reform was vividly demonstrated in 1859 by a renegade clutch of Mexico City clergymen. These priests could trace their own theological allegiance back to the reformed piety's turn-of-the-century heyday, but the revitalized ultramontane current had the upper hand in the capital's archbishopric. Alarmed by the archbishop's "incendiary pastorals," the priests sent a representative, Rafael Díaz Martínez, to the Liberal Party's camp in Veracruz to request aid in their battle with the church hierarchy. The Liberals, they hoped, would support their struggle to wean the faithful away from the "seditious ramblings of false ministers" and toward a true understanding of the sacrifice of the original martyr for democracy, Jesus Christ.[48]

Díaz Martínez received a warm welcome in Veracruz among the liberal defenders of "true religion." At his behest, these liberals extended the mantle of their protection to clergymen who dedicated themselves to "administering to souls and cultivating the Lord's vineyard."[49] Melchor Ocampo, later to be remembered as the father of the Mexico's civil marriage laws and for his role in the wartime Juárez administration, was among the liberals camped out in the port city. In contrast to his well-known denunciations of parish priests who indebted the poor with high fees for parish services, Ocampo enthusiastically lauded these virtuous lower clergy who "consoled the poor, visited the sick, and, in keeping with their ministry, tried to end hunger, nudity, and misery." These reformed clergy, Ocampo predicted, would improve that favorite liberal cause, public education, because instead of learning "rancid silliness and ultramontanism, the young would imbibe morality."[50]

The liberals sheltering in Veracruz further decreed that as the government's agent in this endeavor, Díaz Martínez should encourage his fellow reformed prelates to win their flocks to the liberal Constitution of 1857. The priests could reassure the public that the document adhered to Christian principles and that the new laws issued from Veracruz represented the triumphant return of the church's primitive democratic doctrines—an timeworn reformist argument frequently heard during the 1857 Constitutional Convention. Signed by Melchor O'Campo, the founding document of the Constitutional Clergy made vague references to state salaries for these liberal priests but it also underlined the liberals' commitment to the separation of church and state. Thus it firmly promised little more than government protection from decidedly antagonistic ecclesiastical superiors, and their "ultramontane ideas" and "intolerable despotism."[51]

Returning to Mexico City with the triumphant liberal forces on January 1, 1861, Díaz Martínez and nine other priests petitioned for three centrally located churches, citing as justification their efforts to procure peace in the republic and a record of blessing without charge over 400 civil marriages as well as numerous baptisms and burials. The parishes of La Merced, San Hipólito, and La Santísima were quickly turned over to them in early January.[52]

The opposition to this reform proved fast and fierce, and, as it had in El Salvador, control over the sacraments became a particular flashpoint. In January of 1861, the lay voice of the ultramontane forces, *El Pájaro Verde*, informed the public that La Merced offered the sacraments without the ecclesiastical authorities' approval and that at least one priest had no license; La Santísima was now under civil, not ecclesiastical, jurisdiction, the paper added.[53] The Cathedral Chapter, which had prudently followed the archbishop's advice to stop sermons during such trying times, now counseled a return to preaching to combat "the dissidents in La Merced who were leading even stalwart women away from true belief."[54]

Defenders of the conservative church even hovered outside the reformers' church doors before Mass, waylaying the faithful and informing them that the Constitutional Clergy had been officially excommunicated.[55] The conservative laity also stood firm, petitioning the government to keep the Constitutional Clergy out of the parishes of San Miguel and Santa Veracruz.[56] Pasquinades attacking these liberal clerics as schismatics and Protestants appeared on church doors one Sunday in February; in response, the following Sabbath churchgoers were greeted with a retraction. The Cathedral Chapter forcefully disavowed authorship of the preceding week's screed and noted that the laity committed no error in patronizing the dissidents, who were indeed true Catholics and strictly adhered to church dogma. While the liberal press gloatingly chalked up a victory for the "truly religious" in their battle with the "fanaticism" of the "vulgar superstitious," *El Pájaro Verde* stiffly noted that the Cathedral Chapter would not have voiced their opinions with a clandestine press; the retraction was entirely apocryphal.[57]

Not surprisingly, the forces arrayed against the dissidents in Mexico City took their cue from the church hierarchy, many of whom had been exiled by the victorious liberals.[58] From the very moment of the Constitutional Clergy's 1859 inception, the hierarchy had decried the reformed clerics' threat. Here was Satan's synagogue, a gathering place for the followers of Luther and Calvin, an invention of Jansenism and Regalism, the hierarchy warned, and "the true Catholic would not be prisoner to this schismatic and impious propaganda . . . [but would instead] close his ears to the pompous prating of the demagogic reformers and obey only the authorized voice of his pastors."[59]

With these clear instructions, the impassioned conservative newspapers *La Unidad Católica* and *El Pájaro Verde* defended the faith in the bishops' absence, publishing lists of priests and deacons who had strayed from Mother Church as well as the subsequent retractions, retorts, and wavering of many of those same priests and deacons. When the liberal press called for a public discussion the accuseds'q errors, the conservative newspapermen fired back that there was nothing to discuss: the dissidents disagreed with their bishops and no less an authority than San Cipriano made it clear that when a schism occurred those who broke with the hierarchy were the schismatics. The Constitutional Clergy were no longer Roman Catholics.[60]

After four tense months, in early May the Constitutional Clergy beat a temporary retreat from their three parishes in Mexico City, not returning again until September. The now-chastened clerics confessed that they were few and that, alas, as the conservative Catholic press suggested, they might indeed fail on this second attempt to establish churches in the city. But they attributed this possibility not to the tepid lay enthusiasm charged by *La Unidad Católica*, but to clerical intrigue, the official church's overwhelming wealth, and the continued disrespect for freedom of religion. Intrigue was hardly the worst of it: the conservative clergy were in fact plotting a Saint Bartholomew Day type massacre, the liberals announced, an orgy of violence in which they would "bathe themselves in the liberal heretics' blood, as the fanatical French Catholics did in the blood of the Huguenots."[61]

Here the clerics expressed rumors that had earlier ricocheted around the nervous city.[62] In a provocative move, the *Pájaro Verde* had earlier denounced the Huguenot violence that had provoked what they insinuated was a legitimate French Catholic outburst—the convents sacked, the priests strung up, the faithful murdered during solemn processions through the streets.[63] Clearly both sides of this civil war likewise felt that they skirmished in a larger religious war.

The repression of external religious frivolities, the Constitutional Clergy's favorite battle in this war, must be seen in light of this long transatlantic struggle for the soul of the church itself. In December of 1860, the victorious liberals prohibited the public procession of the Host to the homes of the sick and dying.[64] Liberal writers applauded the move: Constitutional Clergy leader and *Monitor Republicano* editorialist Juan N. Enríquez Orestes burlesqued the communicants at the cathedral who on their knees worshipped "the mules and the driver, who, with his hat on, drove the carriage that conveyed the Host." These fervent Mexicans reminded him of the "Israelites who worshipped the golden calf"— those oft-invoked idolaters.[65] He himself took the Host to the sick under his robes.[66]

In a world where religion was politics and politics had such deep religious hues, the law against the Eucharist's public procession and the Constitutional Clergy's naked satire quickly became a flashpoint of conservative resistance. To the accusation that the lights, mules, sacristans, priests, and bells that accompanied the Eucharist dignified "the most indifferent things and suffocated good sentiment," *El Pájaro Verde* took up cudgels in what they cast as a classic Catholic battle against heretics: the defense of Christ's real presence in the Eucharist. "Although God might be everywhere," they responded to the liberals' insinuations of exactly that, "He that is in the Host is not only God, but the man called Christ."[67]

But rather than addressing the Eucharistic issue with the rationalist arguments against transubstantiation, the liberal press took great pains to underscore that they challenged only the exterior trappings of religion and never the essential sacraments and doctrines themselves. The criticism stung nonetheless, as they were widely perceived to be attacking the central mystery of the faith, in the tradition of the Protestant heretic John Calvin. *La Unidad Católica* made sure readers understood this connection, noting that even the French Luis XIV softened a law of religious tolerance by decreeing that Calvinists cease and desist from their provocative singing when the Eucharist passed; more recently, Napoleon made Jews and Protestants adorn their houses for Eucharistic processions, the paper added.[68] The wars of religion raged on, far from Wittenberg and Geneva.

THE PIOUS WOMEN OF MEXICO

While the liberal and conservative newspapers wrangled, the female faithful took to the streets to defend the ultramontane church, just as their foresisters had in Mérida and in San Salvador. Upward of 150 women from the parish of San Miguel petitioned the president to accompany the Host in January of 1861, an event widely reported in the papers. Even after the government flatly denied their request and reiterated its prohibition of public religious acts, the nocturnal processions continued.[69] In early February of 1861, the priest of Santa Veracruz Parish was imprisoned and released the next day after an animated group of his female parishioners accompanied the Host out of the parish church into the streets.[70] Shortly thereafter, a neighborhood inspector arrested and imprisoned twenty-one women, one layman, and a priest as they amassed near the door of San Juan de Díos parish awaiting the Host's exit so they could "continue their scandals."[71]

Radical liberals no doubt remembered the petitions signed by thousands of Mexico City women who, along with groups of women from the provinces, had rallied to defend the bishops and church wealth and defeat the cause of religious freedom in 1856.[72] Over 800 Morelia women asked the government to release Clemente de Jesús Munguia and return him to his bishopric, noting that although laws and government were not the domain of the their sex, they could indeed attest to his unassailable character.[73] The *"beatas fanáticas"* and *"ancianas supersticiosas"* who haunted liberals were all too real.[74]

The Mexico City women who processed with the Eucharist were simply one brigade in the larger battle between the sexes. "Who had not heard a seditious sermon, who did not have a wife, daughter, or mother who from the confessional brought discord into the domestic home," asked the *Boletín del Ejército Federal* in response to its own question of who sustained the reactionaries.[75] Cultivated ladies crowned the brows of the assassins of Tacubaya the day of their triumphal entry into Mexico City, the two liberal luminaries lamented, "while scapulars and crosses reflected the animated gazes and furtive kisses." Women were mixed up in all of the reactionaries' endeavors, Ramírez and Prieto reported, so that if "we cease to combat them, we shall face the complete triumph of the reaction."[76]

As historian Margaret Chowning demonstrates, one of the mid-century liberals' favorite tactics for discrediting the church was to associate it with women and effeminacy, as had their pre- and post-independence intellectual precursors.[77] To express his staunch support for *La Reforma*, for example, a prominent editor distanced himself from its self-evident enemies: "[N]either friars, sacristans nor skirts have influenced me," he insisted, "I am not Samson . . . and no Delilah's skirts have twisted my reason to prevent me from supporting the destruction of convents."[78] The public celebration of religious holidays and customs like Day of the Dead not only threatened freedom of conscience, it provided an opportunity for women and effeminate men (*petimetres*) to strut and display themselves, liberal intellectual Guillermo Prieto opined.[79] Balandro and Prieto's portrayal of the *Reforma* as a rational masculine force pitted against a superstitious and feminized enemy was a frequent trope in liberal publications: the *Boletín del Ejército Federal* saw in the current agitation of the patria "a sign of virility, a powerful force to break the bonds of religious superstition that have impeded its forward march."[80]

Liberal intellectuals Ignacio Ramírez and Guillermo Prieto joined the newspapers in noting women's treacherous support for their opponents. The conservatives were awash in feminine silliness, they charged, and peddling superstition—water from San Ignacio for one sickness, earth from the Christ of Chalma for another.[81] "Fanatical *beatas* and vulgar old women" served as the *Unidad Católica's* oracles, the *Monitor Republicano* reported.[82] In important ways, this war of religion was also a battle of the sexes.

THE REFORMERS LOSE GROUND

The conservative press boldly declared it was winning this war. *La Unidad Católica* noted that when the liberals declared freedom of worship, no Protestants, Jews, or Muslims rushed to create their own temples. So, their opponents contested, the liberals had rifled through eighteenth-century French history to hit on a solution: the Constitutional Clergy, an influential group who had championed the French Constitution of 1791, with its mandate for a non-hierarchical church, elected church, and simpler worship. This "exotic plant," this French import, was failing to thrive in Mexican soil, the conservative paper reported, and its ministers thus resorted to tactics such as the forced conscription of the faithful for the Mass; despite these radical measures, the pews remained sparsely populated.[83]

The conservatives may have been right. In Mexico City and in many of the provinces, the reformers appeared to be too few and far between to combat the church's vocal criticism and the laity's considerable hostility. A Guanajato crowd pelted the constitutional clerics with rocks when they sallied into the streets.[84] A liberal law of 1861 decreed that the churches confiscated from the regular orders should be occupied by priests who supported the constitution, but local authorities found ways to subvert the requirement. Chiapas officials finessed the issue, for example, by noting that an "ancient and clearly democratic" priest was indeed available. But given his weak eyesight and advanced age he simply could not fill the post.[85] They had a point: within the year he was dead, leaving instructions that he was to be buried with "a cross in his right hand, the 1857 Constitution in the left, and letters from Benito Juárez under his robes."[86] Meanwhile, Chiapas could side-step the federal requirement.

While certainly a clerical minority and often the object of popular indifference and even hostility, however, these pro-*Reforma* fishers of men were neither numerically insignificant nor entirely lacking in influence. Ever keen to downplay their rivals' numbers, *La Unidad Católica* estimated that in all of Mexico only about 100 clerics supported the Reform Laws. Of those, they further asserted, merely a dozen of these used the press or the pulpit to promote the reformed church, and those few hailed from only a few states. This is clearly a partisan underestimate: the capital's press, even the conservative press, regularly reported the activities of reformers in many other parts of the republic.[87]

Although perhaps not filling the pews, the Constitutional Clergy dominated another important pulpit during the liberals' brief stint in Mexico City: the press. The newspapers' importance in the battle for hearts and minds was certainly not lost on contemporaries. When the conservatives captured and summarily executed liberal luminary Melchor Ocampo in early June of 1861, a mob chanting a popular couplet by liberal leader and writer Guillermo Prieto sacked the ultramontanist *Pájaro Verde*, throwing the press into the street and burning it as an indifferent police force watched.[88] And when in December 1861 *La Unidad Católica* urged readers to defend the pope's temporal power, suggestively noting that he was surrounded by exiled clerics, they ran smack into Mexico City's press censorship tribunal, the Jurado de Imprenta, who accused them of inciting the public against the Reform Laws. The eleven-man committee—which included liberal *Siglo Diez y Nueve* editor Francisco Zarco, who had been arrested by the conservatives in 1858 and in 1860, and Federal District Governor Juan José Baz—imprisoned author Florentino Saucedo and seized dozens of the offending articles.[89] The reformist and satirical *La Orquesta* opined that the press tribunal's agent had knocked on these conservative Catholics' door and awakened them from a dream that they were in Rome, not Mexico.[90] It was in front of this passionately contested tribunal of the reading public that reformist Catholic liberals spelled out the tenets of this simple, ethic-based Christianity.

Under the leadership of Juan N. Enríquez Orestes, the Constitutional Clergy's rhetorical flash lit up the headlines of the *Monitor Republicano*. No stranger to controversy, as a parish priest and later as a St. Vicent de Paul mission preacher in Zimapán, Enríquez Orestes had incurred the wrath of both the brothers and his own superiors Archbishop Lázaro de la Garza y Ballesteros and Bishop of Linares

FIGURE 8.1 Melchor Ocampo, one of the most revered liberal intellectuals of the Mexican Reforma and an author of the 1857 Constitution, was killed by conservative guerillas a few months after returning to private life to clear the field for Benito Juárez's presidency. A former seminarian and a lifelong proponent of Reform Catholicism, he is often misread in retrospect as a secularist. Nineteenth-century lithograph (artist unknown). World History Archive/Alamy Stock Photos.

Francisco de Paula Verea y González. These run-ins, he felt, sprang from the hierarchy's aversion to his simple sermons on the scriptural truths of equality and fraternity—sermons which won him a loyal following in Tulancingo, Zimapán, Jacala, Alfajayucan, and Mineral del Monte.[91]

CLERICAL CELIBACY

In 1861, with the liberals firmly in control of the capital city, the liberal *Monitor Republicano* and the conservative *La Cruz* squared off on the issue of clerical celibacy. Predictably, as had the intelligentsia of an earlier iteration of the Reform Catholic International in Central America and elsewhere, Enríquez Orestes argued that clerical marriage flowered during the church's early years; celibacy was an accretion of the centuries and contravened the wisdom of the early church councils. The truth of democratic doctrines found in the early church councils was an argument frequently heard from liberals during the 1857 Constitutional Convention.[92]

Celibacy, Enríquez Orestes noted, was a seductive fantasy: in reality, lascivious priests "menaced girls, prostituted widows, corrupted married women, and threatened virginal purity."[93] Their motivation for insisting on their celibacy? These sensual men, he claimed, refused to submit to the divine law of chaste and honest matrimony in order to keep concubines and avoid "the commitment to one woman" and the nuisance of caring for their children."[94] *La Unidad Católica* fired back that Enríquez Orestes merely propagated the usual drivel spewed by Catholicism's enemies.[95]

The hero priest of liberal novelist and pamphleteer Nicolás Pizarro's 1861 *El Monedero* is a literary case in point. Together with a virtuous Indian artisan initially scorned by a beautiful aristocrat, Father Luis establishes La Nueva Filadelfia, a "fraternal colony" of hearty yeoman liberated from grasping foreign merchants and huge landowners. These humble republicans labor to their physical capacity and receive an education centered on the exact sciences and strict morality; a solid piety free of "superstitions" and the constant practice of mutual Christian love suffuses their brotherly interactions in this pastoral community.

No one abandoned this Christian utopia, the author explains, "because outside of it they could never find so much brotherly protection and such simple and true sociability purified by the truly divine influence of Christian love."[96] The simple injunction to love thy neighbor was emblazoned in gold on the community rotunda. Other than an avaricious Yankee named William Walker and the country's political chaos, the only menace to this idyll is the celibate priest's natural sexual urges; the approving author marries him to a devoted wife at the story's end. And indeed, although women farmed alongside the men, Nueva Filadelfia lacked the sexual edginess of some of its European utopian counterparts. This was no Fourierian phalanx: the patriarchal household reigned supreme, and women could not attend a community gathering unless a husband, brother, or father accompanied them.[97]

Particularly in the north, the reformed church scored major successes, and its opposition to celibacy was key to some of this support. Tamaulipas' liberal legislature granted a petition by Santa Bárbara parish priest and *hacienda* owner Ramón Lozano to legitimize his three children in March of 1861. This event was widely applauded in the state's liberal press and just as loudly decried as a scandal by Mexico City's *Pájaro Verde*.[98] The bishop of Linares promptly prohibited the town's parishioners from any communication with the "disgraced priest Lozano" and declaring the sacraments he administered invalid.[99]

Lozano, however, was not backing down, despite a small clutch of his own parishioners who circulated the bishop's edict to discourage church attendance. He noted that his clerical predecessors in the thriving town of perhaps 10,000 had been as fragile as he on the celibacy issue. Perhaps more importantly, his children's legitimacy was guaranteed by the Reform Laws, which he held in high regard.[100]

SCHISM

With the hierarchy poised to oust him from his post over celibacy, on May 12, 1861, Lozano issued a manifesto of the new *Iglesia apostólica Mexicana de Santa Bárbara de Tamaulipas (Apostolic Mexican Church of Santa Bárbara, Tamaulipas)*, noting in his parish baptismal record that his church had forever changed that day "ceasing to be Romish." Fifty-three parishioners promptly signed this rousing statement.[101] The hierarchy behaved like wolves among sheep, the proclamation declared, and it was no longer possible to live in open struggle against conscience. This liberty of conscience and true Catholicism formed the cornerstones of the new church. Church canons that clashed with the Reform Laws were all banned. The Santa Bárbara rebels would indeed recognize Bishop Francisco de Paula's authority, but only after he had sworn to uphold the 1857 Constitution and the Reform Laws— an unlikely event indeed, as the bishop had worked assiduously and quite publicly to combat those same laws. In the meantime, Lozano would serve as head and "true pope" of his flock.[102]

Lozano's break with the official church sent shock waves through the hierarchy. From the archbishopric of Monterrey came a June pastoral letter warning parishioners that Lozano could no longer administer the sacraments; they would have to go to nearby Tula or Jicotencal. The edict begged those parishioners "who were still real Catholics" to help remove all obstacles to the reception of a new priest.[103] Monclova parish priest Narciso Villarreal urged the parishioners to request a new priest and leave "the new Holiness to his fanatical delirium."[104] Although the hierarchy did eventually finagle a new priest into the parish in late July, Lozano refused to disappear, whipping off a spirited reply to Villarreal.[105] Bishop Veréa had no jurisdiction over him and thus no right to suspend him for sexual incontinence: the

Mexican constitution had eliminated special tribunals and privileges. And in a
pair of statements that would have earned the approbation of Mier, Cañas, and
Delgado, Lozano insisted that the scriptures and the example of the early church
placed priests on the level of the bishops. His parishioners—Catholics, not fanatics, he insisted—understood dogma and their own consciences well enough to
know that the hierarchy erred.[106]

Outright schismatics like Lozano were joined by numerous clerics who most
decidedly aided the liberals, though their exact relationship to the official schism
remains cloudy. The church hierarchy charged a Taxco priest, Manuel Gómez, with
revealing the conservative army's position to liberal leader Juan Alvarez in 1858.
Gómez later reported in *El Movimiento* that the conservatives clapped him in leg
irons; after reiterating the tenets of the reformed faith, he begged the readership
to exempt him from those priests who had been indifferent to the country's destruction at conservative hands, reminding them that he had earlier defended the
true faith in Morelia's liberal press.[107] A Tepanco parish priest refused to raise funds
for the conservatives, and the liberals did not harass him as they did other priests,
the church courts reported; he had even organized dances and other festivities for
the liberal troops. Another priest proclaimed his support for the constitutionalists
and harbored soldiers in his home in San José Miahuatlán. When his superiors
summoned him, he refused to appear, continuing with his ministry while he hid in
Puebla. And instead of calming passions in the tiny town of Nextlalpan, one Father
Rafael Rodríguez encouraged villagers' "anti-ecclesiastical and communist ideas"
and refused to persuade his parishioners that the liberals coveted their land.[108]

Constitutional cleric Enríquez Orestes' counterpart in the provinces, Francisco
de P. Campa of Zacatecas, eagerly swore the oath to the 1857 Constitution and,
until his dramatic public retraction, regularly contributed pro-liberal, anti-church
hierarchy editorials to four area newspapers, two of which were under his leadership; his ultramontanists detractors fired back in spirited exchanges reminiscent
of Central America's pamphlet wars between Catholics.[109] Suspended by the hierarchy, Linares' liberal army chaplain Vicente Guevara was a cause célèbre with the
Constitutional Clergy. During Ignacio Comonfort's brief reign, he had confessed
several liberal luminaries shunned by the church and had then paid for his heroism,
suffering prison and mistreatment after the conservative victory in 1858; he later
contributed pro-reform articles to Mexico City's liberal press in 1861.[110] When
Zacatecas parish priest Juan José de Orellano ignored the bishop of Guadalajara's
instructions to resist state seizure of church property, the church attempted to
remove him from his post. Secular officials in this liberal redoubt designated the
hand-picked church investigator as "a cleric of dubious antecedents because of his
fanaticism, superstition, and ignorance."[111] He would no doubt foment sedition

against the secular authorities, the city council felt, and they prevented him from removing Orellano. In short, struggles over observance and authority within the church occupied a central role in the liberal-conservative competition for Mexico's hearts and minds.

And indeed the Constitutional Clergy—like so many reformist Catholics before them—would reiterate this conviction that they represented a valiant effort to restore the church rather than abandon it. As did many of the Constitutional Clergy after 1862, Enríquez Orestes sought financing from a nineteenth-century version of the NGO: Protestant missionaries from the colossus of the north, in this case the Episcopal Church.[112] But although his would-be patrons had high hopes for a church on Mexican soil, what shines out in the priest's rather shadowy funding quest is a man whose desire to reform the Catholic Church never wavered; he was no closet Protestant, although it is certainly not far-fetched to say that reformist Catholicism—with its distrust of excessive clerical and saintly mediation with the Divine—helped create the theological and cultural preconditions for others' conversion.

Enríquez Orestes and several colleagues had arrived in New York in 1864 highly touted by their sponsors as "men of intelligence and probity, and deserving of high regard."[113] Eerie tensions soon developed. The Mexican priests refused to say the Mass with their hosts, who found their actions and intentions "inscrutable"; would these erstwhile allies really "hold up a piece of dough and say it was Christ?," the gringos wondered, concluding that they might indeed: Enríquez Orestes had defended the Catholic sacraments as indispensable to salvation and seemed more versed in "papal dogmatics" than his colleagues.[114] Body and blood of Christ, Enríquez Orestes so believed; the Host was not a symbol of Christ's sacrifice, but the sacrifice itself. Some of the more astute Episcopalian missionaries grasped that their Mexican allies had no intention of ushering in a Protestant reformation: in 1864 Ciudad Victoria, where Enríquez Orestes had been so warmly received, Reverend A. E. Longson was introduced to a liberal army official in 1865 as an "anti-papist priest."[115]

REFORM IN RETREAT

The Constitutional Clergy counted staunch and influential liberal intellectuals like Ocampo, Prieto, Pizarro, and Ramírez in their camp. Liberal pamphlets and even the federal army's own official bulletin rehearsed the fundamental tenets of the faith; under the fiery leadership of the prolific Enríquez Orestes they were a major presence in the 1861 and 1862 liberal press in Mexico City. Yet for all this, even by their own reckoning they failed, for with few exceptions Mexico City congregants stayed away in droves. The hierarchy's vocal enmity, the satire heaped on them by *El Pájaro Verde* and *La Unidad Católica*, and, perhaps, equally important, the implacable distrust of this heresy displayed by many women—all of this proved too much to overcome.

Their own aversion to accumulation played a part as well; apostolic poverty was all very well in theory, but certainly no way to run a movement. "For supporting the Reform laws, where God's splendor shines," they explained, they had been reduced to penury. They feared ending up as "ashes in the Laguna of Texcoco" although, like good Christian martyrs they vowed not to falter.[116] Although, as we have seen, the liberals offered explicit blueprints for proper priestly comportment and for the church's internal reorganization, starting with the pope's demotion, the reform laws nevertheless aimed at the separation of church and state, and at least a few liberals were unwilling to violate this tenet. As Francisco Zarco carefully explained, "Although the schismatics might rant and rave, and although we support their ideas, the government's job is not to endorse a particular sect."[117] Without government salaries or private donations, they had no way to support themselves.

This is hardly surprising given reformist Catholicism's stress on freedom of conscience and each enlightened individual's direct relationship with God. Priests— even virtuous fellow-traveler priests—were no godlier than liberal laymen, and except for the sacraments that these priests could provide, they were not really needed for real religion to flourish. As the liberal hero of Nicolas Pizarro's *La Coqueta* tells a benighted elderly woman (almost a redundancy in liberal discourse), "Priests are not religion . . . religion is the belief that each person has in the Divinity and in the mode in which to best honor Him . . . religion is good and necessary to society—priests are some good, some bad."[118]

France's Constitutional Clergy had to contend with nonjuring priests and their often female allies in places like the Vendée, but also with the official Cult of Reason, with its tendentiously secular rituals and de-Christianization campaigns. Perhaps ironically, the absolute centrality of Christian humanism to Mexican liberal discourse and the intellectual leadership's eloquent and oft-repeated defense of reformist Catholicism and embeddedness in the Reform Catholic International ensured that Mexico's Constitutional Clergy would be helpmeets rather than leaders in this religious movement. It was Mexico's enlightened laity who led a godly campaign to save their simple ethical religion from the church. And if their own piety suggested to them that ordained priests were not absolutely central to this religion, an army to fight their dogged opponents most certainly was.

ONWARD CHRISTIAN SOLDIERS? REFORMED RELIGION AND
THE LIBERAL ARMY

"We find ourselves in one of the phases of the great religious revolution that has agitated society since the sixteenth century," announced the Liberal army's official publication, the *Boletín del Ejército Federal*, in 1858. The soldiers, it explained, were enrolled in a fight that started with Martin Luther's protest:

> [T]he Dominican Tetzel's scandalous sale of indulgences encouraged another religious, a professor of theology in Witberg to take up the standard of reform and inspire Germany and all of Europe to combat Rome . . . their spirits were ready to fight this force that had corrupted even the purest Christians. The religious revolution then followed a slow path, conquering the sacred right of freedom of conscience . . . putting clerical riches into circulation . . . and reducing Rome to the point that it ceased to terrify Christian Nations. And when the revolution marches forward? What do Mexican clerics do? They ignite religious hatred, formulating anathemas against the innocent and denying them the sacraments. This clerical misconduct has irritated these families, and they have fled their altars; these people look for an asylum against this tyranny and disdain in God's great *misercordia*, in the reading of the holy writings where every unfortunate finds consolation and where doctrines abound to help them separate what truly comes from Jesus Christ and what comes from clerical passions and interests.[119]

According to some of Mexico's most distinguished historians, this Christian army had a general befitting its stated religious mission. In his position as a commander of the liberal army, Santos Degollado "was a new incarnation of the armed man of religion," writes Enrique Krauze, and "the finest example of the fusion between inner Catholicism and political liberalism." This assessment is shared by Justo Sierra, who asserts that the general trusted the Reform Laws to resurrect "the Church's prestige through returning it to the Gospel, poverty, charity love, and the good."[120]These characterizations are no less than what Degollado himself inscribed in the record: in a letter to his son in September of 1860, the general, temporarily out of favor with Juárez, lamented the "ingratitude, reproaches, and calumniations" he had suffered at the hands of "our co-religious." He reiterated, however, that "the sanctity of the cause" gave him courage. "We should die like Hidalgo and Morelos died, because our blood falling on the eyes of the people (like that of the Divine Redeemer on those of the blind man's) will open them forever."[121] Just three days after accepting his position as general of the federal army in 1858, Degollado told the troops that "if the people ask me to lay down my arms, I will. But not to those adventurers who want to return to the status of Spanish colony; not to the privileged classes. . . not to those who would keep men's thoughts and actions in perpetual tutelage; not, in short to those hypocritical Pharisees who invoke the religion of Jesus Christ without really believing in it or observing its maxims of fraternity and peace."[122] The liberals, he roundly concluded in a March 1859 speech, were the true defenders of "the religion of The Crucified."[123]

Much more difficult to determine, however, is the degree to which the liberal troops shared Degollado's particular brand of religious passion. Neither side in the War of the Reform inspired mass participation: liberals and conservatives alike resorted to the draft to stock their ranks, and at no point were there more than twenty-five-thousand soldiers out of a population of some eight million.[124] In Florencia Mallon's analysis, a huge cultural rift thus yawned between the irreligious liberals and the Indian and *mestizo* villagers whose community life centered on more communal Catholicism.[125] Although Mallon underestimates the liberals' religiosity, the point in some ways stands: Reformist Catholic enthusiasts found few friends among a rural population that had long since made the church its own—and decidedly different from that of reformers.

But we may need to disaggregate the liberal army to evaluate its adherents' religious sensibility, perhaps along lines of geography. It would be odd indeed for a general like Degollado to send his troops to battle with rousing rhetoric that reflected little more than his own idiosyncrasies. There are other suggestions of reformist sympathies on the battlefield itself. In June of 1862, Enríquez Orestes joined the liberal army as a chaplain. In the *Monitor Republicano* he urged Mexicans to take up arms, likening liberal combatants to "Jesus Christ, who, infused with abnegation, went to Golgotha to offer himself in holocaust."[126]

There is also evidence of popular support for his interpretation. In 1864, during the French imperial intervention, the warrior-priest found himself in conflict with the conservative bishop of Ciudad Victoria. The northerneastern city had been a bastion of liberal resistance to the French, and some of the laity saw in Enríquez Orestes a spiritual leader who shared their piety and politics. Five hundred residents declared that the ultramontane bishop, cooperating with the imperial invaders, had denied them an official parish priest in revenge for their "democratic tendencies." The liberal general had stepped into the void, much to the delight of this crowd. They had "borne witness to the injuries to the God of Charity (Misercordia) enacted by those who titled themselves his ministers" and so a liberal army chaplain fresh from the battlefield was an "evangelical martyr," not the "false, impious imposter" portrayed in official church propaganda. They insisted he stay.[127]

The schismatic cleric Ramón Lozano also found the liberal cause to be a holy one. Made famous by his stand over legitimizing his three children and breaking with the official church, his leadership endured into the years of the French occupation. He effectively led his flock into battle under the banner of his Reform Catholic schism. In early April of 1864, his followers rallied at his *hacienda* near Santa Bárbara, Tamaulipas. There he issued a manifesto against the abuse of the military levy by the district's military and political chief. In place of the abusive official, "citizen" Lozano named himself the new authority. Many who co-signed this proclamation were among the fifty-three men who had signed on to his schismatic church. When the French seized the town a year later, they targeted local liberal leaders, sacking Lozano's house, destroying the *hacienda's* store and ruining his precious library. He likened them to "savage Comanche" outside of the pale of civilization.[128] Later that month, he warned the citizens of the nearby town of Tula that they had but two choices in the battle with the French invaders: a sincere and fraternal embrace with other Tamaulipans who resisted these interlopers, or a war to the death.[129] In 1869, after the liberal liberation of Mexico from French rule, he led a successful movement to change the town's name from Santa Bárbara to Ocampo, after his martyred hero Melchor Ocampo. In the 1870s, he served as a senator in the state legislature.[130]

These are tantalizing hints, but the religious sensibilities of much of the liberal army remains an open question. Radical liberal intellectuals, on the other hand, most assuredly shared Degollado's sense that their crusade was a holy one. Thundering on the Alameda during the independence celebration of 1855, the poet and novelist Guillermo Prieto announced that when God's word first came into the world, force had dominated reason and particular interests reigned over the common good. From the cross Christ proclaimed man's liberty and announced the great revolution of love, fraternity, and equality.[131] This theme was frequently rehearsed. If Hegel's spirit was slowly unfolding through history to liberate mankind from tyranny, for the celebrated pamphleteer and novelist Nicolás Pizarro Suárez this spirit was evangelical Christianity—a promise that gradually unfurled to destroy the despotic power of king's who claimed divine favor.[132] God's will, however, required human agency. This same author's political catechism—adopted under the victorious liberal government as an official school textbook—offered some telling advice on resistance to tyranny to its young audience: "If your country's tyrant threatens you with cruel torments for not obeying his laws, resist, let him see you smile; this is what the first, real Christians practiced as they marched to their martyrdom."[133]

Taking the dais on the Alameda during the 1861 Independence Day celebrations, Ignacio Ramírez informed the crowd that the Roman Catholic Church, "pagan in the time of Cesar, feudal in the middle ages, and monarchical today," had met its match in Mexico's great hope for salvation: "The innumerable and good believers, who, loyal to the standard of the crucified . . . proclaim Him the symbol of love and justice, and not of ambition and rancor; for that reason, they promise us that one day the first clerical blessing will be for democracy and their first anathema for intolerance and despotism."[134] Liberals fought to define God and to reform religious practice in accordance with their definitions. They were the heirs of a Reform Catholic International anchored in the former Spanish Empire, not the secular junior partner of the French Revolution that their conservative foes tried to paint them.

Conclusion

A CATHOLIC CIVIL war rent the Spanish Atlantic world during the Age of Revolution. Both sides in the conflict demonstrated considerable intellectual and cultural creativity. This was not a battle between modernizers and traditionalists, but among religious innovators. In the decades leading up to independence, literate urban lay and clerical reformers throughout the Spanish Empire transformed the Reform Catholic but decidedly regalist doctrines of earlier reformist Catholics into a transnational movement hostile to monarchical absolutism.

Over the course of the eighteenth century, reformist Bourbon bishops and statesmen had crafted an absolutist defense of the sacralized monarchy's prerogatives over those of the papacy. They had championed notions of conciliar authority that reduced the pope's writ. Reformers in places like Mérida and San Salvador, many of them humble lower clergy, embraced these earlier Bourbon reformers' campaigns to decenter the pope in church ecclesiology. Under the new conditions of Ferdinand VII's exile, however, they reacted to the crisis of authority by taking aim against the absolutism of the monarchy itself. They were arrayed against the pope's champions, the ultramontane forces who increasingly supported the concept of absolutist monarchy and embraced reformist Catholics' biggest foes: the Jesuits who had, ironically, earlier crafted elaborate theories of the rights of the people to resist absolutist tyrants.

For God and Liberty. Pamela Voekel, Oxford University Press. © Oxford University Press 2023.
DOI: 10.1093/oso/9780197610190.003.0010

During the time of the Cádiz Cortes, new freedoms of expression and new printing presses provided an early glimpse of the centrality of the two transatlantic church currents to opposing regional and national political factions. These liberals and conservatives continued to battle over crucial questions of religious and political order in Central America during the tumultuous 1820s and 1830s, and during the Mexican War of Reform a generation later. Moreover, the battle lines they drew prefigured the intra-church conflicts of the later nineteenth century across the Catholic world.

Reform Catholicism was truly transnational. It was not centered in Paris, and it arguably reached its most radical form among supporters of the Cortes de Cádiz like the Sanjuanistas and Father Delgado and his coterie in San Salvador, among New Spain's literate rebel intelligentsia, and among liberals in the 1820s and 30s and beyond in Mexico, Colombia, and Central America. The Reform Catholic International was just that: international, with multiple nodes of power in the early nineteenth century rather than a single radiant center. For every French Grégoire we see Latin Americans like Sanjuanista José Matias Quintana and his son the Mexican rebel Andrés Quintana Roo; for every Spanish Juan Antonio Llorente we see a Mexican Fray Servando Teresa de Mier or a Colombian Juan Germán Roscio or an El Salvadoran Isidro Menéndez or a Guatemalan Mariano Gálvez.

The Reform Catholic International that animated republican movements and fought for local control of churches across the Atlantic world was characterized by widely shared transregional intellectual production and by site-specific creativity—hardly surprising given the church's three-century presence in Spanish America. This reformist current of the church provided the language to talk about new forms of representation. Further, it offered the sanctification that justified new political structures like the 1812 Constitution and the liberal republics of the post-independence period.

Reform Catholicism was not a justification for republicanism *ex post facto*, not a religious alibi for a secular politics. Rather, the very conceptualization of individual citizens and representative polities sprang from late eighteenth-century religious configurations with deep roots in theological history, as did notions of civil control over the church. In Central America and Mexico, reformers fought to wield the state against the ultramontane church in order to create godly republics.

Scholars of religion and politics amongst more subaltern groups in Latin America will not be surprised to learn that the intertwined religious and political ideas of ultramontane and reformist Catholics had multiple genealogical strands, and that these groups rewove those strands to produce new ideas in the context of ever-shifting local and global circumstances. As historian and theologian Jennifer Scheper Hughes reminds us, indigenous people in New Spain responded to the demographic crisis of the sixteenth-century church by "actively folding Christian deities, sacred edifices, and rites under their own care and protection," and "leveraging the church" to defend much revered Mesoamerican religious organizations against colonial dispossession. In a state of despair at the mission's failures to counter the overwhelming death toll, a settler colonialist church on the precipice of collapse perforce yielded to indigenous preferences and practices. Indigenous Christians created rival theologies and institutions, ensuring a future for the Mexican church. Tellingly, in his wide-ranging *México Profundo*, Guillermo Bonfil Batalla includes Mesoamerican Catholicism as part of the core of the indigenous Mexico, what he calls the "deep" Mexico, the Mexico continuously assailed and exploited by an elite "imaginary" Mexico comprised over the years of Franciscan friars, Bourbon bureaucrats, nineteenth-century liberals, or PRI technocrats. His account provides a deeply historicist understanding of the processes that allowed Mesoamerican civilization to survive and thrive within a Catholic framework.[1] Seen from this angle, the chief protagonists of *For God and Liberty* were profoundly "imaginary" emanations of a Latin America born in a transatlantic crucible, although they were most certainly homegrown.

The region's subsequent histories offer many examples of this racialized religious conflict. In 1830s Central America, for example, accusations of superstition and fanaticism came easily to liberals' lips after more than a decade of heated confrontations. The indigenous Catholicism of the Guatemalan highlands, where the regular orders had held sway throughout the 1820s, threatened reformist-inflected notions of civilization and rendered the indigenous barbarians in reformers' eyes. The consequences of a decade of religious vitriol can be seen in liberal Alejandro Marure's analysis of the 1837 Santa Rosa uprising. This movement of mostly ladino but also indigenous peasants rose against Guatemalan head of state and reformist stalwart Mariano Gálvez's liberal reforms of 1834. Gálvez purged the liturgical calendar, declared Spanish the national language, banned religious processions, and attracted Protestant immigrants through a misbegotten land give-away to a shady British colonization company.[2]

In reflecting on these developments, the liberal Marure found ample parallels between the Santa Rosa uprising and the rebellion against the French Revolution that flared in the Vendée in 1793, when Catholic peasants wearing images of the Sacred Heart rose up alongside the refractory clergy who had refused to swear the oath to the constitution. The superstitious peasants of the Vendée, a horrified Marure noted, bore relics and saints' images into battle while shouting "My body belongs to the king and my soul to the pope," and they attributed their victories to God's miraculous interventions. Their rural Guatemalan counterparts of 1837, according to Marure, were equally superstitious. To be sure, these peasants resented increased land enclosure, judicial innovations like trial by jury, and haughty medical practitioners who failed to solve the raging cholera epidemic, Marure argued, but the real cause of the violent uprising lay elsewhere. The "mental disposition and religious preoccupations of the masses" fueled their violent rage: this was not a bandit war, but one with intertwined political and religious causes, and one where the contrast between civilization and barbarism was founded in no small part in the three sides conflicting religious proclivities.[3] Leaders garnered recruits by promising the return of the archbishop, the regular orders, and the treasures stolen from the church, as well as the overthrow of the liberals' odious civil marriage and divorce laws. Marure acknowledged, however, that the rebels' grievances went far beyond these unpopular actions, as they continued their struggle even after Gálvez promised to retract these measures.[4]

In fact, in the second half of the nineteenth century, this alliance between elite ultramontane conservatives and the mass of "folk" believers was the deciding realignment within Catholicism—not only in Latin America, but around the world. Writing of this "New Catholicism" in later nineteenth-century Europe, historian Christopher Clark characterizes the increasingly centralized, Romanized church as "marked by a convergence of elite and popular devotions, an interpenetration of lay and clerical organization, a rhetorical vehemence and a resourcefulness in the management of communicative media that impressed contemporaries, whether sympathetic or hostile."[5] All of these developments are visible in the Independence-era religious wars of Latin America a half-century earlier.

Elements of this increasingly decisive relationship took shape at the Vatican level in response to the "Roman question," the long attenuation of papal temporal authority. In successive waves over the course of the middle decades of the century, as the pope's sovereignty over the papal states grew increasingly tenuous, coordinated publicity campaigns sparked outpourings of popular support for the beleaguered pontiff. Letters, petitions, and donations signaled the potential for popular identification with the first celebrity pope. When in 1848 the pope wrote to heads of state requesting statements of support against the encroaching Italian Republic, Mexican President José Joaquín Herrera offered him asylum in Mexico among his six million devoted children. This presidential gesture encouraged a wave of public demonstrations in Mexico.[6]

The state of siege turned a mildly reformist pope into the implacable enemy of liberalism, including its Reform Catholic currents. It also made him an active supporter of popular Catholicism, for with such an uncertain grip on temporal authority, his security lay in pressure on his French defenders from the Catholic masses below. The 1854 declaration of Mary's Immaculate Conception as official dogma epitomized the pope's growing solicitude for popular devotionalism.[7] In

Europe as earlier in Spanish America, too, this growing alliance between the pope and the people turned on constitutional innovations that brought more people than ever before into the realm of overt politics. Likewise, armed conflict on the Italian Peninsula turned popular belief into a resource for holy war. Small voluntary donations by ordinary Catholics, originally destined for the support of the papal troops, grew into a steady stream of operating revenue. To register their resistance to liberal governments, fervent believers of the popular classes poured their modest surplus into the papal treasury—a critical prop to church finances as the revenue-producing papal states were wrenched from its control. The support of "fanatics" in turn strengthened the hand of the ultramontane faction in the intra-church theological battles: Vatican I was a rout for Reform Catholics. And when at the 1870 council's end Pius was forced to flee Rome and surrender temporal power for good, elite lay and clerical ultramontanes turned their experience in mass mobilization to an unprecedented "Black International" of Catholic conservatism high and low.[8]

There were, for example, other possible trajectories for the Catholicism that emerged from the conflict. One of these is discernable in the 1840s Catholic civil war that wracked the Yucatán and the indigenous highlands of Guatemala. In these majority-Maya regions of Central America and Mexico, the deciding factor was neither the reformers nor the elite ultramontane. Rather, the most important protagonists were indigenous Christians who had taken the faith under their protection as the chaos of the Independence era raged around them, and who now wanted to be left alone to worship and farm.[9] As historian Douglass Sullivan Gonzalez makes clear, Conservative *caudillo*—and former swineherd—José Rafael Carrera emerged as a national figure after his leadership of this Santa Rosa rebellion in the east. His swarthy troops occupied the Guatemalan capital in February of 1838 and again in April of 1839. One of his early acts was to re-instate the practice of church burials, outlawed by Gálvez in 1834. Liberals had overseen the construction of suburban cemeteries throughout the indigenous highlands of the west, provoking dogged resistance from Indian communities and often their priests as well. Re-instating church burials was Carrera's opening salvo in a studious and successful effort to win indigenous support through respect for their "traditions"—essentially religious traditions—and their control over spiritual resources through the confraternities that had so irked liberal reformers. Respect for *"usos y costumbres"* became a leitmotif of the savvy Carrera's rule. The liberal cemetery campaign itself, like the resistance it engendered in the highlands, demonstrates the ongoing import of religion to political outcomes throughout the 1830s.[10]

In a development that prefigured Catholic alignments worldwide, this emerging alliance between ultramontane and folk Catholics proved decisive to the expansion of Carrera's insurgency and ultimate victory. With their hands more firmly on the reins of power in 1839, Guatemalan conservatives in the Second Constitutional Assembly systematically rolled back the liberals' religious reforms. In these moves, the Assembly was led by the president, Friar Fernando Antonio Dávila, an ultramontane devotee in the pamphlet wars of the 1820s and a conservative gadfly in the 1824 ANC; and by Vice-President Juan José Aycinena, of the storied conservative family. The assembly lifted the suppression of the religious orders and restored Casaús as a Guatemalan citizen and as the archbishop. Not to be outdone, the federal government suspended earlier liberal decrees on civil marriage and divorce, restored religious holidays to the calendar, and re-instituted religious vows.[11] It was this new and deeply uneasy coalition of conservative ultramontane Catholics and the "superstitious" majority who so irked reformers that finally put reformers on the defensive, decentering the ultramontane disputes with Reform Catholics that had rent the region asunder for more than two decades.

What the indigenous majority in the highlands of Guatemala gained from their alliance with Carrera's forces was the right to be left alone, the right to self-determination, the right to continue their own Catholic intellectual and cultural projects. That elites had expended so much energy in the bloody battles of the ultramontane and reformist Catholic civil war ensured that neither side could claim an outright victory in Central America, and that the Catholicism of those who had mostly avoided the conflagrations of the 1820s would survive and thrive to fight another day in the region's nineteenth century and beyond.

In the Yucatán too, a third Catholic force would prove decisive in the 1840s and beyond into the twentieth century. Unlike in Guatemala, here Maya rebels would not make alliances with a conservative state to win their battle for self-determination but instead remove themselves to autonomous enclaves. Late in 1850 a cross appeared to these Maya rebels at a natural well (*cenote*). The cross spoke in Yucatec Maya and assured listeners of God's favor for their cause. The visitation would prove the beginning of a massive messianic cult that would endure for more than a century, providing spiritual succor for beleaguered rebel troops. The *cruzob*, or "people of the cross," consolidated their position, essentially controlling the modern-day state of Quintana Roo from a town called Chan Santa Cruz or "Little Holy Cross." At one point, after being taken captive, the cross demanded the governor withdraw his troops, release prisoners, and return stolen property. The cross spoke on its own behalf but also in the name of God the Father, God the Son, and God the Holy Spirit, and Mary and Jesus.[12]

This "fanaticism" of the ultramontane and the "superstition" of the indigenous would continue to inform liberals' understanding of past battles and present enemies and justify their social leadership throughout the nineteenth century.

Writing in the late 1870s, for example, liberal chronicler Lorenzo Montúfar recalled that the miraculous nun Teresa de Aycinena had publicly attributed the 1830 earthquake to God's wrath for the expulsion of Archbishop Casaús. "Fanatical" believers had circulated her gloss on the tragedy, as if "by telegraph." If God smote his enemies, Montúfar sarcastically noted, then why had Lutheran firemen saved more people from a burning New York City theater than had the Jesuits from a fire that consumed their church in Santiago de Chile? The fire had killed 2,000 women but just 25 men in 1863. This radical imbalance incited an explosion of reformist commentary on the irrationality of pious women and of their Jesuit influencers. Here and elsewhere Montúfar's late nineteenth-century analysis lined up with that of earlier reformers.[13] The political battles of the nineteenth century were fought under the sacred canopy.

NOTES

ABBREVIATIONS

ACM	Archivo del Catedral de México, Mexico City, Mexico
AD	Archivo Documental
AEC	Archives of the Episcopal Church, Austin, Texas, USA
AGCA	Archivo General de Centro-América, Guatemala City, Guatemala
AGE	Archivo General del Estado, Monterrey, Nuevo León, Mexico
AGEY	Archivo General del Estado, Mérida, Yucatán
AGI	Archivo General de Indias, Seville, Spain
AGN-El Salvador	Archivo General de la Nación, San Salvador, El Salvador
AGN-Mexico	Archivo General de la Nación, Mexico City, Mexico
AHAG	Archivo Histórico de la Arquidiócesis de Guatemala, Guatemala City, Guatemala
AHAY	Archivo Histórico del Arzobispado, Mérida, Yucatán, Mexico
AHCM	Archivo Histórico de la Ciudad de México, Mexico City, Mexico
AHAM Archivo	Histórico de la Arquidiócesis de Monterrey, Monterrey, Nuevo León, Mexico
AHMM	Archivo Histórico de la Municipalidad de Miquihuana, Tamaulipas, Mexico
AHN	Archivo Histórico Nacional, Madrid, Spain
AHPM	Archivo Histórico de Protocolos de Madrid, Madrid, Spain
AN	Archivo de Notarias del Distrito Federal, Mexico City, Mexico
ANC	Asamblea Nacional Constituyente

APSBM	Archivo de la Parroquia de Santa Bárbara Martir, Ocampo, Tamaulipas, Mexico (a repositor of parish records, not an official archive).
AES	Archivo de la Sagrada Congregación de Negocios Eclesiásticos Extraordinarios, Vatican City
ASV	Archivo Secreto Vaticano, Vatican City
BL	British Library, London, UK
BL-UC	Bancroft Library, University of California, Berkeley, California, USA
BLAC	Benson Latin American Collection, University of Texas Libraries, Austin, Texas, USA
BN-Chile	Biblioteca Naciónal de Chile, Santiago, Chile
BN-Colombia	Biblioteca Naciónal de Colombia, Bogotá, Colombia
BN-Guatemala	Biblioteca Naciónal de Guatemala, Guatemala City, Guatemala
BN-Mexico	Biblioteca Naciónal, Mexico City, Mexico
BN-Spain	Biblioteca Naciónal, Madrid, Spain
CAIHY	Centro de Apoyo a la Investigación Histórico de Yucatán
CIESAS	El Centro de Investigaciones y Estudios Superiores en Antropología Social, Guatemala
CIRMA	Centro de Investigaciones Regionales de Mesoamérica, Guatemala
Col.	Column
Condumex	Centro de Estudios Históricos, Condumex, Mexico City, Mexico
Exp.	Expediente (file)
Fol.	Foleto
IIH-UAT	Instituto de Investigaciones Históricos de la Universidad Autónoma de Tamaulipas, Ciudad Victoria, Tamaulipas, Mexico
KS-UK	Special Collections, Kenneth Spencer Research Library, University of Kansas, Lawrence, Kansas, USA
LAL-TU	Latin America Library at Tulane University, New Orleans, Louisiana, USA
MASC-WS	Manuscripts, Archives, and Special Collections, Washington State University, Pullman, Washington, USA
RG	Record group
SC-USC	Special Collections, University of Southern California Library, Los Angeles, California
SCL-UVA	Albert and Shirley Small Collections Library, University of Virginia, Charlottesville, Virginia, USA
Sutro	Sutro Collection, San Francisco State University, San Francisco, California
UCA	Biblioteca "P.Florention Idoate, SJ," Universidad Centroamericana José Simeón Cañas, San Salvador, El Salvador
UNAM	Universidad Nacional Autónoma de México
WRC-RU	Woodson Research Center, Rice University, Houston, Texas, USA
YCM-UA	Yucatán Collection on Microfilm, University of Alabama, Tuscaloosa, Alabama, USA

INTRODUCTION

1. For an erudite treatment of the Reform Catholic International—a term he coined—in Europe, and its conflict with the Jesuits, see Dale Van Kley, *Reform Catholicism and the International Suppression of the Jesuits in Enlightenment Europe* (New Haven, CT.: Yale University Press, 2018). I have adopted this term, and its opposite, the Ultramontane Catholic International, because reformist Catholics in Spain and Latin America recognized their membership in these transatlantic networks and consistently eschewed identification with subsets within the larger group, especially French Jansenists. In the Spanish imperial and then Latin American context, the label "Jansenist" was a pejorative often applied to reformers to discredit them, and almost never an identification they claimed. Reform Catholicism is sometimes identified as "Enlightened Catholicism," but, as Van Kley points out, the Jesuits too were part of the larger Catholic enlightenment, and so the term "Catholic Enlightenment" obscures the two sides' ready identification of the other side as antagonistic, as well as their considerable doctrinal and political differences.

2. On the Mina expedition, see Manuel Ortuño Martínez, *Expedición a Nueva España de Xavier Mina* (Pamplona, ES: Universidad Pública de Navarra, Pamplona, 2006); and his *Vida de Mina. Guerrillero, liberal, insurgente* (Madrid, ES: Trama Editorial, 2008). Also see Jaime Olveda, ed., *La expedición fallida de Xavier Mina* (Zapopan, Jalisco, MX.: El Colegio de Jalisco, 2019).

3. Harris Gaylord Warren, "The Origins of General Mina's Invasion of Mexico" *Southwestern Historical Quarterly* 42, no. 1 (July 1938): 1–20. For more on the community of Spanish exiles organizing resistance efforts from Britain, see Karen Racine, "Nature and the Mother: Foreign Readings and the Evolution of Andrés Bello's American Identity, London, 1810-1829," in *Strange Pilgrimages: Exile, Travel, and National Identity in Latin America, 1800-1990s*, ed. Ingrid Elizabeth Fey and Karen Racine (Wilmington, DE: Scholarly Resources, 2000), 3–19. For more on Britain's relationship to Mexican independence, see Estela Guadalupe Jiménez Codinach, *La Gran Bretaña y la independencia de México (1808-1821)*, trans. Ismael Izarro Suárez and Mercedes Pizarro Suárez (México: Fondo de Cultura Económica, 1991).

4. Alexandre Pétion quoted in Marie Arana, *Bolívar: American Liberator* (New York, NY: Simon and Schuster, 2013), 179. Paul Verna, *Pétion y Bolívar* (Caracas, VE: Ediciones de la Presidencia de la República, 1980 [1969]).

5. William F. Lewis, "Símon Bolívar and Xavier Mina: A Rendezvous in Haiti," *Journal of Inter-American Studies* 11, no. 3 (July 1969): 461. Marie Arana, *Bolívar*, 190–191.

6. On the Haitian slave rebels' universalization of the 1789 French Declaration of the Rights of Man and of the Citizen, see Laurent Dubois, "An Enslaved Enlightenment: Rethinking the Intellectual History of the French Atlantic," *Social History* 31, no. 1 (February 2006): 1–14. For a critique of the notion that the ideologies of subaltern groups merely extend ideologies elaborated by others in the interest of inclusion, see Adom Getachew, "Universalism after the Postcolonial Turn," *Political Theory* 44, no. 6 (December 2016): 821–845. Jean Casimir argues that Haitians crafted more communal notions of identity and sovereignty and were less identified with the notion of the individual that formed the fundamental constituent of the Rights of Man and Citizen, see Jean Casimir, *The Haitians. A Decolonial History*, trans. Laurent Dubois; foreward Walter D. Mignolo (Chapel Hill, NC: University of North Carolina Press, 2020).

7. Ada Ferrer, "Haiti, Free Soil, and Antislavery in the Revolutionary Atlantic," *American Historical Review* 117, no. 1 (February 2012): 40–66. Ada Ferrer, *Freedom's Mirror. Cuba and Haiti in the Age of Revolution* (New York, NY: Cambridge University Press, 2014). Edgardo Pérez

Morales, *No Limits to Their Sway: Cartagena's Privateers and the Masterless Caribbean in the Age of Revolutions* (Nashville, TN: Vanderbilt University Press, 2018).

8. Harris Gaylord Warren, "Xavier Mina's Invasion of Mexico," *Hispanic American Historical Review* 23, no. 1 (February 1943): 52–76; Héctor Cuauhtémoc Hernández Silva, "Las motivaciones políticas de Xavier Mina, sus preparativos en Galveston y su desembarco en el Nuevo Santander en 1817," in *La expedición fallida de Xavier Mina*, ed. Jaime Olveda (Zapopan, Jalisco, MX.: El Colegio de Jalisco, 2019). Pérez Morales, *No Limits*, 6, 110, 115, 124–126.

9. On the idealism and interests fueling small makeshift armies of rebels in this period, see Karen Racine, "Fireworks over Fernandina: The Atlantic Dimension of the Amelia Island Episode, 1817," in *La Florida: 500 Years of Hispanic Presence*, ed. Viviana Díaz-Balsera and Rachel A. May (Gainesville, FL: University Press of Florida, 2014), 171–191.

10. Mexico City, Inquisición de México, Statement by Fray Servando Teresa de Mier, July 15, 1817, in Juan E. Hernández y Dávalos, ed., *Colección de documentos para la historia de la Guerra de Independencia de Mexico de 1808 a 1821*, 6 vols (Mexico: J.M. Sandoval, 1880), 6:854–859. The list of books and papers found in Mier's crates appears as Num. 978, "Inventario de los libros y papeles recogidos al declarante Mier en Soto la Marina y entregados al Tribunal de la Fe," in *Colección*, ed. Hernández y Dávalos, 6:840–854. Christopher Domínguez Michael provides the most comprehensive treatment of the Mexican intellectual's written work and swashbuckling life, see his *Vida de Fray Servando* (México: Ediciones Era, 2004); on the books in Mier's crates, see pp. 547–554.

11. Jaime Rodriguez O. "José Miguel Ramos Arizpe," in *Encyclopedia of Latin American History and Culture*, ed. Barbara A. Tenenbaum and Georgette M. Dorn, 4 vols. (New York: Charles Scribner's Sons, 1996), 4:537. Ramos de Arizpe's report on conditions in his province can be found in his *Memoria, que el doctor D. Miguel Ramos de Arispe, cura de Borbón y diputado en las presentes cortes generales y extraordinarias de España por la Provincia de Cohauila, una de las cuatro internas del oriente en el Reyno de México: presénta á el augusto congreso, sobre el estado natural, político, y civil de su dicha provincia, y los del Nuevo Reyno de León, Nuevo Santander, y los Texas, con exposición de los defectos del sistema general, y particular de sus gobiernos, y de las reformas, y nuevos establecimientos que necesitan para su prosperidad.* (Cádiz, ES: D. José María Guerrero, 1812). For more on Ramos de Arizpe's life, see Carlos González Salas, *Miguel Ramos de Arizpe: Cumbre y camino* (México, D.F.: Porrúa 1978). Alfonso Toro, *Don Miguel Ramos Arizpe,"Padre del Federalismo Mexicano": Biografía* (Saltillo, MX.: Coordinación General de Extension Universitaria y Difusión Cultural, 1992).

12. See, for example, Julio César Pinto Soria, "Los religiosidades indígenas y el estado nación en Guatemala (1800-1850)," in Peer Schmidt, Sebastian Dorsch, and Hedwig Harold-Schmidt, eds., *Religiosidad y clero en América Latina: La época de las revoluciones Átlanticas Religiosity and Clergy in Latin America (1767-18500: The Age of Atlantic Revolutions* (Cologne, DE: Böhlau Verlag, 2011), 307–327. Eric Van Young, *The Other Rebellion. Popular Violence, Ideology, and the Mexican Struggle for Independence, 1810-1821* (Stanford, CA.: Stanford University Press, 2002). Juan Pedro Albán, *Indios rebeldes e idólotras: dos ensayos históricos sobre la rebelión india de Cancuk, Chiapas, acaecida el el año de 1712* (México: CIESAS, 1997). William B. Taylor, *Theater of a Thousand Wonders. A History of Miraculous Images and Shrines in New Spain* (New York, NY: Cambridge University Press, 2016). Nancy M. Farriss, *Maya Society Under Colonial Rule. The Collective Enterprise of Survival* (Princeton, NJ: Princeton University Press, 1984), esp. 256–355.

13. Bartolomé José Gallardo, *Diccionario crítico-burlesco* (Burdeos, ES: Imprenta de Pedro Beaume, 1819). Juan José León Jovo and Juan Francisco de Arizpe Rosales, "Carta Pastoral,"

Villa de Santiago de Nuevo León, 31 May 1817, AHAM, 1 Gobierno, 1 enero 1797 to 1 julio de 1829, fols.132v, 133, 134v, 135.

14. Villa de Santiago de Nuevo León, Cabildo sede vacante to Monterrey, Cadereyta, Guajuco, Pilón, Linares, San Carlos, Santander, Santillán, Soto la Marina, Burgos, Cruxillos, San Fernando, Refugio, Mier, Reinosa, and Carmargo, August 8, 1817, AHAM, 1 Gobierno, 1 Enero 1797 to 1 julio de 1829, fols. 137v-139.

15. Gallardo, *Diccionario*, 70, 73, 74, 82, 84, 85.

16. Villa de Santiago de Nuevo León, Cabildo sede vacante to Monterrey, Cadereyta, Guajuco, Pilón, Linares, San Carlos, Santander, Santillán, Soto la Marina, Burgos, Cruxillos, San Fernando, Refugio, Mier, Reinosa, and Carmargo, 8 August 1817, AHAM, 1 Gobierno, 1 enero 1797 to 1 julio de 1829, fols.137v-139.

17. The works by the Abbé Grégoire found among Mier's possessions were recorded by the Inquisition exactly as follows: *Les ruines de Port-Royal des champs en 1809; De la Constitution Française de l'an 1814;* and *Apologie de Barthelemy de Las-Casas Eveque de Chiapas.* See Num. 978, "Inventario de los libros y papeles recogidos al declarante Mier en Soto la Marina y entregados al Tribunal de la Fe," in Hernández y Dávalos, ed., *Colección de documentos*, 6:843, 847, 849.

18. Voekel, *Alone before God.*

19. Jay Kinsbruner, *Independence in Spanish America: Civil Wars, Revolutions and Underdevelopment* (Albuquerque, NM: University of New Mexico Press, 1994), 88. José Servando Teresa de Mier Noriega y Guerra, *Memoria político-instructiva, enviada desde Filadelfia en agosto de 1821, a los gefes independientes del Anáhuac, llamado por los españoles Nueva España* (Philadelphia, PA: J. F. Hurtel, 1821), 18. Mier refers to Roscio as "my friend, the celebrated Dr. Roscio." I use the term "literate rebels" with some caution; reformist and ultramontanist Catholic tracts and ideas were read from pulpits and ideas spread to and among the illiterate through sermons, rousing exhortations to battle, and participation in particular religious cults, like the Jesuits' Sacred Heart of Jesus, a meme condensing political and religious meaning into a single dynamic image. For a particularly insightful analysis of how ideas circulated among the semiliterate or illiterate during this tumultuous time period, see Cristina Soriano, *Tides of Revolution. Information, Insurgencies, and the Crisis of Colonial Rule in Venezuela* (Albuquerque, NM: University of New Mexico Press, 2018), especially 47–75. Also see Víctor Peralta Ruiz, "Prensa y redes de communicación en el Virreinato del Perú, 1790-1821," *Tiempos de América* 12 (2005): 1–20. Jessica Fowler analyzes how notions of religious heresy traveled around the Atlantic in the early modern world in her "Illuminating the Empire: The Dissemination of the Spanish Inquisition and the Heresy of Alumbradismo, 1525-1600," (Ph.D. diss, University of California, Davis, 2015). S. Elizabeth Penry finds that the networks of the "lettered revolution" extended deep into the Andean countryside and involved letters circulated by literate Andean commoners during the eighteenth century, see her *The People are King: The Making of an Indigenous Andean Politics* (New York, NY: Oxford University Press, 2019), 185–195.

20. Alfonso Múnera, *El fracaso de una nación: región, clase y raza en el Caribe colombiano (1717-1810)* (Havana: Fondo Editorial Casa de las Americas, 2011), 208–211. Brian R. Hamnet, *The End of Iberian Rule on the American Continent, 1770-1830* (New York, NY : Cambridge University Press, 2017), 163–164. Jeremy Adelman, *Sovereignty and Revolution in the Iberian Atlantic* (Princeton, NJ: Princeton University Press, 2006), 272, 274–276. For more on rebel clerics who experienced the Crown's wrath and Pablo Morillo's campaigns, see Ana María Bidegain, "Los apóstoles de la insurrección y el vicariocastrense (1810-1820)," *Boletín de Historia y Antigüedades* (June, 2013): 199–237; Brian R. Hamnett, "The Counter Revolution of Morillo and the Insurgent Clerics of New Granada, 1815-1820," *The Americas* 32, no. 4 (April 1976): 597–617. See also Pablo

Morillo, *Mémoires du Général Morillo, Comte de Carthagègene, Marquis de la Puerta, Rélatifs aux principaux évenements de ses campagnes en Amérique de 1815 à 1821* (Paris, 1826).

21. This notorious group of eight patriots or "monsters," as Spanish officer Domingo Monteverde labeled them, included José Cortés de Madariaga, a Chilean-born priest and doctor of theology, whose 1811 reformist tract rehearsed reformist Catholic denunciations of monastic despotism and lauded the Empire's rebels, including New Spain's reform-minded rebel parish priest Miguel Hidalgo y Costilla; see José Cortés Madariaga, *Diario y observaciones del presbítero José Cortés Madariaga, en su regreso de Santafé á Caracas, por la via de los rios Negro, Meta y Orinoco, despues de haber concluido la comisión que obtuvo de su gobierno, para acordar los tratados de alianza enter ambos estados* (Caracas,VE, 1811), 22. For an informative description of the Ceuta presidio that housed rebels against the Empire during this period, see Charles Walker (with Liz Clarke), *Witness to the Age of Revolution: The Odyssey of Juan Bautista Tupac Amaru* (New York, NY: Oxford University Press, 2020), 43–51.

22. Juan Germán Roscio, *Obras, Tomo I, El Triunfo de la libertad sobre el despotismo*, intro. Augusto Mijares; comp. Pedro Grases (Caracas, VE: Publicaciones del Secretaria General de la Decimal Conferencia Interamericana, 1953 [1817]).

23. Barnaba Niccolò Maria Luigi Chiaramonti, Bishop of Imola, later Pope Pius VII, quoted in Thomas Bokenkotter, *Church and Revolution: Catholics in the Struggle for Democracy and Social Justice* (New York, NY: Doubleday, 1998), 32. Carmen Ruiz Barrionuevo, "Juan Germán Roscio y el pensamiento antiliberal," *Philologia Hispalensis* 25 (2011): 184. Barnaba Niccolò Maria Luigi Chiaramonti, *Homilía del cardenal Chiaramonti, obispo de Imola, actualmente sumo pontifice Pio VII, dirigida al pueblo de su diócesis en la República Cisalpina, el día del nacimiento de J.-C. año de 1797*, trans. Juan Germán Roscio (Philadelphia, PA: J.F. Hurtel, 1817). Barnaba Niccolò Maria Luigi Chiaramonti, *Homélie du Citoyen Cardinal Chiaramonti, Evêque d'Imola, actuellement... Pontife Pie VII, adressée au peuple de son diocèse... le jour de la naissance de Jésus-Christ, l'an 1797*, trans., Abbé Grégoire (Paris, 1814). For more on Pope Pius VII's homily, see Thomas Worcester, "Pius VII: Moderation in an Age of Revolution and Reaction," in *The Papacy Since 1500: From Italian Prince to Universal Pastor*, ed. James Corkery, Thomas Worcester, and Linda Hogan (New York, NY: Cambridge University Press, 2011), 111.

24. The 1819 Congress of Angostura that elected Simón Bolívar President of the Republic of Gran Colombia also elected Roscio vice president of Venezuela. Its preparatory meetings got underway late in 1818. See Jay Kinsbruner, *Independence in Spanish America: Civil Wars, Revolutions and Underdevelopment* (Albuquerque, NM: University of New Mexico Press, 1994), 88. For an insightful review of Roscio's thought, see Ruiz Barrionuevo, "Juan Germán Roscio."

25. On the Synod of Pistoia, see, for example, Shaun Blanchard, *The Synod of Pistoia and Vatican II: Jansenism and the Struggle for Catholic Reform* (New York, NY: Oxford University Press, 2019).

26. Cádiz, Miguel Ramos de Arispe to Mier (note that Arizpe was sometimes, as here, spelled as Arispe), 27 March 1813, "Correspondence Re: The Venezuelan Wars of Independence," SCL-UVA, MSS 3977, pp. 1–2. Arizpe's report on conditions in his province can be found in his *Memoria* . For more on Ramos de Arizpe's life, see Carlos González Salas, *Miguel Ramos de Arizpe: Cumbre y Camino* (México, D.F.: Porrúa 1978). On Arizpe's later encounter with Grégoire, and Grégoire's request that Ramos Arizpe relay information to Bishop Juan José Díaz de Espada y Landa, see Paris, Abbé Henrí Grégoire to Fray Servando Teresa de Mier, 17 March, 1824, reprinted in Miquel I Vergés and Díaz-Thomé, eds., *Escritos inéditos*, 514. The letter was originally written in French and translated by the editors. Ramos de Arizpe gave last rites to Mier in Novemeber of 1827; see Gisella C. Carmona and Armando Artega Santoyo, *Fray*

Servando Teresa de Mier, una vision en los tiempos, 2nd ed. (Monterrey, MX: Ayuntamiento de Monterrey, 2007), 44. The reformist Catholic proclivities of Valentín Gómez Farias' administration and of the public sphere of letters in post-independence Mexico, especially the thought of Liberal luminary José María Luis Mora, is detailed in Voekel, *Alone Before God*, 146–170.

27. Bianca Premo critiques the widely influential notion that Europe exported the Enlightenment to Latin America, arguing that women, slaves, and indigenous peoples generated their own Enlightenment concepts in the empire's late eighteenth-century civil courtrooms. See her *The Enlightenment on Trial: Ordinary Litigants and Colonialism in the Spanish Empire* (New York, NY: Oxford University Press, 2017), especially 8–10 and 229–230. In recent historiographies of the Atlantic world and the Spanish Empire, a process of reorientation is underway. Growing bodies of work on the overlapping and interconnected African, indigenous, and French, Spanish, and even Dutch and Danish Atlantic circuits have begun to return the British Atlantic to a more proportionate role in the historiography. New scholarship centers the transnational networks of ideas generated by often-overlooked subaltern actors like slave women and vodou priests. New works center the Spanish and Portuguese Empires rather than northern Europe as the locus of intellectual production. For critical theoretical framings, see, for example, María Elena Martínez, "Religion, Caste, and Race in the Spanish and Portuguese Empires. Local and Global Dimensions," in *Iberian Empires and the Roots of Globalization*, ed. Anna More, Ivonne del Valle, and Rachel Sarah O'Toole (Nashville, TN: Vanderbilt University Press, 2019), 75–104; Micol Seigel, "Beyond Compare: Comparative Method after the Transnational Turn," *Radical History Review* 91 (2005): 62–90; Ricardo Salvatore, ed., *Los lugares del saber: contextos locales y redes transnacionales en la formación del conocimiento modern* (Buenos Aires: Beatriz Viterbo, 2007); Pamela Voekel, Bethany Moreton, and Michael Jo, "Vaya con Dios: Religion and the Transnational History of the Americas," *History Compass* 5, no. 5 (2007): 1604–1639; Jorge Cañizares-Esguerra and Benjamin Breen, "Hybrid Atlantics: Future Directions for the History of the Atlantic World," *History Compass* 11, no. 8 (2013): 597–609; Ernesto Bassi, "Beyond Compartmentalized Atlantics: A Case for Embracing the Atlantic from Spanish American Shores," *History Compass* 12, no. 9 (2014): 704–716; Ivonne del Valle, *Escribiendo desde los márgenes: Colonialismo y jesuitas en el siglo XVIII* (México, D.F.: Siglo XXI, 2009), esp. 46–63. Paul Gilroy, *The Black Atlantic: Modernity and Double Consciousness* (Cambridge, MA: Harvard University Press, 1995); Serge Gruzinski, "Les mondes mêlés de la monarchie catholique et autres 'connected histories,'" *Annales* 56, no. 1 (2001): 85–117; Walter Mignolo, *Local Histories/Global Designs: Coloniality, Subaltern Knowledges and Border Thinking* (Princeton, NJ: Princeton University Press, 2000); Manuel A. Vásquez and Marie Friedman Marquardt, *Globalizing the Sacred: Religion Across the Americas* (New Brunswick, NJ: Rutgers University Press, 2003), especially 197–222; Michelle A. Stephens, "Black Transnationalism and the Politics of National Identity: West Indian Intellectuals in Harlem in the Age of War and Revolution," *American Quarterly* 50, no. 3 (1998): 592–608. Exemplary works of Atlantic World history in this vein include Jessica Marie Johnson, *Wicked Flesh: Black Women, Intimacy, and Freedom in the Atlantic World* (Philadelphia: University of Pennsylvania Press, 2020); James H. Sweet, *Domingos Álvares, African Healing, and the Intellectual History of the Atlantic World* (Chapel Hill: University of North Carolina Press, 2011); Karen Graubart, "Learning from the *Qadi*: The Jurisdiction of Local Rule in the Early Colonial Andes," *Hispanic American Historical Review* 92, no. 2 (2015): 195–228. Valentina Napolitano, *Migrant Hearts and the Atlantic Return: Transnationalism and the Roman Catholic Church* (New York, NY: Fordham University Press, 2016). Jane E. Mangan, *Transatlantic Obligations: Creating the Bonds of Family in Conquest-era Perú and Spain* (New York, NY: Oxford University Press, 2016). Brandon

R. Byrd demonstrates the dangers of assuming that transnational networks—like the Black International—are exempt from power relations caused by hierarchies among participants, in this case hierarchies within the African diaspora linked to geography, race, religion gender, or class; see his *The Black Republic: African Americans and the Fate of Haiti* (Philadelphia, PA: University of Pennsylvania Press, 2020). Silvia Rivera Cusicanqui points out the lumpiness and inequalities of transnational academic networks in her "*Ch'ixinakax utxiwa*: A Reflection on the Practices and Discourses of Decolonization," *South Atlantic Quarterly* 111, no. 1 (2012): 95–109.

28. Voekel, *Alone before God*; Pamela Voekel, "The Baroque Church," in *The Cambridge History of Religions in Latin America*, ed. Virginia Garrard, Paul Freston, and Stephen C. Dove (New York, NY: Cambridge University Press, 2016), 160-172. Here I part ways with François-Xavier Guerra, who argues that except for a few Latin Americans alert to French or North American ideas, new modern visions of community washed ashore in Spanish America beginning around 1808; he also notes that New Spain's numerous religious tracts as compared to France's indicated modernity's retardation in Mexico. See François-Xavier Guerra, *Modernidad y independencies. Ensayos sobre las revoluciones hispánicas* (México, D.F.: Fondo de Cultura Económica, 1993), 13, 85, 89, 101, 290, 338. On the violence to other ways of being enacted by notions of "universal Man," see Sylvia Wynter, "Unsettling the Coloniality of Being/Power/Truth/Freedom: Towards the Human, after Man, Its Overrepresentation—An Argument," *The New Centennial Review* 3, no. 3 (2003): 257–337. For an astute critique of the notion of modernity as secular and religion as a zone of tradition, and of liberal notions of putatively deracinated individuals as superior to communal identification, see, for example, Saba Mahood, *The Politics of Piety: The Islamic Revival and the Feminist Subject* (Princeton, NJ: Princeton University Press, 2005). Also see Jonathan Sheehan, "Enlightenment, Religion, and the Enigma of Secularization: A Review Essay," *American Historical Review* 108, no. 4 (2003): 1061–1080. The outsized influence of French secular *philosophes* and the French Revolution has been a constant theme in the historiography of ideas in Latin America during the Age of Revolution. Not even the most erudite theologians are spared. Hugh Hamill, for example, underscored the French Revolution and secular French ideas as key to Miguel Hidalgo y Costilla's thought and to New Spain's insurgency. In 1987, an exasperated Carlos Herrejón Peredo noted that French encyclopediasts had no influence on Hidalgo; and the fact that several of the rebel priest's friends read Rousseau did not cancel out the priest's years of theological study. See Hugh Hamill, *The Hidalgo Revolt* (Tallahassee, FL: University of Florida Press, 1966); and Carlos Herrejón Peredo, *Hidalgo: razones de la insurgencia y biografía documental* (México, D.F.: Secretaría de Educación Pública, 1987), 34. For an illuminating critique of the notion that France radiated the Enlightenment outward, see Premo, *Enlightenment on Trial*, passim.

29. Mario Góngora, "Estudios sobre el galicanismo y la 'Ilustración católica' en América española," *Revista Chilena de Historia y Geografia* 125 (1957): 126. Also see George M. Addy, *The Enlightenment in the University of Salamanca* (Durham, NC: Duke University Press, 1966).

30. José Pérez Calama arrived in New Spain with the reformist Bishop of Puebla Francisco Fabían y Fuero in 1765, and served as rector of the Seminario y Colegio de San Nicolás Obispo in Valladolid beginning in 1784, and, starting in 1789, as Bishop of Quito. Calama provides a case in point of how Reform Catholic ideas were disseminated by the clerical hierarchy and then transformed and repurposed for more radical ends by the lower clergy and the literate laity. Calama recommended reformist luminaries Daniele Concina, Luís António Vernei, and Melchor Cano to his professors at the seminary. Rebel priest Miguel Hidalgo y Costilla was heavily influenced by Cano and Vernei while studying at the seminary in Valladolid and wrote

a 1784 thesis entitled *Disertación sobre el verdadero método de estudiar teología escolástica* at the Colegio, where Calama served as director in 1784. Hidalgo's thesis is reproduced in Carmen Rovira, *Pensamiento filosófico méxicano del siglo XIX y primeros años del XX* (México: UNAM, 1988), 163–180.

31. How, then, has the map of the Atlantic world failed to incorporate the fractious empire of faith in its trans-imperial explanations of the Age of Revolution? Two characteristics of the historiography of the independence and immediate post-independence period have limited most scholars' ability to appreciate the context in which this turbulent religious rupture unfolded. First, although there is no more transnational and hydra-headed institution in this era than the Catholic Church, nationally framed studies have rendered invisible this region-wide and pan-Atlantic religious discord at the center of Latin America during the 1790 to 1860 period.The result is a historiography that often imposes national integration backward onto the colonial period and the period when the new republics' boundaries were in flux, or indeed not yet imagined. There are a number of excellent studies of Reform Catholic luminaries and projects in Latin America, the Caribbean, and Spain, but they mostly confine themselves to one country or center on individual thinkers, or fail to examine or fully elaborate this religious current's larger social and political linkages and effects. See, for example, the following: Miguel Figueroa y Miranda, *Religión y política en la Cuba del siglo XIX. El obispo Espada visto á la luz de los archivos romanos, 1802-1832* (Miami, FL: Ediciones Universal, 1975). Guillermo Gallardo, *La política religiosa de Rivadavia* (Buenos Aires: Ediciones Teoría, 1962). Consolación Fernández Mellén, *Iglesia y poder en la Habana. Juan José Díaz de Espada, un obispo ilustrado (1800-1832)* (Bilbao: Universidad del País Vasco, 2014). Ana Carolina Ibarra, "Religión y política. Maneul Sabino Crespo, un cura párroco del sur de México" *Historia Mexicana* 56, no. 1 (July–September 2006): 5–69. Eduardo Torres-Cuevas, ed. and intro., *Obispo Espada. Ilustración, reforma y antiesclavismo. Selección, introducción y notas de Eduardo Torres-Cuevas* (Cuba: Palabra de Cuba, 1990). Brian Larkin, *The Very Nature of God: Baroque Catholicism and Religious Reform in Bourbon Mexico City* (Albuquerque, NM: University of New Mexico Press, 2010). William Elvis Plata Quezada, "El catolicismo liberal (o liberalismo católico) en Colombia decimonónica," *Franciscanum. Revista de las ciencias del espíritu* 51, no. 152 (2009): 71–132. For an interesting examination of the role of "Jansenist episcopalism" in Chile's battle for the *patronato*, see Lucretia Enríquez "El patronato en Chile de Carrera á O'Higgins," *Hispania Sacra* 60, no. 122 (July–December 2008): 507–529. Two works employ a wider framework than the nation-state or region or individual actors, although neither work pursues the wider influence of these ideas on particular sectors of society; see D. A. Brading, *The First America: The Spanish Monarchy, Creole Patriots and the Liberal State 1492-1866* (New York, NY: Cambridge University Press, 1991), 492–514; and Mario Góngora, "Estudios sobre el galicanismo y la 'Ilustración católica' en América española," *Revista Chilena de Historia y Geografía* 125 (1957): 96–151..

32. Works on reformers and Reform Catholicism in Spain are numerous and include the following: María Giovanna Tomisch, *El Jansenismo en España: Estudios sobre las ideas religiosas en la segunda mitad del siglo XVIII*, prologue Carmen María Gaite (Madrid, ES: Siglo Vientiuno España Editores, 1972). Germán Ramírez Aledón, ed., *Valencianos en Cádiz. Joaquin Lorenzo Villanueva y el grupo valenciano en las Cortes de Cádiz* (Cádiz, ES: Biblioteca de la Cortes de Cádiz, Fundación Municipal de Cultura, 2008). Paula Demerson, *María Francisca de Sales Portocarrero: una figura de la Ilustración* (Madrid, ES: Editorial Nacional, 1975). Richard Herr, *The Eighteeenth-Century Revolution in Spain* (Princeton, NJ: Princeton University Press, 1959). Joël Saugnieux, *Un prélat éclairé: Don Antonio Tavira y Almazán, 1737-1807: contribution à l'étude du jansénisme espagnol* (Toulouse, FR: Ibérie Recherche, 1970). Gérard Dufour, *Juan

Antonio Llorente en France (1813-1822): contribution a l'étude du libéralisme chrétien en France et en Espagne au début du XIX siècle (Geneva, CH: Libraire Droz, 1982). Antonio Mestre Sanchís, "Repercusión del sínodo de Pistoia en España," in *Il sinodo di Pistoia del 1786: atti del convegno internazionale per il secondo centerario, Pistoia-Prato, 25-27 settembre 1986*, ed. Claudio Lamioni (Rome, IT: Herder, 1991): 425–439. Andrea J. Smidt, "Bourbon Regalism and the Importation of Gallicanism: The Political Path for a State Religion in Eighteenth-Century Spain," *Anuario de Historia de la Iglesia* 19 (2010): 25–53. Charles Noel, "Clerics and Crown in Bourbon Spain, 1700-1808: Jesuits, Jansenists, and Enlightened Reformers," in Bradley and Van Kley, eds., *Religion and Politics*, 119–154. Manuel Revuelta González, S.J, *Politica religiosa de los liberales en el siglo XIX* (Madrid: Escuela de Historia Moderna, 1973). Andrea J. Smidt, "Fiestas and Fervor: Religious Life and Catholic Enlightenment in the Diocese of Barcelona, 1766-1775" (Ph.D Dissertation, Ohio State University, 2006), and her "Josep Climent I Avinent (1706-1781): Enlightened Catholic, Civic Humanist, Seditionist," in *Enlightenment and Catholicism in Europe. A Transnational History*, ed. Jeffrey D. Burson and Ulrich L. Lehner (Notre Dame, IN: University of Notre Dame Press, 2014): 327–353. Ulrich Lerner provides examples of the Catholic Enlightenment from a number of regions, including Spain and Latin America, see his Ulrich L. Lehner, *The Catholic Enlightenment: The Forgotten History of a Global Movement* (New York, NY: Oxford University Press, 2016). William J. Callahan, "Two Spains and Two Churches, 1760-1835," *Historical Reflections-Réflexions Historiques* 2, no. 2 (Winter 1976), 157-181.

33. Giambattista Vico, quoted in Michel Foucault, "What Is Enlightenment?" in *The Foucault Reader*, ed. Paul Rabinow (New York, NY: Pantheon, 1984), 44; Premo, *Enlightenment*, 2.

34. Most recently, Raúl Coronado reinvigorated O. Carlos Stoetzer's earlier work, arguing that at the turn of the nineteenth century, a monolithic Scholastic Church co-existed with scientific rationality and modern philosophy, with the latter two the protagonists of the breakthrough from a world given by God to one amenable to man's agency—that is, a world of new political forms like democracy; see his *A World Not to Come: A History of Latino Writing and Print Culture* (Cambridge, MA: Harvard University Press, 2016). O. Carlos Stoetzer, *The Scholastic Roots of the Spanish-American Revolution* (New York, NY: Fordham University Press, 1979). In another vein, José Carlos Chiriamonte critiques the notion that the Neo-Scholasticism of Franciso Suárez, not what he terms "Enlightenment thought," influenced the protagonists of Argentina's independence; see his "Ensayos sobre la 'Ilustración argentina" (Paraná, Argentina: Facultad de Ciencias de la Educación, Universidad del Litoral, 1962), 76–78; also see his *La Ilustración en el Río de la Plata. cultura eclesiástica y cultura laica durante el virreinato* (Buenos Aires: Editorial SudAmerica, 2007).

35. Alonso Nuñez de Haro y Peralta, *Carta pastoral que el doctor d. Alonso Núñez de Haro y Peralta... dirige a todos sus amados diocesanos sobre la doctrina sana en general, contraída en particular á las mas esenciales obligaciones que tenemos para con dios, y para con el rey* (México: Don Felipe de Zúñiga y Ontiveros, 1777), 68.

36. Voekel, *Alone Before God*, 46.

37. E. H. Davenport provides a useful introduction to the ninth-century decretals of Isidore Mercater; these "forgeries" aggrandized the power of Rome over the church; see his *The False Decretals* (Oxford, UK: B.H. Blackwell, 1916). Known as the Pseudo-Isidore these ninth century decretals are not to be confused with the seventh-century collections of canons known as the Hispana and also attributed to St. Isidore of Seville, see Harold J. Berman, *Law and Revolution. The Formation of the Western Legal Tradition* (Cambridge, MA.: Harvard University Press,

1983), 60, fn. 4. J. H. Burns and Thomas M. Izbicki, *Conciliarism and Papalism* (Cambridge, UK: Cambridge University Press, 1997). Dale K. Van Kley, "Catholic Conciliar Reform in an Age of Anti-Catholic Revolution. France, Italy and the Netherlands, 1758-1800," in *Religion and Politics in Enlightenment Europe*, ed. James Bradley and Dale K. Van Kley (Notre Dame, IN: Notre Dame University Press, 2001), 46–118.

38. London, "Carta de Un Americano," November 11, 1811, in *Cartas de Dr. Fray Servando Teresa de Mier (bajo el seudonimo de Un Americano), años de 1811 y 1812* (Monterrey, MX: Tipografia del Gobierno, 1888), 137.

39. See, for example, Lauren G. Kilroy-Ewbank, *Holy Organ or Unholy Idol? The Sacred Heart in Art, Religion, and Culture of New Spain* (Leiden, NL: Brill, 2018).

40. Works that include information on Delgado's schism include the following: Santiago Malaina, S.J., *Historia de la erección de la diócesis de San Salvador* (San Salvador, ELSL: Imprenta Arzobispal, 1944). Mauricio Domínguez T., "El Obispado de San Salvador: foco de desavenencia político-religioso," *Anuario de Estudios Centroamericanos* 1 (1974): 87–132. Carlos Meléndez Chaverri, *El presbítero y doctor don José Matías Delgado, en la forja de la nacionalidad Centroamericana* (San Salvador, ELSL: Direction General de Publicaciones del Ministerio de Educación, 1962). Luis Ernesto Ayala Benítez, *La iglesia y la independencia política de Centroamérica: el caso del estado de El Salvador (1808-1832)* (San Salvador, ELSL: Editorial Don Bosco, 2011). Ayala Benítez draws on multiple archival sources to provide a detailed account of the schism's progression. The book contains a useful appendix of primary sources and he quotes at great length from primary sources in the body of the work. Although he recognizes that some priests supported the liberal cause, he does not see two religious factions in the schism or the larger conflicts between reformist and ultramontane Catholics in Central America and the Atlantic world.

CHAPTER 1

1. Chares Esdaile, *The Peninsular War* (London: Penguin Books, 2002), 285.

2. The literature on the Cortes de Cádiz is copious. A good starting point is Manuel Chust's "The Impact of the Cortes de Cádiz on IberoAmerica (1810-1830)," in *Forging Patrias: IberoAmerica 1810-1824: Some Reflections*, ed. Guadalupe Jiménez Codinach (México: Fomento Cultural Banamex, 2010), 403–453. María Teresa García Godoy, *Las cortes de Cádiz y América: el primer vocabulario liberal español y mejicano (1810-1814)* (Sevilla: Diputación de Sevilla 1998). Scott Eastman and Natalia Sobrevilla Perea, eds., *The Rise of Constitutional Government in the Iberian Atlantic World: the Impact of the Cádiz Constitution of 1812* (Tuscaloosa: University of Alabama Press, 2015). Emilio La Parra López and Antonio Mestre, *El primer liberalismo español y la iglesia: las Cortes de Cádiz* (Alicante: Instituto de Estudios Juan Gil-Albert: Diputación Provincial, 1985). Manuel Moreno Alonso, *La Constitución de Cádiz: Una mirada crítica* (Seville: Ediciones Alfar, 2011). Victor Peralta Ruiz, "El impacto de las Cortes de Cádiz: Un balance historiográfico," *Revista de Indias* 68, no. 242 (2008): 67–96. Mario Rodríguez, *The Cádiz Experiment in Central America, 1808–1826* (Berkeley: University of California Press, 1978). Aaron Pollock, "Las Cortes de Cádiz en Totonicapán: Una alianza insólita en un año insólito," *Studia Historica. Historia Contemporánea* 27 (2009): 207–234.

3. On the electoral process, see Matilde Souto Malecón, "El primer ejercicio constitucional en la Nueva España: la elección del ayuntamiento de la ciudad de Veracruz en 1812. Descripción de la mecanica electoral," in *Elecciones en México en el México del siglo veinte. Las prácticas*, ed. Fausta Gantús (México: Instituto Mora, 2016), 55–92. Also see Antonio Annino, *Historia de*

las elecciones en Iberoamérica, siglo XIX: De la formación del espacio político nacional (México, DF: Fondo de Cultura Económica, 1995).

4. See Melchor Campos García and Roger Domínguez Saldívar, *La diputación provincial en Yucatán, 1812-1823. Entre la iniciativa individual y la acción del gobierno* (Mérida, Mx.: Ediciones de la Universidad Autónoma de Yucatán, 2007). Nettie Lee Benson, *The Provincial Deputation in Mexico, Harbinger of Provincial Autonomy, Independence, and Federalism* (Austin, TX: University of Texas Press, 1992). Jaime E. Rodríguez, "Las instituciones gaditanas en Nueva España, 1812-1814," in *Las nuevas naciones, España y México, 1750-1850*, ed. Jaime E. Rodríguez O (Madrid: MAFRE, 2008), 99–124.

5. On the exclusion of African-descended people from citizenship, see David Sartorious, *"Of Exceptions and Afterlives: The Long History of the 1812 Constitution in Cuba,"* in Eastman and Sobrevilla, *The Rise*, 150–176. Also see María Elena Martínez's towering *Geneological Fictions. Limpieza de Sangre, Religion, and Gender in Colonial Mexico* (Stanford, CA: Stanford University Press, 2008). Jessica L. Delgado and Kelsey C. Moss, "Religion and Race in the Early Modern Iberian Atlantic," in *The Oxford Handbook of Religion and Race in American History*, ed. Paul Harvey and Katherine Gin Lum (New York, NY: Oxford University Press, 2018). María Elena Martínez argues that Iberian institutions and agents "generated and circulated information about religion and caste and created networks within, between, and outside the two empires." Racial discourses were "cosmopolitan, and not national, enterprises." See her "Religion, Caste, and Race in the Spanish and Portuguese Empires. Local and Global Dimensions," in *Iberian Empires and the Roots of Globalization*, ed. Anna More, Ivonne del Valle, and Rachel Sarah O'Toole (Nashville, TN: Vanderbilt University Press, 2019), 91. Anna More, Ivonne del Valle, and Rachel O'Toole remind us that the racial configurations and discourses Martínez discusses were always in dialogue with local conditions and understandings, see their *Iberian Empires*, 10. Karen Graubart exemplifies the collective wisdom in her "Learning from the Qadi: The Jurisdiction of Local Rule in the Early Colonial Andes," *Hispanic American Historical Review* 92, no. 2 (2015): 195–228. This reform-inflected notion of virtue was not a European import. Campeche's city council barred the Duke of Estrada from its ranks, for example, citing his African heritage as a justification. Mérida's Sanjuanista-controlled newspaper, *Clamores*, noted that the Campeche councilmen had maligned people "as black in color as they were white in the virtue of their souls." Fortunately, Sanjuanistas judged people by their virtue not their color, the author from Campeche, Emeterio Balius, reported; see Mérida, *Clamores de la Fidelidad Americana Contra la Opressión, o fragmentos para la historia futura* (hereafter *Clamores*) December 29, 1813, Suplemente al Clamor num. VII, 1. On virtue in this time period, see Voekel, *Alone Before God*, 77–105. On citizenship, see Hilda Sabato, ed., *Ciudadanía política y formación de las naciones. Perspectivas históricas de América Latina* (México: Fondo de Cultura Económica and El Colegio de México, 1999); and Erika Pani, "Actors on a Most Conspicuous Stage: The Citizens of Revolution," *Historical Reflections/Reflections Historiques* 29 (2003): 163–188.

6. Voekel, *Alone Before God*, passim. Here I break decisively with historian François Xavier-Guerra, who stresses the French origins of the individual as society's fundamental constituent. He notes that the victorious project in Spain and in Spanish America belonged to "the most radical group, those who adhered essentially to a French revolutionary vision. Namely, that the Nation, in which sovereignty resides—in the strongest sense of the word—consists of equal individuals." See Francois Xavier-Guerra, "The Spanish-American Tradition of Representation and its European Roots," *Journal of Latin American Studies* 26, no. 1 (February 1994): 5. Laura Machuca Gallegos notes that the Sanjuanistas displayed new political sensibilities; their petitions bore the names of male individuals not corporate groups or collectivities;

see her "Opinión pública y represión en Yucatán, 1808-1816," *Historia Mexicana* 66, no. 4 (264) (April–June 2017): 1698, 1747. The Sanjuanistas were the unexpected spawn of the reformist Catholic Bourbon state and church. Other more subaltern groups in the empire had creatively combined strands of Spanish Neo-Scholastic theories of popular sovereignty with Andean or Meso-American or other philosophies. On indigenous Andean commoners who did just that, signing their correspondence collectively as "beloved comunero brothers," or simply "the comun" see, for example, S. Elizabeth Penry, *The People*, especially 13–15, 151–157. I also break with Sylvia Wynter's argument that the path to the sovereign individual subject of liberalism was necessarily a secular one, while agreeing that this notion of the subject violently foreclosed the acceptance of other ways of being human—like those of the comuneros described by Penry; see Sylvia Wynter, "Unsettling the Coloniality."

7. Spanish Jesuit Francisco Suárez argued that political authority derived from God but resided in the people, broadly defined, and remained inalienable; the people could thus transfer their polity to a monarch and recover the sovereignty transferred to a king turned tyrant. Herein lay a justification to overthrow tyrannical rulers, a firm rejection of monarchical absolutism. A fine Spanish translation of Suárez's 1613 *Defensio fidei* can be found in José Ramon Eguiller Muñoz Guren, trans., *Defensa de la fé católica y apostólica contra los errores del anglicanismo* (Madrid, ES: Instituto de Estudios Políticos, 1971). See Leopoldo José Prieto López, "Hechos e ideas en la condena del Parlamento de París de la *Defensio fidei* de Suárez: poder indirecto del papa en temporalibus, derecho de resistencia y tiranicidio," *Relecciones. Revista Interdisciplinaria de Filosofía y Humanidades* 7 (2020): 37–53. The elite urban creoles of the Sanjuanista movement transformed Reform Catholicism; the extant literature suggests that the rural and indigenous or mestizo majority of Mexico did not embrace this reformist church current. See, for example, Terry Rugeley, *Of Wonders and Wise Men: Religion and Popular Cultures in Southeast Mexico, 1800-1876* (Austin, TX: University of Texas Press, 2001).

8. Ana Carolina Ibarra, *Andrés Quintana Roo* (México, D.F.: Senado de la República, 1987). J. Ignacio Rubio Mañé and Emiliano Enrique Canto Mayén, *Andrés Quintana Roo, patriota y literato* (Mérida, Yucatán, México: Ayuntamiento de Mérida, 2010).

9. Lynda Sanderford Morrison notes that a 1795 census put 28,552 people in Merida, and, based on an 1810 census, 500,000 total people in the peninsula, with 375,000 thousand Indians, 7,000 whites, and 55,000 mixed-race people or *castas*; see her "The Life and Times of José Canuto Vela: Yucatan Priest and Patriot (1802-1859)" (PhD diss., University of Alabama, 1993), 84.

10. Mérida, Provincial Deputation, "Informe acerca del estado de la provincia, y el remedio que considera oportuno a los desordenes que indica, quales son la separación del actual gefe superior," July 23, 1813, AGI, Mexico, 3097A. Manuel Ferrer Muñoz details the larger Yucatecan context during the independence era, see his "La coyuntura de la independencia en Yucatán, 1810-1821," in *La independencia en el sur de México,* ed. Ana Carolina Ibarra (Coyoacán, México: UNAM/Instituto de Investigaciones Históricas, 2004), 343–394.

11. Lorenzo de Zavala has inspired numerous biographies. On his early life in the Yucatán, see Marcela González Calderón, *El Yucatán de Zavala: sus primeros años* (México: Secretaría de Educación del Gobierno del Estado de México, 2012). On Quintana, see Laura Machuca Gallegos, "José Matías Quintana: un hombre entre dos tradiciones," in Sergio Quezada and Inés Ortiz Yam, eds., *Yucatán en la ruta del liberalismo mexicano, siglo XIX* (Mérida, MX: Universidad Autónoma de Yucatán, 2008), 141–166.

12. A good summary is found in Madrid, Pedro de Garibay to king, October 14, 1814, AGI, Mexico, 3006.

13. Mérida, "Pedimiento," August 7, 1812, AGN-Mexico, Bienes Nacionales, vol. 1512, exp. 14, fols. 1–2. Also see Mérida, Manuel Artazo to Secretaria del Estado, December 1, 1812, AGI, Mexico, 3010.

14. Mérida, Ángel Alonso y Pantiga, Francisco de Paula y Villegas, and José Manuel Bersumorza to Captain General Manuel Artazo, March 16, 1813, AGI, Mexico, 3046. Mérida, Pedro Agustín Estéves y Ugarte Report, September 25, 1812, AGI, Mexico, 3097A.

15. Perhaps the best known reformist Catholic of the early eighteenth century, the Italian Lodovico Antonio Muratori, criticized the not-yet defined dogma of the Immaculate Conception of Mary and the blood vow the Jesuits took to defend it. Much of his criticism stemmed from reformers' promotion of Christocentric piety and redefintion—but not outright rejection—of Marian devotion and devotion to the saints. See Shaun Blanchard, "Proto Ecumenical Catholic Reform in the Eighteenth Century. Lodovico Muratori as a Forerunner of Vatican II," *Pro Ecclesia* 25, no. 1 (February 2016): 86–89. Paola Vismara, "Ludovico Antonio Muraroti (1672-1750): Enlightenment in a Tridentine Mode," in *A Companion to the Catholic Enlightenment*, ed. Ulrich L. Lehner and Michael Pinty (Leiden, NL: E.J. Brill, 2010), 249–268. Andres Quintana Roo, José Matias Quintana's son, co-edited the *Semanario Patriótico Americano*, an insurgent newspaper. The paper pointed to "the wise Muratori" as an intellectual font for its notions of sovereigny. See the *Semanario Patriótico Americano*, August 9, 1812, no. 4, p. 4.

16. Mérida, Pedro Obispo de Mérida, September 28, 1812, AGI, Mexico, 3097A. In response to the bishop's censure of Sanjuanista gatherings, both Vicente Velázquez and José Francisco Bates petitioned the captain general for permission to gather to discuss the constitution in their homes, see AGEY, Apartado Colonial, Ramo Correspondencia de Gobernadores, vol. 1, exp. 4, imagenes 016–018.

17. On Hidalgo, see Gabriel Méndez Plancarte, *Hidalgo, reformador intelectual* (Mexico: Ediciones Letras de México, 1945); and Hamill, Jr., *Hidalgo Revolt.* . On Morelos, see Julio Zárate, *José María Morelos: ensayo biográfico* (México: Porrúa, 1987). Numerous works treat the insurgency. See, for example, Van Young, *The Other Rebellion.* ; and his "The Limits of Atlantic World Nationalism in a Revolutionary Age: Imagined Communities and Lived Communities in Mexico, 1810–1821" in *Empire to Nation. Historical Reflections on the Making of the Modern World*, ed. Joseph Eshrick, Hasan Kayali, and Eric Van Young (New York, NY: Rowman and Littlefield, 2006), 34–67. Guedea, *En busca.* Read together, Guedea and Van Young underscore the diversity of the insurgents' ideologies, especially along class and racial lines.

18. Mérida, Josef Martínez de la Pedrera, Ángel Alonso y Pantiga, and Pedro Manuel de Regil, May 15, 1813, AGI, México, 1822.

19. Mérida, Ángel Alonso y Pantiga, Francisco de Paula y Villegas, et. al. to Captain General Artazo, March 16, 1813, AGI, Mexico, 3046.

20. Mérida, Captain General Artazo to Señores electores de partidos reunidos en esta capital, July 10, 1813, AGI Mexico, 3046. Mérida, Ángel Alonso y Pantiga, Francisco de Paula de Villegas, and José Manuel Bersumorza to Manuel Artazo, March 16, 1813, AGI, Mexico, 3046. Mérida, José Matías Quintana to Captain General Manuel Artazo, April 12, 1813, AGI, Mexico, 3046. Artazo had been present in 1789 during the Tupac Amaru revolt in the Andes. Perhaps not surprisingly, he understood the Sanjuanistas for what they were: champions of an empire-wide constitutional monarchy, not insurgent rebels bent on rupture with Spain. On Artazo's long service to the king, see J. Ignacio Rubio Mañé, "El gobernador, capitán general e intendente de Yucatán, mariscal don Manuel Artazo y Barral, y la jura de la constitución

español en Mérida, el año de 1812," in *Boletín del Archivo General de la Nación* 9, nos. 1–2 (1968): 59–60.

21. Mérida, "Articulo Comunicado," *El Aristarco Universal. Periódico Critico-Satirico é Instructivo de Mérida de Yucatán*, May 14, 1813, no. 7, p.1.

22. Mérida, José Matías Quintana and Josef Francisco Bates to Sr. Ministro de la Gobernación de Ultramar, July 10, 1813, AGI, Mexico, 3046. On the 1812 violence during a city council election in Veracruz, see Matilde Souto Mantecón, "1812: Un año crítico. Violencia y elecciones en Veracruz," in *Cuando las armas hablan, los impresos luchan, la exclusión agreda . . . Violenca electoral en México, 1821-1921*, ed. Fausta Gantús Innureta and Alicia Salmerón Castro (San Juan Mixcoac, Ciudad de México: Instituto Mora, 2016), 39–72. On conflicts between reformist and conservative Catholics in Veracruz during the late colonial period, see Voekel, *Alone Before God*, 106–145.

23. Mérida, Capitan General de El Yucatán to Consejo de la Regencia, no date, AGI, Mexico, 3046.

24. Cádiz, Cortes de Cádiz Edict, November 9, 1812, Arrigunaga Collection, BLAC, Box 1, Folder 15. Cádiz, November 9, 1812, AGI, Mexico, 3046. Mérida, José Matías Quintana and Josef Francisco Bates to Sr. Ministro de Ultramar, July 10, 1813, AGI, Mexico, 3046. On the economic consequences of the ban on obventions, see Lorgio Cobá Noh, *El "indio ciudadano:" La tributación y la contribución personal directa en Yucatán, 1786-1825* (Mérida, México: Universidad Autónoma de Yucatán, 2009), esp. 122–124, 127. William B. Taylor cites disputes over parish fees as the most ubiquitous conflict between priests and their indigenous parishioners in the eighteenth century, see his *Magistrates of the Sacred. Priests and Parishioners in Eighteenth-Century Mexico* (Stanford, CA: Stanford University Press, 1996), 424–447.

25. Mérida, Andrés Marino Peniche, May 8, 1813, AGI, Mexico, 3097A.

26. Mérida, Juan José Duarte, José Ortiz, José María Dominguez, and Ignaico Manzanilla, March 3, 1814, AGN-México, Bienes Nacionales, vol. 1245, exp. 8, fols. 3–4.

27. Víctor M. Suárez Molina, ed. and intro., *Estado de la industria, comercio y educacion de la provincia de Yucatán en 1802 y causas de la pobreza de Yucatán en 1821* (Mérida, Yucatán, MX: Ediciones Suárez, 1955).

28. Mérida, *El Redactor Méridano. Periódico del MIA de Esta Ciudad*, August 13, 1813, no. 14, p. 5.

29. Mérida, José Matiás Quintana and Josef Francisco Bates to Sr. Ministro de la Gobernación de Ultramar, July 10, 1813, AGI, Mexico, 3046. In this document Quintana and Bates note that *El Aristarco* of April 21, 1813, no. 23, and of May 14, 1813, no. 7, ran a report where Villegas boasted about beating Indians and another in which O'Horán said he administered 2,000 lashes to his charges. For a representation from Indians from Sisal de la Villa de Valladolid describing priests beating "citizens," see Mérida, City Council Records, March 13, 1813, transcribed in Betty Luisa de María Auxiliadora Zanolli Fabila, "*La alborada del liberalismo Yucateco*: El I *Ayuntamiento Constitucional de Mérida (1812-1814)*" (MA thesis., 2 vols., UNAM, Facultad de Filosofía y Letras, 1993), 2:320–321.

30. Mérida, "Articulo Comunicado," *El Aristarco Universal. Periódico Critico-Satirico é Instructivo de Mérida de Yucatán*, May 14, 1813, no. 7, p. 1. Captain General Artazo complained to authorities in Spain about Villegas and O'Horán's cruelty to Indians and the incessant conflicts they provoked as members of the Provincial Deputation; see Mérida, Captain General Artazo to Secretario del Estado y del Despacho de la Gobernación de Ultramar, AGI, Mexico, 3046.

31. Cura de Hoctum Raymundo Pérez, *Yucatecos* (Mérida, Yucatán: J.E. Bates Impresor, 1813).

32. Terry Rugeley, *Yucatán's Mayan Peasantry and the Origins of the Caste War* (Austin, TX: University of Texas Press, 1996), 43.

33. Ibid., 47.

34. Bartolomé José del Granado Baeza, *Informe del cura de Yaxcabá* (Yucatán, 1813). On Granado Baeza, see Gustavo Martínez Alomía, *Historiadores de Yucatán. Apuntes biográficos y bibliográficos de los historiadores de esta peninsula desde su descubrimiento hasta fines del siglo XIX* (Campeche, Yucatán: Tipografia "El Fénix," 1906), 103. On the Sanjuanistas' critique of *rutinero* clerics' violence toward their Indian charges, see Mérida, José Matías Quintana and Josef Francisco Bates to Sr. Ministro de Ultramar, July 10, 1813, AGI, Mexico, 3046.

35. Mérida, José Ortiz, José María Dominguez, and Ignacio Manzanilla, March 3, 1814, AGN-México, Bienes Nacionales, vol. 1512, exp. 8, fols. 1–2.

36. Archbishop of Mexico Francisco Antonio de Lorenzana and Bishop of Puebla Francisco Fabián y Fuero both championed historical scholarship on the early church while members of Toledo's cathedral chapter between 1750 and 1762, see Luis Sierra Nava, *El cardenal Lorenzana y la Ilustración* (Madrid: Fundación Universitaria Española, Seminario Cisneros, 1975), 93.

37. Mérida, *Clamores*, April 25, 1814, no. 24, p.1; reproduced in María del Carmen Ruiz Castañeda, ed., *Clamores de la Fidelidad Americana Contra la Opression o Fragmentos para la Historia Futura* (México, DF: UNAM, 1986), 105.

38. Tomisch, *El jansenismo*, 21. Lucienne Domergue, "De Erasmo a George Borrow: Biblia y secularización de la cultura española en el Siglo de la Luces," in *La secularización de la cultura española en el Siglo de la Luces: Actas del Congreso de Wolfenbüttel*, ed. Manfried Tietz (Weisbaden, DE: Herzog August Bibliothek Wolfenbüttel, 1992), 57–90. The work of Jacques Bénigne Bossuet provides a perfect case in point of Bourbon church hierarchs increasing emphasis on biblical exegesis and the extreme regalism they often surmised from the Holy Book. Bossuet was frequently read and cited by Bourbon reformers. See his oft-cited *Política deducida de las propias palabras de la Sagrada Ecritura, revisada y traducida por Miguel Joseph Fernández*, 3 vols. (Madrid, ES: Andrés Ortega, 1768). Three works by Bossuet, including the *Política deducida*, were found in rebel leader Miguel Hidalgo y Costilla's library, see Roberto Ramos V, *Libros que leyó don Miguel Hidalgo y Costilla* (México: Editorial Jus, S.A., 1969), 14.

39. Góngora, "Estudios sobre el galicanismo,"126. Mónica Hidalgo Pego, "Formando ministros útiles: inculcación de hábitos y deberes trasmitidos en el Colegio de San Ildefonso (1768-1816)," in *Espacios de saber, espacios de poder. Iglesia, universidades y colegios en Hispanoamérica, siglos XVI–XIX*, ed. Rodolfo Aguierre Salvador (México: Universidad Autónoma de México, 2013), 378–379.

40. Francisco Antonio Lorenzana, "Carta pastoral, santa visita del Pueblo de Zaqualpán," October 12, 1767, Biblioteca Virtual, Patrimonio Bibliográfico, Gobierno de España, 1. On the campaign against Probabilism, see John Tate Lanning, *The Eighteeenth-Century Enlightenment in the University of San Carlos de Guatemala* (Ithaca, NY: Cornell University Press, 1956), 140. Mónica Hidalgo Pego, "Formando ministros," 383. Archbishop Alonso Núñez de Haro y Peralta felt truly moral priests must learn to detest Probabilism, the theory so dear to the Jesuits, and fiercely embrace Probabiliorism, see "Constituciones XXX. De los estudios," in his *Sermones escogidos, pláticas espirituales privadas, y dos pastorales, anteriormente impresas en México: con el retrato del autor, y un resúmen histórico de su vida* (Madrid: Imprenta de la Hija de Ibarra, 1807), 159. Anti-Probabilism was on full display at the 1772 Third Lima Conciliar Assembly. On the spirited works championing both sides of the debate circulated in the city, see Victor Ruiz de Peralta, "Las razones de la fé. La iglesia y la Ilustración en el Perú, 1750-1800," in *El Perú en el siglo XVIII: La era Borbónica*, ed. Scarlett O'Phelan Godoy (Lima, PE: Pontifica Universidad Católica del Perú, Instituto Riva Agüero, 1999), 177–204.

41. Francisco Antonio Lorenzana, "Carta pastoral, Santa visita del pueblo de Zaqualpán," October 12, 1767, Biblioteca Virtual, Patrimonio Bibliografico, Gobierno de Espana, 1.

42. Real Cedula of 1768 cited in Silvado G. A. Benito Moya, "La cultura teológico de las elites letradas. ¿Especulación teórico o pragmaticismo en el Tucumán del siglo XVIII?" *Hispana Sacra* 65, no. 131 (January–June 2013), 342. Natal Alexander (or Nöel Alexandre) was an appellant against the Bull Unigentius. John Tate Lanning and Rafael Heliodoro Valle, intro. and eds., *Reales cedulas de la Real y Pontifica Universidad de México de 1551 á 1816* (México: Imprenta Universitaria, 1946), 213–214. George M. Addy, *The Enlightenment in the University of Salamanca* (Durham, NC: Duke University Press, 1966), 114, 236. José Carlos Chiaramonte, *La Ilustración,75.*

43. Antonio de Tavira y Almazán, Bishop of Canarias, February 15, 1792, "Carta Pastoral," Biblioteca Virtual, Patrimonio Bibliografico, Gobierno de Espana, pp. 2–3.

44. Daniele Cóncina, *Historia del probabilisimo y rigorismo. Disertaciones teologicas, morales, y criticas, en que se explican, y defienden de las sutilezas de los modernos probabilistas los principios fundamentales de la theologia Christiana, Tomo 1*, trans. *Mathias Joachin de Imaz* (Madrid, ES: En la Oficina de la Viuda de Manuel Fernández, 1772). The original work in Italian apparently dated from 1743; see Daniele Concina, *Della storia del probabilismo y del rigorismo: Dizzertazione teologiche, morali y critiche* (Venice, IT: Simon Occhi, 1743), and his *Letter teologico-morali in cointinuazione della difesa della storia del probabilismo e rigorismo, ecc. del P. Daniele Concina: Overro confutazione della riposte pubblicata dal M.R.P.B. dell Compangnia [di jesú]*, 6 vols. (Venice, IT: Simone Occhi, 1751-1754).

45. For more on the changes in Catholic practice and thought among the laity in Mexico City and Veracruz caused in part by the Bourbon state and church's reformist Catholic campaigns, see Voekel, *Alone Before God*, passim.

46. "Dr. Fr. José Nicolás de Lara. Noticia biográfica sobre este celebre yucateco," *Registro Yucateco* 2 (1845): 92–93, 99, 103.

47. Mérida, "Noticias," *El Redactor Méridano. Periodico del MIA de Esta Ciudad*, June 24, 1813, no. 14. The "Noticias" are from Santiago de Cuba, February 12, 1813.

48. Mérida, "Vindicación de los Sanjuanistas sobre la excommunion," *Clamores*, March 1, 1814, no. 19, reproduced in Ruiz Castañeda, *Clamores*, 81.

49. Tlalpujahua y Huichapa, *Semanario Patriótico Americano*, no. 18, November 5, 1812, pp. 2–5.

50. Tomisch, *El jansenismo*, 50. Herr, *Eighteenth-Century Enlightenment*, 17–18.

51. Jaujilla, "Fragmento de las notas en que San Martín confiesa su vocación insurgente," 1817; Juan Hernández y Dávalos, *Colección de documentos*, 6:227.

52. Tecpan, "Statement of Nicolás Ochoa Garibay," 1817, AGN-México, Inquisición, vol. 1416, exp. 21, fols. 269r–270v.

53. Josef Eduardo de Cardenas, *Memoria a favor de la provincia de Tabasco, en la Nueva España, presentado a S.M Las Cortes Generales Extraordinaras por el Dr. D. Josef Eduardo de Cardenas. Diputado en ellas por dicho providencia* (Cádiz, ES: En la Imprenta Ðel Estado Mayor General, 1811), 26, 79.

54. Manuel Sabino Crespo quoted in Ibarra, "Religión y política," 36.

55. Oaxaca, *Correo Americano del Sur*, num. 24, August 5, 1813, 1.

56. Ibarra, "Religión y política," 5–69.

57. Fray Servando Teresa de Mier, *Memorias*, ed. Antonio Castro Leal, 2 vols. (México: Porrúa, 1946), 1:206–207.

58. Mérida, José Matías Quintana, *Clamores*, no. 23, April 18, 1814, p. 1, reproduced in Ruiz Castañeda, *Clamores*, 97. On the funeral of Matías Quintana's daughter Tomasa, see *El Misceláneo*, no. 96, November 13, 1813, p. 2. On Quintana's daughter-in-law, see José Martînez Pichardo, Enrique Peña Nieto, and V. Humberto Benítez Treviño, *Leona Vicario: grandeza de una mujer de su tiempo en la lucha por la Independencia* (Toluca de Lerdo, Estado de México: Gobierno del Estado de México, 2008). Erika Pani, "'Ciudadana y muy ciudadana'? Women and the State in Independent Mexico, 1810–1830," *Gender & History* 18, no. 1 (April 2006): 9.

59. Mérida, José Matías Quintana, *Clamores*, no. 1124, January 1814, p. 4, reproduced in Ruiz Castañeda, *Clamores*, 51.

60. Bustamante's letter to José Matías Quintana was dated May 11, 1812, see Carlos María de Bustamante, *El indio mexicano o avisos al rey Fernando septimo para la pacificación de la America Septentrional. Obra redactada en dos opúsculos durante la permanencia del autor en la prisión del castillo de San Juan de Ulúa en los años 1817-1818. Seguidos del discurso Motivos de mi afecto a la constitución*, ed. Manuel Arellano Zavaleta (México: Instituto Mexicano del Seguro Social, 1981), lv.

61. Mérida, José Matías Quintana, *Clamores*, no. 2, November 22, 1813, p. 8, and no. 3, November 29, 1813, pp. 9–12.

62. José Matías Quintana, *Clamores*, no. 15, February 21, 1814, in Ruiz Castañeda, *Clamores*, 95.

63. José Matías Quintana, *Clamores*, no. 18, March 14, 1814, pp. 2–3, transcribed in Ruiz Castañeda, *Clamores*, 78–79. On Quintana's public protest against the bishop of Puebla, Manuel Ignacio Gonzales del Campillo, see *Clamores*, no. 15, February 24, 1814, p. 2, transcribed in Ruiz Castañeda, *Clamores*, 96.

64. José Matías Quintana, *Clamores*, no. 18, March 14, 1814, pp. 2–3, transcribed in Ruiz Castañeda, *Clamores*, 78–79.

65. José Matías Quintana, *Clamores*, no. 19, March 21, 1814, p. 3, transcribed in Ruiz Castaneda, *Clamores*, 83.

66. Tlalpujahua y Huichapa, *Semanario Patriótico Americano*, no. 18, November 5, 1812, p. 8.

67. For a more detailed examination of the context of the Noris case, see Schmidt, "Bourbon Regalism," 33–34. In front of the Inquisition in 1820, Fray Servando Teresa de Mier mentioned the Noris case as part of an argument about the injustices surrounding the "Index Librorum Prohibitorum," or "Index of Prohibited Books." The list, he argued, unjustly targeted reformist works, see his "Carta del Dr. Mier al inquisidor Dr. D. José Antonio Tirado y Priego, 28 May 1820," in *Colección de documentos para la historia de la Guerra de Independencia de México de 1808 á 1821*, vol. 4, ed. Juan E. Hernández y Dávalos (Nendeln, LI: Kraus, 1968), 838.

68. Góngora, "Estudios sobre el galicanismo," 126.

69. Andrea J. Smith, "Bourbon Regalism," 43.

70. Burns and Izbicki, *Conciliarism*. Also see Van Kley, "Catholic Conciliar Reform," 46–118.

71. Tlalpujahua y Huichapa, *Semanario Patriótico Américano*, November 5, 1812, num. 18, p. 6.

72. Eamon Duffy, *Saints and Sinners*, 195.

73. Francisco Martí Gilabert, *La abolición de la Inquisición en España* (Pamplona, ES: Ediciones Universidad de Navarra, 1975), 90. Eugenio López-Aydillo, *El obispo de Orense en la regencia del año 1810* (Madrid: Imprenta de Fortanet, 1918), 49–50, 58–59, 76–77. José Ramón Hernández Figueiredo, *El cardenal Pedro de Quevado y Quintano en las Cortes de Cádiz* (Madrid: Biblioteca de Autores Cristianos, 2012).

74. López-Aydillo, *Obispo de Orense*, 79; Esdaile, *Peninsular War*, 281, 306.

75. Pedro, obispo de Orense, *Representación del Ecmo. Sr. obispo de Orense, dirigida al supremo consejo de Regencia* (Cádiz, ES: D. Antonio de Murguía, 1812), 4–7. Obispo de Orense et.al, *Manifiesto del obispo de Orense á la nación Española* (Valencia, ES: Imprenta de Francisco Brusola, 1814), 1, 11. Marcelino Menéndez Pelayo, *Historia de los heterodoxos españoles, vol. V, Heterodoxia en el siglo XIX*, ed. Enrique Sánchez Reyes, 2nd ed. (Madrid: Consejo Superior de Investigaciones Científicas, 1946), 44–45.

76. Pedro, Obispo de Orense, *Representación*, 4–7. Obispo de Orense, et.al, *Manifiesto*, 1, 11. Marcelino Menéndez Pelayo, *Historia*, 44–45.

77. Mérida, *El Redactor Méridano*, June 10, 1813, no. 4, p. 14. Mérida, City Council Minutes, June 1, 1813, transcribed in Zanolli Fabila, "La Alborada," vol. 2, 379. The document that the constitutional city council referred to was Pedro, Obispo de Orense, *Representación*.

78. Provincial Deputation, *Proclama de la diputación provincial de Yucatan á sus habitantes* (Mérida, Yucatán: Imprenta del Gobierno, 1814), 1. The provincial deputation's proclamation was signed by Manuel Artazo, Juan José Duarte, Manuel Pacheo, José Joaquín Pinto, Francisco Ortiz, José Francisco de Cicero, and Pedro Manuel Escudero on July 25, 1814. It was reprinted in Madrid and Caracas. See Madrid, *Atalaya de la Mancha*, no. 246, December 24, 1814, pp. 1–7; and Caracas, *Gazeta de Caracas*, no. 10, April 5, 1815, pp. 1–6.

79. The Provincial Deputation reported that Sanjuanistas Pablo Moreno, Vicente Velázquez, and Alexandro Montore sent Agustín de Zavala to Cádiz as their spokesman. See Mérida, January 13, 1814, Manuel Pacheco, Francisco de Paula Villegas, Juan José Duarte, et al. to Sn. Secretaria de Estado y del Despacho de la Gobernación de Ultramar, AGI, Mexico, 3032.

80. Miguel Ramos de Arizpe presented Zavala's claims of electoral fraud to the Cádiz Cortes on July 26, 1813. See Cortes, *Diario de las discusiones y actas de las cortes. Tomo XXI* (Cádiz, ES: Imprenta Nacional, 1813), 38. For more on Zavala's complaints as they wended their way through the Cortes, see Cortes, *Actas de las sesiones de la legislatura ordinario de 1813* (Madrid, ES: Imprenta y Fundación de las Viudas y Hijos de J. Antonio García, 1876), 192; and Cortes, *Actas de las sesiones de la legislatura ordinaria de 1814* (Madrid, ES: Imprenta y Fundación de las Viudas y Hijos de J. Antonio García, 1876), 42.

81. Cádiz, *El Procurador General de la Nación y del Rey*, August 10, 1813, no. 314, p. 1. Cádiz, *El Conciso*, August 29, 1813, no. 29, p. 2. For further analysis of the two papers, see María Rodríguez Gutiérrez, "Las modalidades literarias en la prensa de las Córtes de Cádiz: el caso de *El Procurador General de la Nación y del Rey* (1812-1813)," in *La guerra de pluma. Estudios sobre la prensa de Cádiz en el tiempo de la Cortes(1810-1814). Tomo primero. Imprentas, literatura y periodismo*, ed. Marieta Cantes Casenave, Fernando Dúran López, and Alberto Romero Ferrer (Cádiz, ES: Servicio de Publicaciones de la Universidad de Cádiz, 2006), 305–389. Beatriz Sánchez Hita, "La imprenta en Cádiz durante la Guerra de la Independencia y su relación con la prensa periódica," in Casenave et. al, *La guerra de pluma*, 50–51.

82. Cádiz, "Articulo remitido," *El Duende de los Cafés*, December 22, 1813, no. 144, pp. 1–4. For more on *El Duende de los Cafés*, see Sánchez Hita, "La imprenta," 82–83.

83. Mérida, Pedro Agustín Obispo de Yucatán to Antonio Cano Manuel, July 30, 1813, AGI, Mexico 3032. Zavala sailed to Havana out of Sisal on April 23, 1813, with a passport apparently surreptitiously issued to him by Captain General Manuel Artazo's secretary, Sanjuanista Pablo Moreno. See Mérida, Manuel Artazo to Bishop Estéves y Ugarte, 1 May 1813, AGI, Mexico, 3032; and Bishop Estéves y Ugarte to Captain General Artazo, May 1, 1813, AGI, Mexico, 3032.

84. Cádiz, "Articulo remitido," December 22, 1813, *El Duende de los Cafés*, no. 144, pps. 1–4.

85. Cádiz, *Diario Mercantil de Cadiz*, August 27, 1813, no. 307, pp. 2–3.

86. The copious correspondence between imperial authorities and Yucatán conservatives is summarized in Madrid, Pedro de Garibay to King, October 14, 1814, AGI, Mexico, 3006.

87. Mérida, Francisco de Paula Villegas, Ángel Alonso y Pantiga, José Manuel Bersumorza, Captain General Manuel Artazo, April 2, 1813, AGI, Mexico, 3046. Madrid, R to Provisor y Vicario General Interino de la Diócesis de Cádiz, February 22, 1814, AGI Mexico, 3097A. Cádiz, "Articulo remitido," *El Duende de los Cafés*, December 22, 1813, no. 144, pps.1–4. Salvador Bernabéu Alberti and Daniel García de la Fuente, "Un Comanche en las Cortés de Cádiz: los informes y trabajos de Ramos Arizpe," *Revista de Historia de la Educación Latinoamericana* 16, no. 23 (July–December 2014): 217–230, esp. 223 n. 19.

88. Cádiz, Regencia del Reyno, Juan María Villavicencio, February 23, 1813, AGAY, Cabildo Diocesano. Documentos Gubermentales y Papeles Recibidos, 1720-1832, exp. 2, no. 168. *Discusión del proyecto de decreto sobre el Tribunal de la Inquisición* (Cádiz, ES: Imprenta Nacional, 1813). P. Manuel Revuelta, "Las dos supresiones de la Inquisición durante la Guerra de la Independencia," *Miscelánea Comillas* 71, no. 139 (2013): 221–263. On the establishment of the new tribunals in New Spain, see J. L. Quezada Lara, *¿Una Inquisición constitucional? El Tribunal Protector de la Fé del Arzobispado de México, 1813-1814* (Zamora, MX: El Colegio de Michoacán, 2016).

89. María Ángeles Casado and Emilio La Parra, *La inquisición en España. Agonía y abolición* (Madrid: Catarata, 2013), 99–100. Roberto López Vela, "La jurisdicción inquisitorial y la eclesiástica en la historiografía," *Espacio, Tiempo y Forma, Historia Moderna* 7 (1994): 383–408. Juan Antonio Llorente, *Memoria histórica sobre cuál ha sido la opinión nacional de España acerca del Tribunal de la Inquisición* (Madrid: Imprenta de Sancha, 1812).

90. Cádiz, Luis de Borbón, Cardenal de Escala y Archobispo de Toledo, "Circular de la regencia contra el nuncio," April 1813, reprinted in London, *El Español*, May 1813, pp. 58–65. Cádiz, Juan María Villavivencio to Cabildo Diocesano, February 23, 1813, AGAY, Documentos Gubermentales y Papeles Recibidos 1720-1832, exp. 2, no. 168.

91. Pedro Gravina, *Manifiesto del arzobispo de Nicea don Pedro Gravina, nuncio y legado de su santidad sobre las ocurrencias de su extrañamiento* (Madrid: Repullés, 1814), 3, 12, 22, 36, 55.

92. Cádiz, "Mi primera visita á la tertulia de los Serviles," *El Duende de los Cafés*, August 8, 1813, no. 8, pp. 3–4; Mérida, *El Misceláneo*, September 18, 1813, no. 30, p. 1; Valencia, *Gazeta de Valencia*, July 30, 1813, no. 6, p. 1.

93. Fernando Peña Rambla, *La inquisición en las Cortes de Cádiz. Un debate para la historia* (Castelló de la Plana, ES: Universitat Jaime I, 2016), 290–291. Roberto Calvo Torre, *Belezos: Revista de Cultura Popular y Tradiciones de La Rioja*, no. 7 (2008), 67–73.

94. Manuel García-Herreros, *Reflexiones sobre la protesta del M.R. arzobispo de Nicea D. Pedro Gravina* (Madrid, ES, 1814), 2, 5, 8. Madrid, Manuel García Herreros to Obispo de Yucatán, February 26, 1814, AGAY, Documentos Varios, vol. 1. His full name is Manuel Antonio García-Herreros y Saénz de Tejada.

95. Manuel García-Herreros, *Reflexiones*, 1.

96. Peña Rambla, *La Inquisición*, 290–291. Calvo Torre, *Belezos*, 67–73. Cristobal Robles Muñoz, "La reforma eclesiástica en las Cortes de Cádiz," in *La iglesia en los orígenes de la España contemporánea*, ed. José María Magaz Fernández (Madrid, ES: Publicaciones San Dámaso, 2009), 178–184.

97. On the divided Catholic Church in Spain, see William J. Callahan, "Two Spains and Two Churches 1760–1835," *Historical Reflections/Réflexions Historiques* 2, no. 2 (1976): 157–181.

98. Mérida, *El Miscelaneo*, September 18, 1813, no. 80, p. 2. Denis Gwynn, "Henry Grattan and Catholic Emancipation," *Studies: An Irish Quarterly Review* 18, no. 72 (1929): 590–591.

99. Mérida, *El Misceláneo*, August 15, 1813, no. 74, p. 6. Mérida, *El Misceláneo*, September 1, 1813, no. 76, p. 2.

100. Mérida, *Clamores*, January 24, 1814, no. 11, reproduced in Ruiz Casteñada, *Clamores*, 49–50.

101. Mérida, *El Misceláneo*, September 1, 1813, no. 76, pp.1–2.

102. Bishop Esteves y Ugarte described Santander's assailant as a "traitor to the king" serving time in San Juan de Ulúa prison, see Mérida, Bishop Esteves y Ugarte to King, October 10, 1814, AGI, México, 2597. Santander preached a series of sermons in honor of Ferdinand VII and against "insurgents" and "libertines" in 1814. See, for example, Leonardo Santander de Villavivencio, *Sermón que en la solemne función celebrada por la excelentísima Diputacion Provincal de Yucatán con asistencia de todas las corporaciones, en la santa iglesia catedral de Mérida el domingo 26 de Junio de 1814, en acción de gracias por el dichoso, y plausible regrego de nuestro muy amado y católico monarca el Dr. don Fernando 7 al territorio español predicó con tres dias de termino, el D. Leonardo Santander y Villavicencio, del clausto y gremio de la Real Universidad de Sevilla en el de sagrada teologia, canonigo magistral de dicha ciudad, y actualmente prebendado de esta santa iglesia catedral de Mérida, y catedratico de oprima de teologia en el seminario conciliar de ella* (Mérida, Yucatán: Imprenta del Gobierno, 1814). Other conservatives also recommended Santander to the king, noting he had been maligned by Napolean and by Mérida's liberals; see Mérida, Sala Capitular de Mérida de Yucatán to king, November 25, 1814, AGI, Mexico 2597.

103. The interrogation of Estéban Rejón dates from August 11, 1814, and is signed by Vicar General of the Bishopric Juan María Herrero and excerpted in J. Ignacio Rubio Mañe, *Los Sanjuanistas de Yucatan. Manuel Jimenez Solis, El padre Justis* (México: Boletín del Archivo General de la Nación, 9, 1–2, 1968b), 272.

104. Mérida, Capitan General Manuel Artazo, "Oficio," August 3, 1814, AGN-México, Bienes Nacionales, vol. 42, exp. 1, fols. 10v–11. On Esteban Rejón's Sanjuanista sympathies, see Rugeley, *Origins*, 51–52. Velázquez was heir to his father's estate in the town of Yaxcabá. In an 1813 publication, the town's priest, Bartolomé José del Granado, reported that of the town's 8,591 souls, 7,442 were Indians, 70 were creoles, and none were European. Everyone spoke Mayan, he reported, and only a few people spoke Spanish. See his *Informe del cura de Yaxcabá* (Yucatán, 1813), pp.1–2. Renán Irigoyen Rosaldo, *La Constitución de Cádiz de 1812 y los Sanjuanistas de Mérida* (Mérida, Yucatán: Ayuntamiento de Mérida, 1980), 28.

105. Mérida, Cathedral Chapter, October 18, 1813, AGI, Mexico, 3097A (signed by Don Santiago Martínez de Peralta, B. Manuel Josef González, Ignacio de Zepeda, Joseph de Zavalegui, and D. Leonardo Santander y Villavicencio). Mérida, Manuel de Zepeda to Palacio, January 28, 1814, AGI, Mexico, 3097A.

106. Mérida, Francisco de Paula Villegas, "Remitido," *El Misceláneo*, April 21, 1813, no. 23, p. 4.

107. Valladolid, Miguel Hidalgo y Costilla, "Manifesto del Sr. Hidalgo contestando los cargos que le hizo la inquisición," December 15, 1810, Document 164, in Juan Hernández y Dávalos, *Colección de documentos para la historia de la Guerra de Independencia*, vol. 2 (Mexico: Imprenta de José María Sandoval, 1877–1882), 2:301.

108. Mérida, "Acuerdos del MIA," *El Redactor Méridano*, October 7, 1813, no. 21. The paper reported receiving four official notices from the Secretaria de Gobernación de Ultramar about the Cortes' appointment of censorship board members for the province. Appointees included José María Calzadilla, Vicente María Velázquez, Pablo Moreno, Lorenzo de Zavala, and Pedro Almeida (Almeyda) with Manuel Ximenez, José Matías Quintana, and Jayme Tinto (Jaime) serving as *suplementes*. The original Cortes order appointing these men is found in Cádiz, Sr. Presidente de la Cortes, Edict, July 30, 1813, YCM-UA, roll 2.

109. Lorenzo de Zavala, Manuel Ximenes (Ximenez), Vicente María Velásquez (Velásquez), Pedro Almeida, José María Quintana, "*Junta Censoria*," July 20, 1814 (Mérida: Oficina P y L de D. José Francisco Bates, 1814).

110. These two were Manuel García y Sosa and Ildéfonso Montoré; see Mérida, *Alcance al Misceláneo*, July 20 1814, no. 166, p. 1. Mérida, Juan de Diós Henriquez, José Francisco Negroe, Vicente María Velásquez, Manuel García y Sosa, Domingo de Lara, Lorenzo de Zavala, Ildefonso Montoré, Joaquin Correa, Francisco Antonio del Canto, Ambrocio María Pinelo, Ignacio Marchena, José Anastacio Medina, Antonio del Valle, José Policarpo Tenorio, Juan José Espejo, Miguel de Peraza, Simón de Vargas, Lorenzo Argaiz, José Ignacio Méndez, Rafael Aguallo, Bernabe Negroe, José Peon, Alejandro Montoré, Fautismo Ikan, Manuel Iman, Nicolás Remires, José Lazaro Mena, Domingo Canton, Agustín de Zavala, Francisco del Castillo, "Power of Attorney Given to Pedro Almeyda," September 28, 1812, AGI, Mexico, 3097A.

111. Mérida, Minutes of the Mérida City Council, July 26, 1814, transcribed in Zanolli Fabila, "Alboratas," 2:618. Captain General Artazo's order to end the use of the *rutinero* and Sanjuanista labels in all public speech is found in Mérida, Capitan General Manuel Artazo y Terredemer, Bando, July 27, 1814, YCM-UA, Roll 9.

112. Henry Charles Lea, *A History of the Inquisition of Spain*, vol. 4 (New York, NY: Harper and Brothers, 1887), 424.

113. Germán Ramírez Aledón, ed., *Valencianos en Cádiz. Joaquin Lorenzo Villanueva y el grupo valenciano en las Cortes de Cádiz* (Cádiz, ES: Biblioteca de la Cortes de Cádiz, Fundación Municipal de Cultura, 2008), 29.

114. Mérida, Manuel Artazo, August 13, 1814, AGI, Mexico 3032.

115. Veracruz, Josef Francisco Bates to King Ferdinand VII, July 25, 1816, AGI, Mexico, 3097A.

116. Veracruz, "Dirijiendo las representaciones de don Lorenzo de Zavala, D. Matías Quintana, y Don Josef Francisco Bates, remitidos de Yucatán, y presos en el Castillo de San Juan Ulúa," AGI, Mexico, 3097A. This letter is signed by Lorenzo de Zavala and addressed to the King and dated July 22, 1816.

117. Veracruz, José María Quintana to King Ferdinand VII, August 29, 1816, AGI, Mexico, 3097A.

118. The Vicar General of the Bishopric is Juan María Herrero y Ascaró. Capitan General Manuel Artazo y Terredemer, AGN, Bienes Nacionales, leg. 42, exp. 1. Signed by Herrero on August 10, 1817.

119. Mérida, Manuel Artazo, "Oficio," 3 Aug.1814, AGN- México, Bienes Nacionales, vol. 42, exp. 1.

120. Mérida, "Causa criminal seguida en el Tribunal Eclesiástico contra el Pbro. Don Manuel Ximénez, Año de 1814," June 18, 1817, AGN-México, Bienes Nacionales, leg. 42, exp. 1 (signed by Vicar General of the Bishopric Herrero, 10 August, 1817). Also see Mérida, Miguel de Castro y Araoz to S.M, May 24, 1817, AGN-México, Bienes Nacionales, leg. 42, exp. 1; and Mérida, doctor Herrero to Manuel Ximenéz, August 1817, AGN-México, Bienes Nacionales, leg. 42, exp. 1.

121. Madrid, King to Captain General of the Yucatán, June 8, 1815, AGI, Mexico, 3097A. Madrid, Duque de Moctezuma, Antonio Gansos, Francisco Xavier Vega, Francisco Viana, Francisco Ybanez Leyba, El Marques de Sobremonte, Bruno Ballarino, October 18, 1814, AGI, Mexico, 1822.

122. Veracruz, Josef Dávila (Gobernador de Veracruz) to Sr. Ministro de Gracia y Justicia, "Dirijiendo las representaciones de Don Lorenzo Zavala, D. Matías Quintana, y Don Josef Francisco Bates, remitidos de Yucatán, y presos en el Castillo de San Juan Ullua," August 31,

1816, AGI, Mexico 3097A. That Artazo had the three men taken to San Juan Ulúa is confirmed in AGN-México, Infidencias, vol. 151, exp. 96, fol. 442.

123. Laura Machuca Gallegos details the events during and after the Sanjuanistas' arrest, see her "Opinión pública," 1732–1744.

124. Mérida, Tómas Quintana to King Ferdinand VII, August 22, 1814, AGI, México, 3032.

125. "Solicitud de Ildefonso Montoré, preso por ser adicto á la constitución, del año de 14 que lo dejen libre," Biblioteca Virtual de Yucatán, CAIHY manuscript 126. bibliotecavirtuald-eYucatán.com.mx, images 34 and 35. On a man that Velázquez and Quintana referred to as José Almeyda, see *La Diputación Provincial de Yucatán. Actas de sesiones, 1813-1814, 1820-1821*, intro. María Cecilia Zuleta (México, D.F: Instituto de Investigaciónes Dr. José María Luis Mora, 2006), 332, 360.

126. Mérida, Pedro Josef de Lapeda and Louis Rodríguez Correa, "Solicitud de los curas del sagrario de la catedral sobre no haber cumplido que en las iglesias auxiliaries no se cante misa sin su licencia,"November 17, 1815, AGAY, Asuntos Terminados, vol. 10, 1810-1819. Mérida, Pedro Agustín y Ugarte, November 17, 1815, AGAY, Asuntos Terminados, vol. 10, 1810–1819.

127. Real Palacio de México, Real Cedula, October 7, 1815, BLAC, Arrigunaga Collection, Box 1, Oversized, fol.1. Mérida, D. Miguel de Castro y Aroaz, Bando, January 17, 1816, BLAC, Arrigunaga Collection, Box 1, folder 47.

128. *Representación y manifiesto que algunos diputados á las cortes ordinarias firmaron en los mayores apuros de su opresión en Madrid, para que la magestad del señor D. Fernando el VII á la entrada en España de vuelta de su cautividad, se penetrase del estado de la nación, del deseo de sus provincias, y del remedio que creian oportuno; todo fue presentado á S.M. en Valencia por uno de dichos diputados, y se imagine en cumplimiento de real órden* (Madrid, 1814), 20, 36–37. José Matías Quintana later fingered Álonso y Pantiga as his principal accuser and referred to him as "the Persa" for signing the representation to the king signed by sixty-nine conservative Cortes' deputies; see Mérida, José Matías Quintana to Nicolás María del Castillo, March 4, 1820, AGEY, C12, 01, 021, 007-009. The sixty-nine conservative Cortes' deputies were known as "Las Persas" because the manifesto opened with an analogy between Persia and Spain, see Laura Machuca Gallegos, "Yucatan and Campeche Deputies in Cadiz and their idea about the Yucatán Peninsula, 1810-1814," *Anuario de Estudios Americanos* 69, no. 2 (July–December 2012): 711. For one of the original accusations against the Sanjuanistas, see Josef Martínez de la Pedrera, Ángel Alonso y Pantiga, and Pedro Manuel de Regil, "Expediente de los excesos de una facción conocida con el nombre de Sanjuanistas que introduce el desorden en aquella provincia," AGI, Mexico, 1822.

129. Félix María Calleja, *Bando publicado en México el 7 de octubre de 1815 por el virrey de la Nueva España Félix María Calleja del Rey insertando la cedula real expedida el 31 de enero de 1815 por el rey Fernando VII que le fue dirigida por el Real y Supremo Consejo y Camara de Indias en el sentido de que habiendose hecha presente por el diputado de Yucatán Ángel Alonso y Pantiga los perjuicios que se expeimentabn por haber abolido las Cortes los servicios que hacían los indios* (México, 1815).

130. David Morgan, *The Sacred Heart of Jesus: The Visual Evolution of a Devotion* (Amsterdam, NL: Amsterdam University Press, 2008), 5–11.

131. Lauren Grace Kilroy, "Dissecting Bodies, Creating Cults: Imagery of the Sacred Heart of Jesus in New Spain (PhD diss., UCLA, 2009), 172. Kilroy-Ewbank, *Holy Organ.* .

132. Kilroy, "Dissecting Bodies," 133, 143. For some serious sensorial pious imagery, see Ignatius of Loyola, *The Spiritual Exercises and Selected Works*, ed. George E. Ganss S.J. (New York: Paulist Pess, 1991), 121–128, 41.

133. Kilroy, "Dissecting Bodies," 60.

134. Ibid., 135–136.

135. Reverend Henry M. Baird, ed., *The Christian World: American and Christian Foreign Union*, vol. 26 (January–December 1875) (New York: American Foreign and Christian Union, 1875), 116–117.

136. Kilroy, "Dissecting Bodies," 195.

137. Raymond Jonas, *France and the Cult of the Sacred Heart: An Epic Tale for Modern Times* (Berkeley: University of California Press, 2000), 3.

138. Elizabeth Perry, "Coronation of the Virgin and the Saints," in *Painting a New World: Mexican Art and Life, 1521-1821*, ed. Rogelio Ruiz Goman, Donna Pierce, and Clare Bargellini (Austin: University of Texas Press; and Denver, Co.: Frederick and Jan Mayer Center for Pre-Columbian and Spanish Colonial Art at the Denver Art Museum, 2004), 216–218.

139. Kilroy, "Dissecting Bodies," 60.

140. Ibid., 203.

141. See, for example, Mexico City, "Declaración of Gregorio García Valdemora," August 1, 1768, AGN, Inquisición, vol. 1521, exp. 9; Mexico City, "Declaración de Teodesia González de Cedillo," August 26, 1767, AGN, Inquisición, vol. 1521, exp. 7. Eva María Mehl, "La expulsión de los jesuitas y la represión del jesuitismo en Nueva España," in Rodolfo Aguirre Salvador, ed., *Espacios de saber*, 332.

142. Salvador Bernabéu Alberti, "El vacío habitado. Jesuitas reales y simulados en México durante los años de la supresión (1767-1816)," *Historia Mexicana* (April–June 2009): 1273, 1285–1286, 1291.

143. Duffy, *Saints and Sinners*, 249.

144. Scipione de' Ricci cited in Charles A. Bolton, *Church Reform in 18th Century Italy: The Synod of Pistoia, 1786* (The Hague, NL: Martinus Nijhoff, 1969), 10.

145. Jonas, *France*, 139.

146. Kilroy, "Dissecting Bodies," 118, 69. On the continued popularity of Our Lady of the Light in Spain after the Jesuits' expulsión, see Enrique Jiménez López, "La devoción a la Madre Santísima de la Luz: un aspecto de la represión del jesuitismo en la Epaña de Carlos III," in Enrique Jiménez López, *Expulsión y exilio de los jesuitas españoles* (Alicante, ES: Universidad de Alicante, 1997), 213–228.

147. Immaculada Fernández de Arrillaga, "Profecías, coplas, creencias y devociones de los jesuitas expulsos durante su exilio en Italia," *Revista de Historia Moderna* 16 (1997): 92–93.

148. Duffy, *Saints and Sinners*, 269–272.

149. Kilroy, "Dissecting Bodies," 273. Fewer than twenty Jesuits worked in the Yucatán; they were drastically outnumbered by Yucatán's Franciscans, who numbered over one hundred at their peak. The Yucatán was not a site of major conflict between the two orders. See Mark Lentz, "The Mission That Wasn't: Yucatán's Jesuits, the Mayas, and El Peten, 1703-1767," *World History Connected* (October 2013) at http://worldhistoryconnected.press.illinois.edu/10.3/forum_lentz.html.

150. Santa Maria la Mayor Bajo del Anillo del Pescador (Rome), H. Cardenal Consalvo, July 6, 1817, AGAY, Gobierno Pastoral del Senor Estéves y Ugarte, exp. 2, no. 2. "Sobre el reestablecimiento de la Compania de Jesús," AGAY, Gobierno Pastoral del Senor Estéves y Ugarte, exp. 6, no. 25. The document includes letters from the bishops of Durango and Guanajuato urging the return of the Jesuits. Estéves y Ugarte was in favor of their return.

151. Cresencio Carrrillo y Ancona, *El Obispado de Yucatán. Historia de su fundación y de sus obispos. Desde el siglo XVI hasta el XIX. Seguida de las constituciones sindocales de la diócesis y otros documentos relativos* (Mérida, Yucatán: Imprenta y Litografia "R.Caballero," 1895), 957.

152. Juan Antonio de Castro y Toledo, *Varias poesias que en obsequio del sacratisimo Corazón de Jesús compuso Juan Antonio de Castro y Toledo* (Mérida, Yucatán: Imprenta del Gobierno, 1814).

153. Cristobal Rosel, ed., *Devoción á la Escala Santa. Su origen, translaciones y culto* (Reissued in the Yucatán) (Mérida, Yucatán: Imprenta del Gobierno, 1816), 1–2.

154. Anonymous, *Devoción cotidiana a los santos apostoles* (Mérida, 1816), YCM-UA, roll 15.

155. Un Sacerdote, *Novena de la sacratisima Virgin de Ytzmal. Esto es, á obsequio de la milagrosa imágen de nuestra señora, que baxo de este nombre se venera en su santuario del pueblo de Ytzmal, distante 15 leguas de la capital de Mérida* (Mérida, Yucatán: D. Andrés Martín, 1816), 4.

156. Mérida, Pedro, Bishop of Yucatán, February 9,1814, AGI, Mexico, 3097A.

157. Duffy, *Saints and Sinners*, 212–213.

158. Pedro Agustín Estévez y Ugarte, *Sermón predicado en la santa iglesia catedral de Mérida de Yucatán el día quince de octubre de 1815 por el illmo. don Pedro Agustín Estévez y Ugarte* (Mérida, Yucatán: Oficina del Gobierno, 1815), 5, 12–13, 20, 25.

159. M.L., *Resumen histórico del viage y cautiverio de Pio VII desde su partida de Roma hasta su regreso á esta ciudad o sea hasta su entera libertad*, trans. D.V.X.C.G. Mérida, 1816). [Reprint]

160. On lay women's piety, and women's often close relationships to clergy during the colonial period, see Jessica L. Delgado, *Laywomen and the Making of Colonial Catholicism in New Spain, 1630-1790* (New York, NY: Cambridge University Press, 2018). Delgado argues that if we regard colonial Catholicism as an institution almost uniformly oppressive to women, we "cannot fully understand the phenomenon of so many ordinary women publicly defending the church in the early national period," 2. On the feminization of piety in Mexico City, see Margaret Chowning, "La feminización de la piedad en México: Género y piedad en las cofradías de españoles: tendencias coloniales y pos-coloniales en los arzobispados de Michoacán y Guadalajara," in *Religión, política e identidad en la Independencia de México*, ed. Brian Connaughton (México D.F.: Universidad Autónoma Metropolitana de México, 2010). Also see Elizabeth O'Brien, "'If They Are Useful, Why Expel Them?' Las Hermanas de la Caridad and Religious Medical Authority in Mexico City Hospitals, 1861-1874," *Mexican Studies/Estudios Mexicanos* 33, no. 3 (2017): 417–442; Silvia Arrom, *Volunteering for a Cause: Gender, Faith, and Charity in Mexico from the Reform to the Revolution* (Albuquerque: University of New Mexico Press, 2016); Silvia Arrom, "Las Señoras de la Caridad: pioneras olvidadas de la asistencia social en México, 1863-1910" *Historia Mexicana* 226 (2007): 445–490; Silvia Arrom, "Mexican Laywomen Spearhead a Catholic Revival: The Ladies of Charity, 1863-1910," *Religious Culture in Modern Mexico*, ed. Martin A. Nesvig (Lanham, MD: Rowman & Littlefield, 2007), 50–77.

161. On the event in the Spanish papers, see, for example, Seville, "Arguelles quemado en figura en Mérida Yucatán," *Diario Critico General de Sevilla por el Setabiense*, February 1, 1815, no. 26, p. 1. Seville, *La Tía Norica á los Criticos del Malecón*, no. 29, 1815, p. 1. Also see the *Gaceta de Caracas*, no. 10, April 5, 1815, p. 1.

162. Mérida, *El Sabatino, Periodico Instructivo y Crítico de Mérida de Yucatán*, August 6, 1814, no. 32, p. 2, col. 2. Mérida, Deputation Provincial, July 23, 1813, AGI, Mexico, 3097A.

163. Mérida, Report of the Deputation Provincial, reprinted in Madrid, "Proclama," *Atalaya de la Mancha en Madrid*, December 24, 1814, no. 246, p. 4. The report was also reprinted in Mexico City, *Gazeta del Gobierno de México*, October 28, 1814, no. 648, pp. 1–6.

164. Sevilla, "Argüelles quemado en figura en Mérida Yucatán," *Diario Critico General de Sevilla por el Setabiense*, February 1, 1815, no. 26, p. 1, See, for example, Agustín Argüelles, author, and Francisco Tomás Valiente, ed., *Discursos* (Oviedo, ES: Junta General del Principado de Asturias, 1995).

165. Mérida, *El Sabatino. Periodico Instructivo y Crítico de Mérida de Yucatán*, August 6, 1814, no. 32, p. 2, col. 2. Mérida, Deputation Provincial, July 23, 1813, AGI, México, 3097A.

166. Subdelegado de Mama, "Manifiesto Viva Fernando VII," September 12, 1814, AGI, Mexico, 3032.

167. Manuel Cresencio Rejón, *Discursos parlamentarios (1822-1847). Compilación, notas y reseña biográfica por Carlos A. Achanove Trujillo* (México: Secretaría de Educación Pública, 1943), 67–69.

168. On influential reformist Catholics like Mier, José María Luis Mora, and Joaquin Lizardi, and Reform Catholic influence on politics and the public sphere of letters in the young republic, see Voekel, *Alone Before God*, 146–170.

169. Pablo Franco, José María Iturralde, Félix Osores, Joaquín Román, and Servando de Mier, *Dictamen de la comisión de patronato, leído en session pública, del soberano congreso mexicano. Se imprime de orden de su soberanía* (México: Imprenta Nacional del Supremo Goberino en Palacio, 1823).

CHAPTER 2

1. Dominican Archbishop Casáus was an exemplary Bourbon churchman; while in Mexico, he defended the ethical probabiliorist position against what reformers saw as the Jesuits' moral laxism, their probabilist ethics, and gave an invited eulogy at the funeral of reformist firebrand Bishop Alonso Núñez y Haro y Peralta's funeral. Like the reform-minded bishops appointed by the Bourbons, Casáus would later condemn the radicalism of the lower clergy and laity who transformed the Reform Catholicism of the late Spanish Empire away from its episcopalism and regalism and toward a more radically democratic church under civil auspices. In response to the rebel movement led by parish priest Miguel Hidalgo y Costilla and in light of Ferdinand VII's ultramontanism, Casáus would, like Yucatán's conservatives, evolve away from his reformist Bourbon stance and into a royalist then conservative ultramontanist. On his earlier intellectual trajectory in Mexico, see Mauricio Beuchot, "Algunos fuentes de la filosofía social de fray Ramón Casáus, catedrático de la Universidad de México y el autor de El Anti-Hidalgo," in *Los Dominicos insurgentes y realistas de México y Río de la Plata*, ed. Fray Eugenio Torres Torres (Santiago de Queretaro, Queretero, México: D.R. Instituto Dominicano de Investigaciones Históricas), 383–394.

2. The 1784 report is introduced and transcribed in Robert S. Smith, "Forced Labor in the Guatemalan Indigo Works," *The Hispanic American Historical Review* 36, no. 3 (August 1956), 319–328.

3. Guatemala City, Antonio González to Secretary of State, October 14, 1803, AGI, Guatemala 668.

4. Juan Carlos Sarazúa, "Recolectar, administrar y defender: la construcción del estado y las resistencias regionales en Guatemala, 1800-1871" (PhD diss., Universitat Pompeu Fabra, 2013), 33. Virginia Garrard-Burnett, "Indigo," in *Encyclopedia of Latin American History and Culture*, vol. 3, ed. Jay Kinsbruner and Erick D. Langer, 2nd ed., (Detroit, MI: Charles Scribner's Sons, 2008), 829–830. Madrid, Consejo de Indias, April 18, 1817, AGI, Guatemala, 668. José Antonio M. Fernández, *Pintando el mundo de azul: El auge añilero y el mercado centroaméricano, 1750–1810* (San Salvador: Dirección de Publicaciones e Impresos, Consejo Nacional para la Cultura y el Arte, 2003). Adrian C. Van Oss rejects the idea that Central America's economy revolved around exports. Central America's only monocrop, he notes, was corn grown for domestic consumption, see his "A Far Kingdom: Central American Autarky at the End of the Eighteenth

Century," in his *Church and Society in Spanish America* (Amsterdam, NL: CEDLA, 2003), 7. The *intendencia* of San Salvador in 1807 was home to 4,729 Spaniards; 71,715 *indios*; and 89,374 *mestizos*, see Xiomara Avendaño Rojas and Norma Hernández Sánchez, *¿Independencia o autogobierno? El Salvador y Nicaragua, 1786-1811* (Managua, NIC: LEA Grupo Editorial, 2014), Table 14, p.145. Carlos Meléndez Chaverri cites the following population statistics for 1811 San Salvador: 614 Spaniards, 585 *indios*, and 10,600 inhabitants classified as of mixed ancestry; see his *José Matías Delgado, prócer centroamericano,* 2nd ed. (San Salvador: Dirección de Publicaciones e Impresos, 2000), 86.

5. Troy Floyd, "The Indigo Merchant: Promoter of Central American Economic Development, 1750-1808," *Business History Review* 39, no. 4 (winter, 1965): 466–488.

6. Jeremy Baskes, *Staying Afloat: Risk and Uncertainty in Spanish Atlantic World Trade, 1760-1820* (Stanford CA: Stanford University Press, 2013); and Xabier Lamikiz, *Trade and Trust in the Eighteenth-Century Atlantic World: Spanish Merchants and their Overseas Networks* (Suffolk, UK: Boydell Press, 2013). Geoffrey A. Cabot, "The consolidation of 1804 in Guatemala," *The Americas, Academy of American Franciscan History* 29, no. 1 (1971): 20–38.

7. The pattern of economic tension between centers and peripheries has been widely noted by scholars of Latin America. In places like Veracruz, Mexico; Venezuela; and the Palatine lowlands, a "liberal crescent" housed new mercantile groups who had grown sleek under Bourbon auspices and who now vigorously advocated for free trade. They squared off against the colonial highlands, places like the central Andes and central Mexico, where entrenched merchants and artisans sought tariff protection. In short, the theory holds, conservative Catholic highlands battled liberal, anticlerical trading ports. This pattern is typically represented in the literature as reflecting the strength of "the church" in the central areas, and its weakness on the coast and frontier; see, for a summary of this literature, Alan Knight, "The Peculiarities of Mexican History: Mexico Compared to Latin America, 1821-1992," *Journal of Latin American Studies* 24 (quincentenary supplement 1992): 120–122. However, as my *Alone Before God* demonstrated for Veracruz and Mexico City, and as *For God and Liberty* demonstrates more broadly, the conflict is bettered explained by investigating *which* church current was most influential where, and among whom. Reformist Catholics were in influential in Veracruz, and many of them were merchants, Voekel, *Alone Before God*, passim, but especially 123–145 and 223.

8. Floyd, "The Indigo Merchant," 471–472. Richmond F. Brown, *Juan Fermín de Aycinena. Central American Colonial Entrepreneur, 1729-1796* (Norman, OK: University of Oklahoma Press, 1997),15. See also Robert W. Patch, "Imperial Politics and Local Economy in Colonial Central America, 1670–1770," *Past and Present* 143 (1994): 77–107.

9. Brown, *Juan Fermín*, 34, 96. Brown refers to the Monte Pío de Cosecheros de Añil as the "Indigo Growers' Fund." The body's statutes organized the growers as a guild and established a fund under its administration to be used for financing production. It was headquartered in San Vicente, the heart of El Salvador's indigo producing region. The royal treasury loaned the guild 100,000 pesos, backed by a new export duty of 4 pesos per *zurron* (214 pounds) of indigo. Though never enough to meet all the growers' demands, this fund reduced their dependence on the merchants until the industry collapsed later in the nineteenth century under pressure from new synthetic dyes; see Ralph Lee Woodward, Jr., "Economic and Social Origins of the Guatemalan Political Parties (1773-1823)," *Hispanic American Historical Review* 45, no. 4 (November 1965): 547.

10. San Salvador, Don Pedro Delgado to Señores Cosecheros don Alexandro Sanz de Verugo and Vocales, January 2, 1794, AGI, Guatemala 668. Guatemala, Monte Pio Cosecheros de Añil, Guatemala y El Salvador, 1782 á 1819, AGI, Guatemala, 668; San Salvador, Pedro Delgado to

Señor Presidente Gobernador y Capitan General Dn. Bernardo Froncoso, January 13, 1794, AGI, Guatemala, 668. For more on the merchants' guild, see Ralph Lee Woodward, Jr., *Class Privilege and Economic Development: The Consulado de Comercio of Guatemala, 1793–1871* (Chapel Hill: University of North Carolina Press, 1966).

11. Madrid, Consejo de Indias, April 17, 1817, AGI, Guatemala, 668. See also Guatemala, Antonio González to Secretary of State, October 14, 1803, AGI, Guatemala 668.

12. The Bourbon reforms liberalized interoceanic commerce, increasing commercial interchange between and within Iberia and New World imperial possessions. Merchant tribunals were organized in Carácas (1793), Guatemala City (1793), Buenos Aires (1794), Havana (1794), Cartagena (1795), Chile (1795), Veracruz (1795), and Guadalajara (1795); see Matilde Souto Mantecón, *Mar abierto. La política y el comercio del Consulado de Veracruz en el ocaso del sistema imperial* (Mexico: El Colégio de México, Instituto Mora, 2001), 49.

13. Guatemala City, Antonio González to Secretary of State, October 14, 1803, AGI, Guatemala 668.

14. On the Reform Catholic influence on the increasingly vocal antipathy to excessive luxury in the late eighteenth century and beyond into the mid-nineteenth century, see Voekel, *Alone Before God, passim*, but especially 43–76, and 156–160.

15. Romero del Alamo, *Efectos perniciosos del lujo: Las cartas de D. Manuel romero del Alamo al Memorial Literario de Madrid (1789)*, ed. Elvira Martínez Chacón (Oviedo, ES: Universidad de Oviedo, Servicio de Publicaciones, 1985), 624–638, 19, 426, 432. Gaspar Melchor de Jovellanos, "Población de España," in Biblioteca de autores Españoles desde la formación del lenguaje hasta nuestros días. Obras públicas y inéditas de Don Gaspar Melchor de Jovellanos, multiple vols., ed. D. Miguel Artola (Madrid: Ediciones Atlas, 1961), 56:595.

16. Oviedo, May 6, 1782, Gaspar Melchor de Jovellanos, "Discurso pronunciado por el señor Gaspar de Jovellanos del Consejo de S.M. de la Real Sociedad de Amigos del País del Principado de Asturias y su actual director," in Ramon Jordan de Urries, ed., *Cartas entre Campomanes y Jovellanos* (Madrid: Fundación Universitaria Español, 1975), 32–33.

17. For a suggestive argument about the rise of individual aesthetic taste as a marker of social status, see Michael Kwass, "Big Hair: A Wig History of Consumption in Eighteenth-Century France" *American Historical Review* 111, no. 3 (June 2006): especially 644, 656–658. On fashion and discourses on luxury and status, see Tamara J. Walker, *Exquisite Slaves. Race, Clothing, and Status in Colonial Lima* (Cambridge, UK: Cambridge University Press, 2017). Marta V. Vicente, *Clothing the Spanish Empire: Families and the Calico Trade in the Early Modern Atlantic World* (New York: Palgrave MacMillan, 2006), 65–84. Rebecca Earle, "Luxury, Clothing and Race in Colonial Spanish America," in *Luxury in the Eighteenth Century. Debates, Desires, and Delectable Goods*, ed. Maxine Berg and Elizabeth Eger (Houndmills, UK: Palgrave Macmillan, 2003): 219–227. Silvia Hunold Lara, "The Signs of Color: Women's Dress and Racial Relations in Salvador and Rio de Janeiro, ca 1750–1815," *Colonial Latin American Review* 6, no. 2 (1997): 205–222.

18. Anonymous, *España triumfante del ocio, del lujo, y de ciertas preocupaciones, bajo el gobierno de la constitucion política de la monarquía por un español amante de su patria* (Madrid: Imprenta de Fuenebro, 1820), 33.

19. Ibid.

20. Ibid., 11, 15, 31–34, 37, 39, 45. Bernard Mandeville, *The Fable of the Bees: or Private Vices, Publick Benefits*, ed. F.B. Kaye (Indianapolis: University of Indiana Press, 1988 [org.1714]). The poem dates from 1705.

21. Humberto Tandron, *El comercio de Nueva España y la controversia sobre la libertad de comercio, 1796-1821* (México, D.F.: Instituto Mexicano de Comercio Exterior, 1976), 9–10. Eduardo

Arcila Farías, *Reformas económicos del siglo XVIII en la Nueva España* (México, D.F.: SepSetentas, 1984), 1:106, 132.

22. Mérida, Yucatán, February 3, 1814, "Consulta de la Diputación Provincial de Yucatán en el expediente de comercio libre," BLAC, Arrigunaga Collection, Box 1, Folder 24.

23. On the insurgent press in the larger context of newspaper production during the Independence period, see Virginia Guedea, "Las publicaciones periódicas durante el proceso de independencia (1808-1821)," in *La república de las letras. Asomos a la cultura escrita del México decimonónico*, ed. Belem Clark de Lara and Elisa Speckman Guerra (México, D.F.: UNAM, 2005), esp. 30.

24. Oaxaca, *Correo Americano del Sur*, October 13, 1813, no. 33, p. 4

25. *Ilustrador Americano*, October 3, 1812, no. 2, p. 2.

26. Ibid.

27. *Seminario Patriótico Americano*, August 16, 1812, no. 5, p. 6.

28. Mérida, Yucatán, *El Yucateco o El Amigo del País. Periódico de Mérida*, May 17, 1828, p. 1.

29. Anonymous, "Medidas politícas que deben tomar los jefes de los ejércitos americanos para lograr su fin por medios llanos y seguros, evitando la efusión de sangre de una y otra parte," 1812, AGN-México, Historia, vol. 116, fols. 89r–90v.

30. Valladolid, Miguel Hidaldo y Costilla, "A todos los habitantes de América" (December 15, 1810), *El Despertor Americano*, December 20, 1810, no. 1, p. 3.

31. *Seminario Patriótico Americano*, August 9, 1812, no. 4, p. 4.

32. *Seminario Patriótico Americano*, December 6, 1812, no. 21, p. 1.

33. *Seminario Patriótico Americano*, January 10, 1813, no. 26, p. 4.

34. Mérida, *Clamores de la fidelidad americana contra la opresión o fragmentos para la historia futura*, January 17, 1814, reproduced in Ruiz Castañeda, ed., *Clamores* ,45.

35. François-Xavier Guerra notes that on November 7, 1811, 7,000 copies of the *Diario de México* were distributed in Mexico City alone, enough for one out of twenty of the capitol's 140,000 persons to have their own copy, see his *Modernidad e independencia*, 281.

36. Mexico City, *Diario de México*, August 13, 1811; Voekel, *Alone Before God*, 160.

37. *Concilio Provincial Mexicano IV: Celebrado en la ciudad de México el año de 1771* (Queretero, México: Escuela de Artes, 1898), 182. D. Alonso Núñez de Haro y Peralta, "Edicto de 20 de octubre de 1774 communicando al clero de su diócesis que con motivo de su próxima visita a la misma ha dispuesto no se le hagan festejos de ninguna especie," BN-México, Lafragua Collection, vol. 100, p. 7. Lorenzana and Fabian y Fuero both promoted scholarship on early church history while serving in the cathedral chapter in Toledo, Spain, between 1750 and 1762. See Luis Sierra Nava, *El cardenal Lorenzana y la Ilustración* (Madrid: Fundación Universitaria Española, Seminario Cisneros, 1975), 93.

38. José Eduardo de Cárdenas, *Memoria a favor de la provincia de Tabasco, en la Nueva España, presentado a S.M. y Las Cortes Generales Extraordinarias por el Dr. d. Josef Eduardo de Cárdenas, diputado en ellas por dicha providencia.* (Cádiz, ES: Imprenta de Estado Mayor General, 1811), 6, 26, 67, 70.

39. Ibid., 67.

40. Ibid., 26.

41. Mérida, "Legislativo," *El Redactor Méridano* no. 14 (August 13, 1813): 54–55.

42. Ibid., 54.

43. Cárdenas, *Memoria*, 6. For more on the association of luxury with femininity and with women, and on the masculinity of reformist Catholicism, see Voekel, *Alone Before God*, 143–146, 157–160.

44. Cárdenas, *Memoria*, 36.

45. Mexico City, *Diario de México*, November 22, 1805, vol. 1, no. 54, pp. 3–4.

46. Miguel Hidalgo y Costilla, "A los habitantes de América" *El Despertor Americano*, December 20, 1810, no. 1, p. 3.

47. The question of women's exclusion from citizenship and from the category of individuals in the nineteenth century is complex. See for example, Erika Pani, "'Ciudadana y muy ciudadana'? Women and the State in Independent Mexico, 1810–30" *Gender & History* 18, no. 1 (April 2006): 5–10. Ana Lidia García, *El fracaso del amor: género e individualismo en el siglo XIX mexicano* (México, D.F.: El Colegio de México and Toluca, MX: Universidad Autónoma del Estado de México, Centro de Estudios Históricos, 2006).

48. On the composition of the growers' union, the Junta de Cosecheros, in 1812, see Sajid Alfredo Herrera Mena, "Luchas de poder, practicas políticas y lenguaje constitucional. San Salvador a fines de 1821," *Hacer historia en El Salvador. Revista Electrónico de Estudios Históricos*, no. 1, año 1, p. 3.

49. Timothy Hawkins, *José de Bustamante and Central American Independence. Colonial Administration in an Age of Imperial Crisis* (Tuscaloosa: The University of Alabama Press, 2004), 103. Sajid Alfredo Herrera details the historiography of the uprising in his "1811. Relectura de los levantamientos y protestas en la provincia de San Salvador," *Revista La Universidad* 16 (2011): 111–126.

50. Rodolfo Baron Castro, *José Matías Delgado y el movimiento insurgente de 1811* (San Salvador: Ministerio de Educación, Dirección General de Publicaciónes, 1962), 145–158. Also see Sajid Alfredo Herrera Mena, "Escenarios de lealtad e infidencia durante el régimen constitucional gaditano: San Salvador, 1811–1814," in *Mesoamérica* 32, no. 53 (June–December 2011): 200–210.

51. Roberto Turcios, *Los primeros patriotas. San Salvador en 1811* (San Salvador: Ediciones Tendencias, 1995). On the 1811 uprisings in other El Salvadoran towns, see Elizet Payne Iglesias, "¡No hay rey, no se pagan tributos! La protesta communal en El Salvador. 1811," *Intercambio* 4, no. 5 (2007): 15–43. Payne Iglesias notes that the 1811 protests in Usulután, Zacatecoluca, Santiago Nonualco, Santa Ana, and Metapán centered on fiscal grievances conditioned by a town's particular ethnic makeup. Aaron Pollack similarly notes that many of the uprisings before Independence centered on linked economic and racial grievances rather than on political autonomy from imperial authorities; see his *La época de las independencias en Centroamérica y Chiapas: procesos políticos y sociales* (México: Instituto Mora and Universidad Autónoma Metropolitana, Unidad Iztapalapa, 2013); and Aaron Pollack, ed., *Independence in Central America and Chiapas, 1770-1823, trans. Nancy Hancock* (Norman, OK: University of Oklahoma Press, 2019).

52. San Salvador, José Matías Delgado, "Manifesto del padre vicario y cura de San Salvador doctor don José Matías Delgado, leído en su iglesia parroquial en la solemne festival del domingo veinte y dos de diciembre," December 22, 1811, AGI, Guatemala, 495. Rodolfo Baron Castro provides an astute reading of Delgado's sermon; see his, *José Matías Delgado*, 180–186; the sermon is reproduced on pages 207–209, n. 19.

53. San Salvador, José Matías Delgado, "Manifesto del padre vicario y cura de San Salvador doctor don José Matías Delgado, leído en su iglesia parroquial en la solemne festival del domingo veinte y dos de diciembre," December 22, 1811, AGI, Guatemala, 495.

54. Timothy Hawkins, *José de Bustamante*.

55. J. M. Peinado, October 20, 1812 (Cádiz: Imprenta Nacional, 1813). For an example of a humble Reform Catholic cleric sermonizing on the Constitution of 1812 in Spain, see

Juan António Posse, *Memorias del cura liberal don Juan Antonio Posse con su discurso sobre la constitución de 1812, ed. Richard Herr* (Madrid: Siglo Veintiuno de Espana, 1984), especially 251–293.

56. Cádiz, José Ignacio Avila, n.d. "Moción del diputado don José Ignacio Avila sobre erección de la Diócesis de San Salvador," reproduced in Santiago Malaina, *Historia de la erección de la Diocesis de San Salvador* (San Salvador, C.A., 1944), 51.

57. San Salvador, Constitutional City Council to King, July 4, 1813, AGCA, Signatura B1.13, exp. 483, leg.16, fol. 11v.

58. Jorge García Laguardia, *CentroAmérica en las Cortes de Cádiz* (México: Fondo de Cultura Ecónomica, 1994), 23.

59. Guatemala, *Real Audiencia*, "Sobre averiguar la conducta de don Simón Villegas en punto al estado de insurreción que se recela en esta capital," October 23, 1808, AGCA, Signatura B 2.7, leg. 34, exp. 777, fols. 1, 22–24. For more on Simón Bergaño y Villegas' journalism and poetry in Guatemala and Cuba, see Catherine Poupney Hart, "Parcours journalistiques en régime colonial: José Rossi y Rubí, Alejandro Ramírez et Simón Bergaño," *El Argonauta Español* 6 (2009), at http://jounrals.openedition.org/argonauta/603, [1–28], 14–19. Jordana Dym, "Conceiving Central America: A Bourbon Public in the *Gazeta de Guatemala* (1797-1807)," in *Enlightened Reform in Southern Europe and its Atlantic Colonies, ca. 1750-1830*, ed. Gabriel Paquette (Farnham, UK: Ashgate, 2009), 99–118; and Severo Martínez Peláez, "Simón Bergaño y Villegas, periodista y prócer," *Revista de la Asociación de Periodistas de Guatemala*, no. 34 (November 1971): 107–113. Clerical celibacy provoked debate throughout Latin America in this period; see, for example, Robert di Stefano, "El debate sobre el celibato sacro y los enclaustramientos forzados en el Río de la Plata revolucionario," *Jahrbuch für Geschichte Lateinamerikas—Anuario de Historia de America Latina* 44, no. 1, https://doi.org/10.7767/jbla.2007.44.1.207, published December 18, 2013. The Bourbons increasingly saw population density and health, not gold or silver, as the key to national wealth. Discourses about the regular orders' sterility and clerical celibacy should be read in this context. See, for example, Conde de Pedro Rodríguez Campomanes, *Discurso sobre la educación popular y fomento de la industria popular* (Madrid: Don Antonio de la Sancha, 1744), cxxxvi.

60. Juan José Díaz de Espada y Landa, *Carta pastoral que el ilustrísimo señor don Juan Joseph Díaz de Espada y Landa... dirige á sus diocesanos sobre las falsas doctrinas contrarias á nuestros dogmas y costumbres cristianas impresas en varios papeles del Correo de las Damas de esta ciudad* (Havana: Imprenta de la Curia Episcopal, por D.E.J. Boloña, 1811).

61. Simón Bergaño y Villegas, *Manifiesto que pública uno de los editores del Correo de las Damas, D. Simón Bergaño y Villegas, para sincerer su opinion vulnerada en la pastoral impresa el dos de septiembre, contra el rasgo filosófico de Dorila, y la persona del autor* (Palma de Mallorca, ES: Imprenta de Miguel Ramos, 1813), 14, 20–21. On Mexico's Tenth Muse, Sor Juana Inés de la Cruz, see Octavio Paz, *Sor Juan Inés de la Cruz o Las trampas de la fé* (México: Fondo de Cultura Económica, 1995). For Sor Juana's lyrical critique of the sexual double standard, see her poem "Hombres necios," (Foolish Men), in Sor Juana Inés de la Cruz, *Obras completas*, ed. Alfonso Méndez Plancarte (México, D.F.: Porrúa, 1997), 109.

62. "*Nos don Francisco Javier Mier y Campillo, obispo de Almería é inquisidor general a todos los fieles, Sabed: por el espacio de cinco años se vió nuestra nación inundada de folletos, periódicos y papeles perversos* [Texto impreso]," Madrid, Francisco Javier, Obispo Inquisidor General, July 22, 1815, BN-Spain, Consejo de Inquisición (España), R/62470/5, 1815, pp. 2–5.

63. Hawkins, *José de Bustamante*, 164–165.

64. Guatemala City, José de Bustamante to Regency, "Manifiesto documentado del gefe político superior de Guatemala sobre instalación de la diputación provincial (reservado)," September 18, 1813, AGI Guatemala, 531.

65. Ramón López Jiménez, *José Simeón Cañas. Su obra, su verdadera personalidad y su destino* (San Salvador: Dirección General de Cultura, Dirección de Publicaciones, 1970), 344.

66. Guatemala, Jose de Bustamante to Regency, "Informe reservado del gefe superior de Guatemala sobre varios incidencias occurridas en la diputacion provincial," October 23, 1813, AGI, Guatemala, 531.

67. Mexico City, D. Fr. Ramón Casaús y Torres to Bernardo Ruiz de Medina, December 20, 1800, reproduced in Ramón Casaús Torres y Las Plazas, *El anti-Hidalgo* (Morelia, MX: Universidad Michoacana de San Nicolás de Hidalgo, 1988), 18–19, and passim. Fr. Ramón Casaús y Torres, *El párroco americano contra el apóstata de los párrocos americanos 10 Miguel Hidalgo Costilla* (Oaxaca, 1811), 3. For more on Casaús' contretempts with Miguel Hidalgo y Costilla, see Beuchot, "Algunos fuentes" and Casaús, *El anti-Hidalgo*.

68. Ramón Casaús y Torres, *El arzobispo electo de Guatemala á sus diocesados de San Salvador* (Guatemala: Imprenta de Arévalo, 1811), 1–4.

69. Fr. José Mariano Vidaurre, *Sermón que en las exequias funebres que se hicieron en la ciudad de San Salvador a la venerable memoria del señor Dr. D. Isidro de Sicilia y Montoya, cura propio que fue de la misma ciudad y sus anexos, provisor vicario general y governador de este arzobispado de Guatemala, y dean dignidad de la santa iglesia metropolitana de esta diócesis* (Guatemala: Don Manuel de Arévalo, 1812), 27.

70. Ramón Casaús y Torres, *Sermon de Nuestra Señora de el Rosario predicado en la iglesia de Santo Domingo de Guatemala día 6 de octubre de 1811 por el Dr. D. Fr. Ramón Casaús y Torres, obispo de Rosen y arzobispo electo de esa metropoli, del consejo de S.M. lo publica la Archicofradia del Santisimo Rosario* (Guatemala: Oficina de Don Manuel Arévalo, 1811), 20.

71. Guatemala, Fr. Alonso Escobar to Real Audiencia, January 5, 1810, AGCA, Signatura A.1, leg. 6927, exp. 56921, fol. 2. Guatemala City, Fr. José de Santiago to Audiencia, May 6, 1810, AGCA, Signatura A.1, leg. 6927, exp. 56921, fol. 7. Guatemala City, Fr. Juan de Dios Campos to Audiencia, no date, AGCA, Signatura A.1, leg. 6927, exp. 56921, fol. 9.

72. Guatemala City, José de Bustamante, September 16, 1813, AGCA, Signatura B, Leg. 34, exp. 796, fols. 84–85v. At this time, Guatemala City was by far the largest city in Central America with some 25,000 inhabitants. Other major Central American cities like Granada, León, Comayagua, Ciudad Real, and Cartago had populations under 9,000; San Salvador had roughly 12,000 inhabitants. See Brown, *Juan Fermín ,*16–17.

73. Hawkins, *José de Bustamante*, 160–164. Laughlin, *Beware,*108–109.

74. The other two men who signed the letter to José María Morelos were Santiago Celis and Juan Manuel Rodriguez, see "Testimonio de los pedimientos del senor fiscal del crimen y minuta del Real acuerdo en las causas de infidencia de la ciudad de San Salvador," July 7, 1818, AGCA, Sig. B 2.6, leg. 30, exp. 763, fols.10v and 13–13v. Carlos Meléndez Chaverri, *José Matías Delgado*, 193–194.

75. Cardenas, *Memoria*, 26, 79.

76. Testimony of Luciana Roque, Antonia Magaña, and María del Pilar Cornejo; Juzgado Primero Constitucional de San Vicente, San Vicente [El Salvador], August 3, 1813, AGCA, Signatura B, leg. 34, exp. 796, fols. 76–80. San Vicente, El Salvador, Manuel Cárcamo to José María Peinado, August 16, 1813, AGCA, Signatura B, leg. 34, exp. 796, fols. 64–65v.

77. On the titles given to Molina and Cárcamo by the Spanish Regency, see AGCA, B2.9, exp. 878, leg. 38.

78. See Guatemala, José de Bustamante to Council of the Regency, March 3, 1813, reproduced in the *Revista de la Academia Hondureña de Geografia e Historia*, 55 (January–June 1972), 59.

79. San Salvador, José María Peinado, August 21, 1813, AGCA, Signatura B, leg. 34, exp. 796, fol. 92. San Salvador, Manuel Aguilar, August 21, 1813, AGCA, Signatura B, leg. 34, exp. 796, fol. 94.

80. The rebel city council claimed that Manuel Aguilar's arrest and a summons issued to his brother Nicolás spurred the short uprising. Captain General Bustamante regarded these events as insignificant, pointing instead to more longstanding grievances. See Guatemala, José de Bustamante to Council of the Regency, March 3, 1813, reproduced in the *Revista de la Academia Hondureña de Geografia e Historia*, vol. 55 (January–June 1972): 62.

81. San Salvador, Manuel Aguilar, August 21, 1813, AGCA, Signatura B, leg. 34, exp. 796, fol. 94.

82. San Salvador, Manuel Aguilar, "Sermón," February 28, 1813, quoted in Meléndez Chaverri, *El Presbitero*, 215.

83. Ibid.

84. San Salvador, José Maria Peinado to Captain General Bustamante, February 28, 1814, AGN-El Salvador, Fondo Colonial, caja 4, exp. 27, fols. 1–4.

85. Guatemala, Fr. José Buenaventura Villageliu to Fr. Ramón Casaús, Third Informe, December 20, 1821, 53–58, find at http://site.madremariateresa.org/index.php/documentos/informes-villageliu. The same year, 1816, Archbishop Casaús licensed Jesuit José Ángel de Toledo's *Día feliz consagrado a los cultos del Corazón de Jesús. Por el padre José Ángel de Toledo de la Compañia de Jesús, natural de Guatemala* (Guatemala: Beteta, 1817), 1, 32. Toledo wrote the work for his sister, who wanted to dedicate a day each month to the Sacred Heart of Jesus. He dedicated it to the women of all of the religious orders. The special oration to Mary opens with a line about her immaculate conception. Also see P. F. Francisco Viteri, *Exercicio devoto para el primer viernes de cada mes dedicado al culto del santisimo Corazón de Jesús extractado para fomento de la devoción . . . por el P. F. Francisco Viteri* (Guatemala: Imprenta de D. Manuel de Arévalo, 1818).

86. Guatemala, Fr. José Buenaventura Villageliu to Fr. Ramón Casaús, Third Informe, December 20, 1821. Found at http://site.madremariateresa.org/index.php/documentos/infor mes-villageliu, 2020, pp. 53–58.

87. "Los Editores," reproduced in Miguel Ángel García, *Diccionario histórico enciclopédico de la República de El Salvador. El Doctor José Matías Delgado. Homenaje en el primer centenario de su muerte, 1832-1932. Documentos para el studio de su vida y de su obra*, vol. 2 (El Salvador: Imprenta Nacional, 1939), [393–396], 394–395. Signed by "Los Editores."

88. Brianna Leavitt-Alcántara, *Alone at the Altar. Single Women and Devotion in Guatemala, 1670-1870* (Stanford, CA: Stanford University Press, 2018),157–60. For more on the Royal Order to remove prominent creoles from the city council in 1815, and on the 1817 Royal Order to reinstate them, see Hawkins, *José de Bustamante*, 189–206.

89. Fray Servando Teresa de Mier, *The Memoirs of Fray Servando Teresa de Mier*, ed. Susan Rotker, trans. Helen Lane (Cambridge, UK: Oxford University Press, 1998), 140–141.

90. Vicente Pazos Kanki, *Letters on the United Provinces of South America Addressed to the Hon. Henry Clay, Speaker of the House of Representatives of the U. States by Don Vicente Pazos*, trans. Platt H. Crosby (New York: J. Seymour, 1819), 103.

91. See also Horacio Rodriguez Plata, *Andrés María Rosillo y Meruelo* (Bogotá, Col.: Editorial Cromos, 1963), 195–200.

92. Manuel Plata, *Apología de la provincial del Socorro, sobre el crimen de cismatica que se la imputa por la erección de obispado, en Santafé de Bogotá año de 1811* (Imprenta Real de Don Bruno Espinosa de los Monteros, 1811).

93. Ibid., 19. On "Jansenist episcopalism" in Chile's battle for the *patronato*, see Lucretia Enríquez "El patronato en Chile de Carrera á O'Higgins," *Hispania Sacra* 40, no. 122 (July–December 2008): 507–529.

94. Juan Bautista Pey de Andrade and José Domingo Duquesne, Número 9. Cisma del Socorro, "Final de la pastoral de los gobernadores del arzobispado," reprinted in José Manuel Groot, *Historia eclesiástica y civil de nueva Granada escrita sobre documentos auténticos*, vol. 3, 2nd ed. (Bogotá: Casa Editorial de M. Rivas y Cia, 1891), appendix, xv–xvi. Paulina Castañeda Delgado, "El cisma del Socorro y sus protagonistas," in *Homenaje al Dr. Muro Orejón*, 2 vols. (Sevilla: Uiversidad de Sevilla, 1979), 1:262. Castañeda Delgado argues that schism protagonists relied on secular, regalist authors to justify their exercise of the patronato; she does not recognize Reform Catholicism as an influence on the schism. For a short basic outline of some of the events surrounding the schism, see José Manuel Groot, *Historia eclesiástica*, 86–92. Also see Rodriguez Plata, *Andres María Rosillo*, 195–210.

95. Plata, *Apologia*, 4, 3.

96. José Antonio de Torres y Peña, *Precaución contra el manifiesto, que trata de alucinár á los senicllos y cohonestár el císma del Socorro. Lo ofrece á los verdaderos fieles don Jose Antonio de Torres y Peña, cura de Tabio* (Bogotá: Imprenta Patriótica de D. Nicolás Calvo y Quixano, 1811), 11, 14, 15, 19, 84.

97. See Bogotá, Andrés María Rosillo to Vice President of Colombia, October 29, 1822, in Francisco José Otero et. al., *Sobre el patronato: publicación de los dictámenes de algunas personas de rango, de conocida literature y fama, con el objetivo de que la opinión se ilustre en una matería que todavía no se ha dado sufiiciementement á la luz* (Bogotá: Imprenta de la República por N. Lora, 1823), 21. *Sobre el patronato* includes texts solicited by congressional leaders and executive branch officials eager to inform the public about the *patronato* debate. The small book contains entries by Francisco José Otero, Andrés María Rosillo y Meruelo, Ignacio de Herrera, Francisco de Paula y Santander, and Juan José Osio. Rosillo's manifesto that he accused Torres of forwarding to hostile authorities in Madrid was entitled "Manifiesto de los derechos, fundamentos, y razones que persuaden hallarse las supremas juntas, y pueblos del Nuevo Reino de Granada lejitimamente autorizados para usar del patronato, respecto de todas las Iglesias, cuidar del culto, proveer toda clase de ministros eclesiasticos y socorrér de todos modos á la iglesia de Jesuscirsto," *Sobre el patronato*, 21.

98. Bishop of Palencia Narciso Coll y Pratt to Santiago Guistiani, Archbishop of Tiro and Apostolic Nuncio, December 16, 1825, ASV, Archivo de la Nunciatura de Madrid, Scatola 270. Coll y Pratt was the archbishop of Caracas before moving to his position as bishop of Palencia. Here he is discussing the actions of archbishop of Santa Fé Juan Bautista Sacristán y Galeano. For a well-documented account of Sacristán's eleven-year odyssey that prevented the archbishop from taking up residence in the Audienca de Santa Fé until 1816, see Castañeda Delgado, "El cisme," 272–279.

99. John Leddy Phelan, *The People and the King: The Comunero Revolution in Colombia, 1781* (Madison: University of Wisconsin Press, 1978), 45. Guillermo Hernández de Alba and Fabio Lozano y Lozano, eds., *Documentos sobre el doctor Vicente Azuero* (Bogotá: Imprenta Nacional, 1944), x.

100. Juan N. Azuero Plata, *Respuesta a un papel que, con el titulo de verdadera vindicación de esta ciudad de Bogotá y su cabildo en las pesonas del procurador general y padre de menores en el año*

1816, han publicado los doctores Ignacio Herrera y José Ignacio San Miguel (Bogotá: Imprenta del Estado, 1823).

101. On the creation of a governing *junta* in Santa Fé de Bogotá and *juntas* in other regions of Latin America, see John Lynch, *The Spanish Revolutions* (New York, NY: W.W. Norton, 1983); and Manuel Chust Calero, *1808, la eclosión juntera en el mundo hispano* (México, D.F.: Fondo de Cultura Económica, 2007).

102. Santa Fé, Viceroy Antonio Amat to Benito Hermida, March 19, 1810, AGI, Santa Fé, 629. On Rosillo's imprisonment, see Santa Fé de Bogotá, *Diario Político de Santafé de Bogotá*, no. 4, September 4, 1810, pp. 1–2. On the dramatic events of July 20, see, for example, Bogotá, *La Constitución Feliz. Periódico Político y Económico de la Capital del Nuevo Reyno de Granada*, August 17, 1810, no. 1, passim. On Bogotá's lower classes in the July 20 movement, see Manuel Pareja Ortiz, "El pueblo bogotano en la revolución del 20 de julio de 1810," *Anuario de Estudios Americanos* 71, no. 1 (January–June 2014): 281–311.

103. Anonymous, "Relación del acaesido en la capital de Santa Fé desde el memorable 20 de julio hasta el día de la fecha," AGI, Santa Fé, 745.

104. This account of Azuero's actions around July 20 is that of General Antonio Obando, quoted at length in Roberto M. Tisnés, *Historia eclesiástica. Historia Extensa de Colombia, Vol. 13, Tomo 4. El clero y la independencia en Santafé, 1810-1815* (Bogotá: Ediciones Lerner, 1971).

105. Groot, *Historia eclesiástica*, 60.

106. José Manuel Restrepo, *Historia de la revolución de la República de Colombia en la América Meridional*, vol. 1 (Colombia: Imprenta de José Joaquin Besanzon, 1858 [org.1827], 81. Patricia Cardona Zuluaga, "José Manuel Restrepo y la historia de la República de Colombia: Testimonios y documentos," *Araucaria. Revista Iberoamericana de Filosofía, Política y Humanidades* 16, no. 31 (January–June 2014): 223–231.

107. Juan N. Azuero Plata, *Respuesta a un papel que, con el titulo de Verdadera vindicación de esa ciudad de Bogotá y su cabildo en las pesonas del procurador general y padre de menores en el año 1816, han publicado los doctores Ignacio Herrera y José Ignacio San Miguel* (Bogotá: Imprenta del Estado, 1823), 19, 20.

108. Manuel Maria Mallarino. *Juan N. Azuero Plata* (Bogotá: Imprenta de Echeverría Hermanos, 1857), 16.

109. Madrid, Bishop of Palencia Narciso Coll y Pratt to Papal Nuncio, November 11, 1822, ASV, Archivo de la Nunciatura de Madrid, Scatola 270, fols. 4, 4v, 5. On Coll y Pratt's testimony, see Mireya Sosa de León, "La disolución del orden civil durante la guerra de independencia en el testimonio del arzobispo Narciso Coll y Pratt, 1810-1816," *Ensayos históricos*, 2a Etapa, no. 19, (2007): 89–118.

110. Andrés María Rosillo y Meruelo, *Representación apologética, y demostrativa de los motivos que urgen sobre que se llame al ilustrisimo señor arzobispo doctor don Juan Bautista Sacristán* (Santa Fe: Imprenta del Sol, 1812), 3–5, 23.

111. Santa Fé, Andrés María Rosillo y Meruelo, "Dad al Cesar lo que es de Cesar, y a dios lo que es de dios," 1815, Documentos de la Biblioteca Nacional de Colombia, Colección F. Pineda, vol. 361, fols. 22–27, 43. For more on the context of the tithe debate, see Rodriguez Plata, *Andres María Rosillo y Meruelo*, 241–246.

112. Santander, Andrés María Rosillo to King, July 11, 1817, AGI, Santa Fé, 973.

113. Ramon Eguiguren, *Manifiesto en que el doctor J.R. Equiguren, cura de manta, opositor a la prebenda doctoral, para la cual había sido propuesto en primer lugar con todos los votos del Illmo. Cabildo Metropolitano, hace presente sus méritos y servicios en las tres carreras eclesiástica, literaria y política* (Bogotá, Col.: Imprenta de la República, 1825), 16–18.

114. See Bogotá, Andrés María Rosillo to Vice President of Colombia, October 29, 1822, in Otero et. al., *Sobre el patronato*, 22.

115. Castañeda Delgado "El cisme," 269–270.

116. Miguel Rosillo to Andrés Rosillo, December 16, 1817, AGI, Estado, 105.

117. Santa Fé de Bogotá, Andrés María Rosillo y Meruelo to Juan Bautista Sacristán, October 19, 1813, AGI, Santa Fé, 747. On Sacristán's disrust of Rosillo, see Santiago de Cuba, Juan Bautista Sacristán to minister of grace and justice, December 30, 1813, AGI, Santa Fé, 747; and Santiago de Cuba, Juan Bautista Sacristán to minister of grace and justice, July 30, 1814, AGI, Santa Fé, 747. Brian R. Hamnett treats exiled ecclesiastics and Pablo Morillo's campaigns in his "The Counter Revolution of Morillo and the Insurgent Clerics of New Granada, 1815-1820," *The Americas* 32, no. 4 (April 1976), 597–660. Also see Ana Maria Bidegain, "Los apóstoles de la insurrección y el vicariocastrense (1810-1820)," *Boletín de Historia y Antigüedades* (June 2013), 199–237. See also Morillo, *Mémoires du Géneral.* . For Rosillo's report to Ferdinand VII, see Santander, Andrés María Rocillo (*sic*) to King, January 15, 1818, AGI, Santa Fé, 973; the report is summarized in Palacio, Juan Lozano de Torres to Secretary del Despacho del Estado, March 2, 1818, AGI, Estado, 57. On the Council of the Indies' quip about the early church and the *patronato*, see Consejo de Indias, Sala de Justicia, July 1, 1818, AGI, Santa Fé, 973.

118. See Bogotá, Andrés María Rosillo to Vice President of Colombia, October 29, 1822, in Otero et. al., *Sobre el patronato*, 21–22.

119. Arana, *Bolívar*, 113, 117, 175, 178–179, 186, 193–194, 226.

120. Santa Fé, Report of the Audiencia, October 20, 1809, reproduced in Rodriguez Plata, 86–88.

121. See Bogotá, Andrés María Rosillo to Vice President of Colombia, October 29, 1822, in Otero et. al., *Sobre el patronato*, 16, 24–25.

122. Andres Rosillo, *Venganza de la justicia por la manifestación de la verdad en orden al patronato de la iglesia, que se atribuye a la suprema potestad de Colombia. Escrita por el señor doctor Andrés Rosillo dean de la misma iglesia, en representación que tenia dispuesta el muy venerable sr. dean y cabildo de esta capital para el senado, y ofrecida en otra que se dío á la misma corporación* (Caracas, VE: Valentín Espinal, 1824), 3, 8–10, 22–23, 35, 54. Also see José David Cortés Guerrero, "Las discusiones sobre el patronato en Colombia en el siglo xix," *Historia Crítica* 52 (January–April 2014): 99–122.

123. On Madariaga's considerable achievements while in Santiago de Chile, see Madrid, Vicente Joaquín Maturana, "Relaciones de los meritos, y servicios del doctor Don Josef Cortés y Madariaga, Canóningo de la Iglesia Catedral de la Ciudad de Santiago de Chile," February 26, 1803, BN-Chile, Sala de Microfilmatos.

124. Cortés Madariaga, *Diario y observaciones*, 22. For more on Francisco Miranda, see Racine, *Francisco Miranda*.

125. Madariaga, *Diario y observaciones*, 8.

126. Madariaga, *Diario y observaciones*, 28.

127. Lima, Viceroy Joseph Abascal to Minister of Grace and Justice Nicolás María Sierra, January 8, 1811, AGI, Lima, 741.

128. Public Prison, Cádiz, Joseph Cortés Madariaga to Dear Friend, February 16, 1813, "Correspondence Re: the Venezuelan Wars of Independence," SCL-UVA, MSS 3977, 1–2.

129. Ibid.

130. Kingston, Jamaica, José Cortés Madariaga to Joaquín López de Sotomayor, November 22, 1817, BN-Chile, Sala de Microfilmatos, vol. 72, pp. 1–2.

131. Cádiz, Miguel Ramos de Arispe to Mier (note that Arizpe was sometimes, as here, spelled as Arispe), 27 March 1813, "Correspondence Re: the Venezuelan Wars of Independence," SCL-UVA, MSS 3977, pp. 1–2. Arizpe's report on conditions in his province can be found in his *Memoria*. For more on Arizpe's life, see González Salas, *Miguel Ramos de Arizpe*. On Arizpe's later encounter with Gregoire, see Paris, Abbé Henrí Grégoire to Fray Servando Teresa de Mier, March17, 1824, reprinted in Miquel I Vergés and Díaz-Thomé, eds., *Escritos inéditos*, 514. The letter was originally written in French and translated by the editors.

132. Kinsbruner, *Independence*, 88. For a comprehensive introduction to Roscio's piety and political activities, see Carmen Ruiz Barrionuevo, "Juan Germán Roscio," 181–200.

133. Nancy Vogeley, *The Bookrunner: A History of Inter-American Relations—Print, Politics and Commerce in the United States and Mexico, 1800-1830* (Philadelphia, PA: American Philosophical Society, 2011), 161–162.

134. Vogeley, *Bookrunner*, 166, 159.

135. Juan Germán Roscio, *Obras*, vol. 1: *El Triunfo de la libertad sobre el despotismo*, prologue by Augusto Mijares, compilation by Pedro Grases (Caracas, VE: Publicaciones del Secretaría General de la Decimal Conferencia Interamericana, 1953), 336–337, 236, 239.

CHAPTER 3

1. Jorge Luján Muñoz, "La Asamblea Nacional Constituyente Centroamericana de 1823-24" *Revista de Historia de América* 94 (July–December 1982): 60–61, 67.

2. Arturo Taracena Arriola, "La mirada de tres actores guatemaltecos sobre la Guerra Federal de 1826-1829: Montúfar y Coronado, Córdova, y García Granados. Reflexiones metodológicas sobre un conflicto armado," in *La primera guerra federal centroamericana, 1826-1829. Nación y estados, republicanismo y violencia*, ed. Arturo Taracena Arriola (México: Universidad Rafael Landívar, 2015), [55–86]; 56–58. Sajid Alfredo Herrera Mena, "La invención liberal de la identidad estatal salvadoreña 1824-1839," *Estudios Centroamericanos. Revista de Extensión Cultural de la Universidad Centroamericana "José Simeón Cañas,"* no. 684 (2005): 913–936.

3. Ayala Benítez, *La iglesia*, 139, 151. Malaina, S.J., *Historia de la erección*, 54. Miguel Angel García, *Diccionario histórico enciclopédico de la República de El Salvador. El doctor José Matías Delgado. Homenaje en el primer centenario de su muerte, 1832-1932. Documentos para el estudio de su vida y de su obra, Tomo II.* (El Salvador: Imprenta Nacional, 1939), 118–119. The appointment was later formally decreed by El Salvador's state government on May 4, 1824.

4. León, Nicaragua, Julián Podi de Penaquila and Tomás Delgado de Santa Columba to Fray Nicolás García de Jeréz, September 28, 1823, in José D. Gámez, ed., *Archivo histórico de la República de Nicaragua por José D. Gámez*, vol. 1: *1821-1826* (Managua, NIC: Tipografía Nacional, 1896), 123; note that this page is incorrectly marked as page 9 in the book, but is followed by page 124. Chester Zalaya Goodman mentions that León's clergy were reluctant to sign, see his *Nicaragua en la Independencia* (San José, CR: Editorial Universitaria Centroamericana, 1971), 216. On September 19, 1823, the city of León swore allegiance to the Asamblea Nacional Constituyente. Clerics overwhelmingly declined to sign. On September 22, Bishop García Jeréz had sent the Junta Gobernativa de León a memorandum explaining why he would not pledge his obedience to the ANC. On October 5, 1823, the ANC confirmed that the clerics of the diocese, including those in convents, had signed; see Guatemala, October 6, 1823, Article 4 of *Actas de la Asamblea Nacional Constituyente de las provincias unidas del Centro de América, año 1823* (Guatemala: Editorial Ejercito, 1971), 4. For more on García Jeréz's earlier political

actions, see J. C. Pinto Soria, *Centroamérica de la colonia al estado nacional* (Guatemala: Editorial Universitaria, 1986), 135–136.

5. León, Nicaragua, Julián Podi de Penaquila and Tomás Delgado de Santa Columba to Fray Nicolás García de Jeréz, September 28 1823, in Gámez, ed., *Archivo histórico*, 123–125. On an earlier oath-swearing campaign to the legitimacy of independence, see Xiomara XiomaraAvendaño Rojas, "Theaters of Power in 1821. Swearing Loyalty to Independence in the Province of Guatemala," *Independence in Central America and Chiapas, 1770-1823*, ed. Aaron Pollack, trans. Nancy T. Hancock (Norman, OK: University of Oklahoma Press, 2019), 81–99; this information is on page 93. Eusebio Arzate encouraged his initially suspicious flock in Jacaltenango in the district of Huehuetenango to pledge their allegiance to Independence. Over a decade later, Casaús would put Arzate on a short list of dangerous clerics he sent to the pope. See Casaús to Pope Gregorio XVI, May 28, 1833, AES, Guatemala, 1831-1836, Pos. 7-10, Fasc. 512, fol. 21.

6. León, Nicaragua, Julián Podi de Penaquila and Tomás Delgado de Santa Columba to Fray Nicolás García de Jeréz, September 28, 1823, in Gámez, ed., *Archivo Histórico*, 123–125.

7. León, Nicaragua, Julián Podi de Penaquila, and Tomás Delgado de Santa Columba to Fray Nicolás García de Jeréz, September 28, 1823, in Gámez, ed., *Archivo Histórico*, [123–125], 151, 157.

8. Guatemala, Palacio Nacional, Francisco Esteban Milla and Juan Hernández to Secretaria del Estado y Despacho General, November 19, 1823; and Francisco Esteban Milla and Juan Hernández to Secretaria del Estado y Despacho General, AGN-El Salvador, Manuscritos, Tomo 1, Caja 13, exp. 13, fols. 1,-1v, 3, 5,-5v, 6, 11, 11–12. Milla and Hernández both held the title of Secretary in the ANC. Alejandro Marure asserts that this erudite reformist report compiled by the ANC commission to address García de Jeréz's recalcitrance was authored by Dr. Mariano Gálvez and was sent to the bishop, see Marure, *Bosquejo histórico de las revoluciones de Centro-América, desde 1811 hasta 1834* (New York City: Wentworth Press Reprint, 2018 [org. 1837]), 81–82.

9. Mestre Sanchis, "La influencia," *Revista Historia Moderna, Anales de la Universidad de Alicante*, 19 (2001): 125–127.

10. Palacio Nacional, Guatemala, Francisco Esteban Milla and Juan Hernández to Secretaria del Estado y Despacho General, November 19, 1823, AGN-El Salvador, Manuscritos, Tomo 1, Caja 13, exp. 13, fols. 1, 1v, 3, 5, 5v, 6, 11, 11v, 12.

11. Anonymous, *En oficio de 19 del que rige recibido por el correo de hoy, participa el gefe político de León ciudadano José Carmen Salazar al S.P.E lo que sigue* (Guatemala: Arévalo, 1823). León, Nicaragua, Ciudadano José Carmen Salázar to Superior Poder Executivo, December 24, 1823, BN-Guatemala, Fondo Antiguo. Registro No. 1946, Folder de hojas sueltas de 1821, 1822, y 1823.

12. Luján Muñoz, "La Asamblea," 58. Marure *Bosquejo histórico*, 101.

13. Asamblea Nacional, *Actas de la Asamblea Nacional Constituyente de las Provincias Unidas del Centro de América* (Guatemala: Editorial Ejercito, 1971), 225. Davila served as the treasurer of the cathedral chapter in Chiapas prior to serving as president of the ANC in 1824, see Robert M. Laughlin, *Beware*, 97. Alejandro Marure reports that *El Indicador* first appeared in the waning months of 1824, led by an editorial team consisting of José Francisco Cordova; Juan Francisco Sosa; Manuel Montúfar; Fernando Antonio Dávila, a prominent conservative participant in the pamphlet war; José María Castilla; and the printer José Beteta. According to Marure, liberals founded *El Liberal* in 1825 as a counterweight to the conservative *El Indicador*. San Salvador's *Semanario Político Mercantil* first appeared in late July of 1824; Marure, *Bosquejo histórico*, 104–105. When conservative Rafael Carrera regained control of the liberal stronghold of Los Altos, Guatemala in 1840, he appointed Dávila to replace the liberal priests Urbano

Ugarte and José María Aguilar; see Arturo Taracena Arriola, *Invención criollo, sueño ladino, pesadilla indigena, Los Altos de Guatemala de región á estado, 1740-1871* (Guatemala: CIRMA, 1999), 240–241. Fernando Antonio Dávila also published his own pamphlet in response to Cañas' *Segunda advertencia patriótica*; see his *Satisfacción a la segunda advertencia del presbitero doctor Jose Simeón Cañas por el presbitero Fernando Antonio Dávila* (Guatemala: Imprenta de Beteta, 1824), 9–10.

14. Asamblea Nacional, *Actas de la Asamblea*, session of June 30, 1823; the debate on church and state is on pages 301–303.

15. Antigua, Guatemala, "Al Congreso Constituyente de este estado en sesión de 21 de septiembre 1824 se presentó por su presidente el C. José María Chacón, una proposición que entre otros artículos contenía el que sigue,"AHAG, *Fondo diócesano, Colección de decretos, Asamblea Nacional Constituyente 1821-1844*, fol. 16.

16. Antigua, Guatemala, Decreto #14, September 30, 1824, *AHAG. Fondo diócesano, Colección de decretos, Asamblea Nacional Constituyente, 1821-1844*, fol. 31.

17. Van Oss, *Catholic Colonialism*, 50, 137–141. On the Franciscans and Dominicans' ongoing presence in parishes in the indigenous western highlands of Guatemala, see the list of clerics manning the parishes in Guatemala and El Salvador in January of 1829 in AHAG, Fondo Diócesano, Cartas, enero de 1829, exp. 32. Of the 136 parishes, 20 were manned by friars, all of them in the vicarates of Momostenango, Verapaz, and Huehuetenango (spelled Gueguetenango in the document).

18. Caroyln Hall and Héctor Pérez Brignoli, with John V. Carter, Cartographer, *Historical Atlas of Central America* (Norman, OK: University of Oklahoma Press, 2003), 91, 86, 111. Fray Eugenio Torres Torres notes that the Dominicans in Peru, Quito, and New Grenada lost their indigenous *doctrinas* during the Bourbon secularization movement of the mid-eighteeenth century, while the process of dispossession was much slower in the Kingdom of Guatemala; see Torres Torres, ed., *Los Dominicos insurgentes* 10–11.

19. Antigua Guatemala, September 30, 1824, Decreto no. 14, AHAG. *Fondo Diócesano, Colección de Decretos, Asamblea Nacional Constituyente, 1821-1844*, fols. 3, 31.

20. Santa Ana, José León Díaz to José Matías Delgado, January 28, 1824, AHAG, Fondo Diocesano, Correspondencia, Cartas, January 1824. Santa Ana, José Crisanto Salazar to *jefe político* Miguel Elizondo, February 11, 1824, AHAG, Fondo Diocesano, Correspondencia, Cartas, February 1824. Santa Ana, Hipolito Montenegro to Arzobispo Ramón Casaús, February 18, 1824, AHAG, Fondo Diocesano, Correspondencia, Cartas, February 1824. Santa Ana, Hipolito Montenegro to Miguel Elizondo, February 12, 1824, AHAG, Fondo Diocesano, Correspondencia, Cartas, February 1824, exp. 41. Miguel Elizondo to Hipolito Montenegro, February 12, 1824, AHAG, Fondo Diocesano, Correspondencia, Cartas, February 1824, Exp. 41. Miguel Elizondo to Mariano Prado, February 12, 1824, AHAG, Fondo Diocesano, Correspondencia, Cartas, February 1824, Exp. 41. Santa Ana, Ypolito Montenegro to Provisor y Vicario General de este Arzobispado, April 23, 1824, AHAG, Fondo Diocesano, Correspondencia, Cartas, April 1824, exp. 17. Ahuachapán, José Antonio Aguilar and Sisto Padilla to presbitero Carlos José Telles, May 10, 1824, AHAG, Fondo Diocesano, Correspondencia, Cartas, May 1824, exp. 31. Aguilar and Sisto wrote to Telles to request that he serve as parish priest. Hipólito Montenegro was also spelled Ypólito Montenegro in the documents.

21. Ahuachapán, José Antonio Aguilar and Sisto Padilla to presbitero Carlos José Telles, May 10, 1824, AHAG, Fondo Diocesano, Correspondencia, Cartas, May 1824.

22. It was reformist intellectual Isidro Menéndez who nominated Aguachapán for the distinction; see the session of July 29, 1823, in Asamblea Nacional, *Actas de la Asamblea*, 532.

23. Chalchuapa, Ignacio Perdomo to Ypólito Montenegro, March 8, 1824, AHAG, Fondo Diocesano, Correspondencia, Cartas, March 1824.Aguachapán, Municipio de Aguachapán to Ypólito Montenegro, 9 March 1824, Fondo Diocesano, Correspondencia, Cartas, Marzo 1824. Santa Ana, Ypólito [elsewhere "Hipolito"] Montenegro to Municipio de Aguachapán, March 9, 1824, Fondo Diocesano, Correspondencia, Cartas, March 1824. A summary of the scramble to place a priest in Aguachapán's parish pulpit can be found in Santa Ana, José Mariano Herrarte to Archbishop Casaús, January 2, 1825, AHAG, Fondo Diocesano, Cartas, January 1825. Archbishop Casaús's reply to this report can be found in Guatemala City, Archbishop Casaús, January 15, 1825, AHAG, Fondo Diocesano, Cartas, January 1825. Ahuachapán, José Antonio Aguilar and Sisto Padilla to presbitero Carlos José Telles, May 10, 1824, AHAG, Fondo Diocesano, Correspondencia, Cartas, May 1824.

24. Chalchaupa, Ignacio Perdomo to Bernardo Dighero, July 14, 1824, AHAG, Fondo Diocesano, Correspondencia, Cartas, July 1824.

25. San Salvador, Report of Alejandro Escalante, May 24, 1824, AGCA, Signatura B 10.7, leg. 185, exp. 4041, fol. 3r. Palacio de Guatemala, Report of Marcial Zabadua, Secretary of Relations of Justice and Ecclesiastical Affairs, to Jefe pólitico de Guatemala, June 8, 1824, Signatura B 10.7, leg. 185, exp. 4041, fol. 21.

26. Miguel Muñoz, *Vindicación del Ilmo. Sr. obispo de San Salvador y defensa de la disciplina de la sta. iglesia católica, por el R. padre D. Miguel Muñoz* (Guatemala: Imprenta de Luna, 1862), 7–8.

27. Jutiapa, Francisco Estévan López to Archbishop Casaús, July 13, 1824, AHAG, Fondo Diocesano, Correspondencia, Cartas, July 1824.

28. Asunción Izalco, Alcalde Num. 1 y toda la municipio [sic] junto con el común, May 22, 1824, AHAG, Fondo Diocesano, Correspondencia, Cartas, May 1824. On Saldaña's arrival in Antigua's Convent of Belén, see Muñoz, *Vindicación*, 9.

29. Muñoz, *Vindicación*, 9.

30. José Ignacio Saldaña, Tomás Miguel Saldaña, Francisco Estévan López, *Invitación al venerable clero, secular y regular* (Guatemala: Juan José Arévalo, 1824), 2.

31. Miguel Muñoz and Tomás Miguel Pineda y Saldaña, *Carta católica romana á los fieles del estado de San Salvador* (Guatemala: Juan José de Arévalo, 1824), 6.

32. Fernando Antonio Dávila, *Esposición del ciudadano Fernando Antonio Dávila, representante en la Asamblea Constituyente de estos estados por el Partido de Sacatepeque. Leída en la sesión pública del 5 de julio [1824] del corriente año en que se comenzó a discutir la ley fundamental de la nación* (Guatemala: Beteta, 1824), 2–3.

33. Fernando Antonio Dávila, *Esposición*, 10.

34. Mexico City, Fray Servando Teresa de Mier, April 17, 1823, *Diario de las sesiones del Congreso Constituyente de México, tomo IV,* cited in Jesús Reyes Heroles, *El liberalismo mexicano, Tomo I: Los orígenes* (México: Fondo de Cultura Económica, 1974), 288. Central American reformers cited the 1823 Mexican commission and invoked Spanish reformist institutions like the Colegio de San Isidro. They also invoked Spanish church councils, like that of Toledo in the seventh century, see, for example, the pseudononomous Su Guanaco's *Chocollos* (San Salvador: Imprenta del Gobierno, 1825), 2–4.

35. San Salvador, Guillen, San Martín, and Miguel Castro, October 11, 1824, ASV, Segr. Stato Esteri, 1823-1845, rubrica 279, busta 592.

36. Palacio Nacional, November 19, 1823, Francisco Esteban Milla and Juan Hernández to Secretaria del Estado y Despacho General, AGN-El Salvador, Manuscritos, Tomo 1, Caja 13, exp.13.

37. Anonymous, *Aviso oportuno á las autoridades y al pueblo* (El Salvador: Imprenta del Gobierno, 1825), 1–4.

38. R. M. and B. P., *Refutación á los enemigos encubiertos de la patria y manifiestos calumniadores del Estado del Salvador por los diputades de su congreso constituyente* (San Salvador: Imprenta Liberal del Gobierno del Estado del Salvador, 1825), 9–15. R. M. and B. P are almost certainly Ramón Meléndez and Bonifacio Paniagua, the only two deputies serving in El Salvador's congress with these initials; see Congreso Constituyente del Estado de El Salvador, "Actas de las sesiones del primer Congreso Constituyente del Estado de El Salvador, 17 de abril al 29 de mayo de 1824," in Carlos Cañas Dinarte, ed., *Boletín* (Asociación para el Fomento de los Estudios Históricos en Centroamérica/AFEHC), no. 25 (2006): passim. For short biographies of statesmen Meléndez and Paniagua, see *Carlos Cañas Dinarte, Violeta Scarlet Cortez, and Gilbert Águilar Avilés, Historia del órgano legislativo de la República de El Salvador, 1824-1864,* vol. 1 (San Salvador: Junta Directiva Órgano Legislativo, 2006), 150, 159.

39. See, for example, Constitutional City Council of Sensuntepeque to Deputation Provincial, July 6, 1821, AGI, Guatemala, 654; Constitutional City Council of San Miguel to Deputation Provincial, August 12, 1821, AGI, Guatemala 654; Ramón Francisco Casaús y Torres to Deputation Provincial, September 1,1821, AGI, Guatemala 654. For more on the centrality of the municipalities as loci of identity and political action see Sajid Alfredo Herrera Mena, *El ejercicio de gobernar: Del cabildo borbónico al ayuntamiento liberal. El Salvador, 1750–1821* (Castellón, Spain: Universitat Jaume I, 2014); and Jordana Dym, *From Sovereign Villages to National States. City, State, and Federation in Central America, 1759–1839* (Albuquerque, NM: University of New Mexico Press, 2006).

40. Ruth María de los Angeles Tenorio Góchez, "Cuan rápidos pasos de esta pueblo hácia la civilización européa: Periódicos y cultura impresa en El Salvador (1824-1850)," (PhD diss., Ohio State University 2006), 96–97, 101, 105. Jorge Lardé y Larín, *Orígenes del periodismo en El Salvador* (El Salvador: Ministerio de Cultura, 1950), 46, 53–55.

41. Henry Dunn, *Guatimala [sic], or, the United Provinces of Central America, in 1827-8; Being Sketches and Memorandums Made During a Twelve Months' Residence in that Republic* (New York, NY: C.&C. Carvill, 1828), 119.

42. Guatemala, "Constestación," *El Indicador*, November 29, 1824, p. 3, cols. 1–3.

43. On the signature campaign in support of the *Carta católica*, see Ciriaco Villacorta, *Discurso pronunciado en el Congreso Federal por el licenciado Ciriaco Villacorta, diputado por el estado de El Salvador, en 18 de julio, á tiempo que discutia el dictámen de las comisiones unidas sobre erección de silla episcopal en aquel estado* (San Salvador: Imprenta del Gobierno, 1826), 2.

44. José Ignacio Saldaña et.al., *Invitación al venerable*, 4–5.

45. Muñoz, *Carta católica*, 1.

46. Dr. Juan Nepomuceno Azuero, *Dr. Merizalde y el Notícíozote* (Bogotá: F.M. Stokes, 1825), 14. The doctor in the title was Dr. José Felix Merizalde.

47. Vicente Azuero, *Representación dirigida al Supremo Poder Ejecutivo contra el presbítero doctor Francisco Margallo, por el doctor Vicente Azuero* (Bogotá, 1826), reprinted in Guillermo Hernández de Alba and Fabio Lozano y Lozano, eds., *Documentos sobre el doctor Vicente Azuero* (Bogotá: Imprenta Nacional, 1944), 293.

48. Dr. Juan Nepomuceno Azuero, *Dr. Merizalde*, 39.

49. Ibid., 24.

50. Vicente Azuero, *Representación dirigida*, 297. For more on the new bible society, see "William Elvis Plata Quezada, "El catolocismo liberal (o liberalismo católico) en Colombia decimonónica," *Franciscanum* 51, no. 152 (July–December 2009): 96–101.

51. José Ignacio Saldaña, *Justa repulsa de iniquias acusaciones, ó entiéndase respuesta que se dá al impreso anónimo de San Salvador intitulado Contestación al manifesto de Saldaña* (Guatemala: Imprenta de Arévalo, 1825), 3. Santa Rosa Parroquia, January 10, 1826, José Ignacio Zaldaña, "Paisano," found in ASV, Arch. Segr. Stato Esteri, 1823-1845, rub. 279, busta 592.

52. San Salvador, "Al autor o autores de la *Carta católica*," *Semanario Político Mercantil de San Salvador* no. 5 (August 28,1824): 4, cols. 1–2. Other reformist works also singled out Devoti for particular criticism, see, for example, R. M. and B. P., *Refutación*, 15.

53. Gelasio Galán y Jurco, *Instituciones canónicas de Juan Devoti, obispo de Aragni. Divididos en cuatro libros. Puestos en Castellano y reducidas puramente de la parte doctrinal, en benefico, comodidad y mas fácil uso de los jovenes que se dedícan al estado* (Valencia, ES: Imprenta de Cabrerizo, 1839), 2, 6–8.

54. San Salvador, "Al autor o autores de la Carta Católica," *Semanario Político Mercantil de San Salvador*, no. 5 (August 28, 1824): 4, cols. 1–2. On Climent's ties to French Jansenists and general theology and pastoral practice, see Smidt, "Fiestas and Fervor,"and her "Josep Climent," 327–353 and especially 331–334.

55. Van Oss, *Catholic Colonialism*, 79–89, 137.

56. See Timothy Tackett, *Religion, Revolution and Regional Culture in Eighteenth-Century France. The Ecclesiastical Oath of 1791* (Princeton, NJ: Princeton University Press, 1986), xv, 3, 5, 11, 14, 16. Eamon Duffy, *Saints and Sinners: A History of the Popes*, 3rd ed. (New Haven, CT: Yale University Press, 1997), 254–255. Also see Joseph F. Burns, *Priests of the French Revolution: Saints and Renegades in a New Political Era* (University Park, PA: Pennsylvania State University Press, 2014).

57. Dale Van Kley, "The Ancien Régime, Catholic Europe, and the Revolution's Religious Schism," in *A Companion to the French Revolution*, ed. Peter McPhee (Chichester, UK: John Wiley & Sons, 2013), 128.

58. Pius VI, "A nuestros amados hijos los cardenales de la S.I.R., y á nuestros venerables hermanos los arzobispos y obisopos y á nuestros amados hijos los cabildos, clero y pueblo de Francia," in Pío VI, *Colección de los breves é instrucciones de nuestro santo padre el papa Pio VI relativos a la Revolución francesa desde el año 1790 hasta el de 1796, traducidos al español por el Dr. D. Pedro Zarandia, canónigo de la santa iglesia catedral de Jaca, y examinador sinodal de su obispado, Tomo II* (Zaragoza, ES: Imprenta de Polo y Mongre, 1829), 31, 46, 49, 55.

59. José Ignacio Saldaña, Tomás Miguel Saldaña, Francisco Estevan López, *Verdaderas razones conra las aparentes que contiene el manifiesto de cuatro de mayo último del director del estado de San Salvador, sobre erección de iglesia y elección de obispo hecho en el doctor José Matías Delgado* (Guatemala: J.J. Arévalo, 1824), 11. The document was signed on September 4, 1824, in the town of Atescatempa in the parish of Jutiapa.

60. Ramón López Jiménez, *José Simeón Cañas. Su obra, su verdadera personalidad y su destino* (San Salvador: Dirección General de Cultura, Dirección de Publicaciones, 1970), 344, 347, 372, 381. Guatemala, Captain General José de Bustamante to Regency, "Informe reservado del gefe superior de Guatemala sobre varios incidencias occurridas en la diputación provincial," October 23, 1813, AGI, Guatemala, 531.

61. José Simeón Cañas, *Advertencia patriótica* (Guatemala: Imprenta Nueva, 1824), 1–3, 8, 20.

62. San Salvador, *Semanario Político Mercantíl de San Salvador*, "Articulo comunicado," October 2, 1824, p. 3, col. 2

63. Cañas, *Advertencia*, 18, 5, 8–9.

64. Basilio Zeceña, *Carta al hermano autor del libelo Adivinanza piadosa* (Guatemala: Antonio Beteta, 1825), 2. Victor Castrillo, *Adivinanza piadosa* (San Salvador: Imprenta del Gobierno,

1824), 1, 3, 4. Ramón López Jimenez and Rafael Díaz report that Victor Castrillo authored the unsigned *Adivinanza piadosa*, see their *Biografia de José Simeón Cañas* (San Salvador: Imprenta Nacional, 1968), 117. Zeceña's earlier work that Castrillo referenced was Presbiterio Dr. Basilio Zeceña, *Observaciones sobre la Advertenica patriótica públicada bajo el nombre del doctor Cañas* (Guatemala: Beteta, 1824).

65. Fernando Antonio Dávila, Dr. Ángel María Candina, and Antonio González, *A la Advertencia patriótica del doctor José Simeon Cañas, contestación de los presbiterios Fernando Antonio Dávila, Dr. Ángel María Candina y Dr. Antonio González* (Guatemala: Imprenta de Beteta, 1824), 24–28 37, 49. Doctor of Theology Candina served as the rector of the University of San Carlos in 1822 and again in 1828 when conservatives controlled appointments. Morazan imprisoned him in 1829; see Christophe Belaubre, "Candida, Ángel María," AFEHC, Ficha no. 151, at https://www.afehc-historia centroamericana.org/diccionario2/diccionario_fiche_id_151. html. Fernando Antonio Dávila published in response to Cañas' *Segunda advertencia patriótica*, noting that El Salvador's attempts to prevent the circulation of ecclesiastical edicts contravened the liberals' own insistence on press freedom, making them hypocrites, see Fernando Antonio Dávila, *Satisfaccion a la Segunda advertencia del presbitero Doctor José Simeón Cañas por el presbitero Fernando Antonio Dávila* (Guatemala: Beteta, 1824), 9–10. El Salvador's government prohibited the circulation of papal bulls and edicts without prior government approval, and, according to Alejandro Marure, mandated the death penalty, exile, or prison—depending on the case—for those found guilty; people who intercepted these papal communications and brought them to the attention of state authorities were to be thanked in a public ceremony. See Alejandro Marure, *Efemérides de los hechos notables acaecidos en la república de Centro-América, desde el año de 1821 hasta el de 1842. Seguidas de varios catálogos de presidentes de la república, jefes de estado, etc.* (Guatemala: Imprenta de la Paz, 1844).

66. On Barruel as a formidable "enemy of the Enlightenment," see Darrin M. McMahon, *Enemies of the Enlightenment: The French Counter-Enlightenment and the Making of Modernity* (New York, NY: Oxford University Press, 2001), 112–114.

67. Abbé Augustin Barruel, *Historia del clero en el tiempo de la Revolución francesa* (Mexico: M.J. de Zúñiga, 1800), 75–76. José Mariano Herrarte, *Adverencia patriótica* (Guatemala: Imprenta, J.J. de Arévalo, 1824), 1–2. José Andrés de Santa María pointed readers to the edicts and pastoral letters of French clergy who resisted the Civil Constitution of the Clergy, noting that Barruel had collected and published these oppositional tracts, see his *Desengaño religioso al pueblo de Guatemala* (Guatemala: Beteta, 1825), 31.

68. José Simeon Cañas, *Segunda advertencia patriótica del doctor Cañas* (Guatemala: Imprenta Nueva á cargo de J.J. de Arévalo, 1824), 1, 8. Signed by the author on October 28, 1824.

69. Presbiterio Dr. Basilio Zeceña, *Observaciones sobre la advertenica patiótica públicada bajo el nombre del doctor Cañas* (Guatemala: Beteta, 1824), 8–9.

70. Alyssa Goldstein Stepinwall, *The Abbé Grégoire and the French Revolution: The Making of Modern Universalism* (Berkeley, CA: University of California Press, 2005), 111 and passim.

71. Henrí Grégoire, *Lettre circulaire de M. Grégoire, évêque du départemente de Loir e Cher, à ses diocésains, pour la convocation des elèves au séminaire de Blois* (July 7, 1791) (n.p., 1791), 2–3; cited in Goldstein Stepinwall, *Abbé Grégoire*, 112.

72. Henrí Grégoire, *Memoria sobre el clero escrita por el celebre obispo H. Grégoire*, translated by José María del Barrios (San Salvador: Imprenta del Gobierno, 1826), 8–9, 12, 14. A note at the beginning of the book states that Ciriaco Villacorta gave Barrios' Spanish translation of the pamphlet to the El Salvadoran government, who gave the order to print and disseminate the translated work.

73. Fr. Ramón Casaús y Torres, *Sermón tercero de San Pedro Mártir de Verona, predicado en 29 de abril de 1807 por el ilustrísimo y reverendísimo Fr. Ramón Casaús y Torres en la fiesta que el illmó. y santo Tribunal de la Inquisición con su ilustre cofradia celebró en la iglesia de la imperial convento de nuestro padre Santo Domingo de México* (México: Oficina de D. Juan Bautista de Arizpe, 1807), 38. In this sermon Casaús provided a historical explanation for the good done by the Inquistion; see especially pp. 38–41.

74. Grégoire, *Memoria sobre el clero*, 14. On Grégoire's despair about the repression that an aging Constitutional Clergy faced in 1820s France, see his letter to Fray José Servando Teresa de Mier of March 17, 1824, reprinted in Miquel i Vergés and Díaz-Thomé, eds., *Escritos inéditos*, 512–515, especially 514.

75. Grégoire's new work was his *Essai historique sur les libertés de l'Église gallicane et des autres églises de la catholicité, pendant les deux derniers siècles* (Paris: Censeur, 1818). Guatemala City, "Noticias Nacionales," *El Indicador*, March 24, 1825, no. 23, p. 1, col. 2. Guatemala City, *El Liberal*, No. 11, June 6, 1825, p. 1, col. 1. Paris, Abbè Henrí Grègoire to Fray Servando Teresa de Mier, September 30, 1825, reprinted in Vergés and Díaz-Thomé, eds., *Escritos inéditos*, 515.

76. Paris, Abbé Henrí Grégoire to Fray Servando Teresa de Mier, March 17, 1824, reprinted in Miquel I Vergés and Díaz-Thomé, eds., *Escritos inéditos*, 513. The editors translated the letter from French to Spanish.

77. Cañas, *Segunda advertencia*, 9.

78. José Andrés de Santa María, *Carta critica al doctor Simeon Cañas sobre los fundamentos de su Advertencia patriótica* (Guatemala: Impresa de Beteta, 1824), 12. Santa María quotes 1 Timothy 6:8, in Latin.

79. Santa María, *Carta critica*, 12–14.

80. 1 Timothy 6:8–10.

81. "Noticias curiosas. El asunto del obispado y otros, en el Seminario político" reproduced in Garcia, *Diccionario histórico*, 418.

82. Anselmo Ortiz quoted in Kimberly Sue Olson, "Crucifixion, 5, 84, 86.

83. Pamphlet in Miguel Ángel García, *Diccionario histórico*, 395.

84. Anselmo Ortiz quoted in Olson, "Crucifixion," 5, 84, 86. Miguel José de Aycinena authored a defense of ecclesiastical and lay religious resources from state extractions, see his Fr. Miguel José de Aycinena, "Procedimintos de la Provincia de Predicadores de Guatemala en la exacción del 7 por 100 impuesta por la Asamblea Nacional Constituyente de las Provincias Unidas de Centro de América sobre el valor liquido de las fincas de comunidades eclesiásticas seculars y regulares y sobre capitales de cofadías, hermandades, y obras pías" (Guatemala: J.J. de Arévalo, 1824).

85. San Salvador, *Semanario Politico Mercantil de San Salvador*, July 31, 1824, p. 4, col. 1. Parish priest Leonicio Dominguez also asserted that Delgado's usurpation of the Holy Father's prerogatives made him a wolf in sheeps' clothing, see Pbro. Leoncio Dominguez, *El párroco de Coxutepeque á sus feligreses* (Guatemala: Imprenta de Arévalo, 1825), 1–2.

86. Guatemala, José Matías Delgado to Ramón Casuas, July 21, 1824, and and Guatemala, Ramón Casaús to José Matías Delgado, July 28, 1824, in José Ignacio Marticorena, "Testimonio del expediente que obra en esta secretaría del gobierno del Estado del Salvador, sobre erirígir en diócesis su teritorio; y nombramiento y presentación del Obispo," ASV, Arch. Segr. Stato Esteri, 1823-1845, rub. 279, busta 592.

87. San Salvador, Juan José Salázar to Arzobispo Casaús, 29 June 1824, AHAG, Fondo Diocesano, Correspondencia, Cartas, July 1824, exp. 90.

88. San Salvador, "Policia de Seguridad," *Semanario Político Mercantil de San Salvador*, August 7, 1824, p. 8, col. 2. Salazar's name later appeared on a list of priests expelled by Delgado from El Salvador, see El Amigo de la Verdad, *A los editors del periodico titulado Semanario Politico Mercantil de San Salvador* (Guatemala: Imprenta de la Union), 2. On September 25, 1824, the *Semanario* reported that the government had dissolved a *junta* that met in the Convent of Santo Domingo. Ortiz, the guardian of the Franciscan convent, and parish priest of Ylobasco Juan José Salazar comprised the *junta*. Ortiz, the paper reported, had been expelled, but similarly dangerous juntas existed in Jutiapa and Ylobasco. Casaús protected both of these juntas, the *Semanario* asserted; see *Semanario Politico Mercantil de San Salvador*, September 25, 1824, p. 2, col. 2, n. 2.

89. The 21 June 1824 edict is discussed in a letter dated October 11, 1824, that Casaús sent to the pope. The letter is reproducd in Miguel Ángel García, *Diccionario histórico*, 350–351. Salázar noted that he had received a message from Ortiz delivered by a third party while the cleric was detained in El Salvador. Ortiz ordered Salázar not to disseminate Casuas' June 21 edict, fearing it was too incendiary and that Delgado's many supporters would turn against the church hierarchy; see San Salvador, Juan José Salázar to Arzobispo Casaús, June 29, 1824, AHAG, Fondo Diocesano Correspondencia, Cartas, July 1824.

90. San Salvador, José Ignacio Marticorena, "Testimonio del expediente que obra en esta secretaría del gobierno del Estado del Salvador, sobre erirígir en díocesis su teritorio; y nombramiento y presentación del obispo," April 12, 1825, ASV, Arch. Segr. Stato Esteri, 1823–1845, rub. 279, busta 592.

91. San Salvador, "S.S.Q.B.S.M." *Semanario Político Mercantil de San Salvador* August 28, 1824, p. 1.

92. San Salvador, "Gobierno del Estado," Alexandro Escalante, Intendente gefe político, July 28, 1824, in *Semanario Politico Mercantil de San Salvador*, August 7, 1824, p. 5, col. 1. Ortiz and Casaús loyalist Juan José Salazar, the elderly priest from Llobasco, later offered to disseminate the June 21 edict condemning Delgado; see San Salvador, Juan José Salázar to Arzobispo Casaús, June 29, 1824, AHAG, Correspondencia, Cartas, July 1824. Puebla, México, El Ciudadano General de Brigada Vicente Filísola to José Francisco Barrundia, October 2, 1824, reproduced in *Miguel Ángel García, Diccionario histórico*, [3–64], 26.

93. Pueblo de San Miguel de Llobasco, Juan José Salazar to Arzobispo Casaús, March 7, 1825, AHAG, Correspondencia, Cartas, July 1824.

94. Pedro de Lara, LLobasco, "Libro de Baustismos, 1824-1827," reproduced in Santiago Malaina, *Historia de la erección*, 56, Document 5.

95. Llobasco, Maximo Pineda to Dr. José Matías Delgado, February 20, 1827, AHAG, Fondo Diocesano, Cartas, Correspondencias, 1827.

96. Guatemala City, José María Herrarte to parroco de S. Luis Xilotepeque, January 30, 1826, AHAG, Fondo Diocesano, Secretaría, Cartas 1826.

97. Guatemala, José Mariano Herrarte to Sacristan Mayor Teodoro Franco, June 9, 1829, AHAG, Edictos, Decretos Pastorales, 1748–1845, expediente 34.

98. Llobasco, Maximo Pineda to Dr. José Matías Delgado, February 20, 1827, AHAG, Fondo Diocesano, Cartas, Correspondencias, 1827.

99. A Casaús loyalist made "citizen priest" and Delgado appointee Mariano Carillo's request for a baptismal certificate required for a marriage contingent on proof that he labored in the lord's vineyard with Casaús' blessing. Xilotepec, Pbro. don José Ignacio Marin á un sacerdote del intruso de El Salvador, February 5, 1826, AHAG, Fondo Diocesano, Secretaría, Cartas 1826, Carta 27. The priest who received the letter is identified as Mariano Carrillo.

100. The parish priest of Chiquimula, Julian Alfaro, wrote to Casaús for permission to send the parish priest of Metapán, José Ignacio Rendon, a baptismal certificate for a marriage applicant. Alfaro inquired if Rendon occupied his position with Casaús's blessing; see Chiquimula, "Oficio del parroco de Chiquimula, sobre una solicitud del parroco de Metapán, de San Salvador," February 10, 1826, AHAG, Fondo Diocesano, Secretaría, Cartas, 1826.

101. San Salvador, *Semanario Político Mercantil de San Salvador*, August 7, 1824, Alcance al Numero 2, p. 9, col. 2.

102. Saldaña, Saldaña, and López, *Invitación*.

103. *Carta en que se hacen algunas observaciones sobre un papel titulado Informe que el Dr. Juan Nepomuceno Azuero y Plata, cura y superintendente de su cantón, dió a la vice-presidencia de la Nueva Granada* (Santiago de Chile: Imprenta Nacional, 1825), 5, n. 4.

104. Juan Nepomuceno Azuero y Plata, *Informe que el Dr. Juan Nepomuceno Azuero Plata, cura de Sota y vicario superintendente de su cantón, dió a la vice-presidencia de la Nueva Granada, a principios de 1820, sobre los derechos del gobierno, en la provisión de beneficios eclesiásticos y otros puntos de inmúnidad* (Bogotá: Imprenta Nacional, 1824), 4–6.

105. Azuero y Plata, *Informe*, 14.

106. Ibid., 15.

107. Ibid., 19, 20.

108. José Andrés de Santa María, *Desengaño*, 10.

109. Ibid., 10, 30–31.

110. Miguel José Aycinena, *El ex-provincial del Orden de Predicadores Fr. Miguel José de Aycinena explica los motivos y fundamentos de su circular de 6 de febrero de 1825 expedidas a los religiosos de su provincia por donde deben recibir los derechos y ordenes de las autoridades civiles* (Guatemala: Imprenta Nueva de C. Arévalo, 1826), 6.

111. Guatemala City, "Un acomedido á los editors del *Indicador*," *El Indicador*, November 22, 1824, No. 7, p. 4, cols. 1–2; direct quote in col. 2.

112. San José, Costa Rica, José Guerrero, Manuel Aguilar and Pedro Zeledón, "Estado de Costa Rica. A la Asamblea del Estado se presente al siguiente voto particular," September 2, 1825, reproduced in Miguel Ángel García, *Diccionario histórico,*[423–429], 425. Casaús warned Rome that Costa Rica could produce a schism like that of El Salvador, see, for example, Rome, "Affari eccla straordinari. Sicsma de Guatimala," August 13, 1826, ASV, Arch. Segr. Stato Esteri, 1823–1825, rub. 279, busta 592. Guatemala, Archbishop Casaús to Pope, March 13, 1826, reproduced in Miguel Ángel García, *Diccionario histórico* [385–387], 387. On attempts to establish a bishopric in Costa Rica during this time, see José Bernal Rivas Fernández, "En busca de la independencia ecclesiática de Costa Rica," *AHIg* 11 (2002): [239–278], 243–247.

113. José Ignacio Saldaña, *Contestación al anónimo impreso en San Salvador con fecha de Guatemala de 10 de octubre de 1825* (Guatemala: Imprenta Nueva, C. C. Arévalo, 1826), 14–16. José Ignacio Saldaña signed the work in Santa Rosa Parish on January 10, 1826.

CHAPTER 4

1. Victor Castrillo received power of attorney to represent Delgado in Rome in front of a notary in San Salvador on July 12, 1825. See San Salvador, José Matías Delgado and Pedro Miguel López, July 12, 1825, ASV, Arch. Segr. Stato Esteri, 1823–1825, rubrica 279, busta 592. Also see Guatemala City, *El Redactor General*, November 3, 1825, no.19, p. 2, col. 1.

2. Roberto Regoli, "La Congregación Especial para los Asuntos Eclesiásticos de España durante el trienio liberal (1820-1833)" *Anuario de Historia de la Iglesia* 19 (2010): 141–166. On

the radical ecclesiastical reforms hatched during the 1820 to1823 period, see Manuel Revuelta Gonzalez, "Los planes de reforma eclesiástica durante el trienio constitucional," *Miscelánea Comillas* 56–57 (1972): 93–124.

3. On Delgado's appointment of Castrillo as his ambassador, see Guatemala City, *El Redactor General*, November 3, 1825, no. 19, p. 2, col. 1. On Castrillo's time in Rome, see Ayala Benítez, *La iglesia*, 187–188.

4. Their release was secured by an 1817 royal order. On the Belén Conspiracy, so named because it took place in the Convent of Belén, see Hubert Howe Bancroft, *History of the Pacific States of North America, Vol. 3, Central America, 1801-1887* (San Francisco, CA: The History Company, 1887), 18–19. Alfred de Valois, *Mexique, Havane, et Guatemala. Notes de Voyage* (Paris, 1861), 220–221. Christophe Belaubre, "Al cruce de la historia social y política: un acercamiento crítico a la 'conjuación' de Belén, Guatemala (1813)," in *Revoluciones, guerras y revoluciones políticas en la América hispano-portuguesa, 1808-1824*, ed. Sajid Alfredo Herrera Mena (El Salvador: Universidad Centroamericana, 2013), 9–29. Mario Rodríguez, *La conspiración de Belén en nueva perspectiva* (Guatemala: Ministerio de Educación, 1965). Information on Castrillo's 1819 release can be found in Guatemala City, "El reo de la causa llamada de Belén . . . es indultado de los cargos," December 13, 1819, AGCA, Sig. B2.5, exp. 758, leg. 29, fol. 14.

5. María M. de Lines, "Movimientos precursors de la independencia el el Reino de Guatemala," *Revista de la Universidad de Costa Rica* 31 (1971): 34.

6. Guatemala City, José Victor Castrillo to Capitan General José de Bustamante, December 20, 1817, AGCA, Sig. B 2.5, leg. 29, exp. 754, fols.1–2. Guatemala City, Fr. Luis García to Capitan General José de Bustamante, January 3, 1818, AGCA, Sig. B 2.5, exp. 754, fol.3. Real Palacio, Guatemala City, Capitan General José de Bustamante, January 12, 1818, AGCA, Sig. B 2.5, exp. 754, fol. 4.

7. Guatemala City, Provincial de la Merced to Archbishop Casaús, August 18, 1824, AGCA, Sig. B-1, leg. 3594, exp. 82461, fol. 1.

8. Valerio Ignacio Rivas, *Discurso pronunciado por el ciudadano Valerio Ignacio Rivas en la tertulia patriótica de Guatemala en la acción de la noche del jueves 19 de enero del corriente año* (Guatemala: Imprenta de la Union: 1826), 5. Magda Aragon Ibarra reports that in 1837 and 1838 Valerio Ignacio Rivas worked as a land surveyor near Totonicapán, and incurred the community's wrath for his actions, see her "El trabajo de los agrimensores en Guatemala, siglo XIX," *Anuario Revista de Estudios Cuarta* 1 (2016): 163–165. Guatemala, "Decreto," July 28, 1829, BN-Guatemala, Fondo Antigo, Registro 1952. On the Assemblea Nacional Constituyente's (ANC'S) 1823 degree establishing *tertulias patrióticas* in every municipality, see AHAG, Fondo Diocesano, Secretaría. Impresos, leyes y decretos. Año 1823, No. 34, pp. 1–5. In 1826, Sonsonate's city council proposed the establishment of a *tertulia patriótica* to instruct the youth of the city, see Sajid Alfredo Herrera Mena, "Orden corporativo en tiempos republicanos: las municipalidades salvadoreñas (1824-1838)," in *Diálogo historiográfico Centroamérica-México*, ed. Brian Connaughton (México, D.F.: Universidad Autónoma Metropolitana and Editorial Gedisa, 2017), 193–194.

9. Guatemala, Victor Castrillo to Archbishop Casaús, February 1825, AHAG, Correspondencia, Fondo Diocesano, Correspondencia, Cartas, 1825. Granada, City Council Report, November 12, 1824, included in Guatemala, Victor Castrillo to Archbishop Casaús, 1825, AHAG, Correspondencia, Fondo Diocesano, Cartas, February 1825.

10. Ibid.

11. José D. Gámez, *Nicaragua desde los tiempos prehistóricos hasta 1860, en sus relaciones con España, México, y Centro-América* (Nicaragua: Tipografía El Pais, 1889), 374. Ayala Benítez, *La iglesia*,178.

12. Central America, Victor Castrillo to Pope Leo XII, July 20, 1826. The original letter in Latin is reproduced in full in Ayala Benítez, *La iglesia*, 284–297. David Chu translated the letter from Latin to English at my behest.

13. Paris, Fr. Victor Castrillo to Escamilla, March 12, 1827, ASV, Archivo Segreterio Stato Esteri, Años 1823–1845, Rubrica 279, Busta 592.

14. Villacorta's letter to the Holy Father also highlighted Casaús' malice, evidenced by the clandestinely circulated edicts he issued against the actions of Delgado's coterie. Striking a lighter tone, the *jefe supremo* also praised Delgado's twenty-eight-year-stint as San Salvador's parish priest, attributing his success to his ability to align evangelical morality with El Salvadorans' enthusiasm for independence from Spain. San Salvador, Juan Vicente Villacorta to Pope Leo XII, July 13, 1825, ASV, Archivo Segreterio Stato Esteri, Años 1823–1845, Rubrica 279, Busta 592; and San Salvador, José Matias Delgado to Pope Leo XII, July 10, 1825, ASV, Archivo Segreterio Stato Esteri, Años 1823–1845, Rubrica 279, Busta 592.

15. Guatemala City, October 11, 1824, Fr. Ramón Francisco, Arzobispo de Guatemala to Pope Leo XII, reproduced in Miguel Ángel García, *Diccionario histórico enciclopédico de la República de El Salvador. El doctor José Matías Delgado. Homenaje en el primer centenario de su muerte, 1832-1932. Documentos para el estudio de su vida y de su obra. Tomo II* (El Salvador: Imprenta Naciónal, 1939), 350–351. For more on Rome's exchange with Casaús and others on the schism, see Ayala Benítez, *La iglesia*, 167–174.

16. Guatemala City, October 11, 1824, Fr. Ramón Francisco, Arzobispo de Guatemala to Pope Leo XII, reproduced in Miguel Ángel García, *Diccionario histórico*, 350–351.

17. Brown, *Juan Fermín de Aycinena*, 199–201.

18. Cádiz, José Aycinena to Santiago Guistiani, Archbishop of Tiro and Apostolic Nuncio, December 16, 1825, ASV, Archivo de la Nunciatura de Madrid, Scatola 270, ff. 1-1v. Rome, Cardinale della Somagalia to Monginor Nunzio, May 30, 1826, ASV, Archivo de la Nunciatura de Madrid, Scatola 270, ff. 1. Brown, *Juan Fermín de Aycinena*, 199–201. Guatemala City, "Dictámen aprobado por el Congreso Federal de la República de Centro-América, expedida por el Congreso sobre este asunto," July 19, 1825; and Guatemala City, "Dictámen de las Comisiones reunidas de puntos constitucionales, de justicia y negócios ecclesiásticos, sobre erección de obispado, y nombramiento y posesión de obispo en el estado de El Salvador, presentado y leído en el Congreso Federal, en los días 27 y 28 de junio de 1825 y señalado para su discusión el 28 del mismo mes," in García, Diccionario histórico, 142 and 143–153. Guatemala City, Cathedral Chapter, *Informe que el cabildo eclesiástico de la catedral de Guatemala dió al actual prelado de esta santa iglesia metropolitana, Dr. y Mtro Fr. Ramón Francisco Casaús y Torres sobre la erección de obispado y nombramiento de obispo que hizo el estado de S. Salvador, en la conformidad que se manifesta por los tres exemplares impresos en aquella ciudad: Estos se han reimpreso al fin de este informe; así por lo que conducen á su recta inteligencia, tambien porque se citan en él muchos de sus lugares* (Guatemala: Imprenta Nueva, J. J. de Arévalo, 1825).

19. See El Patriota's squib is reproduced in Miguel Angel García, *Diccionario histórico*, 414–415.

20. Rome, Pope Leo XII to Jefe del Gobierno de El Salvador Villacorta, September 24, 1826, reproduced in Ramón López Jiménez, *Mitras salvadoreñas* (San Salvador: Ministerio de Cultura, Departamento Editorial, 1960), 27–29.

21. Rome, Pope Leo XII to José Matías Delgado, September 24, 1826, reproduced in López Jiménez, *Mitras*, 30–32.

22. Guatemala City, Ramón Casaús, Pastoral Letter, August 31, 1827, cited in Ayala Benítez, *La iglesia*, 206.

23. [Valentín] Gómez Farías, [José Sixto] Berduzco, [José Loreto] Barraza, [Francisco] García [Salinas], [José Francisco] Quintero, [Florentino] Martínez, "Dictámen de las comisiones unidas eclesiáticas y de relaciones de la cámara de senadores sobre las instrucciones que deben dar al enviado á Roma, leído y mandado a imprimir en sessión secreta de 2 de marzo de 1826," in *Colección eclesiástica mejicana*, vol. 2, [13–61], 16, 17, 28, 37, 59, 60.

24. See Rome, "Nuova Republica del Messico. Tratative della s. sede con la republica del Messico," AES, Congregation for Extraordinary Ecclesiastical Affairs, Sessione 103, September 9, 1826. Also see Guatemala City, "Copia de un artículo publicado en un periódico de Paris, titulado *El Amigo de la Religion y del Rei* y en el *Conservador Belga*, que se publicó en la ciudad de Lieja en los Paises-Bajos," *El Indicador*, October 15, 1827, no.153, p. 3, col. 2 and p. 4, col. 1. See Paris, *Le constitutionnel*, "Extérieur Amerique Meridionale," August 15, 1826, p. 1, cols. 1–2. On September 3, 1826, *Le constitutionnel* reported that Guatemalan ecclesiastics opposed the schism in El Salvador, see p. 1, col. 1. Spain's papal nuncio sent the Cádiz paper, which he referred to as the "Giornale di Cadiz," on to Rome; he glossed the report as "having interesting information on religious affairs in America, particularly Mexico"; see Madrid, March 9, 1826, D.V.E to Card. Segr. De Stato Roma, no. 663, ASV, Archivo de la Nunciatura de Madrid, Scatola 270.

25. On the Congregation for Extraordinary Ecclesiastical Affairs, see Owen Chadwick, *The Pope*, 552–553. Alfonso Alcala Alvarado offers the most complete account of the early Mexican republic's interactions with the papacy around the patronato and other issues, see his *Una pugna diplomatica ante la Santa Sede. El restablecimiento del episcopado en México, 1825-1831* (México: Editorial Porrúa, 1967), esp. 41–61.

26. Rome, Council for Extraordinary Ecclesiastical Affairs, AES, Sessione no. 103, September 24, 1826, Nuova Republica de Messico, fols. 3–4.

27. For more on José Maria Luis Mora as a reform Catholic and the religious nature of the public sphere of letters in the decades immediately after Mexico's 1821 independence, see Voekel, *Alone Before God*, 146–170. On Gómez Farías' secularization of the northern missions in 1833, see Robert H. Jackson and Edward Castillo, *Indians, Franciscans, and Spanish Colonization. The Impact of the Mission System on California Indians* (Albuquerque, NM: University of New Mexico Press, 1995), especially 87–90. On Quintana Roo's actions as minister of justice, see Ibarra, ed., *Andrés Quintana Roo*, 153–158. On Mora, see Charles Hale, *Mexican Liberalism in the Age of Mora* (New Haven, CT: Yale University Press, 1968). For a brief synopsis of the reforms enacted in Mexico in 1832 and 1833, see J. Lloyd Mecham, *Church and State in Latin America. A History of Politico-Ecclesiasical Relations* (Chapel Hill, NC: University of North Carolina Press, 1966 [1934]), 348–350.

28. Franco, Pablo, et.al, *Dictámen de la comisión*, 7–13. For more on the committee's report, which called for elections of clerics, see Voekel, *Alone Before God*, 155–156.

29. Jean-Francois Briere, "Abbé Grégoire and Haitian Independence," *Research in African Literatures* 35, no. 2 (summer 2004), 37. Madison Smartt Bell, *Touissant Louverture*, 194–195. For more on Grégoire's relationship to Haitian rulers, see Goldstein Sepinwall, *Abbé Grégoire*, 181–198.

30. Abbé Henrí Grégoire to Fray Servando Teresa de Mier, March 17, 1824, reprinted in Miquel I Vergés and Díaz-Thomé, eds., *Escritos inéditos*, 513. The letter was originally written in French and translated by the editors. Fagoaga hailed from one of New Spain's wealthiest silver mining and merchant families. He first met Mier in London and helped finance the Mina expedition; he also assisted the friar in 1820 as he languished in prison in San Juan de Ulúa; see Dominguez Michael, *Vida*, 486. Also see Jiménez Codinach, *La Gran Bretaña*.

31. Paris, Abbé Henrí Grégoire to Fray Servando Teresa de Mier, September 30, 1825, reprinted in Miquel I Vergés and Díaz-Thomé, eds., *Escritos inéditos*, 517. The letter was originally written in French and was translated into Spanish by the editors.

32. On the trustee system in the early Republic of the United States, see Patrick Carey, *People, Priests, and Prelates: Ecclesiastical Democracy and the Tensions of Trusteeism* (Notre Dame, IN: Notre Dame University Press, 1987). For more on the role of Spanish speakers like Mier in the transformation of Catholicism in Philadelphia during this period, see Richard A. Warren, "Displaced 'Pan-Americans' and the Transformation of the Catholic Church in Philadelphia, 1789-1850," *The Pennsylvania Magazine of History and Biography* 127, no. 4 (October 2004): 343–366. For more on Mier's participation in the St. Mary's parish schism, see Domínguez Michael, *Vida*, 608–612.

33. Servando Teresa de Mier, *The Opinion of the R. Rev. Servandus A. Mier, Doctor of Sacred Theology in the Royal and Pontifical University of Mexico, and Chaplain of the Army of the Right, First Army of the Peninsula, on Certain Queries Proposed to Him by the Rev. William Hogan, Pastor of St. Mary's Church* (Philadelphia: n.p., 1821), 4–6.

34. Servando Teresa de Mier, *A Word Relative to an Anonymous Pamphlet Printed in Philadelphia Entitled "Remarks on the Opinion of the Rt. Rev. Servandus A. Mier, Doctor of Sacred Theology, on Certain Queries Proposed to Him by Rev. Wm. Hogan* (Philadelphia, n.p., 1821), 4.

35. Patrick W. Carey, "John F.O. Fernandez: Enlightened Lay Catholic Reformer, 1815-1820" *The Review of Politics* 43, no. 1 (January 1981): 112–114. Gerald P. Fogarty, S.J., *Commonwealth Catholicism. A History of the Catholic Church in Virginia* (Notre Dame, IN: University of Notre Dame Press, 2001), 33–41.

36. St. Bernard, Espistol. Ad Eugen: Papam, 238 cited in John F. O. Fernandez, *Letter Addressed to the Most Reverend Leonard Neale, Archbishop of Baltimore. By a Member of the Roman Catholic Congregation of Norfolk, Virginia* (Norfork, 1816), 5, 21; quoted portion on pages 9–10.

37. Amrose Maréchal, *Pastoral Letter of the Archbishop of Baltimore, to the Roman Catholicks [sic] of Norfolk, Virginia* (Baltimore: J. Rosinson, 1819), 24.

38. Fogarty, S.J., *Commonwealth Catholicism*, 44–45.

39. Dale B. Light, *Rome and the New Republic. Conflict and Community in Philadelphia Catholicism between the Revolution and the Civil War* (Notre Dame, IN: University of Notre Dame Press, 1996), 226. Rodney Hessinger, "'A Base and Unmanly Conspiracy": Catholicism and the Hogan Schism in the Gendered Religious Market of Philadelphia," *Journal of the Early Republic* 31, no. 3 (fall 2011): 357–396.

40. Fray Servando Teresa de Mier, *Discurso del Dr. D. Servando Teresa de Mier sobre la encíclica del Papa León XII. Quinta impression revisada y corregida por el autor* (México: Imprenta de la Federación, 1825), 31, 19, 12, 26. The edict Mier references is from August 27, 1808.

41. Regoli, "La Congregación, 161.

42. See, for example, Emilio La Parra López and Antonio Mestre Sanchís, *El primer liberalismo español y la iglesia* (Alicante: Instituto de Cultura Juan Gil-Albert, 1985). Luis Barbastro Gil, *Revolución liberal y reacción (1808-1833): protagonismo ideológico del clero en la sociedad valenciana* (Alicante, ES: Caja de Ahorros Provincial, 1987). Revuelta, *Política religiosa*.

43. Regoli, "La Congregación," 15, 153.

44. Royal Decree of September 5, 1799 cited in Gérard Dufour, "Las ideas político-religiosas de Juan Antonio Llorente," *Cuadernos de Historia Contemporánea* 10 (1998): 14. Mariano Luis de Urquio, *Apuntes para la memoria sobre mi vida política, persecuciones y trabajos padecidos en ella*, ed. Aleix Romero Peña (Madrid, ES: Editorial Siníndice, 2010), 32.

45. Villanueva, *Vida literaria*, 310–311.

46. Villanueva, *Vida Literaria*, vol. 1, 70. For more on Villanueva, see Hamnett, "Joaquin Lorenzo Villanueva," 19–41. Joaquin Villanueva, *Vida Literaria*, 63.

47. Juan Antonio Llorente, *Anales secretos de la inquisición* (Madrid: Imprenta de Ibarra, 1812), 60. José Espiga was denounced by the Inquisition as a Jansenist in 1799; see Paula Demerson, *María Francisca de Sales Portocarrero: una figura de la Ilustración* (Madrid: Editorial Nacional, 1975), 298.

48. Herr, *The Eighteeenth-Century Revolution in Spain*, 426–427.

49. Juan Antonio Llorente, *Colección diplomatica de various papeles antiguos y modernos sobre dispensas matrimoniales y otros puntos de disciplina eclesiástica* (Madrid: Imprenta de Ibarra, 1809), 72, 73, 96, 111, 165, 168, 169; the testimony of San Isidro professor and Calahorra cathedral canon Blas Aguiriano appears on pages 90–123. Saugnieux, *Un prélat éclairé*. . Barcelona's bishop is identified as Pedro Díaz de Valdés by Saugnieux, see his *Un prélat éclairé*, 165–169. Gaspar Melchor de Jovellanos, whom historian David A. Brading calls "a leader of the Jansenist party," appointed Tavira to Salamanca's bishopric. Jovellanos had hoped that Tavira would transform the University of Salamanca, which he regarded as tragically beset by "the usurpations of the Roman Curia; their aversion to the sovereign authority and its regalias; and their ambition to dominate the schools and preserve the influence of the religious orders and, in a word, to perpetuate ignorance." Jovellanos concluded that "Tavira is our Bossuet and ought to be the reformer of our Sorbonne"; Jovellanos quoted in D. A. Brading, *First America*, 509.

50. Joaquin Villanueva, *Vida Literaria*, vol. 1, 64. *Gérard Dufour, Juan Antonio Llorente en France: (1813-1822): contribution a l'étude du libéralisme chrétien en France et en Espagne au début du XIX siècle* (Geneva, CH: Libraire Droz, 1982), 14–16. Antonio Pereira de Figueiredo, *Demonstração theologica, canonica, e historica do direito dos metropolitanos de Portugal para confirmarem, e mandarem sagrar os bispos suffraganeos nomeados por sua magestade e do direito dos obispos de cada provincia para confirmarem, e sagrarem os seus respectivos metropolitanos, tambem nomeados por sua magestade ainda fóra do caso de rotura com a corte de Roma* (Lisbon: Regia Officina Typografica, 1769). A Spanish translation of the book was printed in Lima, Perú in 1833. On the title page, the translator is referred to as "Un amante de la ilustración Americana;" see António Pereira de Figueiredo, *Demostración teólogica, canónica e histórica, del derecho de los metropolitanos de Portugal para confirmar y mandar consagrar a los obispos sufraganeos nombrados por su magestad* (Lima: Imprenta de la Patria de T. López, 1833).

51. Van Kley, *Reform Catholicism*, 30–31, 55, 156–157. Evergton Sales Souza, *Jansénisme et réforme de l'église dans l'empire portugais* (Lisbon, PT: Fundação Calouste Gulbenkian, Centre Culturel Calouste Gulbenkian, 2004). Samuel J. Miller, *Portugal and Rome C. 1748–1830: An Aspect of the Catholic Enlightenment* (Rome, IT: Università Gregoriana Editrice, 1978), 152, 169–178, 212.

52. Henry Kamen, *The Disinherited: Exile and the Making of Spanish culture, 1492-1975* (New York, NY: HarperCollinsPublisher, 2008), 180–184. On Llorente's influence on radical Argentine reformers like Bernardino Rivadavia, who oversaw a 1822 reform of the regular orders and the church in line with Reform Catholic tenets, see Gallardo, *La política religiosa*, 41–66. Nancy Vogely notes that much of Llorente's work that circulated in the Americas was printed in northern Spain and France; see her "Llorente's Readers in the Americas," in *Liberty! Égalité! Independencia!*, ed. David S. Shields (Worchester, MA: American Antiquarian Society, 2007), 375–393. Fray Servando Teresa de Mier mentions personal contacts as key distributors of his works: in a letter to Andrés Bello, he notes that Manuel Pinto ferried 600 copies of his *Historia de la revolución de la Nueve España* to South America, while another acquaintance traveled with 170 copies, see Phildelphia, "Carta a Andrés Bello," October 7, 1821, in Fray

Servando Teresa de Mier, *La Revolución y la fe. Una antología general*, ed. Begoña Pulido Herráez (Mexico: Fondo de Cultura Económica; Fundación para las Letras Méxicanas; and UNAM, 2013), 387–389. On Bello's intellectual impact in the Atlantic world, see Karen Racine, "Nature and the Mother: Foreign Readings and the Evolution of Andrés Bello's American Identity, London, 1810-1829," in *Strange Pilgrimages: Exile, Travel, and National Identity in Latin America, 1800-1990s*, ed. Ingrid Elizabeth Fey and Karen Racine (Wilmington, DE: Scholarly Resources, 2000), 3–19. Bello chided Mier for sending 750 copies of one of his works to Buenos Aires— most likely the 770 books Mier mentioned to him in his October 7, 1821, letter—noting that "50 copies would have been excessive, and I'm sure that not twenty have sold"; Bello quoted in Angel Rama, *La crítica de la cultura en America Latina* (Lima, Perú: Biblioteca Ayacucho, 1985), 69.

53. Ever the satirist, Mier described *Auctorem fidei*'s detailed examination of Reform Catholic errors as "the best possible defense of the Council." Mier also recounted a visit to the Synod's convener, Scipione de' Ricci, during a trip to Italy; the pope had tricked Ricci into retracting his radical positions by erasing the caveats that Ricci had carefully appended to his formal written retraction; Mier, *Memoirs*, 92. On the considerable influence of the Synod of Pistoia in Spain, see Mestre Sanchís, "Repercusión del sínodo," 425–439. Also see F. Díaz de Cerio, "Jansenimso histórico y regalismo borbónico español a finales del siglo XVIII," *Hispana Sacra* 33, no. 67 (1981): 102.

54. In his 1806 memoir, Urquio blamed Spain's papal nuncio and the court's shadowy "Jesuit party" for his misfortunes. The reform party's conflicts with the Jesuits were the true motor of Spanish history, Urquio argued, an intriguing gloss indeed. When he began as minster of state, the kingdom was wracked by "religious schisms" led by recently returned ex-Jesuits who "inundated" streets and plazas with their writings; Urquio ordered these "worthless scribblings" confiscated; see Mariano Luis de Urquio, *Apuntes para la memoria sobre mi vida política, persecuciónes y trabajos padecidos en ella*, ed. and intro. by Aleix Romero Peña (Madrid, ES: Editorial Siníndice, 2010), 36, 39, 76–78.

55. Andrea J. Smidt, "Bourbon Regalism," 50–51. Aleix Romero Peña, "Caída y persecución del ministro Urquijo y de los jansenistas españoles," *Revista Historia Autónoma* 2 (March 2013): 76.

56. Mier, *Memoirs*, 11. Joaquin Villanueva reported that Urquijo was only released from the Fortress in Pamplona in March of 1808, see his *Vida literaria*, 65.

57. Herr, *Eighteenth-Century Revolution*, 430–431. Sanjuanista Lorenzo de Zavala's Mexico City newspaper, an organ of the York Right Masons called *El Aguila Mexicana*, reported that the Count of Montijo had been caught in a dragnet of Spanish liberals and languished in an Inquisition dungeon until 1820; See Mexico City, *El Aguila Mexicana*, July 17, 1825, p. 2, col. 3.

58. Fray Servando, *Memoirs*, 134, 34, 76–77, 90–92.

59. Demerson, *María Francisca*, 261–284. Mestre Sanchis, "La influencia," 51.

60. Dufour, "Las ideas," 14.

61. Cortes de Cádiz, *Diario de las sesiones de Cortes*, Sesion del día 27 de Agosto de 1820, pp. 682–684, at https://app.congreso.es/est_sesiones, accessed on 1/4/2021.

62. Joaquin Villanueva, *Vida literaria*, 255, 262. Dictamen dated March 13, 1821.

63. Rome, Pope Pius VII to King Ferdinand, August 30, 1821, in *Colección eclesiástica Española comprensiva de los breves de S.S., notas del R. Nuncio, representaciones de los SS obipos á las cortes, pastorales, edictos, y con otros documentos relativos á las inovaciones hechas por los constitucionales en materias eclesiáticas desde el 7 de marzo de 1820*, Tomo I (Madrid: Imprenta de E. Aguado, 1823), 39–45. Cortes de Cádiz, *Actas de las sesiones secretas de las cortes ordinarias*

y extraordinarias de los años 1820 y 1821, de las años 1822 á 1825 y de las celebradas por las diputaciones permanentes de las mismas cortes ordinarias (Madrid: J. Antonio García, 1874), 224, 250. Villanueva, *Vida literaria*, vol. 2, 247, 251. Manuel Revuelta Gonzalaez, S.J, *Politica religiosa*, 343–345. For more on Muñoz Torrero, see Juan García Pérez, *Diego Muñoz Torrero. Ilustración, religiosidad y liberalism* (Mérida, Badajoz, ES: Editora Regional de Extremadura, 1989).

64. Carlos Le Brun, *Retratos de la revolución de España, ó de los principales participantes que han jugado en ella, muchos de los cuales están sacados en caricaturas en lo rídiculo en que ellos mismos se habían puesto, cuando el retrasista los iba sacando; con unas observaciónes políticas al fin sobre la misma;y la resolución sobre la question de por qué se malogró ésta y no lo de los Estados-Unidos* (Philadelphia, PA., 1826), 19–20.

65. Carlos Le Brun, *Vida de Fernando septimo, rey de España; ó coleccion de anecdotas de su nacimiento y de su carrera privada y política, publicadas en castellano por Dn. Carlos Le Brun* (Philadelphia, PA, 1826), 201.

66. Madrid, *El Universal*, July 23, 1821, p. 2, cols. 2–3. Madrid, *El Universal*, March 9, 1822, p. 1, col. 2; Madrid, *El Universal*, November 26, 1822, p. 2, col. 3.

67. London, *Ocios de Españoles Emigrados* 8 (November 1824) in *Ocios de Españoles Emigrados*, vol. 2 (London: A. Macintosh, 1824), 303–304. The newspaper *Ocios* was written in London from 1824 to 1827 by a group of exiled Spanish liberals and edited by the Villanueva brothers.

68. Villanueva, *Vida Literaria*, 62.

69. Joaquin Lorenzo Villanueva, *Dictámen del Sr. D. Joaquín Lorenzo Villanueva, diputado en Cortes por Valencia, acerca de la segunda proposición preliminar del proyecto de decreto sobre los tribunales protectores de la religion, leído en las sesiones del 20 y 21 de enero* (Cádiz, ES: Imprenta de D. Diego García Campoy, 1813), 75, n. 1.

70. Consolación Fernández Mellén, *Iglesia y poder en la Habana. Juan José Díaz de Espada, un obispo ilustrado (1800-1832)* (Bilbao, ES: Universidad del País Vasco, 2014), 259.

71. Miguel Figueroa y Miranda, *Religión y política en la Cuba del siglo XIX. El obispo Espada visto á la luz de los archivos romanos,1802-1832* (Miami, FL: Ediciones Universal, 1975), 16, 33, 260–269. Eduardo Torres-Cuevas, ed. and intro., *Obispo Espada. Ilustración, reforma y antiesclavismo. Selección, introducción y notas de Eduardo Torres-Cuevas* (Cuba: Palabra de Cuba, 1990), 167–168, 94–98. On Archbishop Antonio Jorge Galban's anti-Jesuit sentiments, see Antonio Mestre and Rafael Benítez Sánchez Blanco, *La iglesia en la España de los siglos XVII y XVIII* (Madrid: La Editorial Católica, 1979), 622.

72. Eduardo Torres-Cuevas, Jorge Ibarra Cuesta, and Mercedes García Rodríguez, eds. and intro., *Félix Varela. El que nos enseño primero en pensar. Obras. Tomo I* (Havana, Cuba: Editorial Cultura Popular, 1997), xxiv. Félix Varela, *Miscelánea filosófica. Tercera edición por Felix Varela* (New York, NY: Imprenta de Enrique Newton, 1827).

73. Hidalgo y Costilla, *Disertación*, 163–180.

CHAPTER 5

1. Dym, *From Sovereign Villages* .

2. Ibid.

3. Manuel Montúfar y Coronado, *Memorias para la historia de la revolución de Centro América (Memorias de Jalapa), Recuerdos y anecdotas, tomo 1, vol. 65 Biblioteca Guatemalteca de Cultura Popular* (Guatemala: Centro Editorial José de Pineda Ibarra, 1963 [original 1832]), 93, 95–96.

4. Francisco Morazán, *Memorias de David. Manifiesto del pueblo centroamérico* (Teguicigalpa, HOND: Instituto Morazánico de Honduras, 1953 [orginal 1841]), 36.

5. Sajid Alfredo Herrera Mena, "La invención liberal de la identidad estatal salvadoreña 1824-1839," *Estudios Centroamericanos. Revista de Extensión Cultural de la Universidad Centroamericana "José Simeón Cañas,"* 60, no. 684 (2005): 16–19.

6. Hazel Marylyn Bennett Ingersoll, "The War of the Mountain. A Study of Reactionary Peasant Insurgency in Guatemala, 1837-1873" (PhD diss., George Washington University, 1972), 7–14. On the effects of the British debt on Central American politics, see Mario Rodríguez, *A Palmerstonian Diplomat in Central America, Frederick Chadfield, Esq.* (Tucson, AZ: The University of Arizona Press, 1964), 114–120 and passim. On the insect plague see Luis Alberto Arrioja Díaz Viruell, "Guatemala y Nueva España: historia de una plaga compartida, 1798-1807," *Revista de Historia Moderna* 33 (October 2015): 309–323. On resource conflicts between the states and the federal government, see Xiomara Avendaño Rojas, "Fiscalidad y soberanía. Dos puntos críticos del gobierno federal en Centroamérica, 1824-1838," *Relaciones. Revista del Colegio de Michoacán* 12, nos. 67/68 (1996): 105–125; Robert Smith, "El financiamiento de la Federación Centroamericana, 1821-1838," in *Lecturas de historia de Centroamérica*, ed. Luis René Cáceres (San José, CR: Banco Centroamericano de Integración Económica, 1989), 439–468; and Pedro Joaquín Chamorro, *Historia de la federación de la América Central, 1823-1840* (Madrid, ES: Cultura Hispanica, 1951). Historian Clara Pérez Fabrigat notes three principal causes of the region's post-Independence instability: the states' unwillingness to support the federal government's fiscal demands; the cost of passifying the conflict between Grenada and León with troops from eastern El Salvador; and resentment towards Guatemala's large contingent of representatives in the federal assembly, see Clara Pérez Fabregat, "Apuntes socioeconómicos sobre la Guerra Federal de 1826 a 1829. La experiencia salvadoreña en clave regional," in *La primera guerra federal centroaméricana, 1826-1829*, ed. Arturo Taracena Arriola (Guatemala: Editorial Cara Parens, 2015), 141; and Clara Pérez Fabrigat, *San Miguel y el oriente salvadoreño. La construcción del estado de El Salvador, 1780-1865* (El Salvador: Universidad Simeón Cañas Editores, 2018), 153–186.

7. As historian Charles Walker has argued vigorously, characterizing the post-Independence era in Latin America under the catch-all term "instability" is too often a means of avoiding historical analysis. He writes that "the dizzying change of presidents and other signs of turmoil" after independence "have led scholars to interpret the post-Independence period as mere chaos or elite machinations and lower-class failures" rather than "illuminat[ing] the logic and nature of these struggles." Charles F. Walker, *Smoldering Ashes: Cuzco and the Creation of Republican Peru, 1780-1840* (Durham, NC: Duke University Press, 1999), 4. Arguably, the very form of the question takes stability as an assumed norm. And indeed, as Donald Stevens notes, explanations for the perceived failure of former New Spain clustered around, on the one hand, a diagnosis of fiscal frailty, and, on the other, a personalization that painted local strongmen—*caudillos*—as something akin to non-ideological, self-interested mafiosi. Stevens' cliometric analysis disproved any direct relationship between convulsions in Mexican leadership and either declining federal income or fluctuating foreign trade between Independence and the Reforma; Donald Fithian Stevens, *Origins of Instability in Early Republican Mexico* (Durham, NC: Duke University Press, 1991), 2. Bristling with terms like "barbarian" and "primitive," the early search for universal principles to explain an alleged pan-regional weakness for charismatic authoritarians subsequently gave way more nuanced explanations for *caudillismo* as at least a rational patron-client relationship. As historian Natalia Sobrevilla Perea points out, however, any effort to collapse the specificities of post-Independence leadership into a single category will inevitably miss the actual politics of alliances, policy, and military power. Natalia

Sobrevilla Perea, *The Caudillo of the Andes: Andrés de Santa Cruz* (Cambridge, UK: Cambridge University Press, 2011).

8. Xilotepec, José Ignacio Martín to ciudadano presbítero Mariano Carillo, February 5, 1826, AHAG, Fondo Diocesano, Secretaría, Cartas 1826. Chiquimula, "Oficio del parroco de Chiquimula, sobre una solicitud del parroco de Metapán, de San Salvador," February 10, 1826, AHAG, Fondo Diocesano, Secretaría, Cartas, 1826.

9. San Salvador, Ignacio Perdomo to Archbishop Casaús, January 26, 1826, AHAG, Fondo Diocesano, Correspondencia, Cartas, 1826. Carcel General de San Salvador, Ignacio Perdomo to Archbishop Casaús, October 13, 1825, AHAG, Fondo Diocesano, Correspondencia, Cartas, 1825. Carcel General de San Salvador, Ignacio Perdomo to Archbishop Casaús, October 19, 1825, AHAG, Fondo Diocesano, Correspondencia, Cartas, 1825. Carcel General de San Salvador, Ignacio Perdomo to Archbishop Casaús, December 1, 1825, AHAG, Fondo Diocesano, Correspondencia, Cartas, exp. 18. Carcel General de San Salvador, Ignacio Perdomo to Archbishop Casaús, November 15, 1825, AHAG, Fondo Diocesano, Correspondencia, Cartas, 1825. Carcel General de San Salvador, Ignacio Perdomo to Archbishop Casaús, October 13, 1825, AHAG, Fondo Diocesano, Correspondencia, Cartas, 1825.

10. Carcel General de San Salvador, Ignacio Perdomo to Archbishop Casaús, September 15, 1825, AHAG, Fondo Diocesano, Secretaría, Cartas, 1825.

11. Guatemala, *El Indicador*, June 20, 1825, fol. 3, col. 2.

12. Carcel General de El Estado de San Salvador, Ignacio Perdomo to Casaús, October 19, 1825, AHAG, Fondo Diocesano, Secretaria, Cartas,1825.

13. Carcel General de El Estado de San Salvador, Ignacio Perdomo to Casaús, November 15, 1825, AHAG, Fondo Diocesano, Secretaria, Cartas, 1825.

14. Ignacio Perdomo to Ignacio Herrarte, January 22, 1827, AHAG, Fondo Diocesano, Secretaria, Cartas, 1826.

15. Mauricio Domínguez T., "El obispado de San Salvador: Foco de desavenencia político-religioso," *Anuario de Estudios Centroamericanos* 1 (1974): 114.

16. Manuel José Arce, *Memoria de la conducta pública y administrativa de Manuel J. Arce durante el periodo de su presidencia* (México: Imprenta de Galván, 1830), 15.

17. On Elizondo's boast to Mariano Prado, see Santa Ana, Elizondo to Mariano Prado, February 12, 1824, AHAG, Correspondencia, Cartas, February 1824. Anonymous "C.C.E.E.," December 1, 1825, reproduced in García, *Diccionario histórico*, 400–401.

18. Guatemala City, "Voto particular de C.A. Alvarado, senador del estado libre de Costa Rica, discutido en el senado de 10 de deciembre 1825," in García, *Diccionario histórico* [136–142]: 140, 142.

19. Anonymous "C.C.E.E.," December 1, 1825, reproduced in García, *Diccionario histórico*, 400–401.

20. Arce, *Memoria*, 15. Philip F. Flemion, "State's Rights and Partisan Politics: Manuel José Arce and the Struggle for Central American Union," *Hispanic American Historical Review* 53, no. 4 (Nov. 1973): 612–613.

21. Arce, *Memoria*, 15.

22. Q.B.S.M-L.E.L, "Que se sirven inserter en su periódico esa representación con sus notas les suplica su atento servidor," reproduced in García, *Diccionario histórico* [403–408], 405.

23. Mary Wilhelmine Williams, "The Ecclesiastical Policy of Francisco Morázan and the other Central American Liberals," reprint pamphlet from the *Hispanic American Historical Review* 3, no. 2 (May 1920): 122–123.

24. Palacio Nacional de Guatemala, January 11, 1826, Juan Francisco de Sosa to Secretario del Senado, AGN-El Salvador, Fondo Federación, caja 8, año de 1826.

25. Guatemala, "Noticias nacionales," *El Indicador*, February 28, 1825, num. 20, fols. 1–2. Notably, this article was reprinted in Mexico City's conservative *El Sol* in an act of ultramontane collaboration; Mexico City, *El Sol*, "Guatemala 28 de Febrero," April 1, 1825, fol. 2, cols. 1–3. Alejandro Marure reports that *El Indicador* first appeared in the waning months of 1824, led by an editorial team consisting of José Francisco Cordova; Juan Francisco Sosa; Manuel Montúfar; Fernando Antonio Dávila; José María Castilla; and the printer José Beteta. Marure reports that liberals founded *El Liberal* in 1825 as a counterweight to the conservative *El Indicador*. San Salvador's *Semanario Politico Mercantil* first appeared in late July of 1824. See Alejandro Marure, *Bosquejo histórico de las revoluciones de Centro-América desde 1811 hasta 1834*, vol. 1 (Guatemala: Imprenta de la N. Academia de Estudios, 1837), 185–186.

26. Fr. Manuel Garcia, *Reflecsiones [sic] sobre el articulo primero del decreto emitido por la Asamblea de Guatemala en veinte de julio de 1826 por Fr. Manuel Garcia, lego de S. Francisco* (Guatemala: Imprenta Mayor, Casa de Porras, 1826), 1–3. Also see *Cuerpo y alma del decreto de julio del corriente año relativa a profesiones. Conversación de dos amigos don Cazcarria y don Zurriago* (Guatemala: Imprenta Mayor, Casa de Porras, 1826). On the decree's revocation, see Guatemala City, "Comunicado," *El Indicador*, September 18, 1827, num. 149, pp. 2–3; and Guatemala City, "Estado de Guatemala," *El Indicador*, October 8, 1827, num. 152, pp. 2–3.

27. San Salvador, "Al Jefe político accidental de S. Vicente," March 31, 1827, AGN-El Salvador, caja 2, exp. 1.

28. Greg Grandin, *The Blood of Guatemala: A History of Race and Nation* (Durham NC: Duke University Press, 2000), 77. Douglass Sullivan-Gonzalez, *The Black Christ of Esquipulas: Religion and Identity in Guatemala* (Lincoln, NE: University of Nebraska Press, 2016), 64.

29. Voekel, *Alone Before God*, passim.

30. Grandin, *Blood*, 76–77, 101.

31. For a vivid description of the lead-up to Flores' death and the crowd's actions, see Sullivan-Gonzalez, *Black Christ*, 60–66. On the liberals' decision to move the seat of state government to Quetzaltenango, see Flemion, "State's Rights," 600–618. Also see Leslie Bethel, *Central America Since Independence* (New York, NY: Cambridge University Press, 1991), 12–13.

32. San Salvador, Al padre provincial de SF fray Pedro José Méndez, February 13, 1827, AGN-El Salvador, caja 2, exp. 1. San Salvador, 3 March 1827, Al jefe del departamento de Sonsonate, AGN-El Salvador, caja 2, exp. 1. San Salvador, March 21, 1827, Al jefe político de Sonsonate, AGN-El Salvador, caja 2, exp. 1.

33. San Salvador, "Noticias Frescas" *El Salvadoreño*, July 20, 1828, no. 14, pg. 2, col. 2, and "Variedades," p. 3, cols. 1–2.

34. Nacaome, Silvestre Tome to padre arzobispo ciudadano Ramón Casaús y Torres, November 18, 1825, AHAG, Fondo Diocesano, Correspondencia, Cartas, 1825. The press reported that Delgado held clerical prisoners in San Salvador, see, for example, Guatemala City, *El Redactor General*, November 3, 1825, No. 19, p. 2, col. 1.

35. San Salvador, Al padre obispo electo, December 24, 1826, AGN-El Salvador, Fondo Federación, caja 2, exp. 1. San Salvador, Al Padre obispo electo, January 8, 1826, AGN-El Salvador, Fondo Federación, caja 2, Exp. 1

36. San Salvador, "A los ciudadanos, alcaldes, juntas y regimento de Titiguapa (Titihuapa)," December 29, 1826, AGN-El Salvador, Fondo Federación, Caja 2, Exp. 1. San Salvador, January 8, 1827, Al Padre obispo electo, AGN-El Salvador, Fondo Federación, caja 2, exp. 1.

37. San Salvador, Al Jefe político e intendente de este departamento, January 20, 1827, AGN-EL Salvador, caja 2, exp. 1. Other cases reveal that local and state officials kept tabs on priests. Cleric Tomás Bermúdez left El Salvador in 1825, a report detailed. He appealed to the head of state to return to visit his ailing mother and was granted a passport on the condition that he check in with San Salvador's department head and place himself under Delgado's orders. When he deviated from his announced itinerary, a state official asked San Miguel's *jefe político* to locate him; see "Al jefe político de San Miguel," September 26, 1827, AGN-El Salvador, Fondo Federación, Caja 2, exp. 1, carta 1.13. On November 13, 1827, El Salvador's vice-jefe gave cleric Diego Mariano de Arce, apparently a parish priest in San Vicente, twenty-four hours to appear in San Salvador or incur a 500 pesos fine, see San Salvador, "Vice jefe to presbítero Diego Mariano de Arce," November 13,1827, ANES, caja 2, exp. 1. On October 17, 1827, a state official told San Vicente's jefe politico that the ecclesiastical authorities knew that priest Buenaventura Guerrero had caused problems in Sensuntopeque, and were monitoring the situation, "To Jefe Político de San Vicente," October 17 1827, AGN-El Salvador, caja 2, exp. 1.

38. Jutiapa, Francisco Esteban López to Casaús, April 26, 1826, AHAG, Fondo Diocesano, Correspondencia, Cartas, April 1826, exp. 104.

39. San Miguel Petapa, November 16, 1825, Ponciano Garrote and Municipio de Santa Inés to Casaús, AHAG, Fondo Diocesano, Correspondencia, Cartas, 1825.

40. Santa Inés, José Tomas Calderón (for the municipality) to Casaús, November 18, 1825, AHAG, Fondo Diocesano, Correspondencia, Cartas, Cartas November 1825.

41. El Salvador, Al Padre obispo electo, October 10, 1827, AGN-El Salvador, Fondo Federación, caja 2, exp. 1. Tiburcio Hernández, José Torres de León y Ramón Romero had journeyed to El Salvador and directed themselves to the government in El Salvador.

42. Tecapa, Martín Torres, 12 Feb. 1826, AHAG, Fondo Diocesano, Secretaría, Cartas, 1826.

43. Guatemala, J.M.H.S. to P. Zaldaña don Thomas, August 4, 1827, AHAG, Fondo Diocesano, Secretaria de Gobierno Eclesiastico, Serie Larrazabal, Tomo 18, fol. 140. Guatemala, José María Herrarte, 3 August 1827, AHAG, Fondo Diocesano, Secretaria de Gobierno Eclesiastico, Serie Larrazabal, Tomo 18, fols. 149v. On Monteros returning to San Salvador, see Sonsonate, Juan Felix Belado to Archbishop Casaús, July 29, 1827, AHAG, Fondo Diocesano, Secretaria de Gobierno Eclesiástico, Serie Larrazabal, Tomo 18, No. 26. On Monteros' suspension, see Palacio Nacional, August 4, 1827, AHAG, Fondo Diocesano, Secretaria de Gobierno Eclesiástico, Serie Larrazabal, Tomo 18, fol. 109.

44. José Francisco Aqueche to Casaús, September 26, 1827, AHAG, Fondo Diocesano, Correspondencia, Cartas, exp. 244. Guatemala City, Casaús to José Francisco Aqueche, September 26, 1827, AHAG, Fondo Diocesano, Correspondencia, Cartas, exp. 244. Doug Sullivan Gonzalez, *Piety*, 82.

45. Cuartel General de Mejicanos, "Manuel de Arzú al Secretario de Estado y del Despacho de la Guerra sobre que el supremo Gobierno le concede al presbítero Isidro Menéndez el curato de Caluca," March 6, 1828, AGN-El Salvador, caja 9, exp. 1–42.

46. Santa Catalina, Mariano Solis to Casaús, May 28, 1827, AHAG, Fondo Diocesano, Correspondencia, Cartas, May 1827, exp. 123. Also see Guatemala City, Casaús to José Francisco Aqueche, September 26, 1827, AHAG. Fondo Diocesano, Correspondencia, Cartas, September 1827, exp. 244, and ibid, José Francisco Aqueche to Casaús, n.d.

47. Isalco, Pablo de Sagastume to José Mariano Herrarte, May 19, 1828, AHAG, Fondo Diocesano, Secretaría, Cartas, 1828. Sagastume penned a widely circulated pamphlet that denounced the schism; see Pablo M. Sagastume, *Satisfación* (Guatemala: Imprenta Nueva, 1825).

48. *Obispo y obispado: doctrina de la iglesia católica sobre esta materia* (Guatemala: Imprenta de la Unión, á cargo de Juan José de Arévalo, 1825), 9, 10. José María Santa María noted that the Council of Trent prescribed excommunication for laymen who robbed the church of the tithe, see his *Impugnación del manifiesto del gobierno de San Salvador sobre la justificación de la erección de aquel nuevo obispado, y elección del Dr. Delgado para esta nueva dignidad: á la que se añadirá la ninguna razon que tiene aquel gobierno para apropiarse los diezmos de aquella provincial, e invertirlos en los usos que le parezca* (Guatemala: Beteta, 1824).

49. Santa Catalina, Mariano Solís to Casaús, May 28, 1827, AHAG, Fondo Diocesano, Correspondencia, Cartas, May 1827, exp. 123. Mariano Solís to José Mariano Herrarte, AHAG, Fondo Diocesano, Correspondencia, Cartas, May 1827. Casaús to Mariano Solís, June 2, 1827, AHAG, Fondo Diocesano, Correspondencia, Cartas, May 1827.

50. Coatepeque, Ciriaco Antonio Xirón to Casaús, September 1, 1827, AHAG, Fondo Dicoesano, Correspondencia, Cartas, September 1827. El Salvador, "Al jefe político de San Vicente," October 17, 1827, AGN-El Salvador, caja 2, exp. 1. Nejapa, ciudadano presbítero secretario José Mariano Herrarte, April 28, 1827, AHAG. Fondo Diocesano, Correspondencia, Cartas, April 1827.

51. Historian Douglass Sullivan-González places Muñoz in Esquipulas from August of 1824 to March of 1830; see his *Black Christ*, 73, 78.

52. Esquipulas, Miguel Muñoz to Casaús, February 7, 1827, AHAG, Fondo Diocesano, Correspondencia, Cartas, February 1827.

53. Antonio R. Vallejo, *Compendio de la historia social y política de Honduras: aumentada con los acontecimientos de Centro-América*, vol. 1 (Tegucigalpa, HOND: Tipografía Nacional, 1886), 144. Esquipulas, Miguel Muñoz to Mariano Herrarte, February 7, 1827, AHAG, Fondo Diocesano, Secretaria del Gobierno Eclesiastico, Correspondencia, Cartas, February 1827. In the later part of the nineteenth century, the ultramontane would prevail over reformist Catholics on a global scale in part because they incorporated rather than attacked popular piety like pilgrimage sites centered on miraculous apparitions, see for example, David Blackbourn, *Marpingen: Apparitions of the Virgin Mary in the Nineteenth Century* (New York, NY: Knoft, 1994).

54. Esquipulas, Miguel Muñoz to Mariano Herrarte, February 7, 1827, AHAG, Fondo Diocesano, Secretaria del Gobierno Eclesiastico, Correspondencia, Cartas, February 1827.

55. Comayagua, Ministro General del Gobierno Supremo del Estado de Honduras to Gobierno Supremo de Guatemala, November 10, 1826, AGCA, Signatura B 10.8, leg. 3483, exp. 79641, fols. 756–756v. Comayagua, Ministro General del Gobierno Supremo del Estado de Honduras to Gobierno Supremo de Guatemala, October 10, 1826, AGCA, Signatura B 10.8, Leg. 3483, exp. 79641, fols. 733–733v. Comayagua, HOND, Dionisio de Herrera to José del Valle, November 10, 1826, reproduced in Lois E. Bumgartner, "The Attempted Assasination of Honduran President Dionisio de Herrera, November 3, 1826," *Hispanic American Historical Review* 42, no. 1 (Feb. 1962): 60–62. Also see Montúfar y Coronado, *Memorias*, 61. For a basic introduction to Herrera's political career, see Rafael Heliodoro Valle, "Dionisio de Herrera, 1783-1850. A Centennial Tribute," *Hispanic American Historical Review* 30, no. 4 (Nov. 1950): 554–558.

56. José Ignacio Zaldaña noted that Delgado appointed his "inept" relative, Inocente Escolan, to the parish of Tonacatepequez, thereby impeding Francisco Estevan López from occupying the position, see his "Paisano" Santa Rosa Parroquia, January 10, 1826, p. 12, found in ASV, Arch. Segr. Stato Esteri, Rub. 279, Busta 592. López teamed up with Zaldaña and Tomás Miguel Saldaña to pen their *Verdaderas razones contra las aparentes que contiene el manifiesto de cuatro de mayo último del director del Estado de S. Salvador, sobre erección de iglesia y elección de obispo hecho en el doctor José Matías Delgado* (Guatemala: Imprenta de J.J. Arévalo, 1824). Carcel

General de San Salvador, Ignacio Perdomo to Archbishop Casaús, September 15, 1825, AHAG, Fondo Diocesano, Secretaría, Cartas 1825.

57. León, Nicaragua, Fr. Juan de Dios Campos Diez to Real Audiencia, August 4, 1813, AGCA, Signatura B 2.2, leg. 24, exp. 710, fol. 1. Carcel General del Estado de San Salvador, Ignacio Perdomo to Ramón Casaús, November 15, 1825, AHAG, Fondo Diocesano, Secretaría, Cartas 1826.

58. George Andrew Thompson, *Narrative of an Official Visit to Guatemala from Mexico* (London, UK: John Murray, 1829), 232.

59. Guatemala City, Palacio del Gobierno, Ejército Federal de Operaciones to Secretario de Estado y del Despacho de Guerra, September 8, 1828, AGN-El Salvador, Fondo Federación, caja 9, 1828.

60. San Salvador, J. Mayorga to Tata P. Campos, February 18, 1828; LAL-TU, Central American Printed Ephemera Collection, 1745-2005, Folder 15, Politics (1827-1828), pp. 1–2

61. Ahuachapán, Commander General of Operations R. Merino to Fr. Juan de Dios Campos, December 26, 1827; Ahuachapán, Fr. Juan de Dios Campos to Commander General of Operations R. Merino, December 26, 1827; San Salvador, M. Prado to Fr. Juan de Dios Campos, January 12, 1828; San Salvador, M. Prado to Fr. Juan de Dios Campos, January 17, 1828; San Salvador, J. Mayorga to Tata P. Campos, February 18, 1828; these letters are found in LAL-TU, Central American Printed Ephemera Collection, 1745-2005, Folder 15, Politics (1827-1828), pp. 1–4. English traveler George Andrew Thompson reported dining with Menéndez at President Arce's home in 1825; see his *Narrative*, 232. Historian Philip F. Flemion notes that conservatives embraced Arce as the candidate most likely to respect the congress' decisions regarding the Delgado schism without presidential interference; see his "States' Rights," 608–609. Menéndez's friendship with Arce apparently continued for a time, despite his own political and theological support for Delgado. Manuel Montúfar notes that when Arce was forced out of El Salvador, he asked the vice-president to intervene with Casaús to ensure that Menéndez could return with him to Guatemala; Casaús instead suspended the priest. Menéndez reconciled with Delgado and returned to El Salvador, apparently choosing ideological and religious commitment over his loyalty to the compromised Arce; see Montúfar y Coronado, *Memorias*, 73–74. On December 11, 1828, San Salvador's liberal paper *El Salvadoreño* ran a letter from an Ahuachapán reader accusing Menéndez of tampering with local elections to advance Arce's political party. The letter accused him of close relations with Arce, see San Salvador, December 11, 1828, Q.P., "Communicado" *El Salvadoreño*, December 14, 1828, num. 25, p. 2, col. 2; p. 3, col. 1.

62. San Salvador, Al padre fray Luis (sic) de Dios Campos Diez, cura de Santa Ana, March 31, 1827, AGN-El Salvador, Fondo Federación, caja 2, exp. 1. And San Salvador, Al jefe político de Sonsonate, 31 March 1827, AGN-El Salvador, caja 2, exp. 1. On the March 1827 El Salvadoran invasion of Guatemala, see Arturo Taracena Arriola, "La Mirada de tres actores guatemaltecos sobre la Guerra Federal de 1826 a 1829: Montúfar y Coronado, Córdova, y García Granados. Reflexiones metodológicas sobre un conflict armado," in *La primera guerra*, ed. Taracena Arriola, 59.

63. Anonymous, *Apologia laconica de un cura contra la locura de algunos curas* (Guatemala: Imprenta Nueva a dirección de Cayetano de Arévalo, 1825), 1. In August of 1826, José Bernardo Dighero informed the public that clerics from Nicaragua augmented the horror occurring in El Salvador, specifically the administration of sacraments. The following clerics from Nicaragua operated in El Salvador without permission, he explained: Luciano Alaro,

Nasario Rosales, Anastasio Aguilar, Miguel González, Manuel Romero, José María Arias, Tomás Muños, Eucébio Lanuza, Anselmo Velásques, Fr. Pedro Reina (Franciscan), Fr. Juan de Dios Campos, and Fr. Ramón Jalon. Archbishop Casaús, Dighero reported, had declared the sacraments these immigrant clerics administered worthless and the clerics excommunicated; see El Gobierno Metropolitano, August 9, 1826, No Title (Guatemala: Imprenta de la Unión, 1826). Signed by José Bernardo Dighero.

64. Sagastume, *Satisfacción*, 1–2.

65. José Mariano Herrarte, *Advertencia patriótica* (Guatemala: Imprenta Nueva, 1824), 1–2.

66. José Ignacio Saldaña, "Manifiesto," August 5, 1825, printed in the *Gazeta Diario de México*, October 26, 1825, no. 152, p. 1, col. 1.

67. Ahuachapán, Fray Juan de Dios Campos Diez to Casaús, June 30, 1826, AHAG, Fondo Diocesano, Correspondencia, Cartas, April 1826.

68. Chalchaupa, Ignacio Perdomo to Bernardo Dighero, July 14, 1824, AHAG, Correspondencia, Cartas, July 1824.

69. Guatemala, Eúsebio María Menéndez to Casaús, April 27, 1827, AHAG, Fondo Diocesano, Secretaría, Cartas 1827, Carta #94. Guatemala City, José Ignacio Figueroa to Casaús, November 22, 1827, AHAG, Fondo Diocesano, Secretaría, Cartas 1827, Carta #94.

70. On Menéndez's original cooperation with Delgado, see San Salvador, José Matias Delgado to Br. Eusébio María Menéndez, April 6, 1826, AHAG, Fondo Diocesano, Secretaría, Cartas 1826, Carta #92. It is unclear how and why Menéndez got to Guatemala City, but his superiors reported on his steady rehabilitation and dedication to penance. See, for example, José Ignacio Figueroa to Casaús, November 22, 1827, AHAG, Fondo Diocesano, Secretaría, Cartas 1827. Also see Eusebio María Menéndez to Casaús, April 27, 1827, AHAG, Fondo Diocesano, Secretaría, Cartas 1827.

71. Anonymous, *Ciudadanos ¡compasion! Que los cismaticos quieren perseguirnos con furor. Apología de los curas y demás eclesiásticos perseguidos en el Estado de El Salvador, por no reconocer un obispado y un obispo de nueva invención anti-católica. Uno de los perseguidos la dedica a los mismos perseguidores* (Guatemala: Imprenta Nueva, 1825), 1–2v. Miguel Castro was Miguel José Castro y Lara, the editor of the *Semanario Político Mercantil*; Lara y Larín, *Origenes*, 46. Castro later served as the editor of *El Salvadoreño*; see María Eugenia Claps-Arenas, "*El Salvadoreño* y la formación de opinión pública en el contexto de la primera guerra federal centroamericana, 1828-1829" *Liminar* 17, no. 1 (January–June 2019), at http://dx.doi.org/10.29043/liminar.v17i1.644.

72. Accusations that Casaús ordered the clerical exodus were reportedly printed in El Salvador's *Seminario político Mercantil*; see the response to these liberal claims in El Amigo de la Verdad, "A los editores del periodico titulado *Semanario Político Mercantil* de San Salvador" (Guatemala: Imprenta de la Unión, n.d.), 1–2.

73. Palacio Arzobispal de Guatemala, Ramón Casaús y Torres to Ciudadano Secretario del Gobierno del Estado, January 13, 1826, ASV, Arch. Segr. Stato Esteri, Rub. 279, Busta 592.

74. Ibid.

75. Palacio del Arzobispado de Guatemala, Joseph Bernardo Digheno, AGCA, Signatura B.1, leg. 1126, exp. 25633. Palacio del Arzobispado de Guatemala, Bernardo Digheno to Parroco Vicario de Mico, AGCA, Signatura B.1, leg. 1126, exp. 25633. Also see Chimaltenango, vicario de Chimaltenango Pedro Paiz Monteceros to parrocos del Vicario de Chimaltenango, April 2, 1827, AHAG, Fondo Diocesano, Correspondencia, Cartas, June 1827. Chimaltenango, Monteceros to cuidadanos parrocos del Vicario de Chimaltenango, December 29, 1827, AHAG, Fondo Diocesano, Correspondencia, Cartas, December 1827.

76. Sacatepeque, Casaús to parroco de Mixco, April 4, 1827, AHAG, Fondo Diocesano, Correspondencia, Cartas, April 1827.

77. Cobán, signed by Mariano Iglesias, Matías Torres, and twenty-three others, February 9, 1828, AGCA, Signatura B 8.1, legajo 1124, exp. 25457, fols. 1 and 3v. During the colonial period, the Crown banned Indians from bearing arms. Even large Indian towns like Quetzaltenango, which only set up a Spanish and Ladino city council in 1806, housed militias made up of Blacks, mulatoes and Spaniards; jittery whites called in militias to put down Indian uprisings in the highlands. During the first federal war, both sides recruited Indians, who often resisted enlistment, especially, perhaps, in Los Altos. Historians Juan Carlos Sarazúa and Arturo Taracena Arriola both suggest that *castas—mestizos, pardos, mulatos—* predominated in both armies. See Juan Carlos Sarazúa Pérez, "Política y etnicidad y servicio militar. Dos experiencias paralelas en MesoAmérica. Chiapas y Guatemala, 1808-1871" *Revista Historia de América* no. 152 (January–December 2016), 144, 147,153; and his "Recolectar, administrar y defender: la construcción del estado y las resistencias regionales en Guatemala, 1800-1871" (PhD diss., Barcelona, Universitat Pompeu Fabra, 2013), 276–278. Taracena Arriola, "Mirada," 76–77. Also see Juan Carlos Sarazúa Peréz, "Desertores y rebeldes. Dos formas de entender la militarización en Guatemala y Chiapas, 1825-1859," *Prohistoria* 20, no. 28 (December 2017): 105–106. Clara Pérez Fabregat reports that Indians in El Salvador participated in the war as soldiers and as providers of services like ditch digging, see her "Apuntes socioeconómicos sobre la Guerra Federal de 1826 á 1829: la experiencia salvadoreña en clave regional," in Arturo Taracena Arriola, ed., *La primera guerra*, 132–133. That Cobán's indigenous people spoke little Spanish, and that the town's multiple confraternities held significant control over access to the sacred, is unsurprising. Adrian C. van Oss notes that priests often "could do nothing without the confraternities" because they refused resources to clerics who contravened their agendas; he concludes that the confraternities engaged Catholicism on their own terms; Van Oss, *Catholic Colonialism*, 137–140, 150–151.

78. Guatemala City, *El Indicador*, March 31, 1827, num. 125, p. 2, col. 2.

79. Henry Dunn, *Guatimala [sic], or, the United Provinces of Central America, in 1827-8; Being Sketches and Memorandums Made During a Twelve Months Residence in that Republic* (New York, NY: C &C Carvill, 1828), 120.

80. Palacio de Guatemala, Fray Ramon Francisco Casaús y Torres, August 31, 1827, "Fray Ramon Francisco Casaús y Torres por la gracia de dios y la santa sede apostólica arzobispo de Goatemala (*sic*) á nuestros amados diocesanos salud, paz, y unidad en Jesus Cristo," BN-Guatemala, Fondo Antiguo, Colección Valenzuela, Registro No. 3317.

81. Guatemala City, "Necrologia," *El Indicador*, August 27, 1827, num. 146, p. 4, col. 2.

82. Sensuntepeque, July 6, 1821, Constitutional City Council of Sensuntepeque to City Council of San Salvador, AGI, Guatemala 654; José Ignacio Zaldaña, "Paisano," Santa Rosa Parroquia, January 10, 1826, p. 6, found in ASV, Arch. Segr. Stato Esteri, Rub. 279, Busta 592.

83. Guatemala City, "Necrologia," *El Indicador*, August 27, 1827, num. 146, p. 4, col. 2. That parishioners in one town had backed Molina, not Delgado, for the position of Bishop of El Salvador is discussed in José Ignacio Saldaña, *Justa repulsa de iniquas acusaciones: o entiéndase respuesta que se dá al impreso anónomio de San Salvador titulado Contestación al manifiesto del P. Saldaña* (Guatemala: Imprenta Nueva, 1825), 8.

84. Guatemala City, Gobierno to Casaús y Torres, Dr. Fr. Ramon, January 7, 1828, "El gobierno del estado agradezca al arzobispo el donativo de las arañas de plata, cuyo product era invertido en los gastos de la guerra con El Salvador," B 10.8, exp. 79643, leg. 3485, fol. 6. Guatemala, "El arzobispo informa al gobierno del estado, haber dado instrucciones a las

comunidades religiosas, para que cedan en calidad de donativo, objetos de plata, para cubrir con su venta los gastos de la guerra con El Salvador," Guatemala, AGCA, Signatura B 10.8 exp. 79643, leg. 3485, fol. 5.

85. El Salvador, Mariano Prado to Casaús, April 26, 1827, AHAG, Fondo Diocesano, Correspondencia, Cartas, Cartas 1827.

86. Esquipulas, Miguel Muñoz to Casaús, January 24, 1826, AHAG, Fondo Diocesano, Cartas, January 1826.

87. San Salvador, Delgado to Fulgencio González, April 6, 1827, AHAG, Fondo Diocesano, Corresondencia, Cartas, January 1827. San Salvador, Faustino Camacho, January 10, 1827, AHAG, Fondo Diocesano, Correspondencia, Cartas, January 1827.

88. F. Morázan to Ministro del Estado de Guatemala, August 6,1829, AGCA, Sig. B, leg. 2434, exp. 51475, fols. 2, 3–4v; Felix Mejia, August 25, 1829, fol. 14.

89. Guatemala Jose Mariano Herrarte to los ciudadanos párrocos y sectores de las iglesias del margen, November 29, 1827, AHAG, Fondo Diocesano, Correspondencia, Cartas 1827.

90. Anonymous, *Vuestros mandarinas os están engañando para perderos* (Guatemala: Beteta, 1827).

91. Pope Leo XII, December 1, 1826, reproduced in Marure, *Bosquejo histórico I*, xxv–xxvii, Documento no. 9; and Ayala Benítez, *La iglesia*, 194–195.

CHAPTER 6

1. The literature on the rise of a public sphere of letters during the Age of Revolution is copious. A starting point for many authors is Jürgen Habermas, *The Structural Transformation of the Public Sphere: An Inquiry into a Category of Bourgeois Society*, trans. Thomas Burger (Cambridge, MA: MIT Press, 1989); and François-Xavier Guerra *Modernidad e independencies. Ensayos sobre las revoluciones hispánicas* (Madrid: Editorial Mapfre, 1992), 13, 85, 89, 101, 290, 338. Also see Christopher Belaubre, "Opinión pública," in Jordana Dym y Sajid Herrera Mena (coords.), *Centroamérica durante las revoluciones atlánticas: el vocabulario político, 1750-1850* (San Salvador: IEESFORD Editores, 2014), 181–197. Guerra sees New Spain's numerous religious tracts as compared to France as indications of modernity's retardation in Mexico. On the religious nature of the public sphere of letters in Mexico after independence, see Voekel, *Alone Before God*, 146–170. Adrian C. Van Oss notes that of the 2,700 works printed in colonial Guatemala, "80 percent were ecclesiastical or devotional works or theses defended at the theologically oriented University of San Carlos as opposed to only 13 percent civil or military decrees"; see his "A Far Kingdom: Central American Autarky at the End of the Eighteenth Century," in *Church and Society in Spanish America* (Amsterdam, NL: CEDLA, 2003), 18. Erica Pani notes the limited role of women in this Republic of Letters underscoring that the catalogue of the enormous Lafragua Collection in Mexico's National Library contains only two female authors and two pamphlets written solely by women during the years 1808 to 1821, see her "Ciudadana," 11. On the politics of printing across Mexico's long nineteenth century see Zeltsman, *Ink.* .

2. In the public Guatemalan legislative session of August 20, 1825, José María Santa Cruz decried the disparities of wealth between the upper and lower clergy and pointed to biblical precedence for state-salaried clerics; the war of words, he noted, threatened to end in an armed confrontation, see Guatemala City, *El Liberal*, September 18, 1825, no. 23, pp. 1–2.

3. L.E.L, "Comunicados. Revolucionaba en el siglo 10," signed in Usulután on November 27, 1825, and reproduced in García, *Diccionario histórico*, 422–423.

4. Anonymous, *Contestación al comunicado que comienza Revolucionaba en el siglo X el arzobispo de Milan, incerto en el numero 71 del Seminario del Estado de el Salvador en que con hechos traidos por la malicia, se exorta al pueblo pacífico de Guatemala á revolucionar contra su digno prelado; por que evitando los abusos y desordenes religiosos promueve el honor de los gobiernos y de toda la república* (Guatemala: Imprenta de la Union, a cargo de Juan José Arévalo, 1826), 1–2. Signed with the initials D.U.C.Y.G.J.M.G.M. On Berber Christian bishop Donatus Magnus and the Donatist schism, see Richard Miles, *The Donatist Schism: Controversy and Contexts* (Liverpool, UK: Liverpool University Press, 2018). On the Babylonian prophet Mani, see Johannes van Oort, *Mani and Augustine. Essays on Mani, Manicheasism, and Augustine* (Leiden, NL: Brill, 2020); and Ian Gardner, *The Founder of Manicheaeism: Rethinking the Life of Mani* (Cambridge, UK: Cambridge University Press, 2020).

5. San Salvador, José Mariano Rey Carillo to Casaús, August 8, 1826; and Guatemala, Casaús to José Mariano Rey Carillo, August 30, 1826, AHAG, Fondo Diocesano, Correspondencia, Cartas, August 1826, exp. 161, fols. 1-1v.

6. José Andrés de Santa María, *Apóstrofe a los ministros del sanctuario*, March 1, 1826, found in his *Preservativo contra el impio e irreligioso folleto Aviso oportuno a las autoridades y al pueblo y Satisfacción a los cargos de dicho author y el comunicado del Semanario Mercantil de San Salvador de febrero de 1826 hacen al padre Santa María y a su religion* (Guatemala: Imprenta de la Unión, 1826), 31–32.

7. Ibid., 31–32.

8. San Salvador, "Guatemala," *El Salvadoreño*, July 27, 1828, no. 16, p. 1, col. 2. Antonio García Redondo, *Soberanía é independencia de la iglesia católica en el desempeño del ministerio que la confió su divino fundador Jesús Cristo* (Guatemala: Imprenta de la Unión, 1825).

9. San Salvador, Gobierno Supremo del Estado to jefe político de San Miguel, December 29, 1826, AGN-El Salvador, Fondo Federación, caja 2, exp. 1.

10. Juan José de Aycinena and José Mariano Domínguez, "Guatemala," December 20, 1825; reproduced in García, *Diccionario histórico*, 402–403.

11. Dym, *From Sovereign Villages*, 212–213, 245–246.

12. See the undated squib signed by "Los Editores" reproduced in García, *Diccionario histórico*, 393–396. Also see the undated "Communicado," signed by "Un Progimo," reproduced in García, *Diccionario histórico*, 408–411. "Progimo" received a response from Fray José Andres de Santa María; see Santa María's *Satisfaccion al comunicado del Semanario Político Mercantil de San Salvador de ocho de febrero de 1826* (Guatemala: Imprenta de la Unión, 1826), especially 39.

13. Santa Rosa Parish, José Ignacio Saldaña, "Untitled [first word: Paisano]," January 10, 1826, ASV, Segr. Stato Esteri, años 1823-1845, rubrica 279, busta 592.

14. "Un Progimo," "Communicado," reproduced in García, *Diccionario histórico*, 408–411.

15. "Los Editores" reproduced in García, *Diccionario histórico*, [393–396], 395.

16. *Novena al sacratisimo Corazón de Jesús. Sacada de un libro, su titulo Tesoro escondido en el Corazón de Jesús, que salió á luz para su culto, y venerable erección en nuestra España* (Guatemala: D. Manuel Arévalo, 1823), 3. The pamphlet was an extract from Spaniard and cult-propagator Juan de Loyola's 1734 book *Thesoro escondido en el corazón de Jesús, descubierto a nuestra España en la breve noticia de su culto ... su autor el padre Juan de Loyola, de la Compañia de Jesús, 3rd edition* (Madrid, ES: Imprenta de Manuel Fernández, 1736). The book was released in Mexico as *Novena al sacratísimo Corazón de Jesús: sacada de las sólidas prácticas de un libro que con el título de: Tesoro escondido en el corazón de Jesús, ha salido nuévamente á luz para dar noticia de su sagrado culto á nuestra España* (México: Imprenta de D.S. Valdes, 1821). *Devoción al Sagrado Corazón de Jesús, para todos los viernes del año, particularmente para el primero de cada mes, con la invocación*

de su santísimo nombre, que se puede decir todos los dias (México: Imprenta de D. Alejandro Valdés, 1821).

17. Anonymous, *Aviso oportuno á las autoridades y al pueblo* (El Salvador: Imprenta del Gobierno, 1825), 2–4. Quote on p. 4.

18. Anonymous, *Aviso oportuno*, 6, n. 3.

19. José Andrés de Santa María, *Preservativo,*10.

20. Ibid., 3, 7, 8, 10, 12.

21. José Andrés de Santa María, *Satisfación al comunicado* (Guatemala: Imprenta de la Unión, 1826), 39.

22. On the church of Utrecht and its far-flung European correspondents, see Douglas Bradford Palmer "The Republic of Grace: International Jansenism and the Age of Enlightenment and Revolution" (PhD diss., Ohio State University, 2004), 1, 18.

23. Guatemala, Jose Mariano Herrarte, March 6, 1828, ASV, Rubrica 279, Busta 529.

24. A federal army report from 1828 refers to Meléndez's prior post in Culaco; see Cuartel General de Mejicanos, Manuel de Azmita, April 28, 1828, AGN-El Salvador, Fondo Federación, Caja 9, 1828. Christophe Belaurbe, "Menéndez, don Isidro," AFEHC, Ficha no. 658, at https://www.afehc-historia-centroamericana.org/index_action_fi_aff_id_658.html, accessed on 1 March 2020.

25. Guatemala City, Isidro Menéndez, "Exposición que formó y leyó en el senado general el presbítero doctor don Isidro Menéndez, cuando se trató del sanción legal del decreto y orden que expidio el Congreso General de San Salvador el 18 de julio de 1825, sobre la mitra del estado," in García, *Diccionario histórico*, 181–232. The El Salvadoran government reprinted the speech as Isidro Menéndez, *Exposición del senador por el Estado de Nicaragua P.C.L.D.C. Isidro Menéndez: hecha en el senado á 10 de agosto de 1825 al deliberar sobre el proyecto de decreto y órden del Congreso federal en el negocio de obispado de S. Salvador: se publíca de órden del gobierno del estado con las notas oficiales del autor que la remite, la de contestación del gobierno, y las en que éste reclamó oportunamente al congreso y senado a no pertenecer éste negocio á la Federacion* (San Salvador: Imprenta del Gobierno, 1825).

Cortes, *Dictámen de la comisión eclesiástica encargada del arreglo definitivo del clero de España. Impreso por órden del Córtes* (Madrid: Imprenta de D. Tomas Alban y Compañia, 1825).

26. Guatemala City, "Dictamen aprobado por el Congreso Federal de la República de Centro-América, expedida por el Congreso sobre este asunto," July 19, 1825; and Guatemala City, July 20, 1825, "Dictamen de las comisiones reunidas de puntos constitucionales, de justicia y negócios ecclesiásticos, sobre erección de obispado, y nombramiento y posesión de obispo en el estado de El Salvador, presentado y leído en el Congreso Federal, en los días 27 y 28 de junio de 1825 y señalado para su discusión el 28 del mismo mes," in García, *Diccionario histórico*, 142 and 143–153.

27. Menéndez, *Exposición*, 17.

28. "*Dictámen de la comisión eclesiástica*," 4.

29. *Ibid.*, 6, 8, 16. An earlier Cortes de Cádiz report from 1813 argued that Rome had usurped the right to consecrate bishops, a right that had been granted to all of the apostles, not just Peter, see *Dictámenes del Consejo de Estado y de las Comisiones Eclesiástica y de Justicia reunidas sobre el modo de suplir las confirmaciones de los obispos electos durante la actual incomunicación con la Silla Apostólica* (Cádiz: Imprenta Nacional, 1813), especially p. 13.

30. Juan Antonio Llorente, *Notas al dictamen de la comision eclesiástica, encargada del arreglo definitive del clero de España* (Madrid: Alban, 1823). John-Baptiste Say, *Political Economy; Or the Production, Distribution, and Consumption of Wealth*, trans. C. R. Prinsep and intro.

Clement C. Biddle (Philadelphia, PA: Lippincott; Grambodo, Grigg, Elliott &Company, 1851 [original 1803]), 50.

31. Juan Antonio Llorente, *Disertación sobre el poder que los reyes españoles ejercieron hasta el siglo duodecimo en la division de obispados, y otros puntos conecsos de disciplina eclesiástica; con un apendice de escrituras en que constan los hechos citados en la Disertación* (Madrid: Imprenta de Ibarra, 1810). For the dates of the documents in the appendix, see pp. 87–245. Menéndez, *Exposición*, 19.

32. Ciriaco Villacorta, *Discurso pronunciado en el Congreso Federal por el licendiado Ciriaco Villacorta, diputado por el estado de El Salvador, en 18 de julio, á tiempo que discutia el dictamen de la comisiones unidas sobre erección de la silla episcopal en aquel estado* (San Salvador, Imprenta del Gobierno, 1826), 3. Signed by Villacorta in Guatemala on July 15, 1825.

33. Ibid., 6, 7, 9.

34. "El Amigo de la Verdad," *Á los editores del periódico titulado Semanario Político Mercantil de San Salvador* (Guatemala: Imprenta de la Unión, 1826), 3. Francisco Alvarado, *Carta crítica de un Filosofo Rancio que impugna à la española antigua y no à la francesa el discurso del señor diputado Argüelles sobre contribución de diezmos y los dictámenes de otros varios señores diputados que distraen á las Cortes de su principal objecto* (Isla de Leon, 1811), especially 4 and 6. Javier Lasarte, "Los diezmos ante la contribución extraordinaria propuesta por carga de Argüelles a las Cortes de Cádiz. El Filósofo Rancio arremete contra Argüelles y desata la polémica," *Revista de estudios regionales* 95 (2012): 203–273. For more on the conservative faction in the Cortes, see Julio Herrera González, *¡Serviles! El grupo reaccionario de las Cortes de Cádiz* (Málaga, ES: Servicio de Publicaciones de Unicaja Fundación, 2007).

35. For Villacorta's speech, see, for example, Guadalajara, *El Nivel*, no. 261, April 30, 1826, pp. 1–2; Guadalajara, *El Nivel*, no. 262, May 2, 1826, pp. 1–4; Guadalajara, *El Nivel*, no. 263, May 4, 1826, pp. 1–3. For *El Nivel's* more general critiques of their ultramontane foes' religiosity and statements of their own reform beliefs, see, for example, Guadalajara, *El Nivel*, no. 211, January 3, 1826, pp. 1–2; Guadalajara, *El Nivel*, no. 212, January 5, 1826, pp. 1–2; Guadalajara, *El Nivel*, no. 210, January 24, 1826, pp. 2–3; Guadalajara, *El Nivel*, no. 156, August 28, 1825, pp. 1–2. Guadalajara, *El Nivel*, no. 137, July 14, 1825, pp. 1–3. For more on radical federalists in Guadalajara's lively public sphere of letters, see Adrián Acosta, "Una reflexión sobre 'cultura política' e 'ideopraxias' en los escritos de Los Polares. Guadalajara, 1821-1826" *Historias 86* (September–December 2013): 47–72.

36. Guadalajara, *El Nivel*, November 12, 1825, no. 189, pp. 1–2.

37. I.I.M.J.E.A., *Á los fieles del estado del Salvador* (Guatemala: Imprenta de la Union, 1825), 99.

38. Santa-María, *Preservativo*, 24.

39. Fr. José Andrés de Santa-María, *Reconvención amistosa al senador Isidro Menéndez por Fr. José Andres de Santa-Maria, maestro y regente de los estudios del convento de Santo Domingo de Guatemala* (Guatemala: Imprenta Mayor, 1826), 1, 15.

40. José Andres de Santa María, *Catecismo teológico* (Guatemala: Imprenta Mayor, 1825), 5–6.

41. Ibid., 18–19, 8.

42. Un Prógimo, "Comunicado," in García, *Diccionario histórico*, 408–411.

43. J. Lloyd Mecham, *Church and State in Latin America: A History of Politico-Ecclesiastical Relations*, revised edition (Chapel Hill, NC: The University of North Carolina Press, 1966), 19–25. Also see Antonio Joaquín de Rivadeneyra y Barrientos, *Manual compendio del regio patronato indiano* (Madrid, ES: Antonio Marin, 1755). Brian Connaughton, "República Federal y patronato. El ascenso y descalabro de un proyecto," *Estudios de Historia Moderna y Contemporánea*

de México 39 (2010): 6–70. Teófanes Egido, "El Real Patronato," in *Iglesia y sociedad en el Reino de Granada (siglos XVI–XVIII)*, ed. Antonio Luis Cortés Peña and Guadalupe Muñoz, et.al. (Granada: Universidad de Granada), 9–21. Lucrecia Raquel Enríquez, "El patronato de la monarquía católica a la república católica chilena (1810–1833)," in *Normatividades e instituciones eclesiásticas en el Virreinato del Perú, siglos XVI–XIX*, ed. Otto Danwerth and Benetta Albani (Berlin, DE: Max Planck Institute for Legal History and Legal Theory, 2019), 223–243.

44. "La encíclica 'Etsi longissimo' de 30 de enero de 1816" reproduced in Pedro de Leturia, *La acción diplomática de Bolivar ante Pio VII; a la luz del Archivo Vaticano* (Venezuela: Gran Palperia de Libros, 1984), 281–282.

45. Mecham, *Church and State*, 76.

46. Ibid., 61–62.

47. Lucas Ayarragaray, *La iglesia en América y la dominación Española: Estudio de la época colonial* (Buenos Aires: Lajouane, 1920), 259–260.

48. Mexico City, *Correo de la Federacion Mexicana*, April 21, 1827, num. 172. Tomo 2, 2.

49. Ibid., 1–3.

50. Guadalajara, *El Defensor de la Religion*, September 7, 1827, p. 2, cols. 1–2; p. 3, col. 1. The paper criticized Quintana's intervention in the debate.

51. For more on José Guadalupe Gómez Huerta (1783–1836), see *Diccionario Porrúa de historia, biografía, y geografía de México*, vol. 3 (Mexico: Porrúa, 1995), 1508. On Gómez Huerta's 1827 proposal to Zacatecas' congress to establish a bishopric separate from Guadalajara as well as the feverishly federalist context of Zacatecas, see Rosalina Ríos Zúñiga, "El ejercicio del patronato y la problemática eclesiástica en Zacatecas durante la Primera República Federal (1824-1834)," *Historia Critica*, 52 (January–April 2014): 53–55.

52. José Miguel Godoa, March 2, 1827, "Informe que el Sr. Dr. D. José Miguel Gordoa, gobernador de la diócesis de Guadalajara, obispo despues de la misma, dirigió á consulta del honorable congreso de Zacatecas sobre algunas proposiciones presentados á aquella asamblea," in *Colección eclesiástica mexicana*, vol. 2, 298–321 (Mexico: Imprenta de Galvan, 1834), quote on page 303. Also see "Un Hombre de Bien," *El cisma religiosa casaurá el político* (Mexico: Imprenta del Ciudadano Alejandro Valdés, 1827). The author conceded that wrongheaded reformers like José María Alpuche and Gómez Huerta influenced public opinion. Luckily, he noted, the Holy Father's defenders outnumbered the reformers; see p. 7.

53. José Guadalupe Gómez Huerta, *Discurso pronunciado por el Sr. Huerta en la sesión secreta del 15 de Mayo, en favor del dictamen de la comisión eclesiástica, sobre arreglo de patronato* (Guadalajara: Imprenta del C. Urbano Sanroman, 1827), 8.

54. Ibid., 9.

55. Guadalajara, *El Defensor de la Religion*, October 19, 1827, no. 80, p. 2, cols. 1–2. For the larger press context, see Celia del Palacio Montiel, *La disputa por las conciencias: los inicios de la prensa en Guadalajara, 1809-1835* (Guadalajara, MX.: University of Guadalajara, 2001).

56. Guadalajara, *El Defensor de la Religion*, April 13, 1827, no. 26, p. 3, cols. 1–2; p. 4, col. 1. For more on the *Defensor*'s critiques of Llorente's and Gómez Huerta's theories of church and state governance, see, for example, Guadalajara, *El Defensor de la Religion*, no. 24, April 6, 1827, p. 4, col. 1; Guadalajara, *El Defensor de la Religion*, no. 82, October 26, 1827, p. 2, cols. 1–2, p. 3, cols. 1–2, p. 4, col. 1; Guadalajara, *El Defensor de la Religion*, no. 28, April 20, 1827, p. 2, col. 2, p. 3, cols. 1–2. Guadalajara, *El Defensor de la Religion*, April 27, 1827, p. 2, col. 2, p. 3, cols.1–2.

57. Juan Antonio Llorente, *Discurso sobre una constitución religiosa, considerada como parte de la civil nacional, su autor un americano, los da á luz D. Juan Antonio Llorente, doctor en sagrados*

cánones (Paris, FR: Imprenta de Stahl, 1820), 10, 12, 16, 18, 167. For a brief description of the work's reception in Spain, see P. Marcelino Menéndez y Pelayo, *Historia de los heterodoxos españoles*, vol. 3 (Madrid: Librerá Católica de San José, 1880), 425–428.

58. Ramón Casaús, Edict of May 8, 1828, AHAG, Fondo Diocesano, Secretaria de Gobierno Eclesiastico, Serie Larrazabal, Tomo 2. Llorente, *Discurso sobre una constitución*.

59. Roberto Regoli, "La Congregación Especial para los Asuntos Eclesiásticos de España durante el trienio liberal (1820-1823)," *Anuario de Historia de la Iglesia* 19 (2010): 154–155.

60. Guadalajara, *El Defensor de la Religion*, no. 49, July 3, 1827, p. 2, col. 2; p. 3, cols. 1–2. Mexico City, *El Sol*, no. 1441, October 23, 1827, p. 2, cols. 2–3; p. 3, col. 1. San Salvador, *El Salvadoreño*, August 7, 1828, no. 19, p. 2, col. 2; p. 3, col. 1. Guatemala's liberal *Redactor General* also found *El Sol* and *El Indicador*' conservatism troubling, see Guatemala City, *El Redactor General*, num. 19, November 3, 1825, p. 1, col.1.

61. Mexico City, *El Sol*, no. 1608, p. 1, cols 2–3; p. 2, cols. 1–3, and p. 4, cols. 1–2. Casaús' pastoral letter was dated August 31, 1827; Pope Leo XII's letter to Delgado was dated December 1, 1826.

62. On Lizardi's reformist Catholicism, see Voekel, *Alone Before God*, 146–170.

63. On Lizardi's pamphlet trade outside the doors of the Mexican Senate, see Rafael Rojas, *La escritura de la Independencia: el surgimiento de la opinión pública en México* (México, D.F: Taurus/Centro de Investigación y Docenia Económicas, 2003), 49, 51. On Lizardi's excommunication, see Silvia Juliana Rocha Dallos, "Oiga el público verdades: los panfletos de Fernández de Lizardi (1820-1827)," *Ulúa* 27 (2016): 242.

64. José Joaquín Fernández de Lizardi, *Horrorosos atentados de una parte del clero de Goatemala* [sic] *contra la independencia general o sea el genio de la anarquia* (México, DF: Oficina de Ontiveros, 1826), 3–5, 6 n. 3. An 1826 pamphlet by the pseudonymous "El Amigo de la Verdad" listed Parish Priest of Chinameca Crespin as one of the parish priests exiled from El Salvador; "El Amigo de la Verdad," *Á los editores*, 2. On Lizardi's conflicts with Bernardo Martínez y Ocejo, the bishop of Sonora, see Lizardi, *El sedicioso manifiesto del Obispo de Sonora. Impugnado por el Pensador en la sexta Conversación del Payo y el Sacristán* (1825) in Lizardi, *Obras V*, 328–329. Lizardí was responding to Martínez y Ocejo's *Soberanía del Altísimo defendida por el Illmo. Sr. D. Fr Bernardo del Espírit Sano ausado como reo á la Superioridad* (Guadalajara, México: Viuda de Romero, 1824). For cleric Dionisio Crespin's own take on how he became the Guatemalan army's chaplan, see Prison de Sonsonate, August 7, 1829, Statement of Dionisio Crespin, AGCA, Signatura B, leg. 2434, exp. 51477, fols. 1–2v.

65. José María de Aza, *Horrorosos atentados del Pensador Mexicano contra el clero de Guatemala. O sea El genio de la anarquia* (México: Imprenta del Cuidadano Juan Cabrera, 1826), passim. For more on Aza and his dispute with Lizardi, see Torcuato Di Tello, *Política nacional y popular en México, 1820-1847*, 1st edition (México: Fondo de Cultura Económica, 1994), 107. Around the same time, Aza accused Lizardi of assaulting him in Juan Cabrera's printing office and brandishing two pistols at him after he handedly repelled the assault. The *Aguila Mexicana* noted that Lizardi denounced Aza for libel to a censorship board. Aza was jailed but the board released him and ordered his bond returned to Juan Cabrera. See José María de Aza, *Muerte del escudero Aza, atentada por El Pensador Mexicano en la Imprenta de Cabrera* (Mexico: Imprenta de C. Juan Cabrera, 1826), 2. Mexico City, *El Aguila Mexicana*, June 6, 1826, no. 37, pp. 2–3.

66. For more on both Montúfar and his liberal nemesis in the world of letters Alejandro Marure, who labeled the Aycineas "The Family," see Timothy Hawkins, "A War of Words: Manuel Montúfar, Alejandro Marure, and the Politics of History in Guatemala," *The Historian* 64, nos. 3/ 4 (spring/summer 2002): 518–519. Marure was the author of *Bosquejo histórico de la revoluciones*

de Centro-América. The work was commissioned by Mariano Galvez in 1833 and published in 1838 as an antidote to Montúfar's interpretation of the post-independence era. See Fernando Cruz and Antonio Machado, *José Batres Montúfar y Alejandro Marure* (Guatemala: Ministerio de Educación Pública, 1957), 106–107;; Alejandro Marure, *Bosquejo histórico de las revoluciones de Centroamérica desde 1811 a 1834*, 2 vols. (Guatemala: Ministerio de Educación Pública, 1960).

67. Manuel Montúfar y Coronado, *Memorias para la historia de la revolución de Centro-América (Memorias de Jalapa), Recuerdos y anecdotas, Biblioteca Guatemalteca de Cultura Popular, tomo 1, vol. 65 [1832]* (Guatemala: Centro Editorial José de Pineda Ibarra, 1963), 93, 95–96.

68. Marure, *Bosquejo histórico.*

69. For more on the 1820 uprising in Totonicapán, see Aaron Pollock, *Levantameinto K'iche en Totonicapán 1820. Los lugares de las políticas subalternas* (Guatemala: Asociación para el Avance de las Ciencias Sociales de Guatemala, 2008).

70. Juan Carlos Sarazúa Pérez, "Fuerzas militares para defender al Estado: Guatemala, 1823-1863," in *Las fuerzas de guerra en la construcción del estado: America Latina siglo XIX*, ed. Juan Carlos Garavaglia, Juan Pro Ruíz y Eduardo Zimmerman (Rosario, Argentina: Prohistoria ediciones, 2012), 35–36, 40, 44–45. Juan Carlos Sarazúa, "Política y etnicidad y servicio militar. Dos experiencias paralelas en MesoAmérica. Chiapas y Guatemala, 1808-1871" *Revista Historia de América* 152 (January–December 2016): 142, 144–145, 147, 135–162. Juan Carlos Sarazúa, "Recolectar, administrar y defender: la construcción del estado y las resistencias regionales en Guatemala, 1800-1871" (PhD diss., Universitat Pompeu Fabra, 2013), 276–277.

71. Arturo Taracena Arriola, "La mirada de tres actores Guatemaltecos sobre la Guerra Federal de 1826 á 1829: Montufar y Coronado, Córdova y García Granado. Relexiones metodológicas sobre un conflict armado," in *La primera guerra federal centroamericana, 1826-1829. Nación y estados, republicanismo y violencia*, ed. Arturo Taracena Arriola (Mexico City: Universidad Autónoma Metropolitana, Unidad Iztapalapa, 2005), 76–77.

72. Juan Carlos Sarazúa Pérez, "Recolectar, gastar, y reclutar en tiempos de guerra: financas públicas y servicio military indígena en Guatemala durante la Guerra Federal de 1826 á 1829," in *La primera guerra*, ed. Taracena Arriola, 104–105.

CHAPTER 7

1. Guatemala, Mariano Gálvez, June 6, 1829, AGCA, Carp. 10, Signatura B, leg. 2552, exp. 60054. On the reforms, see Sullivan Gonzalez, *Piety, Power*, 8. Jorge Luis Arriola, *Gálvez en la encrucijada. Ensayo crítico en torno al humanismo político de un gobernante* (Guatemala: Editorial Cara Parens, 2012). Holleran, *Church and State.*

2. Sullivan Gonzalez, *Piety*, 8. Also see Jorge Luis Arriola, *Gálvez*. Holleran, *Church and State.*

3. Historian Douglass Sullivan-González places Muñoz in Esquipulus from August of 1824 to March of 1830, see his *The Black Christ*, 73, 78.

4. Christophe Belaubre, "Miguel Muñoz," AFEHC, Ficha no. 685, at https://www.afehc-histo ria-centroamericana.org/index_action_fi_aff_id_685, accessed on November 25, 2017.

5. Comayagua, Ministro General del Gobierno Supremo del Estado de Honduras to Gobierno Supremo de Guatemala, November 10, 1826, AGCA, Signatura B 10.8, leg. 3483, ex 79641, fols. 756–756v. Comayagua, Ministro General del Gobierno Supremo del Estado de Honduras to Gobierno Supremo de Guatemala, October 10, 1826, AGCA, Signatura B 10.8, Leg. 3483, exp. 79641, fols. 733–733v. Comayagua, Dionisio de Herrera to José del Valle, Nov. 10 1826; reproduced in Lois E. Bumgartner, "The Attempted Assassination of Honduran President Dionisio de Herrera, 3 November 1826," *Hispanic American Historical Review* 42, no. 1 (February

1962): 60–62. Montúfar, *Memorias*, 61. For a basic introduction to Herrera's political career, see Rafael Heliodoro Valle, "Dionisio de Herrera, 1783-1850. A Centennial Tribute," *Hispanic American Historical Review* 30, no. 4 (November 1950): 554–558.

6. Marquez had been part of the committee that wrote the *Proyecto de bases constitucionales para las Provincias Unidas del Centro de América* along with Delgado, Isidro Menéndez, and Pedro Molina; he also served on the committee that penned the 1824 Constitution alongside Menéndez and Delgado and others. He presided over a liberal Honduran assembly in 1829; the assembly ended ecclesiastical immunity from secular law (the *fuero*), declared civil matrimony, and made it possible for clerics to marry; see Alberto Membreño *Aztequismos de Honduras* (Mexico: Imprenta de Ignacio Escalante, 1907), 16, 19.

7. Miguel Muñoz, *Defensa de las llaves de San Pedro en la autoridad diocesana y breves noticias de los cismas del Arzobispado de Guatemala y del de la iglesia sufraganea de Honduras: por el Presbítero Miguel Muñoz del obispado de Nicaragua* (New York NY: Imprenta Española de D. Juan de la Granja, 1834), 80.

8. Miguel Muñoz, *Defensa*, 7–8, 82, 84. Montúfar, *Memorias*, 169–170. In August of 1832, the *jefe político* of Chiquimula reported his failure to capture Irías and Muñoz in Honduras; see Chiquimula, Jefe Político to Secretaria del Gobierno Supremo del Estado, August 16, 1832, AGCA, Signatura B 118.14, leg. 2478, ex 54744, fol. 1.

9. Montúfar, *Memorias*, 172. On the Franciscans and Dominicans' control of parishes in the indigenous western highlands of Guatemala, see the list of clerics manning these and other parishes in January of 1829 in AHAG, Fondo Diocesano, Correspondencia, Cartas, January 1829. Of the 136 total Guatemalan and El Salvadoran parishes listed, twenty were manned by friars, all of them in the vicarates of Momostenango, Verapaz, and Huehuetenango (spelled Gueguetenango in the document).

10. Guatemala, *El Indicador*, August 24, 1826, no. 94, p. 2, cols 1–2. Here *El Indicador* reproduced the text of the July 20, 1826 decree issued by the Guatemalan legislature. The paper criticized the decree.

11. Guatemala City, "Comunicado" *Siglo de Layfayette*, January 14, 1832, no. 12.

12. Guatemala, Gefe del Estado, "Decree of 28 July 1829," August 16, 1829, BN-Guatemala, Fondo Antigua, Registro no. 1952. Signed Juan M. Rodriguez.

13. Guatemala City, José Miguel Aguirre to Supreme Government, 1829, AGCA, Signatura B83.12m, leg. 1124, exp. 25494, fol. 1.

14. Guatemala, C. Juana María Mansila, "La C. Juana María Mansila solícita permiso para que pueda regresar su hijo Pedro Peres y Mansilla," AGCA, B 83.13, leg. 1124, ex 25489, fols. 1-1v. So comprehensive was the expulsion decree that even Juan de Dios Campos Diez had to appeal to stay in Guatemala; see Juan de Dios Campos Diez to Gefe del Estado Pedro Molina, Guatemala, 12 Sept.1829, AGCA, Sig. B, Leg. 2435, fols. 1-2; Juan de Dios Campos Diez to J. Manuel Rodríguez, Guatemala, September 12, 1829, AGCA, Sig. B, Leg. 1112, exp. 24867, fols. 1-1v.

15. Guatemala, José Antonio Alcayaga, "Presentación que el provisor hace al gobierno en favor de los regulares," August 7, 1829, AGCA, B83.1, leg. 1124, ex 25486, fol. 2.

16. Guatemala, José Clemente López, Fernando Valero, and Eusenio Zelaya, July 27, 1829, Signatura B.83.12, leg. 1124, exp. 25477, fols. 2, 3, 4.

17. Guatemala, Gefe del Estado de Guatemala to Jefe Departamental de Querala, June 3, 1829, AGCA, Carpeta 11, Signatura B, Leg. 2432, exp. 51100, fol. 2v.; Signatura B 83.12, leg. 1124, exp. 25483.

18. Guatemala, Gobierno Supremo del Estado to Provisor y Vicario General de Guatemala, September 29, 1829, AGCA, Signatura B, leg. 3593, exp. 82454.

19. Guatemala, El Gobierno del Estado to Villa de Zacapa, 21 Feb. 1838, AGCA, Signatura B 119.2, leg. 2523, exp. 57201, fol. 1. In Victor Castrillo's lengthy defense of his actions in the Zacapa area, he refers to a provisional junta that persecuted him as "the actual inquisition of Chiquimula"; see his *Maravillas de Zacapa y sus contornos* (Guatemala: Imprenta de A. de Estudios, 1838), 2; Castrillo signed the work on May 3, 1838.

20. Guatemala, AGCA, Carpeta 8, Signatura B, leg. 2433, exp. 51169.

21. George Alexander Thompson, *Narrative of an Official Visit to Guatemala from Mexico* (London, UK: John Murray, 1829), 219. The journal entry was dated June 9, 1827.

22. Guatemala, María Dolores Roma to Secretaria General del Gobierno de este Estado, October 17, 1829, AGCA, Carpeta 1, Signatura B, Leg. 1112, exp. 24871, fol. 2.

23. Zeceña, *Observaciones*; signed on October 22, 1824.

24. Victor Castrillo, *Adivinanza piadosa* (San Salvador: Imprenta del Gobierno, 1824).

25. Guatemala City, Mariano Gálvez to Ciudadano Gefe Departamental de esta Corte, May 18, 1829, AGCA, Carpeta 10, Signatura B 119.4, leg. 2552, exp. 60054, fol. 2.

26. Basilio Zeceña, *Al público respectable* (Guatemala: Imprenta de la Unión, 1829), 1.

27. Guatemala, Basilio Zeceña, September 7, 1829; J. A. Alcayaga to Secretaria General del Gobierno de este estado, October 12, 1829; Provincial Vicar General, October 13, 1829—all found in AGCA, Carpeta 1, Signatura B, Leg. 1112, ex 24865, fols. 2, 2v, 3. Morazán appears to have sprung José Antonio Alcayaga from prison, where the government had placed him after he refused to pay a required 100 peso fee to support the conservatives' war effort. Under pressure from Morazán, Casaús initially approved Alcayaga's appointment as vicar general. One in Havana, he retracted his approval, citing Alcayaga's history of support for Delgado, which included naming him vicar general of El Salvador in 1830; see Christophe Belaubre, "José Antonio Alcayaga," AFEHC, ficha no. 1328 at https://www.afehc-historia-centroameric ana.org/index_action_fi_aff_id_1328, accessed on 2/23/2020. Miguel Muñoz, *Defensa*, 8.

28. Zeceña served alongside Delgado and Cañas in the Provincial Deputation in 1821, and as the parish priest of Chalchuapa, a small town near Santa Ana, in 1820. In 1828, he was the parish priest of San Juan de Sacatepéquez, Guatemala; see Christophe Belaubre, "Zeceña y Fernández de Córdova, Basilio," AFEHC, ficha no. 84, at https://www.afehc-historia cen-troamericana.org/diccionario2/diccionario_fiche_id_84.html Basilio Zeceña y Fernández de Córdoba. Accessed on 2/27/2020.

29. Fernández de Lizardi, *Horrorosos atentados*. For more on Lizardi as a Reform Catholic intellectual, see Pamela Voekel, *Alone Before God*, 123–145. On his life and works, see Nancy Vogely's *Lizardi and the Birth of the Novel in Spanish America* (Gainesville: The University Press of Florida, 2001). Carcel de Sonsonate, August 7, 1829, Statement of Dionisio Crespin, AGCA, Signatura B, leg. 2434, exp. 51477, fols. 1-2v. El Amigo de la Verdad, *A los editors del periodico titulado Semanario Politico Mercantil de San Salvador* (Guatemala: Imprenta de la Unión, n.d.), 2. Perdomo identified Ramón Soltis as a Casaús supporter.

30. Havana, Cuba, Casaús to Francisco Pablo Vasquez, January 27, 1830, AES, Guatemala, Anno 1828-1831, Pos. 4-6, Fasc. 511. On Alcayaga's rationale for appointing Delgado, see Palacio Arzobispal de Guatemala, José Antonio Alcayaga, October 5, 1829, BN-Guatemala, Valenzuela Collection, Fondo Antiguo, Registro 1952, Folder de Ojas Sueltas 1829. On the October 14 announcement of Delgado's appointment as vicar and the swearing-in ceremony in San Salvador on October 18, 1829, see San Salvador, José Matías Delgado, José Simeón Cañas, Pedro Lara,

and Pablo Fernández, October 18, 1829, BN-Guatemala, Valenzuela Collection, Fondo Antiguo, Registro 1952, Folder de Ojas Sueltas 1829.

31. El Salvador, J. Antonio Alcayaga to C. Manuela Castañeda, LAL-TU, Tulane Ephemera, Central American Printed Emphemera Collection, 1715-2005, Folder 151, Politics 1827–1828, 1.

32. Havana, Archbishop Casaús to Francisco Pablo Vasquez, January 27, 1830, AES, Guatemala, Anno 1828-1831, Pos. 4-6, Fasc. 511.

33. José Antonio Alcayaga, *Carta del ex-gobernador del arzobispado protestando por su destitución con motivo de haber nombrado el Delgado provisor y vicario provincial de San Salvador. Hace al propio tiempo vicario a cargo á Casaús* (Guatemala: Imprenta de Lorenzana, 1830), 1–2, 7–8. The document is dated April 14, 1830 and addressed to Casaús.

34. The Cathedral Chapter penned an eighty-page pamphlet that responded in part to El Salvadoran conservatives who accused them of enacting a church schism; see *Cabildo de la S.I.M, Impugnación al impreso que se publicó en S. Salvador con este titulo: "El Monstruo de dos cabezas." Y defensa de la sinceridad y rectitud de los procediminetos del Cabildo de la S.I.M. de Guatemala, con motivo de la elección de provisor y vicario . . . la dan a luz los individuos del propio cabildo que la subscriben* (Guatemala: Imprenta Nueva, 1831). Signed on August 31, 1831.

35. Muñoz, *Defensa*, iii, iv. Félix Amat de Palau y Font, *Observaciones pacíficas sobre la potestad eclesiástica*, vol.1 (reprint Salt Lake City, Utah: Nabu Press, 2002 [Original 1817]), 1.

36. Joaquín Lorenzo Villanueva, *Vida literaria de Dn. Joaquín Lorenzo Villanueva: o, memoria de sus escritos y de sus opiniones eclestiásticas y políticas, y de algunos sucesos notables de su tiempo. Con un apéndice de documentos relativos a la historia del concilio de Trento, tomo 1,* (London: Dulau and Company, 1825), 68–69.

37. Holleran, *Church and State*, 113. José Ignacio Ávila served as a representative of El Salvador in the Cortes de Cádiz, and proposed the establishment of a bishopric in El Salvador; see, for example José María García León, *Los diputados doceañistas*, vol. 1 (Cádiz: Ayuntamiento, 2006), 279–280.

38. Madrid, Tiberi to Polidori, March 1, 1831, in Vicente Cárcel Ortí, *Correspondencia diplomatica del Nuncio Tiberi (1827-1834) (Documentos para la historia de las relaciones iglesia-estado en la España del siglo XIX, Serie I, iv)* (Pamplona, ES: Ediciones Universidad de Navarra, 1976), 561–562.

39. Guatemala City, Calixto García Goyena, Guatemalan Assembly, June 1830, AGCA, B.118.15, exp. 54949, leg. 2484. The Guatemalan government declared Casaús a traitor to the nation on June 13, 1830, see AGCA, B83.12, exp. 25466, leg. 1124, fol. 24.

40. Excerpted in Ayala Benítez, *La iglesia*, 236–237.

41. Rome, Polidori to Tiberi, March 31, 1831, in Cárcel Ortí, *Correspondencia*, 561–562, n. 2.

42. Gregorio XVI's 1799 book was reprinted after he became pope, see his *Il trionfo della Santa Sede e della Chiesa contro gli assalti dei novatori combattuti e respinti colle stesse loro armi* (Venezia, IT: Guiseppe Battaggia, 1832).

43. See for example, Guatemala, Mariano Turabanino, "Congreso Federal: Ponencias," July 14, 1830, AGCA, Sig. B 7.4, exp. 3120, leg. 130, fol. 4.

44. Mexico City, *Registro Oficial del Gobierno de los Estados-Unidos Mexicanos*, August 20, 1830, num. 17, año I, Tomo II, p. 2, col. 2. Madrid, Spanish Papal Nuncio Tiberi to Polidori, March 1, 1831, in Vicente Cárcel Ortí, *Correspondencia*. On discussions of clerical marriage in the federal congress, see Mariano Turabanino to Federal Congress, Guatemala City, July 14, 1830, AGCA, B 7.4, ex 3120, leg. 130, fol.4.

45. Mier, *Memoirs*, 35.

46. Vicente Pazos Kanki, trans., *Observaciones sobre los inconvenientes del celibato de los clerigos* (London, 1815); the translation was of Jacques Maurice Gaudin's *Les inconvéniens du célibat de prêtres: prouvés par des recherches historiques* (Geneva, CH: Chez J.L. Pellet, Imprimeur de la République, 1781). On the contents of Mier's crates of books, see "Inventario de los libros y papeles recogidos al declarante Mier en Soto la Marina y entregados al Tribunal de la Fe" in *Colección de documentos para la historia de la Guerra de Independencia de Mexico de 1808 a 1821*, vol. 4, ed. Juan E. Hernández y Dávalos (Mexico: J.M. Sandoval, 1880), [840–847], 841, 843. Newspaper editor and Doctor of Theology Pazos Kanki energetically circulated *Observaciones* in Buenos Aires and environs. The work was bound with an essay by an anonymous local author that assailed the pope's authority through a parable of a society where blindfolded people unquestionably follow a small group of men without blindfolds led by a leader called Eyes. A reformist radical, Pazos Kanki explained in an 1819 work that reformers attempted to abolish clerical celibacy in Buenos Aires, and demonstrated that the pope was only bishop of Rome, not the Holy Father of the entire church, which "possessed the right of electing its own pastors"; see his *Letters on the United Provinces of South America Addressed to the Hon. Henry Clay, Speaker of the House of Representatives of the U. States by don Vicente Pazos*, trans. Platt H. Crosby, Esq. (New York, NY, 1819), 103. For more on Aymara-speaker Pazos Kanki's transatlantic life, see Racine "Fireworks over Fernandina." ; and Pablo Martínez Gramuglia and Mariana Rosetti, *Letrado americano, organizador cultural: algunas polémicas de Vicente Pazos Kanki como editor de periódicos rioplatenses (1811-1816)*, at https://doi.org/10.4000/argona uta.2695, accessed on 3/15/2020.

47. Mexico City, *Registro Oficial del Gobierno de los Estados-Unidos Mexicanos*, August 20, 1830, num. 17, año I, Tomo II, p. 2, col. 2.

48. Ibid.

49. Mexico City, *Registro Official del Gobierno de los Estados-Unidos Mexicanos*, August 4, 1830, num. 101, año 1, Tomo 2, p. 4, col. 1.

50. Malacátan, José León Taboada to Casaús, July 2, 1826, AHAG, Fondo Diocesano, Correspondencia, Cartas, July 1826. Guatemala, Gobierno del Estado to Provisor Vicario, February 10, 1830, AHAG, Fondo Diocesano, Correspondencia, Cartas, February 1830.

51. Guatemala, Pablo de Sagastume, January 2, 1827, AHAG, Fondo Diocesano, Secretaría, Cartas, 1827.

52. Zacuapa, Alcalde #1 Dionisio Pineda and Alcalde #2 Saturino Pineda to Ciudadano Provisor y Gobernador, April 29, 1830, AHAG, Correspondencia, Correspondencia, Cartas, March 1830.

53. *Escrito que los vecinos de esta capital presentaron á la A.O.L contra el Dr. José Matías Delgado en obsequio del bien general de la república y particular del estado* (San Salvador: Imprenta Mayor, 1831).

54. "Representacion que los sacerdotes que subscriben han hecho de la A. de E. del Salvador, relativa á la nulidad de las facultades del Dr. José Matias Delgado," BNG, Fondo Antiguo, Registro no. 1954, Folder de Ojas Sueltas 1831, fols. 1–3. Signed by Ramón Aguilar, Marcelo Viles, Francisco Velasco, Fr. Files Antonio Castro, Santiago Rayas, José Huerga, Ecaristo Camacho, and Rafael Rodríguez.

55. Isidro Menéndez, *Censura de la ley de la asamblea de 21 de enero de 1831 que reconoce por legitimo arzobispo al Sr. Casaús* (San Salvador: Imprenta del Estado, 1831).

56. Guatemala City, "Contestación al Redactor Oajaqueño," *El Siglo de Lafayette* no. 8 (December 3, 1831): 4, cols. 1–2.

57. See Mexico City, *El Aguila Méxicana*, July 17, 1825, p. 2, col. 3.

58. Isidro Menéndez, *Censura*, 6–7, 12.

59. Isidro Menéndez, *Contestación del autor de la censura de la ley de 28 de enero de 1831 á los papeles publicados contra ella* (San Salvador: Imprenta del Estado, 1831), 4–5. This pamphlet was signed by Menéndez in Ahuachapán on June 11, 1831. A number of authors weighed in on Delgado's quest for the bishopric and the state's proper relationship to the church and the people in El Salvador. The pseudonymous "La Verguenza" argued for Bishop Delgado's legitimacy because the people elected the legislature and the legislature had named him bishop; see his *Contra la mentira titulada Verdad* (San Salvador: Imprenta del Estado, 1830); also see the pseudonymous "El Honor's" response to "La Verguenza," which asserted that Delgado's use episcopal regalia insulted the people because the pope had rejected his pretensions to the bishopric; "El Honor," *Noticias muy particulares venidas del catolicismo* (San Salvador: Imprenta Mayor, 1830).

60. Isidro Menéndez, *Contestación*, 5–6.

61. Ibid., 6. Pedro Tamburini, *Verdadera idea de la Santa Sede, escrita en Italiano por el presbítero D. Pedro Tamburini de Brescia. Profesor de la Universidad Imperial y Real de Pavia, caballero de la Orden de Hierro, miembro del Instituto Imperial y Real de las Ciencias, y traducida por D. N. Q. S.C. quien la dedica á los pueblos de América* (London: Imprenta Española de M. Calero, 1826), 212–213, 252–253, 257. In this work, Tamburini stressed the Church Fathers' authority, the importance of reading the bible in the vernacular, the corrupt nature of indulgences, the divine right of bishops, and the pope's limited writ. For more on Tamburini, one of the Synod of Pistoia's most important intellectual authors, see Owen Chadwick, *The Popes and European Revolution* (New York, NY: Oxford University Press, 1981), 402–403.

62. De' Ricci cited in Chadwick, *The Popes*, 425.

63. Gaspar Melchor de Jovellanos, "Diario sexto," in *Biblioteca de autores Españoles desde la formación del lenguaje hasta nuestros días. Obras públicas y inéditas de Don Gaspar Melchor de Jovellanos*, multiple volumes, ed. D. Miguel Artola (Madrid: Ediciones Atlas, 1961), 75:240–241.

64. Menéndez, *Contestación*, 19–21; Tamburini, *Verdadera idea*, xvii–xviii.

65. London, *Ocios de Españoles Imigrados. Periódico mensual*, vol. 6 (London, UK: Imprenta de Macintosh, 1824-27), 270–271. This *Ocios* issue appears to be number 30 of September 1826.

66. Warren, "The Origins,"18.

67. Puigblanch cited in Menéndez Pelayo, *Historia de heterodoxias*, 2:662.

68. Villanueva, *Viaje literario de las iglesias de España* (Madrid: Imprenta Real, 1803).

69. Ayala Benítez reproduces both the original Latin and his translation into Spanish of Pope Pius VIII's June 17, 1829, excommunication order against Delgado; see Ayala Benítez, *La Iglesia*, 214–221. He also reproduces both the Latin original and his translation of the June 30, 1829, letter Pope Pius VIII sent to Archbishop Casaús explaining the excommunication decree; see pp. 222–224; the reference to marriage dispensations is in the latter letter and on p. 223.

70. Isidro Menéndez, *Contestación del autor*, 6, 18. Isidro Menéndez cites Llorente, 14.

71. Guatemala City, "Tolerancia," *El Siglo de Layfayette* no. 6 (November 8, 1831): 1, cols. 1–2, and p. 2, col. 1. For more on the paper see María Eugenia Claps Arenas, "*El siglo de Lafayette y su discurso sobre México*," *Revista Pueblos y Fronteras Digital* 12, no. 24 (December 2017–May 2018): 23–42, https://www.redalyc.org/articulo.oa?id=90653647002.

72. Guatemala "Derecho de gentes. Grégoire," *Siglo de Lafayette*, October 27, 1831, no. 4, p. 3, col. 2.

CHAPTER 8

1. An earlier version of this chapter appeared as Pamela Voekel, "Liberal Religion: The Schism of 1861," in *Religious Culture in Modern Mexico*, ed. Martin Austin Nesvig (Lantham: Rowman & Littlefield, 2007), 78–105. The chapter is reproduced by permission here. . For a concise summary of liberals' legal and other campaigns to reform the church in this period, see Gabriela Díaz Patiño, *Católicos, liberales, y protestantes. El debate por las imágenes religiosas en la formación de una cultura nacional (1848-1908)* (Mexico, D.F.: Colegio de México, 2016), 127–143.

2. The classic statement on Mexican liberalism in the nineteenth century is that of Charles Hale; see his *Mexican Liberalism in the Age of Mora* (New Haven, CT: Yale University Press, 1968); and his *The Transformation of Mexican Liberalism in Late Nineteenth-Century Mexico* (Princeton, NJ: Princeton University Press, 1994). Hale reads influential liberal theorist José María Luis Mora, for example, as heavily influenced by utilitarianism and other secular theories, concluding that Mora bent his multiple channels of influence to the task of "fashioning a society where religious values and the Church as an institution would be of little consequence in the action of individuals," p. 160. Although Mora's secular influences are undeniable, for an alternative analysis that argues for theologian Mora's and other reformers' deeply reformist Catholic roots and influences, see Voekel, *Alone Before God*, 148–170. Michael P. Costeloe, *The Central Republic in Mexico: A Study of the Patronage Debate, 1821-1857* (London, UK: Royal Historical Society, 1978). Costeloe depicts liberal reformers enthralled to secular ideologies of European providence, noting that "imbued with and overly dependent upon the utilitarian and rationalist ideologies of Europe," these optimists "constructed a hypothetical model of their society" and quickly realized that the church, with its external piety and socially prestigious but non-elected clergy, was a "relic of a bygone theocratic age that had no place in their modern, progressive, society," p. 75. Jacqueline Covo notes that reformist Catholic ideas surfaced and were influential during debates about the 1857 Constitution; see her *Las ideas de la Reforma en México, 1855-1861* (Mexico City: Universidad Autonoma de México, 1983). Jesús Reyes Heroles provides a comprehensive and favorable look at Mexican liberalism across the nineteenth century; he includes the Sanjuanistas as a key origin point, see his *El Liberalismo Mexicano*, 3 vols. (México: Universidad Nacional de México, Facultad de Derecho, 1957–1961).

3. Historian Dale van Kley, the doyen of the eighteenth-century European branch of the Reform Catholic International, describes the work of Pietro Tamburini and Giuseppe Zola as the "boldest statement in defense of civil toleration to appear under Catholic auspices in the eighteenth century," and a key Catholic intellectual justification for the sanctification of civil over church authority, see Van Kley, *Reform Catholicism*, 55.

4. Although no historical event can be attributed to a single cause, the conflict definitively brought back into open warfare the reformist cause that had drawn blood across Central America earlier in the century It pivoted substantially upon many of the same ecclesiastical issues that had split Mérida into warring factions and transformed Bourbon-era Reform Catholic regalists into doctrinal opponents of the absolutist King Ferdinand VII or, in the case of much of the church hierarchy, into his ultramontane champions. Reformers did battle with a spirited, nuanced, sophisticated and modern ultramontane church hierarchy and movement; on the ultramontane movement, see Pablo Mijangos y González, *The Lawyer of the Church. Bishop Clemente de Jesús Munguía and the Clerical Response to the Mexican Liberal Reforma* (Lincoln: University of Nebraska Press, 2015), passim, but especially 196–198. Mijangos y González cautions that the church's close relationship with the conservatives was not always rosy, in part because conservative politicians raided church coffers to fund their war efforts;

see especially pages 204–214. The Mexican Jesuit historian Mariano Cuevas detailed some of the persecution the ultramontane faced; he wrote from exile in Texas during the religious confrontations of the 1920s; see his *Historia de la iglesia en México*, vol. 5 (El Paso, TX: Editorial "Revista Católica," 1928). David A. Brading, "Ultramontane Intransigence and the Mexican Reform: Clemente de Jesús Munguía," in *The Politics of Religion in an Age of Revival: Studies in Nineteenth-Century Europe and Latin America*, ed. Austen Ivereigh (London, UK: Institute of Latin American Studies, 2000), 115–142. David Allen Gilbert reads the *Reforma* as a battle between conservative ultramontane and liberal anticlerical forces, see his "Long Live the True Religion!" Contesting the Meaning of Catholicism in the Mexican Reforma, 1855-1860" (PhD diss., University of Iowa, 2003). Erika Pani, "Para difundir las doctrinas ortodoxas y vindicarlas de los errores dominantes: Los periódicos católicos y conservadores en el siglo XIX," in *La república de las letras. Asomos a la cultura escrita de México decimonónico*, vol. 2, *Publicaciones periódicos y otros impresos*, ed. Belem Clark de Lara and Elisa Speckman Guerra (Mexico, D.F.: UNAM, 2005). Sol Serrano, *Qué hacer con dios*, especially 81–86; and Francisco Javier Ramón Solans, "The Roman Question in Latin America: Italian Unification and the Development of a Transatlantic Ultramontane Movement," *Atlantic Studies* 18, no. 2 (2021): 129–148.

5. Although given his larger concern with Mexican Protestantism, he can provide only a cursory treatment of Mexico's schismatic Catholic Church, Jean-Pierre Bastian attributes what he sees as the Constitutional Clergy's failure to find support in the provinces to four factors: fear of political reprisals, church unity, scant funds, and little lay support for the movement; Jean-Pierre Bastian, *Los disidentes: Sociedades protestantes y revolución en México, 1872-1911* (México: Colegio de México and Fondo de Cultura Económica, 1993), 34. For more on the Constitutional Clergy's relationship to Protestant efforts in Mexico, see John Steven Rice, "Evangelical Episcopalians and the Church of Jesus in Mexico, 1857-1906" (MA thesis, University of Texas Pan-American, 2000); Fay Sharon Greenland, "Religious Reform in Mexico; The Role of the Mexican Episcopal Church" (MA thesis, University of Florida, 1958); Alpha Gillett Bechtel, "The Mexican Episcopal Church: A Century of Reform and Revolution" (MA thesis, San Diego State College, 1966).

6. Enríque Krauze, *Mexico: Biography of Power. A History of Mexico, 1810-1996* (New York, NY: HarperCollinsPublishers, 1997), 133

7. Jan Bazant, "Mexico from Independence to 1867," in *The Cambridge History of Latin America*, vol. 3, *From Independence to 1870*, ed. Leslie Bethell (Cambridge, UK: Cambridge University Press, 2002), 435–436.

8. Ibid., 439, 443. Also see Michael P. Costeloe, *Church Wealth in Mexico: A Study of the "Juzgado de Capellanías" in the Archbishopric of Mexico, 1800-1856* (Cambridge, UK: Cambridge University Press, 1967). Jan Bazant, *Alienation of Church Wealth in Mexico. Social and Economic Aspects of the Liberal Revolution, 1856-1875* (Cambridge, UK: Cambridge University Press, 1971). Robert J. Knowlton, *Church Property and the Mexican Reform, 1856-1910* (DeKalb, IL.: Northern Illinois University Press, 1976).

9. Krauze, *Mexico*, 149, 166–167; Bazant, "Mexico," 454.

10. Krauze, *Mexico*, 158–159, 168–169; Bazant, "Mexico," 457–459.

11. Bazant, "*Mexico*," 439, 443, 459–462.

12. Krauze, *Mexico*, 170–171.

13. Mexico City, *El Monitor Republicano*, October 9, 1862, p. 1, col. 6.

14. Mexico City, *El Monitor Republicano*, October 20, 1862, p. 2, col. 6.

15. See, for example, Melchor Ocampo, "Representación sobre reforma de aranceles y obvenciones parroquiales, dirigido al H. Congreso del Estado de Michoacán por el ciudadano

Melchor Ocampo y que hizo suya el señor diputado D. Ignacio Cuevas (1851)," in *La religión, la iglesia, y el clero* (México: Empresas Editoriales, 1958), 45. Melchor Ocampo, September 15, 1858, "Discurso de Melchor Ocampo," in *Documentos básicos de la Reforma, 1854-1875*, vol. 2, intro. Mario V. Guzmán Galarza (México: Partido Revolucionario Institucional, 1982), 221–229. For more on Ocampo's life and work, see Raúl Arreola Cortés, *Melchor Ocampo. Vida y obra* (Morelia, MX: Gobierno del Estado de Michoacán, 1988); Mexico City, *El Monitor Republicano*, March 11, 1861, p. 1, cols. 1–3; Mexico City, *El Movimiento*, February 23, 1861, p. 1, col. 3; J. H., *El liberalismo y sus efectos en la República Mexicana* (México: Andrés Boix, 1858), 6; *Caso de conciencia sobre el juramento constitucional. Carta de un párroco Jalíciense* (México: Imprenta de V. García Torres, 1857), 3, 4, 14. Historian Dennis Paul Ricker notes that this pamphlet was rumored to have been written by Francisco Ortiz, a minister in the Sagrario in Guadalajara; see Dennis Paul Ricker, "The Lower Secular Clergy of Central Mexico: 1821-1857" (PhD diss., University of Texas at Austin, 1982), 323–325.

16. Pedro Echeverría, *Catecismo de la doctrina clero-maquiavélica o sea del padre Ripalda según lo observa y prédica el clero mexicano* (México: Imprenta de la Reforma, 1861).

17. Mexico City, *El Heraldo*, November 15, 1861, p. 1, cols.1 and 3.

18. Mexico City, *El Constitucional*, March 19, 1861, p. 1, cols. 3, 4.

19. Mexico City, *El Monitor Republicano*, March 9, 1861, p. 4, col. 2. For other examples of the satirical treatment of miraculous saints and holy men, see Mexico City, *El Heraldo*, April 16, 1861, p. 3, col. 3. Mexico City, *La Orquesta*, April 17, 1861, no.14, p. 3, col. 2. Mexico City, *El Heraldo*, June 13, 1861, p. 3, col. 2. Mexico City, *El Siglo Diez y Nueve*, June 13, 1861, no. 150, p. 3, col. 4.

20. Cuartel General en el Hospital de Belén de Guadalajara, *Boletín del Ejército Federal*, October 9, 1858, p. 2, cols. 2–3:

21. Mexico City, *El Monitor Republicano*, July 10, 1861, no. 3986, p. 1, cols. 5–6; p. 2 cols. 1–3.

22. Mexico City, *El Monitor Republicano*, July 18, 1861, no. 3994, p. 1, col. 1.

23. Ibid.

24. Mexico City, Ponciano Arriaga in *El Monitor Republicano*, March 18, 1861, p. 1, col. 4. Also see Mexico City, Ponciano Arriaga in *El Monitor Republicano*, March 12, 1861, p. 1, cols. 1–4, especially col. 2. Arriaga served as Defensor de los Fondos de Beneficencia under Juárez in 1861–1862; see Silvia Arrom, *Containing the Poor: The Mexico City Poor House, 1774-1871* (Durham, NC: Duke University Press, 2001), 216.

25. Ignacio Manuel Altamirano, *La Navidad en las montañas*, trans. Harvey L. Jonson (Gainesville, FL: University of Florida Press, 1961 [1871]), 12–13. For more examples of this glorification of the reformed lower clergy, see, for example, Guillermo Prieto (Fidel), *Viajes de orden suprema. Años de 1853, 54, y 55*, 3rd edition, (México: Editorial Patria, 1970), 285; Mexico City, *El Monitor Republicano*, September 4, 1856, p. 3, cols. 4, 5, 6; Juan José Baz also placed the virtuous lower clergy at the heart of "the democracy of the republic"; see his *Artículos diversos de la Bandera Roja de Morelia escritos por Juan José Baz en 1859* (México: Imprenta de Vicente García Torres, 1861), 11.

26. Altamirano, *La Navidad*, 37.

27. Ibid., 41.

28. Ibid., 44–45.

29. Mexico City, *El Monitor Republicano*, February 6, 1861, p. 1, cols. 1–4; col. 3.

30. Anonymous, "Arribo y recepción del excelentísimo señor don Benito Juárez, presidente constituciónal, al puerto de Veracruz (en el vapor Tennessee de New Orleáns)," document reproduced in Ernesto de la Torre Villar, ed., *El Triunfo de la república liberal, 1857-1860. Selección*

de testimonios de la Guerra de Tres Años. Con un estudio prelimiar y notas (México: Fondo de Cultura Económica, 1960), 58–60.

31. Mexico City , Emilio Castelar, *El Heraldo*, June 13, 1861, p. 1, col. 3. See also Mexico City, I.A. Montiel, *El Heraldo*, April 26, 1861, p. 3, col. 3. Mexico City , *El Monitor Republicano*, April 18, 1862, num. 4268, p. 2, col. 4.

32. Mexico City , *El Monitor Republicano*, October 14, 1861, no. 4082, p. 1, cols. 4–5. For more on this theme, see Mexico City, *El Monitor Republicano*, July 18, 1861, no. 3994. p. 1, col. 1–4.

33. In 1854, Pope Pious IX declared the dogma of the Immaculate Conception of Mary, an event that became a rallying point for Mexico's ultramontane Catholics; see, for example, Felipe Villarejo, *Sermón pronunciado en la solemne función que el comercio de esta capital dedicó a la declaración dogmática de la Inmaculada Concepción de María Santisima, el 23 de septiembre de 1855* (México: Imprenta de J.M. Andrade y F. Escalante, 1855); Lázaro de la Garza y Ballesteros, *Carta pastoral del Illmo, y Exmo. Sr. Arzobispo de México* (México: Imprenta de Vicente Segura, 1855). The conservative army's official bulletin noted that just as the people began to enthusiastically celebrate the Immaculate Conception of Mary, the liberals erased December 8th, the day of Guadalupe, as a national holiday, see Toluca, *Boletín Oficial del Ejército. Religion, Union, Independencia*, December 16, 1860, p. 1, col. 4. The Month of Mary was also energetically embraced in Mexico; for one example of many, see Mexico City, *La Unidad Católica*, June 4, 1861, p. 2, col. 5. José Alberto Moreno Chávez, *Devociones políticas. Cultura católica y politización en la Arquidiócesis de México, 1880-1920* (México: El Colegio de México, 2013), 56. Díaz Patiño, *Católicos, liberales*, 77–93, 261–262. Matthew Butler demonstrates conservatives' ongoing embrace of the Sacred Heart as a political and religious symbol in the twentieth century, see his "La coronación del Sagrado Corazón de Jesús en la Arquidiócesis de México, 1914," in *Revolución, cultura y religión: nuevas perspectivas regionales, siglo XX*, ed. Yolanda Padilla Rangel, Luciano Ramírez Hurtado y Francisco Javier Delgado Aguilar (Aguascalientes, MX: Universidad Autónoma de Aguascalientes, 2011), 24–68.

34. Mexico City, *La Unidad Católica*, May 29, 1861, p. 1, cols. 1–3. *Suplemento manifestación que hacen al venerable clero y fieles de sus respectivos diócesis y a todo el mundo católico, los Ilmo. Sres. El arzobispo de México y obispos de Michoacán, Linares, Guadalajara, y el Potosí, y el Sr. Dr. D. Francisco Serrano como representante de la mitra de Puebla. En defensa del clero y de la doctrina católica, con ocasión del manifiesto y los decretos expedidos por el. Sr. Lic. D. Benito Juárez en la ciudad de Veracruz en los días 7,12, 13, 23 de julio de 1859* (Celaya, MX.: Imprenta de G. Galván, 1859), 18, 25–26.

35. Voekel, *Alone Before God*, 164–166.

36. Moreno Chávez, *Devociones políticas*, 56. Juan José de Aycinena, *Noticia de las funciones con que se celebró la definición dogmática de la Inmaculada Concepción de la Santísima Virgen María, en la S.M.I. de Santiago de Guatemala... en los dias 20, 21, 22 y 23 de julio de 1855* (Guatemala: En la Oficina de L. Luna, 1855). For more on Aycinena, see Chandler, *Juan José de Aycinena*.

37. Díaz Patiño, *Católicos, liberales*, 77–93, 261–226. On the conditions under which the pope's statements were infallible according to *Paster aeternus*, see John W. O'Malley, *Vatican I: The Council and the Making of the Ultramontane Church* (Cambridge, MA: Harvard University Press, 2018), 193–198.

38. Mexico City, *El Constitucional*, March 18, 1861, p. 1, col. 3.

39. Caroline Ford, *Creating the Nation in Provincial France: Religion and Political Identity in Brittany* (Princeton, NJ: Princeton University Press, 1993), 101–102; Holmes, *Triumph*, 112. Lamennais edited *Le Monde* with George Sand in 1837; see Bernard M. G. Reardon, *Religion in*

the Age of Romanticism. Studies in Early Nineteenth Century Thought (Cambridge, UK: Cambridge University Press, 1985), 202.

40. Holmes, *Triumph*, 76.

41. Mexico City, *El Heraldo*, May 30, 1861, p. 4, col. 1.

42. Joseph Mazzine, "Letter to Abbé Lamennais of 1834," October 12, 1834, in *The Life and Writing of Joseph Mazzine*, 6 vols. (London: Smith, Elder and Company, 1891), 3:42–43.

43. Mexico City, *El Siglo Diez y Nueve*, January 5, 1857, no. 3.005, p. 2, cols. 4; and January 19, 1857, p. 1 col. 2; and January 20, 1857, p. 2, cols. 1–2.

44. Frederick B. Pike, "Heresy, Real and Alleged, in Peru: An Aspect of the Conservative-Liberal Struggle, 1830-1875," *Hispanic American Historical Review* 47, no. 1 (February 1967): 60.

45. Francisco de Paula González Vigil, "Apuntes acerca de mi vida (1857)," reproduced in "Escritos inéditos de Vigil," *Documenta* 3, no. 1 (1951–1955): 454, cited in Pike, "Heresy," 60.

46. José Ignacio Víctor Eyzaguirre, *El catolicismo en presencia de sus disidentes* (Guadalajara, JA, MX: Tipografía de Rodríguez, 1856), 11.

47. Frederick B. Pike, "Heresy," 50–74. For more on González Vigil and reformist Catholicism, see Frederick B. Pike, "Church and State in Peru and Chile since 1840: A Study in Contrasts," *American Historical Review* 73, no. 1 (October 1967): 30–50.

48. Mexico City, August 15, 1859, Rafael Díaz Martínez, Juan Nepomuceno Enríquez Orestes, Juan Francisco Domínguez, Manuel Aguilar, Manuel Estrada, and Cristóbal González Rió (1859), reproduced in Mexico City , *El Monitor Republicano*, October 5, 1861, p. 1, cols. 4–6, p. 2, cols. 1–2. Justo Sierra reports that the Liberal Party contacted the reformist clerics first, not the other way around, see his *Juárez: Su obra y su tiempo*, ed. Arturo Arnáiz y Freg (Mexico: UNAM, 1972), 180–181.

49. Mexico City, President's Order, March 13, 1857, AGN-Mexico, Justicia Eclesiástica, vol. 181, fols. 1–32. This document also contains letters from the bishops confirming their willingness to cooperate in the statistical survey. Veracruz, October 25, 1859,Secretaria del Estado y del Despacho de Gobernación, "Se nombra agente general del gobierno al presbítero d. Rafael Díaz Martínez," in *Documentos básicos de la Reforma*, vol. 3, ed. Mario V. Guzmán Galarza (México: Partido Revolucionario Institucional, 1982), 79.

50. Veracruz, Melchor Ocampo, August 12, 1859, BN-México-Lafragua, vol. 467, fol. 163; Covo, *Las Ideas de la Reforma*. For a summary of Ocampo's famous analysis of exploitative priests, which has been interpreted as his blanket anti-clericalism rather than as a specific critique common to Reform Catholics, see Krauze, *Mexico*, 152–154.

51. Veracruz, Secretaria del Estado y del Despacho de Gobernación, October 25, 1859, "Se nombra Agente General del Gobierno al Presbítero d. Rafael Díaz Martínez," in Mario V. Guzmán Galarza, ed., *Documentos básicos*, 79–83. Veracruz, Melchor Ocampo to Rafael Díaz Martínez, October 25, 1859, AHA, Sección Arzobispado, "Relativo al presbítero Rafael Díaz Martínez, 1859," caja 99, exp. 28, fols. 1–3v. Also see Mexico City, *El Monitor Republicano*, October 7, 1861, p. 1, cols. 3–4, and p. 2, col. 1. If the liberals did pay Díaz Martínez and other priests, it was very little; when the priest fell ill, his mother petitioned the government for funds for his relief, citing his efforts as head of the Constitutional Clergy, see Mexico City, Guadalupe Martínez de Díaz to President Juárez, July 26, 1861, AGN-México, Gobernación, leg.'1153 (1), caja 1389, exp. 23, fol. 6. Melchor Ocampo noted to Díaz Martínez that given the import of church and state separation, he could offer him only the satisfaction of his own conscience and the esteem of the *gente sensata* (reasonable people), see Veracruz, Melchor Ocampo to Rafael Díaz Martínez, October 25, 1859, AHA, Sección Arzobispado, "Relativo al presbiterio Rafael Díaz Martínez, 1859," caja 99, exp. 28, fol. 3v.

52. Mexico City, Justino Fernández to Ministro de Justicia, January 24, 1861, and Mexico City, Ramírez to S. Gobernador del Distrito Federal, January 29, 1861, AGN-México, Gobernación, leg. 1153 (1), caja 1389, exp. 4, no. 43. Mexico City, 29 January 1861, Gobernación, leg. 1153 (2), caja 1390, exp. 13, fols. 1–4v. Mexico City, *La Reforma*, January 20, 1861, p. 2, col. 4. Mexico City, *El Siglo Diez y Nueve*, January 19, 1861, p. 3, col. 1. Meticulous chronicler José Ramón Malo reported on March 1, 1861, that the Bethlehemites' church was also granted to the "apostate clergy"; see his *Diario de sucesos notables (1854-1864)*, ed. Mariano Cuevas, vol. 2 (México: Editorial Patria, 1948), 601.

53. Mexico City, *El Pájaro Verde*, January 24, 1861, p. 2, col. 4. Mexico City, *El Pájaro Verde*, February 9, 1861, p. 2, col. 5. Historian Erica Pani reports that the *Pájaro Verde* got its start up money from the bishop of Michoacan, Monsignor Clemente de Jesus Munguía; see her *Para mexicanizar el Segundo Imperio. El imaginario político de los imperialistas* (México: Colegio de México and Instituto Mora, 2001), 177, fn. 308.

54. Mexico City, February 7, 1861, Archivo Histórico de la Mitra, Actas de Cabildo, libro 87, fol. 11.

55. Mexico City, *El Monitor Republicano*, February 13, 1861, p. 3, col. 4. Constitutional cleric Juan Nepomuceno Enríquez Orestes later reported that the men outside the churches were ex-Mercedarian fathers who informed the faithful that the Constitutional Clergy were "American Jews and Protestants," and ex-communicated, see Mexico City, *El Monitor Republicano*, October 14, 1861, p. 2, cols. 3–4.

56. Mexico City, *El Pájaro Verde*, May 2, 1861, p. 3, col. 1.

57. Mexico City, February 23, 1861, *El Siglo Diez y Nueve*, p. 3, col. 5. Mexico City, *El Movimiento*, February 23, 1861, p. 3, cols. 1–2. Mexico City, *El Movimiento*, February 25, 1861, p. 3, col. 5. Mexico City, *El Monitor Republicano*, February 24, 1861, p. 3, cols. 2, 3. Mexico City, *El Pájaro Verde*, February 23, 1861, no. 43, p. 3, col. 4. News of the exchange of pasquinades in Mexico City reached the provinces, see, for example, Durango, José Y. Gallegos to Francisco Zarco, March 15, 1861, AGN-MEXICO, Gobernación, leg. 1153, caja 1389, exp. 5, no. 13, fols. 1–3v.

58. Brian Hamnett, *Juárez* (New York, NY: Longman, 1994), 112. Archbishop Garza y Ballesteros was expelled on January 17, 1861, along with four colleagues. They were given three days to leave the country.

59. *Suplemento manifestación*, 18, 25–26.

60. Mexico City, *El Pájaro Verde*, May 13, 1861. no. 57, p. 1, col. 1. Mexico City, *El Pájaro Verde*, May 14, 1861, no. 58, p. 2, col. 5. Mexico City, *El Pájaro Verde*, 15 May 1861, p. 2, col. 3. Mexico City, *El Pájaro Verde*, May 17, 1861, num. 61, p. 2, cols. 4–6.

61. José Ramón Malo, May 2, 1861, *Diario de sucesos*, 612. Mexico City, October 10, 1861, *La Unidad Católica*, p. 1, cols. 1–2. Mexico City, October 22, 1861, *La Unidad Católica*, p. 2, col. 4. Mexico City, Juan Nepomuceno Enríquez Orestes, Juan Francisco Domínguez, Manuel Aguilar, Manuel Estrada, Cristóbal González Ríos, October 5, 1861, *El Monitor Republicano*, p. 1, cols. 4–6, p. 2, cols. 1–2.

62. For example, red and green crosses mysteriously painted on doors and windows on the eve of the anniversary of the April 11, 1858, conservative massacre of liberal soldiers and civilians at Tacubaya inspired the Liberal press to wonder if the Liberal Reform Club planned to butcher "the reactionaries," or whether, instead, the symbols were left by conservatives who planned to slaughter liberals. Perhaps, the press mused, the crosses were just an adolescent prank. Mexico City, April 10, 1861, *El Siglo Diez y Nueve*, p. 3, col. 3. Mexico City, April 10, 1861, *La Orquesta*, tomo 1, no. 12, p. 2, col. 3. On the Saint Bartholomew's Day Massacre, see Barbara B. Diefendorf, *Beneath the Cross: Catholics and Huguenots in Sixteenth-Century Paris* (New York, NY: Oxford University Press, 1991), 93.

63. Mexico City, February 22, 1861, *El Pájaro Verde*, no. 15, p. 1 col. 4.

64. Mexico City, January 1861, "Decretos y circulares del Gobierno del Distrito de México," AGN-México, Gobernación s/s, caja 482, exps. 6, 18. Mexico City, January 11, 1861, *El Pájaro Verde*, no. 6, p. 2, col. 4. Also see, Mexico City, September 6, 1862, AGN-México, Gobernación, sec. primera, 1862, caja 25, exp. 59.

65. Mexico City, Juan N. Enríquez Orestes in *El Constitucional*, October 26, 1861, p. 1, col. 3.

66. Mexico City, Juan N. Enríquez Orestes in *El Monitor Republicano*, December 10, 1861, no. 4139, p. 2, cols. 2–3.

67. Mexico City, *El Pájaro Verde*, February 6, 1861, no. 28, p. 1. Responding to an earlier editorial on the Eucharist that had appeared in *El Pájaro Verde*, George M. Mathews, the British Chargé d'Affaires in Mexico City, wrote to Francisco Zarco explaining that the paper went too far and that he had never seen the Eucharist appear publicly in Rome; see Jalapa, George M. Mathews to Francisco Zarco, February 1, 1861, in Lilia Díaz ed. and trans., *Versión francesa de México. Informes diplomáticos, 1858-1862* (México: Colegio de México, 1964), 212.

68. Mexico City, *La Unidad Católica*, May 10, 1861, p. 3, col. 5.

69. Mexico City, Señoras de la parroquia de S. Miguel to señor Presidente, January 1861, AGN-Mexico, Gobernación, Leg. 1153 (1), caja 1389, exp. 4, no. 2, fols. 1–1v. México City, Orden del Gobierno del Distrito, January 31, 1861, AGN-México, Gobernación, leg. 1153 (2), caja 1390, exp. 13, fol. 2v. México City, Miguel Blanco to Ministro de Gobernación, February 4, 1861, AGN-México, Gobernación, leg. 1153, caja 1389, exp. 1, fol. 3. Mexico City, *El Pájaro Verde*, February 8,1861, no. 30, p. 2, col. 6. José Ramón Malo, *Diario de sucesos*, 595–596. Mexico City, *Trait d'Union*, March 11, 1861, p. 1, col. 4.

70. José Ramón Malo, *Diario de sucesos*, 593.

71. Mexico City, *El Siglo Diez y Nueve*, February 11, 1861, tomo 1, no. 28, p. 3, col. 3

72. Mexico City, "Protestan las mujeres contra la venta de los bienes del clero," *El Monitor Republicano*, October 24, 1856, p. 1, col. 1. Mexico City , "La representación de las señoras," *El Monitor Republicano*, July 21, 1856, p. 1, col. 1. Richard Sinkin, *The Mexican Reform, 1856-1876* (Austin, TX: Institute of Latin American Studies, 1979), 139. Silvia Arrom, *The Women*, 42–43. Mexico City, *El Monitor Republicano*, July 6, 1856, num. 3.235, p. 4, col. 4. Mexico City, "Las Mexicanistas vueltas bloomeristas," *El Monitor Republicano*, July 21, 1856, p. 3, cols. 2–4. *Representación que las señoras de Guadalajara dirigen al soberano Congreso Constituyente sobre que en la carta fundamental que se discute, no quede consignada la tolerancia de cultos en la república* (Guadalajara, JA: Tipografía de Rodríguez, 1856).

73. Morelia, "Representación de muchas señoras de Morelia pidiendo se deje en libertad al obispo de aquella diócesis para volver a ella," to Ministro de Justicia y Negocios Eclesiásticos, September 26, 1856, A.G.N, Justicia Eclesiástica, vol. 179, fol. 481.

74. Mexico City, "Protestan las mujeres contra la venta de los bienes del clero," *El Monitor Republicano*, October 24, 1856, p. 1, col. 1. Mexico City, "La representación de las señoras," *El Monitor Republicano*, July 21, 1856, p. 1. Sinkin, *Mexican Reform*, 139; Arrom, *Women*, 42–43.

75. Sayula, *El Boletín del Ejército Federal*, August 11, 1858, num. 14, p. 1, cols. 2–3.

76. Ignacio Ramírez and Guillermo Prieto, August 16, 1861, in Guillermo Prieto, *Obras Completas XXIII. Periodismo político y social*, vol. 3, ed. Boris Rosen Jelomer (México: Consejo Nacional para la Cultura y las Artes, 1997), 332.

77. Margaret Chowning, "Liberals, Women, and the Church in Mexico: Politics and the Feminization of Piety, 1700-1930," unpublished paper delivered to the Harvard Latin American Studies Seminar, 2002, 3–4

78. Mexico City, Darío Balandro to Editors of *El Monitor Republicano*, September 3, 1861, *El Monitor Republicano*, no. 4041, p. 3, cols. 3–4.

79. Guillermo Prieto, "La fiesta de todos santos," in *Obras completas*, 4:321–323.

80. Guadalajara, *Boletín del Ejército Federal*, November 19, 1858, no. 29, p. 1, col. 2.

81. Ignacio Ramírez and Guillermo Prieto, August 16, 1861, Prieto, *Obras Completas*, vol. 3, 332.

82. Mexico City, *El Monitor Republicano*, October 14, 1861, p. 2, cols. 3–4.

83. Mexico City, *La Unidad Católica*, May 29, 1861, p. 1, cols. 1–3. Although they were wrong about the Mexican Constitutional Clergy's origins, the parallel with the French Constitutional Clergy was an apt one. Historian Timothy Tackett reports that for most of these French clerics the stock reasons for swearing the oath to the 1791 Constitution were that it returned the primitive spirit of the church and was consistent with the church councils. See Timothy Tackett, *Religion, Revolution*, , especially 13, 69, 71. The parallel between the French and Mexican Constitutional Clergy was not lost on Mexico City's liberal French language newspaper, *Le Trait d'Union: Journal Français Universal*, who ran a February 12, 1861, editorial lauding the efforts of both groups; see p. 2, col. 2. Jacqueline Covo reports that in 1855, roughly two thousand French nationals in Mexico read the paper, which regularly published a thousand copies; see Jacqueline Covo, "*Le Trait D'Union*, periódico frances de la Ciudad de México, entre la Reforma y la Intervención," *Historia Mexicana* 35, no. 3 (January–March 1986), 464.

84. José Ramón Malo, April 1, 1861, *Diario de sucesos*, 609.

85. San Cristóbal de las Casas, Chiapas, March 7, 1861, [?] to Minister of Justice and Public Instruction, AGN-México, Gobernación, leg. 1153 (1), caja 1389, exp. 10, fol. 1.

86. Mexico City, *La Unidad Católica*, November 27, 1861, p. 3, col. 1. This report was reprinted from *La Tijera de San Cristóbal de las Casas*.

87. Mexico City, *La Unidad Católica*, December 16, 1861, no. 180, p. 1, cols. 1–3. *La Unidad Católica* reported roughly ten Constitutional Clergy operating in the states of Oaxaca, Jalisco, and Zacatecas. For other reports of the activities of the reformed clergy in these states and others, see, for example, Mexico City, *El Pájaro Verde*, May 13, 1861, no. 57, p. 1, col. 1. Mexico City, *El Pájaro Verde*, July 18, 1863, p. 3, cols. 4–5. Mexico City, *El Pájaro Verde*, May 2, 1861, p. 1, col. 1. José Ramón Malo, *Diario de sucesos*, p. 612. Mexico City, *El Siglo Diez y Nueve*, February 12, 1857, no. 3.043, p. 2, col. 1. Mexico City, "Los curas en el estado de México," *El Monitor Republicano*, March 16, 1862, no. 4235, p. 3, col. 3. Mexico City, *El Monitor Republicano*, March 22, 1862, no. 4241, p. 1, cols. 1–6 and p. 2, cols. 1–2. On Padre Guevara in Puebla, see Mexico City, *El Monitor Republicano*, May 22, 1862, no. 4302, p. 1, cols. 1–6, and p. 2, cols. 1–4. Mexico City, "Iglesia mexicana," *El Heraldo*, June 13, 1861, p. 3, col. 3. A clerical supporter of the 1857 Constitution, Ignacio Hernández from Tampico, noted that the church "did not need treasure to comply with its pious obligations," cited in Alfonso Toro, *La iglesia y el estado en México* (México: Talleres Gráficos de la Nación, 1927), 262. Many of the clergy who disobeyed the bishops' instructions to deny the sacraments to those who swore the oath to the 1857 Constitution were suspended; see Walter V. Scholes, "A Revolution Falters: Mexico, 1856–1857," *Hispanic American Historical Review* 32, no. 1 (February 1952): 19, n. 56. More priests resisted the Constitution of 1857 than supported it, of course; for some vivid examples of their opposition see Ricker, "The Lower," 316–319. On clerical opposition to the Reform program more generally, see Robert J. Knowlton, "Clerical Response to the Mexican Reform, 1855-1875," *Catholic Historical Review* 50, no. 4 (January 1965): 509–529; and Robert J. Knowlton, "Some Practical Effects of Clerical Opposition to the Mexican Reform, 1856-1860," *Hispanic American*

Historical Review 45, no. 2 (May 1965): 246–257. Even this obvious undercount of 100 clerics loyal to the 1857 Constitution should be kept in perspective as a proportion of the total clerical ranks in the country at the time: José María Pérez Hernández estimated 1,717 secular and 1,472 regular clergy in Reform-era Mexico; Pérez Hernández, *Estadística de la República Mejicana* (Guadalajara, JA.: Tipografía del Gobierno, 1862), 248. Richard Sinkin reports that in 1850 Mexico had 3,182 secular clergy and 1,193 regular clergy; Sinkin, *Mexican Reform*, 118. In 1856, Miguel Lerdo de Tejada reported 3,320 secular clergy and 1,295 regulars, as well as 1,484 female religious whose convents housed 533 young women and 1,266 maids; see his *Cuadro sinóptico de la república mexicana en 1856, formado en vista de los últimos datos oficiales y otras noticias fidedignas* (México: Ignacio Cumplido, 1856), 80.

88. D. José M. Vigil, *México a través de los siglos*. Vol. 5, *La Reforma*, ed. Vicente Riva Palacio (Barcelona, ES: Espasa y Compania), 477. José Ramón Malo, *Diario de sucesos*, 619. Justo Sierra, *Juárez. Su obra y su tiempo*, ed. Arturo Arnáiz y Freg (Mexico: UNAM, 1972), 282. Melchor Ocampo was killed on June 3, 1861. For more on the politics of printing during the long nineteenth century, see Corrina Zeltsman, *Ink under the Fingernails. Printing Politics in Nineteenth-Century Mexico* (Berkeley, CA: University of California Press, 2021).

89. Mexico City, "Que haremos por el papa," *La Unidad Católica*, December 27, 1861, no. 190, p. 1. Mexico City, Lazo Estrada to President of City Council, December 28, 1861, AHCM, Jurados de Imprenta, 1829 a 1868, vol. 2740, exp. 48, fols. 1, 2, 4 and 6. When Baz, as an official representative of the president, had tried to enter the cathedral during Holy Week in 1857 to demonstrate the nation's patronage over the church, he was met by a humble choirboy who refused him entry; Sinkin, *Mexican Reform*, 135.

90. Mexico City, *La Orquesta*, January 2, 1862, No. 34, p. 2.

91. Mexico City, *El Monitor Republicano*, March 26, 1862, no. 4245, p. 1, col. 4. Mexico City, *El Monitor Republicano*, April 6, 1862, no. 4255, p. 1, cols. 1–6 and p. 2, cols. 1–2. In an act reminiscent of disputes in El Salvador circa 1825, the Jacala city council had gone over the bishop's head to petition the government in 1856 to name Enríquez Orestes as their priest. Less than a year before, this liberal stronghold in Hidalgo had issued its *Acta de Jacala*, which adumbrated the Reform Laws and which historian Jesús Reyes Heroles later dubbed "the most complete document of its type for Mexican liberalism." Jacala, "El ayuntamiento de Jacala pide se nombre para aquel curato al Br. Juan N. Enríquez Orestes," December 6, 1856, AGN-México, Justicia Eclesiástica, vol. 179, fols. 427–428v. Jesús Reyes Heroles cited in Ana Lau Jaiven and Ximena Sepúlveda Otaiza, *Hidalgo, una historia compartida* (México: Instituto de Investigaciones Dr. José María Luis Mora, 1994), 136.

92. Veracruz, October 25, 1859, Secretaria del Estado y del Despacho de Gobernación, "Se nombra agente general,"79–83. Also see Mexico City, *El Monitor Republicano*, October 7, 1861, p. 1, cols. 3–4 and p. 2, col. 1.

93. Mexico City, Juan N. Enríquez, "Editorial: clerigos constitucionales reformistas. Celibato y matrimonio eclesiástico," *El Monitor Republicano*, November 28, 1861, num. 4127. Mexico City, *El Monitor Republicano*, December 13, 1861, no. 4142, p. 1 cols. 1–6. Under Juan N. Enríquez Orestes' leadership, the Constitutional Clergy's rhetorical flash lit up the headlines of the *Monitor Republicano*. No stranger to controversy, as a parish priest and later as a St. Vicent de Paul mission preacher in Zimapán, Enríquez Orestes had incurred the wrath of both the brothers and his own superiors Archbishop Lazaro de la Garza y Ballesteros and Bishop of Linares Francisco de Paula Verea. These run-ins, he felt, sprang from the hierarchy's aversion to his simple sermons on the scriptural truths of equality and fraternity—sermons that won him a loyal following of liberals in Tulancingo, Zimapán, Jacala, Alfajayucan, and Mineral del

Monte. See, for example, Mexico City, *El Monitor Republicano*, March 26, 1862, no. 4245, p. 1, col. 4. Mexico City, *El Monitor Republicano*, April 6, 1862, no. 4255, p. 1, cols. 1–6, and p. 2, cols. 1–2. Mexico City, *La Unidad Católica*, December 24, 1861, p. 1 cols. 1–4.

94. Mexico City, Juan N. Enríquez, "Editorial: clerigos constitucionales reformistas. Celibato y matrimonio eclesiástico," *El Monitor Republicano*, November 28, 1861, num. 4127. Mexico City, *El Monitor Republicano*, December 13, 1861, no. 4142, p. 1, cols. 1–6.

95. Mexico City, "Editorial: El celibato eclesiástico y los clerigos llamados constitucionales," *La Unidad Católica*, December 24, 1861, p.1, cols. 1–4.

96. Nicolás Pizarro, *El Monedero* (México: Imprenta de Nicolás Pizarro, 1861), 226–227. Novelist and pamphleteer Nicolás Pizarro Suárez (1830–1895) worked in public administration in the early 1850s and for the Ministry of Justice under the Liberal Party in Veracruz; see Carlos Illades and Adriana Sandovál, *Espacio social y representación literaria en el siglo XIX* (México: Plaza y Valdés Editores: Universidad Autónoma Metropolitana, Unidad Iztapalapa, 2000), 16. Erika Pani also underscores the important of *caridad* to Pizarro's social vision in *El Modedero*; see her "Para halagar la imaginación': Las repúblicas de Nicolás Pizarro," in *El republicanismo en Hispanoamérica. Ensayos de historia intelectual y política*, ed. José Antonio Aguilar and Rafael Rojas (México: Centro de Investigación y Docena Económicas and Fondo de Cultura Económica, 2002), 424–446, especially 436, 439–440, 444–445. For more on Pizarro Suárez, see Luis Reyes de la Maza, "Nicolás Pizarro, novelista y pensador liberal," *Historia Mexicana* 6, no. 4 (April/June 1957): 572–588.

97. Pizarro, *El Monedero*, 122–123, 377, 588.

98. Tampico, Governor Juan José de la Garza Edict, April 1, 1861, AD-IIH-UAT, Decretos 1851–1929, Decreto no. 10. Ciudad Victoria, *El Rifle de Tamaulipas. Periódico Político y Literario. Segunda Época*, April 20. 1861, p. 1, col. 2. Mexico City, *La Unidad Católica*, May 28, 1861, p. 3, col. 1.

99. Santa Bárbara de Tamaulipas, Ramón Lozano to *El Rifle de Tamaulipas*, June 6, 1861, *printed in Ciudad Victoria, El Rifle de Tamaulipas. Periódico Político y Literario. Segunda Época*, June 22, 1861, p. 2, cols. 1–2. *La Unidad Católica* ran Bishop Verea's suspension of Ramón Lozano; see June 24, 1861, p. 3, cols. 4–5, and p. 5, cols. 1–2.

100. Santa Bárbara de Tamaulipas, Ramón Lozano to *El Rifle de Tamaulipas*, June 6, 1861, printed in Ciudad Victoria, *El Rifle de Tamaulipas. Periódico Político y Literario. Segunda Época*, June 22, 1861, p. 2, cols. 1–2.

101. Santa Bárbara de Tamaulipas, May 12, 1861, APSBM, Ocampo, Tamaulipas (formerly Santa Barbara, Tamaulipas), Libro de Bautismos de 1854-1862, fol. 245. In June of 1861, the bishop of Guadalajara reported that Lozano had declared canonical laws that contravened reform laws invalid, declared himself pope, and refused to recognize Bishop Francisco de Paula y Veréa's authority unless he respected reform laws; see New York, Pedro Obispo de Guadalajara to Sn. Dr. Lazaro de la Garza, June 29, 1861, AHA, Serie Correspondencia, caja 103, exp. 18, fols. 1–6.

102. Mexico City, *El Siglo Diez y Nueve*, June 23, 1861, p. 3, cols. 3–4. Mexico City, *El Heraldo*, June 4, 1861, p. 3, cols. 2–4. Mexico City, *La Unidad Católica*, June 15, 1861, p. 3, col. 4; June 18, p. 1, cols. 3–5. Bishop Francisco de Paula y Verea urged the faithful to not swear the oath to the 1857 Constitution and to resist the state's encroachment on church prerogatives; see, for example, Monterrey, Teran to Ministro de Justicia, July 24, 1857, AGN-México, Justicia Eclesiástica, vol. 181, Ramo Indiferente, exp. 78, fols. 266–267. Monterrey, Francisco de Paula to Ministro de Justicia y Negocios Eclesiásticos, May 16, 1857, "Protesta del Sr. obispo de Linares contra la ley de obvenciones parroquiales," AGN-México, Justicia Eclesiástica, vol. 183, fol. 355.

Monterrey, Francisco de Paula to Ministro de Justicia y Negocios Eclesiásticos, December 29, 1856, AGN-México, Justicia Eclesiástica, vol. 183, fol. 385.

103. Monterrey, June 20, 1861, Circular of the Gobierno Eclesiástico del Obispado de Monterrey, AD-IIH-UAT, sin clasificación.

104. Narciso Villarreal, *Cuatro palabras al presbítero D. Ramón Lozano, cura propio de Santa Bárbara, para que no descanse tranquilo en sus errores* (24 July, 1861) (Monterrey, México: Imprenta de A. Mier, 1861), 4, 7, 10, 13.

105. Santa Bárbara de Tamaulipas, May 12, 1861, APSBM, Ocampo, Tamaulipas, Libro de Bautismos de 1854-1862, fol. 245. On July 31, 1861, a new parish priest begins to record baptisms in the parish's record book. This parish holds parish record books but is not a formal archive.

106. Ramón Lozano, *Contestación á las cuatro palabras del cura de Monclova, D. Narciso Villareal* (Ciudad Victoria: Imprenta de Sebastián Perrillos, 1861), 1.

107. Taxco, Juan de Oehla to Ministro de Justicia, September 7, 1858, AGN-México, Justicia Eclesiástica, tomo 146, fols. 126–131. Mexico City, *El Monitor Republicano*, August 28, 1861, no. 4035, p. 3, cols. 2–3. On Gómez' secularization from the Dominicans in Queretaro, see Queretero, José María Encinos to Consejo del Gobierno, June 13, 1850, AGN-México, Justicia Eclesiástica, vol. 171, fol. 158.

108. Tehuacán, General José Maria Cobos Report, February 4, 1860, AGN-México, Justicia Eclesiástica, tomo 146, fols. 447–449. Tacuba, [?] to Ministro de Justicia, October 29, 1859, AGN-México, Ministerio de Justicia, Negocios Eclesiásticos, y Instrucción Pública, AGN-México, Justicia Eclesiástica, Tomo 19, fols. 341–342. Puebla, "Sobre el conducta observada por el Presb. D. José Joaquín de Herrera," 19 September 1859, Ministerio de Justicia, Negocios Eclesiásticos, y Instrucción Pública, AGN-Mexico, Justicia Eclesiástica, Tomo 19, pp. 311–319; 321–322. On May 13, 1861, the *Pájaro Verde* listed Manuel Gómez and two other Taxco priests as Constitutional Clergy; José Joaquín de Herrera from the Puebla area also appeared on their list, see p. 1, col. 1

109. Francisco P. Campa, *Protesta y retracción del presb. Francisco de P. Campa ante su dignísimo prelado el Illmo. Sr. Dr. D. Francisco de P. Verea, obispo de la diócesis de Linares* (Guadalajara, JA: Imprenta de Rodríguez, 1857), 2. Conservative works disputing Enríquez Ortes' views include *Gran ascención aereostática del presbítero ciudadano Francisco de P. Campa en busca del Espíritu Santo; para que concurra á los juzgados de la República* (Guadalajara, JA.: Imprenta de Dionisio Rodriguez, 1857); and José María P. del Arbol, *Una carta dirigida al P. Campa* (Guadalajara, México: Imprenta de Dionisio Rodriguez, 1857). José Gutierrez Casillas lists priests who supported the ecclesiastical desmortization as well as those who acted as chaplains in the liberal army, including one Ignacio Traspea, who ran with a band who profaned churches, see his *Historia de la iglesia en México* (Mexico: Editorial Porrúa, 1974), 308–310.

110. Mexico City, "El pres. don Vicente Guevara pide se le satisfagan sus sueldos como capellan del 6 batallon de Linea," November 16, 1857, AGN-México, Justicia Eclesiatica, vol. 182, fol. 194. Mexico City, Ministro de Hacienda to Ministro de Justicia, November 19, 1856, AGN-México, Justicia Eclesiástica, vol. 182, fol. 196. Mexico City, *El Monitor Republicano*, May 22, 1862, no. 4302, p. 1, cols. 2–3. On Guevara's press interventions, see, José Rámon Malo, September 9, 1861, *Diario de sucesos*, p. 641.

111. Zacatecas, Jesús Valdez and [?] Zamora to Señor Ministro de Justicia, "El Gobierno de Zacatecas, avisa que el Obispo de Guadalajara trata de separar al cura de aquella ciudad por no haber este cumplido con sus instrucciones respeto de la ley de desamortización," November 26, 1856, AGN-México, Justicia Eclesiástica, vol. 179, fols. 457–458v. The bishop of Guadalajara

suspended parish priest Ramón Valenzuela for ministering to a liberal batallion fighting the "reactionaries" of San Luis Potosí, see Zacatecas, Ramon Valenzuela to Zamora, February 28, 1857, AGN-México, Justicia Eclesiástica, Tomo 181, Exp.11, fols. 458v–459.

112. New York City, October–November 1864, Declaration of Rev. Orestes to Rev. Doctor Cove and Reverend Smith, AEC, National Council RG 73: (Domestic and Foreign Missionary Society)—Mexico Records, 1864–1952, Miscellaneous, 1864–1879, RG 73-15, fol. 1.

113. New Orleans, October 17, 1864, Elijah Guion, Daniel Shaves and A. Vallas to the Bishops, Clergy and Laity of the Protestant Episcopal Church in the United States, AEC, RG 73: Nacional Council (Domestic and Foreign Missionary Society)—Mexico Records, 1864–1952, Miscellaneous, 1864–1879, RG 73-15, fol. 1.

114. Cleveland, Ohio, E. C. Nicholson to S. Dennison, May 1, 1865, AEC, RG 73: Nacional Council (Domestic and Foreign Missionary Society)—Mexico Records, 1864–1952, Miscellaneous, 1864–1879, RG 73-7, E.C. Nicholson Papers, 1864–5, fols. 13–13v, 15.

115. José Miguel Barragán Sánchez, "Pequeño diario portátil 1864. Memorias de un guerrillero durante la intervención francesa," *Archivos de Historia Potosina* 3, no. 8 (January–March 1977): 237. He records that he was in Ciudad Victoria on July 5, 1864.

116. Mexico City, *El Monitor Republicano*, October 7, 1861, p. 1, col. 1. *La Unidad Católica* shredded these men's pretensions to poverty, claiming that in his capacity as an inspector of seized ecclesiastical property Enríquez Orestes obtained the best ornaments and sacred vessels of the entire inventory of La Merced, see Mexico City, *La Unidad Católica*, August 9, 1861, p. 2, col. 4.

117. Mexico CityFrancisco Zarco in *Siglo Diez y Nueve*, June 22, 1861, p. 1, col. 1.

118. Nicolás Pizarro, *La coqueta* (México: Imprenta de Ana Echeverría de Pizarro e Hijas, 1861), 74.

119. Cuartel General en el Hospital de Belén de Guadalajara, *Boletín del Ejército Federal*, October 19, 1858,no. 25, p. 2, cols. 1–3.

120. Enrique Krauze, *Mexico*, 157. Justo Sierra, *Juárez*, 288.

121. Mexico City, *El Monitor Republicano*, August 13, 1862, p. 3, cols. 4–5.

122. Colima, Santos Degollado, "Proclama que el general Degollado dirigió al Ejército Federal con fecha 30 de Marzo de 1858," in Torre Villar, ed., *El Triunfo*, 56–57.

123. Santos Degollado, "Proclama que el general Degollado expidió a los vecinos de la Ciudad de México, el 21 de marzo de 1859" in Torre Villar, ed., *El Triunfo*, 91.

124. Krauze, *Mexico*, 170.

125. Florencia Mallon, *Peasant and Nation: The Making of Postcolonial Mexico and Peru* (Berkeley, CA.: University of California Press, 1995), 93–94. The liberals' stance on local religious rituals was more complicated than unmitigated opposition. They knew that discretion was the better part of valor in the campaign against popular religion. As the federal army's bulletin put it in an 1858 discussion of that year's Virgin of Guadalupe festivities: although we know that "religion loses nothing without fireworks and bell pealing," if we seek to curb these practices "later people murmur that the liberals are to blame and that the heretical government has prohibited a manifestation of reverence." Some liberals did appreciate popular religion as a basis of national folklore. In his insightful work on liberal intellectual Ignacio Manuel Altamirano's 1880s sketches of customs and manners (*cuadros costumbristas*), historian Edward N. Wright-Rios argues that he regarded rural Indian religious festivals "as showcases of authentic Mexicaness." See in this order: Mexico City, *El Monitor Republicano*, June 9, 1862, p. 1, cols. 1–6 and pg. 2, col. 5. Mexico City, *El Monitor Repubicano*, July 10, 1861, no. 3986, p. 1, cols. 5–6, p. 2, cols. 1–3. See also Mexico City, *Siglo Diez y Nueve*, June 15, 1861, no. 152, p.3,

col.3. Guadalajara, *Boletín del Ejército Federal*, December 13, 1858, no. 38, p. 2, col. 4. Edward Wright-Rios, "Indian Saints and Nation-States: Ignacio Manuel Altamirano's Landscapes and Legends" *Mexican Studies/Estudios Mexicanos* 20, no. 1 (winter 2004): 2, 12. Guillermo Prieto, "La fiesta de todos santos," in *Obras Completas*, vol. 4, 321–323.

126. Mexico City, *El Monitor Republicano*, June 9, 1862, p. 1, col. 6.

127. Ciudad Victoria, "Respuesta que los católicos de Ciudad Victoria dan a los avisos que desde Monterrey les dirige el padre d. José María Hinojosa," January 15, 1864, AEC, RG 73: Nacional Council (Domestic and Foreign Missionary Society)—Mexico Records, 1864–1952, Miscellaneous, 1864–1879, RG 73-15, fol. 1.

128. Santa Bárbara de Tamaulipas, Ramón Lozano and Benigno el Valdes (and signed by 500 or so others) to Jefatura Político y Militar, April 3, 1864, original in Archivo Histórico, Municipalidad de Miquihuana, Tamaulipas, Caja 3, fols. 1–4; I thank Juan Díaz Rodríguez, head of the historical collection of the AD-IIH-UAT in Ciudad Victoria, for providing me with a copy of this document. Also see, Ramón Lozano to D. Pedro José Méndez, June 9, 1865, in *Documentos relacionados con la vida militar, política, y familiar de Gral. don Pedro José Méndez*, vol. 2 (Ciudad Victoria: Talleres Linotipograficos del Gobierno del Estado, 1966), 29. On the central place of indigenous peoples to racialized notions of civilization and citizenship in nineteenth-century Mexico, see, for example, María Josefina Saldaña-Portillo, *Indian Given. Racial Geographies Across Mexico and the United States* (Durham, NC: Duke University Press, 2016).

129. Santa Bárbara, May 23, 1865, Ramón Lozano to señor Teofilo Ramírez, in Ciudad Victoria, *Boletín de Campana*, May 31, 1865, p. 2v, col. 2.

130. Joaquín Meade, *La Huasteca tamaulipeca, tomo 2* (Ciudad Victoria: IIH-UAT, 1978), 69. Ciudad Victoria, June 4, 1870, *La Reconstrucción. Periódico Oficial del Gobierno del Estado de Tamaulipas*, p. 2, cols. 2–4, and p. 3, col. 1. Ciudad Victoria, *La Reconstrucción. Periódico Oficial del Gobierno del Estado de Tamaulipas*, January 21, 1871, p. 4, cols. 2–3. Ciudad Victoria, *Seminario de los Debates del Congreso de Tamaulipas*, September 17, 1871, pp. 2–3.

131. Guillermo Prieto, "Oración cívica pronunciado por el ciudadano Guillermo Prieto en la alameda de México, el día 16 de septiembre de 1855," in *Obras Completas*, vol. 4, p. 5.

132. Nicolás Pizarro, *La libertad en el orden. Ensayo sobre derecho puúlico en que se resuelven algunas de las más vitales cuestiones que se agitan en México desde su independencia* (Mexico: Imprenta de Ana Echeverría de Pizarro e Hijas 1855), 9.

133. Nicolás Pizarro, *Catecismo político*, 94.

134. Ignacio Ramírez, "Discurso cívico pronunciado el 16 de septiembre de 1861 en la alameda de México, en memoria de la proclamación de la Independencia," in *Obras de Ignacio Ramírez*, vol. 1, ed. Ignacio M. Altamirano (México: Editora Nacional, 1960), 131.

CONCLUSION

1. Scheper Hughes, *The Church*, 7–8. Guillermo Bonfil Batalla, *México Profundo: Reclaiming a Civilization* (Austin, Tx: University of Texas Press, 1996).

2. Julio César Pinto Soria, "Los religiosidades indígenas y el estado nación en Guatemala (1800-1850)," in *Religiosidad y clero en América Latina: La época de las revoluciones Atlánticas. Religiosity and Clergy in Latin America (1767-1850): The Age of Atlantic Revolutions*, ed. Sebastian Dorsch, Peer Schmidt, and Hedwig Herold-Schmidt (Cologne, DE: Böhlau Verlag, 2011) 316–318. Sullivan Gonzalez, *Piety*, 8.

3. My understanding of the import of religious proclivities to imperialist or elitist delineations of what constitutes civilization vs. barbarism draws on Lorgia García Peña's discussion of

the United States' marines' criminalization of Dominican Blackness, in part through demonization of Afro-religious rituals of possession and Afro-diasporic Catholic saints cults organized through confraternities; see her *The Borders of Dominicanidad. Race, Nation, and Archives of Contradiction* (Durham, NC: Duke University Press, 2016), 56–92. Also see Ivonne del Valle, "A New Moses," 47–73, especially 47–48; Del Valle notes that the core self-understanding of the Christian West "consisted of the myth of a civilization born with monotheism and the abandonment of paganism and idolatry, elements of a rejected past but which, at the moment of the encounter with societies that followed different models of civilization, becomes reactivated and globalized in the form of a presumed 'natural law' applicable to all human groups," 47. Also see Aimée Césaire, *Discourse on Colonialism* (New York, NY: Monthly Review Press, 2001 [original 1950],). Many scholarly explanations of measures of social status and hierarchy in Latin America's colonial period argue for a process of secularization whereby religious categories like *limpieza de sangre* are eclipsed by phenotype and class as the most salient markers of status by the late eighteenth century. See, for example, Martínez, *Geneological Fictions*; and Stuart B. Schwartz, *Blood and Boundaries. The Limits of Religious and Racial Exclusion in Early Modern Latin America* (Waltham, MA: Brandeis University Press, 2020). For God and Liberty argues that religious categories changed significantly by the late eighteenth century rather than simply faded away but remained salient markers of identity.

4. Alejandro Marure. *Memoria sobre la insurrección de Santa Rosa y Mataquescuintla en Centro-América, comparada con la que estalló en Francia, el año de 1790, en los departamentos de la Vendée, etc.* (n.p., 1838), 8, 9, 12.

5. Christopher Clark, "The New Catholicism and the European Culture Wars," *Culture Wars: Secular-Catholic Conflict in Nineteenth-Century Europe, ed. Christopher Clark and Wolfram Kaiser* (New York, NY: Cambridge University Press, 2003), 11. Given the long history of indigenous control of access to the sacred, and of a distinctly localcentric and rural Catholicism in Mexico and Central America the relationship between elite ultramontanism and the popular classes could also be tenuous or even antagonistic. Brian A. Stauffer provides a cautionary tale of assuming ultramontane and popular Catholic alliance rather than antagonism or cooptation; see his *Victory on Earth as in Heaven: Mexico's Religionero Rebellion* (Albuquerque, NM: University of New Mexico Press, 2019), passim. Also see Austen Ivereigh, ed. and intro., *The Politics of Religion in an Age of Revival. Studies in Nineteenth Century Europe and Latin America* (London: Institute of Latin American Studies, 2000), 1–21.

6. Solans, "The Roman Question," 133–134.Peter D'Agostino, *Rome in America: Transnational Catholic Ideology from the Risorgimento to Fascism* (Chapel Hill, NC: University of North Carolina Press, 2004), 26–31.

7. Peter D'Agostino, *Rome in America*, 26–32.

8. John W. O'Malley, *Vatican I: The Council and the Making of the Ultramontane Church* (Cambridge, MA: Harvard University Press, 2018), esp. 55–95. Christopher Clark and Wolfram Kaiser, "Introduction: The European Culture Wars," in Clark and Kaiser, *Culture Wars*, 5. John F. Pollard, *Money and the Rise of the Modern Papacy: Financing the Vatican, 1850-1950* (New York, NY: Cambridge University Press, 2005), 31–35; Emiel Lamberts, *The Struggle with Leviathan: Social Responses to the Omnipotence of the State, 1815-1965* (Leuven, BE: Leuven University Press, 2016), 179–183; Austin Gough, *Paris and Rome: The Gallican Church and the Ultramontane Campaign, 1848-1853* (Oxford, UK: Clarendon Press, 1986).

9. Scheper Hughes, *The Church*. The literature on indigenous Catholicism is copious. Juan Pedro Viqueira Albán notes how Indians brought their own intertwined political and religious meanings to the cult of the saints and holy people in his *Indios rebeldes e idólotras: dos ensayos*

históricos sobre la rebelión India de Cancuk, Chiapas, acaecida el el año de 1712 (México: CIESAS, 1997). Confraternities controlled by indigenous people were particularly important spaces for the practice of indigenous Catholicism; Adrian C. van Oss notes that indigenous confraternities often refused to turn over resources to priests who contravened their agendas; see his *Catholic Colonialism*.; also see John K. Chance and William B. Taylor, Cofradias and Cargos: An Historical Perspective on the Mesoamerican Civil-Religious Hierarchy, *American Ethnologist* 12, no. 1 (1985): 1–26. Aaron Pollock underscores that Lucas Aguilar, second in command during the large-scale 1820 Indian uprising in Totonicapan, originally rose up against the local priest from his position as a leader of a confraternity in 1818; see his *Levantamiento K'iche en Totonicapán. Los lugares de la política subalternas* (Guatemala: Avanasco, 2008), 164. Pinto Soria, "Los religiosidades," 313.

10. In his analysis of the popular religiosity that led to defense of church burials, Sullivan Gonzalez rightly notes that the burial disputes demonstrate the ongoing salience of popular religion for the opponents of the hygienic new cemeteries. But he misses that suburban cemeteries, far from being a secular project, had long been a Reform Catholic cause, as reformers' more Augustinian theology demoted the significance of burial under the protection of a particular saint or near a particular altar and attenuated the connection to the gathered faithful that church burial was meant to safeguard; see Pamela Voekel, *Alone Before God*, passim.

11. Holleran, *Church and State*, 125–126. While Mariano Gálvez led a frontal assault on popular religiosity and pushed for civil control over the church in 1830s Guatemala, the liberal Mexican administration of Vice-President Valentín Gómez Farías and his chief advisor, José María Luis Mora, in 1833 declared monastic vows a matter of conscience, abolished obligatory tithing, and seriously entertained thoughts of whittling down the bloated calendar of saints' festivals. At the same time, liberal state legislatures in Mexico, Puebla, and Veracruz prohibited pilgrimages to shrines, required state approval for confraternities, prohibited the collection of church taxes, and closed convents and church schools. The influential Mora justified the short-lived regime's assault on the church by noting that preaching the divine word, administering the sacraments, and attending to matters directly related to God's cult had been the church's only prerogatives in its early centuries. It was only in the fourth century under the Emperor Constantine that clerics had garnered riches and the right to punish malefactors, as well as other civil privileges. If rights came from temporal powers like Emperor Constantine, Mora concluded, they could be removed by them; see Pamela Voekel, *Alone Before God*, 154. Will Fowler sees Mora as the "anticlerical" administration's most adamant ideologue and Sanjuanista Lorenzo de Zavala as its most radical member; see Will Fowler, "Valentín Gómez Farías: Perceptions of Radicalism in Independent Mexico, 1821–1847," *Bulletin of Latin American Research* 15 (1996): 39–62. For more on Gálvez's reforms, see Jorge Luis Arriola, *Gálvez en la encrucijada. Ensayo crítico en torno al humanismo político de un gobernante* (Guatemala: Editorial Cara Parens, 2012).

12. Don E. Dumond, "The Talking Crosses of Yucatán: A New Look at Their History," *Ethnohistory* 32, no. 4 (1985): 291–308. Other key works on the Caste War of Yucatán include Nelson A. Reed, *The Caste War of Yucatán* (Stanford, CA: Stanford University Press, 2001). Apolinar García García, *Historia de la Guerra de Castas de Yucatán* (Mérida, Yucatán, México: Ediciones de la Universidad Autónoma de Yucatán, 2018). Victoria. Bricker, *The Indian Christ, the Indian King* (Austin: University of Texas Press, 1981). Terry Rugeley, *Yucatan's Maya Peasantry and the Origins of the Caste War* (Austin: University of Texas Press, 1996). Moisés González Navarro, *Raza y tierra: la guerra de castas y el henequén* (México: El Colegio de México, 1979). On the constitutional city councils established by the Cortes de Cádiz and the land

enclosure that whites who often controlled these new councils enacted against Indian communities in the Yucatán leading up to the Caste War, see Karen Caplan, *Indigenous Citizens: Local Liberalism in Early National Oaxaca and Yucatán* (Stanford, CA: Stanford University Press, 2009).

13. Montúfar also rehearsed venerable Reform Catholic wisdom in his 1870s discussion of Guatemala's 1831 declaration of ownership of the patronato, noting that the layity elected bishops in the church's early centuries, and that the pope later usurped this right. The government needed to exercise the patronato to stave off the worst elements of ultramontanism; see Lorenzo Montúfar, *Reseña histórica de Centro América* (Guatemala: Tipografia de El Progreso, 1878–1887), 226, 291. For more on the 1863 fire at the Jesuit church in Santiago, see Sol Serrano's *¿Que hacer con díos en la república? Política y secularización en Chile (1845-1885)* (México: Fondo de Cultura Económica, 2008), 29–30.

BIBLIOGRAPHY

PRIMARY SOURCES

Actas de las sesiones secretas de las Cortes ordinarias y extraordinarias de los años 1820 y 1821, de los años 1822 a 1825 y de las celebradas por las diputaciones permanentes de las mismas Cortes ordinarias. Madrid: J. Antonio García, 1874.

Alcayaga, José Antonio. *Carta del ex-gobernador del arzobispado protestando por su destitución con motivo de haber nombrado el Delgado provisor y vicario provincial de San Salvador. Hace al propio tiempo vicario a cargo de Casáus.* Guatemala: Imprenta de Lorenzana, 1830.

Alvarado, Francisco. *Carta crítica de un filósofo rancio que impugna a la española antigua y no a la francesa el discurso del señor diputado Argüelles sobre contribución de diezmos y los dictámenes de otros varios señores diputados que distraen a las Cortes de su principal objecto.* Isla de León, 1811.

El Amigo de la Verdad. *A los editores del periódico titulado Semanario Político Mercantil de San Salvador.* Guatemala: Imprenta de la Unión, 1826.

Apología lacónica de un cura contra la locura de algunos curas. Guatemala: Imprenta Nueva a dirección de Cayetano de Arévalo, 1825.

Árbol, José María P. del. *Una carta dirigida al P. Campa.* Guadalajara, México: Imprenta de Dionisio Rodríguez, 1857.

Arce, José Manuel. *Memoria de la conducta pública y administrativa de Manuel J. Arce durante el periodo de su presidencia.* México: Imprenta de Galván, 1830.

Argüelles, Agustín. *Discursos.* Edited by Francisco Tomás Valiente. Oviedo, ES: Junta General del Principado de Asturias, 1995.

Asamblea Nacional. *Actas de la Asamblea Nacional Constituyente de las Provincias Unidas del Centro de América.* Guatemala: Editorial Ejército, 1971.

Aviso oportuno a las autoridades y al pueblo. El Salvador: Imprenta del Gobierno, 1825.

Aycinena, Juan José de. *Noticia de las funciones con que se celebró la definición dogmática de la Inmaculada Concepción de la Santísima Virgen María, en la S.M.I. de Santigo de Guatemala ... en los dias 20, 21, 22 y 23 de julio de 1855*. Guatemala: Oficina de L. Luna, 1855.

Aycinena, Miguel José. *El ex-provincial del Orden de Predicadores Fr. Miguel José de Aycinena explica los motivos y fundamentos de su circular de 6 de febrero de 1825 expedidas a los religiosos de su provincia por donde deben recibir los derechos y ordenes de las autoridades civiles.* Guatemala: Imprenta Nueva de C. Arévalo, 1826.

Aycinena, Miguel José de. "Procedimintos de la Provincia de Predicadores de Guatemala en la exacción del 7 por 100 impuesta por la Asamblea Nacional Constituyente de las Provincias Unidas de Centro de América sobre el valor liquido de las fincas de comunidades eclesiásticas seculares y regulares y sobre capitales de cofadías, hermandades, y obras pías. Guatemala: J.J. de Arévalo, 1824.

Aza, José María de. *Horrorosos atentados del Pensador Mexicano contra el clero de Guatemala. O sea el genio de la anarquía.* Mexico: Imprenta del Ciudadano Juan Cabrera, 1826.

Aza, José María de. *Muerte del escudero Aza, atentada por El Pensador Mexicano en la imprenta de Cabrera.* México: Imprenta de C. Juan Cabrera, 1826.

Azuero, Vicente. *Representación dirigida al Supremo Poder Ejecutivo contra el presbítero doctor Francisco Margallo, por el doctor Vicente Azuero* (Bogotá, 1826)

Azuero Plata, Juan Nepomuceno. *Informe que el Dr. Juan Nepomuceno Azuero Plata, cura de Sota y vicario superintendente de su canton, dió a la vice-presidencia de la Nueva Granada, a principios de 1820, sobre los derechos del gobierno, en la provision de beneficios eclesiásticos y otros puntos de inmunidad.* Bogotá: Imprenta Nacional, 1824.

Azuero Plata, Juan Nepomuceno. *Dr. Merizalde y el Noticiozote.* Bogotá: F.M. Stokes, 1825.

Azuero Plata, Juan Nepomuceno. *Respuesta a un papel que, con el título de Verdadera vindicación de esta ciudad de Bogotá y su cabildo en las personas del procurador general y padre de menores en el año 1816, han publicado los doctores Ignacio Herrera y José Ignacio San Miguel.* Bogotá: Imprenta del Estado, 1823.

Bancroft, Hubert Howe. *History of the Pacific States of North America.* Volume 3, *Central America, 1801-1887.* San Francisco, CA: The History Company, 1887.

Barruel, Abbé Augustin. *Historia del clero en el tiempo de la Revolución francesa.* México: M.J. de Zúñiga, 1800.

Baz, Juan José. *Artículos diversos de la Bandera Roja de Morelia escritos por Juan José Baz en 1859.* México: Imprenta de Vicente García Torres, 1861.

Bossuet, Jacques Bénigne. *Política deducida de las propias palabras de la Sagrada Escritura, revisada y traducida por Miguel Joseph Fernández.* 3 vols. Madrid: Andrés Ortega, 1768.

Calleja, Félix María. *Bando publicado en México el 7 de octubre de 1815 por el virrey de la Nueva España Félix María Calleja del Rey insertando la cédula real expedida el 31 de enero de 1815 por el rey Fernando VII que le fue dirigida por el Real y Supremo Consejo y Cámara de Indias en el sentido de que habiéndose hecha presente por el diputado de Yucatán Ángel Alonso y Pantiga los perjuicios que se experimentaban por haber abolido las Cortes los servicios que hacían los indios.* Mexico City, 1815.

Campa, Francisco P. *Protesta y retracción del Presb. Francisco de P. Campa ante su dignísimo prelado el Illmo. Sr. Dr. D. Francisco de P. Verea, obispo de la Diócesis de Linares.* Guadalajara: Imprenta de Rodríguez, 1857.

Cañas, José Simeón. *Advertencia patriótica.* Guatemala: Imprenta Nueva, 1824.

Cañas, José Simeón. *Segunda advertencia patriótica del doctor Cañas.* Guatemala: Imprenta Nueva de J.J. de Arévalo, 1824.

Cárdenas, Josef Eduardo de. *Memoria a favor de la provincia de Tabasco, en la Nueva España, presentado a S.M. Las Cortes Generales Extraordinarias por el Dr. D. Josef Eduardo de Cárdenas. Diputado en ellas por dicha provincia.* Cádiz, ES: En la Imprenta del Estado Mayor General, 1811.

Carta en que se hacen algunas observaciones sobre un papel titulado Informe que el Dr. Juan Nepomuceno Azuero y Plata, cura y superintendente de su cantón, dió a la vice- presidencia de la Nueva Granada. Santiago de Chile: Imprenta Nacional, 1825.

Casáus y Torres, Ramón. *El arzobispo electo de Guatemala á sus diocesanos de San Salvador.* Guatemala: Arévalo, 1811.

Casáus y Torres, Ramón. *Sermón de Nuestra Señora de El Rosario predicado en la iglesia de Santo Domingo de Guatemala día 6 de octubre de 1811 por el Dr. D. Fr. Ramón Casáus y Torres, obispo de Rosen y arzobispo electo de esa metrópoli, del consejo de S.M. lo publica la Archicofradía del Santísimo Rosario.* Guatemala: Oficina de Don Manuel Arévalo, 1811.

Casaús y Torres, Fr. Ramón. *Sermón tercero de San Pedro Mártir de Verona, predicado en 29 de abril de 1807 por el ilustrísimo y reverendísimo Fr. Ramón Casaús y Torres y Las Plazas ... en la fiesta que el illmó. y santo Tribunal de la Inquisición con su ilustre cofradía celebró en la iglesia de la imperial convento de nuestro padre Santo Domingo de México.* México: Oficina de D. Juan Bautista de Arizpe, 1807.

Casáus y Torres, Ramón. *Oración fúnebre del Exmo. é Illmo. señor doctor don Alonso Nuñez de Haro.* México: Mariano Joseph de Zúñiga y Ontiveros, 1800.

Caso de conciencia sobre el juramento constitucional. Carta de un párroco jalisciense. México: Imprenta de V. García Torres, 1857.

Castrillo, Victor. *Maravillas de Zacapa y sus contornos.* Guatemala: Imprenta de A. de Estudios, 1838.

Castro y Toledo, Juan Antonio de. *Varias poesias que en obsequio del sacratísimo Corazón de Jesús compusó Juan Antonio de Castro y Toledo.* Mérida, Yucatán: Imprenta del Gobierno, 1814.

Chiaramonti, Barnaba Niccolò Maria Luigi, Bishop of Imola. *Homélie du citoyen Cardinal Chiaramonti, evêque d'Imola, actuellement ... Pontife Pie VII, adressée au peuple de son diocèse ... le jour de la Naissance de Jésus-Christ, l'an 1797.* Translated by Abbé Grégoire. Paris: 1814.

Chiaramonti, Barnaba Niccolò Maria Luigi. *Homilía del cardenal Chiaramonti, obispo de Imola, actualmente sumo pontifice Pio VII, dirigida al pueblo de su diócesis en la República Cisalpina, el día del nacimiento de J.-C. año de 1797.* Translated by Juan Germán Roscio. Philadelphia, PA: J.F. Hurtel, 1817.

¡Ciudadanos! ¡Compasión! Que los cismáticos quieren perseguirnos con furor. Apología de los curas y demás eclesiásticos perseguidos en el Estado del Salvador, por no reconocer un obispado y un obispo de nueva invención anticatólica. Uno de los perseguidos la dedica a los mismos perseguidores. Guatemala: Imprenta Nueva, 1825.

Coleccion eclesiástica española comprensiva de los breves de S.S., notas del R. Nuncio, representaciones de los SS. obispos á las Cortes, pastorales, edictos, y con otros documentos relativos á las innovaciones hechas por los constitucionales en materias eclesiásticas desde el 7 de marzo de 1820, Tomo I. Madrid: Imprenta de E. Aguado, 1823-24.

Concilio Provincial Mexicano IV: Celebrado en la ciudad de México el año de 1771. Querétaro, México: Escuela de Artes, 1898.

Concina, Daniele. *Historia del probabilismo y rigorismo. Disertaciones theológicas, morales, y críticas, en que se explican, y defienden de las sutilezas de los modernos probabilistas los principios fundamentales de la theología Christiana. Escrita en idioma italiano por el Rmo. Mrq. fray*

Daniel Concina, del Orden de Predicadores: y traducida al español por el licenciado D. Mathías Joachín de Imaz, canónigo penitenciario, que fue de la Insigne Colegial de Santa María de la ciudad de Vitoria, y abogado de los Reales Consejos. Dividida en dos tomos. Año de 1772. Tomo I. Madrid: En la Oficina de la Viuda de Manuel Fernández, 1772.

Concina, Daniele. *Lettere teologico-morali in cointinuazione della difesa della storia del probabilismo e rigorismo, ec. del P. Daniele Concina: Ovvero confutazione della riposta pubblicata dal M.R.P.B. dell Compangnia [di jesú].* Venice: Simone Occhi, 1751–1754.

Concina, Daniele. *Della storia del probabilismo e del rigorismo: Dizzertazione teologiche, morali y critiche.* Venice: Simon Occhi, 1743.

Contestación al comunicado que comienza Revolucinaba en el siglo X el arzobispo de Milan, incerto en el numero 71 del Seminario del Estado de El Salvador en que con hechos traidos por la malicia, se exorta al pueblo pacífico de Guatemala á revolucionar contra su digno prelado; por que evitando los abusos y desordenes religiosos promueve el honor de los gobiernos y de toda la república. Guatemala: Imprenta de la Union de Juan José Arévalo, 1826.

Cortes. *Actas de las sesiones de la legislatura ordinario de 1813.* Madrid: Imprenta y Fundación de las Viudas y Hijos de J. Antonio García, 1876.

Cortes. *Actas de las sesiones de la legislatura ordinaria de 1814.* Madrid: Imprenta y Fundación de las Viudas y Hijos de J. Antonio García, 1876.

Cortes. *Diario de las discusiones y actas de las Cortes. Tomo XXI.* Cádiz: Imprenta Nacional, 1813.

Cortés Madariaga, José. *Diario y observaciones del presbítero José Cortés Madariaga, en su regreso de Santafé á Caracas, por la via de los rios Negor, Meta y Orinoco, despues de haber concluido la comisión que obtuvo de su gobierno, para acordar los tratados de alianza entre ambos estados.* Caracas: 1811.

Cresencio Rejón, Manuel. *Discursos parlamentarios (1822-1847). Compilación, notas y reseña biográfica por Carlos A. Achanove Trujillo.* México: Secretaría de Educación Pública, 1943.

Cuerpo y alma del decreto de julio del corriente año relativo a profesiones. Conversación de dos amigos don Cazcarria y don Zurriago. Guatemala: Imprenta Mayor, Casa de Porras, 1826.

Dávila, Fernando Antonio. *Exposición del ciudadano Fernando Antonio Dávila, representante en la Asamblea Constituyente de estos estados por el Partido de Sacatepeques. Leída en la sesión pública del 5 de julio [1824] del corriente año en que se comenzó á discutir la ley fundamental de la nación.* Guatemala: Beteta, 1824.

Dávila, Fernando Antonio. *A la Segunda advertencia del presbítero doctor José Simeón Cañas por el presbítero Fernando Antonio Dávila.* Guatemala: Imprenta de Beteta, 1824.

Dávila, Fernando Antonio, Ángel María Candina, and Antonio Gonzales. *A la Advertencia patriótica del doctor José Simeón Cañas. Contestación de los presbiterios Fernando Antonio Dávila, Dr. Ángel Maria Candina y Dr. Antonio Gonzáles.* Guatemala: Imprenta de Beteta, 1824.

Delgado, José Matías. *C.R. Consejo representativo.* San Salvador: Imprenta del Estado, 1831.

Devoción al Sagrado Corazón de Jesús, para todos los viernes del año, particularmente para el primero de cada mes, con la invocación de su santísimo nombre, que se puede decir todos los días. México: Imprenta de D. Alejandro Valdés, 1821.

Dictamen de la comisión eclesiástica encargada del arreglo definitivo del clero de España. Impreso de órden de las Cortes. Madrid: Imprenta de D. Tomás Alban y Compañía, 1825.

Dictamenes del Consejo de Estado y de las Comisiones Eclesiástica y de Justicia reunidas. Cádiz: Imprenta Nacional, 1813.

Discusión del proyecto de decreto sobre el Tribunal de la Inquisición. Cádiz: Imprenta Nacional, 1813.

Domínguez, Leoncio. *El párroco de Coxutepeque á sus feligreses.* Guatemala: Imprenta de Arévalo, 1825.

Dunn, Henry. *Guatimala* [sic], *or, the United Provinces of Central America, in 1827-8. Being Sketches and Memorandums Made During a Twelve Months' Residence in that Republic.* New York, NY: C. & C. Carvill, 1828.

Echeverría, Pedro. *Catecismo de la doctrina clero-maquiavélica o sea del padre Ripalda según lo observa y predíca el clero mexicano.* México: Imprenta de la Reforma, 1861.

Eguiguren, Ramón. *Manifiesto en que el doctor J.R. Eguiguren, cura de Manta, opositor a la prebenda doctoral, para la cual había sido propuesto en primer lugar con todos los votos del Illmo. Cabildo Metropolitano hace presente sus méritos y servicios en las tres carreras eclesiástica, literaria y política.* Bogotá: Imprenta de la República, 1825.

En oficio de 19 del que rige recibido por el correo de hoy, participa el gefe político de León ciudadano José Carmen Salazár al S. P.E lo que sigue. Guatemala: Imprenta de Arévalo, 1823.

España triunfante del ocio, del lujo, y de ciertas preocupaciones, bajo el gobierno de la constitución política de la monarquía por un español amante de su patria. Madrid: Imprenta de Fuentenebro, 1820.

Estévez y Ugarte, Pedro Agustín. *Sermón predicado en la santa iglesia catedral de Mérida de Yucatán el día quince de octubre de 1815 por el illmo. don Pedro Agustín Estévez y Ugarte.* Mérida, Yucatán: Oficina del Gobierno, 1815.

Eyzaguirre, José Ignacio Víctor. *El catolicismo en presencia de sus disidentes.* Guadalajara: Tipografía de Rodríguez, 1856.

Oliveira Fernández, J. A. *Letter, Addressed to the Most Reverend Leonard Neale, Archbishop of Baltimore, by a Member of the Roman Catholic Congregation of Norfolk, in Virginia.* Norfork, 1816.

Fernández de Lizardi, José Joaquín. *Horrorosos atentados de una parte del clero de Goatemala* (sic) *contra la independencia general o sea el genio de la anarquía.* Mexico City: Oficina de Mariano Ontiveros, 1826.

Fernández de Lizardi, José Joaquín. *El sedicioso manifiesto del obispo de Sonora. Impugnado por El Pensador en la Sexta conversación del payo y el sacristán.* Mexico: Imprenta de Mariano Ontiveros, 1825.

Franco, Pablo, José María Iturralde, Félix Osores, Joaquín Román, and Servando de Mier, *Dictamen de la Comisión de patronato, leído en sesión pública del soberano Congreso mexicano. Se imprime de orden de su soberanía.* México: Imprenta Nacional del Supremo Gobierno, 1823.

Galán y Junco, Gelasio. *Instituciones canónicas de Juan Devoti, obispo de Anagni. Divididos en cuatro libros. Puestos en castellano y reducidas puramente á la parte doctrinal, en beneficio, comodidad y mas fácil uso de los jóvenes que se dedican al estudio del derecho canónico.* Valencia, ES: Imprenta de Cabrerizo, 1839.

Gallardo, Bartolomé José. *Diccionario crítico-burlesco.* Burdeos, ES: Imprenta de Pedro Beaume, 1819.

Gámez, José D., editor. *Archivo histórico de la República de Nicaragua por José D. Gámez, Tomo 1, 1821-1826.* Managua, NIC: Tipografía Nacional, 1896.

García, Fr. Manuel. *Reflecsiones* [sic] *sobre el artículo primero del decreto emitido por la Asamblea de Guatemala en veinte de julio de 1826 por Fr. Manuel García lego de S. Francisco.* Guatemala: Imprenta Mayor, Casa de Porras 1826.

García Redondo, Antonio. *Soberanía e independencia de la Iglesia católica en el desempeño del ministerio que la confió su divino fundador Jesucristo.* Guatemala: Imprenta de la Unión, 1825.

García-Herreros, Manuel. *Reflexiones sobre la protesta del M.R. arzobispo de Nicea D. Pedro Gravina.* Madrid, 1814.

Garza y Ballesteros, Lázaro de la. *Carta pastoral del Illmo, y Exmo. Sr. Arzobispo de México.* México: Imprenta de Vicente Segura, 1855.

Gómez Huerta, José Guadalupe. *Discurso pronunciado por el Sr. Huerta en la sesión secreta del 15 de mayo, en favor del dictamen de la comisión eclesiástica, sobre arreglo de patronato.* Guadalajara: Imprenta del C. Urbano Sanromán, 1827.

Gordoa, José Miguel. "Informe que el Sr. Dr. D. José Miguel Gordoa, gobernador de la diócesis de Guadalajara, obispo después de la misma, dirigió a consulta del honorable congreso de Zacatecas sobre algunas proposiciones presentados a aquella asamblea." In *Colección eclesiástica Mejicana*, volume 2, 298–321. México: Imprenta de Galván, 1834.

Granado Baeza, Bartolomé José del. *Informe del cura de Yaxcabá.* Yucatán, 1813.

Gran ascención aereostatica del presbítero ciudadano Francisco de P. Campa en busca del Espíritu Santo; para que concurra á los juzgados de la República. Guadalajara, México: Imprenta de Dionisio Rodríguez, 1857.

Gravina, Pedro. *Manifiesto del Arzobispo de Nicea Don Pedro Gravina, nuncio y legado de su santidad sobre las ocurrencias de su extrañamiento.* Madrid: Repullés, 1814.

Grégoire, Henri. *Essai historique sur les libertés de l'Église gallicane et des autres églises de la catholicité, pendant les deux derniers siècles.* Paris: Censeur, 1818.

Grégoire, Henri. *Memoria sobre el clero escrita por el célebre obispo H. Grégoire*, translated by José María del Barrio. San Salvador: Imprenta del Gobierno, 1826.

Gregorio XVI. *Il trionfo della Santa Sede e della Chiesa contro gli assalti dei novatori combattuti e respinti colle stesse loro armi.* Venezia: Guiseppe Battaggia, 1832.

Groot, José Manuel. *Historia eclesiástica y civil de Nueva Granada escrita sobre documentos auténticos.* Volume 3. Bogotá: Casa Editorial de M. Rivas & Cia, 1891.

Hernández y Dávalos, Juan, editor. *Colección de documentos para la historia de la Guerra de Independencia de México de 1808 a 1821.* Mexico: J.M. Sandoval, 1880.

Herrarte, José Mariano. *Advertencia patriótica.* Guatemala: Imprenta Nueva, 1824.

Un Hombre de Bien, *El cisma religioso causará el político.* Mexico: Imprenta del Ciudadano Alejandro Valdés, 1827.

"El Honor," *Noticias muy particulares venidas del catolocismo.* San Salvador: Imprenta Mayor, 1830.

Impugnación al impreso que se publicó en S. Salvador con este título: "El Monstruo de dos cabezas." Y defensa de la sinceridad y rectitud de los procedimientos del Cabildo de la S.I.M. de Guatemala, con motivo de la elección de provisor y vicario . . . la dan a luz los individuos del propio Cabildo que la subscriben. Guatemala: Imprenta Nueva, 1831.

Interpelación que hacen los infrascriptos individuales del estado de El Salvador, presos en S. Francisco de Guatemala, al pueblo soberano de Centro-América. Guatemala: Imprenta de la Unión, 1833.

J.H. *El liberalismo y sus efectos en la República Mexicana.* Mexico: Andrés Boix, 1858.

Le Brun, Carlos. *Retratos de la revolución de España, ó de los principales personages que han jugado en ella, muchos de los quales están sacados en caricaturas por lo ridículo en que ellos mismos se habían puesto, quando el retratista los iba sacando; con unas observaciones políticas al fin sobre la misma; y la resolución sobre la qüestión de por qué se malogró esta, y no la de los Estados Unidos.* Philadelphia, 1826.

Le Brun, Carlos. *Vida de Fernando séptimo, rey de España; ó colección de anécdotas de su nacimiento y de su carrera privada y politica, publicadas en castellano por Dn. Carlos Le Brun.* Philadelphia, PA, 1826.

Llorente, Juan Antonio. *Colección diplomática de varios papeles antiguos y modernos sobre dispensas matrimoniales y otros puntos de disciplina eclesiástica.* Madrid: Imprenta de Ibarra, 1809.

Llorente, Juan Antonio. *Discurso sobre una constitución religiosa, considerada como parte de la civil nacional, su autor un americano, los da á luz D. Juan Antonio Llorente, doctor en sagrados cánones.* Paris: Imprenta de Stahl, 1820.

Llorente, Juan Antonio. *Disertación sobre el poder que los reyes españoles ejercieron hasta el siglo duodécimo en la división de obispados, y otros puntos conecsos [sic] de disciplina eclesiástica; con un apéndice de escrituras en que constan los hechos citados en la disertación.* Madrid: Imprenta de Ibarra, 1810.

Llorente, Juan Antonio. *Memoria histórica sobre cuál ha sido la opinión nacional de España acerca del Tribunal de la Inquisición.* Madrid: Imprenta de Sancha, 1812.

Llorente, Juan Antonio. *Notas al dictamen de la comisión eclesiástica, encargada del arreglo definitivo del clero de España.* Madrid: Imprenta de Alban, 1823.

Llorente, Juan Antonio. *Anales secretos de la Inquisición española; memoria histórica sobre la Inquisición española.* Madrid: Libería Bergua, 1932.

Loyola, Juan de. *Thesoro escondido en el Corazón de Jesús, descubierto a nuestra España en la breve noticia de su culto ... su autor el padre Juan de Loyola, de la Compañia de Jesús.* Madrid: Imprenta de Manuel Fernández, 1736.

Lozano, Ramón. *Contestación a las cuatro palabras del cura de Monclova, D. Narciso Villareal.* Ciudad Victoria: Imprenta de Sebastián Perrillos, 1861.

Mallarino, Manuel María. *Juan N. Azuero Plata.* Bogotá, CO: Imprenta de Echeverría Hermanos, 1857.

Maréchal, Ambrose. *Pastoral Letter of the Archbishop of Baltimore, to the Roman Catholicks (sic) of Norfolk, Virginia.* Baltimore, ML: J. Robinson, 1819.

Martínez y Ocejo, Bernardo. *La soberanía del Altísimo.* Guadalajara, México: Imprenta de la Viuda de Romero, 1824.

Marure, Alejandro. *Efemérides de los hechos notables acaecidos en la república de Centro-América, desde el año de 1821 hasta el de 1842. Seguidas de varios catálogos de presidentes de la república, jefes de estado, etc.* Guatemala: Imprenta de la Paz, 1844.

Marure, Alejandro. *Memoria sobre la insurrección de Santa Rosa y Mataquescuintla en Centro América, comparada con la que estalló en Francia, el año de 1790, en los departamentos de la Vendée, etc.* Guatemala, 1838.

Mayorga, Juan de Dios. *Exposición del origen, progreso y estado actual de las incidencias ocurridas en S. Salvador.* México: Oficina de José María Ramos Palomero, 1822.

Mazzine, Joseph. *The Life and Writing of Joseph Mazzine.* London, UK: Smith, Elder and Company, 1891.

Menéndez, Isidro. *Censura de la ley de la Asamblea de 21 de enero de 1831 que reconoce por legítimo arzobispo al Sr. Casáus.* San Salvador: Imprenta del Estado, 1831.

Menéndez, Isidro. *Contestación del autor de la censura de la ley de 28 de enero de 1831 a los papeles publicados contra ella.* San Salvador: Imprenta del Estado, 1831.

Menéndez, Isidro. *Exposición del senador por el Estado de Nicaragua P.C.L.D.C. Isidro Menéndez: hecha en el senado á 1° de agosto de 1825 al deliberar sobre el proyecto de decreto y órden del Congreso federal en el negocio de obispado de S. Salvador: se publíca de órden del gobierno del estado con las notas oficiales del autor que la remite, la de contestación del gobierno, y las en que éste reclamó oportunamente al congreso y senado a no pertenecer éste negocio á la Federacion.* San Salvador: Imprenta del Gobierno, 1825.

Menéndez y Pelayo, Marcelino. *Historia de los heterodoxos españoles*. 3 vols. Madrid: Librería Católica de San José, 1880–1882.

Mier Noriega y Guerra, José Servando Teresa de. *Cartas de Dr. Fray Servando Teresa de Mier (bajo el seudónimo de Un americano), años de 1811 y 1812*. Monterrey, Mx.: Tipografía del Gobierno, 1888.

Mier Noriega y Guerra, José Servando Teresa de. *Discurso del Dr. D. Servando Teresa de Mier sobre la encíclica del papa León XII. Quinta impresión revisada y corregida por el autor*. México: Imprenta de la Federación, 1825.

Mier Noriega y Guerra, José Servando Teresa de. *Memoria político-instructiva, enviada desde Filadelfia en agosto de 1821, a los gefes independientes del Anáhuac, llamado por los españoles Nueva España*. Philadelphia: J. F. Hurtel, 1821.

Mier Noriega y Guerra, José Servando Teresa de. *The Opinion of the R. Rev. Servandus A. Mier, Doctor of Sacred Theology in the Royal and Pontifical University of Mexico, and Chaplain of the Army of the Right, First Army of the Peninsula, on Certain Queries Proposed to Him by the Rev. William Hogan, Pastor of St. Mary's Church*. Philadelphia: n.p., 1821.

Mier Noriega y Guerra, José Servando Teresa de. *A Word Relative to an Anonymous Pamphlet Printed in Philadelphia Entitled "Remarks on the Opinion of the Rt. Rev. Servandus A. Mier, Doctor of Sacred Theology, on Certain Queries Proposed to Him by Rev. Wm. Hogan."* Philadelphia: n.p., 1821.

M.L. *Resúmen histórico del viage y cautiverio de Pio VII desde su partida de Roma hasta su regreso á esta ciudad; ó sea hasta su entera libertad. Traducido del francés al castellano por D.V.X.C. de G. Reimpreso en Mérida*, 1816.

Montúfar, Lorenzo. *Reseña histórica de Centro-América*. 7 vols. Guatemala: Tipografía El Progreso/La Unión, 1878–1887.

Montúfar, Manuel. *Memorias para la historia de la revolución de Centro-América por un guatemalteco*. Jalapa, México: Impreso por Aburto y Blanco en la Oficina del Gobierno, 1832.

Morazán, Francisco. *Memorias de David. Manifiesto del pueblo centroamérico*. Teguicigalpa: Instituto Morazánico de Honduras, 1953 [1841].

Morillo, Pablo. *Mémoires du Géneral Morillo, Comte de Carthagène, Marquis de la Puerta, Rélatifs aux principaux évenements de ses campagnes en Amérique de 1815 à 1821*. Paris: 1821.

Muñoz, Miguel, and Tomás Miguel Pineda y Saldaña. *Carta católica romana a los fieles del Estado de San Salvador*. Guatemala: Juan José de Arévalo, 1824.

Muñoz, Miguel. *Defensa de las llaves de San Pedro en la autoridad diocesana y breves noticias de los cismas del Arzobispado de Guatemala y de la iglesia sufragánea de Honduras: por el presbítero Miguel Muñoz del Obispado de Nicaragua*. New York, NY: Imprenta Española de D. Juan de la Granja, 1834.

Muñoz, Miguel. *Vindicación del Ilmo. Sr. obispo de San Salvador D. Tomás Miguel Saldaña, y defensa de la disciplina de la Sta. Iglesia católica, por el R. padre D. Miguel Muñoz*. Guatemala: Imprenta de Luna, 1862.

Novena al sacratísimo Corazón de Jesús. Sacada de un librito su titulo Tesoro escondido en el Corazón de Jesús, que salió á luz para su culto y venerable erección en nuestra España. Guatemala: D. Manuel Arévalo, 1823.

Novena al sacratísimo Corazón de Jesús: sacada de las sólidas prácticas de un libro que con el título de: Tesoro escondido en el Corazón de Jesus, ha salido nuévamente á luz para dar noticia de su sagrado culto á nuestra España. México: Imprenta de D.S. Valdes, 1821.

Novena de la sacratísima Virgen de Ytzmal. Esto es, á obsequio de la milagrosa imagen de nuestra señora, que baxo de este nombre se venera en su santuario de Puebla de Ytzmal, distante 15 leguas de la capital de Mérida. Mérida: D. Andrés Martín, 1816.

Núñez de Haro y Peralta, Alonso. *Carta pastoral que el illmô doctor D. Alonso Núñez de Haro y Peralta ... dirige a todos sus amados diocesanos sobre la doctrina sana en general, contraída en particular á las mas esenciales obligaciones que tenemos para con dios, y para con el rey.* México: Don Felipe de Zúñiga y Ontiveros, 1777.

Núñez de Haro y Peralta, Alonso. *Sermones escogidos, pláticas espirituales privadas, y dos pastorales, anteriormente impresas en México. . . Con el retrato del autor, y un resúmen histórico de su vida.* Madrid: Imprenta de la Hija de Ibarra, 1807.

Obispo y obispado: doctrina de la Iglesia católica sobre esta materia. Guatemala: Imprenta de la Unión, á cargo de Juan José de Arévalo, 1825.

Obispo de Orense, et.al, *Manifiesto del Obispo de Orense á la nación española.* Valencia: Imprenta de Francisco Brusola, 1814.

Observaciones sobre los inconvenientes del celibato de los clérigos. London: Imprenta de Carlos Wood, 1815.

Ocampo, Melchor. "Discurso de Melchor Ocampo." In *Documentos básicos de la Reforma, 1854-1875,* volume 2, introduced by Mario V. Guzmán Galarza. México: Partido Revolucionario Institucional, 1982.

Ocampo, Melchor. *La religión, la iglesia, y el clero.* Reprint. México: Empresas Editoriales, 1958 [1858].

Otero, Francisco José, Andrés María Rosillo, Juan José Osio, and Ignacio de Herrera. *Sobre el patronato: publicación de los dictámenes de algunas personas de rango, de conocida literatura y fama, con el objetivo de que la opinión se ilustre en una materia que todavía no se ha dado suficientemente a la luz.* Bogotá, CO: Imprenta de la República por N. Lora, 1823.

Palau y Font, Félix Amat de. *Observaciones pacíficas sobre la potestad eclesiástica.* Salt Lake City, UT: [Reprint], Nabu Press, 2002 [1817].

Pazos Kanki, Vicente. *Letters on the United Provinces of South America Addressed to the Hon. Henry Clay, Speaker of the House of Representatives of the U. States by D. Vicente Pazos. Translated from the Spanish by Platt H. Crosby, Esq.* New York, NY: J. Seymour; London: J. Miller, 1819.

Pereira de Figueiredo, Antonio. *Demonstração theologica, canonica, e historica do direito dos metropolitanos de Portugal para confirmarem, e mandarem sagrar os bispos suffraganeos nomeados por sua magestade e do direito dos obispos de cada provincia para confirmarem, e sagrarem os seus respectivos metropolitanos, tambem nomeados por sua magestade ainda fóra do caso de rotura com a corte de Roma.* Lisbon, PT: Regia Officina Typografica, 1769.

Pereira de Figueiredo, Antonio. *Demostración teólogica, canónica e histórica, del derecho de los metropolitanos de Portugal para confirmar y mandar consagrar a los obispos sufraganeos nombrados por su magestad.* Lima, PE: Imprenta de la Patria de T. López, 1833.

Pérez Hernández, José María. *Estadística de la República Mejicana.* Guadalajara: Tipografía del Gobierno, 1862.

Pius VI, *Colección de los breves é instrucciones de nuestro santo padre el Papa Pío VI relativos a la Revolución francesa desde el año 1790 hasta el de 1796, traducidos al español por el Dr. D. Pedro Zarandia, canónigo de la Sta. Iglesia Catedral de Jaca, y Examinador sinodal de su obispado. Tomo II.* Zaragoza, ES. : Imprenta de Polo y Monge, Hermanos, 1829.

Pizarro Suárez, Nicolás. *Catecismo político constitucional.* México: Imprenta de Ana Echeverría de Pizarro e hijas, 1861.

Pizarro Suárez, Nicolás. *La Coqueta.* México: Imprenta de Ana Echeverría de Pizarro e Hijas, 1861.

Pizarro Suárez, Nicolás. *La libertad en el orden. Ensayo sobre derecho público en que se resuelven algunas de las más vitales cuestiones que se agitan en México desde su independencia.* Mexico: Imprenta de Ana Echeverría de Pizarro e Hijas, 1855.

Pizarro Suárez, Nicolás. *El Monedero.* Mexico: Imprenta de Nicolás Pizarro, 1861.

Plata, Manuel. *Apología de la provincia del Socorro, sobre el crimen de cismática que se la imputa por la erección de Obispado, en Santafé de Bogotá año de 1811.* Bogotá: Imprenta Real de Don Bruno Espinosa de los Monteros, 1811.

Prieto, Guillermo. *Obras Completas.* T. XXIII. Volume 3, *Periodismo político y social.* Edited by Boris Rosen Jélomer. México: Consejo Nacional para la Cultura y las Artes, 1997.

Quevedo y Quintana, Pedro. *Representación del Ecmo. Sr. obispo de Orense, dirigida al Supremo Consejo de Regencia.* Cádiz: D. Antonio de Murguía, 1812.

Quintana, José Matías. *Manifiesto, de las notorias infracciones, con que los Sres. capitanes generales de las provincias de N.E. y península de Yucatán D. Félix María Calleja y D. Manuel Artazo, insultan descaradamente la Constitución, y las leyes pisándolas y quebrantándolas, más escandalosa, y criminalmente que los rebeldes Morelos, Toledo y demás caudillos de la insurrección, con inserción de los documentos que lo califican; para que vistos los hechos, decida el español imparcial, si esta parte de la América septentrional, tiene razón para resentirse de los golpes despóticos, y arbitrarios con que la tiranizan sus principales mandones.* Mérida, Yucatán: Imprenta Patriótica de D. José Francisco Bates, 1813.

Ramírez, Ignacio. *Obras de Ignacio Ramírez.* Volume 1. México: Editora Nacional, 1960.

Ramos Arizpe, Miguel. *Memoria, que el doctor D. Miguel Ramos de Arizpe, cura de Borbón, y diputado en las presentes Cortes Generales y Extraordinarias de España por la Provincia de Coahuila, una de las cuatro internas del oriente en el Reyno de México, presenta á el augusto congreso, sobre el estado natural, político, y civil de dicha provincia, y los del Nuevo Reyno de León, Nuevo Santander, y los Texas, con exposició de los defectos del sistema de las reformas, y nuevos establecimientos que necesítan para su prosperidad.* Cádiz: Imprenta de D. José María Guerrero, 1812.

R. M. and B. P. *Refutación á los enemigos encubiertos de la patria y manifiestos calumniadores del Estado de El Salvador por los diputades de su congreso constituyente.* San Salvador: Imprenta Liberal del Gobierno del Estado de El Salvador, 1825.

Representación y manifiesto que algunos diputados a las Cortes ordinarias firmaron en los mayores apuros de su opresión en Madrid, para que la majestad del señor D. Fernando el VII a la entrada en España de vuelta de su cautividad, se penetrase del estado de la nación, del deseo de sus provincias, y del remedio que creían oportuno; todo fue presentado a S.M. en Valencia por uno de dichos diputados, y se imagine en cumplimiento de real orden. Madrid, ES, 1814.

Representación que las señoras de Guadalajara dirigen al soberano Congreso Constituyente sobre que en la carta fundamental que se discute, no quede consignada la tolerancia de cultos en la república. Guadalajara, MX: Tipografía de Rodríguez, 1856.

Restrepo, José Manuel. *Historia de la revolución de la República de Colombia en la América Meridional.* Volume 1. Besanzon, France: Imprenta de José Jacquin, 1858 [1827].

Rivadeneyra y Barrientos, Joaquín de. *Manual compendio del regio patronato indiano.* Madrid, ES: Antonio Marin, 1755.

Rosillo y Meruelo, Andrés María. *Representación apologética, y demostrativa de los motivos que urgen sobre que se llame al ilustrísimo señor arzobispo doctor don Juan Bautista Sacristán.* Santa Fé de Bogotá: Imprenta del Sol, 1812.

Un Sacerdote. *Novena de la sacratísima Virgin de Ytzmal. Esto es, á obsequio de la milagrosa imagen de nuestra señora, que baxo de este nombre se venera en su santuario de Puebla de Ytzmal, distante 15 leguas de la capital de Mérida.* Mérida, Yucatán, MX: D. Andrés Martín, 1816.

Sagastume, Pablo M. *Satisfacción*. Guatemala: Imprenta Nueva, 1825.

Saldaña, José Ignacio . *Contestación al anónimo impreso en San Salvador con fecha de Guatemala de 10 de octubre de 1825*. Guatemala: Imprenta Nueva, C. C. Arévalo, 1826.

Saldaña, José Ignacio. *Justa repulsa de iniquas acusaciones, ó entiendase respuesta que se dá al impreso anónimo de San Salvador intitulado Contestación al manifiesto de Saldaña*. Guatemala, Imprenta de Arévalo, 1825.

Saldaña, José Ignacio, Tomás Miguel Saldaña, and Francisco Estevan López. *Invitación al venerable clero, secular y regular*. Guatemala: Juan José Arévalo, 1824.

Saldaña, José Ignacio, Tomás Miguel Saldaña, and Francisco Estevan López. *Verdaderas razones contra las aparentes que contiene el manifiesto de cuatro de mayo ultimo del director del Estado de San Salvador, sobre erección de iglesia y elección de obispo hecho en el doctor José Matías Delgado*. Guatemala: J.J. Arévalo, 1824.

Santa María, José Andrés de. *Carta crítica al doctor Simeón Cañas sobre los fundamentos de su Advertencia patriótica*. Guatemala: Impresa de Beteta, 1824.

Santa María, José Andrés de. *Catecismo teológico*. Guatemala: Imprenta Mayor, 1825.

Santa María, José Andrés de. *Desengaño religioso al pueblo de Guatemala*. Guatemala: Beteta, 1825.

Santa María, José Andrés de. *Impugnación del manifiesto del gobierno de San Salvador sobre la justificación de la erreción de aquel nuevo obispado, y elección del Dr. Delgado para esta nueva dignidad: á la que se añadirá la ninuna razon que tiene aquel gobierno para apropiarse los diezmos de aquella provincial, e invertirlos en los usos que le parezca*. Guatemala: Beteta, 1824.

Santa María, José Andrés de. *Preservativo contra el impio e irreligioso folleto "Aviso oportuno a las autoridades y al pueblo": y Satisfacción a los cargos que dicho autor y el comunicado del Semanario Mercantil de San Salvador de febrero de 1826, hacen al padre Santa María y a su religión*. Guatemala: Imprenta de la Unión, 1826.

Santa María, José Andrés de. *Reconvención amistosa al senador Isidro Menéndez por Fr. José Andrés de Santa-María, maestro y regente de los estudios del convento de Santo Domingo de Guatemala*. Guatemala: Imprenta Mayor, 1826.

Santa María, José Andrés de. *Satisfacción al comunicado del Semanario Político Mercantil de San Salvador de ocho de febrero de 1826*. Guatemala: Imprenta de la Unión, 1826.

Santander de Villavivencio, Leonardo. *Sermón que en la solemne función celebrada por la excelentísima Diputacion Provincal de Yucatán, con asistencia de todas las corporaciones, en la santa iglesia catedral de Mérida el domingo 26 de Junio de 1814, en acción de gracias por el dichoso, y plausible regrego de nuestro muy amado y católico monarca el Dr. don Fernando 7 al territorio español predicó con tres dias de termino, el D. Leonardo Santander y Villavicencio, del clausto y gremio de la Real Universidad de Sevilla en el de sagrada teologia, canónigo magistral de dicha ciudad, y actualmente prebendado de esta santa iglesia catedral de Mérida, y catedrático de oprima de teologia en el seminario conciliar de ella*. Mérida: Imprenta del Gobierno, 1814.

Say, John-Baptiste. *Political Economy; Or the Production, Distribution, and Consumption of Wealth*. Translated by C. R. Prinsep. Introduction by Clement C. Biddle. Philadelphia, PA: Lippincott; Grambodo, Grigg, Elliott &Company, 1851 [1803].

Suplemento manifestación que hacen al venerable clero y fieles de sus respectivas diócesis y a todo el mundo católico, los Ilmos. Sres. Arzobispo de México y obispos de Michoacán, Linares, Guadalajara, y el Potosí, y el Sr. Dr. D. Francisco Serrano como representante de la mitra de Puebla. En defensa del clero y de la doctrina católica, con ocasión del manifiesto y los decretos expedidos por el. Sr. Lic. D. Benito Juárez en la ciudad de Veracruz en los días 7, 12, 13, 23 de julio de 1859. Celaya: Imprenta de G. Galván, 1859.

Tamburini, Pedro. *Verdadera idea de la Santa Sede, escrita en italiano por el presbítero D. Pedro Tamburini de Brescia. Profesor de la Universidad Imperial y Real de Pavia, caballero de la Orden de Hierro, miembro del Instituto Imperial y Real de las Ciencias, y traducida por D. N. Q. S.C. quien la dedica á los pueblos de América.* London: Imprenta Española de M. Calero, 1826.

Tejada, Miguel Lerdo de. *Cuadro sinóptico de la República mexicana en 1856, formado en vista de los últimos datos oficiales y otras noticias fidedignas.* México: Ignacio Cumplido, 1856.

Thompson, George Andrew. *Narrative of an Official Visit to Guatemala from Mexico.* London, UK: John Murray, 1829.

Torres y Peña, José Antonio de. *Precaución contra el manifiesto, que trata de alucinar a los sencillos y cohonestar el cisma del Socorro. Lo ofrece a los verdaderos fieles don José Antonio de Torres y Peña, cura de Tabio.* Bogotá, CO: Imprenta Patriótica de D. Nicolás Calvo y Quixano, 1811.

Valois, Alfred de. *Mexique, Havane, et Guatemala. Notes de voyage.* Paris, FR, 1861.

Varela, Félix. *Miscelánea filosófica. Tercera edición por Félix Varela.* New York, NY: Imprenta de Enrique Newton, 1827.

Venganza de la justicia por la manifestación de la verdad en orden al patronato de la Iglesia, que se atribuye a la suprema potestad de Colombia. Escrita por el señor doctor Andrés Rosillo, dean de la misma iglesia, en representación que tenía dispuesta el muy venerable sr. dean y cabildo de esta capital para el senado, y ofrecida en otra que se dio a la misma corporación. Caracas, VE: Valentín Espinal, 1824.

La Vergüenza. *Contra la mentira titulada Verdad.* San Salvador: Imprenta del Estado, 1830.

Verney, Luis António. *Método verdadeiro de estudar, para ser util à Republica, e à Igreja: proporcionado ao estilo, e necesidade de Portugal, exposto em varias cartas, escritas polo [sic] R.P. Barbadinho.* 2 vols. Nápoles, IT: Genaro e Vicenzo Muzio, 1746.

Verney, Luis António. *Verdadero método de estudiar, para ser útil á la República y á la Iglesia: proporcionado al estilo y necessidad de Portugal, expuesto en varias cartas, escritas en idioma portugués por el R.P Bernardiño. . . Traducido del portugués por don Joseph Maimó y Ribes.* 5 vols. Madrid: Joaquín de Ibarra, 1760–1768.

Vidaurre, Fr. José Mariano. *Sermón que en las exequias fúnebres que se hicieron en la ciudad de San Salvador a la venerable memoria del Señor Dr. D. Isidro de Sicilia y Montoya, cura propio que fue de la misma ciudad y sus anexos, provisor vicario general y governador de este arzobispado de Guatemala, y dean dignidad de la santa iglesia metropolitana de esta diócesi.* Guatemala: Don Manuel de Arévalo, 1812.

Villacorta, Ciriaco. *Discurso pronunciado en el Congreso Federal por el licenciado Ciriaco Villacorta, diputado por el estado de El Salvador, en 18 de julio, á tiempo que discutia el dictamen de las comisiones unidas sobre erección de silla episcopal en aquel estado.* San Salvador: Imprenta del Gobierno, 1826.

Villanueva, Joaquín Lorenzo. *Vida literaria de Dn. Joaquín Lorenzo Villanueva, o memoria de sus escritos y de sus opiniones eclesiásticas y políticas, y de algunos sucesos notables de su tiempo, Tomo 1.* London, UK: Imprenta de A. Macintosh, 1825.

Villarejo, Felipe. *Sermón pronunciado en la solemne función que el comercio de esta capital dedicó a la declaración dogmática de la inmaculada concepción de María santísima, el 23 de septiembre de 1855.* Mexico: Imprenta de J. M. Andrade y F. Escalante, 1855.

Villareal, Narciso. *Cuatro palabras al presbítero D. Ramón Lozano, cura propio de Santa Bárbara, para que no descanse tranquilo en sus errores.* Monterrey: Imprenta de A. Mier, 1861.

Zeceña, Basilio. *Al público respetable.* Guatemala: Imprenta de la Unión, 1829.

Zeceña, Basilio. *Carta al hermano autor del libelo Adivinanza piadosa.* Guatemala: Antonio Beteta, 1825.

Zeseña, Basilio. *Observaciones sobre la Advertencia patriótica publicada bajo el nombre del doctor Cañas.* Guatemala: Beteta, 1824.

SECONDARY SOURCES

Acosta, Adrián. "Una reflexión sobre 'cultura política' e 'ideopraxias' en los escritos de *Los polares.* Guadalajara, 1821–1826." *Historias 86* (September–December 2013): 47–72.

Addy, George M. *The Enlightenment in the University of Salamanca.* Durham, NC: Duke University Press, 1966.

Adelman, Jeremy. *Sovereignty and Revolution in the Iberian Atlantic.* Princeton, NJ: Princeton University Press, 2006.

Albán, Juan Pedro. *Indios rebeldes e idólotras: dos ensayos históricos sobre la rebelión india de Cancuk, Chiapas, acaecida el el año de 1712.* México: CIESAS, 1997.

Alcalá, S. Alfonso. *Una pugna diplomática ante la Santa Sede. El restablecimiento del episcopado en México 1825-1831.* México: Porrúa, 1967.

Altamirano, Ignacio Manuel. *La Navidad en las montañas.* Edited and translated by Harvey L. Johnson. Gainesville, FL: University of Florida Press, 1961.

Arana, Marie. *Bolívar: American Liberator.* New York: Simon and Schuster, 2013.

Arcila Farías, Eduardo. *Reformas económicas del siglo XVIII en la Nueva España.* México: SepSetentas, 1984.

Argüelles, Agustín. *Discursos.* Edited by Francisco Tomás Valiente. Oviedo, ES: Junta General del Principado de Asturias, 1995.

Annino, Antonio. *Historia de las elecciones en Iberoamérica, siglo XIX: De la formación del espacio político nacional.* México, DF: Fondo de Cultura Económica, 1995.

Arreola Cortés, Raúl. *Melchor Ocampo. Vida y obra.* Morelia, MX.: Gobierno del Estado de Michoacán, 1988.

Arrioja Díaz Viruell, Luis Alberto. "Guatemala y Nueva España: historia de una plaga compartida, 1798-1807." *Revista de Historia Moderna* 33 (October 2015): 309–323.

Arriola, Luis. *Gálvez en la encrucijada. Ensayo crítico en torno al humanismo político de un gobernante.* Guatemala: Editorial Cara Parens, 2012.

Arrom, Silvia. *Containing the Poor. The Mexico City Poor House, 1774-1871.* Durham, NC: Duke University Press, 2001.

Arrom, Silvia. "Mexican Laywomen Spearhead a Catholic Revival: The Ladies of Charity, 1863-1910." In *Religious Culture in Modern Mexico,* edited by Martin A. Nesvig, 50–77. Lanham, MD: Rowman & Littlefield, 2007.

Arrom, Silvia. "Las Señoras de la Caridad: pioneras olvidadas de la asistencia social en México, 1863-1910." *Historia Mexicana* 226 (2007): 445–490.

Arrom, Silvia. *The Women of Mexico City, 1790-1857.* Stanford, CA: Stanford University Press, 1985.

Arrom, Silvia. *Volunteering for a Cause: Gender, Faith, and Charity in Mexico from the Reform to the Revolution.* Albuquerque, NM: University of New Mexico Press, 2016.

Avendaño Rojas, Xiomara. "Fiscalidad y soberanía. Dos puntos críticos del gobierno federal en Centroamérica, 1824-1838." *Relaciones. Revista del Colegio de Michoacán* 17, nos. 67/68 (1996): 105–125.

Avendaño Rojas, Xiomara. "Theaters of Power in 1821. Swearing Loyalty to Independence in the Province of Guatemala." In *Independence in Central America and Chiapas, 1770-1823,* edited by Aaron Pollack and translated by Nancy T. Hancock, 81–99. Norman: University of Oklahoma Press, 2019.

Ayala Benítez, Luis Ernesto. *La iglesia y la independencia política de Centroamérica: "El caso del Estado de El Salvador" (1808-1832)*. San Salvador: Editorial Universidad Don Bosco, 2011.

Ayarragaray, Lucas. *La iglesia en América y la dominación española: Estudio de la época colonial*. Buenos Aires: Lajouane, 1920.

Barbastro Gil, Luis. *Revolución liberal y reacción (1808-1833): protagonismo ideológico del clero en la sociedad valenciana*. Alicante: Caja de Ahorros Provincial, 1987.

Barón Castro, Rodolfo. *José Matías Delgado y el movimiento insurgente de 1811*. San Salvador: Ministerio de Educación, Dirección General de Publicaciones, 1962.

Barragán Sánchez, José Miguel. "Pequeño diario portátil 1864. Memorias de un guerrillero durante la intervención francesa." *Archivos de Historia Potosina* 3, no. 8 (January–March 1977).

Baskes, Jeremy. *Staying Afloat: Risk and Uncertainty in Spanish Atlantic World Trade, 1760-1820*. Stanford, CA.: Stanford University Press, 2013.

Bassi, Ernesto. "Beyond Compartmentalized Atlantics: A Case for Embracing the Atlantic from Spanish American Shores." *History Compass* 12, no. 9 (2014): 704–716.

Bastian, Jean-Pierre. *Los disidentes. Sociedades protestantes y revolución en México, 1872-1911*. México: Colegio de México and Fondo de Cultura Económica, 1993.

Bazant, Jan. *Alienation of Church Wealth in Mexico. Social and Economic Aspects of the Liberal Revolution, 1856-1875*. Cambridge, UK: Cambridge University Press, 1971.

Bazant, Jan. "Mexico from Independence to 1867." In *The Cambridge History of Latin America*, volume 3, *From Independence to 1870*, edited by Leslie Bethell, 43–470. Cambridge, UK: Cambridge University Press, 1985.

Bechtel, Alpha Gillett. "The Mexican Episcopal Church: A Century of Reform and Revolution." MA thesis, San Diego State University, 1966.

Belaubre, Christophe. "Opinión pública." In *Centroamérica durante las revoluciones atlánticas: el vocabulario político, 1750-1850*, edited by Jordana Dym and Sajid Alfredo Herrera Mena, 181–197. San Salvador: IEESFORD Editores, 2014.

Belaubre, Christophe. "Candida, Ángel María," AFEHC, Ficha no. 151, at https://www.afehc-historia-centroamericana.org/diccionario2/diccionario_fiche_id_151.html, accessed 26/7/2022.

Belaurbe, Christophe. "Menéndez, don Isidro."AFEHC, Ficha no. 658, at https://www.afehc-historia-centroamericana.org/index_action_fi_aff_id_658.html, accessed on 1/3/2020.

Bell, Madison Smartt. *Toussaint Louverture. A Biography*. New York, NY: Random House, 2007.

Benito Moya, Silvano G. A. "La cultura teológica de las elites letradas. ¿Especulación teórica o pragmatismo en el Tucumán del siglo XVIII?" *Hispana Sacra* 55, no. 131 (January–June 2013): 309–359.

Benson, Nettie Lee. *The Provincial Deputation in Mexico, Harbinger of Provincial Autonomy, Independence, and Federalism*. Austin, TX: University of Texas Press, 1992.

Berman, Harold J. *Law and Revolution. The Formation of the Western Legal Tradition*. Cambridge, MA: Harvard University Press, 1983.

Bernabéu Alberti, Salvador, and Daniel García de la Fuente. "Un Comanche en las Cortes de Cádiz: los informes y trabajos de Ramos Arizpe." *Revista de Historia de la Educación Latinoamericana* 16, no. 23 (July–December 2014): 217–230.

Bernabéu Alberti, Salvador. "El vacío habitado. Jesuitas reales y simulados en México durante los años de la supresión (1767-1816)." *Historia Mexicana* 58, no. 4 (April-June 2009): 1261–1303.

Bethel, Leslie. *Central America Since Independence*. Cambridge, UK: Cambridge University Press, 1991.

Bidegain, Ana María. "Los apóstoles de la insurrección y el vicario castrense (1810-1820)." *Boletín de Historia y Antigüedades* 100, no. 856 (June 2013): 199–237.

Blackbourn, David. *Marpingen: Apparitions of the Virgin Mary in the Nineteenth Century.* New York, NY: Knoft, 1994.

Blanchard, Shaun. "Proto Ecumenical Catholic Reform in the Eighteenth Century. Lodovico Muratori as a Forerunner of Vatican II." *Pro Ecclesia* 25, no. 1 (February 2016): 71–89.

Blanchard, Shaun. *The Synod of Pistoia and Vatican II. Jansenism and the Struggle for Catholic Reform.* New York, NY: Oxford University Press, 2019.

Bokenkotter, Thomas. *Church and Revolution: Catholics in the Struggle for Democracy and Social Justice.* New York, NY: Doubleday, 1998.

Bolton, Charles. *Church Reform in Eighteenth-Century Italy (The Synod of Pistoia, 1786).* The Hague: Martinus Nihhoff, 1969.

Bonfil Batalla, Guillermo. *México Profundo: Reclaiming a Civilization.* Austin, TX: University of Texas Press, 1996.

Brading, D. A. *Church and State in Bourbon Mexico. The Diocese of Michoacán.* Cambridge, UK: Cambridge University Press, 1994.

Brading, D. A. *The First America: The Spanish Monarchy, Creole Patriots and the Liberal State 1492-1866.* Cambridge, UK: Cambridge University Press, 1991.

Brading, D. A. "Liberal Patriotism and the Mexican Revolution." *Journal of Latin American Studies* 20, no. 1 (May 1988): 27–48.

Brading, D. A. *Miners and Merchants in Bourbon Mexico, 1763-1810.* Cambridge, UK: Cambridge University Press, 1971.

Brading, David A. "Ultramontane Intransigence and the Mexican Reform: Clemente de Jesús Munguía." In *The Politics of Religion in an Age of Revival: Studies in Nineteenth-Century Europe and Latin America,* edited by Austen Ivereigh, 115–142. London, UK: Institute of Latin American Studies, 2000.

Bricker, Victoria. *The Indian Christ, the Indian King.* Austin, TX: University of Texas Press, 1981.

Brière, Jean-François. "Abbé Grégoire and Haitian Independence." *Research in African Literatures* 35, no. 2 (Summer 2004): 34–43.

Brown, Richmond F. *Juan Fermín de Aycinena. Central American Colonial Entrepreneur, 1729-1796.* Norman, OK: University of Oklahoma Press, 1997.

Bumgartner, Lois E. "The Attempted Assassination of Honduran President Dionisio de Herrera, November 3, 1826." *Hispanic American Historical Review* 42, no. 1 (February 1962): 60–62.

Burns, J. H., and Thomas M. Izbicki. *Conciliarism and Papalism.* Cambridge, UK: Cambridge University Press, 1997.

Burns, Joseph F. *Priests of the French Revolution. Saints and Renegades in a New Political Era.* University Park: Pennsylvania State University Press, 2014.

Bustamante, Carlos María de. *El indio mexicano o avisos al rey Fernando séptimo para la pacificación de la América Septentrional. Obra redactada en dos opúsculos durante la permanencia del autor en la prisión del Castillo de San Juan de Ulúa en los años 1817-1818. Seguidos del discurso Motivos de mi afecto a la Constitución.* Edited by Manuel Arellano Zavaleta. México: Instituto Mexicano del Seguro Social, 1981.

Butler, Matthew. "La coronación del Sagrado Corazón de Jesús en la Arquidiócesis de México, 1914." In *Revolución, cultura y religión: nuevas perspectivas regionales, siglo XX,* edited by

Yolanda Padilla Rangel, Luciano Ramírez Hurtado, and Francisco Javier Delgado Aguilar, 4–68. Aguascalientes, México: Universidad Autónoma de Aguascalientes, 2011.

Byrd, Brandon R. *The Black Republic: African Americans and the Fate of Haiti*. Philadelphia, PA: University of Pennsylvania Press, 2020.

Callahan, William J. *Church, Politics, and Society in Spain, 1750-1874*. Cambridge, MA: Harvard University Press, 1984.

Callahan, William J. "Two Spains and Two Churches 1760-1835," *Historical Reflections/ Réflexions Historiques* 2, no. 2 (Winter 1976): 157–181.

Calvo Torre, Roberto. *Belezos: Revista de Cultura Popular y Tradiciones de La Rioja*, no. 7 (2008): 67–73.

Campos García, Melchor, and Roger Saldívar. *La diputación provincial en Yucatán, 1812-1823. Entre la iniciativa individual y la acción del gobierno*. Mérida, MX: Ediciones de la Universidad Autónoma de Yucatán, 2007.

Cañas Dinarte, Carlos, Violeta Scarlet Cortez, and Gilbert Ágular Avilés. *Historia del órgano legislativo de la República de El Salvador, 1824-1864*. Volume 1. San Salvador: Junta Directiva Órgano Legislativo, 2006.

Cañizares-Esguerra, Jorge, and Benjamin Breen. "Hybrid Atlantics: Future Directions for the History of the Atlantic World." *History Compass* 11, no. 8 (2013): 597–609.

Caplan, Karen. *Indigenous Citizens: Local Liberalism in Early National Oaxaca and Yucatán*. Stanford, CA: Stanford University Press, 2009.

Cárcel Ortí, Vicente. *Correspondencia diplomática del Nuncio Tiberi (1827-1834)*. Pamplona, ES: Ediciones Universidad de Navarra, 1976.

Carey, Patrick W. "John F.O. Fernandez: Enlightened Lay Catholic Reformer, 1815-1820." *The Review of Politics* 43, no. 1 (January 1981): 112–129.

Carey, Patrick W. *People, Priests, and Prelates: Ecclesiastical Democracy and the Tensions of Trusteeism*. Notre Dame, IN: Notre Dame University Press, 1987.

Carmona, Gisella C., and Armando Arteaga Santoyo, eds. *Fray Servando Teresa de Mier, una visión en los tiempos*. Monterrey, México: Ayuntamiento de Monterrey, 2007.

Carrrillo y Ancona, Crescencio. *El Obispado de Yucatán. Historia de su fundación y de sus obispos. Desde el siglo XVI hasta el XIX. Seguida de las constituciones sindocales de la diócesi y otros documentos relativos*. Mérida, Yucatán: Imprenta y Litografia "R. Caballero," 1895.

Casimir, Jean. *The Haitians: A Decolonial History*. Translated by Laurent Dubois. Introduced by Walter D. Mignolo. Chapel Hill: University of North Carolina Press, 2020.

Castañeda Delgado, Paulina. "El cisma del Socorro y sus protagonistas." In *Homenaje al Dr. Muro Orejón*, volume 1, edited by Luis Navarro García, 257–280. Seville, Spain: Universidad de Sevilla, 1979.

Césaire, Aimé. *Discourse on Colonialism*. New York, nY: Monthly Review Press, 2001 [1950].

Chadwick, Owen. *The Popes and European Revolution*. Cambridge, UK: Clarendon Press and Oxford University Press, 1981.

Chamorro, Pedro Joaquín. *Historia de la federación de la América Central, 1823-1840*. Madrid, ES: Cultura Hispanica, 1951.

Chance, John K., and William B. Taylor, "Cofradias and Cargos: An Historical Perspective on the Mesoamerican Civil-Religious Hierarchy." *American Ethnologist* 12, no. 1 (1985): 1–26.

Chandler, David Lee. *Juan José de Aycinena. Idealista conservador de la Guatemala del siglo XIX*. Antigua, Guatemala: Centro de Investigaciones Regionales de Mesoamérica, 1988.

Chiaramonte, José Carlos. *Ensayos sobre la 'Ilustración' argentina*. Paraná, AR: Facultad de Ciencias de la Educación, Universidad del Litoral, 1962.

Chiaramonte, José Carlos. *La Ilustración en el Río de la Plata: cultura eclesiástica y cultura laica durante el virreinato.* Buenos Aires, AR: Editorial Sudamericana, 2007.

Chowning, Margaret. "La feminización de la piedad en México: Género y piedad en las cofradías de españoles: tendencias coloniales y pos-coloniales en los arzobispados de Michoacán y Guadalajara." In *Religión, política e identidad en la Independencia de México,* coordinated by Brian Connaughton, 475–514. México, D.F.: Universidad Autónoma Metropolitana and Benémerita Universidad Autónoma de Puebla, Instituto de Ciencias Sociales y Humanidades Alfonso Vélez Pliego, 2010.

Chowning, Margaret. "Liberals, Women, and the Church in Mexico: Politics and the Feminization of Piety, 1700–1930." Unpublished paper delivered to the Harvard Latin American Studies Seminar, Cambridge, MA, 2002.

Chust, Manuel."The Impact of the Cortes de Cádiz on IberoAmerica (1810-1830)." In *Forging Patrias: IberoAmerica 1810-1824. Some Reflections,* edited by Guadalupe Jiménez Codinach, 403–453. México: Fomento Cultural Banamex, 2010.

Claps-Arenas, María Eugenia. *"El Salvadoreño* y la formación de opinión pública en el contexto de la primera guerra federal centroamericana, 1828-1829." *LiminaR* 17, no. 1 (2019): 33–47. http://dx.doi.org/10.29043/liminar.v17i1.644

Claps-Arenas, María Eugenia. *"El Siglo de Lafayette* y su discurso sobre México." *Revista Pueblos y Fronteras Digital* 12, no. 24 (December 2017-May 2018): 23–42.

Clark, Christopher. "The New Catholicism and the European Culture Wars." In *Culture Wars: Secular-Catholic Conflict in Nineteenth-Century Europe,* edited by Christopher Clark and Wolfram Kaiser, 11–46. New York: Cambridge University Press, 2003.

Clark, Christopher, and Wolfram Kaiser. "Introduction: The European Culture Wars." In *Culture Wars: Secular-Catholic Conflict in Nineteenth-Century Europe,* edited by Christopher Clark and Wolfram Kaiser, 1–10. New York: Cambridge University Press, 2003.

Cobá Noh, Lorgio. *El "indio ciudadano": La tributación y la contribución personal directa en Yucatán, 1786-1825.* México: Universidad Autónoma de Yucatán and Instituto de Investigaciones Dr. José Luis Mora, 2009.

Connaughton, Brian. "República federal y patronato. El ascenso y descalabro de un Proyecto." *Estudios de Historia Moderna y Contemporánea de México,* 39 (2010): 6–70.

Coronado, Raúl. *A World Not to Come: A History of Latino Writing and Print Culture.* Cambridge, MA: Harvard University Press, 2016.

Cortés Guerrero, José David. "Las discusiones sobre el patronato en Colombia en el siglo XIX." *Historia Crítica* 52 (January–April 2014): 99–122.

Costeloe, Michael P. *The Central Republic in Mexico: A Study of the Patronage Debate, 1821-1857.* London, UK: Royal Historical Society, 1978.

Covo, Jacqueline. *"Le Trait d'Union,* periódico francés de la Ciudad de México, entre la Reforma y la Intervención." *Historia Mexicana* 35, no. 3 (January–March 1986): 461–476.

Cruz, Fernando, and Antonio Machado. *José Batres Montúfar y Alejandro Marure.* Guatemala: Ministerio de Educación Pública, 1957.

Cuevas, Mariano. *Historia de la iglesia en México.* Volume 5. El Paso, TX: Editorial "Revista Católica," 1928.

D'Agostino, Peter. *Rome in America: Transnational Catholic Ideology from the Risorgimento to Fascism.* Chapel Hill, NC: University of North Carolina Press, 2004.

Davenport, E.H. *The False Decretals.* Oxford, UK: B.H. Blackwell, 1916.

Delgado, Jessica L. *Laywomen and the Making of Colonial Catholicism in New Spain, 1630-1790.* New York, NY: Cambridge University Press, 2018.

Delgado, Jessica L., and Kelsey C. Moss, "Religion and Race in the Early Modern Iberian Atlantic." In *The Oxford Handbook of Religion and Race in American History*, edited by Paul Harvey and Katherine Gin Lum. New York, NY: Oxford University Press, 2018.

Demerson, Paula de. *María Francisca de Sales Portocarrero: una figura de la Ilustración*. Madrid, ES: Editorial Nacional, 1975.

Díaz López, Lilia, ed. *Versión francesa de México. Informes diplomáticos, Volume 2, 1858-1862*. México, D.F.: Colegio de México, 1964.

Díaz Covarrubias, Juan. *Obras completas*. Volume 2. Edited by Clementina Díaz de Ovando. México: UNAM, 1959.

Diáz Patiño, Gabriela. *Católicos, liberales, y protestantes. El debate por las imágenes religiosas en la formación de una cultura nacional (1848-1908)*. México, D.F.: Colegio de México, 2016.

Diccionario Porrúa de historia, biografía y geografía de México. 6th edition. Mexico: Porrúa, 1995.

Diefendorf, Barbara B. *Beneath the Cross: Catholics and Huguenots in Sixteenth-Century Paris*. New York, NY: Oxford University Press, 1991.

Di Stefano, Robert. "El debate sobre el celibato sacro y los enclaustramientos forzados en el Río de la Plata revolucionario." *Jahrbuch für Geschichte Lateinamerikas/Anuario de Historia de América Latina* 44, no. 1 (2007): 207–234.

Di Tello, Torcuato. *Política nacional y popular en México, 1820-1847*. México: Fondo de Cultura Económica, 1994.

Documentos relacionados con la vida militar, política, y familiar de Gral. don Pedro José Méndez. Volume 2. Ciudad Victoria, México: Talleres Linotipográficos del Gobierno del Estado, 1966.

Domergue, Lucienne. "De Erasmo a George Borrow: Biblia y secularización de la cultura española en el Siglo de la Luces." In *La secularización de la cultura española en el Siglo de la Luces: Actas del Congreso de Wolfenbüttel*, edited by Manfried Tietz, 57–90. Weisbaden, DE: Herzog August Bibliothek Wolfenbüttel, 1992.

Domínguez Michael, Christopher. *Vida de Fray Servando*. México: Ediciones Era, 2004.

Domínguez T., Mauricio. "El Obispado de San Salvador: Foco de desavenencia político-religioso." *Anuario de Estudios Centroamericanos* 1 (1974): 87–133.

Dubois, Laurent. "An Enslaved Enlightenment: Rethinking the Intellectual History of the French Atlantic." *Social History* 31, no. 1 (February 2006): 1–14.

Duffy, Eamon. *Saints and Sinners. A History of the Popes*. New Have: Yale University Press, 1997.

Dufour, Gérard. "Las ideas político-religiosas de Juan Antonio Llorente." *Cuadernos de Historia Contemporánea* 10 (1988): 11–22.

Dufour, Gérard. *Juan Antonio Llorente en France (1813-1822): contribution a l'étude du libéralisme chrétien en France et en Espagne au début du XIX siècle*. Geneva, CH: Libraire Droz, 1982.

Dumond, Don E. "The Talking Crosses of Yucatán: A New Look at Their History." *Ethnohistory* 32, no. 4 (1985): 291–308.

Dym, Jordana. "Conceiving Central America: A Bourbon Public in the Gazeta de Guatemala (1797-1807)." In *Enlightened Reform in Southern Europe and its Atlantic Colonies, ca. 1750-1830*, edited by Gabriel Paquette, 99–118. Farnham, UK: Ashgate, 2009.

Dym, Jordana. *From Sovereign Villages to Nation States: City, State, and Federation in Central America, 1759-1839*. Albuquerque, NM: University of New Mexico Press, 2006.

Dym, Jordana. "The State, the City, and the Priest: Political Participation and Conflict Resolution in Independence-Era Central America." In *City and Nation: Rethinking Place and*

Identity: Comparative Urban and Community Research, volume 7, edited by Michael Peter Smith and Thomas Bender, 136–180. New Brunswick, NJ: Transaction Publishers, 2001.

Earle, Rebecca. "Luxury, Clothing and Race in Colonial Spanish America." In *Luxury in the Eighteenth Century: Debates, Desires, and Delectable Goods*, edited by Maxine Berg and Elizabeth Eger, 219–227. Houndmills, UK.: Palgrave Macmillan, 2003.

Eastman, Scott, and Natalia Sobrevilla Perea, eds. *The Rise of Constitutional Government in the Iberian Atlantic World: the Impact of the Cádiz Constitution of 1812*. Tuscaloosa, AL: University of Alabama Press, 2015.

Egido, Teófanes. "El Real Patronato." In *Iglesia y sociedad en el Reino de Granada (siglos XVI–XVIII)*. Coordinated by Antonio Luis Cortés Peña and Guadalupe Muñoz et al., 9–21. Granada, ES: Universidad de Granada, 2003.

Suárez, Francisco. *Defensa de la fé católica y apostólica contra los errores del Anglicanismo*. Edited by José Eguiller Muñioz Guren. Madrid: Instituto de Estudios Políticos, 1971 [1613].

Enríquez, Lucrecia Raquel. "El patronato en Chile de Carrera a O'Higgins." *Hispania Sacra* 60, no. 122 (July–December 2008): 507–529.

Enríquez, Lucrecia Raquel. "El patronato de la monarquía católica a la república católica chilena (1810–1833)." In *Normatividades e instituciones eclesiásticas en el Virreinato del Perú, siglos XVI–XIX*, edited by Otto Danwerth and Benetta Albani, 223–243. Berlin, DE: Max Planck Institute for Legal History and Legal Theory, 2019.

Esdaile, Chares. *The Peninsular War*. London, UK: Penguin Books, 2002.

Farriss, Nancy M. *Maya Society Under Colonial Rule. The Collective Enterprise of Survival*. Princeton, NJ: Princeton University Press, 1984.

Fernández Arrillaga, Immaculada. "Profecías, coplas, creencias y devociones de los jesuitas expulsos durante su exilio en Italia." *Revista de Historia Moderna: Anales de la Universidad de Alicante* 16 (1997): 83–98.

Fernández, José Antonio M. *Pintando el mundo de azul: El auge añilero y el mercado centroamericano, 1750–1810*. San Salvador: Dirección de Publicaciones e Impresos, Consejo Nacional para la Cultura y el Arte, 2003.

Fernández Mellén, Consolación. *Iglesia y poder en la Habana. Juan José Díaz de Espada, un obispo ilustrado (1800-1832)*. Bilbao ES: Universidad del País Vasco, 2014.

Ferrer, Ada. *Freedom's Mirror. Cuba and Haiti in the Age of Revolution*. New York, NY: Cambridge University Press, 2014.

Ferrer, Ada. "Haiti, Free Soil, and Antislavery in the Revolutionary Atlantic." *American Historical Review* 117, no. 1 (February 2012): 40–66.

Ferrer Muñoz, Manuel: "La coyuntura de la independencia en Yucatán, 1810-1821." In *La independencia en el sur de México*, edited by Ana Carolina Ibarra, 343–394. Coyoacán, México: UNAM/Instituto de Investigaciones Históricas, 2004.

Figueroa y Miranda, Miguel. *Religión y política en la Cuba del siglo XIX. El Obispo Espada visto a la luz de los archivos romanos, 1802-1832*. Miami, FL: Ediciones Universal, 1975.

Flemion, Philip F. "State's Rights and Partisan Politics: Manuel José Arce and the Struggle for Central American Union." *The Hispanic American Historical Review* 53, no. 4 (November 1973): 600–618.

Floyd, Troy S. "The Indigo Merchant: Promoter of Central American Economic Development, 1750-1808." *Business History Review* 39, no. 4 (winter 1965): 466–488.

Fogarty, Gerald P. *Commonwealth Catholicism. A History of the Catholic Church in Virginia*. Notre Dame, IN: University of Notre Dame Press, 2001.

Ford, Caroline. *Creating the Nation in Provincial France: Religion and Political Identity in Brittany.* Princeton, NJ: Princeton University Press, 1993.

Foucault, Michel. "What Is Enlightenment?" In *The Foucault Reader*, edited by Paul Rabinow, 32–50. New York, NY: Pantheon, 1984.

Fowler, Jessica. "Illuminating the Empire: The Dissemination of the Spanish Inquisition and the Heresy of Alumbradismo, 1525-1600." PhD dissertation, University of California at Davis, 2015.

Fowler, Will. "Valentín Gómez Farías: Perceptions of Radicalism in Independent Mexico, 1821-1847." *Bulletin of Latin American Research* 15 (1996): 39–62.

Gallardo, Guillermo. *La política religiosa de Rivadavia.* Buenos Aires, AR: Ediciones Teoría, 1962.

García, Miguel Ángel. *Diccionario histórico enciclopédico de la República de El Salvador. El doctor José Matías Delgado. Homenaje en el primer centenario de su muerte, 1832-1932. Documentos para el estudio de su vida y de su obra.* Volume 2. El Salvador: Imprenta Nacional, 1939.

García y García, Apolinar. *Historia de la Guerra de Castas de Yucatán.* Mérida, Yucatán, México: Ediciones de la Universidad Autónoma de Yucatán, 2018.

García Godoy, María Teresa. *Las Cortes de Cádiz y América: el primer vocabulario liberal español y mejicano (1810-1814).* Sevilla, ES: Diputación de Sevilla 1998.

García Laguardia, Jorge. *Centroamérica en las Cortes de Cádiz.* Mexico: Fondo de Cultura Económica, 1994.

García León, José María. *Los diputados doceañistas.* Volume 1. Cádiz, ES: Ayuntamiento de Cádiz, 2006.

García Peña, Lorgia. *The Borders of Dominicanidad. Race, Nation, and Archives of Contradiction.* Durham, NC: Duke University Press, 2016.

García Pérez, Juan. *Diego Muñoz Torrero. Ilustración, religiosidad y liberalism.* Extremadura, ES: Editora Regional de Extremadura, 1989.

Gardner, Ian. *The Founder of Manichaeism. Rethinking the Life of Mani.* Cambridge, UK: Cambridge University Press, 2020.

Garrard-Burnett, Virginia. "Indigo." In *Encyclopedia of Latin American History and Culture*, volume 3, edited by Jay Kinsbruner and Erick D. Langer, 829–830. Detroit, MI: Charles Scribner's Sons, 2008.

Getachew, Adom. "Universalism after the Post-colonial Turn." *Political Theory* 44, no. 6 (December 2016): 821–845

Gilbert, David Allen. "'Long Live the True Religion!' Contesting the Meaning of Catholicism in the Mexican Reforma, 1855–1860." PhD dissertation, University of Iowa, 2003.

Gilroy, Paul. *The Black Atlantic: Modernity and Double Consciousness.* Cambridge, MA: Harvard University Press, 1995.

Goldstein Stepinwall, Alyssa. *The Abbé Grégoire and the French Revolution: The Making of Modern Universalism.* Berkeley, CA: University of California Press, 2005.

Góngora, Mario. "Estudios sobre el galicanismo y la 'Ilustración católica' en América española." *Revista Chilena de Historia y Geografía* 125 (1957): 96–151.

González Calderón, Marcela. *El Yucatán de Zavala: sus primeros años.* México: Secretaría de Educación del Gobierno del Estado de México, 2012.

González Navarro, Moisés. *Raza y tierra: la guerra de castas y el henequén.* México: El Colegio de México, 1979.

González Salas, Carlos. *Miguel Ramos de Arizpe: Cumbre y camino.* México: Porrúa 1978.

Gough, Austin. *Paris and Rome: The Gallican Church and the Ultramontane Campaign, 1848-1853.* Oxford, UK: Clarendon Press, 1986.

Grandin, Greg. *The Blood of Guatemala: A History of Race and Nation.* Durham, NC: Duke University Press, 2000.

Graubart, Karen. "Learning from the *Qadi*: The Jurisdiction of Local Rule in the Early Colonial Andes," *Hispanic American Historical Review* 92, no. 2 (2015): 195–228

Greenland, Fay Sharon. "Religious Reform in Mexico: The Role of the Mexican Episcopal Church." MA thesis, University of Florida, 1958.

Gruzinski, Serge. "Les mondes mêlés de la monarchie catholique et autres 'connected histories.'" *Annales* 56, no. 1 (2001): 85–117.

Guedea, Virginia. *En busca de un gobierno alterno: los Guadalupes de México.* México: Instituto de Investigaciones Históricas, UNAM, 1992.

Guedea, Virginia. "Las publicaciones periódicas durante el proceso de independencia (1808-1821)." In *La república de las letras. Asomos a la cultura escrita del México decimonónico,* edited by Belem Clark de Lara and Elisa Speckman Guerra, 29–42. Mexico City: Universidad Nacional Autónoma de México, 2005.

Guerra, François-Xavier. *Modernidad e independencias: ensayos sobre las revoluciones hispánicas.* México D.F.: Fondo de Cultura Económica, 1993.

Guerra, Francois-Xavier. "The Spanish-American Tradition of Representation and its European Roots." *Journal of Latin American Studies,* 26, no. 1 (February 1994): 1–35.

Gutiérrez Casillas, José. *Historia de la iglesia en México.* Mexico: Editorial Porrúa, 1974.

Guzmán Galarza, Mario V. *Documentos básicos de la Reforma, 1854-1875.* México: Partido Revolucionario Institucional, 1982.

Gwynn, Denis. "Henry Grattan and Catholic Emancipation," *Studies: An Irish Quarterly Review* 18, no. 72 (1929): 576–592.

Habermas, Jürgen. *The Structural Transformation of the Public Sphere: An Inquiry into a Category of Bourgeois Society.* Translated by Thomas Burger. Cambridge, MA: MIT Press, 1989.

Hale, Charles. *Mexican Liberalism in the Age of Mora.* New Haven, CT.: Yale University Press, 1968.

Hale, Charles. *The Transformation of Mexican Liberalism in Late Nineteenth-Century Mexico.* Princeton, NJ: Princeton University Press, 1994.

Hall, Caroyln and Héctor Pérez Brignoli, with John V. Carter, Cartographer. *Historical Atlas of Central America.* Norman, OK: University of Oklahoma Press, 2003.

Hamill, Hugh M. *The Hidalgo Revolt: Prelude to Independence.* Gainesville: University of Florida Press, 1966.

Hamnett, Brian R. "The Counter Revolution of Morillo and the Insurgent Clerics of New Granada, 1815-1820." *The Americas* 32, no. 4 (April 1976): 597–617.

Hamnett, Brian R. *The End of Iberian Rule on the American Continent, 1770-1830.* Cambridge, UK: Cambridge University Press, 2007.

Hamnett, Brian R. "Joaquín Lorenzo Villanueva (1757-1837): de 'católico ilustrado' a 'católico liberal'. El dilema de la transición." In *Visiones del liberalismo. Política, identidad y cultura en la España del siglo XIX,* edited by Alda Blanco and Guy Thomson, 19–41. Valéncia, ES: Universitat de Valencia, 2008.

Hamnett, Brian R. *Juárez.* London, UK: Longman, 1994.

Hart, Catherine Poupney. "Parcours journalistiques en régime colonial: José Rossi y Rubí, Alejandro Ramírez et Simón Bergaño." *El Argonauta Español* (June 2009): 1–28. https://doi.org/10.4000/argonauta.603.

Hawkins, Timothy. *José de Bustamante and Central American Independence: Colonial Administration in an Age of Imperial Crisis.* Tuscaloosa, AL: The University of Alabama Press, 2004.

Hawkins, Timothy. "A War of Words: Manuel Montúfar, Alejandro Marure, and the Politics of History in Guatemala." *The Historian* 64, nos. 3/4 (spring/summer 2002): 513–533.

Hendricks, Frances Kellam. "The First Apostolic Mission to Chile," *Hispanic American Historical Review* 22, no. 4 (Nov., 1942): 644–669.

Hernández de Alba, Guillermo, and Fabio Lozano y Lozano, eds. *Documentos sobre el doctor Vicente Azuero.* Bogotá, CO: Imprenta Nacional, 1944.

Hernández Figueiredo, José Ramón. *El Cardenal Pedro de Quevado y Quintano en las Cortes de Cádiz.* Madrid, ES: Biblioteca de Autores Cristianos, 2012.

Hernández y Dávalos, Juan E., ed. *Colección de documentos para la historia de la Guerra de Independencia de México de 1808 a 1821.* Nendeln, LI: Kraus, 1968.

Hernández Silva, Héctor Cuauhtémoc. "Las motivaciones políticas de Xavier Mina, sus preparativos en Galveston y su desembarco en el Nuevo Santander en 1817." In *La expedición fallida de Xavier Mina,* edited by Jaime Olveda. Zapopan, Jalisco, MX: El Colegio de Jalisco, 2019.

Herrejón Peredo, Carlos. *Hidalgo: razones de la insurgencia y biografía documental.* México, D.F.: Secretaría de Educación Pública, 1987.

Herrera González, Julio. *¡Serviles! El grupo reaccionario de las Cortes de Cádiz.* Málaga, ES: Servicio de Publicaciones de Unicaja Fundación, 2007.

Herrera Mena, Sajid Alfredo. "1811. Relectura de los levantamientos y protestas en la provincia de San Salvador." *Revista La Universidad* 16 (October-December, 2011): 111–126.

Herrera Mena, Sajid Alfredo. *El ejercicio de gobernar: del cabildo borbónico al ayuntamiento liberal. El Salvador colonial, 1750–1821.* Castellón, ES: Universitat Jaume I, 2014

Herrera Mena, Sajid Alfredo. "Escenarios de lealtad e infidencia durante el régimen constitucional gaditano: San Salvador, 1811–1814." *Mesoamérica* 32, no. 53 (June–December 2011): 200–210.

Herrera Mena, Sajid Alfredo. "La invención liberal de la identidad estatal salvadoreña 1824-1839." *Estudios Centroamericanos. Revista de Extensión Cultural de la Universidad Centroamericana "José Simeón Cañas"* 60, no. 684 (2005): 913–936.

Herrera Mena, Sajid Alfredo. "Luchas de poder, practicas políticas y lenguaje constitucional. San Salvador a fines de 1821," *Hacer historia en El Salvador. Revista Electrónico de Estudios Históricos* 1, no. 1 (2007): 1–15.

Herrera Mena, Sajid Alfredo. "Orden corporativo en tiempos republicanos: las municipalidades salvadoreñas (1824-1838)." In *Diálogo historiográfico Centroamérica-México,* edited by Brian Connaughton, 177–218. Mexico City: Universidad Autónoma Metropolitana and Editorial Gedisa, 2017.

Herrera Mena, Sajid Alfredo. "Autonomia, independencia, y patronato repúblicano en San Salvador. José Matías Delgado e Isidro Méndez, 1808-1830," 337-355. In *Juristas de la Independencia.* Edited by José María Pérez Callados and Samuel Rodrigues Barbosa. Madrid, ES: Marcial Pons, 2012.

Herr, Richard. *The Eighteenth-Century Revolution in Spain.* Princeton, NJ: Princeton University Press, 1959.

Hessinger, Rodney. "A Base and Unmanly Conspiracy": Catholicism and the Hogan Schism in the Gendered Religious Market of Philadelphia." *Journal of the Early Republic* 31, no. 3 (fall 2011): 357–396.

Hidalgo Pego, Mónica. "Formando ministros útiles: inculcación de hábitos y deberes tras-mitidos en el Colegio de San Ildefonso (1768-1816)." In *Espacios de saber, espacios de poder. Iglesia, universidades y colegios en Hispanoamérica, siglos XVI-XIX,* edited by Rodolfo Aguirre Salvador, 379–395. México: UNAM, 2013.

Holleran, Mary Patricia. *Church and State in Guatemala.* New York, NY: Octagon Books, 1974.

Holmes, J. Derek. *The Triumph of the Holy See: A Short History of the Papacy in the Nineteenth Century.* London, UK: Burns and Oates, 1978.

Ibarra, Ana Carolina, ed. *Andrés Quintana Roo.* México: Senado de la República, 1987.

Ibarra, Ana Carolina. "Religión y política. Manuel Sabino Crespo, un cura párroco del sur de México." *Historia Mexicana* 56, no. 1 (July–September, 2006): 5–69.

Illades, Carlos, and Adriana Sandoval. *Espacio social y representación literaria en el siglo XIX.* México: Universidad Autónoma Metropolitana, 2000.

Ingersoll, Hazel Marylyn Bennett. "The War of the Mountain: A Study of Reactionary Peasant Insurgency in Guatemala, 1837-1873." PhD dissertation, George Washington University, 1972.

Irigoyen Rosaldo, Renán. *La Constitucion de Cadiz de 1812 y los Sanjuanistas de Mérida.* Mérida: Ayuntamiento de Mérida, Yucatán, 1980.

Jackson, Robert H., and Edward Castillo. *Indians, Franciscans, and Spanish Colonization: The Impact of the Mission System on California Indians.* Albuquerque, NM: University of New Mexico Press, 1995.

Jiménez Codinach, Estela Guadalupe. *La Gran Bretaña y la Independencia de México (1808-1821).* Translated by Ismael Izarro Suárez and Mercedes Pizarro Suárez. México: Fondo de Cultura Económica, 1991.

Jiménez López, Enrique. "La devoción a la Madre Santísima de la Luz: un aspecto de la represión del jesuitismo en la España de Carlos III." In *Expulsión y exilio de los jesuitas españoles,* edited by Enrique Jiménez López, 213–228. Alicante, ES: Universidad de Alicante, 1997.

Johnson, Jessica Marie. *Wicked Flesh: Black Women, Intimacy, and Freedom in the Atlantic World.* Philadelphia, PA: University of Pennsylvania Press, 2020.

Jonas, Raymond. *France and the Cult of the Sacred Heart: An Epic Tale for Modern Times.* Berkeley, CA: University of California Press, 2000.

Jovellanos, Gaspar Melchor de. "Discurso pronunciado por el Señor Gaspar de Jovellanos del Consejo de S.M. de la Real Sociedad de Amigos del País del Principado de Asturias y su actual director [1782]." In *Cartas entre Campomanes y Jovellanos,* edited by Ramón Jordán de Urries. Madrid, ES: Fundación Universitaria Español, 1975.

Kamen, Henry. *The Disinherited: Exile and the Making of Spanish Culture, 1492-1975.* New York, NY: HarperCollinsPublisher, 2008.

Kilroy, Lauren Grace, "Dissecting Bodies, Creating Cults: Imagery of the Sacred Heart of Jesus in New Spain." PhD dissertation, University of California at Los Angeles, 2009.

Kilroy-Ewbank, Lauren G. *Holy Organ or Unholy Idol? The Sacred Heart in Art, Religion, and Culture of New Spain.* Leiden, NL: Brill, 2018.

Kinsbruner, Jay. *Independence in Spanish America: Civil Wars, Revolutions and Underdevelopment.* Albuquerque, NM: University of New Mexico Press, 1994.

Knowlton, Robert J. *Church Property and the Mexican Reform, 1856-1910.* DeKalb, IL: Northern Illinois University Press, 1976.

Knowlton, Robert J. "Clerical Response to the Mexican Reform, 1855-1875." *Catholic Historical Review* 50, no. 4 (January 1965): 509–529.

Knowlton, Robert J. "Some Practical Effects of Clerical Opposition to the Mexican Reform, 1856-1860." *Hispanic American Historical Review* 45, no. 2 (May 1965): 246–257.

Krauze, Enrique. *Mexico. Biography of Power. A History of Modern Mexico, 1810-1996.* Translated by Hank Heifetz. New York, NY: Harper Collins Publisher, 1997.

Kwass, Michael. "Big Hair: A Wig History of Consumption in Eighteenth-Century France." *American Historical Review* 111, no. 3 (June 2006): 631–659.

La Parra López, Emilio, and Antonio Mestre, *El primer liberalismo español y la iglesia: las Cortes de Cádiz.* Alicante, ES: Instituto de Estudios Juan Gil-Albert: Diputación Provincial, 1985.

Lamberts, Emiel. *The Struggle with Leviathan: Social Responses to the Omnipotence of the State, 1815-1965.* Leuven, BE: Leuven University Press, 2016.

Lamikiz, Xabier. *Trade and Trust in the Eighteenth-Century Atlantic World: Spanish Merchants and their Overseas Networks.* Suffolk, UK: Boydell Press, 2013.

Lanning, John Tate. *The Eighteenth-Century Enlightenment in the University of San Carlos de Guatemala.* Ithaca, NY: Cornell University Press, 1956.

Lanning, John Tate, and Rafael Heliodoro Valle, eds. *Reales cédulas de la Real y Pontificia Universidad de México de 1551 a 1816.* México: Imprenta Universitaria, 1946.

La Parra López, Emilio, and Antonio Mestre Sanchís. *La inquisición en España. Agonía y abolición.* Madrid, ES: Catarata, 2013.

La Parra López, Emilio, and Antonio Mestre Sanchís. *El primer liberalismo español y la Iglesia.* Alicante, ES: Instituto de Cultura Juan Gil-Albert, 1985.

Lara, Silvia Hunold. "The Signs of Color: Women's Dress and Racial Relations in Salvador and Rio de Janeiro, ca 1750–1815," *Colonial Latin American Review* 6, no. 2 (1997): 205–222.

Lardé y Larín, Jorge. *Orígenes del periodismo en El Salvador.* San Salvador: Ministerio de Cultura, 1950.

Larkin, Brian. *The Very Nature of God: Baroque Catholicism and Religious Reform in Bourbon Mexico City.* Albuquerque, NM: University of New Mexico Press, 2010.

Lasarte, Javier. "Los diezmos ante la contribución extraordinaria propuesta por carga de Argüelles a las Cortes de Cádiz. El filósofo rancio arremete contra Argüelles y desata la polémica." *Revista de estudios regionales* 95 (2012): 203–273.

Lau Jaiven, Ana, and Ximena Sepúlveda Otaiza. *Hidalgo, una historia compartida.* México: Instituto de Investigaciones Dr. José María Luis Mora, 1994.

Laughlin, Robert M. *Beware the Great Horned Serpent: Chiapas Under the Threat of Napoleon.* Albany, NY: Institute for Mesoamerican Studies, 2003.

Lea, Henry Charles. *A History of the Inquisition of Spain.* Volume 4. New York: Harper and Brothers, 1887.

Leavitt-Alcántara, Brianna. *Alone at the Altar. Single Women and Devotion in Guatemala, 1670-1870.* Stanford, CA: Stanford University Press, 2018.

Lehner, Ulrich L. *The Catholic Enlightenment: The Forgotten History of a Global Movement.* Oxford: Oxford University Press, 2016.

Lentz, Mark. "The Mission That Wasn't: Yucatán's Jesuits, the Mayas, and El Peten, 1703-1767." *World History Connected* (October 2013).

Leturia, Pedro. *La acción diplomática de Bolívar ante Pío VII (1820-1823): a la luz del Archivo Vaticano.* Caracas, VE: Ediciones La Gran Pulpería de Libros Venezolanos, 1984.

Lewis, William F. "Simón Bolívar and Xavier Mina: A Rendezvous in Haiti." *Journal of Inter-American Studies* 11, no. 3 (July 1969): 458–465.

Light, Dale B. *Rome and the New Republic. Conflict and Community in Philadelphia Catholicism between the Revolution and the Civil War.* Notre Dame, IN., and London, UK: University of Notre Dame Press, 1996.

Lines, María M. de. "Movimientos precursores de la independencia en el Reino de Guatemala." *Revista de la Universidad de Costa Rica* 31 (1971): 27–40.

López Jiménez, Ramón. *Mitras salvadoreñas.* San Salvador: Ministerio de Cultura, Departamento Editorial, 1960.

López Jiménez, Ramón. *José Simeón Cañas. Su obra, su verdadera personalidad y su destino.* San Salvador: Dirección General de Cultura, Dirección de Publicaciones, 1970.

López Vela, Roberto. "La jurisdicción inquisitorial y la eclesiástica en la historiografía," Espacio, Tiempo y Forma, Serie IV, *Historia Moderna* 7 (1994): 383–408.

López-Aydillo, Eugenio. *El Obispo de Orense en la regencia del año 1810. Plantamiento de los problemas fundamentales de la vida constitucional de España.* Madrid, ES: Imprenta de Fortanet, 1918.

Loyola, Ignatius of. *The Spiritual Exercises and Selected Works.* Edited by George E. Ganss, S.J. Preface by John W. Padberg. New York, NY: Paulist Press, 1991.

Luján Muñoz, Jorge. "La Asamblea Nacional Constituyente Centroamericana de 1823-24." *Revista de Historia de América* 94 (July–December 1982): 33–89.

Lynch, John. *The Spanish Revolutions.* New York, NY: W.W. Norton, 1983.

Machuca Gallegos, Laura. "José Matías Quintana: un hombre entre dos tradiciones." In *Yucatán en la ruta del liberalismo mexicano, siglo XIX,* edited by Sergio Quezada and Inés Ortiz Yam, 141–166. Mérida, MX: Universidad Autónoma de Yucatán, 2008.

Machuca Gallegos, Laura. "Opinión pública y represión en Yucatán, 1808-1816," *Historia Mexicana* 66, no. 4 (April–June 2017): 1687–1757.

Machuca Gallegos, Laura. "Yucatán and Campeche: Deputies in Cadiz and their Ideas About the Yucatán Peninsula, 1810-1814." *Anuario de Estudios Americanos* 69, no. 2 (July–December 2012): 695–722.

Mahood, Saba. *The Politics of Piety: The Islamic Revival and the Feminist Subject.* Princeton, NJ: Princeton University Press, 2005.

Malaina, Santiago. *Historia de la erección de la diócesis de San Salvador.* San Salvador, 1944.

Mallon, Florencia. *Peasant and Nation: The Making of Postcolonial Mexico and Peru.* Berkeley, CA: University of California Press, 1995.

Malo, José Ramón. *Diario de sucesos notables (1854-1864).* Edited by Mariano Cuevas. México: Editorial Patria, 1948.

Mandeville, Bernard. *The Fable of the Bees: or Private Vices, Public Benefits.* Edited by F. B. Kaye. Indianapolis, IN: University of Indiana Press, 1988 [1714].

Mangan, Jane E. *Transatlantic Obligations: Creating the Bonds of Family in Conquest-era Perú and Spain.* New York, NY: Oxford University Press, 2016.

Martí Gilabert, Francisco. *La abolición de la Inquisición en España.* Pamplona, ES: Ediciones Universidad de Navarra, 1975.

Martínez, María Elena. *Geneological Fictions. Limpieza de Sangre, Religion, and Gender in Colonial Mexico.* Stanford, CA: Stanford University Press, 2008.

Martínez, María Elena. "Religion, Caste, and Race in the Spanish and Portuguese Empires. Local and Global Dimensions." In *Iberian Empires and the Roots of Globalization,* edited by Anna More, Ivonne del Valle, and Rachel Sarah O'Toole, 75–104. Nashville, TN: Vanderbilt University Press, 2019.

Martínez Alomía, Gustavo. *Historiadores de Yucatán. Apuntes biográficos y bibliográficos de los historiadores de esta península desde su descubrimiento hasta fines del siglo XIX.* Campeche, Yucatán, MX: Tipografía "El Fénix,"1906.

Martínez Gramuglia, Pablo, and Mariana Rosetti, "Letrado americano, organizador cultural: algunas polémicas de Vicente Pazos Kanki como editor de periódicos rioplatenses (1811-1816)." *In El Argonauta Española 14 (2017)* https://doi.org/10.4000/argonauta.2695.

Martínez Pichardo, José, Enrique Peña Nieto, and V. Humberto Benítez Treviño. *Leona Vicario: grandeza de una mujer de su tiempo en la lucha por la Independencia.* Toluca de Lerdo, Estado de México, MX: Gobierno del Estado de México, 2008.

Marure, Alejandro. *Bosquejo histórico de las revoluciones de Centro-América, desde 1811 hasta 1834.* 2 vols. Guatemala: Ministerio de Educación Pública, 1960.

McMahon, Darrin M. *Enemies of the Enlightenment: The French Counter-Enlightenment and the Making of Modernity.* New York, NY: Oxford University Press, 2001.

Meade, Joaquín. *La Huasteca Tamaulipeca.* Volume 2. Ciudad Victoria, Tamaulipas, Mx.: UAT-IIH, 1978.

Mecham, J. Lloyd. *Church and State in Latin America. A History of Politico-Ecclesiastical Relations.* Chapel Hill, NC: University of North Carolina Press, 1966.

Mehl, Eva María. "La expulsión de los jesuitas y la represión del jesuitismo en Nueva España." In *Espacios de saber, espacios de poder. Iglesia, universidades y colegios en Hispanoamérica siglos XVI-XIX,* edited by Rodolfo Aguirre Salvador, 317–346. México: UNAM, 2013.

Meléndez Chaverri, Carlos. *José Matías Delgado, prócer centroamericano.* 2nd ed. San Salvador: Dirección de Publicaciones e Impresos, 2000.

Meléndez Chaverri, Carlos. *El presbítero y doctor Don José Matías Delgado en la forja de la nacionalidad Centroamericana.* San Salvador: Dirección General de Publicaciones del Ministerio de Educación, 1962.

Marcelino Menéndez Pelayo, *Historia de los heterodoxos españoles.* Volume 5, *Heterodoxia en el siglo XIX,* edited by Enrique Sánchez Reyes. 2nd edition. Madrid: Consejo Superior de Investigaciones Científicas, 1946.

Membreño, Alberto. *Aztequismos de Honduras.* México: Imprenta de Ignacio Escalante, 1907.

Mestre Sanchís, Antonio. "La influencia del pensamiento de van Espen en la España del siglo XVIII." *Revista Historia Moderna, Anales de la Universidad de Alicante* 19 (2001): 405–430.

Mestre Sanchís, Antonio. "Repercusión del sínodo de Pistoia en España." In *Il Sinodo di Pistoia del 1786: atti del convegno internazionale per il secondo centerario, Pistoia-Prato, 25-27 settembre 1986,* edited by Claudio Lamioni, 425–439. Rome, IT: Herder, 1991.

Mestre Sanchís, Antonio, and Rafael Benítez Sánchez-Blanco. *La iglesia en la España de los siglos XVII y XVIII.* Madrid ES: Editorial Católica, 1979.

Mier Noriega y Guerra, José Servando Teresa de. *Escritos inéditos de Fray Servando Teresa de Mier,* edited by J. M. Miquel i Vergés and Hugo Díaz-Thomé. México: El Colegio de México, Centro de Estudios Históricos, 1944.

Mier Noriega y Guerra, José Servando Teresa de. *Memorias.* 2 vols. Edited by Antonio Castro Leal. México: Editorial Porrúa, 1946.

Mier Noriega y Guerra, José Servando Teresa de. *La Revolución y la fé. Una antología general.* Edited by Begoña Pulido Herráez. México: Fondo de Cultura Económica, Fundación para las Letras Mexicanas, and UNAM, 2013.

Mignolo, Walter. *Local Histories/Global Designs: Coloniality, Subaltern Knowledges and Border Thinking.* Princeton, NJ: Princeton University Press, 2000.

Mijangos y González, Pablo. *The Lawyer of the Church. Bishop Clemente de Jesús Munguía and the Clerical Response to the Mexican Liberal Reforma.* Lincoln, NE.: University of Nebraska Press, 2015.

Miles, Richard. *The Donatist Schism: Controversy and Contexts.* Liverpool, UK: Liverpool University Press, 2018.

Montúfar y Coronado, Manuel. *Memorias para la historia de la revolución de Centro América (Memorias de Jalapa), Recuerdos y anécdotas, tomo 1, vol. 65, Biblioteca Guatemalteca de Cultura Popular.* Guatemala: Centro Editorial José de Pineda Ibarra, 1963.

Montúfar, Lorenzo. *Reseña histórica de Centro América.* Guatemala: Tipografia de El Progreso, 1878–1887.

Morán Ortí, Manuel. "Conciencia y revolución liberal: actitudes políticas de los eclesiásticos en las Cortes de Cádiz," *Hispana Sacra* 55, no. 112 (1990): 485–492.

Morazán, Francisco. *Memorias de David [1841]; Manifiesto del pueblo centroaméricano.* Teguicigalpa, HN: Instituto Morazánico de Honduras, 1953.

Moreno Alonso, Manuel. *La constitución de Cádiz: Una mirada crítica.* Sevilla, ES: Ediciones Alfar, 2011.

Morgan, David. *The Sacred Heart of Jesus: The Visual Evolution of a Devotion.* Amsterdam, NL: Amsterdam University Press, 2008.

Múnera, Alfonso. *El fracaso de una nación: región, clase y raza en el Caribe colombiano (1717-1810).* Havana, Cuba: Fondo Editorial Casa de las Américas, 2011.

Napolitano, Valentina. *Migrant Hearts and the Atlantic Return: Transnationalism and the Roman Catholic Church.* New York, NY: Fordham University Press, 2016.

Noel, Charles. "Clerics and Crown in Bourbon Spain, 1700-1808: Jesuits, Jansenists, and Enlightened Reformers." In *Religion and Politics in Enlightenment Europe*, edited by James E. Bradley and Dale K. Van Kley, 119–153. Notre Dame, IN: University of Notre Dame Press, 2001.

O'Brien, Elizabeth. "'If They Are Useful, Why Expel Them?' Las Hermanas de la Caridad and Religious Medical Authority in Mexico City Hospitals, 1861-1874." *Mexican Studies/Estudios Mexicanos* 33, no. 3 (2017): 417–442.

O'Gorman, Edmundo. *La invención de América: el universalismo de la cultura de occidente* Mexico, D.F.: Fondo de Cultura Económica, 1958.

Olson, Kimberly Sue. "Crucifixion, Resurrection, and Reform: A Guatemalan Nun's Path to Power in the Patriarchal Church, 1816-1841." MA thesis, University of Texas-Austin, 1989.

O'Malley, John W. *Vatican I: The Council and the Making of the Ultramontane Church.* Cambridge, MA: Harvard University Press, 2018.

Oort, Johannes van. *Mani and Augustine: Essays on Mani, Manichaeism, and Augustine.* Leiden, NL: Brill, 2020.

Ortuño Martínez, Manuel. *Expedición a Nueva España de Xavier Mina.* Pamplona, ES: Universidad Pública de Navarra, 2006.

Ortuño Martínez, Manuel. *Vida de Mina. Guerrillero, liberal, insurgente.* Madrid, ES: Trama Editorial, 2008.

Oss, Adriaan C. van. *Catholic Colonialism: A Parish History of Guatemala, 1524-1821.* Cambridge, UK: Cambridge University Press, 1986.

Oss, Adrian C. van. "A Far Kingdom: Central American Autarky at the End of the Eighteenth Century." In *Church and Society in Spanish America*, edited by Adrian C. van Oss, 1–24. Amsterdam, NL: CEDLA, 2003.

Palacio Montiel, Celia del. *La disputa por las conciencias: los inicios de la prensa en Guadalajara, 1809-1835*. Guadalajara, MX.: Universidad de Guadalajara, 2001.

Palmer, Douglas Bradford. "The Republic of Grace: International Jansenism and the Age of Enlightenment and Revolution." PhD dissertation, Ohio State University, 2004.

Pani, Erika. "'Actors on a Most Conspicuous Stage': The Citizens of Revolution." *Historical Reflections/Refléctions Historiques* 29 (2003): 163–188.

Pani, Erika. "Ciudadana y muy ciudadana'? Women and the State in Independent Mexico, 1810–30." *Gender & History* 18, no. 1 (April 2006): 5–19.

Pani, Erika. "Para difundir las doctrinas ortodoxas y vindicarlas de los errores dominantes: Los periódicos católicos y conservadores en el siglo XIX." In *La república de las letras. Asomos a la cultura escrita de México decimonónico*, volume 2, *Publicaciones periódicos y otros impresos*, edited by Belem Clark de Lara and Elisa Speckman Guerra, 119–130. México, D.F.: UNAM, 2005.

Pani, Erika. "'Para halagar la imaginación': Las repúblicas de Nicolás Pizarro." In *El republicanismo en Hispanoamérica. Ensayos de historia intelectual y política*, edited by José Antonio Aguilar and Rafael Rojas, 424–446. México: Centro de Investigación y Docencia Económicas and Fondo de Cultura Económica, 2002.

Pani, Erika. *Para mexicanizar el Segundo Imperio. El imaginario político de los imperialistas*. México: Colegio de México and Instituto Mora, 2001.

Pareja Ortiz, Manuel. "El pueblo bogotano en la revolución del 20 de Julio de 1810." *Anuario de Estudios Americanos* 71, no. 1 (January–June, 2014): 281–311.

Patch, Robert W. "Imperial Politics and Local Economy in Colonial Central America, 1670-1770." *Past and Present* 143 (1994): 77–107.

Payne Iglesias, Elizet. "¡No hay rey, no se pagan tributos! La protesta comunal en El Salvador. 1811." *Intercambio* 4, no. 5 (2007): 15–43.

Peña Rambla, Fernando. *La Inquisición en las Cortes de Cádiz. Un debate para la historia*. Castelló de la Plana, ES: Universitat Jaime I, 2016.

Penry, S. Elizabeth. *The People are King: The Making of Indigenous Andean Politics*. New York, NY: Oxford University Press, 2019.

Peralta Ruiz, Víctor. "El impacto de las Cortes de Cádiz: Un balance historiográfico." *Revista de Indias* 68, no. 242 (2008): 67–96.

Peralta Ruiz, Víctor. "Prensa y redes de comunicación en el virreinato del Perú, 1790-1821." *Tiempos de América* 12 (2005): 1–20.

Pérez Fabregat, Clara. "Apuntes socioeconómicos sobre la Guerra Federal de 1826 a 1829. La experiencia salvadoreña en clave regional." In *La primera guerra federal centroaméricana, 1826-1829*, edited by Arturo Taracena Arriola, 119–164. Guatemala: Editorial Cara Parens, 2015.

Pérez Fabrigat, Clara. *San Miguel y el oriente salvadoreño. La construcción del Estado de El Salvador, 1780-1865*. El Salvador: Universidad Simeón Cañas Editores, 2018.

Pérez Morales, Edgardo. *No Limits to Their Sway: Cartagena's Privateers and the Masterless Caribbean in the Age of Revolutions*. Nashville, TN: Vanderbilt University Press, 2018.

Perry, Elizabeth. "Coronation of the Virgin and the Saints." In *Painting a New World: Mexican Art and Life, 1521-1821*, edited by Rogelio Ruiz Goman, Donna Pierce, and Clare Bargellini. Austin, TX: University of Texas Press and Denver, Co: Frederick and Jan Mayer Center for Pre-Columbian and Spanish Colonial Art at the Denver Art Museum, 2004.

Phelan, John Leddy. *The People and the King: The Comunero Revolution in Colombia, 1781*. Madison, WI: University of Wisconsin Press, 1978.

Pike, Frederick B. "Church and State in Peru and Chile since 1840: A Study in Contrasts." *American Historical Review* 73, no. 1 (October 1967): 30–50.

Pike, Frederick B. "Heresy, Real and Alleged, in Peru: An Aspect of the Conservative-Liberal Struggle, 1830-1875." *Hispanic American Historical Review* 47, no. 1 (February 1967): 50–74.

Pinto Soria, Julio César. *Centroámerica de la colonia al estado nacional.* Guatemala: Editorial Universitaria, 1986.

Pinto Soria, Julio César. "Los religiosidades indígenas y el estado nación en Guatemala (1800-1850)." In *Religiosidad y clero en América Latina: La época de las revoluciones Atlánticas. Religiosity and Clergy in Latin America (1767-1850): The Age of Atlantic Revolutions,* edited by Sebastian Dorsch, Hedwig Harold-Schmidt and Peer Schmidt, 307–327. Cologne, DE.: Böhlau Verlag, 2011.

Plata Quezada, William E. "El catolicismo liberal (o liberalismo católico) en Colombia deci-monónica." *Franciscanum. Revista de las Ciencias del Espíritu* 51, no. 152 (2009): 71–132.

Pollack, Aaron ."Las Cortes de Cádiz en Totonicapán: Una alianza insólita en un año insólito," *Studia Historica. Historia Contemporánea* 27 (2009): 207–234

Pollack, Aaron. *La época de las independencias en Centroamérica y Chiapas: procesos políticos y sociales.* México: Instituto Mora and Universidad Autónoma Metropolitana, Unidad Iztapalapa, 2013.

Pollack, Aaron, ed. *Independence in Central America and Chiapas, 1770-1823.* Translated by Nancy Hancock. Norman, OK: University of Oklahoma Press, 2019.

Pollack, Aaron. *Levantamiento K'iche' en Totonicapán 1820. Los lugares de las políticas subalter-nas.* Guatemala: Asociación para el Avance de las Ciencias Sociales de Guatemala, 2008.

Poupeney Hart, Catherine. "Parcours journalistiques en régime colonial: José Rossi y Rubí, Alejandro Ramírez et Simón Bergaño," *El Argonauta Español* 6 (2009) at https://journals. openedition.org/argonauta/621.

Pollard, John F. *Money and the Rise of the Modern Papacy: Financing the Vatican,1850–1950.* New York, NY: Cambridge University Press, 2005.

Premo, Bianca. *The Enlightenment on Trial: Ordinary Litigants and Colonialism in the Spanish Empire.* New York, NY: Oxford University Press, 2017.

Prieto, Guillermo. *Viajes de orden suprema. Años de 1853, 54 y 55.* 3rd ed. Mexico: Editorial Patria, 1970.

Prieto López, Leopoldo José. "Hechos e ideas en la condena del Parlamento de París de la *Defensio fidei* de Suárez: poder indirecto del papa en temporalibus, derecho de resistencia y tiranicidio." *Relectiones. Revista Interdisciplinar de Filosofía y Humanidades* 7 (2020): 37–53.

Quezada Lara, J.L. *¿Una Inquisición constitucional? El Tribunal Protector de la Fe del Arzobispado de México, 1813-1814.* Zamora, MX: El Colegio de Michoacán, 2016.

Racine, Karen. "Fireworks over Fernandina: The Atlantic Dimension of the Amelia Island Episode, 1817." In *La Florida: 500 Years of Hispanic Presence,* edited by Viviana Díaz-Balsera and Rachel A. May, 171–191. Gainesville, FL: University of Florida Press, 2014.

Racine, Karen. *Francisco Miranda: A Transatlantic Life in the Age of Revolution.* Wilmington, DE: Scholarly Resources, 2003.

Racine, Karen. "Nature and the Mother: Foreign Readings and the Evolution of Andrés Bello's American Identity, London, 1810-1829." In *Strange Pilgrimages: Exile, Travel, and National Identity in Latin America, 1800-1990s,* edited by Ingrid Elizabeth Fey and Karen Racine, 3–19. Wilmington, DE: Scholarly Resources, 2000.

Rama, Ángel. *La crítica de la cultura en América Latina.* Edited by Saúl Sosnowski and Tomás Eloy Martínez. Caracas, VE: Biblioteca Ayacucho, 1985.

Ramírez Aledón, Germán, ed. *Valencianos en Cádiz. Joaquín Lorenzo Villanueva y el grupo valen-ciano en las Cortes de Cádiz*. Cádiz: Biblioteca de la Cortes de Cádiz, Fundación Municipal de Cultura, 2008.

Ramón Solans, Francisco Javier. "The Roman Question in Latin America: Italian Unification and the Development of a Transatlantic Ultramontane Movement." *Atlantic Studies* 18, no. 2 (2021): 129–148.

Ramos, Roberto. *Libros que leyó don Miguel Hidalgo y Costilla*. México: Editorial Jus, S.A., 1969.

Reardon, Bernard M. G. *Religion in the Age of Romanticism. Studies in the Early Nineteenth Century Thought*. Cambridge, UK: Cambridge University Press, 1985.

Reed, Nelson A. *The Caste War of Yucatán*. Stanford, CA: Stanford University Press, 2001.

Regoli, Roberto. "La 'Congregación Especial para los Asuntos Eclesiásticos de España' durante el trienio liberal (1820-1833)." *Anuario de Historia de la Iglesia* 19 (2010): 141–166.

Revuelta González, Manuel. "Las dos supresiones de la Inquisición durante la Guerra de la Independencia." *Miscelánea Comillas* 71, no. 139 (2013): 221–263.

Revuelta González, Manuel. "Los planes de reforma eclesiástica durante el trienio con-stitucional." *Miscelánea Comillas* 56–57 (1972), 93–124.

Revuelta González, Manuel. *Política religiosa de los liberales en el siglo XIX*. Madrid, ES: Escuela de Historia Moderna, 1973.

Reyes Heroles, Jesús. *El liberalismo mexicano*. Volume 1, *Los orígenes*. México: Fondo de Cultura Económica, 1974.

Reyes Heroles, Jesús. *El Liberalismo Mexicano*, 3 vols. México: UNAM, Facultad de Derecho, 1957–1961.

Reyes de la Maza, Luis. "Nicolás Pizarro, novelista y pensador liberal." *Historia Mexicana* 6, no. 4 (April/June 1957): 572–588.

Rice, John Steven. "Evangelical Episcopalians and the Church of Jesus in Mexico, 1857-1906." MA thesis, University of Texas Pan-American, 2000.

Ríos Zúñiga, Rosalina. "El ejercicio del patronato y la problemática eclesiástica en Zacatecas durante la Primera República Federal (1824-1834)." *Historia Crítica* 52 (January–April 2014): 47–71.

Riquet, Michel. *Augustine de Barruel: un jésuite face aux jacobins francs-maçons, 1741-1820*. Paris: Beauchesne, 1989.

Rivas Fernández, José Bernal. "En busca de la independencia eclesiástica de Costa Rica," *Anuario de Historia de la Iglesia* 11 (2002): 239–278.

Rivera Cusicanqui, Silvia. "*Ch'ixinakax utxiwa*: A Reflection on the Practices and Discourses of Decolonization." *South Atlantic Quarterly* 111, no. 1 (2012): 95–109.

Rocha Dallos, Silvia Juliana. "Oiga el público verdades: los panfletos de Fernández de Lizardi (1820-1827)." *Ulúa* 27 (2016): 235–257.

Rodríguez, Mario. *A Palmerstonian Diplomat in Central America, Frederick Chadfield, Esq.* Tucson, AZ: The University of Arizona Press, 1964.

Rodríguez, Mario. *The Cádiz Experiment in Central America, 1808–1826*. Berkeley, CA: University of California Press, 1978.

Rodríguez Gutiérrez, María. "Las modalidades literarias en la prensa de las Córtes de Cádiz: el caso de El Procurador General de la Nación y del Rey (1812-1813)." In *La guerra de pluma. Estudios sobre la prensa de Cádiz en el tiempo de la Cortes (1810-1814). Tomo primero Imprentas, literatura y periódismo*, edited by Marieta Cantos Casaneve, Fernando Dúran López and Alberto Romero Ferrer, 305–389. Cádiz, ES: Servicio de Publicaciones de la Universidad de Cádiz, 2006.

Rodríguez O., Jaime. "José Miguel Ramos Arizpe." In *Encyclopedia of Latin American History and Culture*, volume 4, 537. New York: Charles Scribner's Sons, 1998.

Rodríguez O, Jaime E. "Las instituciones gaditanas en Nueva España, 1812-1814." In *Las nuevas naciones, España y México, 1750-1850*, edited by Jaime E. Rodríguez O, 99–144. Madrid: MAFRE, 2008.

Rodríguez Plata, Horacio. *Andrés María Rosillo y Meruelo*. Bogotá, CO: Editorial Cromos, 1963.

Rojas, Rafael. *La escritura de la Independencia: el surgimiento de la opinión pública en México*. México, D.F.: Taurus/Centro de Investigación y Docencia Económicas, 2003.

Romero del Álamo, Manuel. *Efectos perniciosos del lujo: las cartas de D. Manuel Romero del Álamo al Memorial Literario de Madrid (1789)*. Introduced by Elvira Martínez Chacón, prologue by José Luis García Delgado. Oviedo, ES: Universidad de Oviedo, Servicio de Publicaciones, 1985.

Romero Peña, Aleix. "Caída y persecución del ministro Urquijo y de los jansenistas españoles." *Revista Historia Autónoma* 2 (March 2013): 75–91.

Roscio, Juan Germán. *Obras*. Volume 1, *El triunfo de la libertad sobre el despotismo*. Compiled by Pedro Grases, prologue by Augusto Mijares. Caracas, VE: Publicaciones de la Secretaría General de la Décima Conferencia Interamericana, 1953.

Rovira, Carmen. *Pensamiento filosófico mexicano del siglo XIX y primeros años del XX*. Mexico: UNAM, 1988.

Rubio Mañé, Jorge Ignacio. "El gobernador, capitán general e intendente de Yucatán, mariscal don Manuel Artazo y Barral, y la jura de la constitución español en Mérida, el año de 1812." *Boletín del Archivo General de la Nación* 9, nos. 1–2 (1968): 59–60.

Rubio Mañé, Jorge Ignacio: "Los sanjuanistas de Yucatán. Manuel Jiménez Solís, el padre Justis." *Boletín del Archivo General de la Nación* 9, nos. 1–2, (1968ª): 195–243.

Rugeley, Terry. *Of Wonders and Wise Men: Religion and Popular Cultures in Southeast Mexico, 1800-1876*. Austin, TX: University of Texas Press, 2001.

Rugeley, Terry. *Yucatán's Mayan Peasantry and the Origins of the Caste War*. Austin, TX: University of Texas Press, 1996.

Ruiz Barrionuevo, Carmen. "Juan Germán Roscio y el pensamiento antiliberal." *Philologia Hispalensis* 25 (2011): 181–200.

Ruiz Castañeda, María Carmen, ed. *Clamores de la fidelidad americana contra la opresión o Fragmentos para la historia futura*. Mexico: Universidad Autónoma de México, Instituto de Investigaciones Bibliográficas, Hemeroteca Nacional, 1986.

Ruiz de Peralta, Victor. "Las razones de la fé. La iglesia y la Ilustración en el Perú, 1750-1800." In *El Perú en el siglo XVIII: La era Borbónica*, edited by Scarlett O'Phelan Godoy, 177–204. Lima, PE: Instituto Riva Agüero, 1999.

Sabato, Hilda, ed. *Ciudadanía política y formación de las naciones. Perspectivas históricas de América Latina*. México: Fondo de Cultura Económica and El Colegio de México, 1999.

Sánchez Hita, Beatriz. "La imprenta en Cádiz durante la Guerra de la Independencia y su relación con la prensa periódica." In *La guerra de pluma. Estudios sobre la prensa de Cádiz en el tiempo de la Cortes (1810-1814)*, volume 1, *imprentas, literatura y periódismo*, edited by Marieta Cantos Casaneve, Fernando Dúran López, and Alberto Romero Ferrer, 31–111. Cádiz, ES: Servicio de Publicaciones de la Universidad de Cádiz, 2006.

Sabato, Hilda, ed. *Ciudadanía política y formación de las naciones. Perspectivas históricas de América Latina*. México: Fondo de Cultura Económica-El Colegio de México, 1999.

Sarazúa Pérez, Juan Carlos. "Desertores y rebeldes. Dos formas de entender la militarización en Guatemala y Chiapas, 1825-1859." *Prohistoria* 20, no. 28 (December 2017): 99–122.

Sarazúa Pérez, Juan Carlos. "Fuerzas militares para defender al Estado: Guatemala, 1823-1863." In *Las fuerzas de guerra en la construcción del Estado: América Latina siglo XIX*, edited by Juan Carlos Garavaglia, Juan Pro Ruíz, and Eduardo Zimmerman, 33–58. Rosario, AR: Prohistoria Ediciones, 2012.

Sarazúa Pérez, Juan Carlos. "Política y etnicidad y servicio militar. Dos experiencias paralelas en Mesoamérica. Chiapas y Guatemala, 1808-1871." *Revista Historia de América* 152 (2016): 135–162.

Sarazúa Pérez, Juan Carlos. "Recolectar, administrar y defender: la construcción del estado y las resistencias regionales en Guatemala, 1800-1871." PhD dissertation. Barcelona,ES: Universitat Pompeu Fabra, 2013.

Sarazúa Pérez, Juan Carlos. "Recolectar, gastar, y reclutar en tiempos de guerra: finanzas públicas y servicio militar indígena en Guatemala durante la Guerra Federal de 1826 a 1829." In *La primera guerra federal centroamericana, 1826-1829. Nación y estados, republicanismo de violencia*, edited by Arturo Taracena Arriola, 87–118. México: Universidad Autónoma Metropolitana, Unidad Iztapalapa, 2005.

Sartorious, David. "Of Exceptions and Afterlives: The Long History of the 1812 Constitution in Cuba." In *The Rise of Constitutional Government in the Iberian Atlantic World: The Impact of the Cádiz Constitution of 1812*, edited by Scott Eastman and Natalia Sobrevilla Perea, 150–176. Tuscaloosa, AL: The University of Alabama Press, 2015.

Saugnieux, Joël. *Un prélat éclairé: Don Antonio Tavira y Almazán, 1737-1807: contribution à l'étude du jansénisme espagnol*. Toulouse, France: Ibérie Recherche, 1970.

Scheper Hughes, Jennifer. *Biography of a Mexican Crucifix: Lived Religion and Local Faith from the Conquest to the Present*. New York, NY: Oxford University Press, 2009.

Scheper Hughes, Jennifer. *The Church of the Dead: The Epidemic of 1576 and the Birth of Christianity in the Americas*. New York, NY: New York University Press, 2021.

Scholes, Walter V. "A Revolution Falters: Mexico, 1856-1857." *Hispanic American Historical Review* 32, no. 1 (February 1952): 1–21.

Seigel, Micol. "Beyond Compare: Comparative Method after the Transnational Turn." *Radical History Review* 91 (2005): 62–90.

Serrano, Sol. *¿Que hacer con dios en la república? Política y secularización en Chile (1845-1885)*. México: Fondo de Cultura Económica, 2008.

Sheehan, Jonathan. "Enlightenment, Religion, and the Enigma of Secularization: A Review Essay." *American Historical Review* 108, no. 4 (2003): 1061–1080.

Shields, David S., ed. *Liberty! Égalité! Independencia!* Worchester, MA.: American Antiquarian Society, 2007.

Sierra, Justo. *Juárez: Su obra y su tiempo*, edited by Arturo Arnáiz y Freg. México: UNAM, 1972.

Sierra Nava, Luis. *El cardenal Lorenzana y la Ilustración*. Madrid, ES: Fundación Universitaria Española, Seminario Cisneros, 1975.

Sinkin, Richard. *The Mexican Reform, 1856-1876*. Austin, TX.: Institute of Latin American Studies, 1979.

Smidt, Andrea J. "Bourbon Regalism and the Importation of Gallicanism: The Political Path for a State Religion in Eighteenth-Century Spain." *Anuario de Historia de la Iglesia* 19 (2010): 25–53.

Smidt, Andrea J. "Fiestas and Fervor: Religious Life and Catholic Enlightenment in the Diocese of Barcelona, 1766-1775." PhD dissertation, Ohio State University, 2006.

Smidt, Andrea J. "Josep Climent i Avinent (1706-1781): Enlightened Catholic, Civic Humanist, Seditionist." In *Enlightenment and Catholicism in Europe: A Transnational History*, edited by Jeffrey D. Burson and Ulrich L. Lehner, 327–353. Notre Dame, IN: University of Notre Dame Press, 2014.

Smidt, Andrea J. "Piedad e ilustración en relación armónica. Josep Climent i Avinent, Obispo de Barcelona, 1766-1775." *Manuscrits. Revista d'Història Moderna* 20 (2002): 91–109.

Smith, Robert. "El financiamiento de la Federación Centroamericana 1821-1838." In *Lecturas de historia de Centroamérica*, edited by Luis René Cáceres, 439–468. San José, CR: Banco Centroamericano de Integración Económica, 1989.

Sobrevilla Perea, Natalia. *The Caudillo of the Andes: Andrés de Santa Cruz.* Cambridge, UK: Cambridge University Press, 2011.

Soriano, Cristina. *Tides of Revolution. Information, Insurgencies, and the Crisis of Colonial Rule in Venezuela.* Albuquerque: University of New Mexico Press, 2018.

Sosa de León, Mireya. "La disolución del orden civil durante la guerra de independencia en el testimonio del arzobispo Narciso Coll y Pratt, 1810-1816." *Ensayos históricos* 19 (2007): 89–118.

Souto Mantecón, Matilde. "1812: Un año crítico. Violencia y elecciones en Veracruz." In *Cuando las armas hablan, los impresos luchan, la exclusión agreda: Violenca electoral en México, 1821-1921*, edited by Fausta Gantús Innureta and Alicia Salmerón Castro, 39–72. San Juan Mixcoac, Ciudad de México: Instituto Mora, 2016.

Souto Mantecón, Matilde. "El primer ejercicio constitutional en la Nueva España: la elección del ayuntamiento de la ciudad de Veracruz en 1812. Descripción de la mecánica electoral." In *Elecciones en México en el siglo veinte. Las practicas*, edited by Fausta Gantús Innureta, 55–92. México: Instituto Mora, 2016.

Stephens, Michelle A. "Black Transnationalism and the Politics of National Identity. West Indian Intellectuals in Harlem in the Age of War and Revolution." *American Quarterly* 50, no. 3 (1998): 592–608

Stevens, Donald Fithian. *Origins of Instability in Early Republican Mexico.* Durham, NC: Duke University Press, 1991.

Stoetzer, O. Carlos. *The Scholastic Roots of the Spanish-American Revolution.* New York, NY: Fordham University Press, 1979.

Suárez Molina, Víctor M., ed. *Estado de la industria, comercio y educación de la provincia de Yucatán en 1802 y causas de la pobreza de Yucatán en 1821.* Mérida, Yucatán: Ediciones Suárez, 1955.

Sullivan-González, Douglass. *The Black Christ of Esquipulas. Religion and Identity in Guatemala.* Lincoln, NE: University of Nebraska Press, 2016.

Sullivan-González, Douglass. *Piety, Power, and Politics: Religion and Nation Formation in Guatemala, 1821-1871.* Pittsburgh, PA: University of Pittsburgh Press, 1998.

Sweet, James H. *Domingos Álvares, African Healing, and the Intellectual History of the Atlantic World.* Chapel Hill, NC: University of North Carolina Press, 2013.

Tackett, Timothy. *Religion, Revolution and Regional Culture in Eighteenth-Century France. The Ecclesiastical Oath of 1791.* Princeton, NJ: Princeton University Press, 1986.

Tandrón, Humberto and Susana Liberti. *El comercio de Nueva España y la controversia sobre la libertad de comercio, 1796-1821.* México, DF: Instituto Mexicano de Comercio Exterior, 1976.

Taracena Arriola, Arturo. *Invención criolla, sueño ladino, pesadilla indígena. Los Altos de Guatemala: de región a estado, 1740-1871.* Guatemala: CIRMA, 1999.

Taracena Arriola, Arturo. "La mirada de tres actores guatemaltecos sobre la Guerra Federal de 1826-1829: Montúfar y Coronado, Córdova y García Granados. Reflexiones metodológicas sobre un conflicto armado." In *La primera guerra federal centroamericana, 1826-1829. Nación y estados, republicanismo y violencia*, edited by Arturo Taracena Arriola, 55–86. Guatemala: Editorial Cara Parens, 2015.

Taylor, William B. *Magistrates of the Sacred. Priests and Parishioners in Eighteenth-Century Mexico*. Stanford, CA: Stanford University Press, 1996.

Taylor, William B. *Theater of a Thousand Wonders: A History of Miraculous Images and Shrines in New Spain*. New York, NY: Cambridge University Press, 2016.

Tenorio Góchez, Ruth María de los Ángeles. "Cuán rápidos pasos da este pueblo hacia la civilización europea: Periódicos y cultura impresa en el Salvador (1824-1850)." PhD dissertation, Ohio State University 2006.

Tisnés, Roberto M. *El clero y la independencia en Santafé (1810-1815)*. Edited by Luis Martínez Delgado and Abel Cruz Santos. Bogotá, CO: Ediciones Lerner, 1971.

Tomisch, Maria Giovanna. *El Jansenismo en España: Estudios sobre las ideas religiosas en la segunda mitad del siglo XVIII*. Prologue by Carmen Martín Gaite. Madrid, ES: Siglo Veintiuno España Editores, 1972.

Toro, Alfonso. *Don Miguel Ramos Arizpe,"Padre del Federalismo Mexicano": biografía*. Saltillo, Coahuila, México: Coordinación General de Extensión Universitaria y Difusión Cultural, 1992.

Toro, Alfonso. *La Iglesia y el estado en México*. México: Talleres Gráficos de la Nación, 1927.

Torra, Cristina. "Bartolomé José Gallardo y el Diccionario crítico burlesco." In *Estudios sobre el Cortes de Cádiz. Colección histórica de la Universidad de Navarra*, edited by María Isabel Arriazu et. al, 209–272. Pamplona, ES: Universidad de Navarra, 1967.

Torres-Cuevas, Eduardo, Jorge Ibarra Cuesta, and Mercedes García Rodríguez, eds. *Félix Varela. El que nos enseñó primero en pensar. Obras*. Vol 1. La Habana, Cuba: Imágen Contemporánea, 1997.

Torres-Cuevas, Eduardo, ed. *Obispo Espada. Ilustración, reforma y antiesclavismo*. La Habana, Cuba: Editorial de Ciencias Sociales, 1990.

Torres Torres, Fray Eugenio, ed. *Los Dominicos insurgentes y realistas de México y Río de la Plata*. México: D.R. Instituto Dominicano de Investigaciones Históricas, 2011.

Torre Villar, Ernesto de la. *El triunfo de la república liberal, 1857-60*. México: Fondo de Cultura Económica, 1960.

Turcios, Roberto. *Los primeros patriotas. San Salvador en 1811*. San Salvador: Ediciones Tendencias, 1995.

Urquijo, Mariano Luis de. *Apuntes para la memoria sobre mi vida política, persecuciones y trabajos padecidos en ella*, edited by Aleix Romero Peña. Madrid, ES: Editorial Siníndice, 2010.

Valle, Ivonne del. *Escribiendo desde los márgenes. Colonialismo y jesuitas en el siglo XVIII*. México: Siglo XXI Editores, 2009.

Valle, Ivonne del. "A New Moses: Vasco de Quiroga's Hospitals and the Transformation of 'Indians' from 'Barbaros' to 'Pobres.'" In *Iberian Empires and the Roots of Globalization*, edited by Anna More, Ivonne del Valle, and Rachel Sarah O'Toole (Nashville, TN: Vanderbilt University Press, 2019)

Valle, Rafael Heliodoro. "Dionisio de Herrera, 1783-1850. A Centennial Tribute." *Hispanic American Historical Review* 30, no. 4 (November 1950): 554–558.

Vallejo, Antonio R. *Compendio de la historia social y política de Honduras: aumentada con los acontecimientos de Centro-América. Tomo 1*. Tegucigalpa, HD: Tipografía Nacional, 1886.

Van Kley, Dale K. "The *Ancien Régime*, Catholic Europe, and the Revolution's Religious Schism." In *A Companion to the French Revolution*, edited by Peter McPhee, 123–144. Chichester, UK: John Wiley & Sons, 2013.

Van Kley, Dale K. "Catholic Conciliar Reform in an Age of Anti-Catholic Revolution. France, Italy and the Netherlands, 1758-1800." In *Religion and Politics in Enlightenment Europe*, edited by James Bradley and Dale K. Van Kley. South Bend, IN: Notre Dame University Press, 2001.

Van Kley, Dale K. *Reform Catholicism and the International Suppression of the Jesuits in Enlightenment Europe*. New Haven, CT: Yale University Press, 2018.

Van Young, Eric. "The Limits of Atlantic World Nationalism in a Revolutionary Age: Imagined Communities and Lived Communities in Mexico, 1810-1821." In *Empire to Nation. Historical Perspectives on the Making of the Modern World*, edited by Joseph Eshrick, Hasan Kayali, and Eric Van Young, 34–67. New York, NY: Rowman and Littlefield, 2006.

Van Young, Eric. *The Other Rebellion. Popular Violence, Ideology, and the Mexican Struggle for Independence, 1810-1821*. Stanford, CA: Stanford University Press, 2002.

Verna, Paul. *Pétion y Bolívar*. 3rd ed. Caracas, VE: Ediciones de la Presidencia de la República, 1980.

Vicente, Marta V. *Clothing the Spanish Empire: Families and the Calico Trade in the Early Modern Atlantic World*. New York, NY: Palgrave MacMillan, 2006.

Vigil, José María. *México a través de los siglos*. Volume 5, *La Reforma*. Directed by Vicente Riva Palacio. México, D.F.: Ballescá y Compañía; Barcelona, ES: Espasa y Compañía, 1882.

Vismara, Paola. "Ludovico Antonio Muraroti (1672-1750): Enlightenment in a Tridentine Mode." In *A Companion to the Catholic Enlightenment*, edited by Ulrich L. Lehner and Michael Pinty, 249–268. Leiden, NL: E.J. Brill, 2010.

Voekel, Pamela. *Alone before God. The Religious Origins of Modernity in Mexico*. Durham, NC: Duke University Press, 2002.

Voekel, Pamela. "The Baroque Church." In *The Cambridge History of Religions in Latin America*, 160-172, edited by Virginia Garrard, Paul Freston, and Stephen C. Dove. New York, NY: Cambridge University Press, 2016.

Voekel, Pamela. "Liberal Religion: The Schism of 1861." In *Religious Culture in Modern Mexico*, edited by Martin Austin Nesvig, 78–105. Lantham, ML: Rowman & Littlefield, 2007.

Voekel, Pamela, Bethany Moreton, and Michael Jo. "Vaya con Dios: Religion and the Transnational History of the Americas." *History Compass* 5, no. 5 (2007): 1604–1639.

Vogeley, Nancy. *The Bookrunner: A History of Inter-American Relations—Print, Politics and Commerce in the United States and Mexico, 1800-1830*. Philadelphia, PA: American Philosophical Society, 2011.

Walker, Charles F. *Smoldering Ashes: Cuzco and the Creation of Republican Peru, 1780-1840*. Durham, NC: Duke University Press, 1999.

Walker, Charles F., and Liz Clarke. *Witness to the Age of Revolution: The Odyssey of Juan Bautista Tupac Amaru*. New York, NY: Oxford University Press, 2020.

Walker, Tamara J. *Exquisite Slaves. Race, Clothing, and Status in Colonial Lima*. Cambridge, UK: Cambridge University Press, 2019.

Warren, Harris Gaylord. "The Origins of General Mina's Invasion of Mexico." *Southwestern Historical Quarterly* 42, no. 1 (July 1938): 1–20.

Warren, Harris Gaylord. "Xavier Mina's Invasion of Mexico." *Hispanic American Historical Review* 23, no. 1 (February 1943): 52–76.

Warren, Richard A. "Displaced 'Pan-Americans' and the Transformation of the Catholic Church in Philadelphia, 1789-1850." *The Pennsylvania Magazine of History and Biography* 127, no. 4 (October 2004): 343–366.

Williams, Mary Wilhelmine. "The Ecclesiastical Policy of Francisco Morazán and the other Central American Liberals." *Hispanic American Historical Review* 3, no. 2 (May 1920): 119–143.

Woodward, Jr., Ralph Lee. *Class Privilege and Economic Development: The Consulado de Comercio of Guatemala, 1793-1871.* Chapel Hill, NC: University of North Carolina Press, 1966.

Worcester, Thomas. "Pius VII: Moderation in an Age of Revolution and Reaction." In *The Papacy Since 1500: From Italian Prince to Universal Pastor*, edited by James Corkery, Thomas Worcester, and Linda Hogan, 107–125. New York, NY: Cambridge University Press, 2011.

Wright-Rios, Edward. "Indian Saints and Nation-States: Ignacio Manuel Altamirano's Landscapes and Legends" *Mexican Studies/Estudios Mexicanos* 20, no. 1 (winter 2004): 47–68.

Wynter, Sylvia. "Unsettling the Coloniality of Being/Power/Truth/Freedom: Towards the Human, after Man, Its Overrepresentation—An Argument." *The New Centennial Review* 3, no. 3 (2003): 257–337.

Zanolli Fabila, Betty Luisa de María Auxiliadora. "*La alborada del liberalismo yucateco*: El I *Ayuntamiento Constitucional de Mérida (1812-1814)*," MA thesis, 2 vols., UNAM, Facultad de Filosofía y Letras, 1993.

Zárate, Julio. *José María Morelos: ensayo biográfico.* Mexico: M.A. Porrúa, 1987.

Zelaya Goodman, Chester J. *Nicaragua en la Independencia.* San José, CR: Universitaria Centroamericana, 1971.

Zeltsman, Corrina. *Ink under the Fingernails: Printing Politics in Nineteenth-Century Mexico* Berkeley, CA: University of California Press, 2021.

Zuluaga, Patricia Cardona. "José Manuel Restrepo y la historia de la República de Colombia: Testimonios y documentos." *Araucaria. Revista Iberoamericana de Filosofía, Política y Humanidades* 16, no. 31, (January–June 2014): 223–231.

INDEX

For the benefit of digital users, indexed terms that span two pages (e.g., 52–53) may, on occasion, appear on only one of those pages.
Page numbers followed by f indicate figures. Page numbers followed by n indicate notes.

385